# ECONOMICS OF SOVIET REGIONS

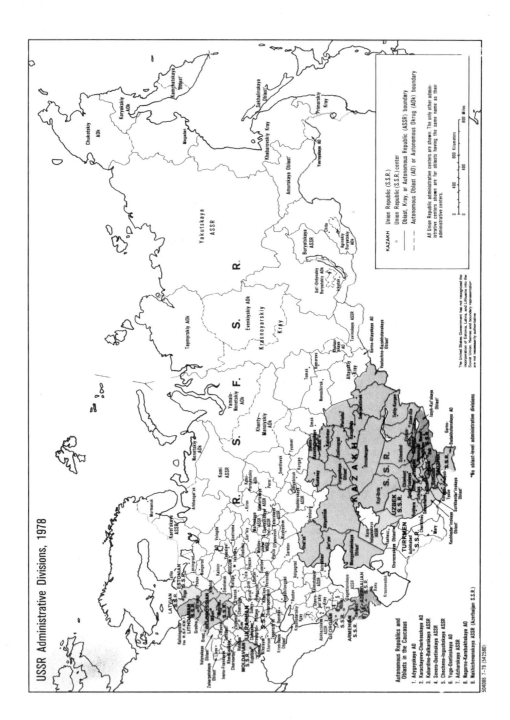

USSR Administrative Divisions, 1978

# ECONOMICS OF SOVIET REGIONS

Edited by
## I. S. Koropeckyj
## Gertrude E. Schroeder

PRAEGER

PRAEGER SPECIAL STUDIES • PRAEGER SCIENTIFIC

**Library of Congress Cataloging in Publication Data**

Main entry under title:

Economics of Soviet regions.

    Bibliography: p.
    Includes indexes.
    Contents: Overview / Alec Nove—Population and
labor force / Warren W. Eason—Growth and
productivity / I. S. Koropeckyj—[etc.]
    1. Soviet Union—Economic conditions—1976-
—Addresses, essays, lectures.  I. Koropeckyj,
I. S.  II. Schroeder, Gertrude E.
HC336.25.E29        330.947′0853         81 5918
ISBN 0-03-059702-1                     AACR2

Published in 1981 by Praeger Publishers
CBS Educational and Professional Publishing
A Division of CBS, Inc.
521 Fifth Avenue, New York, New York 10175 U.S.A.

© 1981 by Praeger Publishers

123456789   145   987654321

Printed in the United States of America

# LIST OF CONTRIBUTORS

JURIS DREIFELDS
  Department of Politics
  Brock University
  St. Catharines, Ontario, Canada

WARREN W. EASON
  Department of Economics
  Ohio State University
  Columbus, Ohio

JAMES W. GILLULA
  Foreign Demographic Analysis Division
  U.S. Department of Commerce
  Washington, D.C.

IHOR GORDIJEW
  Department of Economics
  Macquarie University
  North Ryde, New South Wales, Australia

F. E. IAN HAMILTON
  Department of Geography
  London School of Economics and Political Science
  London, United Kingdom

DAVID S. KAMERLING
  Central Intelligence Agency
  Washington, D. C.

I. S. KOROPECKYJ
  Department of Economics
  Temple University
  Philadelphia, Pennsylvania

IAN M. MATLEY
  Department of Geography
  Michigan State University
  East Lansing, Michigan

ALEC NOVE
    Department of International Economic Studies
    University of Glasgow
    Glasgow, United Kingdom

GERTRUDE E. SCHROEDER
    Department of Economics
    University of Virginia
    Charlottesville, Virginia

F. DOUGLAS WHITEHOUSE
    Central Intelligence Agency
    Washington, D.C.

OLEG ZINAM
    Department of Economics
    University of Cincinnati
    Cincinnati, Ohio

# CONTENTS

# INTRODUCTION

## I. S. Koropeckyj and Gertrude E. Schroeder

The emergence of the USSR as a leading power after World War II led to heightened interest in its socialist economy. This interest was shared by Western scholars, government officials, and the general public. Initially, scholarly interest was centered on developing economic aggregates for the entire USSR in order to make valid comparisons with corresponding aggregates for Western countries, especially the United States. With time, it became apparent that these overall magnitudes obscure considerable variations among regions of the USSR; thus, knowledge of the whole remains incomplete without better understanding of its constituent parts. This situation stems from the fact that the large territory of the USSR comprises regions differing sharply with respect to climate, population density, resource endowment, and level of economic development. Moreover, individual regions are often inhabited by nationalities belonging to different ethnic groups with many languages and cultures, factors that increase diversity among these regions.

The recognition that the USSR cannot be studied meaningfully as a homogeneous entity has produced a number of publications on the ethnic, geographic, and economic aspects of Soviet regions. Up to now, studies of the economic aspects have dealt either with individual regions or with selected problems on an interregional level. No single volume has yet treated comprehensively the most important problems of economic development with respect to all regions. Considering the large scope of the subject and the specificity of economic development in individual regions, such an endeavor would probably be beyond the capability of a single author. Therefore, it is hoped that the present volume, written by specialists in particular fields, will fill this gap. The approach taken here is empirical, with the findings resting on a careful analysis of available data relating to economic development. The discussion is limited to the period after World War II, with only occasional references to earlier periods.

From a solely economic point of view it would be desirable to analyze Soviet regional development on the basis of some well-defined and dimensionally comparable subunits. Unfortunately, Soviet regional statistics, for the most part, are published only for the 15 union republics, formally autonomous constituent political units of the USSR. These republics differ substantially with respect to size, population, and economic potential, making comparisons among them quite difficult. In the case of large republics, such as the Russian Federation, the Ukraine, and Kazakhstan, it would be of interest to treat their subdivisions separately. Nonetheless, the use of republics as units of analysis is not only dictated by data availability, but also corresponds to Soviet practice. Focus on the republics permits a critical examination of such Soviet governmental assertions as all union republics are independent, for all practical purposes, as decision makers, and equalization of their levels of economic development has been "basically" achieved.

The 12 chapters of this volume are divided into two parts: The chapters in the first part deal with selected problems and measures of performance for all republics, and the chapters in the second part are devoted to the analysis of economic development in individual republics. The book begins with an overview chapter discussing methodological problems of regional economics in general, and of some aspects of this field of study specific to the Soviet Union. Among the problems in the center of present attention in the USSR is the declining growth of new entrants to the labor force and the marked differences in these rates among republics. As Chapter 2 shows, this trend has been evident for some time from the differential birth rates in these republics. The growth rates of national income and its individual sectors are the subjects of Chapter 3. These rates have varied among republics; some of the western republics performed best, while the majority of the Central Asian republics showed relatively poor results, except in agriculture. Similar results are found with respect to the growth of total factor productivity and its components: output per worker and per unit of capital. Chapter 4 is concerned with interregional differences and trends in the standard of living. Although levels have risen substantially in all republics since 1950, the differences among them remain significant and have increased during the 1970s. As argued in Chapter 5, high rates of capital formation have prevailed throughout the period in all republics, with characteristic emphasis on growth of industrial capital stock. As a result, little change has taken place in economic structures among republics.

The second part of this book focuses on the individual republics. Although separate chapters for each republic might have been preferable, considerations of expediency dictated grouping of geographically close republics for purpose of description and analysis of economic performance. In the case of the large and diverse RSFSR, some separation seemed required. Accordingly, Chapter 6 treats the western part of this republic with a long history of economic development within the framework of the entire European part of the USSR. The Asiatic part of the Russian Federation is investigated in Chapter 7, which describes the problems facing central planners in their attempt to develop this resource-rich region that is sparsely settled, has an inhospitable climate, and is far removed from traditional centers of economic activity.

The remaining 14 republics are treated as follows: the Ukraine and Moldavia, separately, in Chapters 8 and 9; the Baltic republics of Lithuania, Latvia, and Estonia, and neighboring Belorussia in Chapter 10; the three Transcaucasian republics of Georgia, Azerbaidzhan, and Armenia in Chapter 11; and, finally, ethnically heterogeneous and economically diverse Kazakhstan with the four Central Asian republics of Uzbekistan, Kirgizstan, Tadzhikistan, and Turkmenistan in Chapter 12. In general, an attempt was made to discuss the following aspects of economic development, although not necessarily in this order: the present importance and specialization of a given republic in the overall USSR economy; the pattern of economic development that might have occurred in a given republic if it had developed as an independent country, irrespective of the kind of economic system; the impact of existing institutions and economic policy on economic performance; comparison with the economic experience in neighboring countries; and financial relations with other republics and the central government in Moscow (possible only in the case of the Ukraine). In individual cases, the extent of discussion of these questions depended greatly on the availability of necessary statistics and the results of previous research. The chapters show that differences among individual republics with respect to these variables are often quite substantial.

The editors realize that not all important problems of regional-republic development in the USSR have been treated in this volume, and that some of those considered have not been treated exhaustively. The reasons, as already mentioned, concerned limitation of space, unavailability of needed data, and, in some cases, absence of relevant previous research. Thus, in many ways the present volume is pioneering in nature. The editors would be pleased if this initial effort were to stimulate further research on these republics, for much remains to be done. As can be judged from the meagre available research, the political and economic importance of the constituent republics of the USSR has not yet been sufficiently recognized and appreciated in the West.

# 1

## OVERVIEW
### Alec Nove

The study of Soviet regions is a comparatively underdeveloped area of Western scholarship. Yet here is a country covering a sixth of the world's surface, containing within its borders a wide range of climate, soil, national cultures, resource endowment, at greatly differing levels of development. While it is often appropriate to generalize about the Soviet Union as a whole, one must also ask oneself, Are there not wide differences among areas, even if the economic systems are formally identical?

It is also important not to lose sight of the comparative perspective. Regional problems are not peculiar to the USSR. They would doubtless have existed in acute form if an imaginary Nicholas III were now ruling the Russian Empire. We see many instances in which economic and political tensions are linked with national (or tribal) issues: Canada (Quebec), Belgium (Flemish versus Walloon interests), France (Corsica), Spain (Basques and Catalans), Yugoslavia, Nigeria, Pakistan. Whether developed or underdeveloped, socialist or nonsocialist, many countries face problems of this sort. Tensions arising from unevenness of development also can occur in countries where local nationalisms are not an issue: thus one has the problems of the South of Italy, and the unbalanced development of Mexico. In Great Britain there has long been a problem of the depressed areas of the North, with the added complication in recent years of Scottish and Welsh nationalisms.

There is also the widespread problem of the role of regional authorities. In "capitalist" countries much of industry is owned and managed by large corporations with central headquarters outside of the host region—in some cases outside the host country.

Their decisions can greatly affect the host region's economic welfare. Whose administrative task is it to handle this? What powers
of action, inducement, prohibition should this authority have?
Should it be the concern of the center (for instance, Italian government agencies in Rome concern themselves with setting up new industries in the depressed South), or should there be a regional
(provincial, state) authority with the necessary powers? (Some
would say these powers are unnecessary, since private enterprise,
left to itself, will solve all problems. We will ignore this argument
in the present context. Most "capitalist" countries that suffer from
regional imbalances recognize that they are not self-curing, and
may even be cumulative. Were it otherwise, there would be no
regional problem.) But, in any case, in the Soviet Union there is
virtually no private enterprise, and these questions are handled by
state institutions or they are not handled at all.

This, indeed, is one characteristic of the problem in its
Soviet setting, and it is important enough to analyze further. With
few exceptions, goods and services are produced, delivered, transported, utilized throughout the Soviet Union in accordance with a
centralized plan. True, there are some local industries, and
agricultural activities are partially undertaken to cover local needs.
True, also, there are republican, provincial, and municipal authorities with their own budgets and with, on paper, considerable powers
(to be dealt with later). But the logic and nature of the Soviet economic system are strongly centralizing. Market forces are weak.
They are replaced by "the plan"—or, to be precise, a multiplicity
of plans and instructions, which pass down the hierarchical ladder
and are obligatory. These are plan-orders, and the system is
"directive planning." The plans supposedly reflect the needs of
society, and for this purpose resources are allocated and sub-
allocated on an all-union scale.

In a complex and interlinked industrial economy, the deter-
mination of need and the production and allocation decisions that
flow from it are necessarily centralized. If a factory in Kharkov
makes a product utilized in many parts of the USSR, and uses a
dozen inputs made in other parts of the USSR, its output and inputs
clearly cannot be planned by an authority in the Kharkov region.
We know, from the experience of the sovnarkhozy in Khrushchev's
time, that regional authorities endowed with powers tend (understandably) to divert resources from other regions to their own, a
practice that has to be prevented so as to avoid disintegration of the
industrial planning system. Hence, we return to the more familiar
centralized structure reestablished in 1965.

The reader unfamiliar with Soviet-type economies might
demur. After all, why shouldn't the enterprise in Kharkov negotiate

contracts with its customers all over the USSR, and similarly negotiate to secure its own supplies? This is indeed an alternative
model, but is inapplicable to the Soviet case. This is a market
model, and in the USSR management receives instructions on both
output and inputs (and much besides) from planning officials; only
then is it allowed to negotiate detailed contracts. Under these conditions centralization has its own potent logic. This in turn emas-
culates whatever regional organs there may be. The bulk of the
important decisions are not taken at the regional level.

Matters are made worse by another highly relevant phenomenon. The center, overwhelmed by the magnitude of its task, is
necessarily divided into subunits. Industrial ministries administer
enterprises, directly or through "associations" (obiedineniia), with
Gosplan as the principal coordinating organ. In some instances
there is also a ministry at republican level (of which more in a
moment). Factories in (say) the Kharkov region receive commands
from a large number of different ministries. These ministries
naturally consider their particular industry's problems, rather than
the development of the region as such.

A large number of quotations can be assembled from the
Soviet press to show the ministries' awareness of the weakness of
regional and urban planning: they can ignore local planners'
schemes, and in practice the plan for the region can be simply the
sum total of the separate decisions taken by remote ministries on
the basis of "departmental" (vedomstvennye) considerations. Apart
from its effects on regional plans, this situation is a cause of much
duplication and inefficiency. Each ministry can, and often does,
set up its own component plants to supply "its own" enterprises and
no others—and in Siberia it was reported that in a new town each
ministry organized its own separate telephone network.

The USSR is formally a federation, and on paper the 15 union
republics have considerable powers. However, from the standpoint
of regional planning the republics are often quite unsuitable in size
and boundaries. Some, like Estonia and Moldavia, are very small.
One, the Russian Republic (RSFSR), covers a large part of the
USSR's territory from the Baltic Sea to the Pacific Ocean. The
boundary between the RSFSR and the Ukraine cuts through the industrial complex based on Donets coal. Nor are provincial (oblast')
boundaries in any way related to natural or economic regions.
There are "large regions"—at present 17—but these are adapted to
existing boundaries, and in any event no executive power resides in
them: they are a convenient unit for central planners of regional
development.

Although the republics have their own planning organs, and a
number of industrial ministries, they have only limited powers. In

the case of enterprises subordinated to all-union ministries, orders
flow direct from Moscow without even passing through the republican
capitals. Union-republican ministries exist both at the center and
in the republics, the latter being under "dual subordination"—under
both the republican government and the analogous central ministry.
This in practice means that Moscow's will predominates, particularly since the planning and supply organs at republican level are in
the same position as the union-republican ministries. Furthermore,
since all important material resources are centrally allocated, the
existence of republic or provincial budgets does not of itself give
power to decide on spending, except within narrow limits. Money
is not enough: to acquire material means for action requires the
consent of those who allocate—usually at the center, in Moscow.

Finally, the Party is a centralized institution. Party organs
and officials in the republics and provinces are under the authority
of the Central Committee in Moscow and its apparatus. Since the
Party machine dominates all political, economic, and cultural institutions, and makes all appointments of significance (under the
nomenklatura system), centralization is further reinforced.

This said, it is necessary to enter a caveat. As in any very
large hierarchical organization, the nominally total power of the
central organs is not as absolute as it might seem. It is physically
impossible to control and supervise everything. Local organs and
local management do in fact have some room for maneuver, a
range of decisions to take within necessarily rather broad (and
sometimes contradictory) guidelines from Moscow. Furthermore,
republican and provincial party secretaries are not just the appointed agents of central authority. They also represent local
interest at the center in a struggle for scarce resources, advocat-
ing that more be done in their areas. Brezhnev, like Khrushchev
before him, has complained of mestnichestvo ("localism") and of
the diversion of resources by local officials to projects not regarded
by the center as being of high priority. The fact that great powers
reside in Moscow does not mean that they can be used continuously.
Thus, in Georgia under Mzhavanadze, local officials made large-
scale corruption a way of life, and Moscow intervened only when
the situation became truly scandalous. But intervene it did, and
appointed the former KGB chief, Shevardnadze, to clean up the
mess.

But enough of organizational matters. What of regional
problems?

There is, first, the national question. It concerns not only
the nationalities of the union-republics but many others too: Tatars,
Bashkirs, Iakuts, Chechens are nationalities that have autonomous
republics within the RSFSR. (Crimean Tatars were deported in

1944, and have been vainly claiming the right to return to the Crimean.) In considering their grievances, where these exist, we should distinguish between who decides and what is decided. In some instances what is resented is the fact that the decision is taken by others—by Moscow—rather than the nature of the decision. The same decision, if taken in Kiev or Tbilisi, might well be more readily accepted.

But of course the content of decisions can be important also. Republics (and regions) are unevenly developed. As in other countries (Italy and Yugoslavia, for instance), there is a contradiction between the policy of evening out regional differences and the efficient use of investment resources. Industrial development is far below the all-union average in Central Asia, Azerbaidzhan, and Moldavia. In Central Asia there is a high rate of population growth and relative rural overpopulation. However, for reasons to be discussed in a moment, it is urgent to devote resources to Siberia. Industrial investment in (for instance) Central Asia would be remote from the main markets and increase the strain on transportation, thus yielding a lower rate of return than investment in already developed areas.

This situation presents the central planners with a dilemma. On the one hand there is a shortage of labor and a low birth rate, except in Central Asia. On the other, the native populations tend to cling to rural areas, and industrial investment has attracted migrants from other republics. It might seem a possible solution to persuade the Central Asians to work where labor is scarce—for instance, in Siberia—but they plainly do not wish to leave their homes, and there is no intention to force them. In recent years the Central Asian republics have received a less-than-proportionate share of total investments, and are doubtless pressing for more.

The level of development of different republics has been the subject of a number of studies. It is generally agreed that the Baltic states are first, by almost any indicator of welfare. The Central Asian republics come low on a per capita basis, but this is because there are so many children; their situation is much improved if calculations are made per working person. Indeed, since there is a wage scale common to most of the USSR, levels of wage income do not differ widely. Correction must also be made for availability, especially of food; in this respect Central Asia and Transcaucasia are superior to many areas of the RSFSR, where food shortages have been common in recent years. There is, of course, much more that bears on the economics of the national question, in the contributions to the present volume.

A different problem is that of small towns. The problem arises out of the tendency to have large production units. This tendency is attributable not only to gigantomania, but also to the difficulty for a centralized planning system to manage a very large number of enterprises. Whatever the reasons, the fact remains that few small factories are built, and the average size of industrial establishment is many times larger in the USSR than in any Western country. This has created difficulties in small towns in such regions as Belorussia and the western Ukraine; a town of 20,000-30,000 inhabitants is unlikely to be an adequate base for a factory employing several thousand, even though there may be 100 or more available workers. Since there is officially no unemployment, nor unemployment compensation—and also no compulsory transfer of labor—the local authorities may insist on local workers' being employed even when they are surplus to the local managers' requirements.

This issue is related to another, the tendency for planners and ministries to direct investment to already developed industrial areas. The motive is understandable, and is encountered in all systems: it seems economical to put new factories where the infrastructure and social overhead capital already exist, near the location of major customers and suppliers. But such a policy conflicts with the declared objective of evening out, or at least not enhancing, differences of development among regions.

The drive toward cost-saving, and toward fulfillment of short-run plans, is also responsible for neglect of conservation and environmental protection. The most accessible forests are cut down, the most conveniently located mines and oil wells speedily and ruthlessly exploited. Some industrial regions suffer greatly from pollution. Serious ecological damage is done to rivers.

It is partly the exhaustion of more accessible resources, and partly the great potential riches of the area, that presents the USSR today with its greatest regional development challenge: Siberia. This region has been described as the greatest (certainly the largest) underdeveloped area in the world. Its mineral and forestry resources are vast. It is already producing the major part of Soviet oil and natural gas, and an increasing share of its coal. However, population is sparse, communications are inadequate, many of the most valuable minerals and fuels are in the frozen North, where new towns have to be built and to which it is necessary to move food, building materials, machines, and people over trackless wastes and at very heavy cost.

It has been calculated that about 90 percent of the fuel reserves of the USSR are east of the Urals, but 90 percent of the industry and people are west of the Urals. All this adds up to a vast transportation problem. While the new Baikal-Amur trunk line, soon to be completed, will facilitate movement from central

Siberia to the Pacific, and open up new mineral-rich areas of southern Iakutia, it will do nothing to relieve the grossly over-loaded line from central Siberia westward. All this presents a for-midable challenge: organizational, technological, social. People have to be persuaded to go east, and to stay there, without the use of force. High wages alone will not be enough: living conditions must be created that will compensate for the harsh climate.

This brings one back to the problems of regional planning. Numerous reports speak of the fragmentation of what should be a coordinated effort. Each ministry builds its own houses, canteens, factories, road links, supply depots. Often there is no one in charge of the project as a whole, be it a petrochemical complex or the building of a new town. There are delays because the work is not done in the proper sequence: each ministry has its own time-table and priorities. Journals such as EKO (the organ of the Eco-nomic Institute of the Siberian Academy of Sciences) have reported many such difficulties, and efforts are being made to overcome them by the creation of "territorial production complexes" (TPK) that transcend both ministerial and local-government jurisdictions.

The difficulty is how to "fit" this regional authority into a structure based on industrial and construction ministries, which appoint managers, fix plan targets, suballocate materials, and finance investments. Who at the center is to be the superior of a TPK? Gosplan? But this body is already overwhelmed with its regular planning duties. We may soon see a determined effort to redefine or perhaps even to supplant the ministerial structure, with powers for supermanagers of regionally based industrial and agro-industrial complexes. But such a change will be resisted by exist-ing ministerial and territorial authorities, which would lose power through such an arrangement. Moreover, such a development would do nothing to ease the troubles of urban planning, which are due to the priority of production, and of ministries in charge of production. The local soviet has planning powers on paper, but many reports show that it is often overruled or simply ignored.

Two other matters are worth mentioning here. One is the frequently criticized tendency to ignore regional or climatic differ-ences when designing products. Thus vehicles and other machines fail to stand up to the severe climate of Siberia, while at the other extreme the buses supplied to semitropical Ashkhabad have too much glass and too little ventilation, causing acute discomfort to passengers. The needs of the temperate zone predominate in de-sign bureaus, another instance of the lack of users' influence on production decisions.

The second matter relates to agriculture. Space forbids de-tailed analysis of the many "regional" difficulties. Some relate to machinery: special circumstances are too often ignored—as is shown, for instance, by a decade of complaint about the type of plows supplied to the formerly virgin lands of northern Kazakhstan. There are also complaints about inflexible plans imposed from above, which stand in the way of profitable specialization and, naturally, are unlikely to fit the quite varied soil and climate of a vast land area, though in this respect there has been some improvement. Instead of being ordered to grow almost every crop and keep almost every kind of animal, some areas have been encouraged, or allowed, or sometimes even ordered, to specialize. Thus the Baltic states have concentrated on meat and dairy produce, and do not have to sell grain. No longer does everyone have to sow corn, as they had to do in Khrushchev's time. Prices paid to farms are now much higher, and so are farm incomes, throughout the USSR. The evidence suggests that republican and local officials have a much larger role in agriculture than their equivalents do in industry, vis-à-vis both the center and the managers. It must be added that poor distribution, lack of transport and packaging materials, and irrationally low retail prices cause great unevenness in food supplies and serious shortages, especially in Russia proper (other than in the favored cities of Moscow and Leningrad).

These, then, are some of the problems that the USSR faces with regard to regional planning and development. I hope that setting them out, though in very general terms, will help the reader to appreciate the detailed studies that follow. Let no one doubt that the difficulties of devising, justifying, and enforcing regional policy are great, and not only in the Soviet Union. It is therefore useful to try always to distinguish those problems that are common to many countries and systems from those that relate specifically to the Soviet economic and political system.

# I
# SELECTED PROBLEMS
# OF REGIONAL DEVELOPMENT
# IN THE USSR

# 2

# POPULATION AND LABOR FORCE

## Warren W. Eason

For some time, any discussion of the economics of Soviet labor has focused on the impending "crisis" in labor supply. In fact, by the nature of demographic processes—involving intergenerational cohort links and changing spatial relationships over time—the crisis, and in particular its regional manifestations, has been predictable for more than 20 years.[1]

The dimensions of the crisis are, therefore, well known: a slowdown in the growth of labor supply in overall quantitative terms; a drying up of traditional sources of supply (from agriculture); and an aggravation of long-standing regional disparities in labor supply, with which the system continues to experience great difficulty in dealing. Furthermore, what had been an impending crisis in Soviet labor supply is now a current event.

The present chapter is concerned with the fundamentals of the crisis in terms of the underlying demographic variables, examined on a region-by-region basis, although it is understood that the real crisis is not in demographic change per se but in the pressures generated with respect to labor policies and practices. In response to these pressures, major accommodations will have to be introduced to increase the effectiveness with which the given labor force is developed, distributed, and utilized on the job. In other words, greater attention will have to be paid to increasing productivity, if the decline in the rate of growth of the labor force and the persistent misallocation of labor are not to be translated into a decline in the rate of growth of production.

The present chapter is concerned with the underlying demographic variables on a region-by-region basis, because it is in these terms that some indication of the scope and severity of the crisis can be given in quantitative terms. Recognizing the growing

11

body of literature on the subject,[2] the chapter develops some new measures, in some instances from old data, and reexamines existing measures from different perspectives. The result is to indicate with some precision the paths that the regions seem to be taking as they move into the crisis period so long predicted, and to outline in the same quantitative terms some of the options that may be open to the respective regions in response to the shifting patterns of labor supply.

The chapter is organized around three interrelated sources of demographic influence on Soviet labor supply by regions: the population of working ages; the distribution of employment between agricultural and nonagricultural occupations; and the rural–urban distribution of the population as the basis for projecting regional labor supply differentials.

LABOR SUPPLY AND THE POPULATION
OF WORKING AGES

Given relative stability, at fairly high levels, in the proportion of the Soviet (adult) population in the labor force (a characteristic of Soviet experience that antedates the Soviet era), and given also the insignificance of external migration, the size and structure of the total labor force as a measure of total labor supply is very much a function of the size and structure of the population of working ages.[3] Thus the decline in the rate of growth of the Soviet labor force, presently under way, may be seen as a decline in the rate of growth of the population of working ages; and the latter, in turn, may be seen as reflecting past trends in fertility and mortality, particularly in fertility.

Population fertility at different times in the past influences the rate of growth of the working-age population through its effect on the numbers entering (at age 16) and leaving (at age 55 for females and 60 for males) during the given year. For most of the years under consideration here (1976-2016), the pattern of growth tends to be dominated by the number entering the working ages, primarily because the number leaving is relatively small. Those leaving, at the upper age limits, between 1976 and 2016 are the ones born between 1916/1921 and 1946/1951, the cohorts of which were decimated (some repeatedly) by reduced births and increased deaths, caused mainly by the two world wars and their aftermath, but also by the turmoil attending collectivization in the early 1930s.

The dominant effect of recent fertility trends on the growth of the working-age population, for the country as a whole as well as for each of the republics, is shown in Figure 2.1, where the annual

## FIGURE 2.1

The Crude Birth Rate (Births per 1,000 Population), as Reported
and Projected, Compared with the Annual Percentage Change
in the Population of Working Ages 16 Years Later, as
Projected from 1970 Census Data:
USSR and Republics, 1950–2000

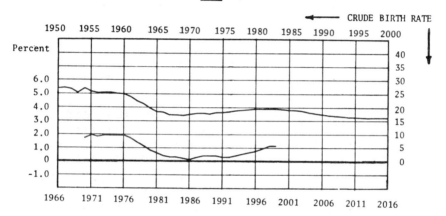

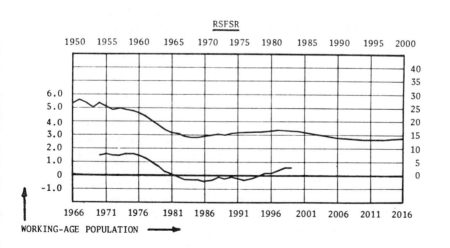

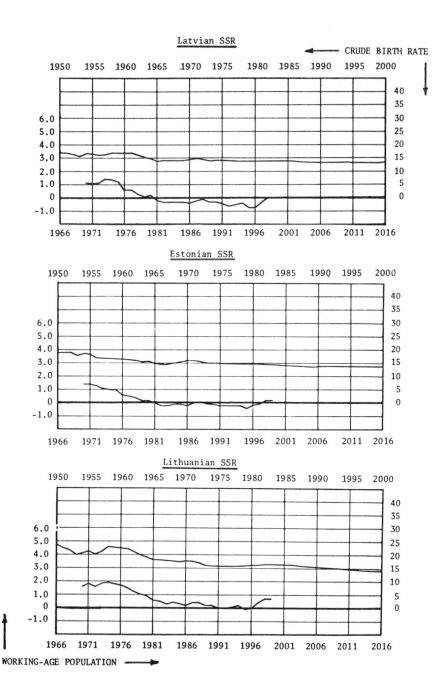

Latvian SSR

CRUDE BIRTH RATE

Estonian SSR

Lithuanian SSR

WORKING-AGE POPULATION

14

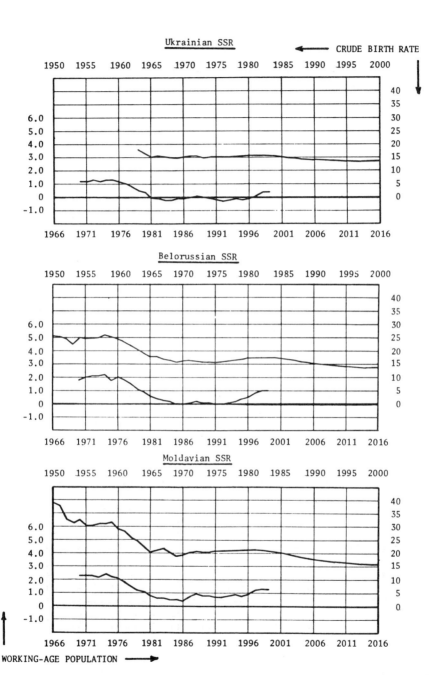

Ukrainian SSR

Belorussian SSR

Moldavian SSR

CRUDE BIRTH RATE

WORKING-AGE POPULATION

15

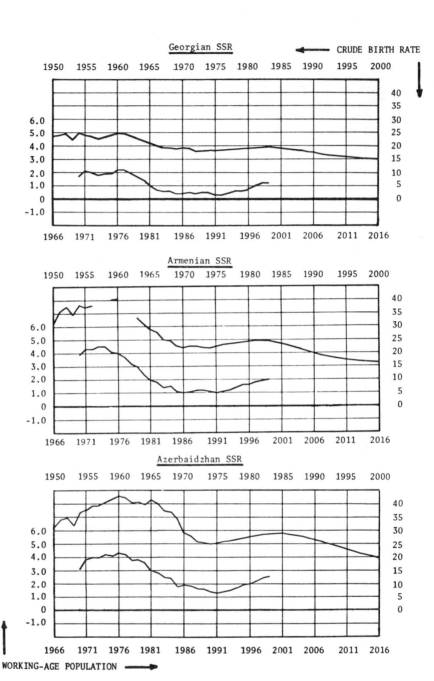

Georgian SSR

CRUDE BIRTH RATE

Armenian SSR

Azerbaidzhan SSR

WORKING-AGE POPULATION

16

## Kazakh SSR

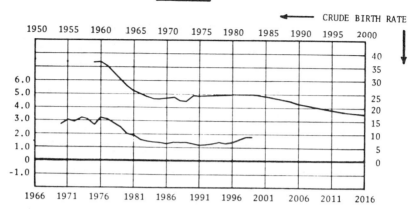

CRUDE BIRTH RATE

## Kirgiz SSR

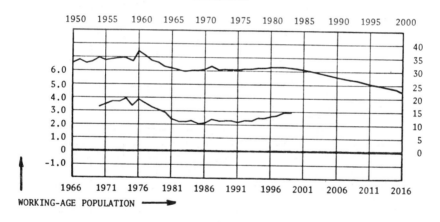

WORKING-AGE POPULATION ➤

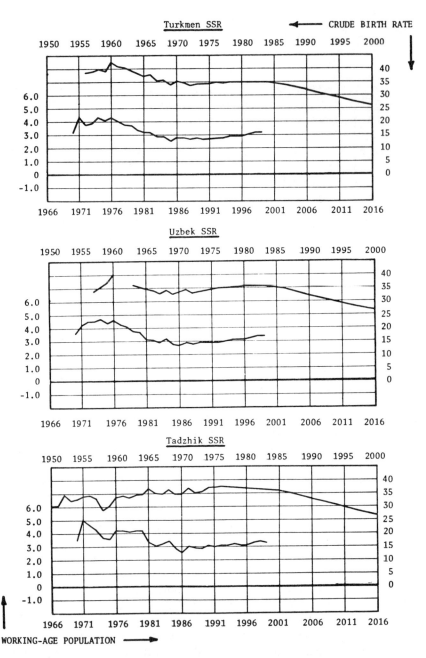

Note: In each graph, the top curve represents the crude birth rate for the respective region, read across the top and down the right side, and the bottom curve represents the corresponding annual percentage change in the population of working ages, read across the bottom and up the left side.

Source: Appendix Table 2.1.

18

crude birth rates, as reported for 1950 through 1975 and projected from 1976 to 2000, are compared with the annual percentage change in the working-age population 16 years later. For the USSR as a whole (the first graph in Figure 2.1), the rate of growth of the working-age population shows a decline—from about 2 percent per year in the 1960s and 1970s to only 0.1 or 0.2 percent in the 1980s—followed by a "recovery," to about 1 percent per year, during the 1990s. From 1970 to 1986 the indicated trends are reasonably firm "predictions" of reality, because they are based on data by age groups from the 1970 Soviet census, projected according to age-specific mortality assumptions in which the margin of uncertainty is relatively small. Trends are also reasonably firm from 1987 to 1992, because they incorporate crude birth rates as reported from 1971 to 1976. After 1992, however, trends in the growth of the working-age population are more difficult to predict, because they require an assumption about fertility after 1976. The assumption used in the projections from which Figure 2.1 is constructed is that fertility will decline by 6 percent overall in the country as a whole between 1976 and 2000. Derived from the projections based on this assumption, the crude birth rate will "peak" in the early 1980s and then decline again, to a level by the end of the century that is almost 5 per 1,000 below the peak.

With a lag of 16 years, the rate of growth of the working-age population will reach what appears to be a "peak" around the year 2000. And if we follow the implications of the fertility projections further than drawn in Figure 2.1, the rate of growth of the working-age population will probably show a decline once again after 2000, reaching perhaps zero growth, or even becoming negative, in the second decade of the twenty-first century. Beginning about 2006, moreover, the decline in the rate of growth in the number entering the working ages, suggested by the assumed 6 percent fertility decline after 1976, may very well be aggravated by the growing number leaving the working ages—males born after 1946 and females born after 1951, when birth rates were recovering to moderately high levels and infant mortality was declining.

To summarize, the pattern of change in the working-age population for the USSR as a whole, for the next three or four decades, will likely be in the form of mild "cyclical" movement around a long-term average that is only slightly on the positive side, perhaps no more than 0.5 percent per year. Such a prospect contrasts sharply with the long-term average of 1.5 percent that has existed (in peacetime) since the 1920s (except for the short-term dip in 1958-62 caused by reduced births during the war).[4]

In these terms, the emerging pattern of labor supply will be fundamentally different from anything the Soviets have experienced

since the beginning of rapid industrialization in 1928. And because
the decline in the rate of growth of the working-age population that
has ushered in the new era has taken place in a relatively short
period of time, the transformation has been dramatic: from a country where labor has been the relatively "abundant" resource and
labor policies and practices have reflected this abundance, to one
where labor is relatively "scarce" and must be treated as such if
economic performance is not to suffer.

So much for recent and prospective trends in the working-age
population for the country as a whole. What about the regions of
the country? Regional trends are also shown in Figure 2.1, comparing crude birth rates with the corresponding change in the
working-age population for each of the 15 republics. Trends for
the RSFSR closely parallel those for the country as a whole, not
surprising since the bulk of the population lives in the RSFSR.
Taken by itself, however, the crude birth rate is somewhat lower
than for the whole country and the rate of growth of the working-
age population also is lower, declining absolutely by up to 0.5 percent per year from 1982 to 1994. For the other republics there are
both similarities and differences compared with the national figures.
For one thing, every republic shows a decline in the crude birth
rate from about 1960.[5] The universal nature of the decline is understandable because it has its roots in the lowered fertility during
World War II, which all segments of the population experienced,
and which, in turn, caused a relative decline in the population of
prime reproductive ages (prospective parents) during the 1960s.

Every republic, therefore, also shows a decline in the rate of
growth of the working-age population beginning in the mid-1970s.
The pattern of the decline in the growth rates is shown in Table 2.1,
where, for each republic, the highest growth rate in the high-growth
years of the mid-1970s is compared with the lowest growth rate of
the low-growth years of the 1980s and early 1990s, and each set is
arrayed in descending order. The corresponding percentage-point
difference between the highest and lowest rates is also given. Two
characteristics of regional growth of the working-age population
emerge from the data in Table 2.1. The first is the wide divergence
among republics in their respective growth rates, ranging, during
the highest growth years of the 1970s, from 5.0 percent in the
Tadzhik to 1.3 percent in the Ukrainian SSR, and during the lowest
growth years of the 1980s and early 1990s, from 2.9 percent in the
Tadzhik to -0.7 percent in the Latvian SSR. The second characteristic among republics is a uniformity in the magnitude of decline
from the highest to the lowest growth years; in most cases growth
rates declined by very close to 2 percentage points. The exceptions
are the Armenian and Azerbaidzhan SSRs, which show a greater

percentage decline (3.5 and 3.0 percentage points) than the others, in all likelihood because of a decline in age-specific fertility in the 1960s that reinforced the decline in the number of prospective parents experienced by all republics, and the Ukrainian SSR, which shows a decline of only 1.6 percentage points. The uniformity of decline among republics in terms of percentage points means, of course, that the degree of divergence between republics with relatively high and low growth levels (see Table 2.1) will tend to increase over the period 1991-96.

What are the implications of these regional patterns of growth of the working-age population for regional labor supply? It depends on whether one focuses on divergent levels of growth in the 1980s and early 1990s or on changes in these levels. Most discussions have focused on the levels of growth, as expressed in Table 2.1 in terms of the absolute changes in the working-age population from 1980 to 1995, comparing the two groupings of republics. All of the growth in the working-age population in the period 1980-95 will take place in the republics with relatively high growth levels, while the population of working ages in the other republics will decline by 1,551,000.

These developments will greatly aggravate the imbalance in labor supply that already exists between the republics with relatively high and those with low growth levels. The implication is that there will be greatly increased pressure on Soviet planners to get labor to move from the one cluster of republics to the other—or to redirect investment in that direction—if productivity is not to suffer. The focus, in other words, is on the growing surplus of labor in certain areas of the country, and the central question is whether it may be tapped in order to achieve a more effective utilization of human resources in the national economy.

If one focuses, on the other hand, on the changes in the rate of growth of the working-age population, then it must be asked whether the fairly precipitous decline in the rate at which labor is becoming available for work—by two or more percentage points per year—might not have a "tightening" effect on labor supply even in the republics with relatively high levels of population growth. After all, if the institutions of labor supply and utilization in a given republic are accustomed to increases in the stock of labor of 3-5 percent per year (as in Central Asia, Armenia, and Azerbaidzhan), might not rates of 1-3 percent represent a considerable downward shift in their pattern of labor supply?

What we are dealing with here are differentials in the rate of growth of the working-age population over time as well as over space. Over space, the RSFSR and most of the rest of European USSR are projected to experience growth in the working-age popula-

# TABLE 2.1

Changes in Growth Rate of Working-Age Population, and Absolute Changes, 1975-95

| Highest Percentage of High Growth Years | | Lowest Percentage of Low Growth Years | | Percentage-Point Difference Between Highest and Lowest |
|---|---|---|---|---|
| Republics with Relatively High Growth Levels | | | | |
| Tadzhik SSR | 5.0 | Tadzhik SSR | 2.9 | -2.1 |
| Uzbek SSR | 4.7 | Uzbek SSR | 2.7 | -2.0 |
| Armenian SSR | 4.5 | Turkmen SSR | 2.6 | -1.7 |
| Azerbaidzhan SSR | 4.3 | Kirgiz SSR | 2.1 | -1.8 |
| Turkmen SSR | 4.3 | Azerbaidzhan SSR* | 1.3 | -3.0* |
| Kirgiz SSR | 3.9 | Kazakh SSR | 1.2 | -2.0 |
| Kazakh SSR | 3.2 | Armenian SSR* | 1.0 | -3.5* |

Total Working-Age Population (Jan 1)

| | | |
|---|---|---|
| 1975 | 22,106,000 | |
| 1980 | 26,428,000 | (1975-95) +14,794,000 (+67.0%) |
| 1995 | 36,900,000 | (1980-95) +10,472,000 (+39.6%) |

Republics with Relatively Low Growth Levels

| Republic | | Republic | |
|---|---|---|---|
| Moldavian SSR | 2.4 | Moldavian SSR | -2.0 |
| Georgian SSR | 2.2 | Georgian SSR | -1.9 |
| Belorussian SSR | 2.2 | Belorussian SSR | -2.2 |
| USSR | 1.9 | USSR | -2.0 |
| Lithuanian SSR | 1.9 | Lithuanian SSR | -2.0 |
| RSFSR | 1.6 | Ukrainian SSR | -1.6* |
| Estonian SSR | 1.4 | RSFSR | -2.0 |
| Latvian SSR | 1.4 | Estonian SSR | -1.8 |
| Ukrainian SSR | 1.3 | Latvian SSR | -2.1 |

| | | Republic | |
|---|---|---|---|
| 0.4 | Moldavian SSR | | |
| 0.3 | Georgian SSR | | |
| 0.0 | Belorussian SSR | | |
| -0.1 | USSR | | |
| -0.1 | Lithuanian SSR | | |
| -0.3 | Ukrainian SSR | | |
| -0.4 | RSFSR | | |
| -0.4 | Estonian SSR | | |
| -0.7 | Latvian SSR | | |

*Total Working-Age Population (Jan 1)*

| 1975 | 120,911,000 | |
|---|---|---|
| 1980 | 128,377,000 | (1975-95) + 3,859,000 (+3.2%) |
| 1995 | 126,826,000 | (1980-95) - 1,551,000 (-1.2%) |

USSR: *Total Working-Age Population (Jan 1)*

| 1975 | 143,018,000 | |
|---|---|---|
| 1980 | 156,806,000 | (1975-95) +20,710,000 (+14.5%) |
| 1995 | 163,728,000 | (1980-95) + 6,922,000 (+4.4%) |

*Republics with exceptional changes in growth rates.
Sources: Figure 2.1; Appendix Table 2.1.

tion that is (algebraically) considerably less than that in Central Asia and the Transcaucasus. Over time, each republic in the Soviet Union will experience a slowdown in the rate of growth compared with that in its own historical past. Every region, therefore, can be thought of as experiencing, to some degree, a growing labor "shortage" in its own terms.

The view across space sees the pressures of a "shortage" developing in European USSR alone, and the solution lying partly in the movement of labor from the labor-surplus areas of Central Asia and the Transcaucasus to the labor-deficit areas further north. The view across time sees elements of "shortage" appearing everywhere, where "shortage" is defined as a marked slowdown in the rate of growth of underlying labor supply compared with what it had been and in terms of which patterns of utilization of labor had been well established. Labor "market" and planning institutions accommodated to a 4 percent rate of growth of labor, for example, will now have to contend with 2 percent or less. Exactly what kind of pressures or constraints this situation will generate is difficult to say without being able to relate the changed labor flows to the underlying production-function relationships in the given area. Nevertheless, reduced flows of labor would seem to place additional obstacles in the way of releasing labor for the benefit of the "deficit" areas of the country.


LABOR SUPPLY AND THE DISTRIBUTION OF
EMPLOYMENT BETWEEN AGRICULTURAL
AND NONAGRICULTURAL OCCUPATIONS

The size and rate of growth of total labor supply in the USSR are primarily functions of the size and growth rate of the population of working ages, but the size and rate of growth of labor supply to nonagricultural occupations are also functions of distribution between agricultural and nonagricultural occupations and the rate of population movement from the one to the other.

During the first peacetime decades of development, nonagricultural employment increased at the relatively high rates of 8-10 percent per year in the 1930s and 3-5 percent in the 1950s and 1960s, as a result of a 1.5 percent average increase in the working-age population; a very high proportion of the population in agriculture, starting at 85 percent in 1928 and remaining above 50 percent until the late 1950s; and regular population migration to urban areas. It was because of such a large pool of human resources in agriculture, and steady growth in the working-age population, that the Soviet economy was able to keep its rapidly growing nonagricultural sectors supplied with labor during the first three decades of industrialization, and at the same time absorb the catastrophic demographic effects of World War II.[6]

The 1950s ended with a spurt of growth in nonagricultural employment (10.9 percent in 1960), joined to an equally sharp decrease in agricultural employment (-7.8 percent) while total employment increased by 3.9 percent (see Appendix Table 2.2). Such exceptional changes in employment in one year were evidently a reaction to the slowdown in the rate of growth of the working-age population, and with it of employment, that had been caused by the entry into the working ages (in 1958-62) of the cohorts born during the war.

After 1960 the growth rates of nonagricultural employment declined, returning gradually to "normal," but then continued to decline into the 1970s. And the declining trend took place not only on the average for the USSR as a whole, but in every republic as well. The trends for the republics are shown in Figure 2.2 in the form of three-year moving averages of annual percentage increases in average annual employment in nonagricultural occupations for each of the 15 republics from 1958 to 1974 (annual data from 1957 to 1975). From peak increases in or around 1960—from 8 or 9 percent per year in Central Asia to 5 or 6 percent in European USSR—the moving averages show a declining rate of increase thereafter, reaching 3 or 4 percent in Central Asia and 1 or 2 percent in European Russia by 1974. The declines registered by the republics from the early 1960s to the mid-1970s are on the order of four or five percentage points.

The rates of growth of nonagricultural employment at the end of the period of decline are quite low by the historical experience of the respective republics, and this may explain why the series on employment, by republic, from which the growth rates were derived, ceased publication after 1975. From the data for the USSR as a whole, however, which continue to be published, growth of nonagricultural employment continues on a slightly downward path, holding at 2.1 percent in 1977 and 1978 (the latest years available; see Appendix Table 2.2). Considering that nonagricultural employment—jobs paying wages and salaried positions in state enterprises—which the series in Figure 2.2 represents, constitutes a priority sector in labor allocation, the authorities may very well feel that the slowdown indicated by the recent data, and the likelihood that it will continue, requires concealment.

It is entirely possible that a serious slowdown in the rate of growth of nonagricultural employment may set in after 1980, as an indirect result of the slowdown in the growth of the working-age population. But in fact it began to appear ten years earlier, when the rate of growth of the working-age population in the various

# FIGURE 2.2

## Annual Percentage Change in Average Annual Employment in Nonagricultural Occupations: By Republics, According to Three-Year Moving Averages, 1958-74

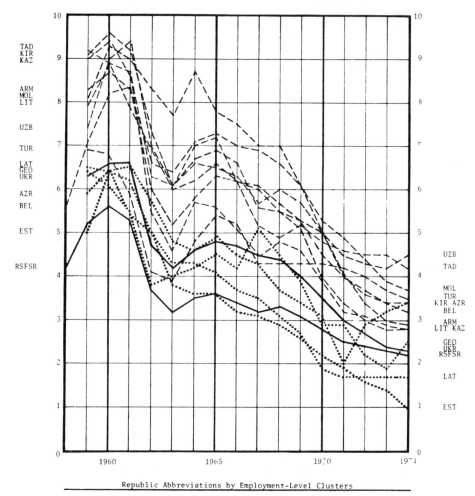

Republic Abbreviations by Employment-Level Clusters

| Lithuanian SSR | LIT | Russian | | Latvian SSR | LAT |
|---|---|---|---|---|---|
| Belorussian SSR | BEL | Soviet | | Estonian SSR | EST |
| Armenian SSR | ARM | Federated Socialist | | Georgian SSR | GEO |
| Moldavian SSR | MOL | Republic | RSFSR | Azerbaidzhan SSR | AZR |
| Kazakh SSR | KAZ | Ukrainian SSR | UKR | | |
| Uzbek SSR | UZB | | | | |
| Turkmen SSR | TUR | | | | |
| Tadzhik SSR | TAD | | | | |
| Kirgiz SSR | KIR | | | | |

Source: Derived from annual percentages in Appendix Table 2.2.

republics was running at historical highs of 1-4 percent per year. What it may reflect, therefore, is growing difficulty, after 1960, of getting labor to move from agricultural to nonagricultural occupations. We may infer this possibility from the data in Figure 2.3, where annual percentage changes in total and agricultural as well as nonagricultural employment are compared for each republic (and the USSR) from 1957 through 1975. (The three-year moving-average increases in nonagricultural employment in Figure 2.2 were derived from the annual increases in Figure 2.3 and Appendix Table 2.2.) Figure 2.3 also reproduces time series on agricultural employment as a percentage of total employment for each republic.

Note from Figure 2.3, first, that the exceptional characteristics of the years 1959-61, referred to above, hold for each of the individual republics as well: an exceptionally high rate of increase of nonagricultural employment (dotted lines); a relatively high rate of increase of total employment (solid lines); and an absolute decrease in agricultural employment. Even in the republics of Central Asia and the Transcaucasus, the large increase in nonagricultural employment in these years could be supported only through an absolute decrease in the number employed in agriculture.

After 1959-61 the increases in nonagricultural employment for each republic tend to move downward. In those republics where the growth of total employment is relatively low (RSFSR, Baltic republics, and the Ukraine), it requires a decrease in agricultural employment for most years to support even a declining rate of growth of nonagricultural employment. In those republics where the growth of total employment is relatively high (Central Asia, Azerbaidzhan, and Armenia), agricultural employment increases for most years along with nonagricultural employment. But the trend line of growth in nonagricultural employment for these republics is nevertheless downward.

The downward trend line suggests that even in these republics a certain "tightening" of labor supply sets in before the effects of the slowdown in the rate of growth of the working-age population are felt (after 1980). The explanation probably lies with agricultural employment as a percentage of total employment, which not only is declining but also is beginning to reach levels in these republics that will have an increasingly constraining effect on the supply of labor to the nonagricultural sectors. The percentage for 1975 for each republic (from Figure 2.3 and Appendix Table 2.2) is as follows:

| | |
|---|---|
| Moldavian SSR | 44.4 |
| Turkmen SSR | 39.0 |
| Uzbek SSR | 37.7 |
| Tadzhik SSR | 37.1 |

## FIGURE 2.3

### Percentage Change in Average Annual Employment, and Agricultural Employment as a Percentage of Total: By Republics, 1955-78

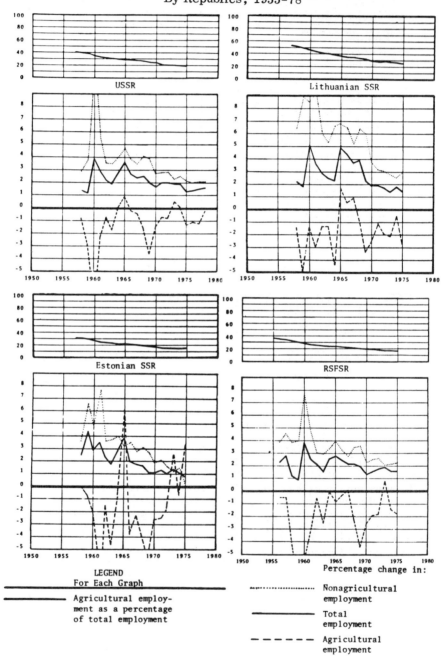

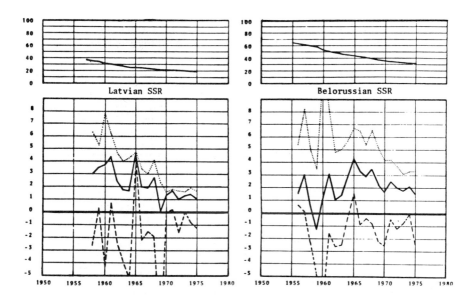

Latvian SSR          Belorussian SSR

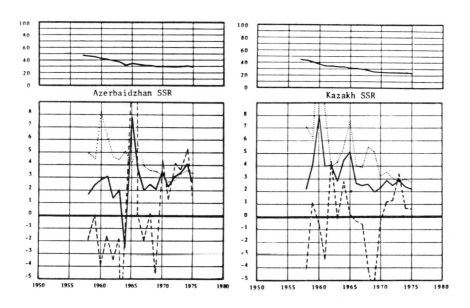

Azerbaidzhan SSR          Kazakh SSR

29

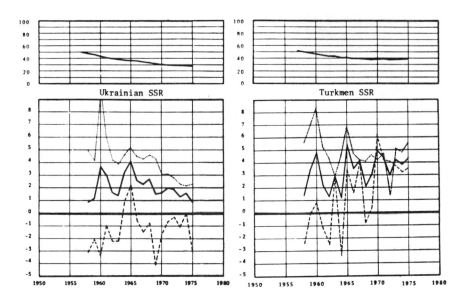

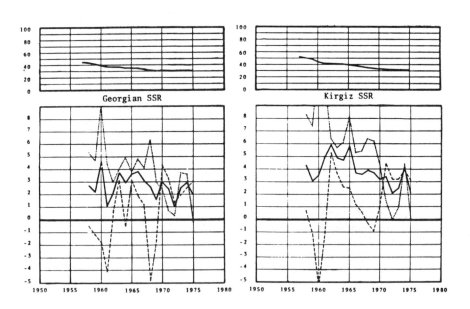

30

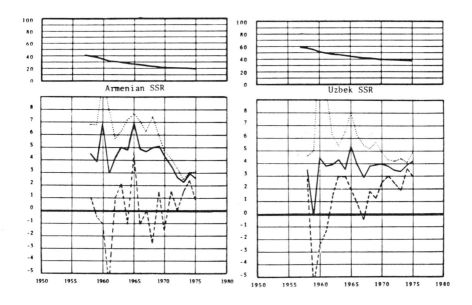

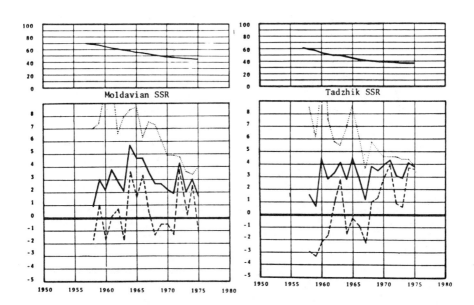

Source: Appendix Table 2.2.

31

| | |
|---|---|
| Kirgiz SSR | 31.1 |
| Belorussian SSR | 31.0 |
| Georgian SSR | 30.2 |
| Azerbaidzhan SSR | 29.7 |
| Ukrainian SSR | 27.0 |
| Lithuanian SSR | 25.4 |
| Kazakh SSR | 23.8 |
| USSR | 20.8 |
| Armenian SSR | 19.6 |
| Latvian SSR | 19.1 |
| Estonian SSR | 17.4 |
| RSFSR | 16.5 |

Except for the four republics at the top of the list, the share of employment in agriculture in the others is less than one-third; and this means, ignoring growth in total employment, that it tends to take twice as large a percentage from agriculture to yield a given percentage increase in nonagricultural employment. But even if the growth of total employment is taken into account, it is true that the smaller the proportion of employment in agriculture, the greater the strain on the agricultural sector to support a given percentage rate of growth of nonagricultural employment.

Thus, the republics with 31 percent or less of employment in agriculture, tending also to be those with a low rate of growth of total employment, required a decrease in agricultural employment in the mid-1970s to support even a modest increase in nonagricultural employment. Exceptions are the Estonian SSR, where nonagricultural employment increased by only 0.3 percent, and the Kazakh, Armenian, and Azerbaidzhan SSRs, where higher rates of growth of total employment permitted small increases in agricultural employment. The four republics at the top of the list, tending to be those with high rates of growth of total employment, continue to support high rates of growth of both agricultural and nonagricultural employment. But for these the trend line of growth of nonagricultural employment in the 1960s and early 1970s is downward, and the rates themselves, by 1975, though high in relation to the other republics, are not exceptional compared with the earlier decades of Soviet development.

The conclusion to be reached from the series in Figure 2.3 is that the tightening of labor supply has come earlier than expected and that it has appeared to some degree in virtually all regions of the country. As a result of reaching certain stages of constraint in labor supply from agricultural occupations, a declining growth trend for nonagricultural employment has already set in that might not have appeared until the 1980s, when it would have been due to the projected slowdown in the rate of growth of the working-age population.

The joint effects on labor supply of a slowdown in the growth of the working-age population and a drying up of agriculture as a source of labor, as noted at the outset of the chapter, have been predicted. It is simply that the constraints from agriculture within the various republics, documented here for the first time, appear to have set in sooner and more uniformly than expected on the basis of earlier predictions. Thus each republic is already experiencing, and will continue to experience, a deepening slowdown in the rate of growth of overall labor supply and its allocation to various sectors. Intraregional pressures from a growing "shortage" of labor over time will therefore mount, and at the same time, interregional differences in the stock and flow of labor are likely to increase. The need to redistribute labor among the regions in the interests of greater efficiency, in order to counter the depressing effects on production and productivity that will otherwise follow the declining growth rates of labor supply, takes on a growing urgency. We turn to this question in the next section of the chapter.

LABOR SUPPLY AND THE RURAL-URBAN DISTRIBUTION
OF THE POPULATION AS THE BASIS FOR PROJECTING
REGIONAL LABOR SUPPLY DIFFERENTIALS

We have already established a basic projection of Soviet labor supply in terms of the working-age population, by republics on an annual basis, to the year 2000 (see Figure 2.1 and Appendix Table 2.1). We would like to create from that base a projection of the labor force and also of employment, in total and by agricultural and nonagricultural occupations, for each of the major regions of the USSR. The results, based on assumptions about the relationships between the population, labor force, and employment, would enable us to chart intraregional changes in labor supply and also give some indication of prospects for interregional movement of labor from surplus to deficit areas.

Unfortunately, past data on the labor force and employment are not sufficient to establish the relationships to the population base on which a projection by regions can be carried out. Data on the labor force (defined as the number of individuals having an occupation on the census date) from the censuses of 1939, 1959, and 1970 are not completely reported by regions, and data on employment (defined as the average number of individuals having a job, on a daily or monthly basis, as reported by various production units[7]) are available by regions only for certain years, as pointed out in connection with Figures 2.2 and 2.3, and have not been published since 1975.

In the absence of required data from the past on which to establish the statistical relationships required for projections, we can utilize available data that will usefully approximate what we need. In place of measures of the total labor force, we can use the population of working ages, and for agricultural/nonagricultural data on the labor force and employment, we can substitute rural/urban data on the population. The results can be only approximate, but by utilizing these surrogates, we will be able to suggest orders of magnitude for the labor supply problem at a more or less uniform and consistent regional level throughout the country. In particular, we will be able to trace the implications, in terms of regional labor supply potential (LSP), of some plausible assumptions about component rates of growth on an annual basis until the year 2000.[8]

We begin with what we know about trends in the distribution and component rates of growth of the total, urban and rural populations (all ages) of each of the oblasts, autonomous republics, and krais of the RSFSR and each of the 14 other republics. Data at this level of detail are available for 1959 and annually thereafter for 1961-65 and 1967-78 (January 1). Using this total urban-rural population breakdown as a crude surrogate for a total-agricultural-nonagricultural labor force breakdown, in the sense described above, we look to the trends in these components to suggest the extent to which given regions may or may not be considered to have a certain LSP for ultimate transfer to the nonagricultural sectors of their own or other regions.

A scan of the percentage of the population in rural areas in 1978 (the latest year available at this writing) reveals considerable variation by region—from over 60 percent in some of the Central Asian republics to around 20 percent in parts of the RSFSR. Having in mind the general relationships set forth above about the effect on labor supply of different proportions of the population in agriculture, it is possible to group the regions of the country (as of 1978) into three categories in terms of their LSP. Those regions with 20-35 percent of the population in rural areas in 1978 are designated as regions of low LSP; those with 35-50, medium LSP; and those with 50-65, high LSP. The results of these designations are pictured in Map 2.1.

It will be noted that the region of low LSP, except for the Volga-Don territory, lies essentially north of the 45th parallel of latitude, including some of the most industrialized and urbanized— and the least hospitable—parts of the country. The region of medium

MAP 2.1

Regions of Low, Medium, and High Labor Supply Potential, According
to Percentage of Population in Rural Areas:  USSR, 1978

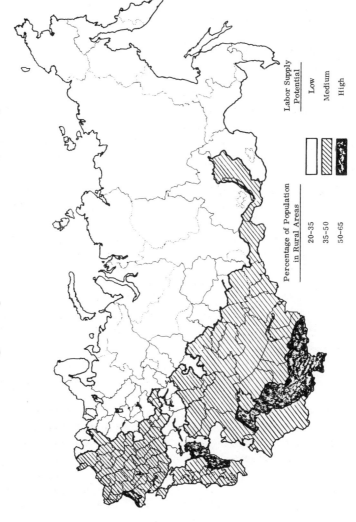

Percentage of Population
in Rural Areas

20-35

35-50

50-65

Labor Supply
Potential

Low

Medium

High

LSP lies south of the 45th parallel, and encompasses the relatively small region of high LSP. The latter includes the Uzbek, Tadzhik, Kirgiz, and Moldavian republics, as well as the Dagestan and Checheno-Ingush autonomous republics of the RSFSR, most of which still have 60 percent or more of their population in rural areas. The Turkmen, Armenian, and Azerbaidzhan republics, although displaying relatively high fertility rates and population growth through the recent past, nevertheless fall within the "medium" range.

Having defined the three regions of LSP in terms of the rural population (all ages) as a percentage of the total, a surrogate for the unavailable data on the labor force within these regions is designated in terms of the population of working ages. As a starting point toward quantification, absolute measures of the total, urban, and rural populations—all ages as well as working ages—may be derived for each of the three regions of LSP for 1959 and 1970, from regional census data reported in Volume II of the 1970 census. And from these data, in turn, it is possible to calculate the respective average annual percentage rates of change between the two censuses. The results, reproduced in Table 2.2, reveal two growth patterns.

First, for each of the three regions taken as a whole, the working-age population increases by less than that of all ages, reflecting the decline and recovery in the rate of growth of the population of working ages that was already under way at the time of the 1959 census but continued to have its effect in the intercensal period.

Second, the intercensal changes in the working-age population of the urban and rural areas separately reflect the different interrelationships in LSP by which the regions are defined. Regions of low LSP show a relatively low rate of growth of the working-age population in urban areas (+1.6) as well as of the total (+0.7), and a relatively small decline in the rural (-1.1), while the rural working-age population as a percentage of the total declines from 34.6 to 28.4. Regions of medium LSP, on the other hand, with the same total growth (+0.7) as the regions of low LSP but a higher percentage in the rural areas (56.8 in 1959 and 42.0 in 1970), show a much higher average rate of growth in the urban areas (+3.4). In regions of high LSP, an even greater increase in the working-age population of urban areas (+4.0) is coupled with an absolute increase in the rural areas (+0.6), a relationship that reflects not only the relatively high rate of growth of the total (+2.0) but also the high percentage in rural areas (64.3 in 1959 and 56.7 in 1970).

Pending the publication of the results of the 1979 census, which (one hopes) will contain adequate data for another pivotal year, we can move forward from 1959-70 on the basis of two sets of data that are available: the annual population (all ages) of rural and urban areas reported for most years since 1959 in sufficient

TABLE 2.2

Total Urban and Rural Population, Percentage Rural, and Average
Annual Intercensal Rates of Change: USSR, 1959 and 1970

|  |  | 1959 | Annual Average Percentage Change | 1970 |
|---|---|---|---|---|
|  | Regions of Low Labor Supply Potential |  |  |  |
|  | Urban | 32,667 | +1.6 | 38,329 |
|  | Rural | 17,301 | -1.1 | 15,290 |
| Working ages | Total | 49,968 | +0.7 | 53,619 |
|  | Percentage rural | 34.6 |  | 28.4 |
|  | Urban | 51,304 | +2.2 | 65,316 |
|  | Rural | 32,369 | -1.4 | 27,735 |
| All ages | Total | 83,673 | +1.0 | 93,051 |
|  | Percentage rural | 38.7 |  | 29.7 |
|  | Regions of Medium Labor Supply Potential |  |  |  |
|  | Urban | 26,443 | +3.4 | 38,321 |
|  | Rural | 34,781 | -2.0 | 27,760 |
| Working ages | Total | 61,224 | +0.7 | 66,081 |
|  | Percentage rural | 56.8 |  | 42.0 |
|  | Urban | 43,282 | +3.3 | 61,967 |
|  | Rural | 64,720 | -0.3 | 62,578 |
| All ages | Total | 108,002 | +1.3 | 124,545 |
|  | Percentage rural | 59.9 |  | 50.2 |
|  | Regions of High Labor Supply Potential |  |  |  |
|  | Urban | 3,078 | +4.0 | 4,628 |
|  | Rural | 5,552 | +0.6 | 6,061 |
| Working ages | Total | 8,630 | +2.0 | 10,689 |
|  | Percentage rural | 64.3 |  | 56.7 |
|  | Urban | 5,392 | +4.6 | 4,708 |
|  | Rural | 11,670 | +2.5 | 15,416 |
| All ages | Total | 17,062 | +3.3 | 20,124 |
|  | Percentage rural | 68.0 |  | 63.9 |

Source: From data in TsSU, Itogi vsesoiuznoi perepisi naseleniia 1970
goda, vol 2 (Moscow), pp. 12-162.

detail that it can be recombined into the regions of low, medium, and high LSP; and single-year estimates (1970-75) and projections (1976-2000) of the population—all ages and working ages—of each of the "economic regions" of the RSFSR and each of the 14 other republics, prepared by Godfrey Baldwin of the Foreign Demographic Analysis Division.[9] With some minor assumptions to establish consistent territorial boundaries, it is possible to assemble the estimated and projected series into regions of low, medium, and high LSP.

These available data leave us in the following position with respect to each of the three regions of LSP: we know the average interrelationships and annual rates of change for the total, urban, and rural populations of all ages and working ages for the intercensal period 1959-70; we can carry these changes forward to 1978 in terms of the total, urban, and rural populations of all ages; and we can estimate (with Baldwin) the natural increase of the total populations of all ages and working ages from 1970 to 1977, and we can project that to 2000.

The question is this: How can we estimate the working-age population in the urban and rural areas separately for each of the three regions from 1970 to 1977, and project the same to 2000—in such a way that it will reflect a plausible, if not likely, pattern of growth rates in terms of their implications for potential labor supply? As far as estimates from 1970 to 1977 are concerned, the answer is that we can carry the 1959-70 average trends forward, modified by the changes that are suggested by the available series on the total, urban, and rural populations of all ages. For projections to 2000, we can extrapolate the trends of the recent past, given the projected total working-age population of each region, by setting the following limiting conditions:

Condition 1. The rate of growth of the urban working-age population can be expected to decrease after the 1970s, but not to a level below +1.0 percent per year. Maintaining such a minimal rate reflects what may well turn out to be the intention of the planners, and it is a rate that is supportable among the regions in terms of the other parameters of change that must be taken into account. A generally higher limit would require unrealistic assumptions about the prospects for the release of labor from agricultural occupations and rural areas. A lower limit, or no growth at all, would signify the failure of the system to capture the LSP of the various parts of the country.

Condition 2. The rural working-age population in the regions of low and medium LSP can be expected to decline absolutely, but not by more than -2.5 percent per year. To decrease by less over most of the period would mean that labor could not be supplied other than out of the region of high LSP at a sufficiently high rate to meet the deficit of the region of low LSP. To decrease by more over any length of time would require unreasonable assumptions about the growth of productivity in agriculture.

Condition 3. The percentage of the working-age population in rural areas can be expected to decline, but not to below about 15 percent in the region of low LSP and 20 percent in the region of medium LSP by the turn of the century. Together with the limit of a +1.0 percent rate of increase in the urban component and a -2.5 percent decrease in the rural, the gradual decline of the percentage rural to 15-20 percent (outside of the region of high LSP), it is felt, would be broadly consistent with the achievement of developmental goals based on substantial but not impossible increases in labor productivity in both urban and rural areas.

The actual calculations of the projections for each region were carried out by hand, adjusting by trial and error to stay within the limits of the conditions set forth above. (The results are reproduced in Figure 2.4 and Appendix Table 2.3, in terms of the annual percentage rates of change and the percentage of the population in rural areas.)

The end result of the projects is the emergence of measures of a labor "deficit" in the regions of low LSP, and the "balancing" of the deficit with "surpluses" from the other two regions—measuring the "deficit" from a zero base in the 1970s (that is, over and above any "shortages" of labor in this region that may already have existed).

It is shown that the deficit in this sense can initially be met, from 1980 to 1983, by the surplus from the region of medium LSP alone. From 1984 to 1988, the region of high LSP must also contribute from its surplus, reaching the point (in 1988) where about half of the cumulative deficit in the region of low LSP has been covered by each of the other two regions. From 1991 to 1995 the region of medium LSP becomes a "deficit" area, but from 1996 to the end of the century, under the rates of growth in urban and rural areas assumed here, the surplus expands in both the medium and high LSP regions—more than enough to cover the projected deficit in the other.

These figures thus open the possibility that about half of the labor deficit of the region of low LSP until about 1990 could be met from the potential surplus of the region of medium LSP, entailing less ambitious assumptions about the policies and practices of labor mobility than if the region of high LSP alone were involved, as is

# FIGURE 2.4

Annual Percentage Rates of Change in Total, Urban, and Rural Population
of All Ages and Working Ages, and Implied Labor-Supply Deficits and
Surpluses: USSR, 1959 and 1970–77, with Projections to 2000

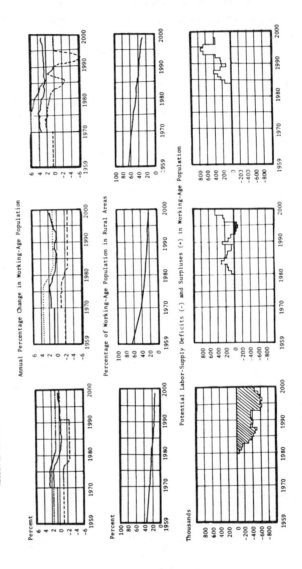

Source: Appendix Table 2.3.

implied by the data of Table 2.1. In other words, subject to the limiting conditions listed above, the region of medium LSP appears capable of meeting its own needs for labor as well as of supplying labor to the region of low LSP, well into the 1980s. Whether Soviet authorities would be able to take advantage of this approach to a labor "balance" is debatable, but the possibilities of moving labor from the medium LSP region to the low LSP region would seem to entail fewer institutional and cultural difficulties than from the region of high LSP alone.

The possibility of labor surpluses in the region of medium LSP also provides time in which to develop and introduce methods for drawing labor from the region of high LSP, recognizing the fact that by the early 1990s the latter will have to be the sole source of additional labor. As shown in Figure 2.4, the needs of the region of low LSP for labor from outside sources continue into the next century—at about 500,000 persons per year, based on the assumption of a 1.0 percent increase in the urban working-age population and no change in the rural after 1991. Beginning about 1995, however, trends in the growth of the working-age population everywhere reverse; the prospect for a "surplus" in the region of medium LSP reappears, and that in the region of high LSP sharply increases (shown in Figure 2.4 as an "extra" surplus after 1996 beyond that needed to "balance" the deficit in the region of low LSP). Figures this far in the future, it must be pointed out, are illustrative, but they cannot be taken too seriously, because they are based on the arbitrary use of one of four fertility variants for the late 1970s on which the projections (from Foreign Demographic Analysis Division) are calculated.

It should also be stressed that all of the projections in Figure 2.4 are not to be considered "predictions" of what will happen or is likely to happen. They are offered as one plausible scenario for regional supply relationships over the next two decades that tries to take into account a more discriminating regional breakdown than heretofore attempted. Other scenarios, of course, are possible. Furthermore, it must be remembered that the data on which the labor surpluses and deficits are based are surrogates for what we would really like to be able to project. The surpluses and deficits are expressed in terms of the working-age population of the rural and urban areas of given regions, whereas we would like to express them in terms of the labor force and employment in agricultural and nonagricultural occupations.

Can we assume that any regularities exist between, say, the agricultural labor force or employment and the corresponding rural population? Perhaps, although the relationships would certainly vary by regions, but the real problem concerns the availability of past data. As far as labor force measures are concerned, which would be preferable for the relationship, Soviet censuses have not reported sufficient (or any) data on the labor force by the rural and urban areas of regions since the census of 1926. The establishment of any relationships or statistical regularities between the labor force and the corresponding population on a consistent regional basis is out of the question.

But we do have measures of average annual employment in agriculture by republics (with no breakdown within the RSFSR, however), as shown in Figure 2.3 and Appendix Table 2.2. From these it is possible to determine average annual employment in agriculture, as a percentage of the corresponding rural population, for each of the 15 republics from about 1957 through 1975. The resulting percentages are set forth in Figure 2.5 and Appendix Table 2.4.

Several characteristics of the percentage ratios emerge:

First, there is a general decline in the percentages, by up to ten percentage points, for each republic between the late 1950s and early 1970s. This is probably due to the high level of rural-urban migration in and around 1960 (reflected in the data of Figure 2.4), which involved a high proportion of adults.

FIGURE 2.5

Average Annual Agricultural Employment as a Percentage
of Rural Population: USSR and Republics, Years
for Which Data Are Available, 1950-78

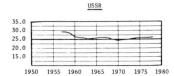

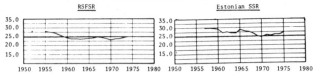

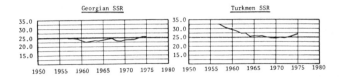

Republics whose percentage is greater
than average for USSR as a whole

Republics whose percentage is less
than average for USSR as a whole

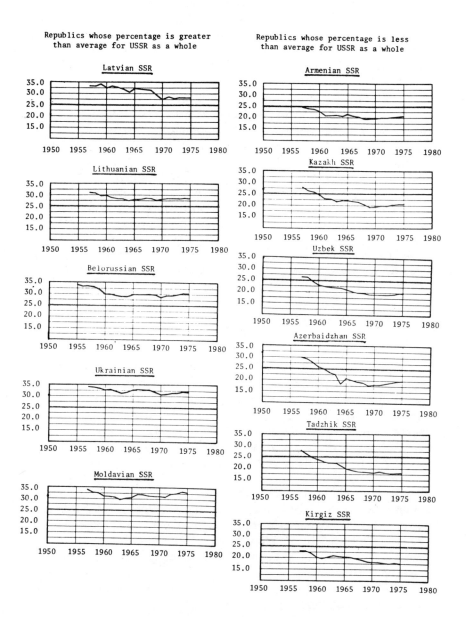

Source: Appendix Table 2.4.

43

Second, on the average for the USSR, agricultural employment is about 25 percent of the rural population, and the percentages displayed by the republics of European USSR are equal to or
somewhat greater than the average. This could reflect a higher
proportion of adults in the rural population, due to a relatively low
birth rate, and an above-average or more intense utilization of
farm labor on a year-round or month-to-month basis. It also could
reflect a higher proportion of the rural population in farming (that
is, a smaller rural nonfarm population), but if anything, the reverse would be the case in the republics of European USSR. The
presence of the Georgian SSR with these European USSR republics
is not unusual, because in a number of other demographic aspects
the Georgian Republic resembles European USSR more than the
Transcaucasus; but the presence of the Turkmen SSR in this group
is difficult to explain. Third, republics with percentages below
average are those in Central Asia and the Armenian and Azerbaidzhan
SSRs. The reasons are probably a smaller proportion of adults in the
rural population, due to a relatively high birth rate, and a higher degree of underemployment and underutilization of farm labor than in
the other republics.

The broad similarity of the trend lines by republics in Figure
2.5 suggests that we may be justified in using the rural population
as a surrogate for agricultural employment and the labor force as
in Figure 2.4. That is, while the figures on surpluses and deficits
(in Figure 2.4) cannot be taken as absolute magnitudes (since they
refer to the working-age population rather than to the labor force
or employment), the distribution between regions of low, medium,
and high LSP may very well be a reasonable indication of the prospects for labor movement in the years ahead.

The configuration in Map 2.1 provides a more graded con-
tinuum of possibilities, compared with the two-part distribution between "surplus" and "deficit" areas. On the other hand, whether
the degrees of surplus or deficit indicated by Map 2.1 can be translated into availability of labor is at best problematical. For the
potential so indicated to be realized requires an understanding of
the potential for moving labor from rural to urban areas (agricultural to nonagricultural occupations) in one and the same region,
and from urban areas in one region to urban areas in another—all
of which raises questions of policies and practices affecting the
distribution and movement of labor that are not considered in this
chapter.

What this chapter has done is to indicate the several degrees
in which the "shortage" of labor within the various regions has developed because of a tightening of labor supply from agricultural
occupations sooner and more generally than predicted, an effect

that will be compounded in the 1980s and 1990s by the predictable slowdown in the growth of the working-age population in all regions; and to show the possibilities for a more discriminating view of labor resources when the RSFSR is subdivided, which tends to increase the prospects for the movement of labor to where it can do the most good. How the authorities will respond to the greater pressures for labor and the greater possibilities for the amelioration of these pressures that this chapter identifies, remains to be seen.

Crude Birth Rate (Births per Thousand Population), as Reported and
Projected, Compared with Annual Percentage Change in Population
of Working Ages 16 Years Later, as Projected from 1970 Census
Data: USSR and Republics, 1950-2000

| Crude Birth Rate | | Population of Working Ages | | | Crude Birth Rate | |
|---|---|---|---|---|---|---|
| Year of Birth | Rate | Year Age 16 | Population (January 1) (thousands) | Percentage Change During Year | Year of Birth | Rate |
| 1950 | 26.7 | 1966 | USSR | | 1984 | 19.1 |
| 1951 | 27.0 | 1967 | | | 1985 | 18.9 |
| 1952 | 26.5 | 1968 | | | 1986 | 18.6 |
| 1953 | 25.1 | 1969 | 130,589 | | 1987 | 18.2 |
| 1954 | 26.6 | 1970 | 132,782 | 1.7 | 1988 | 17.9 |
| 1955 | 25.7 | 1971 | 135,249 | 1.9 | 1989 | 17.6 |
| 1956 | 25.2 | 1972 | 137,733 | 1.8 | 1990 | 17.3 |
| 1957 | 25.4 | 1973 | 140,308 | 1.9 | 1991 | 17.0 |
| 1958 | 25.3 | 1974 | 143,018 | 1.9 | 1992 | 16.8 |
| 1959 | 25.0 | 1975 | 145,745 | 1.9 | 1993 | 16.6 |
| 1960 | 24.9 | 1976 | 148,499 | 1.9 | 1994 | 16.4 |
| 1961 | 23.8 | 1977 | 150,993 | 1.7 | 1995 | 16.3 |
| 1962 | 20.4 | 1978 | 153,078 | 1.4 | 1996 | 16.2 |
| 1963 | 21.2 | 1979 | 154,806 | 1.1 | 1997 | 16.1 |
| 1964 | 19.6 | 1980 | 156,123 | 0.8 | 1998 | 16.1 |
| 1965 | 18.4 | 1981 | 157,014 | 0.6 | 1999 | 16.1 |
| 1966 | 18.2 | 1982 | 157,601 | 0.4 | 2000 | 16.1 |
| 1967 | 17.3 | 1983 | 158,042 | 0.3 | | |
| 1968 | 17.2 | 1984 | 158,455 | 0.3 | | |
| 1969 | 17.0 | 1985 | 158,787 | 0.2 | | |
| 1970 | 17.4 | 1986 | 159,025 | 0.1 | | |
| 1971 | 17.8 | 1987 | 159,522 | 0.3 | | |
| 1972 | 17.8 | 1988 | 160,184 | 0.4 | | |
| 1973 | 17.6 | 1989 | 160,796 | 0.4 | | |
| 1974 | 18.0 | 1990 | 161,417 | 0.4 | | |
| 1975 | 18.1 | 1991 | 161,866 | 0.3 | | |
| 1976 | 18.4 | 1992 | 162,283 | 0.3 | | |
| 1977 | 18.6 | 1993 | 162,893 | 0.4 | | |
| 1978 | 18.8 | 1994 | 163,728 | 0.5 | | |
| 1979 | 19.0 | 1995 | 164,708 | 0.6 | | |
| 1980 | 19.2 | 1996 | 165,791 | 0.7 | | |
| 1981 | 19.3 | 1997 | 167,255 | 0.9 | | |
| 1982 | 19.3 | 1998 | 169,074 | 1.1 | | |
| 1983 | 19.3 | 1999 | 170,968 | 1.1 | | |

(continued)

Appendix Table 2.1, continued

RSFSR

| Crude Birth Rate | | Population of Working Ages | | | Crude Birth Rate | |
|---|---|---|---|---|---|---|
| Year of Birth | Rate | Year Age 16 | Population (January 1) (thousands) | Percentage Change During Year | Year of Birth | Rate |
| 1950 | 26.9 | 1966 | | | 1984 | 16.2 |
| 1951 | 27.1 | 1967 | | | 1985 | 15.9 |
| 1952 | 26.7 | 1968 | | | 1986 | 15.5 |
| 1953 | 25.1 | 1969 | | | 1987 | 15.1 |
| 1954 | 26.8 | 1970 | 73,032 | 1.5 | 1988 | 14.8 |
| 1955 | 25.6 | 1971 | 74,099 | 1.6 | 1989 | 14.4 |
| 1956 | 24.4 | 1972 | 75,288 | 1.5 | 1990 | 14.1 |
| 1957 | 24.7 | 1973 | 76,430 | 1.5 | 1991 | 13.9 |
| 1958 | 24.2 | 1974 | 77,617 | 1.6 | 1992 | 13.7 |
| 1959 | 23.7 | 1975 | 78,835 | 1.6 | 1993 | 13.6 |
| 1960 | 23.2 | 1976 | 80,138 | 1.5 | 1994 | 13.5 |
| 1961 | 21.9 | 1977 | 81,382 | 1.3 | 1995 | 13.5 |
| 1962 | 20.2 | 1978 | 82,446 | 1.0 | 1996 | 13.5 |
| 1963 | 18.8 | 1979 | 83,236 | 0.7 | 1997 | 13.5 |
| 1964 | 16.9 | 1980 | 83,791 | 0.3 | 1998 | 13.6 |
| 1965 | 15.8 | 1981 | 84,066 | 0.1 | 1999 | 13.7 |
| 1966 | 15.4 | 1982 | 84,139 | -0.1 | 2000 | 13.8 |
| 1967 | 14.5 | 1983 | 84,019 | -0.3 | | |
| 1968 | 14.2 | 1984 | 83,802 | -0.3 | | |
| 1969 | 14.2 | 1985 | 83,543 | -0.3 | | |
| 1970 | 14.6 | 1986 | 83,253 | -0.4 | | |
| 1971 | 15.1 | 1987 | 82,900 | -0.3 | | |
| 1972 | 15.3 | 1988 | 82,685 | -0.1 | | |
| 1973 | 15.0 | 1989 | 82,590 | -0.2 | | |
| 1974 | 15.6 | 1990 | 82,462 | -0.1 | | |
| 1975 | 15.7 | 1991 | 82,373 | -0.2 | | |
| 1976 | 15.4 | 1992 | 82,183 | -0.3 | | |
| 1977 | 16.1 | 1993 | 81,959 | -0.2 | | |
| 1978 | 16.3 | 1994 | 81,832 | 0.0 | | |
| 1979 | 16.5 | 1995 | 81,817 | 0.2 | | |
| 1980 | 16.6 | 1996 | 81,948 | 0.2 | | |
| 1981 | 16.7 | 1997 | 82,111 | 0.4 | | |
| 1982 | 16.6 | 1998 | 82,441 | 0.6 | | |
| 1983 | 16.5 | 1999 | 82,934 | 0.6 | | |
| | | | 83,449 | | | |

| Crude Birth Rate | | Population of Working Ages | | | Crude Birth Rate | |
|---|---|---|---|---|---|---|
| Year of Birth | Rate | Year Age 16 | Population (January 1) (thousands) | Percentage Change During Year | Year of Birth | Rate |

Latvian SSR

| Crude Birth Rate | | Population of Working Ages | | | Crude Birth Rate | |
|---|---|---|---|---|---|---|
| 1950 | 17.0 | 1966 | | | 1984 | 13.9 |
| 1951 | 16.7 | 1967 | | | 1985 | 13.8 |
| 1952 | 16.3 | 1968 | | | 1986 | 13.7 |
| 1953 | 15.6 | 1969 | 1,330 | | 1987 | 13.5 |
| 1954 | 16.6 | 1970 | 1,344 | 1.1 | 1988 | 13.4 |
| 1955 | 16.4 | 1971 | 1,359 | 1.1 | 1989 | 13.4 |
| 1956 | 16.0 | 1972 | 1,374 | 1.1 | 1990 | 13.3 |
| 1957 | 16.3 | 1973 | 1,393 | 1.4 | 1991 | 13.3 |
| 1958 | 16.8 | 1974 | 1,413 | 1.4 | 1992 | 13.3 |
| 1959 | 16.7 | 1975 | 1,430 | 1.2 | 1993 | 13.3 |
| 1960 | 16.7 | 1976 | 1,438 | 0.6 | 1994 | 13.3 |
| 1961 | 16.7 | 1977 | 1,446 | 0.6 | 1995 | 13.2 |
| 1962 | 16.1 | 1978 | 1,450 | 0.3 | 1996 | 13.2 |
| 1963 | 15.4 | 1979 | 1,451 | 0.1 | 1997 | 13.2 |
| 1964 | 14.8 | 1980 | 1,454 | 0.2 | 1998 | 13.2 |
| 1965 | 13.9 | 1981 | 1,451 | -0.2 | 1999 | 13.2 |
| 1966 | 14.1 | 1982 | 1,447 | -0.3 | 2000 | 13.3 |
| 1967 | 14.0 | 1983 | 1,442 | -0.3 | | |
| 1968 | 14.1 | 1984 | 1,437 | -0.3 | | |
| 1969 | 14.0 | 1985 | 1,433 | -0.3 | | |
| 1970 | 14.5 | 1986 | 1,427 | -0.4 | | |
| 1971 | 14.7 | 1987 | 1,424 | -0.2 | | |
| 1972 | 15.6 | 1988 | 1,422 | -0.1 | | |
| 1973 | 13.9 | 1989 | 1,418 | -0.3 | | |
| 1974 | 14.2 | 1990 | 1,414 | -0.3 | | |
| 1975 | 14.0 | 1991 | 1,408 | -0.4 | | |
| 1976 | 13.9 | 1992 | 1,400 | -0.6 | | |
| 1977 | 13.8 | 1993 | 1,393 | -0.5 | | |
| 1978 | 13.8 | 1994 | 1,388 | -0.4 | | |
| 1979 | 13.8 | 1995 | 1,378 | -0.7 | | |
| 1980 | 13.9 | 1996 | 1,369 | -0.7 | | |
| 1981 | 13.9 | 1997 | 1,365 | -0.3 | | |
| 1982 | 13.9 | 1998 | 1,365 | 0.0 | | |
| 1983 | 13.9 | 1999 | 1,365 | 0.0 | | |

(continued)

# Appendix Table 2.1, continued

| Crude Birth Rate | | Population of Working Ages | | | Crude Birth Rate | |
| Year of Birth | Rate | Year Age 16 | Population (January 1) (thousands) | Percentage Change During Year | Year of Birth | Rate |
|---|---|---|---|---|---|---|
| | | | Estonian SSR | | | |
| 1950 | 18.7 | 1966 | | | 1984 | 14.3 |
| 1951 | 18.8 | 1967 | | | 1985 | 14.1 |
| 1952 | 18.9 | 1968 | | | 1986 | 14.0 |
| 1953 | 17.8 | 1969 | | | 1987 | 13.9 |
| 1954 | 18.4 | 1970 | 763 | 1.4 | 1988 | 13.8 |
| 1955 | 18.2 | 1971 | 774 | 1.4 | 1989 | 13.7 |
| 1956 | 16.9 | 1972 | 785 | 1.3 | 1990 | 13.7 |
| 1957 | 16.8 | 1973 | 795 | 1.1 | 1991 | 13.7 |
| 1958 | 16.7 | 1974 | 804 | 1.0 | 1992 | 13.7 |
| 1959 | 16.6 | 1975 | 812 | 1.0 | 1993 | 13.7 |
| 1960 | 16.6 | 1976 | 820 | 0.6 | 1994 | 13.7 |
| 1961 | 16.2 | 1977 | 825 | 0.5 | 1995 | 13.7 |
| 1962 | 15.8 | 1978 | 829 | 0.4 | 1996 | 13.7 |
| 1963 | 15.4 | 1979 | 832 | 0.2 | 1997 | 13.7 |
| 1964 | 15.5 | 1980 | 834 | 0.2 | 1998 | 13.7 |
| 1965 | 14.8 | 1981 | 836 | 0.0 | 1999 | 13.7 |
| 1966 | 14.4 | 1982 | 836 | -0.2 | 2000 | 13.7 |
| 1967 | 14.4 | 1983 | 834 | -0.2 | | |
| 1968 | 15.1 | 1984 | 832 | -0.1 | | |
| 1969 | 15.5 | 1985 | 831 | -0.1 | | |
| 1970 | 15.8 | 1986 | 830 | -0.2 | | |
| 1971 | 16.0 | 1987 | 828 | 0.0 | | |
| 1972 | 15.6 | 1988 | 828 | 0.1 | | |
| 1973 | 15.0 | 1989 | 829 | -0.1 | | |
| 1974 | 15.1 | 1990 | 828 | -0.1 | | |
| 1975 | 14.9 | 1991 | 827 | -0.2 | | |
| 1976 | 14.8 | 1992 | 825 | -0.2 | | |
| 1977 | 14.7 | 1993 | 823 | -0.2 | | |
| 1978 | 14.7 | 1994 | 821 | -0.2 | | |
| 1979 | 14.6 | 1995 | 819 | -0.4 | | |
| 1980 | 14.6 | 1996 | 816 | -0.2 | | |
| 1981 | 14.5 | 1997 | 814 | -0.1 | | |
| 1982 | 14.4 | 1998 | 813 | 0.2 | | |
| 1983 | 14.4 | 1999 | 815 | 0.2 | | |
| | | | 817 | | | |

| Crude Birth Rate | | Population of Working Ages | | | Crude Birth Rate | |
| Year of Birth | Rate | Year Age 16 | Population (January 1) (thousands) | Percentage Change During Year | Year of Birth | Rate |
|---|---|---|---|---|---|---|
| | | | Lithuanian SSR | | | |
| 1950 | 23.6 | 1966 | | | 1984 | 16.4 |
| 1951 | 22.5 | 1967 | | | 1985 | 16.3 |
| 1952 | 21.7 | 1968 | | | 1986 | 16.2 |
| 1953 | 20.0 | 1969 | | | 1987 | 16.0 |
| 1954 | 20.6 | 1970 | 1,679 | 1.6 | 1988 | 15.9 |
| 1955 | 21.1 | 1971 | 1,706 | 1.8 | 1989 | 15.7 |
| 1956 | 20.1 | 1972 | 1,736 | 1.6 | 1990 | 15.5 |
| 1957 | 21.1 | 1973 | 1,764 | 1.8 | 1991 | 15.4 |
| 1958 | 22.8 | 1974 | 1,795 | 1.9 | 1992 | 15.2 |
| 1959 | 22.7 | 1975 | 1,830 | 1.8 | 1993 | 15.0 |
| 1960 | 22.5 | 1976 | 1,863 | 1.7 | 1994 | 14.9 |
| 1961 | 22.2 | 1977 | 1,894 | 1.5 | 1995 | 14.7 |
| 1962 | (21.0) | 1978 | 1,923 | 1.2 | 1996 | 14.5 |
| 1963 | 19.7 | 1979 | 1,946 | 1.0 | 1997 | 14.3 |
| 1964 | 19.1 | 1980 | 1,965 | 0.9 | 1998 | 14.2 |
| 1965 | 18.1 | 1981 | 1,982 | 0.6 | 1999 | 14.1 |
| 1966 | 18.0 | 1982 | 1,994 | 0.5 | 2000 | 14.0 |
| 1967 | 17.7 | 1983 | 2,003 | 0.3 | | |
| 1968 | 17.6 | 1984 | 2,010 | 0.4 | | |
| 1969 | 17.4 | 1985 | 2,018 | 0.3 | | |
| 1970 | 17.6 | 1986 | 2,024 | 0.2 | | |
| 1971 | 17.6 | 1987 | 2,028 | 0.4 | | |
| 1972 | 17.0 | 1988 | 2,036 | 0.4 | | |
| 1973 | 16.0 | 1989 | 2,044 | 0.2 | | |
| 1974 | 15.8 | 1990 | 2,045 | 0.2 | | |
| 1975 | 15.7 | 1991 | 2,052 | 0.0 | | |
| 1976 | 15.7 | 1992 | 2,053 | 0.0 | | |
| 1977 | 15.7 | 1993 | 2,053 | 0.1 | | |
| 1978 | 15.8 | 1994 | 2,055 | 0.2 | | |
| 1979 | 16.0 | 1995 | 2,059 | -0.1 | | |
| 1980 | 16.1 | 1996 | 2,057 | 0.0 | | |
| 1981 | 16.3 | 1997 | 2,058 | 0.4 | | |
| 1982 | 16.4 | 1998 | 2,066 | 0.7 | | |
| 1983 | 16.4 | 1999 | 2,080 | 0.7 | | |
| | | 2000 | 2,094 | | | |

(continued)

51

Appendix Table 2.1, continued

| Crude Birth Rate | | Population of Working Ages | | | Crude Birth Rate | |
| Year of Birth | Rate | Year Age 16 | Population (January 1) (thousands) | Percentage Change During Year | Year of Birth | Rate |
|---|---|---|---|---|---|---|
| | | | Ukrainian SSR | | | |
| 1950 | 22.5 | 1966 | | | 1984 | 15.4 |
| 1951 | — | 1967 | | | 1985 | 15.2 |
| 1952 | — | 1968 | | | 1986 | 14.9 |
| 1953 | — | 1969 | | | 1987 | 14.7 |
| 1954 | — | 1970 | 26,214 | 1.2 | 1988 | 14.4 |
| 1955 | — | 1971 | 26,532 | 1.2 | 1989 | 14.2 |
| 1956 | 20.2 | 1972 | 26,842 | 1.3 | 1990 | 14.0 |
| 1957 | — | 1973 | 27,186 | 1.2 | 1991 | 13.9 |
| 1958 | — | 1974 | 27,524 | 1.3 | 1992 | 13.8 |
| 1959 | — | 1975 | 27,896 | 1.3 | 1993 | 13.7 |
| 1960 | 20.5 | 1976 | 28,268 | 1.2 | 1994 | 13.6 |
| 1961 | — | 1977 | 28,616 | 1.0 | 1995 | 13.5 |
| 1962 | — | 1978 | 28,903 | 0.8 | 1996 | 13.5 |
| 1963 | 17.9 | 1979 | 29,128 | 0.5 | 1997 | 13.5 |
| 1964 | 16.5 | 1980 | 29,289 | 0.4 | 1998 | 13.5 |
| 1965 | 15.3 | 1981 | 29,396 | 0.0 | 1999 | 13.6 |
| 1966 | 15.6 | 1982 | 29,401 | -0.1 | 2000 | 13.6 |
| 1967 | 15.1 | 1983 | 29,366 | -0.2 | | |
| 1968 | 14.9 | 1984 | 29,314 | -0.2 | | |
| 1969 | 14.7 | 1985 | 29,250 | -0.1 | | |
| 1970 | 15.2 | 1986 | 29,229 | -0.1 | | |
| 1971 | 15.5 | 1987 | 29,196 | 0.0 | | |
| 1972 | 15.5 | 1988 | 29,197 | 0.1 | | |
| 1973 | 14.9 | 1989 | 29,232 | 0.0 | | |
| 1974 | 15.1 | 1990 | 29,237 | -0.1 | | |
| 1975 | 15.1 | 1991 | 29,220 | -0.2 | | |
| 1976 | 15.1 | 1992 | 29,157 | -0.3 | | |
| 1977 | 15.2 | 1993 | 29,067 | -0.2 | | |
| 1978 | 15.3 | 1994 | 29,003 | -0.1 | | |
| 1979 | 15.5 | 1995 | 28,975 | -0.2 | | |
| 1980 | 15.6 | 1996 | 28,924 | -0.1 | | |
| 1981 | 15.6 | 1997 | 28,886 | 0.1 | | |
| 1982 | 15.6 | 1998 | 28,928 | 0.4 | | |
| 1983 | 15.5 | 1999 | 29,039 | 0.4 | | |
| | | 2000 | 29,159 | | | |

| Crude Birth Rate | | Population of Working Ages | | | Crude Birth Rate | |
|---|---|---|---|---|---|---|
| | | Year | Population (January 1) | Percentage Change During | | |
| Year of Birth | Rate | Age 16 | (thousands) | Year | Year of Birth | Rate |

Belorussian SSR

| Year of Birth | Rate | Year Age 16 | Population (January 1) (thousands) | Percentage Change During Year | Year of Birth | Rate |
|---|---|---|---|---|---|---|
| 1950 | 25.5 | 1966 | | | 1984 | 17.4 |
| 1951 | 25.2 | 1967 | | | 1985 | 17.2 |
| 1952 | 24.4 | 1968 | | | 1986 | 16.8 |
| 1953 | 22.5 | 1969 | | | 1987 | 16.5 |
| 1954 | 24.7 | 1970 | 4,766 | 1.8 | 1988 | 16.1 |
| 1955 | 24.6 | 1971 | 4,854 | 2.0 | 1989 | 15.8 |
| 1956 | (24.8) | 1972 | 4,952 | 2.1 | 1990 | 15.4 |
| 1957 | 25.0 | 1973 | 5,055 | 2.1 | 1991 | 15.1 |
| 1958 | 25.9 | 1974 | 5,163 | 2.2 | 1992 | 14.8 |
| 1959 | 25.2 | 1975 | 5,276 | 1.8 | 1993 | 14.6 |
| 1960 | 24.5 | 1976 | 5,370 | 2.0 | 1994 | 14.3 |
| 1961 | (23.2) | 1977 | 5,480 | 1.8 | 1995 | 14.1 |
| 1962 | (21.9) | 1978 | 5,579 | 1.5 | 1996 | 13.9 |
| 1963 | 20.6 | 1979 | 5,662 | 1.1 | 1997 | 13.8 |
| 1964 | 19.0 | 1980 | 5,727 | 0.9 | 1998 | 13.7 |
| 1965 | 17.9 | 1981 | 5,776 | 0.6 | 1999 | 13.7 |
| 1966 | 17.7 | 1982 | 5,810 | 0.4 | 2000 | 13.7 |
| 1967 | 16.8 | 1983 | 5,832 | 0.3 | | |
| 1968 | 16.5 | 1984 | 5,848 | 0.2 | | |
| 1969 | 15.9 | 1985 | 5,861 | 0.0 | | |
| 1970 | 16.2 | 1986 | 5,864 | 0.0 | | |
| 1971 | 16.4 | 1987 | 5,861 | 0.1 | | |
| 1972 | 16.1 | 1988 | 5,868 | 0.2 | | |
| 1973 | 15.7 | 1989 | 5,879 | 0.1 | | |
| 1974 | 15.8 | 1990 | 5,886 | 0.1 | | |
| 1975 | 15.7 | 1991 | 5,892 | 0.0 | | |
| 1976 | 16.0 | 1992 | 5,889 | 0.0 | | |
| 1977 | 16.3 | 1993 | 5,887 | 0.1 | | |
| 1978 | 16.6 | 1994 | 5,893 | 0.2 | | |
| 1979 | 17.0 | 1995 | 5,908 | 0.4 | | |
| 1980 | 17.3 | 1996 | 5,934 | 0.5 | | |
| 1981 | 17.5 | 1997 | 5,965 | 0.8 | | |
| 1982 | 17.6 | 1998 | 6,011 | 1.0 | | |
| 1983 | 17.5 | 1999 | 6,070 | 1.0 | | |
| | | 2000 | 6,132 | | | |

(continued)

| Crude Birth Rate | | Population of Working Ages | | | Crude Birth Rate | |
|---|---|---|---|---|---|---|
| Year of Birth | Rate | Year Age 16 | Population (January 1) (thousands) | Percentage Change During Year | Year of Birth | Rate |
| Moldavian SSR | | | | | | |
| 1950 | 38.9 | 1966 | | | 1984 | 20.6 |
| 1951 | 37.8 | 1967 | | | 1985 | 20.2 |
| 1952 | 32.7 | 1968 | | | 1986 | 19.7 |
| 1953 | 31.5 | 1969 | | | 1987 | 19.2 |
| 1954 | 32.5 | 1970 | 1,902 | 2.3 | 1988 | 18.7 |
| 1955 | 30.4 | 1971 | 1,945 | 2.3 | 1989 | 18.3 |
| 1956 | 30.3 | 1972 | 1,989 | 2.3 | 1990 | 17.9 |
| 1957 | 31.0 | 1973 | 2,035 | 2.2 | 1991 | 17.5 |
| 1958 | 30.8 | 1974 | 2,080 | 2.4 | 1992 | 17.2 |
| 1959 | 31.5 | 1975 | 2,130 | 2.2 | 1993 | 16.9 |
| 1960 | 29.2 | 1976 | 2,176 | 2.1 | 1994 | 16.7 |
| 1961 | 28.2 | 1977 | 2,221 | 1.8 | 1995 | 16.5 |
| 1962 | 25.6 | 1978 | 2,262 | 1.5 | 1996 | 16.3 |
| 1963 | 24.5 | 1979 | 2,295 | 1.2 | 1997 | 16.2 |
| 1964 | 22.5 | 1980 | 2,325 | 1.1 | 1998 | 16.1 |
| 1965 | 20.4 | 1981 | 2,349 | 0.8 | 1999 | 16.0 |
| 1966 | 21.0 | 1982 | 2,368 | 0.6 | 2000 | 16.0 |
| 1967 | 20.7 | 1983 | 2,383 | 0.6 | | |
| 1968 | 20.0 | 1984 | 2,398 | 0.5 | | |
| 1969 | 19.0 | 1985 | 2,410 | 0.5 | | |
| 1970 | 19.4 | 1986 | 2,422 | 0.4 | | |
| 1971 | 20.2 | 1987 | 2,433 | 0.7 | | |
| 1972 | 20.6 | 1988 | 2,451 | 0.9 | | |
| 1973 | 20.4 | 1989 | 2,473 | 0.8 | | |
| 1974 | 20.4 | 1990 | 2,493 | 0.8 | | |
| 1975 | 20.7 | 1991 | 2,513 | 0.7 | | |
| 1976 | 20.9 | 1992 | 2,531 | 0.7 | | |
| 1977 | 21.0 | 1993 | 2,549 | 0.8 | | |
| 1978 | 21.1 | 1994 | 2,570 | 0.9 | | |
| 1979 | 21.2 | 1995 | 2,593 | 0.8 | | |
| 1980 | 21.3 | 1996 | 2,614 | 0.9 | | |
| 1981 | 21.3 | 1997 | 2,637 | 1.2 | | |
| 1982 | 21.2 | 1998 | 2,668 | 1.3 | | |
| 1983 | 20.9 | 1999 | 2,704 | 1.3 | | |
| | | 2000 | 2,740 | | | |

| Crude Birth Rate Year of Birth | Rate | Population of Working Ages Year Age 16 | Population (January 1) (thousands) | Percentage Change During Year | Crude Birth Rate Year of Birth | Rate |
|---|---|---|---|---|---|---|
| | | | Georgian SSR | | | |
| 1950 | 23.5 | 1966 | | | 1984 | 19.3 |
| 1951 | 23.9 | 1967 | | | 1985 | 19.1 |
| 1952 | 24.6 | 1968 | | | 1986 | 18.8 |
| 1953 | 22.6 | 1969 | | | 1987 | 18.5 |
| 1954 | 24.7 | 1970 | 2,472 | 1.7 | 1988 | 18.1 |
| 1955 | 24.1 | 1971 | 2,514 | 2.1 | 1989 | 17.7 |
| 1956 | 23.7 | 1972 | 2,568 | 2.0 | 1990 | 17.3 |
| 1957 | 23.0 | 1973 | 2,620 | 1.8 | 1991 | 17.0 |
| 1958 | 23.4 | 1974 | 2,667 | 1.9 | 1992 | 16.6 |
| 1959 | 24.2 | 1975 | 2,719 | 1.9 | 1993 | 16.4 |
| 1960 | 24.7 | 1976 | 2,770 | 2.2 | 1994 | 16.1 |
| 1961 | 24.7 | 1977 | 2,831 | 2.2 | 1995 | 15.9 |
| 1962 | 23.8 | 1978 | 2,892 | 1.9 | 1996 | 15.7 |
| 1963 | 22.9 | 1979 | 2,947 | 1.7 | 1997 | 15.5 |
| 1964 | 21.9 | 1980 | 2,997 | 1.4 | 1998 | 15.4 |
| 1965 | 21.0 | 1981 | 3,040 | 1.0 | 1999 | 15.3 |
| 1966 | 20.1 | 1982 | 3,071 | 0.7 | 2000 | 15.3 |
| 1967 | 19.3 | 1983 | 3,093 | 0.6 | | |
| 1968 | 19.1 | 1984 | 3,113 | 0.6 | | |
| 1969 | 18.7 | 1985 | 3,132 | 0.4 | | |
| 1970 | 19.2 | 1986 | 3,143 | 0.4 | | |
| 1971 | 19.0 | 1987 | 3,155 | 0.5 | | |
| 1972 | 18.0 | 1988 | 3,170 | 0.4 | | |
| 1973 | 18.2 | 1989 | 3,184 | 0.5 | | |
| 1974 | 18.3 | 1990 | 3,199 | 0.5 | | |
| 1975 | 18.2 | 1991 | 3,214 | 0.3 | | |
| 1976 | 18.4 | 1992 | 3,224 | 0.3 | | |
| 1977 | 18.6 | 1993 | 3,234 | 0.4 | | |
| 1978 | 18.8 | 1994 | 3,248 | 0.6 | | |
| 1979 | 19.0 | 1995 | 3,267 | 0.6 | | |
| 1980 | 19.2 | 1996 | 3,287 | 0.7 | | |
| 1981 | 19.3 | 1997 | 3,310 | 1.0 | | |
| 1982 | 19.4 | 1998 | 3,342 | 1.2 | | |
| 1983 | 19.4 | 1999 | 3,382 | 1.2 | | |
| | | 2000 | 3,423 | | | |

(continued)

| Crude Birth Rate | | Population of Working Ages | | | Crude Birth Rate | |
|---|---|---|---|---|---|---|
| Year of Birth | Rate | Year Age 16 | Population (January 1) (thousands) | Percentage Change During Year | Year of Birth | Rate |

Armenian SSR

| Year of Birth | Rate | Year Age 16 | Population (January 1) (thousands) | Percentage Change During Year | Year of Birth | Rate |
|---|---|---|---|---|---|---|
| 1950 | 31.5 | 1966 | | | 1984 | 24.0 |
| 1951 | 35.5 | 1967 | | | 1985 | 23.5 |
| 1952 | 37.4 | 1968 | | | 1986 | 22.8 |
| 1953 | 34.5 | 1969 | | | 1987 | 22.1 |
| 1954 | 37.9 | 1970 | 1,206 | 3.9 | 1988 | 21.3 |
| 1955 | 37.4 | 1971 | 1,253 | 4.3 | 1989 | 20.6 |
| 1956 | 37.9 | 1972 | 1,307 | 4.3 | 1990 | 19.9 |
| 1957 | — | 1973 | 1,363 | 4.5 | 1991 | 19.2 |
| 1958 | — | 1974 | 1,425 | 4.5 | 1992 | 18.6 |
| 1959 | 40.2 | 1975 | 1,489 | 4.1 | 1993 | 18.1 |
| 1960 | 40.3 | 1976 | 1,550 | 4.0 | 1994 | 17.7 |
| 1961 | — | 1977 | 1,612 | 3.7 | 1995 | 17.3 |
| 1962 | — | 1978 | 1,671 | 3.2 | 1996 | 17.0 |
| 1963 | 33.1 | 1979 | 1,725 | 3.0 | 1997 | 16.7 |
| 1964 | 30.7 | 1980 | 1,776 | 2.4 | 1998 | 16.6 |
| 1965 | 29.1 | 1981 | 1,819 | 2.0 | 1999 | 16.4 |
| 1966 | 27.7 | 1982 | 1,855 | 1.8 | 2000 | 16.3 |
| 1967 | 25.0 | 1983 | 1,888 | 1.4 | | |
| 1968 | 24.6 | 1984 | 1,915 | 1.5 | | |
| 1969 | 22.8 | 1985 | 1,943 | 1.1 | | |
| 1970 | 22.1 | 1986 | 1,964 | 1.0 | | |
| 1971 | 22.6 | 1987 | 1,983 | 1.1 | | |
| 1972 | 22.5 | 1988 | 2,005 | 1.2 | | |
| 1973 | 22.1 | 1989 | 2,029 | 1.2 | | |
| 1974 | 21.9 | 1990 | 2,053 | 1.1 | | |
| 1975 | 22.4 | 1991 | 2,075 | 1.0 | | |
| 1976 | 23.0 | 1992 | 2,096 | 1.1 | | |
| 1977 | 23.4 | 1993 | 2,119 | 1.2 | | |
| 1978 | 23.7 | 1994 | 2,145 | 1.4 | | |
| 1979 | 24.1 | 1995 | 2,174 | 1.6 | | |
| 1980 | 24.4 | 1996 | 2,208 | 1.6 | | |
| 1981 | 24.6 | 1997 | 2,244 | 1.8 | | |
| 1982 | 24.5 | 1998 | 2,284 | 1.9 | | |
| 1983 | 24.4 | 1999 | 2,328 | 2.0 | | |
| | | 2000 | 2,374 | | | |

|  | Population of Working Ages |  |  |  |  |  |
| Crude Birth Rate | | Year | Population (January 1) (thousands) | Percentage Change During Year | Crude Birth Rate | |
| Year of Birth | Rate | Age 16 |  |  | Year of Birth | Rate |
| --- | --- | --- | --- | --- | --- | --- |
| | | | Azerbaidzhan SSR | | | |
| 1950 | 31.2 | 1966 |  |  | 1984 | 28.7 |
| 1951 | 33.4 | 1967 |  |  | 1985 | 28.7 |
| 1952 | 34.5 | 1968 |  |  | 1986 | 28.5 |
| 1953 | 32.0 | 1969 | 2,244 |  | 1987 | 28.2 |
| 1954 | 36.5 | 1970 | 2,314 | 3.1 | 1988 | 27.8 |
| 1955 | 37.8 | 1971 | 2,403 | 3.8 | 1989 | 27.2 |
| 1956 | 39.6 | 1972 | 2,500 | 4.0 | 1990 | 26.6 |
| 1957 | 39.4 | 1973 | 2,600 | 4.0 | 1991 | 25.9 |
| 1958 | 40.5 | 1974 | 2,709 | 4.2 | 1992 | 25.1 |
| 1959 | 41.5 | 1975 | 2,820 | 4.1 | 1993 | 24.4 |
| 1960 | 42.6 | 1976 | 2,941 | 4.3 | 1994 | 23.6 |
| 1961 | 42.2 | 1977 | 3,064 | 4.2 | 1995 | 22.8 |
| 1962 | 40.3 | 1978 | 3,183 | 3.8 | 1996 | 22.1 |
| 1963 | 40.4 | 1979 | 3,305 | 3.8 | 1997 | 21.4 |
| 1964 | 39.6 | 1980 | 3,423 | 3.6 | 1998 | 20.8 |
| 1965 | 36.4 | 1981 | 3,527 | 3.0 | 1999 | 20.3 |
| 1966 | 35.2 | 1982 | 3,625 | 2.8 | 2000 | 19.8 |
| 1967 | 32.4 | 1983 | 3,714 | 2.5 |  |  |
| 1968 | 31.9 | 1984 | 3,804 | 2.4 |  |  |
| 1969 | 29.3 | 1985 | 3,871 | 1.8 |  |  |
| 1970 | 29.2 | 1986 | 3,943 | 1.9 |  |  |
| 1971 | 27.8 | 1987 | 4,014 | 1.8 |  |  |
| 1972 | 25.6 | 1988 | 4,080 | 1.6 |  |  |
| 1973 | 25.3 | 1989 | 4,145 | 1.6 |  |  |
| 1974 | 25.0 | 1990 | 4,203 | 1.4 |  |  |
| 1975 | 25.1 | 1991 | 4,258 | 1.3 |  |  |
| 1976 | 25.7 | 1992 | 4,318 | 1.4 |  |  |
| 1977 | 26.1 | 1993 | 4,384 | 1.5 |  |  |
| 1978 | 26.6 | 1994 | 4,459 | 1.7 |  |  |
| 1979 | 27.1 | 1995 | 4,545 | 1.9 |  |  |
| 1980 | 27.6 | 1996 | 4,638 | 2.0 |  |  |
| 1981 | 28.0 | 1997 | 4,742 | 2.2 |  |  |
| 1982 | 28.4 | 1998 | 4,857 | 2.4 |  |  |
| 1983 | 28.6 | 1999 | 4,977 | 2.5 |  |  |
|  |  | 2000 |  |  |  |  |

(continued)

| Crude Birth Rate | | Population of Working Ages | | | Crude Birth Rate | |
|---|---|---|---|---|---|---|
| Year of Birth | Rate | Year Age 16 | Population (January 1) (thousands) | Percentage Change During Year | Year of Birth | Rate |
| Kazakh SSR | | | | | | |
| 1950 | 37.6 | 1966 | | | 1984 | 24.5 |
| 1951 | — | 1967 | | | 1985 | 24.1 |
| 1952 | — | 1968 | | | 1986 | 23.7 |
| 1953 | — | 1969 | | | 1987 | 23.2 |
| 1954 | — | 1970 | 6,491 | 2.7 | 1988 | 22.6 |
| 1955 | 36.9 | 1971 | 6,666 | 3.0 | 1989 | 22.1 |
| 1956 | — | 1972 | 6,865 | 2.9 | 1990 | 21.5 |
| 1957 | — | 1973 | 7,064 | 3.2 | 1991 | 21.0 |
| 1958 | — | 1974 | 7,287 | 3.1 | 1992 | 20.5 |
| 1959 | 36.6 | 1975 | 7,516 | 2.7 | 1993 | 20.0 |
| 1960 | 36.7 | 1976 | 7,718 | 3.2 | 1994 | 19.5 |
| 1961 | 35.3 | 1977 | 7,968 | 3.1 | 1995 | 19.1 |
| 1962 | 32.9 | 1978 | 8,218 | 2.8 | 1996 | 18.7 |
| 1963 | 30.4 | 1979 | 8,452 | 2.5 | 1997 | 18.4 |
| 1964 | 27.8 | 1980 | 8,664 | 2.0 | 1998 | 18.1 |
| 1965 | 26.2 | 1981 | 8,841 | 1.9 | 1999 | 17.8 |
| 1966 | 25.1 | 1982 | 9,010 | 1.6 | 2000 | 17.6 |
| 1967 | 24.0 | 1983 | 9,159 | 1.5 | | |
| 1968 | 23.2 | 1984 | 9,301 | 1.4 | | |
| 1969 | 23.3 | 1985 | 9,436 | 1.4 | | |
| 1970 | 23.4 | 1986 | 9,568 | 1.3 | | |
| 1971 | 23.8 | 1987 | 9,689 | 1.4 | | |
| 1972 | 23.5 | 1988 | 9,824 | 1.4 | | |
| 1973 | 23.2 | 1989 | 9,964 | 1.4 | | |
| 1974 | 24.1 | 1990 | 10,106 | 1.3 | | |
| 1975 | 24.1 | 1991 | 10,240 | 1.2 | | |
| 1976 | 24.4 | 1992 | 10,365 | 1.2 | | |
| 1977 | 24.4 | 1993 | 10,491 | 1.3 | | |
| 1978 | 24.6 | 1994 | 10,628 | 1.4 | | |
| 1979 | 24.7 | 1995 | 10,780 | 1.3 | | |
| 1980 | 24.8 | 1996 | 10,926 | 1.4 | | |
| 1981 | 24.9 | 1997 | 11,081 | 1.6 | | |
| 1982 | 24.9 | 1998 | 11,260 | 1.8 | | |
| 1983 | 24.8 | 1999 | 11,462 | 1.8 | | |
| | | 2000 | 11,671 | | | |

| Crude Birth Rate | | Population of Working Ages | | | Crude Birth Rate | |
|---|---|---|---|---|---|---|
| | | | Population | Percentage Change | | |
| Year of | | Year | (January 1) | During | Year of | |
| Birth | Rate | Age 16 | (thousands) | Year | Birth | Rate |

Kirgiz SSR

| Year of Birth | Rate | Year Age 16 | Population (January 1) (thousands) | Percentage Change During Year | Year of Birth | Rate |
|---|---|---|---|---|---|---|
| 1950 | 32.9 | 1966 | | | 1984 | 31.0 |
| 1951 | 33.8 | 1967 | | | 1985 | 30.6 |
| 1952 | 32.7 | 1968 | | | 1986 | 30.1 |
| 1953 | 33.4 | 1969 | 1,325 | | 1987 | 29.6 |
| 1954 | 34.8 | 1970 | 1,369 | 3.3 | 1988 | 29.1 |
| 1955 | 34.0 | 1971 | 1,417 | 3.5 | 1989 | 28.6 |
| 1956 | (34.3) | 1972 | 1,469 | 3.7 | 1990 | 28.1 |
| 1957 | (34.6) | 1973 | 1,524 | 3.7 | 1991 | 27.6 |
| 1958 | 34.8 | 1974 | 1,583 | 3.9 | 1992 | 27.2 |
| 1959 | 33.6 | 1975 | 1,637 | 3.4 | 1993 | 26.7 |
| 1960 | 36.8 | 1976 | 1,699 | 3.8 | 1994 | 26.1 |
| 1961 | 35.5 | 1977 | 1,761 | 3.6 | 1995 | 25.6 |
| 1962 | 33.6 | 1978 | 1,819 | 3.3 | 1996 | 25.1 |
| 1963 | 33.0 | 1979 | 1,876 | 3.1 | 1997 | 24.6 |
| 1964 | 31.4 | 1980 | 1,931 | 2.9 | 1998 | 24.1 |
| 1965 | 31.0 | 1981 | 1,977 | 2.4 | 1999 | 23.6 |
| 1966 | 30.3 | 1982 | 2,021 | 2.2 | 2000 | 23.2 |
| 1967 | 29.5 | 1983 | 2,066 | 2.2 | | |
| 1968 | 30.1 | 1984 | 2,114 | 2.3 | | |
| 1969 | 30.1 | 1985 | 2,159 | 2.1 | | |
| 1970 | 30.5 | 1986 | 2,205 | 2.1 | | |
| 1971 | 31.6 | 1987 | 2,257 | 2.4 | | |
| 1972 | 30.5 | 1988 | 2,309 | 2.3 | | |
| 1973 | 30.6 | 1989 | 2,363 | 2.3 | | |
| 1974 | 30.5 | 1990 | 2,418 | 2.3 | | |
| 1975 | 30.4 | 1991 | 2,471 | 2.2 | | |
| 1976 | 30.7 | 1992 | 2,527 | 2.3 | | |
| 1977 | 30.8 | 1993 | 2,586 | 2.3 | | |
| 1978 | 31.1 | 1994 | 2,650 | 2.5 | | |
| 1979 | 31.3 | 1995 | 2,717 | 2.5 | | |
| 1980 | 31.5 | 1996 | 2,788 | 2.6 | | |
| 1981 | 31.5 | 1997 | 2,864 | 2.7 | | |
| 1982 | 31.5 | 1998 | 2,946 | 2.9 | | |
| 1983 | 31.3 | 1999 | 3,030 | 2.9 | | |
| | | 2000 | | | | |

(continued)

| Crude Birth Rate | | Population of Working Ages | | | Crude Birth Rate | |
|---|---|---|---|---|---|---|
| Year of Birth | Rate | Year Age 16 | Population (January 1) (thousands) | Percentage Change During Year | Year of Birth | Rate |

Turkmen SSR

| Year of Birth | Rate | Year Age 16 | Population (January 1) (thousands) | Percentage Change During Year | Year of Birth | Rate |
|---|---|---|---|---|---|---|
| 1950 | 38.2 | 1966 | | | 1984 | 34.8 |
| 1951 | — | 1967 | | | 1985 | 34.5 |
| 1952 | — | 1968 | | | 1986 | 34.2 |
| 1953 | — | 1969 | | | 1987 | 33.7 |
| 1954 | — | 1970 | 948 | 3.2 | 1988 | 33.2 |
| 1955 | — | 1971 | 978 | 4.3 | 1989 | 32.7 |
| 1956 | 38.5 | 1972 | 1,020 | 3.8 | 1990 | 32.1 |
| 1957 | 39.0 | 1973 | 1,059 | 3.9 | 1991 | 31.5 |
| 1958 | 39.8 | 1974 | 1,100 | 4.3 | 1992 | 30.8 |
| 1959 | 39.3 | 1975 | 1,147 | 4.1 | 1993 | 30.2 |
| 1960 | 42.4 | 1976 | 1,194 | 4.3 | 1994 | 29.6 |
| 1961 | 41.0 | 1977 | 1,245 | 4.0 | 1995 | 29.0 |
| 1962 | (40.3) | 1978 | 1,295 | 3.8 | 1996 | 28.4 |
| 1963 | 39.5 | 1979 | 1,344 | 3.7 | 1997 | 27.8 |
| 1964 | 38.1 | 1980 | 1,394 | 3.4 | 1998 | 27.2 |
| 1965 | 37.2 | 1981 | 1,442 | 3.2 | 1999 | 26.7 |
| 1966 | 37.7 | 1982 | 1,488 | 3.2 | 2000 | 26.2 |
| 1967 | 35.6 | 1983 | 1,535 | 2.9 | | |
| 1968 | 35.7 | 1984 | 1,579 | 2.9 | | |
| 1969 | 34.3 | 1985 | 1,625 | 2.6 | | |
| 1970 | 35.2 | 1986 | 1,667 | 2.8 | | |
| 1971 | 34.7 | 1987 | 1,713 | 2.8 | | |
| 1972 | 33.9 | 1988 | 1,761 | 2.7 | | |
| 1973 | 34.3 | 1989 | 1,809 | 2.8 | | |
| 1974 | 34.3 | 1990 | 1,860 | 2.7 | | |
| 1975 | 34.4 | 1991 | 1,911 | 2.7 | | |
| 1976 | 34.9 | 1992 | 1,962 | 2.8 | | |
| 1977 | 34.8 | 1993 | 2,017 | 2.8 | | |
| 1978 | 34.9 | 1994 | 2,074 | 2.9 | | |
| 1979 | 34.9 | 1995 | 2,134 | 2.9 | | |
| 1980 | 35.0 | 1996 | 2,196 | 2.9 | | |
| 1981 | 35.0 | 1997 | 2,260 | 3.1 | | |
| 1982 | 35.0 | 1998 | 2,329 | 3.2 | | |
| 1983 | 34.9 | 1999 | 2,403 | 3.2 | | |
| | | 2000 | 2,479 | | | |

| Crude Birth Rate | | Population of Working Ages | | | Crude Birth Rate | |
|---|---|---|---|---|---|---|
| Year of Birth | Rate | Year Age 16 | Population (January 1) (thousands) | Percentage Change During Year | Year of Birth | Rate |
| | | | Uzbek SSR | | | |
| 1950 | 30.9 | 1966 | | | 1984 | 35.4 |
| 1951 | — | 1967 | | | 1985 | 35.0 |
| 1952 | — | 1968 | | | 1986 | 34.6 |
| 1953 | — | 1969 | | | 1987 | 34.0 |
| 1954 | — | 1970 | 4,989 | 3.6 | 1988 | 33.5 |
| 1955 | — | 1971 | 5,168 | 4.2 | 1989 | 32.9 |
| 1956 | — | 1972 | 5,385 | 4.5 | 1990 | 32.2 |
| 1957 | 33.8 | 1973 | 5,625 | 4.5 | 1991 | 31.6 |
| 1958 | (35.5) | 1974 | 5,877 | 4.7 | 1992 | 31.0 |
| 1959 | 37.2 | 1975 | 6,155 | 4.4 | 1993 | 30.3 |
| 1960 | 39.9 | 1976 | 6,427 | 4.6 | 1994 | 29.7 |
| 1961 | — | 1977 | 6,720 | 4.3 | 1995 | 29.1 |
| 1962 | — | 1978 | 7,008 | 4.1 | 1996 | 28.6 |
| 1963 | 36.2 | 1979 | 7,292 | 3.8 | 1997 | 28.0 |
| 1964 | 35.4 | 1980 | 7,571 | 3.7 | 1998 | 27.5 |
| 1965 | 34.7 | 1981 | 7,848 | 3.2 | 1999 | 27.0 |
| 1966 | 34.1 | 1982 | 8,101 | 3.1 | 2000 | 26.6 |
| 1967 | 33.0 | 1983 | 8,349 | 2.9 | | |
| 1968 | 34.1 | 1984 | 8,595 | 3.2 | | |
| 1969 | 32.7 | 1985 | 8,867 | 2.8 | | |
| 1970 | 33.6 | 1986 | 9,114 | 2.7 | | |
| 1971 | 34.5 | 1987 | 9,358 | 2.9 | | |
| 1972 | 33.2 | 1988 | 9,629 | 2.8 | | |
| 1973 | 33.7 | 1989 | 9,898 | 2.9 | | |
| 1974 | 34.2 | 1990 | 10,183 | 2.9 | | |
| 1975 | 34.5 | 1991 | 10,476 | 2.9 | | |
| 1976 | 35.0 | 1992 | 10,755 | 2.9 | | |
| 1977 | 35.1 | 1993 | 11,090 | 3.0 | | |
| 1978 | 35.3 | 1994 | 11,423 | 3.1 | | |
| 1979 | 35.5 | 1995 | 11,777 | 3.1 | | |
| 1980 | 35.6 | 1996 | 12,139 | 3.1 | | |
| 1981 | 35.7 | 1997 | 12,518 | 3.3 | | |
| 1982 | 35.7 | 1998 | 12,929 | 3.4 | | |
| 1983 | 35.6 | 1999 | 13,367 | 3.4 | | |
| | | 2000 | 13,822 | | | |

(continued)

| Crude Birth Rate Year of Birth | Rate | Population of Working Ages Year Age 16 | Population (January 1) (thousands) | Percentage Change During Year | Crude Birth Rate Year of Birth | Rate |
|---|---|---|---|---|---|---|
| | | | Tadzhik SSR | | | |
| 1950 | 30.4 | 1966 | | | 1984 | 36.2 |
| 1951 | 30.5 | 1967 | | | 1985 | 35.9 |
| 1952 | 34.4 | 1968 | | | 1986 | 35.5 |
| 1953 | 32.4 | 1969 | | | 1987 | 35.0 |
| 1954 | 32.9 | 1970 | 1,225 | 3.5 | 1988 | 34.4 |
| 1955 | 33.8 | 1971 | 1,268 | 5.0 | 1989 | 33.8 |
| 1956 | 34.2 | 1972 | 1,332 | 4.6 | 1990 | 33.1 |
| 1957 | 33.1 | 1973 | 1,393 | 4.3 | 1991 | 32.4 |
| 1958 | 29.0 | 1974 | 1,453 | 3.7 | 1992 | 31.7 |
| 1959 | 30.3 | 1975 | 1,507 | 3.6 | 1993 | 31.0 |
| 1960 | 33.5 | 1976 | 1,562 | 4.2 | 1994 | 30.3 |
| 1961 | 34.0 | 1977 | 1,628 | 4.2 | 1995 | 29.7 |
| 1962 | 33.5 | 1978 | 1,697 | 4.1 | 1996 | 29.0 |
| 1963 | 34.3 | 1979 | 1,767 | 4.2 | 1997 | 28.4 |
| 1964 | 34.6 | 1980 | 1,842 | 4.2 | 1998 | 27.8 |
| 1965 | 36.5 | 1981 | 1,920 | 3.4 | 1999 | 27.2 |
| 1966 | 35.1 | 1982 | 1,986 | 3.1 | 2000 | 26.6 |
| 1967 | 34.9 | 1983 | 2,048 | 3.2 | | |
| 1968 | 36.5 | 1984 | 2,113 | 3.4 | | |
| 1969 | 34.7 | 1985 | 2,184 | 2.9 | | |
| 1970 | 34.7 | 1986 | 2,247 | 2.6 | | |
| 1971 | 36.8 | 1987 | 2,305 | 3.0 | | |
| 1972 | 35.3 | 1988 | 2,374 | 2.9 | | |
| 1973 | 35.6 | 1989 | 2,442 | 2.9 | | |
| 1974 | 37.0 | 1990 | 2,513 | 3.1 | | |
| 1975 | 37.1 | 1991 | 2,590 | 3.0 | | |
| 1976 | 37.5 | 1992 | 2,668 | 3.1 | | |
| 1977 | 37.4 | 1993 | 2,750 | 3.1 | | |
| 1978 | 37.3 | 1994 | 2,836 | 3.2 | | |
| 1979 | 37.1 | 1995 | 2,926 | 3.1 | | |
| 1980 | 36.9 | 1996 | 3,018 | 3.1 | | |
| 1981 | 36.7 | 1997 | 3,113 | 3.3 | | |
| 1982 | 36.5 | 1998 | 3,215 | 3.4 | | |
| 1983 | 36.4 | 1999 | 3,323 | 3.3 | | |
| | | 2000 | 3,434 | | | |

Note: Figures in parentheses are interpolated.

Sources: Data on crude birth rate from issues of Narkhoz for the USSR and the respective republics, for years through 1976; data on population of working ages, 1970-2000, and on crude birth rate after 1976, from projections made by Godfrey S. Baldwin, Population Projections by Age and Sex: For the Republics and Major Economic Regions of the USSR, 1970 to 2000 (Washington, D.C.: U.S. Government Printing Office, 1979). The latter reproduces data from the projection for every five years; annual data in the present table were supplied by Mr. Baldwin from his worksheets. The "medium" fertility assumption is used. TsSU, Narodnoe khoziaistvo SSSR (Moscow, various years) (hereafter Narkhov).

Total Agricultural and Nonagricultural Average Annual Employment,
Percentage Change in Average Annual Employment, and Agricultural
Employment as Percentage of Total: By Republics, 1955-78

| Year | Average Annual Employment* | | | Percent Agr. | Annual Percentage Change | | |
|------|-------|---------|--------|------|-------|---------|------|
|      | Total | Nonagr. | Agr.   |      | Total | Nonagr. | Agr. |

|      |       |         | USSR   |      |       |         |      |
|------|-------|---------|--------|------|-------|---------|------|
| 1955 |       |         |        |      |       |         |      |
| 1956 |       |         |        |      |       |         |      |
| 1957 | 78,598 | 46,355 | 32,243 | 41.0 |       |         |      |
| 1958 | 79,680 | 47,700 | 31,980 | 40.1 | 1.4 | 2.9 | -0.8 |
| 1959 | 80,610 | 49,492 | 31,118 | 38.6 | 1.2 | 3.8 | -2.8 |
| 1960 | 83,765 | 54,902 | 28,863 | 34.5 | 3.9 | 10.9 | -7.8 |
| 1961 | 86,184 | 57,982 | 28,202 | 32.7 | 2.9 | 5.6 | -2.3 |
| 1962 | 88,084 | 60,081 | 28,003 | 31.8 | 2.2 | 3.6 | -0.7 |
| 1963 | 89,724 | 62,187 | 27,537 | 30.7 | 1.9 | 3.5 | -1.7 |
| 1964 | 92,259 | 64,706 | 27,553 | 29.9 | 2.8 | 4.0 | 0.1 |
| 1965 | 95,543 | 67,747 | 27,796 | 29.1 | 3.6 | 4.7 | 0.9 |
| 1966 | 98,167 | 70,417 | 27,750 | 28.3 | 2.7 | 3.9 | -0.2 |
| 1967 | 100,501 | 72,858 | 27,643 | 27.5 | 2.4 | 3.5 | -0.4 |
| 1968 | 103,054 | 75,850 | 27,204 | 26.4 | 2.5 | 4.1 | -1.6 |
| 1969 | 105,095 | 78,839 | 26,256 | 25.0 | 2.0 | 3.9 | -3.6 |
| 1970 | 106,901 | 81,006 | 25,895 | 24.2 | 1.7 | 2.7 | -1.4 |
| 1971 | 109,299 | 83,303 | 25,997 | 23.8 | 2.2 | 2.8 | 0.4 |
| 1972 | 111,442 | 85,595 | 25,847 | 23.2 | 2.0 | 2.8 | -0.6 |
| 1973 | 113,566 | 87,581 | 25,985 | 22.9 | 1.9 | 2.3 | 0.5 |
| 1974 | 115,680 | 89,678 | 26,002 | 22.5 | 1.9 | 2.4 | 0.1 |
| 1975 | 117,560 | 91,639 | 25,921 | 22.0 | 1.6 | 2.2 | -0.3 |
| 1976 | 119,235 | 93,468 | 25,767 | 21.6 | 1.4 | 2.0 | -0.6 |
| 1977 | 120,993 | 95,394 | 25,599 | 21.2 | 1.5 | 2.1 | -0.7 |
| 1978 | 122,916 | 97,358 | 25,558 | 20.8 | 1.6 | 2.1 | -0.2 |

(continued)

Appendix Table 2.2, continued

| Year | Average Annual Employment | | | Percent | Annual Percentage Change | | |
|------|-------|---------|--------|---------|-------|---------|------|
|      | Total | Nonagr. | Agr.   | Agr.    | Total | Nonagr. | Agr. |

RSFSR

| Year | Total | Nonagr. | Agr. | Agr. | Total | Nonagr. | Agr. |
|------|--------|---------|--------|------|-------|---------|------|
| 1955 | 43,691 | 27,936 | 15,755 | 36.1 |      |      |      |
| 1956 | 44,688 | 29,018 | 15,670 | 35.1 | 2.3  | 3.9  | -0.5 |
| 1957 | 45,929 | 30,344 | 15,585 | 33.9 | 2.8  | 4.6  | -0.5 |
| 1958 | 46,477 | 31,517 | 14,960 | 32.2 | 1.2  | 3.9  | -4.2 |
| 1959 | 46,914 | 32,773 | 14,141 | 30.1 | 0.9  | 4.0  | -5.8 |
| 1960 | 48,731 | 35,335 | 13,396 | 27.5 | 3.9  | 7.8  | -5.6 |
| 1961 | 50,024 | 37,058 | 12,966 | 25.9 | 2.6  | 4.9  | -3.3 |
| 1962 | 51,109 | 38,209 | 12,900 | 25.2 | 2.2  | 3.1  | -0.5 |
| 1963 | 51,948 | 39,361 | 12,587 | 24.2 | 1.6  | 3.0  | -2.5 |
| 1964 | 53,294 | 40,701 | 12,593 | 23.6 | 2.6  | 3.4  | 0.0  |
| 1965 | 54,802 | 42,314 | 12,488 | 22.8 | 2.8  | 4.0  | -0.8 |
| 1966 | 56.180 | 43,725 | 12,455 | 22.2 | 2.5  | 3.3  | -0.3 |
| 1967 | 57,432 | 44,959 | 12,473 | 21.7 | 2.2  | 2.8  | 0.1  |
| 1968 | 58,708 | 46,520 | 12,188 | 20.8 | 2.2  | 3.5  | -2.3 |
| 1969 | 59,857 | 48,183 | 11,674 | 19.5 | 2.0  | 3.6  | -4.4 |
| 1970 | 60,876 | 49,295 | 11,581 | 19.0 | 2.1  | 3.0  | -1.2 |
| 1971 | 61,870 | 50,508 | 11,362 | 18.4 | 1.6  | 2.5  | -1.9 |
| 1972 | 62,971 | 51,818 | 11,153 | 17.7 | 1.8  | 2.6  | -1.8 |
| 1973 | 64,140 | 52,898 | 11,242 | 17.5 | 1.9  | 2.1  | 0.8  |
| 1974 | 65,141 | 54,052 | 11,089 | 17.0 | 1.6  | 2.2  | -1.4 |
| 1975 | 66,162 | 55,269 | 10,893 | 16.5 | 1.6  | 2.3  | -1.8 |

| Year | Average Annual Employment | | | Percent | Annual Percentage Change | | |
|---|---|---|---|---|---|---|---|
| | Total | Nonagr. | Agr. | Agr. | Total | Nonagr. | Agr. |

Lithuanian SSR

| Year | Total | Nonagr. | Agr. | Agr. | Total | Nonagr. | Agr. |
|---|---|---|---|---|---|---|---|
| 1957 | 980 | 456 | 524 | 53.5 | | | |
| 1958 | 1,002 | 485 | 517 | 51.7 | 2.2 | 6.4 | -1.4 |
| 1959 | 1,020 | 528 | 492 | 48.2 | 1.8 | 8.9 | -5.1 |
| 1960 | 1,072 | 573 | 499 | 46.6 | 5.1 | 8.5 | -1.4 |
| 1961 | 1,111 | 626 | 485 | 43.7 | 3.6 | 9.2 | -2.9 |
| 1962 | 1,143 | 664 | 479 | 41.9 | 2.9 | 6.1 | -1.3 |
| 1963 | 1,172 | 699 | 473 | 40.4 | 2.5 | 5.3 | -1.3 |
| 1964 | 1,199 | 745 | 454 | 37.9 | 2.3 | 6.6 | -4.2 |
| 1965 | 1,258 | 796 | 462 | 36.7 | 4.9 | 6.8 | 1.8 |
| 1966 | 1,313 | 848 | 465 | 35.4 | 4.4 | 6.5 | 0.6 |
| 1967 | 1,361 | 892 | 469 | 34.5 | 3.7 | 5.2 | 0.9 |
| 1968 | 1,414 | 949 | 465 | 32.9 | 3.9 | 6.4 | -0.9 |
| 1969 | 1,446 | 996 | 450 | 31.1 | 2.3 | 5.0 | -3.3 |
| 1970 | 1,477 | 1,034 | 443 | 30.0 | 3.2 | 5.3 | -0.9 |
| 1971 | 1,505 | 1,067 | 438 | 27.1 | 1.9 | 3.2 | -1.1 |
| 1972 | 1,530 | 1,100 | 430 | 28.1 | 1.7 | 3.1 | -1.9 |
| 1973 | 1,552 | 1,131 | 421 | 27.1 | 1.4 | 2.8 | -2.1 |
| 1974 | 1,580 | 1,161 | 419 | 26.5 | 1.8 | 2.6 | -0.5 |
| 1975 | 1,603 | 1,195 | 408 | 25.4 | 1.5 | 2.9 | -2.7 |

(continued)

Appendix Table 2.2, continued

| Year | Average Annual Employment | | | Percent | Annual Percentage Change | | |
|------|-------|---------|------|------|-------|---------|------|
| | Total | Nonagr. | Agr. | Agr. | Total | Nonagr. | Agr. |

Estonian SSR

| Year | Total | Nonagr. | Agr. | Agr. | Total | Nonagr. | Agr. |
|------|-------|---------|------|------|-------|---------|------|
| 1957 | 495 | 339 | 156 | 31.5 | | | |
| 1958 | 507 | 351 | 156 | 30.7 | 2.5 | 3.6 | 0.0 |
| 1959 | 529 | 374 | 155 | 29.3 | 4.4 | 6.6 | -0.7 |
| 1960 | 544 | 392 | 152 | 27.9 | 2.9 | 4.9 | -2.0 |
| 1961 | 563 | 422 | 141 | 25.0 | 3.5 | 7.7 | -7.8 |
| 1962 | 576 | 437 | 139 | 24.1 | 2.3 | 3.6 | -1.5 |
| 1963 | 568 | 453 | 133 | 22.7 | 1.8 | 3.7 | -4.6 |
| 1964 | 603 | 471 | 132 | 21.9 | 2.9 | 4.0 | -0.8 |
| 1965 | 626 | 486 | 140 | 22.4 | 3.9 | 3.2 | 6.1 |
| 1966 | 638 | 503 | 135 | 21.2 | 2.0 | 3.5 | -3.7 |
| 1967 | 649 | 517 | 132 | 20.3 | 1.8 | 2.8 | -2.3 |
| 1968 | 660 | 533 | 127 | 19.2 | 1.7 | 3.1 | -4.0 |
| 1969 | 667 | 547 | 120 | 18.0 | 1.1 | 2.7 | -5.9 |
| 1970 | 682 | 557 | 125 | 18.3 | 1.5 | 2.4 | -2.1 |
| 1971 | 691 | 569 | 122 | 17.7 | 1.3 | 2.1 | -2.5 |
| 1972 | 698 | 578 | 120 | 17.2 | 1.0 | 1.6 | -1.7 |
| 1973 | 708 | 585 | 123 | 17.4 | 1.4 | 1.2 | 2.5 |
| 1974 | 716 | 594 | 122 | 17.0 | 1.1 | 1.5 | -0.8 |
| 1975 | 722 | 596 | 126 | 17.4 | 0.8 | 0.3 | 3.3 |

| Year | Average Annual Employment | | | Percent Agr. | Annual Percentage Change | | |
|---|---|---|---|---|---|---|---|
| | Total | Nonagr. | Agr. | | Total | Nonagr. | Agr. |
| | | | | Latvian SSR | | | |
| 1957 | 856 | 536 | 320 | 37.4 | | | |
| 1958 | 882 | 570 | 312 | 35.4 | 3.0 | 6.3 | -2.6 |
| 1959 | 913 | 600 | 313 | 34.3 | 3.5 | 5.3 | 0.3 |
| 1960 | 947 | 647 | 300 | 31.7 | 3.7 | 7.8 | -4.3 |
| 1961 | 989 | 687 | 302 | 30.5 | 4.4 | 6.2 | 0.7 |
| 1962 | 1,014 | 719 | 295 | 29.1 | 2.5 | 4.7 | -2.4 |
| 1963 | 1,032 | 748 | 284 | 27.5 | 1.8 | 4.0 | -3.9 |
| 1964 | 1,050 | 780 | 270 | 25.7 | 1.7 | 4.3 | -5.2 |
| 1965 | 1,098 | 817 | 281 | 25.6 | 4.6 | 4.7 | 4.1 |
| 1966 | 1,120 | 845 | 275 | 24.6 | 2.0 | 3.4 | -2.2 |
| 1967 | 1,141 | 870 | 271 | 23.8 | 1.9 | 3.0 | -1.5 |
| 1968 | 1,172 | 906 | 266 | 22.7 | 2.7 | 4.1 | -1.9 |
| 1969 | 1,173 | 927 | 246 | 21.0 | 0.1 | 2.3 | -8.1 |
| 1970 | 1,190 | 942 | 248 | 20.8 | 1.6 | 2.7 | -2.4 |
| 1971 | 1,210 | 959 | 251 | 20.7 | 1.7 | 1.8 | 1.2 |
| 1972 | 1,222 | 975 | 247 | 20.2 | 1.0 | 1.7 | -1.6 |
| 1973 | 1,238 | 991 | 247 | 20.0 | 1.3 | 1.6 | 0.0 |
| 1974 | 1,255 | 1,010 | 245 | 19.5 | 1.4 | 1.9 | -0.8 |
| 1975 | 1,269 | 1,027 | 242 | 19.1 | 1.1 | 1.7 | -1.2 |

(continued)

Appendix Table 2.2, continued

| Year | Average Annual Employment | | | Percent | Annual Percentage Change | | |
|------|-------|---------|------|---------|--------|---------|------|
|      | Total | Nonagr. | Agr. | Agr.    | Total  | Nonagr. | Agr. |

Azerbaidzhan SSR

| Year | Total | Nonagr. | Agr. | Agr. | Total | Nonagr. | Agr. |
|------|-------|---------|------|------|-------|---------|------|
| 1957 | 1,137 | 593 | 544 | 47.8 | | | |
| 1958 | 1,156 | 622 | 534 | 46.2 | 1.7 | 4.9 | -1.9 |
| 1959 | 1,184 | 650 | 534 | 45.1 | 2.4 | 4.5 | 0.0 |
| 1960 | 1,217 | 703 | 514 | 42.2 | 2.8 | 8.2 | -3.9 |
| 1961 | 1,255 | 749 | 506 | 40.3 | 3.1 | 6.5 | -1.6 |
| 1962 | 1,273 | 784 | 489 | 38.4 | 1.4 | 4.7 | -3.5 |
| 1963 | 1,299 | 819 | 480 | 37.0 | 2.0 | 4.5 | -1.9 |
| 1964 | 1,267 | 861 | 406 | 32.0 | -2.5 | 5.1 | -18.2 |
| 1965 | 1,365 | 897 | 468 | 34.3 | 7.7 | 4.2 | 15.3 |
| 1966 | 1,414 | 946 | 468 | 33.1 | 3.6 | 5.5 | 0.0 |
| 1967 | 1,442 | 983 | 459 | 31.8 | 2.0 | 3.9 | -2.0 |
| 1968 | 1,478 | 1,081 | 460 | 31.1 | 2.5 | 3.6 | 0.2 |
| 1969 | 1,494 | 1,054 | 440 | 29.5 | 1.1 | 3.5 | -4.5 |
| 1970 | 1,550 | 1,088 | 462 | 29.8 | 2.5 | 3.9 | -0.3 |
| 1971 | 1,585 | 1,117 | 468 | 29.5 | 2.3 | 2.7 | 1.3 |
| 1972 | 1,635 | 1,148 | 487 | 29.8 | 3.1 | 2.8 | 4.1 |
| 1973 | 1,691 | 1,186 | 505 | 29.9 | 3.4 | 3.3 | 3.7 |
| 1974 | 1,761 | 1,229 | 532 | 30.2 | 4.1 | 3.6 | 5.3 |
| 1975 | 1,809 | 1,271 | 538 | 29.7 | 2.7 | 3.4 | 1.1 |

| Year | Average Annual Employment | | | Percent | Annual Percentage Change | | |
|---|---|---|---|---|---|---|---|
| | Total | Nonagr. | Agr. | Agr. | Total | Nonagr. | Agr. |

Ukrainian SSR

| Year | Total | Nonagr. | Agr. | Agr. | Total | Nonagr. | Agr. |
|---|---|---|---|---|---|---|---|
| 1957 | 16,093 | 8,078 | 8,015 | 49.8 | | | |
| 1958 | 16,246 | 8,472 | 7,774 | 47.8 | 0.9 | 4.9 | -3.1 |
| 1959 | 16,444 | 8,830 | 7,614 | 46.3 | 1.2 | 4.2 | -2.1 |
| 1960 | 17,055 | 9,690 | 7,365 | 43.2 | 3.7 | 9.7 | -3.4 |
| 1961 | 17,570 | 10,275 | 7,295 | 41.5 | 3.0 | 6.0 | -1.0 |
| 1962 | 17,845 | 10,707 | 7,138 | 40.0 | 1.6 | 4.2 | -2.2 |
| 1963 | 18,104 | 11,121 | 6,983 | 38.6 | 1.4 | 3.9 | -2.2 |
| 1964 | 18,679 | 11,631 | 7,048 | 37.7 | 3.2 | 4.6 | 0.9 |
| 1965 | 19,439 | 12,238 | 7,201 | 37.0 | 4.1 | 5.2 | 2.2 |
| 1966 | 19,955 | 12,795 | 7,160 | 35.9 | 2.6 | 4.5 | -0.6 |
| 1967 | 20,407 | 13,352 | 7,055 | 34.6 | 2.3 | 4.3 | -1.5 |
| 1968 | 20,961 | 13,962 | 6,999 | 33.4 | 2.7 | 4.6 | -0.8 |
| 1969 | 21,283 | 14,558 | 6,725 | 31.6 | 1.5 | 4.3 | -4.1 |
| 1970 | 21,647 | 15,017 | 6,630 | 30.6 | 2.1 | 4.1 | -1.6 |
| 1971 | 22,070 | 15,485 | 6,585 | 29.8 | 2.0 | 3.1 | -0.7 |
| 1972 | 22,483 | 15,918 | 6,565 | 29.2 | 1.9 | 2.8 | -0.3 |
| 1973 | 22,774 | 16,282 | 6,492 | 28.5 | 1.3 | 2.3 | -1.1 |
| 1974 | 23,131 | 16,639 | 6,492 | 28.1 | 1.6 | 2.2 | 0.0 |
| 1975 | 23,331 | 17,028 | 6,303 | 27.0 | 0.9 | 2.3 | -3.0 |

(continued)

Appendix Table 2.2, continued

| Year | Average Annual Employment | | | Percent Agr. | Annual Percentage Change | | |
|------|-------|---------|------|------|-------|---------|------|
|      | Total | Nonagr. | Agr. | Agr. | Total | Nonagr. | Agr. |

Belorussian SSR

| Year | Total | Nonagr. | Agr. | Agr. | Total | Nonagr. | Agr. |
|------|-------|---------|------|------|-------|---------|------|
| 1955 | 3,006 | 1,071 | 1,935 | 64.4 | | | |
| 1956 | 3,052 | 1,129 | 1,923 | 63.0 | 1.5 | 5.4 | 0.6 |
| 1957 | 3,143 | 1,222 | 1,921 | 61.1 | 3.0 | 8.2 | 0.1 |
| 1958 | 3,160 | 1,283 | 1,877 | 59.4 | 0.5 | 5.0 | -2.3 |
| 1959 | 3,120 | 1,328 | 1,792 | 57.4 | -1.3 | 3.5 | -4.7 |
| 1960 | 3,156 | 1,498 | 1,658 | 52.5 | 1.1 | 12.8 | -8.0 |
| 1961 | 3,253 | 1,621 | 1,632 | 50.2 | 3.1 | 8.2 | -1.6 |
| 1962 | 3,290 | 1,699 | 1,591 | 48.4 | 1.1 | 4.8 | -2.6 |
| 1963 | 3,336 | 1,784 | 1,552 | 46.5 | 1.4 | 5.0 | -2.5 |
| 1964 | 3,432 | 1,885 | 1,547 | 45.1 | 2.9 | 5.7 | -0.3 |
| 1965 | 3,581 | 2,011 | 1,570 | 43.8 | 4.3 | 6.7 | 1.5 |
| 1966 | 3,698 | 2,142 | 1,556 | 42.1 | 3.3 | 6.5 | -0.9 |
| 1967 | 3,806 | 2,257 | 1,549 | 40.7 | 2.9 | 5.4 | -0.4 |
| 1968 | 3,941 | 2,404 | 1,537 | 39.0 | 3.5 | 6.5 | -0.8 |
| 1969 | 4,033 | 2,529 | 1,504 | 37.3 | 2.3 | 5.2 | -2.2 |
| 1970 | 4,116 | 2,636 | 1,480 | 36.0 | 2.7 | 5.3 | -1.1 |
| 1971 | 4,219 | 2,747 | 1,472 | 34.9 | 2.5 | 4.2 | -0.5 |
| 1972 | 4,304 | 2,849 | 1,455 | 33.8 | 2.0 | 3.7 | -1.2 |
| 1973 | 4,381 | 2,937 | 1,444 | 33.0 | 1.8 | 3.1 | -0.8 |
| 1974 | 4,475 | 3,033 | 1,442 | 32.2 | 2.1 | 3.3 | -0.1 |
| 1975 | 4,541 | 3,133 | 1,408 | 31.0 | 1.5 | 3.3 | -2.4 |

| Year | Average Annual Employment | | | Percent | Annual Percentage Change | | |
|------|-------|---------|-------|------|-------|---------|------|
|      | Total | Nonagr. | Agr.  | Agr. | Total | Nonagr. | Agr. |

Kazakh SSR

| Year | Total | Nonagr. | Agr. | Agr. | Total | Nonagr. | Agr. |
|------|-------|---------|------|------|-------|---------|------|
| 1957 | 3,116 | 1,740 | 1,376 | 44.2 | | | |
| 1958 | 3,185 | 1,864 | 1,321 | 41.5 | 2.2 | 7.1 | -4.2 |
| 1959 | 3,315 | 1,980 | 1,335 | 40.3 | 4.1 | 6.2 | 1.1 |
| 1960 | 3,579 | 2,251 | 1,328 | 37.1 | 8.0 | 13.7 | -0.5 |
| 1961 | 3,721 | 2,435 | 1,286 | 34.6 | 4.0 | 8.2 | -3.3 |
| 1962 | 3,874 | 2,532 | 1,343 | 34.6 | 4.1 | 4.0 | 4.4 |
| 1963 | 3,983 | 2,642 | 1,341 | 33.7 | 2.8 | 4.3 | -0.1 |
| 1964 | 4,163 | 2,784 | 1,379 | 33.1 | 4.5 | 5.4 | 2.8 |
| 1965 | 4,376 | 2,994 | 1,382 | 31.6 | 5.1 | 7.5 | 0.2 |
| 1966 | 4,493 | 3,115 | 1,378 | 30.7 | 2.7 | 4.0 | -0.3 |
| 1967 | 4,607 | 3,237 | 1,370 | 29.7 | 2.5 | 3.9 | -0.6 |
| 1968 | 4,729 | 3,414 | 1,315 | 27.8 | 2.6 | 5.5 | -4.2 |
| 1969 | 4,826 | 3,588 | 1,238 | 25.7 | 2.0 | 5.1 | -6.2 |
| 1970 | 4,983 | 3,724 | 1,259 | 25.3 | 2.4 | 3.8 | -1.2 |
| 1971 | 5,128 | 3,854 | 1,274 | 24.8 | 2.9 | 3.5 | 1.2 |
| 1972 | 5,259 | 3,969 | 1,290 | 24.5 | 2.5 | 3.0 | 1.3 |
| 1973 | 5,413 | 4,079 | 1,334 | 24.6 | 2.9 | 2.8 | 3.4 |
| 1974 | 5,543 | 4,200 | 1,343 | 24.2 | 2.4 | 3.0 | 0.7 |
| 1975 | 5,666 | 4,315 | 1,351 | 23.8 | 2.2 | 2.7 | 0.6 |

(continued)

Appendix Table 2.2, continued

| Year | Average Annual Employment | | | Percent | Annual Percentage Change | | |
|------|-------|---------|------|---------|-------|---------|------|
|      | Total | Nonagr. | Agr. | Agr.    | Total | Nonagr. | Agr. |

Georgian SSR

| Year | Total | Nonagr. | Agr. | Agr. | Total | Nonagr. | Agr. |
|------|-------|---------|------|------|-------|---------|------|
| 1957 | 1,303 | 723 | 580 | 44.5 | | | |
| 1958 | 1,338 | 716 | 577 | 43.1 | 2.7 | 5.3 | -0.5 |
| 1959 | 1,367 | 797 | 570 | 41.7 | 2.2 | 4.7 | -1.2 |
| 1960 | 1,430 | 870 | 560 | 39.2 | 4.6 | 9.2 | -1.8 |
| 1961 | 1,446 | 908 | 538 | 37.2 | 1.1 | 4.4 | -4.1 |
| 1962 | 1,476 | 935 | 541 | 36.7 | 2.1 | 3.0 | 0.6 |
| 1963 | 1,530 | 972 | 558 | 36.5 | 3.7 | 4.0 | 3.1 |
| 1964 | 1,575 | 1,020 | 555 | 35.2 | 2.9 | 4.9 | -0.5 |
| 1965 | 1,631 | 1,059 | 572 | 35.1 | 3.6 | 3.8 | 3.1 |
| 1966 | 1,693 | 1,110 | 583 | 34.4 | 3.8 | 4.8 | 1.9 |
| 1967 | 1,745 | 1,155 | 590 | 33.8 | 3.1 | 4.1 | 1.2 |
| 1968 | 1,791 | 1,228 | 563 | 31.4 | 2.6 | 6.3 | -4.8 |
| 1969 | 1,819 | 1,265 | 554 | 30.5 | 1.6 | 3.0 | -1.6 |
| 1970 | 1,879 | 1,296 | 583 | 31.0 | 2.8 | 4.1 | 0.3 |
| 1971 | 1,926 | 1,339 | 587 | 30.5 | 2.5 | 3.3 | 0.7 |
| 1972 | 1,945 | 1,356 | 589 | 30.3 | 1.0 | 1.3 | 0.3 |
| 1973 | 1,993 | 1,382 | 611 | 30.7 | 2.5 | 1.9 | 3.7 |
| 1974 | 2,050 | 1,417 | 633 | 30.9 | 2.9 | 2.5 | 3.6 |
| 1975 | 2,091 | 1,459 | 632 | 30.2 | 2.0 | 3.0 | -0.2 |

| Year | Average Annual Employment | | | Percent Agr. | Annual Percentage Change | | |
|------|-------|---------|------|---------|-------|---------|------|
|      | Total | Nonagr. | Agr. |         | Total | Nonagr. | Agr. |

Moldavian SSR

| Year | Total | Nonagr. | Agr. | Agr. | Total | Nonagr. | Agr. |
|------|-------|---------|------|------|-------|---------|------|
| 1957 | 1,051 | 316   | 735 | 69.9 |     |      |      |
| 1958 | 1,061 | 338   | 723 | 68.1 | 0.9 | 7.0  | -1.7 |
| 1959 | 1,093 | 363   | 730 | 66.8 | 3.0 | 7.4  | 1.0  |
| 1960 | 1,117 | 399   | 718 | 64.3 | 2.2 | 9.9  | -1.7 |
| 1961 | 1,160 | 441   | 719 | 62.0 | 3.8 | 10.5 | 0.1  |
| 1962 | 1,194 | 470   | 724 | 60.6 | 2.9 | 6.6  | 0.7  |
| 1963 | 1,219 | 507   | 712 | 58.4 | 2.1 | 7.9  | -1.7 |
| 1964 | 1,288 | 550   | 738 | 57.3 | 5.7 | 8.5  | 3.6  |
| 1965 | 1,348 | 598   | 750 | 55.6 | 4.7 | 8.7  | 1.6  |
| 1966 | 1,411 | 636   | 775 | 54.9 | 4.7 | 6.3  | 3.3  |
| 1967 | 1,462 | 684   | 778 | 53.2 | 3.6 | 7.5  | 0.4  |
| 1968 | 1,502 | 734   | 768 | 51.1 | 2.7 | 7.3  | -1.3 |
| 1969 | 1,543 | 779   | 764 | 49.5 | 2.7 | 6.1  | -0.5 |
| 1970 | 1,585 | 817   | 768 | 48.4 | 3.1 | 6.4  | 0.3  |
| 1971 | 1,615 | 857   | 758 | 46.9 | 1.9 | 4.9  | -1.3 |
| 1972 | 1,685 | 898   | 787 | 46.7 | 4.3 | 4.8  | 3.8  |
| 1973 | 1,719 | 930   | 789 | 45.9 | 2.0 | 3.6  | 0.2  |
| 1974 | 1,771 | 962   | 809 | 45.7 | 3.0 | 3.4  | 2.5  |
| 1975 | 1,801 | 1,001 | 800 | 44.4 | 1.7 | 4.0  | -1.1 |

(continued)

Appendix Table 2.2, continued

| Year | Average Annual Employment | | | Percent Agr. | Annual Percentage Change | | |
|------|-------|---------|------|------|-------|---------|------|
|      | Total | Nonagr. | Agr. |      | Total | Nonagr. | Agr. |

Armenian SSR

| Year | Total | Nonagr. | Agr. | Percent Agr. | Total | Nonagr. | Agr. |
|------|-------|---------|------|------|-------|---------|------|
| 1957 | 514   | 307     | 207  | 40.3 |       |         |      |
| 1958 | 537   | 328     | 209  | 38.9 | 4.5   | 6.8     | 1.0  |
| 1959 | 558   | 350     | 208  | 37.3 | 3.9   | 6.7     | -0.5 |
| 1960 | 596   | 390     | 206  | 34.6 | 6.8   | 11.4    | -1.0 |
| 1961 | 614   | 421     | 193  | 31.4 | 3.0   | 7.9     | -6.7 |
| 1962 | 640   | 445     | 195  | 30.5 | 4.2   | 5.7     | 1.0  |
| 1963 | 672   | 473     | 199  | 29.6 | 5.0   | 6.3     | 2.1  |
| 1964 | 704   | 507     | 197  | 28.0 | 4.8   | 7.2     | -1.0 |
| 1965 | 752   | 546     | 206  | 27.4 | 6.8   | 7.7     | 4.6  |
| 1966 | 789   | 585     | 204  | 25.9 | 4.9   | 7.1     | -1.0 |
| 1967 | 826   | 622     | 204  | 24.7 | 4.7   | 6.3     | 0.0  |
| 1968 | 867   | 668     | 199  | 23.0 | 5.0   | 7.4     | -2.5 |
| 1969 | 911   | 709     | 202  | 22.2 | 5.1   | 6.1     | 1.5  |
| 1970 | 943   | 743     | 200  | 21.2 | 4.6   | 6.3     | -0.6 |
| 1971 | 977   | 774     | 203  | 20.8 | 3.6   | 4.2     | 1.5  |
| 1972 | 1,003 | 800     | 203  | 20.2 | 2.7   | 3.4     | 0.0  |
| 1973 | 1,026 | 820     | 206  | 20.1 | 2.3   | 2.5     | 1.5  |
| 1974 | 1,056 | 845     | 211  | 20.0 | 2.9   | 3.0     | 2.4  |
| 1975 | 1,084 | 871     | 213  | 19.6 | 2.6   | 3.1     | 0.9  |

| Year | Average Annual Employment | | | Percent Agr. | Annual Percentage Change | | |
|------|-------|---------|------|------|-------|---------|------|
|      | Total | Nonagr. | Agr. | Agr. | Total | Nonagr. | Agr. |

Turkmen SSR

| Year | Total | Nonagr. | Agr. | Agr. | Total | Nonagr. | Agr. |
|------|-------|---------|------|------|-------|---------|------|
| 1957 | 486 | 234 | 252 | 51.9 |     |     |      |
| 1958 | 493 | 247 | 246 | 49.9 | 1.4 | 5.6 | -2.4 |
| 1959 | 510 | 264 | 246 | 48.2 | 3.4 | 6.9 | 0.0  |
| 1960 | 534 | 286 | 248 | 46.4 | 4.7 | 8.3 | 0.8  |
| 1961 | 546 | 301 | 245 | 44.9 | 2.2 | 5.2 | -1.2 |
| 1962 | 553 | 314 | 239 | 43.2 | 1.3 | 4.3 | -2.5 |
| 1963 | 569 | 323 | 246 | 43.2 | 2.9 | 2.9 | 2.9  |
| 1964 | 576 | 338 | 238 | 41.3 | 1.2 | 4.6 | -3.4 |
| 1965 | 607 | 361 | 246 | 40.5 | 5.4 | 6.8 | 3.4  |
| 1966 | 628 | 378 | 250 | 39.8 | 3.5 | 4.7 | 1.6  |
| 1967 | 654 | 394 | 260 | 39.8 | 4.1 | 4.2 | 4.0  |
| 1968 | 668 | 410 | 258 | 38.6 | 2.1 | 4.1 | -0.8 |
| 1969 | 688 | 429 | 259 | 37.6 | 3.0 | 4.6 | 0.4  |
| 1970 | 725 | 447 | 278 | 38.3 | 3.5 | 4.3 | 2.3  |
| 1971 | 757 | 466 | 291 | 38.4 | 4.4 | 4.2 | 4.7  |
| 1972 | 780 | 295 | 485 | 37.8 | 3.0 | 4.1 | 1.4  |
| 1973 | 813 | 503 | 310 | 38.1 | 4.2 | 3.7 | 5.1  |
| 1974 | 844 | 519 | 325 | 38.5 | 3.8 | 3.2 | 4.8  |
| 1975 | 880 | 343 | 537 | 39.0 | 4.3 | 3.5 | 5.5  |

(continued)

Appendix Table 2.2, continued

| Year | Average Annual Employment | | | Percent | Annual Percentage Change | | |
|------|-------|---------|------|---------|-------|---------|------|
|      | Total | Nonagr. | Agr. | Agr.    | Total | Nonagr. | Agr. |

Tadzhik SSR

| Year | Total | Nonagr. | Agr. | Agr. | Total | Nonagr. | Agr. |
|------|-------|---------|------|------|-------|---------|------|
| 1957 | 575 | 223 | 352 | 61.2 | | | |
| 1958 | 584 | 242 | 342 | 58.6 | 1.6 | 8.5 | -2.9 |
| 1959 | 588 | 257 | 331 | 56.3 | 0.7 | 6.2 | -3.3 |
| 1960 | 614 | 290 | 324 | 52.8 | 4.4 | 12.8 | -2.2 |
| 1961 | 631 | 312 | 319 | 50.6 | 2.8 | 7.6 | -1.6 |
| 1962 | 652 | 330 | 322 | 49.4 | 3.3 | 5.8 | 0.9 |
| 1963 | 679 | 348 | 331 | 48.7 | 4.1 | 5.5 | 2.8 |
| 1964 | 698 | 372 | 326 | 46.7 | 2.8 | 6.9 | -1.5 |
| 1965 | 729 | 404 | 325 | 44.6 | 4.4 | 8.6 | -0.3 |
| 1966 | 751 | 429 | 322 | 42.9 | 3.0 | 6.2 | -0.9 |
| 1967 | 760 | 445 | 315 | 41.4 | 1.2 | 3.7 | -2.2 |
| 1968 | 789 | 471 | 318 | 40.3 | 3.8 | 5.8 | 1.0 |
| 1969 | 817 | 495 | 322 | 39.4 | 3.5 | 5.1 | 1.3 |
| 1970 | 852 | 518 | 334 | 39.2 | 3.0 | 5.0 | 0.4 |
| 1971 | 889 | 542 | 347 | 39.0 | 4.3 | 4.6 | 3.9 |
| 1972 | 917 | 567 | 350 | 38.2 | 3.1 | 4.6 | 0.9 |
| 1973 | 944 | 592 | 352 | 37.3 | 2.9 | 4.4 | 0.6 |
| 1974 | 983 | 618 | 365 | 37.1 | 4.1 | 4.4 | 3.7 |
| 1975 | 1,020 | 378 | 642 | 37.1 | 3.8 | 3.9 | 3.6 |

| | Average Annual Employment | | | Percent | Annual Percentage Change | | |
| Year | Total | Nonagr. | Agr. | Agr. | Total | Nonagr. | Agr. |
|---|---|---|---|---|---|---|---|
| | | | Uzbek SSR | | | | |
| 1957 | 2,365 | 986 | 1,379 | 58.3 | | | |
| 1958 | 2,448 | 1,031 | 1,417 | 57.9 | 3.5 | 4.6 | 2.8 |
| 1959 | 2,422 | 1,083 | 1,339 | 55.3 | -1.1 | 5.0 | -5.8 |
| 1960 | 2,528 | 1,220 | 1,308 | 51.7 | 4.4 | 12.6 | -2.4 |
| 1961 | 2,625 | 1,334 | 1,291 | 49.2 | 3.8 | 9.3 | -1.3 |
| 1962 | 2,727 | 1,418 | 1,309 | 48.0 | 3.9 | 6.3 | 1.4 |
| 1963 | 2,843 | 1,495 | 1,348 | 47.4 | 4.3 | 5.4 | 3.0 |
| 1964 | 2,944 | 1,592 | 1,352 | 45.9 | 3.6 | 6.5 | 3.0 |
| 1965 | 3,100 | 1,721 | 1,379 | 44.5 | 5.3 | 8.1 | 2.0 |
| 1966 | 3,220 | 1,828 | 1,392 | 43.2 | 3.9 | 6.2 | 0.9 |
| 1967 | 3,314 | 1,928 | 1,386 | 41.8 | 2.9 | 5.5 | -0.4 |
| 1968 | 3,440 | 2,029 | 1,411 | 41.0 | 3.8 | 5.2 | 1.8 |
| 1969 | 3,574 | 2,144 | 1,430 | 40.0 | 3.9 | 5.7 | 1.3 |
| 1970 | 3,684 | 2,228 | 1,456 | 39.5 | 3.7 | 5.3 | 1.5 |
| 1971 | 3,823 | 2,323 | 1,500 | 39.2 | 3.8 | 4.3 | 3.0 |
| 1972 | 3,956 | 2,420 | 1,536 | 38.8 | 3.5 | 4.2 | 2.4 |
| 1973 | 4,092 | 2,527 | 1,565 | 38.2 | 3.4 | 4.4 | 1.9 |
| 1974 | 4,252 | 2,631 | 1,621 | 38.1 | 3.9 | 4.1 | 3.6 |
| 1975 | 4,431 | 2,761 | 1,670 | 37.7 | 4.2 | 4.9 | 3.0 |

(continued)

Appendix Table 2.2, continued

| Year | Average Annual Employment | | | Percent | Annual Percentage Change | | |
|------|-------|---------|------|---------|-------|---------|------|
|      | Total | Nonagr. | Agr. | Agr.    | Total | Nonagr. | Agr. |

Kirgiz SSR

| Year | Total | Nonagr. | Agr. | Agr. | Total | Nonagr. | Agr. |
|------|-------|---------|------|------|-------|---------|------|
| 1957 | 579   | 276     | 303  | 52.3 |       |         |      |
| 1958 | 604   | 299     | 305  | 50.5 | 4.3   | 8.3     | 0.7  |
| 1959 | 623   | 321     | 302  | 48.5 | 3.1   | 7.4     | -1.0 |
| 1960 | 645   | 358     | 287  | 44.5 | 3.5   | 11.5    | -5.2 |
| 1961 | 677   | 393     | 284  | 42.0 | 5.0   | 9.8     | -1.1 |
| 1962 | 717   | 418     | 299  | 41.7 | 5.9   | 6.4     | 5.3  |
| 1963 | 752   | 442     | 310  | 41.2 | 4.9   | 5.7     | 3.7  |
| 1964 | 787   | 469     | 318  | 40.4 | 4.7   | 6.1     | 2.6  |
| 1965 | 833   | 507     | 326  | 39.1 | 5.8   | 8.1     | 2.5  |
| 1966 | 864   | 534     | 330  | 38.2 | 3.7   | 5.3     | 1.2  |
| 1967 | 895   | 563     | 332  | 37.1 | 3.6   | 5.4     | 0.6  |
| 1968 | 930   | 599     | 331  | 35.6 | 3.9   | 6.4     | -0.3 |
| 1969 | 964   | 636     | 328  | 34.0 | 3.7   | 6.2     | -0.9 |
| 1970 | 998   | 664     | 334  | 33.5 | 3.6   | 5.4     | 0.5  |
| 1971 | 1,032 | 693     | 339  | 32.8 | 3.4   | 4.4     | 1.5  |
| 1972 | 1,054 | 715     | 339  | 32.2 | 2.1   | 3.2     | 0.0  |
| 1973 | 1,080 | 738     | 342  | 31.7 | 2.5   | 3.2     | 0.9  |
| 1974 | 1,124 | 767     | 357  | 31.8 | 4.1   | 3.9     | 4.4  |
| 1975 | 1,148 | 791     | 357  | 31.1 | 2.1   | 3.1     | 0.0  |

*Employment data are in thousands.

Sources: Employment data prior to 1970 from issues of Narkhoz for the USSR and the respective republics; employment data for 1970-75 from Stephen Rapawy, "Regional Employment Trends in the U.S.S.R.: 1950 to 1975," in U.S. Congress, Joint Economic Committee, Soviet Economy in a Time of Change, Vol. 1 (Washington, D.C.: U.S. Government Printing Office, 1979), pp. 600-17.

Annual Percentage Rates of Change in Total, Urban, and Rural Populations
of All Ages and Working Ages: Regions of Low, Medium, and High LSP,
USSR, 1959 and 1970-77, with Projections to 2000

| | Region of Low LSP | | | | | | | | |
|---|---|---|---|---|---|---|---|---|---|
| | All Ages | | | | Working Ages | | | | Labor |
| Year | Total | Urban | Rural | Percent Rural | Total | Urban | Rural | Percent Rural | Supply Deficit[a] |
| 1959 | | | | 38.7 | | | | 34.6 | |
| | +1.0 | +2.2 | −1.4 | | +0.7 | +1.6 | −1.1 | | |
| 1970 | — | — | — | 29.6 | +1.5 | +2.4 | −1.0[c] | 28.4 | |
| 1971 | +0.8 | +2.0 | −2.3 | 29.0 | +1.6 | +2.6 | −1.0[c] | 27.7 | |
| 1972 | +0.8 | +2.1 | −2.2 | 28.1 | +1.6 | +2.5 | −1.0[c] | 27.0 | |
| 1973 | +0.8 | +2.1 | −2.5 | 27.2 | +1.7 | +2.6 | −1.0[c] | 26.3 | |
| 1974 | +0.9 | +2.1 | −2.6 | 26.3 | +1.6 | +2.5 | −1.0[c] | 25.6 | |
| 1975 | +0.9 | +2.0 | −2.6 | 25.4 | +1.7 | +2.6 | −1.0[c] | 25.0 | |
| 1976 | +0.9 | +1.6 | −2.2 | 24.6 | +1.5 | +2.3 | −1.0[c] | 24.3 | |
| 1977 | +0.9 | +1.6 | −1.3 | 24.1 | +1.2 | +2.0[c] | −1.3 | 23.7 | |
| 1978 | | | | | +0.9 | +1.8[c] | −2.3 | 23.0 | |
| 1979 | | | | | +0.6 | +1.6 | −2.5[c] | 22.4 | |
| 1980 | | | | | +0.3[b] | +1.3[c] | −2.5[c] | 21.7 | 71 |
| 1981 | | | | | 0.0 | +1.0[c] | −2.5[c] | 21.1 | 139 |
| 1982 | | | | | −0.2 | +1.0[c] | −2.5[c] | 20.5 | 157 |
| 1983 | | | | | −0.3 | +1.0[c] | −2.5[c] | 20.0 | 311 |
| 1984 | | | | | −0.4 | +1.0[c] | −2.5[c] | 19.4 | 392 |
| 1985 | | | | | −0.4 | +1.0[c] | −2.5[c] | 18.9 | 432 |
| 1986 | | | | | −0.5 | +1.0[c] | −2.5[c] | 18.4 | 469 |
| 1987 | | | | | −0.2 | +1.0[c] | −2.5[c] | 17.8 | 514 |
| 1988 | | | | | −0.2 | +1.0[c] | −2.5[c] | 17.3 | 349 |
| 1989 | | | | | −0.2 | +1.0[c] | −2.5[c] | 16.9 | 409 |
| 1990 | | | | | −0.2 | +1.0[c] | −2.5[c] | 16.4 | 374 |
| 1991 | | | | | −0.1 | +1.0[c] | −2.5[c] | 15.9 | 357 |
| 1992 | | | | | −0.1 | +1.0[c] | 0.0[c] | 15.5 | 359 |
| 1993 | | | | | −0.1 | +1.0[c] | 0.0[c] | 15.4 | 597 |
| 1994 | | | | | −0.1 | +1.0[c] | 0.0[c] | 15.1 | 632 |
| 1995 | | | | | −0.1 | +1.0[c] | 0.0[c] | 15.0 | 577 |
| 1996 | | | | | 0.0 | +1.0[c] | 0.0[c] | 14.8 | 622 |
| 1997 | | | | | +0.2 | +1.0[c] | 0.0[c] | 14.7 | 582 |
| 1998 | | | | | +0.2 | +1.0[c] | 0.0[c] | 14.6 | 525 |
| 1999 | | | | | +0.2 | +1.0[c] | 0.0[c] | 14.5 | 457 |
| 2000 | | | | | | | | | |

(continued)

| Year | Region of Medium LSP | | | | | | | | |
|---|---|---|---|---|---|---|---|---|---|
| | All Ages | | | | Working Ages | | | | |
| | Total | Urban | Rural | Percent Rural | Total | Urban | Rural | Percent Rural | Labor Supply Surplus[a] |
| 1959 | | | | 59.9 | | | | 65.8 | |
| | +1.3 | +3.3 | −0.3 | | +0.7 | +3.4 | −2.0 | | |
| 1970 | — | — | — | 50.2 | +1.6 | +3.4[c] | −0.9 | 42.0 | |
| 1971 | +0.9 | +3.0 | −1.2 | 48.3 | +1.7 | +3.4[c] | −0.7 | 41.0 | |
| 1972 | +0.7 | +2.7 | −1.4 | 47.4 | +1.7 | +3.4[c] | −0.8 | 40.0 | |
| 1973 | +0.6 | +2.5 | −1.5 | 45.6 | +1.7 | +3.4[c] | −1.0 | 39.0 | |
| 1974 | +0.7 | +2.4 | −1.3 | 45.4 | +1.8 | +3.4[c] | −0.8 | 38.0 | |
| 1975 | +0.6 | +2.4 | −1.6 | 44.8 | +1.7 | +3.4[c] | −1.1 | 37.0 | |
| 1976 | +0.6 | +2.1 | −1.3 | 44.4 | +1.9 | +3.4[c] | −1.0 | 36.0 | |
| 1977 | +0.6 | +1.9 | −1.1 | 43.6 | +1.7 | +3.1[c] | −1.0 | 35.0 | |
| 1978 | | | | | +1.4 | +2.8[c] | −1.2 | 34.1 | |
| 1979 | | | | | +1.1 | +2.3[c] | −1.6 | 33.2 | |
| 1980 | | | | | +0.9[b] | +1.9[c] | −1.8 | 32.3 | 71[c] |
| 1981 | | | | | +0.6 | +1.5[c] | −2.0 | 31.5 | 139[c] |
| 1982 | | | | | +0.4 | +1.1[c] | −2.5 | 30.8 | 157[c] |
| 1983 | | | | | +0.3 | +1.0[c] | −2.5 | 30.1 | 311[c] |
| 1984 | | | | | +0.2 | +1.0[c] | −2.5[c] | 29.3 | 244 |
| 1985 | | | | | +0.2 | +1.0[c] | −2.5[c] | 28.6 | 188 |
| 1986 | | | | | +0.1 | +1.0[c] | −2.5[c] | 27.9 | 154 |
| 1987 | | | | | +0.2 | +1.0[c] | −2.5[c] | 27.2 | 80 |
| 1988 | | | | | +0.4 | +1.0[c] | −2.5[c] | 26.6 | 89 |
| 1989 | | | | | +0.3 | +1.0[c] | −2.5[c] | 25.9 | 292 |
| 1990 | | | | | +0.2 | +1.0[c] | −2.5[c] | 25.2 | 134 |
| 1991 | | | | | +0.1 | +1.0[c] | −2.5[c] | 24.5 | 91 |
| 1992 | | | | | +0.1 | +1.0[c] | −2.5[c] | 23.9 | −27 |
| 1993 | | | | | +0.1 | +1.0[c] | −2.5[c] | 23.3 | −74 |
| 1994 | | | | | +0.1 | +1.0[c] | −2.5[c] | 22.7 | −104 |
| 1995 | | | | | +0.5 | +1.0[c] | −2.5[c] | 22.1 | −90 |
| 1996 | | | | | +0.6 | +1.0[c] | −2.5[c] | 21.5 | 236 |
| 1997 | | | | | +0.9 | +1.0[c] | −2.5[c] | 20.9 | 276 |
| 1998 | | | | | +1.1 | +1.0[c] | −2.5[c] | 20.4 | 460 |
| 1999 | | | | | +1.2 | +1.0[c] | −2.5[c] | 20.1 | 457 |
| 2000 | | | | | | | | | |

| | | | | | Region of High LSP | | | | |
|---|---|---|---|---|---|---|---|---|---|
| | | All Ages | | | | Working Ages | | | Labor |
| Year | Total | Urban | Rural | Percent Rural | Total | Urban | Rural | Percent Rural | Supply Surplus[a] |
| 1959 | | | | 68.0 | | | | 64.3 | |
| | +3.3 | +4.6 | +2.5 | | +2.0 | +4.0 | +0.6 | | |
| 1970 | — | — | — | 63.9 | +3.3 | +6.0$^c$ | +1.2 | 56.7 | |
| 1971 | +2.0 | +3.1 | +4.2 | 63.7 | +3.8 | +6.0$^c$ | +2.1 | 55.6 | |
| 1972 | +2.5 | +4.2 | +1.5 | 63.3 | +3.9 | +6.0$^c$ | +2.2 | 54.6 | |
| 1973 | +2.5 | +3.6 | +1.8 | 62.7 | +3.9 | +6.0$^c$ | +2.1 | 53.7 | |
| 1974 | +2.5 | +3.8 | +1.7 | 62.3 | +4.0 | +6.0$^c$ | +2.3 | 52.8 | |
| 1975 | +2.3 | +3.6 | +1.5 | 61.8 | +3.7 | +6.0$^c$ | +1.6 | 51.9 | |
| 1976 | +2.4 | +3.1 | +1.9 | 61.1 | +4.0 | +6.0$^c$ | +2.0 | 50.9 | |
| 1977 | +2.1 | +2.7 | +1.7 | 60.8 | +3.7 | +5.6 | +1.8$^c$ | 49.9 | |
| 1978 | | | | | +3.5 | +5.3 | +1.6$^c$ | 49.0 | |
| 1979 | | | | | +3.3 | +5.1 | +1.4$^c$ | 48.1 | |
| 1980 | | | | | +3.2 | +5.0 | +1.2$^c$ | 47.2 | |
| 1981 | | | | | +2.7 | +4.2 | +1.0$^c$ | 46.3 | |
| 1982 | | | | | +2.6 | +4.0$^c$ | +0.8 | 45.5 | |
| 1983 | | | | | +2.5 | +3.8$^c$ | −1.1 | 44.7 | |
| 1984 | | | | | +2.7$^b$ | +3.6$^c$ | −1.8 | 43.5 | 148$^c$ |
| 1985 | | | | | +2.4 | +2.8$^c$ | −2.5 | 42.2 | 244$^c$ |
| 1986 | | | | | +2.3 | +2.0$^c$ | −2.5 | 40.9 | 315$^c$ |
| 1987 | | | | | +2.5 | +2.0$^c$ | −0.1 | 39.7 | 434$^c$ |
| 1988 | | | | | +2.5 | +2.0$^c$ | +2.0 | 39.2 | 260$^c$ |
| 1989 | | | | | +2.5 | +2.0$^c$ | +0.4 | 39.0 | 117$^c$ |
| 1990 | | | | | +2.5 | +2.0$^c$ | +0.2 | 38.8 | 240$^c$ |
| 1991 | | | | | +2.5 | +2.0$^c$ | −1.5 | 38.4 | 266$^c$ |
| 1992 | | | | | +2.6 | +2.0$^c$ | −5.6 | 37.6 | 386$^c$ |
| 1993 | | | | | +2.6 | +2.0$^c$ | −6.7 | 35.8 | 671$^c$ |
| 1994 | | | | | +2.7 | +2.0$^c$ | −5.2 | 33.9 | 736$^c$ |
| 1995 | | | | | +2.7 | +2.0$^c$ | −0.3 | 32.4 | 667$^c$ |
| 1996 | | | | | +2.8 | +2.0$^c$ | 0.0 | 31.9 | 386$^c$ |
| 1997 | | | | | +2.9 | +2.0$^c$ | 0.0$^c$ | 31.3 | 306+87 |
| 1998 | | | | | +3.1 | +2.0$^c$ | 0.0$^c$ | 30.3 | 65+382 |
| 1999 | | | | | +3.1 | +2.0$^c$ | 0.0$^c$ | 29.1 | 0+406 |
| 2000 | | | | | | | | | |

$^a$In thousands.

$^b$After deficits and surpluses appear, total rates refer to changes before implied population transfers, and all other rates and measures to changes after transfers.

$^c$Assumed rates; other rates are either given or derived by arithmetic.

Source: From absolute data according to procedures described in text.

APPENDIX TABLE 2.4

Average Annual Agricultural Employment as Percentage of Rural Population:
By Republics, Years for Which Data Are Available, 1950–75

| Year | Rural Population (thousands) | Agricultural Employment (thousands) USSR | Percent | Rural Population (thousands) | Agricultural Employment (thousands) RSFSR | Percent |
|---|---|---|---|---|---|---|
| 1950 | 109,133 | 31,037 | 28.5 | 57,689 | 15,966 | 27.7 |
| 1955 | | | | 56,232 | 15,755 | 28.0 |
| 1956 | | | | 56,874 | 15,670 | 27.6 |
| 1957 | 110,020 | 32,243 | 29.3 | 57,075 | 15,585 | 27.3 |
| 1958 | 109,349 | 31,980 | 29.2 | 56,650 | 14,960 | 26.4 |
| 1959 | 108,849 | 31,118 | 28.6 | 55,923 | 14,141 | 25.3 |
| 1960 | 108,530 | 28,863 | 26.6 | 55,187 | 13,396 | 24.3 |
| 1961 | 107,823 | 28,202 | 26.2 | 54,343 | 12,966 | 23.9 |
| 1962 | 107,879 | 28,003 | 26.0 | 53,871 | 12,900 | 23.9 |
| 1963 | 108,004 | 27,537 | 25.5 | 53,871 | 12,587 | 23.6 |
| 1964 | 107,712 | 27,553 | 25.6 | 52,803 | 12,593 | 23.8 |
| 1965 | 107,525 | 27,796 | 25.9 | 52,209 | 12,488 | 24.0 |
| 1966 | 106,119 | 27,750 | 26.2 | 51,492 | 12,455 | 24.2 |
| 1967 | (105,936) | 27,643 | 26.1 | (50,645) | 12,473 | 24.7 |
| 1968 | 105,754 | 27,204 | 25.8 | 49,798 | 12,188 | 24.5 |
| 1969 | 104,766 | 26,256 | 25.1 | 48,788 | 11,674 | 24.0 |
| 1970 | 105,745 | 25,895 | 24.5 | 49,106 | 11,384 | 23.2 |
| 1971 | 104,873 | 25,997 | 24.7 | 48,121 | 11,362 | 23.7 |
| 1972 | 103,768 | 25,847 | 24.9 | 47,031 | 11,153 | 23.8 |
| 1973 | 102,526 | 25,985 | 25.3 | 45,892 | 11,242 | 24.5 |
| 1974 | 101,280 | 26,002 | 25.7 | 44,682 | 11,089 | 24.9 |
| 1975 | 100,151 | 25,921 | 25.9 | 43,569 | 10,893 | 25.0 |
| 1976 | 98,934 | 25,599 | 26.1 | | | |

| | Estonian SSR | | | | Georgian SSR | |
|---|---|---|---|---|---|---|
| 1950 | 581 | 169 | 29.1 | 2,253 | 623 | 27.7 |
| — | | | | | | |
| 1957 | 521 | 156 | 29.9 | 2,329 | 580 | 24.9 |
| 1958 | 522 | 156 | 29.9 | 2,312 | 577 | 25.0 |
| 1959 | 521 | 155 | 29.7 | 2,331 | 570 | 24.5 |
| 1960 | 520 | 152 | 29.2 | 2,380 | 560 | 23.5 |
| 1961 | 515 | 141 | 27.4 | 2,380 | 538 | 22.6 |
| 1962 | 504 | 139 | 27.6 | 2,351 | 541 | 23.0 |
| 1963 | 493 | 133 | 27.0 | 2,373 | 558 | 23.5 |
| 1964 | 489 | 132 | 27.0 | 2,397 | 555 | 23.2 |
| 1965 | 485 | 140 | 28.9 | 2,398 | 572 | 23.9 |
| 1966 | 481 | 135 | 28.1 | 2,408 | 583 | 24.3 |
| 1967 | (478) | 132 | 27.7 | (2,414) | 590 | 24.5 |
| 1968 | 474 | 127 | 26.8 | 2,421 | 563 | 23.3 |
| 1969 | 472 | 120 | 25.5 | 2,418 | 554 | 23.0 |
| 1970 | 475 | 117 | 24.7 | 2,447 | 578 | 23.7 |
| 1971 | 473 | 122 | 25.8 | 2,456 | 587 | 23.9 |
| 1972 | 471 | 120 | 25.5 | 2,467 | 589 | 23.9 |
| 1973 | 468 | 123 | 26.3 | 2,478 | 611 | 24.7 |
| 1974 | 464 | 122 | 26.3 | 2,480 | 633 | 25.6 |
| 1975 | 461 | 126 | 27.4 | 2,476 | 632 | 25.6 |

(continued)

83

Appendix Table 2.4, continued

| Year | Rural Population (thousands) | Agricultural Employment (thousands) | Percent | Rural Population (thousands) | Agricultural Employment (thousands) | Percent |
|---|---|---|---|---|---|---|
| | Turkmen SSR | | | Latvian SSR | | |
| 1950 | 764 | 244 | 32.0 | 1,063 | 334 | 20.9 |
| 1957 | 775 | 252 | 32.5 | 957 | 320 | 33.4 |
| 1958 | 791 | 246 | 31.1 | 937 | 312 | 33.3 |
| 1959 | 816 | 246 | 24.8 | 919 | 313 | 34.1 |
| 1960 | 838 | 248 | 29.6 | 920 | 300 | 32.6 |
| 1961 | 854 | 245 | 28.7 | 909 | 302 | 33.2 |
| 1962 | 876 | 239 | 27.3 | 897 | 295 | 32.9 |
| 1963 | 899 | 246 | 27.4 | 884 | 284 | 32.1 |
| 1964 | 928 | 238 | 25.6 | 873 | 270 | 30.9 |
| 1965 | 954 | 246 | 25.8 | 874 | 281 | 32.2 |
| 1966 | 974 | 250 | 25.7 | 862 | 275 | 31.9 |
| 1967 | (1,004) | 260 | 25.9 | (854) | 271 | 31.8 |
| 1968 | 1,034 | 258 | 25.0 | 845 | 266 | 31.5 |
| 1969 | 1,060 | 259 | 24.5 | 839 | 246 | 29.4 |
| 1970 | 1,123 | 275 | 24.5 | 888 | 246 | 27.7 |
| 1971 | 1,160 | 291 | 25.0 | 883 | 251 | 28.5 |
| 1972 | 1,192 | 295 | 24.7 | 879 | 247 | 28.1 |
| 1973 | 1,223 | 310 | 25.3 | 874 | 247 | 28.3 |
| 1974 | 1,248 | 325 | 26.1 | 870 | 245 | 28.2 |
| 1975 | 1,283 | 343 | 26.8 | 855 | 242 | 28.3 |

| Year | | Lithuanian SSR | | | Belorussian SSR | |
|---|---|---|---|---|---|---|
| 1950 | 1,844 | 329 | 17.9 | 6,090 | 1,507 | 24.8 |
| 1956 | 1,685 | 524 | 31.1 | 5,735 | 1,923 | 33.5 |
| 1957 | 1,671 | 517 | 30.9 | 5,714 | 1,921 | 33.6 |
| 1958 | 1,665 | 492 | 29.5 | 5,652 | 1,877 | 33.2 |
| 1959 | 1,679 | 499 | 29.7 | 5,574 | 1,792 | 32.1 |
| 1960 | 1,678 | 485 | 28.9 | 5,520 | 1,658 | 30.0 |
| 1961 | 1,686 | 479 | 28.4 | 5,447 | 1,632 | 30.0 |
| 1962 | 1,673 | 473 | 28.3 | 5,406 | 1,591 | 29.4 |
| 1963 | 1,650 | 454 | 27.5 | 5,376 | 1,552 | 28.9 |
| 1964 | 1,660 | 462 | 27.9 | 5,309 | 1,547 | 29.1 |
| 1965 | 1,652 | 465 | 28.2 | 5,263 | 1,570 | 29.9 |
| 1966 | (1,642) | 469 | 28.6 | 5,230 | 1,556 | 29.8 |
| 1967 | 1,633 | 465 | 28.5 | (5,180) | 1,549 | 29.9 |
| 1968 | 1,617 | 450 | 27.9 | 5,129 | 1,537 | 30.0 |
| 1969 | 1,557 | 439 | 28.2 | 5,050 | 1,504 | 29.8 |
| 1970 | 1,539 | 438 | 28.5 | 5,096 | 1,467 | 28.8 |
| 1971 | 1,516 | 430 | 28.4 | 5,020 | 1,472 | 29.4 |
| 1972 | 1,489 | 421 | 28.3 | 4,933 | 1,455 | 29.5 |
| 1973 | 1,466 | 786 | 28.1 | 4,824 | 1,444 | 30.0 |
| 1974 | 1,441 | 408 | 28.4 | 4,719 | 1,442 | 30.6 |
| 1975 | | | | 4,616 | 1,408 | 30.5 |

(continued)

Appendix Table 2.4, continued

| Year | Rural Population (thousands) | Agricultural Employment (thousands) | Percent | Rural Population (thousands) | Agricultural Employment (thousands) | Percent |
|---|---|---|---|---|---|---|
| | Ukrainian SSR | | | Moldavian SSR | | |
| 1950 | 23,811 | 7,235 | 30.4 | 1,902 | 589 | 31.0 |
| 1957 | 23,416 | 8,015 | 34.2 | 2,159 | 735 | 34.0 |
| 1958 | 22,861 | 7,774 | 34.0 | 2,204 | 723 | 32.8 |
| 1959 | 22,722 | 7,614 | 33.5 | 2,242 | 730 | 32.6 |
| 1960 | 22,521 | 7,365 | 32.7 | 2,300 | 718 | 31.2 |
| 1961 | 22,265 | 7,295 | 32.8 | 2,312 | 719 | 31.1 |
| 1962 | 22,193 | 7,138 | 32.2 | 2,354 | 724 | 30.8 |
| 1963 | 22,192 | 6,983 | 31.5 | 2,387 | 712 | 29.8 |
| 1964 | 22,141 | 7,048 | 31.8 | 2,426 | 738 | 30.4 |
| 1965 | 22,007 | 7,201 | 32.8 | 2,445 | 750 | 30.7 |
| 1966 | 21,801 | 7,160 | 32.9 | 2,415 | 775 | 32.1 |
| 1967 | (21,616) | 7,055 | 32.7 | (2,434) | 778 | 32.0 |
| 1968 | 21,430 | 6,999 | 32.7 | 2,453 | 768 | 31.3 |
| 1969 | 21,140 | 6,725 | 31.9 | 2,454 | 764 | 31.2 |
| 1970 | 21,443 | 6,610 | 30.9 | 2,441 | 760 | 31.2 |
| 1971 | 21,214 | 6,585 | 31.1 | 2,447 | 758 | 31.0 |
| 1972 | 20,885 | 6,565 | 31.5 | 2,446 | 787 | 32.2 |
| 1973 | 20,604 | 6,492 | 31.5 | 2,433 | 789 | 32.5 |
| 1974 | 20,326 | 6,492 | 32.0 | 2,432 | 809 | 33.3 |
| 1975 | 20,066 | 6,303 | 31.5 | 2,432 | 800 | 32.9 |

| | Armenian SSR | | | Kazakh SSR | | |
|---|---|---|---|---|---|---|
| 1950 | 781 | 221 | 28.3 | 4,059 | 1,096 | 27.0 |
| — | | | | | | |
| 1957 | 844 | 207 | 24.5 | 4,925 | 1,376 | 27.9 |
| 1958 | 876 | 209 | 23.9 | 4,980 | 1,321 | 26.5 |
| 1959 | 881 | 208 | 23.6 | 5,117 | 1,335 | 26.1 |
| 1960 | 907 | 206 | 22.7 | 5,376 | 1,328 | 24.7 |
| 1961 | 919 | 193 | 21.0 | 5,619 | 1,286 | 22.9 |
| 1962 | 927 | 195 | 21.0 | 5,902 | 1,343 | 22.8 |
| 1963 | 937 | 199 | 21.2 | 6,171 | 1,341 | 21.7 |
| 1964 | 951 | 197 | 20.7 | 6,235 | 1,379 | 22.1 |
| 1965 | 959 | 206 | 21.5 | 6,277 | 1,382 | 22.1 |
| 1966 | 984 | 204 | 20.8 | 6,343 | 1,378 | 21.8 |
| 1967 | (1,001) | 204 | 20.4 | (6,384) | 1,370 | 21.5 |
| 1968 | 1,018 | 199 | 19.6 | 6,424 | 1,315 | 20.5 |
| 1969 | 1,030 | 202 | 19.7 | 6,398 | 1,238 | 19.9 |
| 1970 | 1,011 | 199 | 19.7 | 6,351 | 1,233 | 19.5 |
| 1971 | 1,018 | 203 | 20.0 | 6,383 | 1,274 | 19.9 |
| 1972 | 1,017 | 203 | 20.0 | 6,528 | 1,290 | 19.7 |
| 1973 | 1,023 | 206 | 20.2 | 6,544 | 1,334 | 20.3 |
| 1974 | 1,029 | 211 | 20.5 | 6,580 | 1,343 | 20.5 |
| 1975 | 1,031 | 213 | 20.7 | 6,618 | 1,351 | 20.5 |

(continued)

Appendix Table 2.4, continued

| Year | Uzbek SSR | | | Azerbaidzhan SSR | | |
|---|---|---|---|---|---|---|
| | Rural Population (thousands) | Agricultural Employment (thousands) | Percent | Rural Population (thousands) | Agricultural Employment (thousands) | Percent |
| 1950 | 4,330 | 1,490 | 34.5 | 1,607 | 515 | 32.1 |
| 1957 | 5,212 | 1,379 | 26.5 | 1,819 | 544 | 29.9 |
| 1958 | 5,370 | 1,417 | 26.4 | 1,884 | 534 | 28.3 |
| 1959 | 5,503 | 1,339 | 24.3 | 1,913 | 534 | 27.7 |
| 1960 | 5,650 | 1,308 | 23.1 | 1,977 | 514 | 26.0 |
| 1961 | 5,748 | 1,291 | 22.5 | 2,012 | 506 | 25.1 |
| 1962 | 5,941 | 1,309 | 22.0 | 2,085 | 489 | 23.5 |
| 1963 | 6,129 | 1,348 | 22.0 | 2,128 | 480 | 22.6 |
| 1964 | 6,238 | 1,352 | 21.7 | 2,195 | 406 | 18.5 |
| 1965 | 6,527 | 1,379 | 21.2 | 2,253 | 468 | 20.8 |
| 1966 | 6,849 | 1,392 | 20.4 | 2,332 | 468 | 20.1 |
| 1967 | (7,031) | 1,386 | 19.8 | (2,381) | 459 | 19.3 |
| 1968 | 7,212 | 1,411 | 19.6 | 2,431 | 460 | 19.0 |
| 1969 | 7,452 | 1,430 | 19.2 | 2,496 | 440 | 17.7 |
| 1970 | 7,599 | 1,466 | 19.3 | 2,550 | 459 | 18.0 |
| 1971 | 7,818 | 1,500 | 19.1 | 2,595 | 468 | 18.1 |
| 1972 | 7,927 | 1,536 | 19.3 | 2,635 | 487 | 18.5 |
| 1973 | 8,070 | 1,565 | 19.3 | 2,669 | 505 | 19.0 |
| 1974 | 8,259 | 1,621 | 19.7 | 2,693 | 532 | 19.8 |
| 1975 | 8,430 | 1,670 | 19.9 | 2,728 | 538 | 19.8 |

| | Tadzhik SSR | | | Kirgiz SSR | | |
|---|---|---|---|---|---|---|
| 1950 | 1,118 | 348 | 31.2 | 1,241 | 318 | 25.7 |
| — | | | | | | |
| 1957 | 1,267 | 352 | 27.8 | 1,322 | 303 | 22.9 |
| 1958 | 1,309 | 342 | 26.1 | 1,330 | 305 | 22.9 |
| 1959 | 1,334 | 331 | 24.8 | 1,370 | 302 | 22.0 |
| 1960 | 1,348 | 324 | 24.0 | 1,407 | 287 | 20.4 |
| 1961 | 1,375 | 319 | 23.2 | 1,447 | 284 | 19.6 |
| 1962 | 1,428 | 322 | 22.5 | 1,458 | 299 | 20.5 |
| 1963 | 1,485 | 331 | 22.3 | 1,483 | 310 | 20.9 |
| 1964 | 1,524 | 326 | 12.4 | 1,553 | 318 | 20.5 |
| 1965 | 1,617 | 325 | 20.1 | 1,597 | 326 | 20.5 |
| 1966 | 1,664 | 322 | 19.4 | 1,632 | 330 | 20.3 |
| 1967 | (1,691) | 315 | 18.7 | (1,683) | 332 | 19.8 |
| 1968 | 1,718 | 318 | 18.5 | 1,734 | 331 | 19.1 |
| 1969 | 1,774 | 322 | 18.2 | 1,778 | 328 | 18.5 |
| 1970 | 1,832 | 331 | 18.1 | 1,835 | 331 | 18.1 |
| 1971 | 1,874 | 347 | 18.5 | 1,872 | 339 | 18.1 |
| 1972 | 1,931 | 350 | 18.1 | 1,910 | 339 | 17.7 |
| 1973 | 1,985 | 352 | 17.7 | 1,950 | 342 | 17.5 |
| 1974 | 2,041 | 365 | 17.9 | 1,991 | 357 | 18.0 |
| 1975 | 2,107 | 378 | 18.0 | 2,037 | 357 | 17.6 |

Note: Figures in parentheses are interpolated.
Sources: Population data from issues of Narkhoz for the USSR and the respective republics; employment data from Appendix Table 2.3.

89

NOTES

1. For example, in Warren W. Bason, "Population Changes," in Allen Kassof, ed., Prospects for Soviet Society (New York: Praeger, 1968), pp. 237-40, employing projections made on the basis of 1959 Soviet census data, the nature of the crisis of the 1980s and 1990s was outlined. It is not much different from that set forth in the present chapter on the basis of more recent information.

2. Recent works include Murray Feshbach, "Manpower Management in the USSR," in W. A. Douglas Jackson, ed., Soviet Resource Management and the Environment (Columbus, Ohio: American Association for the Advancement of Slavic Studies, 1978), pp. 26-44; Murray Feshbach and Stephen Rapawy, "Soviet Population and Manpower Trends and Policies," in U.S. Congress, Joint Economic Committee, Soviet Economy in a New Perspective (Washington, D.C.: U.S. Government Printing Office, 1976), pp. 113-53; Murray Feshbach and Stephen Rapawy, "Labor Constraints in the Five-Year Plan," in U.S. Congress, Joint Economic Committee, Soviet Economic Prospects for the Seventies (Washington, D.C.: U.S. Government Printing Office, 1973), pp. 485-563; Stephen Rapawy, "Regional Employment Trends in the U.S.S.R.: 1950 to 1975," and Murray Feshbach, "Prospects for Outmigration from Central Asia and Kazakhstan in the Next Decade," in U.S. Congress, Joint Economic Committee, Soviet Economy in a Time of Change (Washington, D.C.: U.S. Government Printing Office, 1979), pp. 600-17 and 656-709, respectively; Warren W. Eason, "Demographic Trends and Soviet Foreign Policy," in Seweryn Bialer, ed., Domestic Determinants of Soviet Foreign Policy (Boulder, Colo.: Westview Press, 1980); and Warren W. Eason, "Demographic Divergences at the Republic Level," in NATO, Regional Development in the USSR: Trends and Prospects (Newtonville, Mass.: Oriental Research Partners, 1979), pp. 119-38.

3. For the purpose of this chapter, the "population of working ages," or "working-age population," is meant to refer to what the Soviets call the "able-bodied population," including males aged 16-59 and females aged 16-54. Treating these two expressions more or less synonymously is justified by the fact that the indicated ages more or less correspond to conventional notions of "working ages," and by the fact that Soviet sources provide a reasonable amount of data, over time and by regions, in terms of the "able-bodied population."

4. See Eason, "Demographic Divergences," for a discussion of the earlier decades.

5. The only clear exception is the Tadzhik SSR, which shows a generally rising crude birth rate from 1950 to the late 1970s; but what we are probably seeing here is an improvement in the reporting of births, especially in the rural areas. The fact that the crude birth rate declines by somewhat less than the national average in the Kirgiz, Turkmen, and Uzbek SSRs may also reflect the moderating effect of improved reporting of vital statistics.

6. For a detailed discussion of the earlier years, see Eason, "Demographic Divergences."

7. Nonagricultural employment and agricultural employment on state farms are reported as annual averages of payroll statistics. Agricultural employment on collective farms is calculated as the average of the number of individuals working at least one day in a given month. The average annual employment data in Figures 2.2 and 2.3 and Appendix Table 2.2 are calculated on this basis.

8. Major portions of this section of the chapter are taken from Eason, "Demographic Divergences."

9. As set forth in Godfrey S. Baldwin, Population Projections by Age and Sex: For the Republics and Major Economic Regions of the USSR, 1970 to 2000 (Washington, D.C.: U.S. Government Printing Office, 1979), supplemented with annual data supplied by the author.

# 3

## GROWTH AND PRODUCTIVITY

### I. S. Koropeckyj

INTRODUCTION

In a study published in 1970, this writer investigated the possible objectives of postwar regional policy in the USSR.[1] As in any other country, from a strictly economic point of view, they could have been either equalization of economic development among individual regions or maximization of output for the entire country. Assuming given population mobility, if the productivity of resources was higher in more developed than in less developed regions, then the latter policy alternative would have led to even greater interregional inequality. Of course, a combination of the two objectives might have been a possibility. In view of the scarcity of necessary data, the earlier study was limited to an analysis of the industrial sector, and sometimes had to utilize rather heroic assumptions. Its conclusions were that the USSR had pursued neither interregional equalization nor maximization of the country's total output. Instead, regional policy, primarily through the territorial allocation of investment, had promoted the political and military goals of the Soviet leadership. In other words, geopolitical considerations appeared to be more important than purely economic considerations.[2]

In the meantime, new studies and also more comprehensive data on regional development in the USSR have appeared.[3] These

I am grateful to Daniel Bond, Andrew Buck, and Benjamin Klotz for reading this paper and offering useful comments, and to Sophia Koropeckyj and Hing-Wing Luk for help with research and calculations.

works, and new statistical data in particular, make it possible to reassess the conclusions of the 1970 study. In the following two sections, the equity and efficiency considerations in Soviet regional policy during the 1960s and the first half of the 1970s will be discussed in turn. Since the application of the efficiency criterion requires the consideration of differential productivity levels among union republics, the last section of this chapter will estimate the growth of factor productivity by republics.

The subject of this study is the impact of regional policies on union republics as separate and equal units. Despite great differences among them with respect to the sizes of their economies, the approach of equal treatment of all republics is justified by the political importance of their separate existence. Therefore, only aggregate comparisons will be undertaken here, and the relationships among republics will be shown in terms of aggregate indicators. Specific features of the economic development of individual republics are dealt with in the chapters of this volume devoted to these republics.

Work on this paper was greatly facilitated by the statistical data prepared by Daniel L. Bond for the USSR and 15 union republics for the years 1960-75.[4] The present analysis will be limited to these 15 years, and not broken down into subperiods. Bond divided the entire economy into three major economic sectors: industry, agriculture, and other sectors of material production (construction, transportation, communication, trade, distribution, and miscellaneous). According to Soviet methodology, national income does not include consumer services and the government sector, and is referred to as net material product (NMP). For the most part these data were culled from Soviet statistical yearbooks and other official publications, although in some cases data were estimated by Bond.

Briefly, Bond estimated these data in the following manner. Produced national income (gross output minus the cost of materials and productive services and depreciation allowances) was used as a measure of net output.[5] Such data for the entire economy are available for republics, and are shown in 1965 prices. The corresponding information for individual sectors is only incompletely published in official sources. There are republics for which sectoral data (though for industry and agriculture only) can be found in constant and current prices. By subtracting the data for industry and agriculture from the total, the estimates for other sectors were obtained. Furthermore, on the basis of series in constant and current prices for the same periods of time, the implicit price indexes for individual sectors were derived. These indexes were interpolated for the periods for which the constant-price data were

unavailable, and were used for the adjustment of current-price
series. No sectoral data could be found in constant prices for a
few republics. Therefore, the current-price data were adjusted
with the help of implicit-price indexes of neighboring republics.
To check his estimates, Bond aggregated sectoral data for individual republics and compared such derived output data for the entire
country with the national income data given by official sources.
The results in no case differed by more than 2 percent.

Capital data include only fixed capital: buildings, structures,
equipment, and, in the case of agriculture, livestock and long-term
plantings. These data are gross of depreciation and are as of
January 1 of a particular year.[6] Bond estimated them by using
the values for 1966, derived by James Gillula,[7] and the official
growth indexes of fixed capital for individual sectors. These estimates were then adjusted so that the total for each sector of all
republics corresponded to the value of fixed capital in that sector
for the USSR, as estimated by Constance Krueger.[8]

The data on employment in the state sector (total economy
excluding collective farms) were taken by Bond from official
sources. This indicator represents average annual employment,
adjusted for the number of workdays put in by the labor force.
The data on collective farm employment were also taken from official publications. They were derived by averaging, without
weights, monthly employment data, which included all those who
worked at least one day during the particular month. The data on
collective farm employment probably are less reliable than the
state employment data. Employment in the private sector, predominantly in private agriculture, was not included because of the
lack of information.

Bond's data on output and on inputs suffer from various weak-
nesses. But because these estimates were derived in the same
fashion for all republics, the possible distortions should not affect
all republics much differently.

Throughout the study the 15 republics will be divided into four
groups, according to their geographical location, and listed accordingly. As will be suggested at the end, geographic location
and resulting similarities of political and cultural development are
of importance to the present analysis. The Baltic group includes
Lithuania, Latvia, and Estonia. The second group, called western,
comprises the RSFSR, the Ukraine, Belorussia, and Moldavia.
Although the Russian Federation embraces both Europe and Asia,
the center of its economy and the focus of decision-making power
lie in the west. The Transcaucasian group is less homogeneous
than the others; Georgia and, especially, Armenia are closer to
the west, while Azerbaidzhan in many ways more closely resembles

the Central Asian group. Uzbekistan, Kirgizstan, Tadzhikistan, Turkmenistan, and Kazakhstan belong to the latter group.[9]

The ordering of groups corresponds roughly to their level of economic development as shown by GNP per capita in 1970 (see Table 3.1). They rank in reverse order with respect to the growth of population during the period under discussion. The middle column in the table shows the contribution of each republic to the GNP of the USSR in 1970.

TABLE 3.1

Gross National Product per Capita, Share in the USSR GNP, and Population Growth, by Union Republics

| | GNP per Capita (1970) | Share in Total GNP (1970) | Population (1975) (1960 = 100) |
|---|---|---|---|
| USSR | 100.0 | 100.00 | 119.3 |
| Lithuania | 108.9 | 1.41 | 119.2 |
| Latvia | 118.6 | 1.16 | 117.3 |
| Estonia | 134.4 | .75 | 118.2 |
| RSFSR | 109.5 | 58.92 | 112.5 |
| Ukraine | 101.0 | 19.69 | 115.0 |
| Belorussia | 96.5 | 3.60 | 114.6 |
| Moldavia | 80.6 | 1.19 | 128.4 |
| Georgia | 66.5 | 1.29 | 119.2 |
| Azerbaidzhan | 54.9 | 1.16 | 146.8 |
| Armenia | 74.6 | .77 | 152.7 |
| Kazakhstan | 97.2 | 5.23 | 143.9 |
| Uzbekistan | 56.4 | 2.76 | 163.5 |
| Kirgizstan | 66.4 | .81 | 154.2 |
| Tadzhikistan | 53.4 | .64 | 166.4 |
| Turkmenistan | 69.0 | .62 | 159.9 |

Note: Population data are for the first of the year.
Sources: I. S. Koropeckyj, "National Income of the Soviet Union Republics in 1970; Revision and Some Applications," in Zbigniew M. Fallenbuchl, ed., Economic Development in the Soviet Union and Eastern Europe, vol. 1 (New York: Praeger, 1975), p. 316, Table 11.10; Daniel L. Bond, "Multiregional Development in the Soviet Union: 1960-1975" (Ph.D. diss., University of North Carolina at Chapel Hill, 1979), Table A-16.

EQUALIZATION CONSIDERATIONS

Growth rates of output, labor, and fixed capital are presented in Table 3.2. Three groups of republics may be distinguished with respect to the output growth of the entire economy. The group with the highest growth rates includes Belorussia, Lithuania, and Armenia. The Central Asian republics, except Turkmenistan, and Moldavia fall in the intermediate group. The group with the lowest growth comprises the remaining European republics and Turkmenistan. In the case of industry, the fastest-growing group includes Belorussia, Lithuania, Tadzhikistan, and Moldavia. The remaining republics experienced lower growth rates, and the differences among these republics are not large. Azerbaidzhan is an exception, with the growth rate only slightly above half of that of the fastest-growing republic, Tadzhikistan.

With respect to agricultural growth, the republics can, by and large, be divided into two groups. Such large western republics as the Russian Federation, the Ukraine, Belorussia, and Latvia, with negative growth rates, form one group. Lithuania, whose growth rate is only slightly above zero, can be added. The remaining republics showed positive growth rates, although significantly lower than in the case of industrial output. Two Transcaucasian republics, Azerbaidzhan and Armenia, had the best record with respect to agricultural performance.[10] There is no clear pattern in the other sectors, although in general the growth rate of this group resembles that of industry, and is much higher than that of agriculture. This similarity would suggest that in the USSR development, of other sectors, which are infrastructural in character, is related to industrial development.

At this point it is necessary to make an exception to the analysis of regional development in the USSR within the framework of union republics only. A look at the differential development among regions of the largest republic, the Russian Federation, should help to make understandable the basic considerations in Soviet development strategy. For this purpose, it is sufficient to divide the RSFSR into its European and Asiatic parts. The latter is subdivided for planning purposes into three regions: West Siberia, East Siberia, and the Far East. These Asiatic regions experienced a markedly higher rate of industrial growth than the rest of the republic. While the growth rate for the entire RSFSR was 7.7 percent between 1960 and 1975, it was equal to 8.6 for West Siberia, 9.4 percent for East Siberia, and 8.3 percent for the Far East.[11] These regions, together with the five Central Asian republics, are referred to in Soviet planning as eastern regions. The emphasis on their development, particularly in recent times, can be seen from the fact that

TABLE 3.2

Growth Rates of Output, Labor, and Fixed Capital for
Union Republics, by Economic Sector, 1960-75

| | NMP | Industry | Agriculture | Other Sectors |
|---|---|---|---|---|
| | | Output | | |
| USSR | 6.7 | 9.0 | .1 | 7.0 |
| Lithuania | 8.0 | 11.2 | .3 | 13.6 |
| Latvia | 6.9 | 9.5 | -2.1 | 8.0 |
| Estonia | 6.9 | 9.2 | 1.4 | 9.5 |
| RSFSR | 6.7 | 8.6 | -.5 | 6.7 |
| Ukraine | 6.2 | 8.8 | -.3 | 7.1 |
| Belorussia | 8.0 | 12.5 | -.3 | 9.2 |
| Moldavia | 7.4 | 13.2 | 2.2 | 6.7 |
| Georgia | 6.5 | 9.0 | 1.4 | 6.1 |
| Azerbaidzhan | 5.7 | 7.4 | 3.0 | 5.9 |
| Armenia | 8.6 | 10.1 | 4.1 | 8.1 |
| Kazakhstan | 6.9 | 10.0 | 2.4 | 7.5 |
| Uzbekistan | 7.2 | 10.0 | 2.9 | 9.0 |
| Kirgizstan | 7.1 | 9.4 | 2.1 | 10.1 |
| Tadzhikistan | 7.4 | 13.8 | 2.7 | 7.0 |
| Turkmenistan | 5.3 | 8.9 | 1.6 | 6.5 |
| | | Labor | | |
| USSR | 1.7 | 2.8 | -.8 | 3.5 |
| Lithuania | 2.2 | 5.3 | -1.5 | 4.8 |
| Latvia | 1.4 | 2.5 | -1.6 | 3.0 |
| Estonia | 1.4 | 2.3 | -1.8 | 3.1 |
| RSFSR | 1.5 | 2.3 | -1.4 | 3.1 |
| Ukraine | 1.6 | 3.3 | -1.1 | 3.8 |
| Belorussia | 1.9 | 5.1 | -1.2 | 5.0 |
| Moldavia | 2.6 | 6.5 | .6 | 6.2 |
| Georgia | 2.0 | 2.6 | .7 | 3.4 |
| Azerbaidzhan | 2.1 | 3.0 | .2 | 4.3 |
| Armenia | 3.4 | 5.4 | .1 | 4.8 |
| Kazakhstan | 2.3 | 4.2 | .0 | 3.1 |
| Uzbekistan | 3.1 | 4.3 | 1.5 | 5.6 |

(continued)

|              | NMP  | Industry | Agriculture | Other Sectors |
|--------------|------|----------|-------------|---------------|
| Kirgizstan   | 3.3  | 5.4      | 1.3         | 5.0           |
| Tadzhikistan | 2.7  | 4.9      | .9          | 5.3           |
| Turkmenistan | 2.9  | 2.8      | 2.0         | 4.6           |
| Fixed Capital | | | | |
| USSR         | 9.0  | 9.6      | 8.0         | 8.8           |
| Lithuania    | 10.0 | 12.5     | 8.9         | 8.2           |
| Latvia       | 8.1  | 9.6      | 6.6         | 8.1           |
| Estonia      | 8.2  | 10.6     | 7.7         | 5.9           |
| RSFSR        | 8.8  | 9.4      | 7.9         | 8.5           |
| Ukraine      | 8.7  | 9.0      | 7.5         | 9.4           |
| Belorussia   | 10.1 | 13.8     | 7.7         | 8.7           |
| Moldavia     | 12.2 | 13.7     | 12.2        | 10.7          |
| Georgia      | 7.0  | 7.2      | 5.4         | 8.4           |
| Azerbaidzhan | 6.2  | 5.2      | 7.5         | 7.6           |
| Armenia      | 9.9  | 10.7     | 7.2         | 11.3          |
| Kazakhstan   | 10.3 | 12.6     | 8.3         | 9.8           |
| Uzbekistan   | 11.7 | 12.0     | 10.6        | 12.8          |
| Kirgizstan   | 11.2 | 12.1     | 9.0         | 13.5          |
| Tadzhikistan | 11.2 | 13.1     | 10.0        | 10.6          |
| Turkmenistan | 10.0 | 9.7      | 11.3        | 8.3           |

Note: In order to avoid the annual fluctuations in agriculture and, through them, in the NMP, the indicators for them are the averages of the annual changes. For industry and other sectors, the indicators are compound percentage growth rates.

Source: Daniel L. Bond, "Multiregional Economic Development in the Soviet Union: 1960-1975" (Ph.D. diss., University of North Carolina at Chapel Hill, 1979, Tables A-2, A-3, A-4, A-5, A-18, A-19, and A-20, and worksheet.

between 1971 and 1975, for example, they received 29 percent of all USSR investment, with 56 percent of this sum going to these three Asiatic regions of the RSFSR, 22 percent to Kazakhstan, and 22 percent to the remaining four republics in Central Asia.[12]

Returning to the discussion of interrepublic development, the last two panels of Table 3.2 show growth rates of labor and capital. The pattern of this growth was similar to that of output. The less developed Central Asian republics exhibited generally higher growth rates of inputs than did the more developed republics in the western and Baltic groups. Within the more developed group, however, Belorussia, Moldavia, and Lithuania show growth rates similar to those of the less developed republics. Although Georgia and Azerbaidzhan belong, by all accounts, to the less developed group, their capital growth was the lowest among all republics. In general, capital grew at considerably higher rates than did labor. In fact, the number of agricultural workers in the developed republics declined slightly, while in the less developed group it increased very little.

The faster output growth in Central Asia was accompanied by the highest growth of population among all republics. The opposite was true for most of the western and Baltic republics (see Table 3.1). As a result, the unweighted coefficient of variation[13] of the NMP per capita increased from 0.220 to 0.316 between the benchmark years.[14] This finding shows a continuation of the trend toward greater interrepublic inequality in terms of this indicator, observed by Soviet as well as by Western economists for earlier postwar periods.[15] It can be assumed that the inequality in income per capita among republics is related to the inequality among them in terms of welfare of the population. Because of differential structural changes for individual republics, the change in the coefficient of variation for the overall output per capita differs considerably from the changes in this coefficient for output per capita of major economic sectors. The coefficient for industry and for other sectors increased slightly, from 0.405 to 0.415 and from 0.250 to 0.275, respectively, while for agriculture it declined a little, from 0.339 to 0.323.

Obviously, planners have not succeeded in decreasing interrepublic differences in national income per capita; rather, the opposite is true. But was a decrease their intention? The equalization process could have started primarily through a higher allocation of investment per capita to the less developed republics. Actually, the situation was different. Investment per capita in the more developed republics was, on the average, greater than in the less developed republics during the period. The coefficient of correlation between NMP per capita in 1960, by union republics, and total investment (in material and nonmaterial production sectors) between 1961 and 1975, per average population during this period, is positive and equal to 0.730. This coefficient for material production only is similar in its magnitude, 0.788. However, as a result of differential investment-increase in fixed capital ratio among republics, there is a negative correlation, -0.472, between NMP per capita in 1960 and the growth of fixed capital in material sectors of production. Therefore, the coefficient of variation for fixed capital per capita decreased between 1960 and 1975 by about 10 percent, from 0.313 to 0.283.

On the basis of these indicators, a claim can be made that the planners aimed to speed up the growth of the less developed republics relative to the others, but were frustrated by the faster population growth. But this is not the whole story. Under Soviet conditions, economic development means, above all, industrialization. To accomplish this end, planners allowed industry priority in the allocation of investment, so that the share of industry in total fixed capital increased from 44.7 to 48.5 percent between 1960 and 1975. This additional capital did not go primarily to create new industrial jobs in the less developed republics, as can be seen from only a slight decline in the coefficient of variation for industrial workers per 1,000 population, from 0.428 to 0.402. Rather, it was used primarily to reduce interrepublic differences in the capital-labor ratio in industry. The coefficient of variation for this indicator decreased significantly, from 0.630 to 0.347, while a corresponding decrease for other sectors was more modest, from 0.255 to 0.187, and for agriculture was almost zero, from 0.421 to 0.419.

In this use of investment, planners may have had two objectives in mind. First, since the leaders are primarily interested in defense- and growth-oriented output, they allocated the bulk of investment to capital-intensive heavy industry branches rather than to consumer goods branches. As a result, the share of heavy industry (all branches except light industry, food, glass, ceramics, and china) in fixed capital increased for the entire USSR from 84.7 to 87.1 percent between January 1, 1962, and January 1, 1975.[16] The decrease in the coefficient of variation of the share of heavy industry branches in total industrial capital, from 0.193 to 0.143, for the same period indicates a tendency toward interrepublic equalization in this respect. One of the reasons for this development may have been the above-average growth of heavy industry branches, based on available important natural deposits, in the less developed republics. For example, between 1960 and 1974, 65 percent of industrial investment in Turkmenistan was allocated for oil and gas extraction.[17] But because of great distances, deep drilling requirements, and adverse natural conditions in general,[18] the investment-output ratio was relatively high and the overall effect on industrial output in this republic was not great. Similar conditions existed in other Central Asian republics.

Second, a decrease in the interrepublic inequality in capital per worker appears to be an attempt to equalize the productivity, and consequently the welfare, of industrial workers. The coefficient of variation of productivity of industrial workers among republics decreased by more than one-third, from 0.198 to 0.125, between 1960 and 1975.[19] This policy with respect to productivity equalization has to be viewed, however, in the context of nationality conditions in the USSR. Soviet industry is usually located in urban areas, especially in the less developed republics of Central Asia. For example, in Tadzhikistan in 1978, one-half of all industry was concentrated in two cities, Dushanbe and Leninabad, while 63 percent of the total population lived in the countryside.[20] Among the urban population of this republic, a relatively large number were Russians. Because of their knowledge of the Russian language— dominant in the economic administration—and their modern technical skills,[21] they represented a higher share of industrial workers than their share in Tadzhikistan's total population. Thus the indigenous workers benefited from this improvement in productivity, and subsequently in their welfare, not in spite of, but more likely because of, the presence of a considerable number of Russian co-workers.

Moreover, in order to exploit the mineral wealth of the less developed republics, primarily in Central Asia, more workers are needed, but the local population moves from rural to urban areas only reluctantly.[22] To man the newly constructed plants and mines, workers from Russia are brought in.[23] This phenomenon is not limited to the Central Asian republics; it can be observed in some of the western republics—Moldavia, for example.[24]

It follows that industrialization in the less developed republics often means bringing in both capital and workers, predominantly of Russian nationality.[25] The local population remains unaffected by this kind of industrialization, and continues to live under backward conditions. More ominously, this trend may in the long run mean pushing the titular nationality into the role of ethnic minority in its own territory, a development that has already taken place in Kazakhstan, primarily in its northern part.

All this evidence allows us to conclude that in forming investment policy, planners were little concerned with equalization of economic development among the titular nationalities of the union republics.[26] But whereas in the past this objective was constantly reiterated in official documents and pronouncements, it is now ignored. The official reason for this, pronounced by the highest authorities, is an alleged attainment of interrepublic equalization.[27] The directives for the Tenth Five-Year Plan do not even mention this goal. Instead, the emphasis is on the geographical distribution of investment according to efficiency criteria, mainly through the development of territorial production complexes.[28]

## EFFICIENCY CONSIDERATIONS

Efficiency in regional policy can be understood to mean spatial allocation of resources that maximizes output for the entire country. Because of historical development, natural endowment, and different capital-labor ratios, the productivity of labor and of capital, as well as total factor productivity, differs among individual republics. This holds for aggregate and sectoral production, and for the output of individual products. Obviously, interrepublic distribution of productivity levels at a given point in time can be quite different from the distribution of productivity growth. Only the latter will be of interest in this chapter, for the following reasons. Any aggregate measure of productivity must be based on prices. Since Soviet prices are not equilibrium prices, and production structures are different among republics, interrepublic comparisons of static productivity using such prices can be quite misleading. Furthermore, the preceding objection is much less valid for measures of productivity growth under the assumption that structural changes during the 15-year period were not too great. But in any case, from an efficiency point of view, planners should be guided in resource allocation by the dynamic productivity concept.[29]

It would be of interest to inquire whether interrepublic capital allocation was guided by the productivity growth of resources, primarily of capital. In other words, did the planners allocate capital mainly to those republics in which the increase in output per unit of capital was highest? The emphasis on the efficiency in the allocation of capital rather than of labor is justified by two considerations. First, Soviet planners have relatively little control over interrepublic flows of labor, while they have almost complete control over the allocation of capital. Second, the growth of output in the entire economy and in industry was more correlated with the growth of capital than of labor. The respective coefficients for NMP are 0.469 and 0.254, and for industry, 0.818 and 0.723. In contrast, the supply of labor, rather than of capital, appears to be of greater importance for the growth of agricultural output. The coefficients are 0.666 and 0.334, respectively. For other sectors no significant statistical relationship can be found between the growth of output and either of the two resources; the coefficients of correlation are 0.172 (labor) and 0.092 (capital).

The coefficients of correlation in Table 3.3 suggest an answer to the above question. An inverse relationship between capital growth and productivity growth of capital, labor, and combined resources can be observed for NMP, agriculture, and other sectors. In the case of industry, this relationship is negative for capital productivity but positive for labor productivity, while practically no relationship exists for total factor productivity.

TABLE 3.3

Coefficients of Correlation between Growth Rates of
Capital and Productivity: Union Republics,
by Economic Sector, 1960-75

|  | NMP | Industry | Agriculture | Other Sectors |
|---|---|---|---|---|
| Total factor productivity | -0.233 | 0.081 | -0.181 | -0.397 |
| Labor productivity | -0.033 | 0.380 | -0.101 | -0.218 |
| Capital productivity | -0.864 | -0.683 | -0.641 | -0.634 |

Sources: Tables 3.2, 3.5.

An alternative analysis of efficiency in interrepublic investment distribution can be made in terms of the relationship between capital and labor productivity, on the one hand, and the capital-labor ratio, on the other. In accordance with the efficiency criterion, capital should be substituted for labor in those republics where capital productivity is higher than in other republics. In other words, one should expect a positive relationship between the growth of capital productivity and the increase in the capital-labor ratio, and a negative relationship between labor productivity and the capital-labor ratio. Actually, the results are just the opposite, confirming the finding that an efficiency criterion was not a dominant factor in investment policy. The coefficient of correlation between the increase in the capital-labor ratio and the growth of capital productivity for 1960-75 is -0.780 for NMP, -0.670 for industry, -.0765 for agriculture, and -0.398 for other sectors; between the increase in capital-labor ratio and the growth of labor productivity, it is 0.202 for NMP, 0.608 for industry, 0.014 for agriculture, and 0.012 for other sectors.[30]

As shown earlier in this chapter, particular attention has been paid in recent years to the development of the Asiatic regions of the RSFSR. The conditions in these regions in many ways resemble those in the Central Asian republics. As a result, productivity is likely to be low there, but this cannot be quantitatively estimated because of the lack of the necessary data. Nevertheless, it is highly likely that inefficiencies in spatial investment allocation in the USSR also occur in intrarepublic planning.

Even if efficient investment distribution among republics, in terms of the maximization of output, were an important objective, it would be difficult to implement it. In the USSR the success of this policy would have to depend to a large degree on territorial planning. In other words, territorial planning should make sure that an investment project is not located in isolation from the rest of the economy, but is integrated into the existing and planned economic structure of a given region. However, territorial planning organs are at present insufficiently developed and, in addition, regional planning is subordinated to branch planning.[31] As a result, little attention is paid to this aspect of planning even within the restricted scope allowed by overall planning.[32]

The finding that investment was distributed among republics irrespective of the growth of factor productivity, and in inverse proportion to the growth of capital productivity, suggests that aggregatively the maximization of output for the entire country was not the highest priority of planners. Nor, as shown earlier, was interrepublic equalization of economic development. As in any other aspect of social life, there is no single and direct explanation. The factors behind regional development in the USSR are multiple and complex. But in view of the preceding evidence and of the character of the Soviet state, it seems to this writer that the views expressed by him in the 1970 study are largely still correct. With respect to the development of the union republics during the postwar period, the noneconomic factors called "geopolitical" seem to have been of greater importance to the Soviet leadership than purely economic considerations.

An attempt to explain the specifics of the development of geopolitical factors requires the classification of Soviet republics into the usual North, comprising the Baltic and western republics, and the South, comprising the Transcaucasian and Central Asian republics. To repeat, among the Transcaucasian republics, Georgia and (more especially) Armenia resemble the North, while

Azerbaidzhan resembles the South. Thus, by promoting the development of Belorussia, Moldavia, and Lithuania, the planners succeeded in reducing economic inequality among republics in the more developed area. This policy was probably in response to two non-economic considerations.

First, any past neglect of these republics by the central planners could have been explained to a large extent by their proximity to Western countries and, thus, their vulnerability in time of war. The existence of a <u>cordon sanitaire</u> in the form of other socialist countries after World War II and the changed technology of warfare make this consideration obsolete. Second, the geographical location of these republics may now work to their advantage. Being most exposed to influences from the West and with an expanded flow of information, they may become dissatisfied with their relative backwardness and create political problems for the leadership. In the case of Moldavia, there is the additional consideration of competition between Moscow and Romania, which has not abandoned its claim to this republic.

Fortunately for Soviet planners, these noneconomic considerations coincided with two economic factors favoring development of these republics. As will be shown, productivity growth there was highest among all the republics and, because of their geographical location, they represent an important link in the existing and planned cooperation and integration of the USSR with other European members of the Council of Mutual Economic Assistance.

Among the republics of the Soviet South, Central Asia enjoyed the highest investment growth in the country, after Belorussia and Moldavia. As a result, output growth was high there. At the same time, Central Asian republics, except Tadzhikistan, experienced the highest population growth and the lowest productivity growth in industry and other sectors among all republics. In agriculture, however, they compared favorably with the rest of the country. Nevertheless, the net effect of these trends was a widening of the gap between the North and the South; in terms of NMP per capita, the latter lost to the former (from 77.3 to 59.2 percent between 1960 and 1975).

It is important to note that "other sectors" in Central Asia was the group most favored with respect to investment. The buildup of these sectors, which are basically infrastructural in nature, could be interpreted as an initial step in the modernization effort in this region. But this hypothesis does not correspond to the industrialization experience in the advanced regions of the USSR and other countries with Soviet-type economies, where the development of infrastructure corresponding to the level of industry, if it was ever undertaken, was postponed until the final stage in economic progress.[33] The development of transportation, communication, and similar sectors in the Central Asian republics, as well as in the eastern regions of the Russian Federation, can be explained by the need to exploit important natural deposits in this area and by strategic considerations in regard to neighboring countries, especially China. Investment in agriculture there, although relatively the highest among all republics, was justified on the ground of efficiency, and most benefited the titular nationalities living predominantly in rural areas. However, this policy was not pushed far enough to make a pronounced change in terms of national income per capita.

## ESTIMATION OF PRODUCTIVITY GROWTH

The conclusions about the efficiency (or, rather, the inefficiency) of intestment policy in the preceding part of this paper were derived with reference to the growth of factor productivity in the individual republics. In this section the estimation of productivity measures will be described.

Productivity growth will be designed as the increase in the ratio between net output and inputs that results from all sources other than an increase in inputs of the same quality.[34] If resources are broadly grouped into two categories, labor and capital, then productivity advance will include all improvements in their quality: for example, better education of the labor force, improved technology of capital, and so on. In addition, various extraneous factors are influential, such as the improvement in incentives, the level of economic development, and economies of scale, all of which might influence resource productivity.

The estimation of productivity, in static or dynamic terms, requires a hypothesis about the relationship between output and inputs. A considerable body of literature deals with the advantages of one or another type of production function for analysis of the Soviet economy.[35] Some of these approaches have been applied to the analysis of Soviet regional development.[36] For the present purpose a variant of the Cobb-Douglas production function of the form

$$\Delta A/A = \Delta Q/Q - (a \, \Delta L/L + b \, \Delta K/K)$$

has been selected,[37] where A is productivity, Q is output, L is labor, and K is capital, while coefficient $a + b = 1$. Arithmetic weights are preferable to geometric weights, because they are implicit in real product indexes. The data for Q, L, and K were prepared by Bond; the marginal productivities of labor and capital

or, in aggregate terms, the returns to them can serve as the coefficients a and b, respectively.

The estimation of coefficients a and b can be undertaken using
econometric tools. However, such results vary considerably with
the different specifications of the production function.[38] Therefore,
it appears preferable to use actual returns to labor and capital. In
view of the scarcity of data, such estimates could be made for one
year only, and they must therefore remain constant for the period
under consideration. The point can be raised that this kind of
approach is permissible under the assumption that the ratios between marginal products of labor and capital and between their
prices are equal. Although these conditions probably do not hold
for any country, numerous empirical studies on market and centrally planned economies have been conducted using this methodology.

The returns to labor were estimated for individual republics
for the NMP and three basic sectors in 1970 in an earlier study
containing a detailed description of calculations and sources.[39] It
suffices here to state that the total returns are equal to the sum of
wages in the state and cooperative sectors, income of collective
farm members, income in kind, and social security taxes. The
returns to non-labor resources were not taken from the above-
mentioned study, because more detailed and better estimates have
appeared in the meantime. For example, a 1975 study estimated
the return to fixed and working capital in various economic sectors
in 1970.[40] The total charges for the USSR, for NMP and three
basic sectors, were distributed among republics in proportion to
the value of their fixed capital in these sectors on January 1, 1970.
The assumption of equal returns to capital among republics is quite
unrealistic. But, in view of the lack of data, any adjustment—for
example, along the lines made by this author in the calculation of
republic GNPs in 1970,[41] would be inappropriate in the present
study, which attempts, among other objectives, to estimate the
growth of factor productivity.[42] In any case, the shares of such
derived capital returns and labor returns in the total returns for
NMP and its major subdivisions (see Table 3.4) are used only as
weights for combining the growth rates of labor and capital.

Subtracting the growth rates of combined labor and capital
from the growth rates of output gives the growth rates of factor
productivity (see Table 3.5). The growth rates of partial productivity of labor and capital, listed in the two lower panels of this table,
were derived by subtraction of the respective growth rates from
those of output. Similar estimates of productivity growth were
undertaken by Bond in his econometric study. In general, the results for factor productivity growth in both sectors are very close.
The coefficient of correlation for industry and for other sectors is

TABLE 3.4

Factor Income Shares for Union Republics, by Economic Sector, 1970
(percent)

| | NMP | | Industry | | Agriculture | | Other Sectors | |
|---|---|---|---|---|---|---|---|---|
| | Labor | Capital | Labor | Capital | Labor | Capital | Labor | Capital |
| USSR | 68.3 | 31.7 | 66.0 | 34.0 | 81.0 | 19.0 | 61.3 | 38.7 |
| Lithuania | 73.6 | 26.4 | 71.3 | 28.7 | 80.0 | 20.0 | 67.5 | 32.5 |
| Latvia | 68.4 | 31.6 | 72.8 | 27.2 | 74.7 | 25.3 | 58.7 | 41.3 |
| Estonia | 68.6 | 31.4 | 67.7 | 32.3 | 79.4 | 20.6 | 60.6 | 39.4 |
| RSFSR | 67.0 | 33.0 | 66.6 | 33.4 | 79.6 | 20.4 | 60.6 | 39.4 |
| Ukraine | 70.5 | 29.5 | 66.5 | 33.5 | 83.7 | 16.3 | 61.5 | 38.5 |
| Belorussia | 74.5 | 25.5 | 71.3 | 28.7 | 84.5 | 15.5 | 64.9 | 35.1 |
| Moldavia | 77.0 | 23.0 | 69.0 | 31.0 | 85.5 | 14.5 | 64.9 | 35.1 |
| Georgia | 70.7 | 29.3 | 61.3 | 38.7 | 82.5 | 17.5 | 64.1 | 35.9 |
| Azerbaidzhan | 62.7 | 37.3 | 46.9 | 53.1 | 81.8 | 18.2 | 61.3 | 38.7 |
| Armenia | 72.2 | 27.8 | 68.3 | 31.7 | 79.7 | 20.3 | 71.0 | 29.0 |
| Kazakhstan | 62.6 | 37.4 | 57.0 | 43.0 | 73.1 | 26.9 | 59.3 | 40.7 |
| Uzbekistan | 73.7 | 26.3 | 60.2 | 39.8 | 86.3 | 13.7 | 65.1 | 34.9 |
| Kirgizstan | 71.5 | 28.5 | 66.5 | 33.5 | 79.2 | 20.8 | 66.1 | 33.9 |
| Tadzhikistan | 73.3 | 26.7 | 64.0 | 36.0 | 82.1 | 17.9 | 66.3 | 33.7 |
| Turkmenistan | 67.6 | 32.4 | 52.1 | 47.9 | 74.6 | 25.4 | 67.7 | 32.3 |

Sources: I. S. Koropeckyj, "National Income of the Soviet Union Republics in 1970: Revision and Some Applications," in Zbigniew M. Fallenbuchl, ed., Economic Development in the Soviet Union and Eastern Europe, vol. 1 (New York: Praeger, 1975), Table 11.3 and notes; CIA, USSR: Gross National Product Accounts, 1970 (Washington, D.C.: 1975), Table 8. For description of derivation, see text.

## TABLE 3.5

Growth Rates of Productivity for Union Republics,
by Economic Sector, 1960-75

|  | NMP | Industry | Agriculture | Other Sectors |
|---|---|---|---|---|
| Total Factor Productivity | | | | |
| USSR | 2.7 | 3.9 | -.8 | 1.5 |
| Lithuania | 3.8 | 3.9 | -.3 | 7.7 |
| Latvia | 3.4 | 5.0 | -2.6 | 2.9 |
| Estonia | 3.3 | 4.2 | 1.2 | 5.2 |
| RSFSR | 2.8 | 4.0 | -1.0 | 1.5 |
| Ukraine | 2.6 | 3.6 | -.7 | 1.1 |
| Belorussia | 4.1 | 4.9 | -.5 | 2.9 |
| Moldavia | 2.5 | 4.4 | .1 | -1.1 |
| Georgia | 3.1 | 4.6 | -.1 | .9 |
| Azerbaidzhan | 2.1 | 3.2 | 1.5 | .3 |
| Armenia | 3.4 | 3.0 | 2.6 | 1.4 |
| Kazakhstan | 1.7 | 2.1 | .1 | 1.7 |
| Uzbekistan | 1.9 | 2.7 | .1 | .9 |
| Kirgizstan | 1.6 | 1.7 | -.8 | 2.2 |
| Tadzhikistan | 2.4 | 6.0 | .2 | -.6 |
| Turkmenistan | .1 | 2.8 | -2.7 | .7 |
| Labor Productivity | | | | |
| USSR | 5.0 | 6.2 | .9 | 3.6 |
| Lithuania | 5.8 | 5.9 | 1.8 | 8.8 |
| Latvia | 5.5 | 7.0 | -.5 | 5.0 |
| Estonia | 5.5 | 6.9 | 3.2 | 6.4 |
| RSFSR | 5.2 | 6.4 | .9 | 3.6 |
| Ukraine | 4.7 | 5.5 | .7 | 3.3 |
| Belorussia | 6.1 | 7.4 | .9 | 4.2 |
| Moldavia | 4.8 | 6.7 | 1.6 | .5 |

Table 3.5, continued

|  | NMP | Industry | Agriculture | Other Sectors |
|---|---|---|---|---|
| Georgia | 4.5 | 6.4 | .7 | 2.7 |
| Azerbaidzhan | 3.6 | 4.4 | 2.8 | 1.6 |
| Armenia | 5.2 | 4.7 | 4.0 | 3.3 |
| Kazakhstan | 4.7 | 5.8 | 2.4 | 4.4 |
| Uzbekistan | 4.0 | 5.7 | 1.4 | 3.4 |
| Kirgizstan | 3.8 | 4.0 | .8 | 5.1 |
| Tadzhikistan | 4.7 | 8.9 | 1.8 | 1.7 |
| Turkmenistan | 2.4 | 6.1 | -.4 | 1.9 |
| Capital Productivity | | | | |
| USSR | -2.3 | -.6 | -7.9 | -1.8 |
| Lithuania | -2.0 | -1.3 | -8.6 | -5.4 |
| Latvia | -1.2 | -.1 | -8.7 | -.1 |
| Estonia | -1.3 | -1.4 | -6.4 | 3.6 |
| RSFSR | -2.1 | -.8 | -8.4 | -1.8 |
| Ukraine | -2.5 | -.2 | -7.8 | -2.3 |
| Belorussia | -2.1 | -1.3 | -8.0 | .5 |
| Moldavia | -4.8 | -.5 | -10.0 | -4.0 |
| Georgia | -.5 | 1.8 | -4.0 | -2.3 |
| Azerbaidzhan | -.5 | 2.2 | -4.5 | -1.7 |
| Armenia | -1.3 | -.6 | -3.1 | -3.2 |
| Kazakhstan | -3.4 | -2.6 | -5.9 | -2.2 |
| Uzbekistan | -4.5 | -2.0 | -7.7 | -3.8 |
| Kirgizstan | -4.1 | -2.7 | -6.9 | -3.4 |
| Tadzhikistan | -3.8 | .7 | -7.3 | -3.6 |
| Turkmenistan | -4.7 | -.8 | -9.7 | -1.8 |

Note: See the text for description of derivation.
Sources: Tables 3.2, 3.4.

0.904 and 0.986, respectively. However, for agriculture it is only 0.587. But Bond calculates the growth rates of agricultural output for the period between three-year averages, 1960-62 and 1973-75, whereas in the present study growth rates are the averages of annual changes. Adjusting the latter estimates to Bond's methodology increases the coefficient of correlation for agriculture to 0.819. This close similarity in results obtained by two different methods raises confidence in the results of this study.

Partial productivity trends—for labor and for capital—are of less interest than indicators of total factor productivity. No particular interrepublic pattern can be discerned for either of them. However, with a handful of exceptions, the growth rates of capital productivity in all republics and all sectors are negative. This decline in capital productivity may be an indication of a general difficulty that the Soviet economy experiences in assimilating constantly and substantially growing capital investments.

The growth rates of total factor productivity differ considerably among Soviet republics. Three groups of republics may be distinguished with respect to the productivity growth in NMP. The highest growth rate occurs in the Baltic republics as a group. The western group has generally lower rates, except for Belorussia, which experienced the highest growth rate among all republics. The Central Asian republics, except for Tadzhikistan, show the lowest rates of growth. The Transcaucasian republics are dissimilar in this respect: Georgia and Armenia had high growth rates, while Azerbaidzhan had a significantly lower growth rate.

With respect to the productivity growth in industry, Soviet republics can be divided into two groups. One group, the Soviet North, comprising the Baltic and western republics, shows higher growth rates than those of the less developed Soviet South, to which belong the Transcaucasian and Central Asian republics. Notable exceptions in the latter group are Tadzhikistan and Georgia, whose growth rates are comparable with those of the North. The situation in agriculture is the opposite. In the Baltic and western republics, with the exception of Estonia, agricultural productivity declined slightly, while the less developed South registered slow but positive growth. This progress, however, did not apply to Turkmenistan, Kirgizstan, and Georgia, in which a decline in productivity took place. No clear trend can be observed in the case of other sectors.

As can be seen, there is a relationship between the growth of productivity and geographical location, level of economic development, historical and cultural development, and religious tradition of individual republics, factors that serve as a basis for distinguishing between the Soviet North and South. In order to be more specific about this relationship, the following calculation was undertaken. Taking into account the above factors, the republics were classified on a scale of 1 to 3, with each of the most developed Baltic republics assigned number 3; each of the republics of inter-mediate level—the western and the Transcaucasian—assigned number 2; and each of the least developed Central Asian republics assigned number 1. The coefficients of correlation between this distribution and the growth of productivity in industry and agriculture are as expected, with respect to sign: 0.459 and -0.395, respectively.

It was argued in this paper that interrepublic investment decisions were undertaken in the USSR without regard to the productivity growth in individual republics. Political and defense considerations were of a higher priority to the planners. In the future, however, greater attention may be paid to the equalization and efficiency principles. To avoid a potential conflict between the two objectives, the growth of productivity in the less developed republics would need to be stimulated. This goal would be facilitated if the reasons for differential productivity growth by republics were better understood. The study of the factors determining these trends remains an important task for future research.

NOTES

1. I. S. Koropeckyj, "Industrial Location Policy in the USSR During the Postwar Period," in U.S. Congress, Joint Economic Committee, Economic Performance and the Military Burden in the Soviet Union (Washington, D.C.: U.S. Government Printing Office, 1970).

2. These goals can be summarized as follows: a shift of economic activity from west toward east; territorial dispersal of industry; buildup of regions neighboring China; establishing of economic links between west and east of the country; exploitation of natural wealth in Asiatic regions; and development of industries important for world power politics (armaments, foreign aid, space exploration) located primarily in Moscow, Leningrad, and the Baltic republics. See Koropeckyj, "Industrial Location Policy . . . ," pp. 267 ff.

3. For example, V. N. Bandera and Z. L. Melnyk, eds., The Soviet Economy in Regional Perspective (New York: Praeger, 1973); I. S. Koropeckyj, ed., The Ukraine Within the USSR: An Economic Balance Sheet (New York: Praeger, 1977); James W. Gillula, "Regional Interdependence and Economic Development in the USSR: Interregional Input-Output Analysis" (Ph.D. diss., Duke University, 1978); Daniel L. Bond, "Multiregional Economic

Development in the Soviet Union: 1960-1975" (Ph.D. diss., University of North Carolina at Chapel Hill, 1979); NATO, Economics Directorate, <u>Regional Development in the USSR, Trends and Prospects</u> (Newtonville, Mass.: Oriental Research Partners, 1979).

4. Bond, "Multiregional Economic Development," Appendix tables. For a detailed description of data, see ibid., ch. 3.

5. For a discussion of various Soviet output indicators, see A. Becker, "National Income Accounting in the USSR," in V. G. Treml and J. P. Hardt, eds., <u>Soviet Economic Statistics</u> (Durham, N.C.: Duke University Press, 1972).

6. Fixed capital data in Bond's dissertation are averages for particular years. However, calculations in the present study are based on fixed capital data, referring to January 1, which were prepared by Bond before his dissertation was completed and were given by him to this author. It is believed that the results in the present study would not be much different from the results derived on the basis of an alternative set of data. The source for these data, as well as for some other information not utilized by Bond in his dissertation, will be given as "Bond, worksheet."

7. Gillula, "Regional Interdependence. . . ."

8. Constance Krueger, "Soviet Capital Stock Estimates" (Washington, D.C.: Office of Economic Research, C.I.A., 1977), unpublished paper.

9. The first four Central Asian republics are, in addition to the location and the level of economic development, closely related in terms of race, cultural development, and religious tradition. Kazakhstan, whose native population accounts for only about one-third of its total population, is nevertheless included in this group, because the immigration of Slavs has been insignificant in recent years and is being overshadowed by the population growth of Kazakhs. See Murray Feshbach, "Prospects for Outmigration from Central Asia and Kazakhstan in the Next Decade," in U.S. Congress, Joint Economic Committee, Soviet Economy in a Time of Change (Washington, D.C.: U.S. Government Printing Office, 1979), p. 658, n. 3.

10. These results differ from other Western estimates of agricultural growth in the USSR. For example, the data given by David W. Carey, "Soviet Agriculture: Recent Performance and Future Plans," in U.S. Congress, Joint Economic Committee, <u>Soviet Economy in a New Perspective</u> (Washington, D.C.: U.S. Government Printing Office, 1976), show an average of annual growth rates of 2.7 percent between 1960 and 1975 (Appendix Table 1, p. 596). The difference in the growth rates is mainly due to the difference in definition of the net output of agriculture. As was stated in the text, this study uses the concept of produced

national income, while Carey's output data show agricultural output for sales and home consumption minus farm products used for seed and livestock feed (p. 580, Table 2, n. 1). Thus the latter data include the input of mineral fertilizers, machinery, and other industrial inputs, the supply of which increased considerably in recent times.

11. TsSU, Narodnoe Khoziaistvo RSFSR v 1967a (Moscow, 1968), pp. 46-47 (hereafter Narkhoz RSFSR); Narkhoz RSFSR 75, pp. 47-48.

12. See Gertrude E. Schroeder, "Soviet Regional Development Policies in Perspective," in NATO, Directorate of Economic Affairs, The USSR in the 1980s (Brussels: NATO, 1978), pp. 133-34. According to Schroeder, Soviet regional strategy is now supposed to rely on the development of territorial production complexes. Of thirteen planned complexes, ten are already being developed or are to be developed in the eastern regions: one in West Siberia, five in the Angara-Ienisei river system, three in Kazakhstan, and one in southern Tadzhikistan. To this should be added a number of complexes associated with the construction of the Baikal-Amur railroad, which runs also through RSFSR territory. See ibid., p. 134.

13. As was stated earlier, because interrepublic relations are of interest, the unweighted coefficient of variation will be employed throughout this study (and not the population-weighted, as is often done in regional studies). It is the standard deviation as a percentage of the mean. Compare, on this, Gertrude E. Schroeder, "Soviet Wage and Income Policies in Regional Perspective," The Association for Comparative Economic Studies Bulletin (1974): no. 2, p. 15.

14. Various statistical indicators in this paper are based on the absolute data from Bond, Appendix tables or worksheet. Therefore no source will be cited in such cases.

15. See V. Zlatin and V. Rutgaizer, "Comparison of the Levels of Economic Development of Union Republics and Large Regions," Nauchnye doklady vysshei shkoly—ekonomicheskie nauki (1968): no. 8, translated in Problems of Economics (June 1969): Table 1; I. S. Koropeckyj, "Equalization of Regional Development in Socialist Countries: An Empirical Study," Economic Development and Cultural Change (October 1972): Table 2.

16. TsSU, Narodnoe Khoziaistvo SSSR v 1961a. (Moscow, 1962), p. 187 (hereafter Narkhoz and year); Narkhoz 74, pp. 198-99.

17. James W. Gillula, "The Economic Interdependence of Soviet Republics," in U.S. Congress, Joint Economic Committee, Soviet Economy in a Period of Transition, p. 651, n. 41, quoting a Soviet source.

18. See, for example, B. Geldiev, Ekonomicheskaia gazeta (1974):no. 46; A. Kucherenna, Pravda, April 25, 1975; V. Taldai, Pravda, October 30, 1977.

19. Derived by dividing the output by the number of workers in 1960 and 1975.

20. Kh. Saidmuradov, Sotsialisticheskaia industria, November 25, 1978.

21. For example, in 1970 Russians accounted for 11.9 percent of Tadzhikistan's total population, 30.0 percent of its urban population, and 42.0 percent of the population of its capital, Dushanbe. See TsSU, Itogi vsesoiuznoi perepisi naseleniia 1970 goda, vol. 4 (Moscow, 1972). According to a Soviet estimate cited in Michael Rywkin, "Central Asia and Soviet Manpower," Problems of Communism (January-February 1979):9, Table 2, Tadzhiks accounted for 37 percent of their republic's workers in 1970. The respective percentages were 63 for Kazakhstan, 39 for Uzbekistan, 39 for Kirgizstan, and 32 for Turkmenistan. Rywkin presumably has in mind employment in all sectors other than just agriculture.

22. According to Saidmuradov, Sotsialisticheskaia industria, only 10 percent of the rural population increase in Tadzhikistan moves to the cities.

23. V. Parfenov, Pravda, November 26, 1977, writes: "You cannot deliver human resources to a factory on order, as you can coal or metal. . . . For instance, the natural growth of population in the Central Asian republics is considerably higher than in non-Black-Earth Zone of the Russian Federation, but workers for new enterprises in Dushanbe or Ashkhabad sometimes have to be recruited in Ivanovo, Kalinin, or Vladimir."

24. According to a specialist, "The number of Romanians in industrial production in the Moldavian Republic has remained virtually unchanged since the decision to speed up industrialization, while the influx of non-Romanian specialists in industry and corollary economic activities from other republics has gained momentum since September 1965." See Stephen Fischer-Galati, "The Moldavian Soviet Republic in Soviet Domestic and Foreign Policy," in Roman Szporluk, ed., The Influence of East Europe and the Soviet West on the USSR (New York: Praeger, 1975), p. 246.

25. For an excellent discussion of this problem, see Feshbach, "Prospects for Outmigration . . ."; and Feshbach, "The Structure and Composition of the Soviet Industrial Labor Force," in NATO, The USSR in the 1980s.

26. The lack of convergence among the Soviet republics is not limited to the level of economic development. According to Peter Zwick, "Ethnoregional Socio-Economic Fragmentation and Soviet Budgetary Policy," Soviet Studies (July 1979), the socio-

economic fragmentation among them intensified, if anything, during 1950-70. Furthermore, Zwick argues that if allowance is made for higher population growth in the less developed republics, no attempt was made to alleviate these differences with budget expenditures (pp. 393-94).

27. See Leonid Brezhnev's speech, Komunist Ukrainy (1973): no. 1, p. 40.

28. Pravda, March 7, 1976; "Editorial," Planovoe khoziaistvo (1977):no. 8, pp. 3-4.

29. Soviet scholars recognize the difficulties with cross-section analysis of productivity, also, and recommend only comparisons over time. See V. Kistanov, "Obobschchenie pokazatelei regional'noi effektivnosti proizvodstva," Planovoe khoziaistvo (1976): no. 8, p. 37.

30. See Tables 3.2 and 3.5.

31. See N. Singur and I. Panfilov, "Metodologicheskie i organizatsionnye voprosy territorial'nogo aspekta narodno-khoziaistvennykh planov," Planovoe khoziaistvo (1974): no. 5, p. 28; A. Triakin, "Territorial'nyi aspekt planirovaniia," Planovoe khoziaistvo (1977): no. 8, p. 74.

32. See Hans-Erich Gramatzki, "Regionale Wirtschaftsplanung in UdSSR," Beiheften der Konjunkturpolitik, no. 22 (Berlin: Duncker and Humblot, 1975).

33. See A. Csernok, E. Ehrlich, and Gy. Szilagyi, "A Hundred Years of Infrastructural Development: An International Comparison," Acta Oeconomica (1972): no. 1, p. 10. This is especially true in the case of housing (p. 20).

34. A Soviet specialist argues that, in view of the subordination of a republic's interests to the interests of the entire USSR, net output indicators alone are insufficient for the calculation of economic effectiveness and should be used alongside gross output indicators. See Kistanov, "Obobschchenie pokazatelei regional'noi effektivnosti proizvodstva," p. 38.

35. For example, Martin Weitzman, "Soviet Postwar Economic Growth and Capital-Labor Substitution," American Economic Review (September 1970): Stanislaw Gomulka, "Soviet Postwar Industrial Growth, Capital-Labor Substitution, and Technical Change: A Reexamination," in Zbigniew M. Fallenbuchl, ed., Economic Development in the Soviet Union and Eastern Europe, vol. 2 (New York: Praeger, 1976); Padma Desai, "The Production Function and Technical Change in Postwar Soviet Industry: A Reexamination," American Economic Review (June 1976); Abram Bergson, "Notes on the Production Function in Soviet Postwar Industrial Growth," Journal of Comparative Economics (June 1979).

36. Bond, "Multiregional Economic Development in the Soviet Union."

37. R. R. Nelson, "Aggregate Production Function," American Economic Review (September 1964).

38. See John W. Kendrick, Postwar Productivity Trends in the United States, 1948-1969 (New York: National Bureau of Economic Research, 1973), p. 15.

39. See I. S. Koropeckyj, "National Income of the Soviet Union Republics in 1970: Revision and Some Applications," in Zbigniew M. Fallenbuchl, ed., Economic Development in the Soviet Union and Eastern Europe, vol. 1 (New York: Praeger, 1975), Table 11.3 and notes. However, the data had to be adjusted according to different definitions of the total national income, industry, and other sectors in earlier and present studies.

40. CIA, USSR: Gross National Product Accounts, 1970 (Washington, D.C.: CIA, 1975), Table 8.

41. See Koropeckyj, "National Income," p. 306, Table 11.5 and notes.

42. See Bond, "Multiregional Economic Development in the Soviet Union," pp. 54, 56.

# 4

## REGIONAL LIVING STANDARDS

### Gertrude E. Schroeder

Economic development typically brings with it rising levels of living for the population, and rising incomes are accompanied by familiar shifts in consumption patterns. Within a given country, however, development frequently proceeds unevenly, producing sizable but often diminishing regional disparities in levels of living. The Soviet Union is a socialist state, pursuing development with government ownership of resources and central direction of the production process. Its proclaimed political goals, at least in the postwar period, have been to raise living standards rapidly and to reduce differences of many kinds, including (most notably) differences in levels of development among regions. What has been accomplished, and how do the results compare with those in other industrialized countries?

This inquiry builds upon and extends the author's previous work in this area,[1] as well as that of Alastair McAuley in his meticulous investigation of economic welfare in the Soviet Union.[2] Because of limitations of data, the inquiry focuses on the period 1960-78. Only fragmentary data of the kind required have been published for the USSR's republics before 1960. Nonetheless, inspection of related data available for the 1950s—on growth of industrial and agricultural output, retail sales, and health services—suggests that the picture regarding regional progress in raising living standards generally conforms to that given by data for the later period. The study investigates incomes and consumption in the 15 republics, grouping them into six larger regions: the RSFSR; the western republics—Ukraine, Belorussia, Moldavia; Kazakhstan; Transcaucasia; Central Asia; and the Baltic republics. Although substantial disparities in levels of living exist within individual republics, the paucity of data precludes valid measures for them.

The inquiry first investigates regional differences in the growth of wages and money incomes, with an attempt to describe differences among social groups and to assess the impact of changes in the cost of living. The next section develops a measure of per capita consumption, by region, patterned after that calculated by Western scholars for the USSR as a whole,[3] and compares the results with official Soviet measures. The third section gathers evidence on regional differences in major components of consumption, using various data. The final section summarizes the overall results and makes comparisons with levels and trends in other industrialized countries in the postwar years. The text dispenses to a large degree with methodological details and sources, confining these unexciting but important matters to an appendix.

## PERSONAL INCOMES

Soviet people receive income from a variety of sources. Some two-thirds of total money income comes from wages paid to the state labor force (workers and employees). Collective farmers receive money and in-kind incomes from work for the collective farms. Farm households and many urban ones obtain substantial money incomes and consumption in kind from private agricultural activities. Transfer payments in the form of pensions, allowances, and student stipends provide a growing share of money incomes. Finally, people receive income from interest on savings accounts and state loans, and from other minor sources. Alastair McAuley has painstakingly constructed estimates of total personal incomes and incomes per capita for the USSR and the 15 republics for 1960, 1965, and 1970.[4] This chapter extends these estimates to 1978, using a procedure that is explained in the appendix. The results, with the republics grouped into six larger regions, are presented in Table 4.1.

Personal incomes per capita in current rubles rose more than 2.75 times in the USSR as a whole during the 18-year period under review, an average annual increase of 5.9 percent. Growth was rapid in all regions, the greatest annual gains being made by Moldavia (7.5 percent) and the smallest by Azerbaidzhan (5.2 percent). All components of personal incomes contributed to these gains, with money incomes growing much more rapidly than income in kind, a reflection of the rapid monetization of the agricultural sector and the relative decline of private agriculture.

As shown in Table 4.1, substantial regional disparities in personal incomes have persisted throughout the period. Incomes in the Baltic republics have been well above the national average in each benchmark year, with Lithuania experiencing a significant

TABLE 4.1

Nominal and Real Personal Incomes per Capita:
USSR and Regions, 1960, 1970, 1978

| | Relative Level | | | Index of Real Income (1960 = 100) | |
|---|---|---|---|---|---|
| | 1960 | 1970 | 1978 | 1970 | 1978 |
| USSR (rubles) | 446 | 799 | 1,259 | 157.9 | 218.2 |
| Index (USSR = 100) | 100.0 | 100.0 | 100.0 | | |
| RSFSR | 107.8 | 108.0 | 110.9 | 158.2 | 224.3 |
| Ukraine, Belo- | | | | | |
| russia, Moldavia | 92.9 | 95.9 | 95.8 | 166.6 | 229.5 |
| Ukraine | 94.5 | 97.1 | 95.9 | 162.5 | 221.6 |
| Belorussia | 81.2 | 93.8 | 97.9 | 182.5 | 263.0 |
| Moldavia | 69.9 | 86.0 | 89.9 | 194.2 | 280.4 |
| Kazakhstan | 95.1 | 87.5 | 88.4 | 145.4 | 202.9 |
| Transcaucasia | 82.9 | 79.2 | 79.4 | 148.6 | 206.1 |
| Georgia | 94.2 | 89.4 | 93.6 | 149.9 | 216.8 |
| Azerbaidzhan | 73.0 | 66.0 | 63.3 | 142.6 | 189.9 |
| Armenia | 85.0 | 87.1 | 86.7 | 161.9 | 222.5 |
| Central Asia | 74.6 | 72.8 | 70.0 | 154.6 | 205.1 |
| Uzbekistan | 77.4 | 74.2 | 71.6 | 151.6 | 201.9 |
| Kirgizstan | 71.8 | 72.5 | 69.7 | 159.5 | 211.8 |
| Tadzhikistan | 66.2 | 63.0 | 59.9 | 150.4 | 197.5 |
| Turkmenistan | 74.0 | 78.8 | 75.1 | 168.3 | 221.3 |
| Baltic republics | 118.0 | 123.3 | 117.0 | 165.2 | 216.4 |
| Estonia | 129.0 | 133.2 | 126.9 | 163.1 | 214.8 |
| Latvia | 124.9 | 125.1 | 113.7 | 158.3 | 198.5 |
| Lithuania | 107.8 | 117.7 | 115.1 | 172.3 | 232.8 |

Notes: See appendix for methodology. Indexes of real incomes
represent nominal personal incomes per capita, deflated by a Western-
constructed retail price index. See the text for a discussion of this
index.

Sources: 1960, 1970—Alastair McAuley, Economic Welfare in
the Soviet Union (Madison: University of Wisconsin Press, 1979),
p. 109; 1978—estimated.

relative gain and Latvia a relative decline. Only the RSFSR has managed to approach the affluence of the least affluent of the Baltic republics, and it has gained relatively over the years. The western republics rank next, with incomes in 1978 a little below average and an improved relative position over 1960. The other major regions experienced a relative decline in position. Central Asia ranks lowest, with average personal income in 1978 some 30 percent below the national average. Tadzhikistan in Central Asia and Azerbaidzhan in Transcaucasia are notable, both for their bottom rankings and for the serious deterioration in their relative positions. In contrast, Moldavia's ranking advanced from fourteenth to seventh. Growth in personal incomes was faster in the 1960s than in the 1970s, and the slowdown affected all regions. By 1978 all republics and major regions had average per capita personal incomes above the "poverty level" of 600 rubles per year, an amount deemed by Soviet statisticians to be required to meet a "minimum material subsistence" budget.[5] Yet in 1970 three Central Asian republics and Azerbaidzhan fell below this standard.

In the 1960s political spokesmen repeatedly touted the government's intent to reduce development gaps and to narrow differences in levels of living among regions.[6] As McAuley found, however, no reduction in differentials, as measured by personal money incomes per capita, occurred; in fact the coefficient of variation (weighted by population) rose slightly—from 0.112 to 0.124. In the 1970s this goal was no longer proclaimed, Brezhnev having declared in 1972 that the objective had been essentially achieved.[7] But a wage reform and other incomes policies produced a widening of interrepublic differentials; the coefficient of variation was 0.155 in 1978. Regional variations of these magnitudes are not large by international standards, however, being well within the range found in Western countries.[8]

Up to now the discussion has concerned relative gains in money incomes (including income in kind valued in current prices). Whether their rapid rates of growth imply rapid gains in material well-being depends on changes in taxes and other obligatory payments and on changes in the cost of living. Direct taxes are low in the USSR (less than 10 percent of total money incomes), and, in any event, complete data on direct taxes paid by residents are not available by region. The question of trends in consumer prices is potentially much more decisive. Unfortunately, the Soviet government does not publish cost of living indexes, either for the USSR as a whole or for republics. Indexes of the prices of goods sold at retail are considered unreliable because of their methodological underpinnings.[9] The index for the USSR shows virtually no price change since 1955, a finding that is widely disbelieved—notably by Soviet consumers themselves, if one may judge from émigré statements.[10]

To provide an alternative to the misleading official retail price index, the author of this chapter devised a price index for goods that is implicit in a comparison of household consumption of traded goods measured in constant prices with official Soviet values measured in current prices.[11] This index, which certainly understates the rate of price change, rose at an average annual rate of less than 1 percent in the 1960s and 1.7 percent in the 1970s. In Table 4.1 this index is used to deflate the indexes of nominal incomes, in the belief that some deflation is preferable to none. In view of the evidence belying the official index, trends probably do not differ significantly among republics. The index of real per capita personal incomes for the USSR as a whole more than doubled, rising at an average annual rate of 4.7 percent in the 1960s and 4.1 percent in the 1970s. According to this measure, real personal incomes increased some 29 percent less than nominal incomes in the USSR and its regions during 1960-78. The difference would be greater if income in kind could be fully deflated and if consumer price trends could be measured by procedures used in the West.

The Soviet Union's two major social groups—state employees and collective farmers—did not share equally in these gains in incomes, either nationally or regionally. Moreover, the differences in incomes of the two groups remains sizable, although the gap is diminishing steadily. The most definitive evidence on these points is provided by McAuley for 1960-70.[12] According to his data, per capita personal incomes of state employees rose by two-thirds during the period, while those of collective farmers doubled. For state employees the increases ranged from 36 percent in Tadzhikistan to 99 percent in Belorussia. For collective farmers increases ranged from 52 percent in Uzbekistan to 243 percent in Moldavia. In Uzbekistan and Latvia per capita incomes of state employees rose more rapidly than those of collective farmers. Because of the large share of wages in total personal incomes and the general uniformity of Soviet wage policies, interregional differences in per capita personal incomes of state employees are relatively narrow; in 1970 they ranged from 68 percent of the USSR average in Azerbaidzhan to 124 percent in Estonia. For collective farmers, however, the differences are much wider; incomes ranged from 60 percent of the national average in Tadzhikistan to 202 percent in Estonia. The coefficient of variation for collective farmers' incomes was double that for state employees' incomes. Although diminishing steadily, the gap between the two groups was still large in 1970. For the USSR as a whole, state employees' incomes were 26 percent above collective farmers' incomes, but there was great variation among republics. In the three Baltic republics collective farmers' incomes exceeded those of state employees by 13-22 percent, and in Turkmenia, by 4 percent. In Tadzhikistan, in contrast, incomes of state employees exceeded those of collective farmers by 51 percent. Unfortunately, these comparisons cannot be carried out for 1978 because of lack of data.

Again, we would like to know how interregional disparities in personal incomes in a given year are affected by differences in the cost of living. Unfortunately, the data with which to assess this matter are meager. Soviet sources tell us that prices of many foods and some other products vary modestly among republics because of the system of zonal prices.[13] Collective-farm market prices and prices of personal services also differ regionally, to what extent (on the average) we do not know. On the other hand, most goods and many services have uniform national prices. Soviet economists seem to believe (and this also conforms to the author's impression) that regional income disparities would not be greatly changed by adjustment for price differences. For one thing, regional wage coefficients added to wage rates in the state sector are designed to compensate for regional cost of living differences.

How did the various intergroup and interrepublic disparities change in the 1970s? Unfortunately, McAuley's estimates for 1970 cannot be extended to 1978 with confidence. His estimates rested on a unique body of data on collective farmers' incomes and their structure during 1960-70. Nothing similar is available for later years. Incomes in kind from private agriculture cannot be determined for republics, since there are no data; to assume that 1970 relationships prevailed is to assume the answer to the question one is asking. Moreover, incomes of collective farmers from work in the socialized sector are not available for four republics. Finally, data on transfer payments are far from complete in general, and are not available at all for most republics in 1978. Again, to use past years' relationships and arbitrary values to estimate the missing incomes is to assume away the problem.[14] Complete data are available, however, for average money wages in the state sector; these are presented in Table 4.2. They show the familiar patterns in respect to relative rankings among republics and relatively narrow differences among them.

The differences widened appreciably in the 1970s, however, with the coefficient of variation rising from 0.082 in 1970 to 0.102 in 1978. This widening is accounted for, at least in part, by a general wage reform that was carried out region by region and had not been completed by the end of 1978. What the ultimate results will be in this respect must await data for 1979 and 1980. More data also are needed to determine whether differences between per capita personal incomes of state employees and collective farmers have continued to narrow, and what the pattern of change has been among

TABLE 4.2

Average Annual Wages of State Employees and Savings Deposits per Capita:
USSR and Regions, 1960, 1970, 1978
(rubles)

| | Average Annual Wages of State Employees | | | | Savings Deposits Per Capita | | | |
| --- | --- | --- | --- | --- | --- | --- | --- | --- |
| | 1960 | 1970 | 1978 | Percent Change | 1960 | 1970 | 1978 | Percent Change |
| USSR | 967 | 1,464 | 1,920 | 199 | 51 | 192 | 502 | 984 |
| RSFSR | 997 | 1,513 | 2,016 | 202 | 61 | 216 | 555 | 910 |
| Ukraine, Belorussia, Moldavia | 909 | 1,359 | 1,731 | 190 | 43 | 183 | 540 | 1,256 |
| Ukraine | 940 | 1,382 | 1,752 | 186 | 46 | 193 | 558 | 1,215 |
| Belorussia | 758 | 1,277 | 1,692 | 223 | 31 | 161 | 542 | 1,748 |
| Moldavia | 809 | 1,234 | 1,548 | 191 | 21 | 93 | 305 | 1,452 |
| Kazakhstan | 978 | 1,484 | 1,920 | 196 | 32 | 138 | 336 | 1,050 |

| | | | | | | | | |
|---|---|---|---|---|---|---|---|---|
| Transcaucasia | 911 | 1,335 | 1,675 | 184 | 42 | 187 | 424 | 1,010 |
| Georgia | 900 | 1,272 | 1,608 | 179 | 52 | 247 | 565 | 1,087 |
| Azerbaidzhan | 928 | 1,315 | 1,650 | 178 | 30 | 101 | 228 | 760 |
| Armenia | 905 | 1,476 | 1,836 | 203 | 44 | 249 | 576 | 1,309 |
| Central Asia | 884 | 1,397 | 1,786 | 202 | 25 | 85 | 194 | 776 |
| Uzbekistan | 841 | 1,378 | 1,776 | 211 | 23 | 78 | 186 | 809 |
| Kirgizstan | 899 | 1,351 | 1,722 | 192 | 30 | 102 | 234 | 780 |
| Tadzhikistan | 940 | 1,411 | 1,692 | 180 | 22 | 86 | 169 | 768 |
| Turkmenistan | 1,019 | 1,560 | 2,052 | 201 | 28 | 96 | 217 | 775 |
| Baltic republics | 922 | 1,507 | 1,956 | 212 | 44 | 249 | 720 | 1,636 |
| Estonia | 983 | 1,624 | 2,136 | 217 | 59 | 295 | 695 | 1,178 |
| Latvia | 940 | 1,507 | 1,932 | 206 | 51 | 239 | 592 | 1,161 |
| Lithuania | 869 | 1,435 | 1,890 | 217 | 31 | 236 | 828 | 2,671 |

Sources: Wage data (expressed per month) from annual statistical handbooks published by the USSR and the republics, and (for 1978) from their annual reports on plan fulfillment; data on total savings deposits in TsSU, Narodnoe khoziaistvo SSSR v 1970 g. (Moscow, 1971), p. 564 (publication hereafter cited as Narkhoz), and Narkhoz 78, p. 415.

regions. However, intergroup differences probably continued to narrow, although at a reduced pace. This tentative conclusion is based on the facts that average annual wages paid to collective farmers increased faster than wages of state employees in the USSR as a whole and in nine of the republics for which we have direct information, and that payments and benefits from social consumption funds—the source of transfer payments—expressed per collective farmer participating in the public sector, rose substantially faster than payments and benefits expressed per state employee. These data also suggest that collective farmers in the Baltic republics continue to fare better than state employees, as they did in 1970.

The narrowing of income differences between collective farmers and state employees is a major part of a recent general policy of narrowing differences between agricultural and nonagricultural money wages in general, and also between wages on collective farms and state farms. Reductions have been substantial. In 1960, for the USSR as a whole, average wages in state agriculture were 64 percent of the average nonagricultural wage, and wages on collective farms were 53 percent of those in state agriculture. By 1975 these relationships were 86 percent and 72 percent, respectively. Reductions in these differentials took place in all republics, but at varying rates. The data are not complete enough to sort this out systematically. However, in 1975 state agricultural wages ranged from 63 percent of the nonagricultural wage in Georgia to 109 percent of that wage in Turkmenistan. [15] In that year average wages of collective farmers ranged from 74 percent of wages in state agriculture in the RSFSR to 15 percent above the state level in Armenia; data on this measure are available for only 11 republics. These comparisons, of course, do not take into account the earnings from private activities by the two groups. Both still have substantial shares of their income from that source, but the share is much larger for collective farmers. For the USSR as a whole in 1975, the average family's earnings from private agricultural activity supplemented wages earned in the socialized sector by 58 percent. [16] The supplement for the average state farm family was perhaps half that large.

## TRENDS AND PATTERNS IN REAL CONSUMPTION

Perhaps the best overall measure of changes in levels of living is an index of real per capita consumption of goods and services. In Western accounting practice, such a measure includes household purchases of goods and services for consumption, incomes in kind, imputed rents on owner-occupied housing, and government current expenditures on education, health, and related services. The Soviet government does not publish a comparable measure; its published index of real per capita incomes is based on a Marxist-oriented concept and in any case is believed to overstate improvement in living standards.[17] As already noted, Western scholarship has produced indexes of consumption for the USSR as a whole as components of measures of gross national product (GNP), but no similar measures for republics have yet been developed. McAuley's measures of total incomes pertain to personal incomes (money and in kind), supplemented by government current outlays on communal services, although he also discusses the possible impact of price changes and regional differences in cost of living on these nominal incomes. Working from the expenditure side, Elizabeth Clayton has put together an estimate of per capita consumption in the republics in 1965.[18] Relying on the estimates of total incomes in current rubles put together by McAuley for 1960, 1965, and 1970, we carry these efforts forward by extending McAuley's measures to 1978, then adjusting the estimates for each year to remove nonconsumption expenditures, and finally deflating the results to express them in real terms. The result is a set of indexes of real per capita consumption for 1960-78.

A brief description and evaluation of the procedure for deriving the indexes of real per capita consumption, by republic, is required here; detailed sources and methodology are relegated to the appendix. We start with McAuley's estimates of total current incomes per capita, carried forward to 1978. Total incomes include wages for work in state enterprises, earnings in cash and in kind received for work on collective farms, money incomes and consumption in kind from private agricultural activities, transfer payments (pensions, aid, and stipends), interest on bonds and savings accounts, a small, arbitrary allowance for other unspecified incomes, and government current expenditures and imputed depreciation in respect to provision of health care, education, housing, and other services available without charge or at subsidized prices.

The next step is to convert these measures of total money and in-kind incomes and government outlays to measures of consumption of goods and services. This is accomplished by subtracting from total incomes those elements that do not represent current household consumption in established prices (as conventionally defined in Western national income accounting). The principal items to be deducted are additions to savings, taxes, and other obligatory payments; investment in private housing; and the government housing subsidy. All of these items are available for the republics, or can be estimated with reasonable confidence. The resulting estimates represent money expenditures on goods and services and consumption in kind, expressed in current prices; they include outlays for consumption by both households and the government.

The final step is to deflate these nominal outlays per capita by a price index to obtain an index of real expenditures. The index used is the price index that is implicit in a comparison of our ruble values for the USSR as a whole for 1960-78 with an index of real per capita consumption that measures quantities of goods and services consumed by the population.[19] This index is a component of the overall measure of real GNP. The index derived for the USSR was used to deflate money expenditures for all regions and republics. Compared with no increase at all during 1960-78, shown by the official index of retail prices,[20] the implicit index resulting from such a comparison indicates a price increase of 37.3 percent, probably an understatement. The measures resulting from these procedures are shown in Table 4.3.

In Table 4.3 per capita consumption in current prices for each republic and larger region are given as percentages of the average for the USSR, and derived indexes of real per capita consumption are shown for each region and republic. For each republic the underlying estimates are based almost entirely on official data regarding incomes and government expenditures for communal services. They include the vast bulk of household outlays and all government outlays, and are as complete as possible with existing data. They fit well with various data that can be used as cross-checks. They have been put together to conform as closely as possible to the Western measure of per capita consumption for the USSR. The estimates, of course, contain sins of omission and commission, but these sins are not large, and there is little reason to think that they seriously distort the picture of relative levels and trends among regions. The basic estimates of incomes (expenditures) omit military incomes, imputed rents, and certain other incomes, the nature of which is dimly understood. On the other hand, they include small amounts of imputed depreciation on housing and the capital stock in education and health services; the latter are included in the underlying Soviet expenditure data and cannot be removed with any degree of accuracy.

Finally, deflation of the current price measures by a uniform index assumes that the rate of inflation does not differ regionally. In view of the highly centralized nature of price fixing and administration in the USSR, this seems a reasonable assumption. The question of regional differences in relative prices was discussed above, and it was concluded that, overall, such differences are probably not large in respect to republics (as opposed to the regions within the RSFSR). Moreover, the wage structure includes regional coefficients intended to compensate for cost of living differences.

TABLE 4.3

Indexes and Relative Levels of Real per Capita Consumption:
USSR and Regions, 1960-78

| | Index (1960 = 100) | | | Relative Level (USSR = 100) | | | |
|---|---|---|---|---|---|---|---|
| | 1965 | 1970 | 1978 | 1960 | 1965 | 1970 | 1978 |
| USSR | 112.0 | 143.1 | 176.3 | 100.0 | 100.0 | 100.0 | 100.0 |
| RSFSR | 111.4 | 143.8 | 181.6 | 106.6 | 106.1 | 107.1 | 109.8 |
| Ukraine, Belo-russia, Moldavia | 117.9 | 149.9 | 182.6 | 91.6 | 96.5 | 96.0 | 94.9 |
| Ukraine | 113.8 | 146.8 | 176.0 | 94.3 | 98.0 | 96.6 | 94.1 |
| Belorussia | 121.3 | 161.2 | 205.8 | 84.4 | 91.4 | 95.0 | 98.5 |
| Moldavia | 137.7 | 179.3 | 236.4 | 72.5 | 89.1 | 90.8 | 97.2 |
| Kazakhstan | 107.5 | 136.5 | 166.5 | 95.6 | 91.7 | 91.2 | 90.3 |
| Transcaucasia | 103.7 | 133.7 | 162.5 | 85.7 | 79.4 | 80.1 | 79.0 |
| Georgia | 102.9 | 133.4 | 166.5 | 95.4 | 87.6 | 88.9 | 90.1 |
| Azerbaidzhan | 105.5 | 133.3 | 158.4 | 74.4 | 70.1 | 69.4 | 66.9 |
| Armenia | 104.5 | 140.9 | 170.2 | 87.0 | 81.2 | 85.9 | 84.0 |
| Central Asia | 112.3 | 140.2 | 170.8 | 78.2 | 78.4 | 76.6 | 75.7 |
| Uzbekistan | 106.9 | 139.0 | 171.0 | 80.4 | 76.7 | 78.1 | 78.0 |
| Kirgizstan | 121.5 | 145.8 | 175.1 | 74.7 | 81.0 | 76.1 | 74.2 |
| Tadzhikistan | 122.7 | 135.5 | 160.5 | 70.5 | 77.2 | 66.7 | 64.1 |
| Turkmenistan | 115.3 | 142.8 | 172.5 | 82.4 | 84.8 | 82.2 | 80.6 |
| Baltic republics | 111.3 | 149.5 | 175.1 | 118.7 | 118.0 | 124.0 | 118.6 |
| Estonia | 111.0 | 146.1 | 176.5 | 130.2 | 129.0 | 132.9 | 130.3 |
| Latvia | 107.7 | 141.9 | 162.3 | 127.3 | 122.4 | 126.3 | 117.2 |
| Lithuania | 113.1 | 154.2 | 184.1 | 109.9 | 110.6 | 118.4 | 114.7 |

Source: Author's calculations.

With these caveats, we now turn to an examination of the findings.  According to the data given in Table 4.3, per capita consumption rose quite rapidly in all regions during 1960-78.  Rates of growth ranged from 2.6 percent annually in Azerbaidzhan to 4.9 percent in Moldavia, the average for the USSR being 3.2 percent annually.  In nearly all republics the annual gains were relatively small during 1961-65, largely the result of poor performance in agriculture.  Growth accelerated sharply during 1966-70, thanks in part to good weather for crops and speeded-up resource allocations to agriculture, and partly to faster growth in output of manufactured consumer goods and services.  Progress again slowed noticeably during the 1970s, particularly after 1975.  In all cases the rates of growth of real per capita consumption were significantly slower than those of nominal personal incomes.  The difference helps to explain the rapid growth of per capita savings deposits shown in Table 4.2, and perhaps also a sizable increase in household cash balances, a phenomenon that cannot be measured with available data.

In respect to relative levels, a fairly stable regional hierarchy has prevailed during the period.  All of the Baltic republics have had levels of consumption above the national average by roughly 20 percent, with Lithuania having improved its position, Latvia's position having deteriorated, and Estonia's having remained about the same.  Central Asia as a whole occupied the low end of the scale among major regions, averaging about 25 percent below the national level.  The relative position of all four republics deteriorated during the period, notably in Tadzhikistan.  A similar pattern prevailed, though at a somewhat higher average level, in Transcaucasia.  Kazakhstan's position also fell relatively, while the RSFSR and the western republics experienced small relative gains.  In respect to rankings of individual republics, the Baltic republics and the RSFSR held the highest rankings throughout the period, while Tadzhikistan remained at the bottom.  On the other hand, Moldavia's position rose from fourteenth to sixth.  As measured by the coefficient of variation, there was virtually no change in the degree of regional disparity during the 1960s, and a significant rise during the 1970s.  The weighted coefficients were 0.105 in 1960, 0.107 in 1970, and 0.143 in 1978.  These findings suggest either that the proclaimed policy of reducing interregional disparities was not implemented during the 1960s, or that, if tried, it did not succeed.  The abandonment of that aim in the 1970s was accompanied by a widening of differentials.  Even the greater disparities now prevailing, however, are not especially large by international standards, at least as measured by income comparisons.  The coefficients of variation for per capita consumption are smaller than those for personal incomes, indicating that government provision of health and education services has had an equalizing impact overall.

It is of interest to compare our measures of progress in raising living standards with the measure published by the Soviet government for that purpose: the official indexes of "real incomes of
the population," expressed per capita. These indexes are available
for all republics for the period 1965-78. Although the precise nature and method of calculating the indexes are something of a mys-
tery, [21] they purport to be deflated indexes of money incomes spent
by the population on goods and household utilities and for investment
in private housing, plus incomes in kind and material expenditures
of "institutions serving the population" (providing such services as
transportation, communication, housing, health, education and culture, and recreation. Also included is imputed depreciation on
state-owned housing and on the capital stock of institutions providing services. The deflator is a weighted index of state retail prices,
collective farm market prices, and prices of services. The official
index of real incomes per capita, thus, is a deflated index of consumption and investment in material goods by the population, including imputed depreciation. It differs from conventional Western
measures of real per capita consumption, primarily in that the latter include labor expended in most of the service industries, and
exclude investment of all kinds. Despite the conceptual differences, [22] it is of interest to compare the trends revealed by the two
measures, for both purport to depict trends in the well-being of the
populace.

For the USSR as a whole during 1965-78, the official index of
real per capita incomes shows an increase of 83 percent, compared
with 57 percent shown by our index of per capita consumption. The
former grows more rapidly than the latter in all republics, but the
degree of divergence differs considerably, ranging from 12 percent
in Georgia to 34 percent in Tadzhikistan. For Central Asia as a
whole, the official index gives a 20 percent greater rate of increase
than does the index of per capita consumption. The reasons for
these disparate results are not apparent, and there seems no way
to ferret them out from available information.

## MAJOR COMPONENTS OF CONSUMPTION

Available data do not permit disaggregation of our indexes of
per capita consumption so as to measure changes and relative levels
of major categories of consumption—food, clothing, shelter, and
services. To assess these matters, one must resort to various
physical indicators and a few value measures that are far from
ideal, conceptually. Thus, retail sales per capita are sometimes
used to depict changes in, and relative levels of, consumption of

goods. [23] Although retail sales data are available for all republics, they have serious shortcomings. First, they include a substantial number of sales that do not represent current consumption of goods by the population—sales to state enterprises and institutions, repair services, commission sales, and some investment goods; such items amount to at least 10 percent of retail trade for the USSR, vary from year to year, and differ in shares among republics. The official data in constant prices suffer from the faults of the official retail price indexes. Finally, relative levels of retail sales are highly correlated with levels of urbanization, thus greatly overstating the differentiation of relative levels of consumption. Despite their shortcomings, retail sales per capita do show trends paralleling the growth in personal incomes, and have essentially the same hierarchy of regions in respect to relative levels.

Food

For the USSR as a whole during the period under review, substantial gains were made in all major categories of consumption—food, soft goods, durables, and services. The same undoubtedly holds true for all republics, even though precise measurement is impossible. All of the information available supports this conclusion, but it also indicates that substantial interrepublic differences persist. Food, accounting in 1978 for roughly 45 percent of family expenditures on goods and services in the USSR as a whole, [24] is by far the largest category of consumption expenditures in all republics. As one would expect, its share has been declining with rising incomes, and its composition has been slowly changing in the direction of relatively more meat and dairy products and relatively less bread and potatoes. The best available relevant data are published statistics on consumption of several foods in physical units. Unfortunately, these data are available for only nine republics for various years. Fragmentary though they are, they confirm for the regions the general trends described above and also show large regional disparities. Thus, in 1975 per capita consumption of meat in the Baltic republics exceeded the national average by over 33 percent, and per capita consumption of grain products was about 25 percent below the national average; such a pattern conforms to their status as relatively high-income regions. The reverse pattern is shown by the fragmentary data for some of the low-income republics. In some cases part of this difference is explained by cultural preferences.

Although the caveats noted above should be kept in mind, the data on per capita retail sales shown in Table 4.4 support these general conclusions. They indicate that substantial increases in food purchases were made in all republics, the most rapid being shown by the three republics—Belorussia, Moldavia, and Lithuania—that experienced the most rapid urbanization, and the slowest gains by the more rural Central Asian republics and Azerbaidzhan.

Differences in per capita retail sales are wide—in 1978, for example, per capita food purchases in the Baltic republics were more than double those in Central Asia and nearly double those in Transcaucasia. These disparities were greater than in 1960. Retail sales, of course, do not mirror differences in total per capita consumption of food, because there is substantial home consumption of food produced in private agricultural activity. For the USSR as a whole, the share of consumption in kind in total food consumption fell from 17.5 percent in 1960 to about 12 percent in 1977.[25] However, the importance of this source varies greatly among republics, as does the rate of change. While we can say with confidence from data on retail sales of food that food consumption has risen substantially in all republics and at different rates, we must also conclude that the rates are substantially below those shown by retail sales alone, which reflect, among other things, the shift from home consumption to commercial processing and distribution, as well as price changes. For the USSR as a whole, per capita real consumption of food increased by 55 percent during 1960-78,[26] while per capita retail sales of food rose by 138 percent.

## Other Goods

Per capita retail sales of soft goods, durables, and the like are a much more accurate measure of relative levels and trends in consumption than are sales of food. The principal limitations have to do with inclusion of enterprise purchases and repair services in the data, and the fact that the data are in current prices. Western research has not been able to devise an accurate deflator for nonfood purchases; the "alternative" retail price index used elsewhere in this paper undoubtedly understates the extent of price inflation. For purposes of assessing relative trends and levels of consumption of nonfood goods among regions, however, per capita retail sales data probably are not grossly wrong. The trends in such sales by republic, shown in Table 4.4, correlate closely with trends and relative levels of personal income per capita. As the data indicate, per capita sales of soft goods and durables more than doubled in all regions during 1960-78; they tripled in Lithuania, Belorussia, and Moldavia, where personal incomes and urbanization rose most rapidly. Again, as with incomes, Central Asia trailed the rest. Differences among the republics in 1960 ranged from 51 percent above the

TABLE 4.4

Per Capita Retail Sales of Food and Nonfood Products,
USSR and Regions, 1960-77
(rubles)

| | Food | | | | Nonfood Products | | | |
|---|---|---|---|---|---|---|---|---|
| | 1960 | 1970 | 1978 | Percent Change | 1960 | 1970 | 1978 | Percent Change |
| USSR | 200 | 355 | 482 | 241 | 167 | 284 | 442 | 265 |
| RSFSR | 232 | 497 | 558 | 241 | 175 | 293 | 459 | 262 |
| Ukraine, Belorussia, Moldavia | 152 | 302 | 422 | 278 | 149 | 274 | 432 | 290 |
| Ukraine | 159 | 306 | 419 | 264 | 153 | 276 | 429 | 280 |
| Belorussia | 137 | 314 | 471 | 344 | 132 | 265 | 441 | 334 |
| Moldavia | 95 | 222 | 334 | 352 | 130 | 266 | 442 | 340 |
| Kazakhstan | 176 | 304 | 401 | 228 | 167 | 253 | 394 | 236 |

| | | | | | | | | |
|---|---|---|---|---|---|---|---|---|
| Transcaucasia | 137 | 233 | 315 | 230 | 140 | 223 | 346 | 247 |
| Georgia | 143 | 238 | 347 | 243 | 155 | 254 | 405 | 261 |
| Azerbaidzhan | 129 | 208 | 259 | 201 | 124 | 189 | 281 | 227 |
| Armenia | 141 | 273 | 372 | 264 | 139 | 234 | 376 | 271 |
| | | | | | | | | |
| Central Asia | 134 | 215 | 270 | 201 | 136 | 211 | 318 | 234 |
| Uzbekistan | 133 | 208 | 262 | 197 | 138 | 209 | 311 | 225 |
| Kirgizstan | 138 | 243 | 318 | 230 | 133 | 223 | 342 | 257 |
| Tadzhikistan | 117 | 194 | 238 | 203 | 125 | 202 | 300 | 240 |
| Turkmenistan | 160 | 246 | 293 | 183 | 147 | 220 | 353 | 240 |
| | | | | | | | | |
| Baltic republics | 213 | 431 | 602 | 283 | 212 | 404 | 605 | 285 |
| Estonia | 275 | 505 | 680 | 247 | 247 | 451 | 663 | 268 |
| Latvia | 257 | 477 | 639 | 249 | 253 | 467 | 682 | 270 |
| Lithuania | 153 | 365 | 540 | 353 | 166 | 337 | 522 | 314 |

Note: "Food" includes alcoholic and nonalcoholic beverages. All values are in current prices.
Sources: Narkhoz 60, p. 685; Narkhoz 70, p. 579; Narkhoz 78, p. 435.

135

national average in Estonia to 26 percent below the average in Azerbaidzhan. The differentials widened during the period. In 1978 per
capita sales in Azerbaidzhan were less than two-thirds of the national average. Relative rankings changed somewhat, even though
the Baltic republics remained at the top and Central Asia at the bottom, along with Azerbaidzhan. Belorussia and Moldavia had surpassed the Ukraine.

Retail sales data can be disaggregated to show relative rates
of growth and levels of sales of various kinds of goods. Of special
interest are data pertaining to purchases of consumer durables.
Sales of these symbols of the modern age have grown far more rapidly than sales of nonfood goods as a whole in the USSR and in all
republics, as Soviet policy has belatedly permitted a rapid buildup
of manufacturing capacities for consumer durables from minuscule
levels in the early 1950s. One way to gauge the progress that has
been made is to examine data on household stocks of several kinds
of durables. Unfortunately, data by region are incomplete, but
some examples will illustrate the point. In the USSR as a whole in
1965, only 24 percent of all families had television sets, 11 percent
had refrigerators, and 21 percent had washing machines; in 1977
these percentages were 83, 72, and 69.[27] In the Ukraine in 1965,
21 percent of families had television sets, 8 percent had refrigerators, and 19 percent had washing machines; in 1977 the corresponding shares were 76, 65, and 63.[28] In Uzbekistan in 1965, 20 percent of families had television sets, 13 percent had refrigerators,
and 16 percent had washing machines; in 1977 the corresponding
shares were 68, 66, and 49.[29]

Even though Soviet-made durables are poor in quality and obsolete in design by Western standards, these figures show substantial progress toward the development of a modern, consumer-oriented
society. They also indicate that the gains have been widespread.
Additional data could be presented to buttress this point, but it seems
unnecessary to do so. As for the newest status symbol—the automobile—data are skimpy. However, it is reported that the Baltic republics, Georgia, and Armenia are by far the best provided.[30]

Household Services

In the USSR the service sector has developed in accord with
the priorities of the government rather than in response to private
demand. As a result the sector is relatively backward in comparison with other countries at similar levels of development. This
statement holds, regardless of whether services are taken as a
share of employment, of GNP, or of consumption. Although sys-

tematic data are not available, it is evident that substantial regional differences exist in respect to the provision of services to the population. We define services to include housing, utilities, passenger transportation, communication, repair, personal care, and entertainment and recreation. For the USSR as a whole in 1976, this group accounted for about 10 percent of total consumption. No doubt the shares differ among regions, with larger shares prevailing in the relatively high-income Baltic republics and lower shares in Central Asia and Azerbaidzhan. The availability of such services is strongly correlated with the extent of urbanization, which proceeded unevenly among the republics in the 1960s and 1970s.

To provide an idea of relative trends and levels of household services, Table 4.5 presents data on the progress of urbanization and the provision of one such service—urban housing. As can be observed, there are sharp differences among regions in the rate at which urbanization has proceeded since 1959. The share of urban population in the total rose very rapidly in Belorussia, Moldavia, and Lithuania, which also experienced the most rapid gains in incomes and consumption. Scarcely any urbanization took place in Azerbaidzhan, Tadzhikistan, and Turkmenistan, and not much in Kirgizstan during the 20-year period. Again, these are the regions with the slowest gains in per capita incomes and consumption. At the beginning of 1979, the share of the urban population in the total was highest in Estonia and Latvia, which also have per capita incomes far above average. In contrast, Central Asia, with its relatively low incomes, has only about 40 percent of its population in cities, compared with over 66 percent in the Baltic republics.

As shown in Table 4.5, the availability of urban housing differs substantially among regions. In 1978, Latvia and Estonia enjoyed about 25 percent more housing, measured in square meters of useful space per capita, than was provided in the RSFSR and about 60 percent more than was available in Central Asia. All republics and regions experienced moderate increases in urban housing space per capita during the period, the most rapid gains having been made in the RSFSR and the least rapid in Central Asia. Urban housing is predominantly publicly provided, and rents are highly subsidized and levied at uniform rates. Interesting differences exist among republics, however, in the share of public housing in total urban housing. In Georgia in 1978, only 59 percent of urban housing was state-provided, whereas in the RSFSR the share was 82 percent. The availability of rural housing, overwhelmingly privately owned, apparently is about the same on a per capita basis as urban housing for the USSR as a whole. Whether this relationship holds for the various regions is not known. No data are available on expenditures of households for utilities on a regional basis. However,

## TABLE 4.5

Urbanization and Urban Housing: USSR and Regions, 1959–79

| | Urban Population as Percent of Total Population | | | | Urban Housing Space (sq. m. per capita) | | | |
|---|---|---|---|---|---|---|---|---|
| | 1959 | 1970 | 1979 | Percent Change | 1960 | 1970 | 1978 | Percent Change |
| USSR | 48 | 57 | 62 | 129 | 8.8 | 11.0 | 12.7 | 144 |
| RSFSR | 52 | 63 | 69 | 133 | 8.6 | 11.0 | 12.8 | 149 |
| Ukraine, Belorussia, Moldavia | 42 | 53 | 59 | 140 | 9.6 | 11.7 | 13.4 | 140 |
| Ukraine | 46 | 55 | 61 | 133 | 9.8 | 11.9 | 13.6 | 139 |
| Belorussia | 31 | 45 | 55 | 177 | 8.8 | 10.7 | 12.6 | 143 |
| Moldavia | 22 | 32 | 39 | 177 | 8.4 | 10.1 | 11.3 | 135 |
| Kazakhstan | 44 | 51 | 54 | 123 | 7.9 | 9.8 | 11.4 | 144 |

| | | | | | | | |
|---|---|---|---|---|---|---|---|
| Transcaucasia | 46 | 51 | 56 | 122 | 8.7 | 10.4 | 11.3 | 130 |
| Georgia | 42 | 48 | 52 | 124 | 9.8 | 12.2 | 14.0 | 143 |
| Azerbaidzhan | 48 | 50 | 53 | 110 | 8.1 | 9.3 | 9.7 | 120 |
| Armenia | 50 | 60 | 66 | 132 | 7.9 | 9.6 | 10.5 | 133 |
| | | | | | | | |
| Central Asia | 35 | 38 | 41 | 117 | 7.8 | 8.6 | 9.7 | 124 |
| Uzbekistan | 33 | 36 | 41 | 124 | 7.8 | 8.2 | 9.6 | 123 |
| Kirgizstan | 34 | 38 | 39 | 115 | 7.4 | 8.8 | 9.9 | 134 |
| Tadzhikistan | 33 | 37 | 35 | 106 | 7.9 | 8.8 | 9.5 | 120 |
| Turkmenistan | 46 | 48 | 48 | 104 | 8.4 | 9.8 | 10.4 | 124 |
| | | | | | | | |
| Baltic republics | 48 | 58 | 65 | 135 | 11.0 | 12.8 | 14.5 | 132 |
| Estonia | 56 | 66 | 70 | 125 | 11.5 | 13.7 | 15.8 | 137 |
| Latvia | 56 | 63 | 68 | 121 | 12.2 | 13.9 | 15.3 | 125 |
| Lithuania | 39 | 51 | 61 | 156 | 9.4 | 11.3 | 13.2 | 140 |

Notes: Urban population is as of mid-January of each year. Urban housing is measured in square meters of useful space at end of year.

Sources: Urban population—Narkhoz 70, p. 11; Narkhoz 79, pp. 10-11; urban housing stock—Narkhoz 70, p. 546; Narkhoz 78, p. 398.

rate structures are uniform, and expenditures would be strongly correlated with the level of urbanization. Not only are amenities much more available in cities, but urban residents possess substantially larger stocks of household appliances.

Available data permit us to inspect regional differences in one other kind of service—described in Soviet statistics as "everyday services." They include repair of personal belongings, tailoring, laundry and dry cleaning facilities, barber and beauty shops, photographic services, public baths, and similar services. Provision of such services was long neglected, and despite recent progress their level is still abysmally low by Western standards. In 1978 the volume of such services amounted to a mere 26 rubles per capita; however, in 1960 it was a minuscule 4 rubles per capita. These figures, of course, do not include privately provided services, which are substantial but about which we have little data. Provision of state service has proceeded unevenly among regions, with the most rapid gains being made by republics experiencing rapid urbanization. Levels also differ greatly by region, paralleling the differentials found in retail trade.[31] In 1978 the highest level was in Latvia, where these "everyday services" amounted to 47 rubles per capita. In Azerbaidzhan they amounted to 15 rubles per capita, and in the Central Asian republics they amounted to less than 20 rubles per capita. These data suggest that the USSR and its constituent republics have a long way to go in their halting progress toward the modern, service-oriented economy.

Communal Services

In contrast with household services, the Soviet government has long accorded considerable priority to development of health and education services, which are mainly provided free of direct charge. Large resource allocations have been made over the years, and all regions have shared in them, as the state has sought to develop a healthy and educated work force to staff its rapidly industrializing economy. Unfortunately, the available data do not permit reliable measures of annual current expenditures on these services. Expenditures from republic budgets understate the actual outlays to varying degrees, since they omit expenditures from the all-union budget, as well as outlays by enterprises, collective farms, and other organizations. We do not know how these outlays are distributed among republics. As a substitute one must resort to various physical measures.

Table 4.6 presents data on two key indicators of levels and trends in provision of health services among regions: the number

# TABLE 4.6

Availability of Health Services: USSR and Regions, 1960-78

| | Number of Doctors per 10,000 People | | | Number of Hospital Beds per 10,000 People | | |
|---|---|---|---|---|---|---|
| | 1960 | 1970 | 1978 | 1960 | 1970 | 1978 |
| USSR | 20.0 | 27.4 | 35.4 | 80.4 | 109.2 | 122.0 |
| RSFSR | 20.8 | 29.0 | 38.1 | 82.1 | 112.4 | 126.7 |
| Ukraine, Belo- | | | | | | |
| russia, Moldavia | 19.1 | 27.0 | 33.8 | 77.6 | 106.7 | 121.9 |
| Ukraine | 19.9 | 27.6 | 34.5 | 79.8 | 107.6 | 122.3 |
| Belorussia | 16.4 | 25.8 | 32.3 | 67.9 | 103.8 | 122.0 |
| Moldavia | 14.3 | 20.5 | 29.3 | 72.3 | 102.2 | 116.6 |
| Kazakhstan | 14.1 | 21.8 | 29.8 | 80.6 | 118.2 | 128.7 |
| Transcaucasia | 27.7 | 30.0 | 36.6 | 70.9 | 91.0 | 96.7 |
| Georgia | 33.0 | 36.2 | 43.9 | 73.3 | 91.0 | 105.2 |
| Azerbaidzhan | 23.7 | 25.0 | 31.6 | 69.1 | 93.5 | 96.2 |
| Armenia | 24.0 | 28.8 | 34.4 | 69.1 | 86.0 | 83.1 |
| Central Asia | 14.4 | 19.7 | 26.2 | 79.6 | 101.9 | 107.6 |
| Uzbekistan | 13.8 | 20.1 | 26.7 | 83.6 | 101.8 | 109.0 |
| Kirgizstan | 15.4 | 20.7 | 27.0 | 73.5 | 106.3 | 116.2 |
| Tadzhikistan | 12.7 | 15.9 | 22.6 | 67.1 | 97.9 | 98.4 |
| Turkmenistan | 18.7 | 21.4 | 27.0 | 83.0 | 101.8 | 101.6 |
| Baltic republics | 21.8 | 31.4 | 39.5 | 91.1 | 107.8 | 121.0 |
| Estonia | 23.9 | 33.1 | 39.9 | 94.0 | 110.2 | 115.4 |
| Latvia | 26.4 | 35.6 | 42.6 | 107.2 | 117.9 | 132.3 |
| Lithuania | 17.4 | 27.4 | 37.0 | 77.6 | 99.1 | 115.0 |

Sources: Narkhoz 70, pp. 690, 694; Narkhoz 78, pp. 508, 511.

of doctors and the number of hospital beds per 10,000 population.
As can be seen, all regions and republics made substantial gains on
both measures during the period 1960-78. In respect to availability of doctors, the greatest gains were made by the three republics
experiencing the fastest urbanization: Belorussia, Moldavia, and
Lithuania; the smallest gain was made by Georgia, which, however,
had by far the most doctors per 10,000 people in 1960 and still
occupied the top position in 1978. The other Transcaucasian republics, along with Turkmenistan, also trailed by this measure.
Aside from Georgia, the availability of doctors was greatest in the
Baltic republics and lowest in Central Asia. Differences among republics were fairly sizable, however, ranging in 1978 from 23 in
Tadzhikistan to 44 in Georgia, where many health spas are concentrated. One need not accept the Soviet government's claim to have
more doctors in the nation as a whole, and also in each republic,[32]
than in the United States, to agree that Soviet policy has provided
high levels of doctors and made them widely available. The quality
of their training is another matter. Although Soviet doctors are
poorly trained by Western standards, death rates nonetheless have
been reduced rapidly in all republics and now are in the range characteristic of modern industrialized countries.[33]

An essentially similar picture is given by the other measure
of availability of health care shown in Table 4.6. The number of
hospital beds per 10,000 population increased during 1960-78 by
approximately 33 percent or more in all major regions and by at
least 20 percent in all republics. In 1978, Transcaucasia was least
well off by this measure, and Kazakhstan was best off. Among individual republics, best-provided Latvia had more than half again
as many beds as least-provided Armenia.

In the provision of education, relative progress and achievements of the various regions can be gauged by data on educational
attainment. The usual measure of attainment is median years of
schooling. During 1959-77 median years of schooling in the USSR
as a whole for the population age 16 and over rose from 5.9 to 8.7.[34]
These rapid gains clearly were shared by all republics, but at uneven rates. The level achieved by the USSR means that the average
Soviet adult has completed at least an elementary education, which
in the USSR is seven years. As a substitute for data on median
years of schooling, which are not available by region, Table 4.7
presents statistics regularly published by the Soviet government de-
scribing educational attainment of the population age ten and over
and also of those gainfully occupied. The figures represent the
number of persons per 1,000 population who have completed an elementary education and who have had at least some secondary (high
school) education. Thus, they include all college graduates, as well
as high school dropouts.

TABLE 4.7

Educational Attainment of the Population and Labor Force:
USSR and Regions, 1959-76

| | Number of Persons Age 10 and over with Higher and Secondary Education (per 1,000 population) | | | Number of Gainfully Employed with Higher and Secondary Education (per 1,000 persons) | | |
|---|---|---|---|---|---|---|
| | 1959 | 1970 | 1979 | 1959 | 1970 | 1979 |
| USSR | 361 | 483 | 638 | 433 | 653 | 805 |
| RSFSR | 361 | 489 | 645 | 440 | 656 | 803 |
| Ukraine, Belo- russia, Moldavia | | | | | | |
| Ukraine | 373 | 494 | 630 | 438 | 668 | 813 |
| Belorussia | 304 | 440 | 594 | 331 | 594 | 763 |
| Moldavia | 264 | 397 | 572 | 280 | 508 | 725 |
| Kazakhstan | 347 | 468 | 633 | 447 | 654 | 807 |
| Transcaucasia | | | | | | |
| Georgia | 448 | 554 | 698 | 492 | 711 | 856 |
| Azerbaidzhan | 400 | 471 | 652 | 473 | 674 | 832 |
| Armenia | 445 | 516 | 713 | 527 | 697 | 868 |
| Central Asia | | | | | | |
| Uzbekistan | 354 | 458 | 639 | 447 | 663 | 848 |
| Kirgizstan | 342 | 452 | 614 | 429 | 643 | 804 |
| Tadzhikistan | 325 | 420 | 578 | 407 | 602 | 770 |
| Turkmenistan | 387 | 475 | 620 | 497 | 682 | 823 |
| Baltic republics | | | | | | |
| Estonia | 386 | 506 | 630 | 448 | 660 | 786 |
| Latvia | 431 | 517 | 645 | 502 | 661 | 795 |
| Lithuania | 232 | 382 | 558 | 250 | 496 | 711 |

Note: Figures include both completed and uncompleted education.

Source: Naseleniia SSSR po dannym vsesoivznoi perepisi Naseleniia 1979 goda (Moscow: Politizdat, 1980), pp. 21-22.

Despite their rather peculiar nature, the measures reflect gains for the USSR that are in line with those given by median years of schooling. The data in Table 4.7 indicate unmistakably that educational progress has been widespread. By far the most rapid gains were made by the three republics—Belorussia, Moldavia, and Lithuania—that had the lowest levels in 1959 and that experienced the most rapid urbanization. In these republics, by this measure, educational attainment of the labor force more than doubled, and it almost doubled for the population age ten and over. Nonetheless, in 1979 these republics still ranked at the bottom in educational level of the labor force, and Lithuania ranked lowest for the population in general. The smallest gains on both measures, though substantial, were made by the Transcaucasian republics and by Latvia. However, educational levels in these republics were substantially above the national average in 1959.

As indicated by the range, differences among republics narrowed rapidly during the period. Thus, in respect to education of the population age ten and over, the range was reduced from 93 percent in 1959 to 45 percent in 1970 and to 28 percent in 1979. Corresponding figures in respect to the labor force are 110, 43, and 20. The differentials in 1976 were fairly narrow, when measured for republic populations as a whole. Average educational attainments in all republics, however, mask sharp internal differences in levels achieved by different nationalities. According to census data for 1970, the dominant nationality in each republic had lower attainment than the average for the republic as a whole in all republics except Georgia and Armenia. In all republics the Russians, who in most cases constituted the second largest ethnic group in the non-Russian republics, had far more education than the dominant ethnic group. For example, in Uzbekistan, 598 Russians per 1,000 persons age ten and over had at least some secondary education, compared with 420 Uzbeks on the same measure.[35] Differences were similarly large in most other republics. Substantial differences also existed among republics with respect to relative levels of education attained by men and by women, and also by urban residents compared with rural residents. Despite all these contrasts, significant gains were made everywhere between the census years 1959 and 1979.


AN OVERVIEW

As we have seen, the Soviet population experienced rapid advances in levels of living during the 1960s and 1970s, and this progress was shared by all major regions and republics, although at moderately uneven rates. Gains were made in all major categories of consumption. How do these relative gains compare with those in other countries? The most relevant countries for comparison would seem to be Western and Eastern Europe, Japan, and the United States. During 1960-78, by our measures, per capita consumption in the USSR and its republics grew at average annual rates ranging from 2.6 to 4.9; excluding the front runner, Moldavia, the highest rate was 4.1 percent. Growth in per capita consumption has been calculated using Western procedures for countries of Eastern Europe—Czechoslovakia, Hungary, and Poland—for 1965-78.[36] In each case advances in levels of consumption were below those achieved by the USSR and nearly all republics. Average annual rates of growth in per capita household consumption can be calculated for most OECD countries for 1960-77. These rates, along with those for the USSR and republics, are shown in Table 4.8.

Although, for the most part, rates for OECD countries do not include communal consumption, the weight of the latter in total consumption is small; its inclusion probably would raise the rates somewhat for most countries. In the case of the United States and the United Kingdom, the rate is increased. Inspection of the data given in Table 4.8 indicates that growth rates for per capita consumption achieved by the USSR and constituent regions were modest when compared with most major Western countries. Italy, Japan, France, West Germany, Belgium, and the Netherlands achieved substantially greater gains than any Soviet republic except Moldavia and Belorussia. However, the USSR and nearly all republics gained relative to the United States and the United Kingdom. In general, rates of improvement in levels of living slowed everywhere in the 1970s.

The data presented in Table 4.8 also permit some rough comparisons of relative levels of per capita consumption achieved by the USSR and republics with levels in other countries. To make such comparisons one needs, ideally, calculation of relative purchasing-power parities and expenditures for all countries being compared. A United Nations study done by Irving B. Kravis and Associates provides such measures for 16 countries at widely differing levels of development in 1973.[37] In Table 4.8, we use this study's multilateral comparisons relative to the United States, measured in 1973 "international" prices. A binary comparison is now available for the USSR relative to the United States in 1976.[38] In that year per capita consumption in the Soviet Union, measured in dollar values, was 43 percent that of the United States, the level in rubles was 28 percent, and the geometric mean was 34 percent.

To obtain some notion of how levels of living in the republics might compare with other countries, we can use these international comparisons and the levels of per capita consumption in the republics

TABLE 4.8

USSR and Republics: Comparison of Growth and Relative Levels of
Per Capita Consumption with Selected Countries

| | USSR and Republics | | Other Countries | | |
|---|---|---|---|---|---|
| | Average Annual Rate of Growth 1960–78 | Level as Percent of U.S. in 1976 | | Average Annual Rate of Growth 1960–77 | Level as Percent of U.S. to 1973 |
| USSR | 3.2 | 34.3 | Belgium | 3.7 | 74.8 |
| RSFSR | 3.4 | 37.7 | Colombia | | 18.5 |
| Western Republics | 3.4 | 32.6 | France | 4.2 | 67.9 |
| Ukraine | 3.2 | 32.3 | | | |
| Belorussia | 4.1 | 33.8 | Germany | 3.6 | 63.9 |
| Moldavia | 4.9 | 33.3 | | | |
| | | | Hungary | | 42.0 |
| Kazakhstan | 2.9 | 31.0 | India | | 6.4 |
| Transcaucasia | 2.7 | 27.1 | | | |
| Georgia | 2.9 | 30.9 | Iran | | 23.1 |
| Azerbaidzhan | 2.6 | 22.9 | | | |
| Armenia | 3.0 | 28.8 | Italy | 3.9 | 47.4 |

| | Growth rate | Consumption (Table 4.3) | | Consumption index | Index |
|---|---|---|---|---|---|
| Central Asia | 3.0 | 26.0 | Japan | 7.1 | 53.5 |
| Uzbekistan | 3.0 | 26.8 | Kenya | | 6.1 |
| Kirgizstan | 3.2 | 25.5 | | | |
| Tadzhikistan | 2.6 | 22.0 | Korea | | 14.7 |
| Turkmenistan | 3.1 | 27.6 | | | |
| Baltic republics | 3.2 | 40.7 | Malaysia | | 17.5 |
| Estonia | 3.2 | 44.7 | Netherlands | 3.9 | 60.3 |
| Latvia | 2.7 | 40.2 | | | |
| Lithuania | 3.4 | 39.3 | Philippines | | 13.5 |
| | | | United Kingdom | 1.5 | 62.2 |
| | | | United States | 2.8 | 100.0 |

Sources: Growth rate, USSR—indexes in Table 4.3; consumption levels of republics relative to USSR (for 1978)—Table 4.3; consumption level of USSR relative to U.S. in 1976 dollars (U.S. dollar weights)—Gertrude E. Schroeder and Imogene Edwards, Consumption in the USSR: An International Comparison, U.S. Congress, Joint Economic Committee, Washington, D.C., 1981. OECD, National Accounts of OECD Countries, 1960-1977 (Paris, 1979), Vol. II. Percentages shown are the results given by the comparison carried out in international prices; the percentages do not differ greatly, in most cases, from those given by the geometric mean of the binary comparisons. See Irving B. Kravis and Associates, International Comparisons of Real Product and Purchasing Power (Baltimore: Johns Hopkins University Press, 1978). This work publishes the results of Phase II of the cooperative United Nations, International Comparison Project.

147

relative to the USSR in 1978 as given in Table 4.3. This procedure
assumes that purchasing power parities relative to the United States
in all republics are equal to that calculated for the USSR. Given the
highly centralized nature of Soviet price administration, this assumption does not seem unwarranted. In any event, the resulting estimates of relative levels are meant only to provide rough "ball park"
figures. They reflect goods and services consumed as measured by
data for the "official" economy. How relative levels in the republics would be altered by inclusion of the relevant transactions of the
unofficial or "second" economy is anyone's guess. There is no way
to measure the phenomenon.[39] The author believes that the picture
of relative levels of real consumption given by our measures is not
seriously distorted by omitted "second" economy production. Measures for Western countries do not reflect "second" economies
there either.

   With these caveats, we turn to the data. As Table 4.8 indicates, per capita consumption in the USSR as a whole in 1976 was
only about one-third that of the United States in 1976 and well below
levels achieved in 1973 by all West European countries included in
the UN study, and also below Japan and Hungary. Only Estonia exceeded the level in Hungary and approached the levels in Italy and
Japan. The Hungarian level exceeded that in contiguous Ukraine by
nearly one-fifth. On the other hand, levels in Central Asia were
somewhat above those in neighboring Iran. Roughly speaking, consumption levels in the USSR and most republics are about half those
of West European levels, in Central Asia are about 40 percent, and
in the Baltic republics are roughly two-thirds. Thus, achievement
of even West European living standards, let alone those of the
United States, is only a dream for the peoples of the Soviet Union.
Given the poor prospects for economic growth in the USSR in the
1980s,[40] progress in narrowing the gap, if any, could well be at a
snail's pace.

   We have seen that in the postwar period, levels of income and
consumption per capita have risen substantially and relatively steadily in all regions and republics. Nonetheless, sizable differences
have persisted throughout, and they widened somewhat in the 1970s.
Belated though it may have been, all must agree that the USSR's
disparate republics have made substantial material progress under
a socialist planned economy and as constituents of a single political
entity, the USSR. Large material progress has been made in the
postwar years under other systems, however, by most countries at
intermediate levels of development. In the Soviet republics, material gains have been accompanied by other benefits of socialist
planning—the absence of cyclical mass unemployment and periodic
rampant inflation, provision of education and health care without

direct charge, subsidized housing and food. Although nothing is
known about how the distribution of incomes varies among republics
and over time, it could well be that earned incomes are distributed
more equally in the Soviet Union's republics than in other countries
at comparable levels of development, and that the degree of inequality has decreased markedly since the 1950s. These tentative judg-
ments are based on what has evidently occurred in the USSR as a
whole in recent years[41] and on the high degree of uniformity characteristic of Soviet wage and social policies.

On the other hand, the diverse peoples of the USSR have had
to put up with the familiar deficiencies of Soviet socialism. The
quality of consumer goods and services is notably poor by Western
standards. Retail trade and personal service facilities, long neglected in investment allocations, are abysmally backward by modern standards. The distribution system performs poorly, with
sporadic surpluses and shortages of desired goods a perennial problem. Failure to tailor production to demand and the shortcomings
of the distribution system have spawned endemic corruption and
black markets. Personal and political freedoms have been severely
curtailed. We do not yet know how these assorted systemic costs
differ regionally. One gets the impression from reporting by the
Soviet press and by foreign visitors that systemic ills are least
manifest, in general, in the relatively high-income Baltic republics
and most evident in least affluent Transcaucasia and Central Asia,
where "second economy" activities also seem most prevalent. How
the populations of the different republics tot up the systemic costs
and benefits is a question beyond the grasp of research, as is the
question of how they might have fared under alternative politicoeconomic systems.


## APPENDIX

The purpose of this appendix is to explain more fully the
sources and methodologies used to obtain the ruble values underlying the indexes of real personal incomes and real consumption per
capita shown in Tables 4.1 and 4.3. As noted in the text, the calculations begin with the estimate of total incomes and personal incomes per capita by republic developed by Alastair McAuley for
1960, 1965, and 1970.[42] His estimates are expressed as percentages of the level for the USSR. The derivation of the final values
underlying the indexes in Tables 4.1 and 4.3 involves several steps:
extending McAuley's values to 1978 in respect to total incomes per
capita (including state-provided services); estimating personal incomes per capita in 1978 by deducting state expenditures on services

from total incomes per capita in 1978; reducing the values of total income per capita in each year to remove nonconsumption expenditures, so as to obtain per capita expenditures on goods and services in current established prices; and deflating these current-price values to obtain measures of real per capita personal incomes and expenditures for consumption. The four steps will be described in turn.

Derivation of Total Income per Capita in 1978

The first step in deriving these values was to extend McAuley's values for 1970 to 1978, using the indexes of "real incomes per capita" published by the Soviet government. These indexes can be put together for all republics from data given in their annual statistical handbooks, supplemented by information published in their annual reports of plan fulfillment. Since the government does not admit to the presence of inflation, these indexes are tantamount to measures in current prices. The concept underlying these official indexes differs from McAuley's concept of total incomes, in that the official indexes purport to measure private and state expenditures on material goods and the material outlays involved in the provision of services, whereas McAuley's concept measures all money incomes of the population, including savings and accumulation of cash balances, as well as income in kind and all outlays of the state on communal services (that is, wages of personnel as well as outlays on materials).

Despite these conceptual differences, both measures substantially overlap, in that they both encompass the vast bulk of money incomes (expenditures), along with incomes in kind, and both of them include a substantial share of state outlays on communal services. Therefore, the conceptual differences probably do not significantly distort relative levels and trends among the republics. Imperfect though this procedure is, use of these official indexes is preferable to alternative approaches based on assuming the continuance of past relationships; specifically, the indexes do implicitly measure trends, by republic, in the value of incomes in kind, for which no independent data are available for any year since 1970. They also include all incomes of collective farmers and transfer payments for all republics, for both of which the data are otherwise quite incomplete. The incomes for which data are so incomplete represent large shares of total incomes, and these shares vary by republic and by year.

The second step in deriving final values of total incomes per capita in 1978 is to add to the values obtained in the first step the

1978 increments to savings deposits and to taxes and other obligatory payments. These additions are required because the Soviet indexes of real incomes specifically exclude these items, which represent money incomes received but not spent on consumption. Increments to savings deposits can be calculated from data in Narkhoz.[43] Obligatory payments were estimated for each republic as a uniform percentage (15.5 percent) of its respective state wage and salary bill.[44]

Derivation of Personal Incomes per Capita in 1978

With total incomes per capita estimated as explained above, personal incomes (money and in kind) can be calculated by removing the value of state-provided services (mainly health, education, and the housing subsidy). These expenditures are a major component of a regularly published official statistic labeled "payments and benefits from social consumption funds." These statistics are available for each republic from their reports on plan fulfillment in 1978. Although the shares of services in the totals are not available for 1978, data from which to estimate them with reasonable accuracy are at hand for the USSR and all republics in 1975, 1976, or 1977. The share can be estimated reasonably for Turkmenistan in 1973; in respect to Belorussia, for which no information is available, the share was taken at half the total. The shares of services so calculated do not change greatly from one year to the next, although the shares have tended to decline because of the rapid increase in cash expenditures for pensions and aid. The shares of state-provided services so estimated ranged among republics from 45 to 59 percent of total payments and benefits. The results are not precise, but neither are they seriously in error.

Derivation of Estimates of per Capita Consumption
in Current Prices, 1960-78

The calculations of per capita consumption by region begin with the estimates of total incomes obtained as described above. To estimate consumption of goods and services, it is necessary to remove from these "incomes" all items that do not represent consumption as conventionally defined. The major items are taxes and similar obligations, increments to savings deposits, investment in private housing, and the state housing subsidy. Although allowance should also be made, theoretically, for the change in cash balances, and for other kinds of savings and investment, the paucity of information available precludes doing so. The major deductions can be estimated with considerable confidence. Taxes and other such deductions were estimated for the republics as uniform percentages of their respective wage bills for state employees; the percentage is that for the USSR used in connection with the calculations of total incomes and explained above. Data on increments to savings deposits are available for the USSR and all republics for the years under consideration in Narkhoz.[45] In respect to s960, increments were taken at half the change during 1958-60, adjusted to the change in 1959-60 recorded for the USSR as a whole. The population's investment in privately owned housing is given in Narkhoz.[46] The state housing subsidy for the USSR as a whole is given for 1965, 1970, and 1978 in Narkhoz.[47] The subsidy for 1960 was calculated on the basis of the change in the total stock of public urban housing in 1960-65. Total subsidies were distributed among republics in each year on the basis of their respective shares in the total stock of urban public housing. The data on housing stocks by republic are given in Narkhoz.[48]

Although the final estimates of per capita consumption by region so derived are far from definitive, they probably are not grossly wrong. The ruble values calculated for 1960-78 for the USSR as a whole by this procedure are some 8-9 percent below the values that have been estimated for the USSR by the author in unpublished calculations of GNP in current prices. These estimates include elements that are missing from the calculations in this chapter—military pay and subsistence allowances, imputed rent on owner-occupied housing, privately provided services, and other small items. There is no good way to distribute these additional items of consumption among regions. Their omission probably does not seriously distort the picture of regional differences, which is our concern here. Finally, our estimates of consumption are built up from estimates of incomes, which may be understated. Western estimates of household incomes and expenditures have found an "income gap," relative to measured expenditures, amounting to several billion rubles.[49] In the accounts constructed for 1970 and 1976, the author of this chapter found similar disparities between total expenditures and total incomes. The nature of these missing incomes is dimly understood; it is also possible, of course, that household expenditures are overstated because of incomplete understanding of the contents of the underlying data.

Deflation of Personal Incomes and Consumption

The implicit price index used to deflate our measures of per capita personal incomes is described in the text, and sources are given for its derivation. The index of real per capita consumption that underlies this implicit price index and that is used for comparison with our measures in current prices is also described briefly in the text.[50]

## NOTES

1. Gertrude E. Schroeder: "Regional Differences in Incomes and Levels of Living in the USSR," in V. N. Bandera and Z. Lew Melnyk, eds., The Soviet Economy in Regional Perspective (New York: Praeger, 1973), pp. 167-95; "Soviet Wages and Income Policies in Perspective, ACES Bulletin, Fall 1974, pp. 3-20; "Soviet Regional Development Policies in Perspective," in NATO, The USSR in the 1980s: Economic Growth and Foreign Trade (Brussels: NATO, 1978), pp. 123-42; "Some Indicators of Regional Differences in Incomes in the USSR in the 1970's," in NATO, Regional Development in the USSR (Brussels: NATO, 1979), pp. 25-39.

2. Alastair McAuley, Economic Welfare in the Soviet Union: Poverty, Living Standards and Inequality (Madison: University of Wisconsin Press, 1979).

3. Gertrude E. Schroeder and Barbara S. Severin, "Soviet Consumption and Income Policies in Perspective," in U.S. Congress, Joint Economic Committee, The Soviet Economy in a New Perspective (Washington, D.C.: U.S. Government Printing Office, 1976), pp. 620-60. This source presents indexes of per capita consumption for the USSR for 1950-75. These indexes, part of overall indexes of GNP, follow on the pioneering work of Abram Bergson in measuring Soviet national product by Western concepts and procedures, The Real National Income of Soviet Russia Since 1928 (Cambridge, Mass.: Harvard University Press, 1961), and of Janet G. Chapman in measuring real wages, Real Wages in Soviet Russia Since 1928 (Cambridge, Mass.: Harvard University Press, 1963).

4. McAuley, Economic Welfare in the Soviet Union, p. 109, and appendixes A-E.

5. For a discussion of the "poverty standard," see ibid., pp. 16-20.

6. The objective of narrowing regional gaps in levels of living was stated explicitly in the program of the 22nd Party Congress adopted in 1961 and in the directives for the Eighth Five-Year Plan (1966-70) and somewhat more generally in the directives for the Ninth Five-Year Plan (1971-75).

7. Pravda, December 22, 1972.

8. J. Williamson, "Regional Inequality and the Process of National Development," in L. Needleman, ed., Regional Analysis (Baltimore: Penguin Books, 1968), pp. 99-138.

9. For a critique of the retail price index, see Morris Bonnstein, "Soviet Price Statistics," in Vladimir G. Treml and John P. Hardt, eds., Soviet Economic Statistics (Durham, N.C.: Duke University Press, 1972), pp. 370-78.

10. See, for example, Dimitri K. Simes, "The Soviet Parallel Market," in NATO, Economic Aspects of Life in the USSR (Brussels: NATO, 1976), pp. 91-100; and A. Katsenelinboigen, "Disguised Inflation in the Soviet Union," ibid., pp. 101-12.

11. This index was first published and discussed in Schroeder and Severin, "Soviet Consumption and Income Policies . . . ," pp. 630-32. An updated version of both the underlying consumption index and the price index is given in M. Elizabeth Denton, "Soviet Consumer Policy; Trends and Prospects," in U.S. Congress, Joint Economic Committee, The Soviet Economy in a Time of Change (Washington, D.C.: U.S. Government Printing Office, 1979), pp. 766-68.

12. McAuley, Economic Welfare in the Soviet Union, pp. 123-42.

13. M. V. Kokorev, Tseny na tovary narodnogo potrebleniia (Moscow: Ekonomica, 1978), pp. 184-90.

14. McAuley has extended his estimates of personal incomes by social group to 1974, using partial data and many assumed relationships to fill in the gaps. His results show a large widening of differentials, both among republics and between social groups. See his "Personal Income in the USSR: Republican Variations in 1974," in NATO, Regional Development in the USSR (Brussels: NATO, 1979), pp. 41-58.

15. The available data, gathered from statistical handbooks and plan fulfillment reports, are given in Schroeder, Some Indicators, pp. 32-33.

16. TsSU, Narodnoe khoziaistvo SSSR v 1977 g. (Moscow: Statistika, 1978), p. 410. (Publication hereafter cited as Narkhoz.)

17. For a critique of the official index of real incomes, see Gertrude E. Schroeder, "An Appraisal of Soviet Wage and Income Statistics," in Treml and Hardt, Soviet Economic Statistics, pp. 304-12.

18. Elizabeth M. Clayton, "Regional Consumption Expenditures in the Soviet Union," ACES Bulletin, Winter 1975, pp. 27-46.

19. An updated version of this index of real per capita consumption is given in Denton, "Soviet Consumer Policy," p. 768. The detailed description and evaluation of the index is given in Schroeder and Severin, "Soviet Consumption and Income Policies . . . ," pp. 641-50.

20. Narkhoz 70, p. 602; Narkhoz 78, p. 447.

21. The most complete description of how the published indexes are probably derived is given in Gosplan SSSR, Metodicheskie ukazaniia k sostavleniu-gosudarstvennogo plana razvitiia narodnogo khoziaisva SSSR (Moscow: Ekonomika, 1969), pp. 497-507.

22. The difference in coverage does not account for much of the difference in rates of growth of the two indexes. Investment outlays, which scarcely increased during 1965-78, are less than 1 percent of total household expenditures. Employment in the service industries that are omitted from the Soviet index grew somewhat more slowly than the index of material goods, but, weighted in at 1970 wages, they would have a weight of perhaps 10 percent. The faster growth of the official index of real incomes is believed to lie in a defective deflator, the main component of which is the official index of retail prices.

23. Retail sales were used by Clayton, "Regional Consumption Expenditures . . . ," to measure per capita consumption of goods in the republics in 1965. The shortcomings of this indicator account for much of the difference between her results and those obtained in this chapter.

24. Calculated roughly from data in Narkhoz 78, pp. 391-92.

25. Calculated by the author as components of estimates of Soviet GNP in current prices.

26. Denton, "Soviet Consumer Policy," p. 768.

27. Narkhoz 77, p. 431.

28. TsSU, Narodnoe khoziaistvo Ukrainskoi SSR v 1977a. (Kiev: Technika, 1978), p. 317.

29. TsSU, Narodnoe khoziaistvo Uzbekskoi SSR v. 1977a. (Tashkent: Uzbekistan, 1978), p. 246.

30. A. Avrak, "Ispol'zovanie automobil'ei lichnogo pol'zovaniia," Voprosy ekonomiki (1978): no. 7, p. 134.

31. Most of these "everyday" services, the "productive" services, are actually included in the data on retail sales of nonfood goods. Moreover, the per capita figures given in the text do not accurately represent expenditures by households on these services, because the basic data exclude materials (such as cloth used by tailors) and include purchases of the services by state enterprises and institutions.

32. Narkhoz 77, p. 86. There is considerable doubt as to the comparability of the definitions of "doctors" in this comparison, and there are wide differences in the extent and quality of their training.

33. Ibid., pp. 25, 88.

34. National Foreign Assessment Center, USSR: Trends and Prospects in Educational Attainment, ER79-10344 (Washington, D.C.: the Center, 1979), p. 7.

35. TsSU, Itogi vsesoiuznoi perepisi naseleniia 1970 goda, vol. 4 (Moscow: Statistika, 1972), pp. 484-87.

36. Research Project on National Income in East Central Europe, Czechoslovakia, Hungary and Poland: Domestic Final Uses of Gross Product (New York: LIW International Financial Research, 1979).

37. Irving B. Kravis and Associates, International Comparisons of Real Product and Purchasing Power (Baltimore: Johns Hopkins University Press, 1978). This work publishes the results of Phase II of the cooperative United Nations, International Comparison Project.

38. Gertrude E. Schroeder and Imogene Edwards, Consumption in the USSR: An International Comparison, U.S. Congress, Joint Economic Committee, Washington, D.C., 1981.

39. For an attempt to sort out the issues involved in assessing the impact of the "second economy" on GNP as conventionally measured, see Gertrude E. Schroeder and Rush V. Greenslade, "On the Measurement of the 'Second Economy' in the USSR," ACES Bulletin, Spring 1979, pp. 3-23.

40. U.S. Congress, Joint Economic Committee, Soviet Economic Problems and Prospects (Washington, D.C.: U.S. Government Printing Office, 1977).

41. Peter Wiles and Stefan Markowski, "Income Distribution Under Communism and Capitalism: Some Facts About Poland, the U.K., the U.S.A. and USSR," Soviet Studies, January 1971, pp. 344-69, and April 1971, pp. 487-511; Janet G. Chapman, "Soviet Wages Under Socialism," in Alan Abouchar, ed., The Socialist Price Mechanism (Durham, N.C.: Duke University Press, 1977), pp. 247-81.

42. McAuley, Economic Welfare in the Soviet Union, p. 109.

43. Narkhoz 77, p. 434; Narkhoz 78, p. 415.

44. The percentage for 1977 can be calculated for the USSR from data given in Denton, "Soviet Consumer Policy," and was estimated for 1978 by increasing it by the average annual rate of change during 1976-77.

45. Narkhoz 60, p. 854; Narkhoz 64, p. 897; Narkhoz 70, p. 364; Narkhoz 77, p. 434; Narkhoz 78, p. 415.

46. Narkhoz 70, p. 360; Narkhoz 78, p. 350.

47. Narkhoz 70, p. 541; Narkhoz 78, p. 390.

48. Narkhoz 70, p. 547; Narkhoz 78, p. 399.

49. See, for example, Abraham S. Becker, Soviet National Income, 1958-1964 (Berkeley: University of California Press, 1969), p. 19.

50. For a detailed description and evaluation of both the implicit price index and the index of real consumption, the reader should consult Schroeder and Severin, "Soviet Consumption and Income Policies . . .," pp. 630-32; and Denton, "Soviet Consumer Policy," pp. 766-68.

# 5

# THE GROWTH AND STRUCTURE OF FIXED CAPITAL

## James W. Gillula

In the period from 1960 through 1975 the value of the fixed capital stock of the USSR more than tripled, and in some union republics it increased more than fourfold. This rapid growth—at average annual rates of 6.1-10.4 percent for individual republics—provided the possibility of making substantial changes in the structure of the economies of republics. Information on the ruble values of fixed capital stock is routinely published in the statistical handbooks of only about half of all republics. However, some data included in a 1977 Soviet study have made it possible to derive the values of total fixed capital in branches of material production for all republics in a single year, 1965; and by combining these base-year values with information on growth rates and percentage distributions of branch structure published in the handbooks for the remaining republics, it was possible to estimate the values of fixed capital in major branches of the economy for all republics in most years during the period 1960-75. With additional information published in national statistical handbooks on the branch distribution of industrial fixed capital in all republics, ruble values of capital in individual branches of industry could also be estimated.[1]

This chapter examines structural differences and the extent and nature of structural change in the economies of republics using

The views expressed in this chapter are those of the author, and do not necessarily reflect the official view of the U.S. government. The author would like to thank Dimitri M. Gallik for his helpful comments on an earlier draft of this chapter.

these capital stock data. The analysis focuses in successive sections on the growth and relative levels of total fixed capital in individual republics; the distribution of fixed capital in nonproductive branches of the economy; structural differences in the sphere of material production based on a division into five major branches; and patterns of branch specialization in industry (based on a ten-sector classification) and interrepublic differences in factor intensity in individual branches of industry. The main results of this analysis are summarized in the concluding section.

## TOTAL FIXED CAPITAL

The growth of total fixed capital (both productive and non-productive) in each republic over the period of 1961-75 is summarized by the average annual growth rates presented in Table 5.1. The growth rates were highest over the entire period in a group of republics that by most measures ranked lowest in level of economic development in 1960—the Central Asian republics, Kazakhstan, and Moldavia. The other three republics with above-average rates of growth of fixed capital during these 15 years were Lithuania, Armenia, and Belorussia—republics that experienced the most rapid overall economic growth during this period (as measured by official Soviet national income indexes). One notable trend that is apparent in examining the average growth rates for individual five-year periods is that the rates for 1971-75 in each of the Central Asian republics and Kazakhstan, while remaining above average, were lower than in the 1960s. This trend also applies to Armenia, the one Transcaucasian republic that had above-average rates of growth throughout the period considered.

Although the Central Asian republics had rates of growth of fixed capital among the highest in the country, they also had the highest rates of population growth, and as a result they made little or no gains in their generally low values of fixed capital measured on a per capita basis. This is shown by the indexes of the per capita value of total fixed capital for each republic as a percentage of that for the USSR as a whole, given in Table 5.2. A few comments on the interpretation of these indexes are in order. First, for most purposes it is probably more meaningful to compare some components of fixed capital (particularly certain branches of material production) on the basis of a narrower definition of population, such as the population of working age, since there are substantial differences among republics in the age structure of the population. In such a comparison, for example, the relative levels of total fixed capital in all Central Asian republics and Azerbaidzhan are 10-15 percentage points higher in both 1960 and 1975 than shown in Table 5.2.

TABLE 5.1

Average Annual Rates of Growth of Total Fixed Capital:
USSR and Republics, 1961-75
(percent)

| | 5-Year Averages | | | 15-Year Average |
|---|---|---|---|---|
| | 1961-65 | 1966-70 | 1971-75 | 1961-75 |
| USSR | 8.6 | 7.5 | 7.8 | 8.0 |
| RSFSR | 8.6 | 7.3 | 7.9 | 8.0 |
| Ukraine | 7.9 | 6.9 | 6.9 | 7.2 |
| Moldavia | 9.7 | 9.8 | 9.9 | 9.8 |
| Belorussia | 7.8 | 8.8 | 9.2 | 8.6 |
| Latvia | 7.2 | 6.0 | 6.9 | 6.7 |
| Lithuania | 8.2 | 9.4 | 9.3 | 9.0 |
| Estonia | 7.7 | 6.6 | 7.4 | 7.3 |
| Georgia | 6.6 | 5.9 | 6.0 | 6.2 |
| Armenia | 9.6 | 9.0 | 7.9 | 8.8 |
| Azerbaidzhan | 6.7 | 5.7 | 5.8 | 6.1 |
| Kazakhstan | 11.7 | 9.3 | 8.6 | 9.9 |
| Uzbekistan | 10.2 | 11.4 | 9.7 | 10.4 |
| Kirgizstan | 10.9 | 10.3 | 9.2 | 10.1 |
| Tadzhikistan | 10.6 | 9.4 | 9.2 | 9.7 |
| Turkmenistan | 9.3 | 10.5 | 8.7 | 9.5 |

Source: Calculated from values of fixed capital in 1955 prices from James W. Gillula, The Regional Distribution of Fixed Capital in the U.S.S.R., Foreign Economic Report no. 17 (Washington, D.C.: U.S. Bureau of the Census, Foreign Demographic Analysis Division, 1980), Tables A-1 to A-16.

However, such a change in population base has little effect on the trends (toward or away from the national average) observed in per capita comparisons, and this is true in general of comparisons of republics based on other major economic indicators for this period using alternative population bases.[2] An additional factor to be considered in evaluating indexes of the type given in Table 5.2 is that the RSFSR accounts for an overwhelming share of the Soviet economy (61 percent of total fixed capital), and as a result comparisons of non-Russian republics with the RSFSR rather than with the USSR average can present an even starker contrast. For example, the per capita value of total fixed capital for all non-Russian republics combined was 80 percent of that for the RSFSR in 1960 and 72 percent in 1975.

TABLE 5.2

Per Capita Indexes of Total Fixed Capital in Republics
Relative to USSR Average: 1960, 1965, 1970, 1975

|  | 1960 | 1965 | 1970 | 1975 |
|---|---|---|---|---|
| USSR | 100 | 100 | 100 | 100 |
| RSFSR | 110 | 112 | 113 | 115 |
| Ukraine | 96 | 94 | 92 | 90 |
| Moldavia | 57 | 58 | 63 | 69 |
| Belorussia | 71 | 70 | 74 | 80 |
| Latvia | 138 | 131 | 122 | 117 |
| Lithuania | 88 | 87 | 94 | 101 |
| Estonia | 151 | 147 | 140 | 137 |
| Georgia | 97 | 88 | 82 | 75 |
| Armenia | 81 | 79 | 77 | 73 |
| Azerbaidzhan | 101 | 86 | 73 | 64 |
| Kazakhstan | 93 | 99 | 102 | 102 |
| Uzbekistan | 53 | 52 | 55 | 54 |
| Kirgizstan | 57 | 58 | 60 | 60 |
| Tadzhikistan | 56 | 56 | 54 | 51 |
| Turkmenistan | 80 | 76 | 78 | 73 |

Sources: Calculated from year-end values of fixed capital in
1955 prices from James W. Gillula, The Regional Distribution of
Fixed Capital in the U.S.S.R., Foreign Economic Report no. 17
(Washington, D.C.: U.S. Bureau of the Census, Foreign Demographic Analysis Division, 1980), Tables A-1 to A-16; and from
population figures from Godfrey S. Baldwin, Population Projections
by Age and Sex: For the Republics and Major Economic Regions of
the U.S.S.R., International Population Reports, series P-91, no.
26 (Washington, D.C.: U.S. Bureau of the Census, Foreign Demographic Analysis Division, 1979), pp. 25-57.

This increase in the relative level of the RSFSR in per capita
fixed capital is one of the significant trends apparent from Table
5.2. Among the other republics that made significant gains in the
relative level of per capita fixed capital during this period were
Kazakhstan and Moldavia--two republics where the growth of fixed
capital was sufficient to offset above-average rates of population
growth—and Lithuania and Belorussia. The greatest decline
occurred in Azerbaidzhan. While one might expect that the sharp

drop for the latter republic was due to the decline of its capital-
intensive oil industry, the structural analysis in the following sections indicates that this is at best a partial explanation for Azerbaidzhan's lagging development.

The data presented in Tables 5.1 and 5.2 on the growth and
changes in relative levels of capital stock for republics reflect the
results of 15 years of Soviet investment policy toward republics.
However, the increment to total fixed capital per ruble of total capital investment has not been identical for all republics; in fact, there
have been some systematic differences among republics in this
ratio. It was generally lower in 1961-75 in southern regions—Central Asia, Kazakhstan, and the Transcaucasus—(0.58-0.60) than in
the RSFSR and European regions (0.63-0.65).[3] This presumably is
due in part to the fact that where capital stock has been growing
most rapidly, construction lags are longer and retirement rates
greater, and in part to the fact that there are substantial inter-
branch differences in this ratio. Most of the southern republics
had higher shares of investment and fixed capital in agriculture,
and the ratio for this branch was well below that for all others—0.51
for the USSR as a whole during this period. This point is raised
here since, in order to identify more recent changes in the trends
summarized above, it is necessary to turn to data on the distribution of total capital investment because information on the growth of
fixed capital after 1975 is not available for all republics.

In broad terms the Soviet leadership is faced with the increasingly acute problem of allocating investment that is growing at
a diminishing rate among several priority claimants: the eastern
regions, where an overwhelming proportion of fuel/energy resources
and other raw materials are concentrated; the southern regions,
where most of the growth of the labor force in the 1980s will occur;
and the European USSR, where there will be increasing shortages
of both raw materials and labor but where investment (in the form
of modernization and expansion of existing facilities) should offer a
higher return. The branch structure of investment in different regions (such as the need to focus on labor-intensive branches in
labor-surplus regions) will clearly be an important aspect of the
Soviet response to these competing investment needs, and patterns
of branch specialization will be analyzed in the following sections of
this chapter with an eye toward determining how Soviet development
strategy has responded to the factors mentioned above—at least as
they relate to individual republics.

Since the RSFSR is divided in this broad outline of regional
investment alternatives, some important issues cannot be adequately
treated on the basis of republic data alone. Although data on the
breakdown of total capital investment by economic region and oblast

within the RSFSR are available for the period of 1965-75, they have
not been published since 1975. However, some tentative conclusions
can be drawn by comparing the distribution of investment among six
regional subdivisions of the country during the first four years of
the Tenth Five-Year Plan with the corresponding distribution in the
Ninth Five-Year Plan period and the 1960s (see Table 5.3).

TABLE 5.3

Regional Shares of Total Capital Investment: 1961-79
(percent)

|  | 1961-70 | 1971-75 | 1976-79 |
|---|---|---|---|
| USSR | 100.0 | 100.0 | 100.0 |
| RSFSR | 59.5 | 60.4 | 61.8 |
| Ukraine | 16.7 | 15.9 | 14.9 |
| Other European republics* | 6.9 | 7.6 | 7.4 |
| Transcaucasus | 3.7 | 3.4 | 3.5 |
| Kazakhstan | 7.0 | 6.2 | 6.0 |
| Central Asian | 6.1 | 6.4 | 6.3 |

Note: Column totals may not add to 100 because a small part
of total USSR capital investment is not distributed by region.
    *Moldavia, Belorussia, Latvia, Lithuania, and Estonia.
    Sources: All data for 1961-78 are from various USSR statis-
tical handbooks; data for 1979 are from articles on the fulfillment
of economic plans for that year in the republic press.

It was noted in Table 5.1 that the average rates of growth of
fixed capital in all Central Asian republics declined during the Ninth
Five-Year Plan period, but Table 5.3 shows that at the same time
Central Asia received a slightly higher share of total capital investment in 1971-75 than during the 1960s. Its share then fell
negligibly during 1976-79, but of course the fact that the share of
these four republics in total population continued to increase means
that the level of fixed capital per capita for the region relative to
the national average declined even further. This suggests that
other concerns have, for the time being, taken priority over the
problem of providing the higher levels of investment necessary to
create more jobs in this labor-surplus region.

The investment shares of Kazakhstan, the Ukraine, and other European republics also fell during the first four years of the Tenth Five-Year Plan. However, the share of the Transcaucasus region did not fall, and this must be attributed in part to the above-average overall economic performance of the region. Azerbaidzhan, Georgia, and Armenia ranked first, second, and third among all republics in the growth of national income produced during the first four years of the Tenth Five-Year Plan. The share of the RSFSR in total investment continued to increase—a trend that must be due largely to rapidly growing investment in eastern regions of the republic in connection with the development of fuel and energy resources.

## NONPRODUCTIVE BRANCHES

The collection and reporting of capital stock statistics in the USSR, like all Soviet economic data, are based on the Marxian methodology that distinguishes between branches of material production and the "nonproductive" branches of the economy. The latter include housing, municipal and personal services, health, education, science, culture, and other service activities. Estimates of total nonproductive fixed capital in 1960 and 1975 are available for all republics, but these figures could be broken down only into the shares of housing and of all other nonproductive branches combined.

The value of nonproductive fixed capital grew more slowly than that of fixed capital in the sphere of material production during 1961-75. For the USSR as a whole this resulted in a decline in the share of nonproductive branches in total fixed capital (in constant 1955 prices) from 43 percent in 1960 to 35 percent in 1975. The rank order of republics according to the growth of nonproductive capital during the period differs little from the ranking by growth of total fixed capital. Thus, the overall pattern of changes in the per capita levels of nonproductive fixed capital in republics (see Table 5.4) is quite similar to that for total fixed capital. The index of nonproductive fixed capital per capita increased in the RSFSR, remained at about 50-60 percent of the national average in the Central Asian republics, and declined in all the Transcaucasian republics. Kazakhstan had the largest increase among all republics. Among the European republics, those that made gains according to this measure were Lithuania and Belorussia.

The decline in the share of nonproductive branches in the total fixed capital of the USSR noted above was due primarily to a drop in the share of the housing sector. Investment in housing as a share of total capital investment peaked in the late 1950s at about 23 percent,

# TABLE 5.4

## Per Capita Indexes of Nonproductive Fixed Capital in Republics Relative to USSR Average: 1960 and 1975

| | Total | | Housing | | Other Nonproductive* | |
|---|---|---|---|---|---|---|
| | 1960 | 1975 | 1960 | 1975 | 1960 | 1975 |
| USSR | 100 | 100 | 100 | 100 | 100 | 100 |
| RSFSR | 109 | 118 | 108 | 117 | 113 | 119 |
| Ukraine | 101 | 88 | 104 | 91 | 93 | 84 |
| Moldavia | 63 | 63 | 68 | 61 | 49 | 66 |
| Belorussia | 75 | 77 | 80 | 82 | 63 | 71 |
| Latvia | 153 | 117 | 150 | 120 | 162 | 112 |
| Lithuania | 88 | 96 | 90 | 101 | 81 | 87 |
| Estonia | 150 | 138 | 143 | 133 | 169 | 145 |
| Georgia | 103 | 84 | 101 | 85 | 107 | 83 |
| Armenia | 89 | 81 | 83 | 77 | 107 | 86 |
| Azerbaidzhan | 77 | 56 | 76 | 52 | 81 | 62 |
| Kazakhstan | 75 | 94 | 79 | 98 | 64 | 87 |
| Uzbekistan | 53 | 50 | 53 | 50 | 51 | 50 |
| Kirgizstan | 58 | 60 | 56 | 58 | 64 | 63 |
| Tadzhikistan | 59 | 51 | 57 | 51 | 62 | 51 |
| Turkmenistan | 63 | 55 | 58 | 50 | 77 | 64 |

*Includes municipal and personal services, health, education, science, culture.

Sources: Based on values of fixed capital, in 1955 prices, from James Gillula, The Regional Distribution of Fixed Capital in the U.S.S.R., Foreign Economic Report no. 17 (Washington, D.C.: U.S. Bureau of the Census, Foreign Demographic Analysis Division, 1980), Tables A-17 and A-18, using population figures from Godfrey S. Baldwin, Population Projections by Age and Sex: For the Republics and Major Economic Regions of the U.S.S.R., International Population Reports, series P-91, no. 26 (Washington, D.C.: U.S. Bureau of the Census, Foreign Demographic Analysis Division, 1979), pp. 25-57.

then declined steadily to about 14 percent during the first three years of the Tenth Five-Year Plan.  Fixed capital in "other nonproductive branches" grew at a slightly faster rate than the economy average, however, and as a result its share of total fixed capital increased from 12 percent in 1960 to 14 percent in 1975.  These opposite trends in the shares of the two aggregate branches of nonproductive capital occurred in all republics except Latvia, where the shares of both branches were lower in 1975 than in 1960.  Considerable uniformity is also observed in the changes in the per capita values of both nonproductive branches in each republic.  The per capita indexes for both branches changed in the same direction during this period in all republics except Moldavia and Kirgizstan.

The differences among republics in per capita values of nonproductive fixed capital are, not surprisingly, strongly related to interrepublic differences in the urban share of population.  The rank-correlation coefficient for these two measures in 1975 was 0.84.  Changes in the relative levels of nonproductive capital for republics during 1960-75 were also related in a general way to interrepublic differences in the rate of urbanization.  In six republics that were farther from the national average urban share of population in 1975 than in 1960, the index of per capita nonproductive fixed capital also differed from 100 by a larger margin.  Four other republics moved closer to the national average by both of these measures during this period.  The two significant exceptions to this general relation were Kazakhstan and the Ukraine.  Although the urbanization process in Kazakhstan proceeded at a slightly slower rate than in the nation as a whole, there was a greater increase in per capita nonproductive capital in Kazakhstan than in any other republic.  In the Ukraine the relative level of nonproductive capital per capita dropped sharply even though the republic moved closer to the national average urban share of population.

The explanation for the disproportionately rapid growth of the value of the housing stock and other nonproductive fixed capital in Kazakhstan seems to lie partly in the fact that there were much larger "nonproductive" investments in rural areas of the republic. Data on the distribution of total investment in agriculture between production and nonproduction facilities, which are given in the statistical handbooks of the USSR and most republics, provide an indication of this.  During 1961-75 just over 25 percent of all investment in agriculture in Kazakhstan went for nonproduction facilities, while the corresponding share for the USSR as a whole was 17 percent and no other republic exceeded 20 percent.  This high proportion of investment in nonproduction facilities in Kazakhstan is due in part to the relatively high share of state farm (sovkhoz) agriculture in the republic.  However, given the high national economic priority placed on the development of agriculture in Kazakhstan in the past, it probably also reflects an effort to accommodate and retain a rural work force that includes a large number of migrants from other (mainly Slavic) republics.

The decline in the relative per capita level of nonproductive capital in the Ukraine may well be a reflection of one way in which this republic's economy has been affected by central government policies of redistributing national income among republics. Available evidence indicates that it was primarily the less developed republics of Central Asia, and to some extent Kazakhstan and the Transcaucasus, that benefited from the redistribution of national income through the state budget during the 1960s and the first half of the 1970s, and that the major net outflow of national income throughout this period was from the Ukraine.[4] Furthermore, this income redistribution primarily affected the relative levels of investment in republics, and therefore its effects should show up in the intertemporal comparisons of levels of fixed capital stock made here. In the Ukraine the relative per capita level of productive fixed capital changed little between 1960 and 1975, but there were sharp declines in the relative levels of nonproductive capital—areas that most directly affect the population. As Table 5.4 shows, the per capita value of the housing stock in the republic fell from 104 percent of the national average in 1960 to 91 percent in 1975, and the relative per capita value of "other nonproductive" fixed capital fell from 93 to 84 percent.

Finally, although most of the less developed republics benefited from the central government's income redistribution policies, with the exception of Kazakhstan this redistribution had a smaller effect on the relative levels of fixed capital in nonproductive branches than in branches of material production. In fact, the overall degree of variation among republics in per capita levels of nonproductive fixed capital, as measured by the weighted coefficient of variation, increased from 0.18 in 1960 to 0.23 in 1975.

## MAJOR BRANCHES OF MATERIAL PRODUCTION

Average annual rates of growth of fixed capital in the sphere of material production between 1960 and 1975 are given for all republics in column 1 of Table 5.5. The ranking of republics by these rates is similar to the ranking by total fixed capital given in Table 5.1—the Central Asian republics, Moldavia, and Kazakhstan rank first through sixth, followed by Lithuania and Belorussia. As noted in the previous section, the value of productive capital grew more rapidly than total fixed capital in each republic.

# TABLE 5.5

Average Annual Rates of Growth of Fixed Capital
and Employment in Material Production
for Republics: 1960-75
(percent)

|  | Fixed Capital (1) | Employment (2) | Fixed Capital per Worker (3) |
|---|---|---|---|
| USSR | 8.9 | 1.8 | 7.0 |
| RSFSR | 8.7 | 1.5 | 7.1 |
| Ukraine | 8.5 | 1.6 | 6.8 |
| Moldavia | 11.7 | 2.7 | 8.7 |
| Belorussia | 10.0 | 2.0 | 7.9 |
| Latvia | 8.2 | 1.5 | 6.6 |
| Lithuania | 10.1 | 2.2 | 7.7 |
| Estonia | 8.1 | 1.4 | 6.6 |
| Georgia | 6.9 | 2.1 | 4.8 |
| Armenia | 9.8 | 3.5 | 6.1 |
| Azerbaidzhan | 6.3 | 2.0 | 4.1 |
| Kazakhstan | 10.1 | 2.5 | 7.4 |
| Uzbekistan | 11.7 | 3.2 | 8.2 |
| Kirgizstan | 11.1 | 3.5 | 7.4 |
| Tadzhikistan | 10.9 | 2.8 | 7.8 |
| Turkmenistan | 10.2 | 3.0 | 7.0 |

Sources: Col. (1)—James W. Gillula, The Regional Distribution of Fixed Capital in the U.S.S.R., Foreign Economic Report no. 17 (Washington, D.C.: U.S. Bureau of the Census, Foreign Demographic Analysis Division, 1980), Tables A-17 and A-18; col. (2)—based on the sum of average annual employment in branches of material production in the state sector and on collective farms from Stephen Rapawy, "Regional Employment Trends in the U.S.S.R.: 1950 to 1975," in U.S. Congress, Joint Economic Committee, Soviet Economy in a Time of Change, vol. 1 (Washington, D.C.: U.S. Government Printing Office, 1979), pp. 604, 605, 608 (estimates of the small amount of employment in "other branches," not reported by Rapawy, were also included, but no attempt to estimate employment in private agriculture was made; col. (3)—derived from data used for calculations in cols. (1) and (2).

The growth of capital stock may be expressed as the product of the growth of total employment and the growth of capital per worker—for instance, for the USSR the product of 1.018 and 1.070 (see Table 5.5). A comparison of the latter two rates shows which portion of capital stock growth can be attributed to job creation at the initial level of capital per worker and which portion served to increase the capital/labor ratio. Such a breakdown of the growth of productive fixed capital for union republics is particularly instructive because there were substantial differences among republics in the growth of employment during the period considered here.

The figures in Table 5.5 show that there was less variation among republics in the growth of productive capital per worker than in the absolute growth of total productive capital. Underlying this result is the fact that in republics with the highest rates of growth of productive capital, a larger proportion of capital growth was directed toward expanding employment. Furthermore, a distinction can be made between republics in the southern tier (Central Asia and the Transcaucasus) and those in the European part of the USSR. The share of capital growth that served to increase the capital/labor ratio (column 3 as a percentage of column 1) was uniformly higher for the former than for the latter group of republics, which is evidence of a more capital intensive approach to development in the European USSR. Of course, the effects of structural differences in the economies of republics must also be considered in explaining the growth of the aggregate capital/labor ratio. We will return to this question after examining the extent of structural change between 1960 and 1975.

The shares of fixed capital in five major branches of material production for the USSR and each republic in 1960 and 1975 are given in Table 5.6. For the USSR as a whole there were increases in the shares of industry and construction, accompanied by declines in the shares of agriculture and transportation and communications. Among the individual republics, the two major exceptions to this trend were Azerbaidzhan and Turkmenistan, where the shares of industry dropped and those of agriculture rose. Azerbaidzhan had by far the highest share of productive fixed capital in industry in 1960, due largely to its specialization in the capital-intensive oil industry, and in spite of a drop of eight percentage points by 1975, the share of industry in total productive capital in Azerbaidzhan was still higher than in any other republic. Turkmenistan, by contrast, had below-average shares of fixed capital in industry in both 1960 and 1975, and the trend noted above reflects a continuing if not increasing specialization in agriculture.

Among the remaining republics for which changes in branch shares of fixed capital generally followed the national trends, the

most extensive structural change occurred in Belorussia, which had
the largest increase in the share of industry and the second largest
decrease in the share of agriculture, as well as substantial changes
in the shares of construction and of transportation and communications. Other republics that had significant increases in the share of
industry were Estonia, Lithuania, and Kazakhstan. In the first two,
the increase in the share of industry was largely offset by a fall in
the share of transportation and communications, while in the third
the most significant decline was in the share of agriculture.

Changes in the branch structure of fixed capital in republics
may be viewed as a combination of shifts in the branch distribution
of employment and changes in branch capital/labor ratios. An important issue in the comparison of the economic development paths
of republics is the rate at which labor has been shifted from agriculture to industry. In order to focus on the relative extent of
specialization in these two major branches, the remaining branches
of material production were combined to form a single "other material production" branch, and location quotients based on employment were calculated for all republics. The location quotient relates the share of a particular branch in total production employment in a region to the corresponding share for the country as a
whole:

$$Q_i^r = \frac{L_i^r}{L^r} \; \frac{L_i^u}{L^u} \tag{1}$$

where $L_i^r$ is employment in branch i of republic r; $L^r$ is total employment in republic r; and $L_i^u$ and $L^u$ are the corresponding figures
for the country as a whole. Location quotients for both 1960 and
1975 are given in Table 5.7.

The major trend in the branch structure of employment in
republics identified by these location quotients is the increasing
relative specialization in agriculture in all southern republics except Armenia. There were only small changes in the location quotients for industry in these republics, and their values ranged from
0.40 to 0.73 in 1975. Moldavia remained the republic with the
highest degree of specialization in agriculture ($Q_i^r = 1.89$) but each
of the Central Asian republics, Georgia, and Azerbaidzhan also had
location quotients of 1.40 or more in 1975. An increase in the
quotient for industry accompanied by a decline in that for agriculture is found only in Armenia, Lithuania, and Belorussia, and the
quotient for agriculture in the latter republic was still well above
1.0 in spite of this trend. Although only two republics had location
quotients for industry further from 1.0 in 1975 than in 1960, many

TABLE 5.6

Branch Distribution of Productive Fixed Capital in USSR and Republics: 1960 and 1975
(percent)

1960

| | USSR | RSFSR | Ukraine | Moldavia | Belorussia | Latvia | Lithuania | Estonia |
|---|---|---|---|---|---|---|---|---|
| Industry | 45.5 | 48.1 | 47.2 | 26.6 | 28.4 | 31.8 | 30.6 | 35.0 |
| Agriculture | 23.1 | 18.6 | 26.2 | 44.7 | 37.8 | 33.7 | 41.3 | 26.5 |
| Transportation, communications | 22.3 | 23.6 | 19.3 | 20.2 | 26.1 | 26.6 | 20.9 | 31.9 |
| Construction | 3.3 | 3.6 | 1.9 | 2.2 | 2.4 | 2.8 | 2.6 | 1.7 |
| Trade, distribution, other branches | 5.9 | 6.0 | 5.4 | 6.4 | 5.4 | 5.2 | 4.5 | 4.8 |
| Total | 100.0 | 100.0 | 100.0 | 100.0 | 100.0 | 100.0 | 100.0 | 100.0 |

| | Georgia | Armenia | Azerbaidzhan | Kazakhstan | Uzbekistan | Kirgizstan | Tadzhikistan | Turkmenistan |
|---|---|---|---|---|---|---|---|---|
| Industry | 39.8 | 45.3 | 60.3 | 31.2 | 34.8 | 34.2 | 29.8 | 35.6 |
| Agriculture | 34.4 | 29.2 | 16.3 | 34.4 | 38.6 | 45.2 | 42.5 | 26.6 |
| Transportation, communications | 17.2 | 17.7 | 17.0 | 22.7 | 15.8 | 10.3 | 14.8 | 24.4 |
| Construction | 3.4 | 2.7 | 3.2 | 4.0 | 4.5 | 4.1 | 5.4 | 5.4 |
| Trade, distribution, other branches | 5.1 | 5.1 | 3.2 | 7.6 | 6.2 | 6.3 | 7.4 | 7.9 |
| Total | 100.0 | 100.0 | 100.0 | 100.0 | 100.0 | 100.0 | 100.0 | 100.0 |

## 1975

| | USSR | RSFSR | Ukraine | Moldavia | Belorussia | Latvia | Lithuania | Estonia |
|---|---|---|---|---|---|---|---|---|
| Industry | 49.1 | 51.7 | 49.5 | 31.3 | 44.2 | 38.2 | 40.1 | 45.6 |
| Agriculture | 20.8 | 16.9 | 22.0 | 43.6 | 28.5 | 27.5 | 37.7 | 25.6 |
| Transportation, communications | 20.0 | 20.9 | 19.3 | 15.5 | 17.3 | 25.2 | 12.6 | 20.3 |
| Construction | 4.7 | 4.9 | 3.6 | 3.8 | 4.8 | 3.3 | 4.3 | 3.2 |
| Trade, distribution, other branches | 5.3 | 5.7 | 5.6 | 5.9 | 5.3 | 5.7 | 5.4 | 5.2 |
| Total | 100.0 | 100.0 | 100.0 | 100.0 | 100.0 | 100.0 | 100.0 | 100.0 |

| | Georgia | Armenia | Azerbaidzhan | Kazakhstan | Uzbekistan | Kirgizstan | Tadzhikistan | Turkmenistan |
|---|---|---|---|---|---|---|---|---|
| Industry | 42.1 | 50.8 | 52.3 | 41.4 | 35.1 | 38.5 | 37.2 | 35.1 |
| Agriculture | 28.9 | 21.2 | 19.4 | 27.0 | 35.6 | 34.7 | 35.9 | 31.5 |
| Transportation, communications | 17.6 | 15.1 | 18.7 | 20.2 | 16.8 | 14.4 | 12.9 | 19.8 |
| Construction | 4.3 | 6.2 | 5.8 | 4.3 | 6.8 | 6.0 | 7.3 | 7.6 |
| Trade, distribution, other branches | 7.0 | 6.7 | 3.7 | 7.2 | 5.6 | 6.4 | 6.6 | 6.0 |
| Total | 100.0 | 100.0 | 100.0 | 100.0 | 100.0 | 100.0 | 100.0 | 100.0 |

Note: Columns may not total 100 due to rounding.
Source: James W. Gillula, The Regional Distribution of Fixed Capital in the U.S.S.R., Foreign Economic Report no. 17 (Washington, D.C.: U.S. Bureau of the Census, Foreign Demographic Analysis Division, 1980), Tables A-17 and A-18.

## TABLE 5.7

Location Quotients for USSR and Republics Based
on Employment in Material Production:
1960 and 1975

| | Industry | | Agriculture | | Other Material Production | |
|---|---|---|---|---|---|---|
| | 1960 | 1975 | 1960 | 1975 | 1960 | 1975 |
| USSR | 1.00 | 1.00 | 1.00 | 1.00 | 1.00 | 1.00 |
| RSFSR | 1.18 | 1.13 | .81 | .77 | 1.08 | 1.05 |
| Ukraine | .86 | .95 | 1.22 | 1.19 | .82 | .90 |
| Moldavia | .39 | .58 | 1.76 | 1.89 | .55 | .72 |
| Belorussia | .64 | .87 | 1.46 | 1.37 | .71 | .83 |
| Latvia | 1.10 | 1.10 | .91 | .87 | 1.03 | 1.00 |
| Lithuania | .72 | .96 | 1.33 | 1.14 | .81 | .93 |
| Estonia | 1.11 | 1.10 | .87 | .83 | 1.07 | 1.04 |
| Georgia | .74 | .70 | 1.20 | 1.46 | 1.00 | .95 |
| Armenia | .92 | 1.05 | 1.06 | .95 | 1.00 | .98 |
| Azerbaidzhan | .68 | .68 | 1.25 | 1.40 | .98 | 1.01 |
| Kazakhstan | .66 | .73 | 1.03 | 1.11 | 1.37 | 1.20 |
| Uzbekistan | .54 | .55 | 1.48 | 1.72 | .81 | .89 |
| Kirgizstan | .65 | .73 | 1.32 | 1.43 | .93 | .93 |
| Tadzhikistan | .46 | .53 | 1.53 | 1.70 | .82 | .93 |
| Turkmenistan | .47 | .40 | 1.36 | 1.74 | 1.07 | 1.04 |

Source: Stephen Rapawy, "Regional Employment Trends in the U.S.S.R.: 1950 to 1975," in U.S. Congress, Joint Economic Committee, Soviet Economy in a Time of Change, vol. 1 (Washington, D.C.: U.S. Government Printing Office, 1979), pp. 604, 605, 608.

of the movements toward 1.0 were quite small, indicating that
overall there was only a weak trend toward more balanced industrialization in the sense of equalizing the shares of employment in
industry among republics.[5]

As shown in Table 5.5, there was a substantial increase in
the value of fixed capital per worker in material production for the
USSR as a whole during the 15-year period considered here—an
average annual growth rate of 7.0 percent. Among the major
branches of the economy, the greatest increase in the capital/labor
ratio occurred in agriculture, a 9.0 percent average annual growth
rate, while the value of capital per worker in industry grew at an
average rate of 6.5 percent per year. As a result the capital/labor
ratio in industry exceeded that in agriculture by a factor of 1.8 in
1975, compared with the corresponding figure of 2.6 in 1960. This
relatively more rapid growth of capital per worker in agriculture
than in industry took place in all republics.

Indexes of the capital/labor ratios for republics relative to
the USSR ratios in industry, agriculture, and the entire economy
(sphere of material production) are given in Table 5.8. The
economy-average figures show a sharp drop in the relative levels
of capital per worker in each of the Transcaucasus republics, con-
trasting with increases in the relative positions of Kazakhstan and
the Central Asian republics (except industry and agriculture in
Kirgizstan, and agriculture in Tadzhikistan). The overall capital/
labor ratio grew most rapidly in Moldavia, but it was still the lowest
of all republics in 1975. Much of the difference among republics
in these aggregate capital/labor ratios can be explained by differences in branch structure. For example, the aggregate capital/
labor ratio for a republic ($k^r = K^r/L^r$) may be expressed as a
weighted sum of its individual branch capital/labor ratios with the
shares of employment in each branch as weights:

$$k^r = \sum_i \frac{L_i^r}{L^r} \cdot k_i^r \qquad (2)$$

And the branch shares of employment in the USSR as a whole may
be substituted in this expression as weights for the capital/labor
ratios in each republic in order to examine the effects of branch
structure on the aggregate capital/labor ratio.

Calculations of this type, using national shares of employment in the five major branches of material production as weights
for the branch capital/labor ratios in each republic in 1975, gave
a new aggregate capital/labor ratio that was closer to the actual

TABLE 5.8

Indexes of Capital/Labor Ratios for Republics Relative
to the USSR in Industry, Agriculture, and Entire
Economy: 1960 and 1975

| | Industry (1) | | Agriculture (2) | | Economy (3) | |
|---|---|---|---|---|---|---|
| | 1960 | 1975 | 1960 | 1975 | 1960 | 1975 |
| USSR | 100 | 100 | 100 | 100 | 100 | 100 |
| RSFSR | 96 | 100 | 106 | 114 | 107 | 108 |
| Ukraine | 106 | 90 | 82 | 75 | 88 | 85 |
| Moldavia | 79 | 73 | 58 | 73 | 52 | 66 |
| Belorussia | 64 | 77 | 74 | 75 | 66 | 74 |
| Latvia | 71 | 75 | 179 | 160 | 112 | 106 |
| Lithuania | 82 | 81 | 117 | 153 | 87 | 96 |
| Estonia | 91 | 105 | 174 | 186 | 132 | 124 |
| Georgia | 130 | 99 | 137 | 77 | 110 | 80 |
| Armenia | 105 | 85 | 117 | 92 | 98 | 86 |
| Azerbaidzhan | 297 | 160 | 86 | 68 | 153 | 102 |
| Kazakhstan | 125 | 148 | 173 | 149 | 120 | 128 |
| Uzbekistan | 101 | 110 | 80 | 84 | 71 | 84 |
| Kirgizstan | 90 | 88 | 115 | 95 | 77 | 82 |
| Tadzhikistan | 105 | 118 | 88 | 83 | 73 | 82 |
| Turkmenistan | 184 | 201 | 94 | 96 | 110 | 111 |

Sources: James W. Gillula, The Regional Distribution of
Fixed Capital in the U.S.S.R., Foreign Economic Report no. 17
(Washington, D.C.: U.S. Bureau of the Census, Foreign Demographic Analysis Division, 1980); Stephen Rapawy, "Regional Employment Trends in the U.S.S.R.: 1950 to 1975," in U.S. Congress,
Joint Economic Committee, Soviet Economy in a Time of Change,
vol. 1 (Washington, D.C.: U.S. Government Printing Office, 1979).

USSR ratio for ten republics (see Table 5.9). The significant exceptions to this general result—Azerbaidzhan, Kazakhstan, and Turkmenistan—are republics where there are substantial structural differences within these five major branches, especially industry. Each of these republics has an aggregate capital/labor ratio that is higher than that for the USSR as a whole, but the hypothetical aggregate ratio calculated here is even greater. This result is due largely to a combination of two factors. First, as shown in the following section, these republics have very high capital/labor ratios in industry primarily because they have large shares of capital-intensive extractive branches. Second, the shares of employment in industry in these republics are below the national average. In the calculation of the hypothetical aggregate capital/labor ratio, their high industrial capital/labor ratios are weighted by the higher national average share of employment in industry.

A factor that has a strong influence on this comparison of actual and hypothetical capital/labor ratios is the differing shares of agriculture in the economies of republics. Aggregate capital requirements tend to be reduced by the effects of branch structure (that is, actual capital/labor ratios tend to be lower than they would be on the assumption of USSR structure of employment) in republics with above-average shares of employment in agriculture. This applies to the southern republics (except Armenia), Moldavia, Belorussia, and the Ukraine. Conversely, aggregate capital requirements are increased by branch structure in two republics—the RSFSR and Latvia—that have very low shares of agricultural employment.

It is useful to view the changes in the relative levels of capital per worker in agriculture in light of the trends in the distribution of employment in agriculture summarized above. In six of the nine republics where there was an absolute increase in employment in agriculture (all southern republics plus Moldavia), there was slower-than-average growth of the capital/labor ratio in agriculture. In four of the remining six republics where there was an absolute decline in agricultural employment, the capital/labor ratio in agriculture grew faster than the national average. Of particular note in the latter group is the RSFSR, which had the lowest share of employment in agriculture in both 1960 and 1975 but one of the highest rates of growth of capital per worker in agriculture. These trends suggest that the development of agriculture has in general taken a less capital-intensive form in labor-surplus areas where a higher share of the population remains employed in agriculture.[6] However, a more thorough analysis of factor use in agriculture, which is beyond the scope of this paper, must take into account differences among republics in the intrabranch structure of agriculture, such as

the much higher shares of animal husbandry in the Baltic republics
that contribute to their high capital/labor ratios.

A result that is initially surprising in examining the capital/
labor ratios in industry is the relatively high values in the less
developed republics, while republics that have had the best overall
economic performance, such as Belorussia, Latvia, and Lithuania,
have relatively low values of capital per worker in industry. Of
course such interrepublic differences are greatly influenced by
differences in branch structure within industry, the focus of the
next section.

TABLE 5.9

Actual and Hypothetical Capital/Labor Ratios in Material
Production for USSR and Republics: 1975
(thousands of rubles per employee)

| | Actual | Based on USSR Branch Structure |
|---|---|---|
| USSR | 7.6 | 7.6 |
| RSFSR | 8.2 | 8.0 |
| Ukraine | 6.5 | 6.6 |
| Moldavia | 5.1 | 5.7 |
| Belorussia | 5.7 | 5.9 |
| Latvia | 8.1 | 8.0 |
| Lithuania | 7.3 | 7.3 |
| Estonia | 9.5 | 9.5 |
| Georgia | 6.1 | 6.8 |
| Armenia | 6.6 | 6.7 |
| Azerbaidzhan | 7.8 | 9.2 |
| Kazakhstan | 9.7 | 10.4 |
| Uzbekistan | 6.4 | 7.7 |
| Kirgizstan | 6.3 | 6.6 |
| Tadzhikistan | 6.3 | 7.6 |
| Turkmenistan | 8.5 | 11.8 |

Sources: James W. Gillula, The Regional Distribution of
Fixed Capital in the U.S.S.R., Foreign Economic Report no. 17
(Washington, D.C.: U.S. Bureau of the Census, Foreign Demographic Analysis Division, 1980); Stephen Rapawy, "Regional Employment Trends in the U.S.S.R.: 1950 to 1975," in U.S. Congress,
Joint Economic Committee, Soviet Economy in a Time of Change,
vol. 1 (Washington, D.C.: U.S. Government Printing Office, 1979).

BRANCHES OF INDUSTRY

Patterns of specialization in the industrial structure of republics and trends in the spatial distribution of individual branches
of industry among republics during the 1960s were analyzed in a
paper by Hans-Juergen Wagener.[7] His study was based on two sets
of location quotients for ten or eleven branches of industry, one set
calculated from data in national statistical handbooks on the branch
distribution of industrial fixed capital in each republic at the end of
1961 and 1969, and the other calculated from data in a 1968 hand-
book, Labor in the U.S.S.R., on average annual employment in
industry by republic in 1960 and 1966. Wagener's primary objective
was to evaluate the rationality of the regional distribution of industry from the standpoint of principles governing Soviet industrial
location decisions. Although similar sets of location quotients can
now be calculated for other years as late as 1974 (drawing on the
statistical handbooks of individual republics for employment data),[8]
simply updating Wagener's study adds little to his general conclusions. Since estimates of industrial capital, by branch, for rep-
publics are now available in value terms rather than just percentage
shares, however, his analysis can be extended by examining the
distribution of capital in each branch by republic, and by calculating capital/labor ratios.[9]

During the period for which branch estimates of industrial
capital for republics could be made—1961-74—the shares of industrial fixed capital increased most for the USSR as a whole in the
chemicals, electric power, and machine-building and metalworking
branches, and declined most in the fuels, wood and paper, and food
branches. Two coefficients were defined to measure the extent of
change in the regional distribution of fixed capital in each branch
during this period (see Table 5.10).

First, the similarity of the distribution of fixed capital among
republics in 1961 was compared with the corresponding distribution
in 1974 for each branch, using the coefficient $\lambda(s_i)$, defined as[10]

$$\lambda\left(s_i\right) = \sqrt{\frac{\sum\limits_r \left(s_{ir}^t - s_{ir}^o\right)^2}{\sum\limits_r \left(s_{ir}^o\right)^2}} \tag{3}$$

where $s_{ir}$ is the share of republic r in total fixed capital in branch i
in the year indicated by the superscript—o=1961, t=1974. The
greater this coefficient of comparability, the greater the overall
change in the regional distribution of fixed capital in branch i.

Second, the overall extent of dispersion of fixed capital in each branch among republics in each year was determined using the coefficient H $s_i^t$ , defined as [11]

$$H\left(s_i^t\right) = \sum_r s_{ir}^t \ \log_2 \ \frac{1}{s_{ir}^t} \tag{4}$$

where the superscript t indicates the year, 1961 or 1974. Values of this coefficient of dispersion range from zero, when all capital is concentrated in one republic, to $\log_2 15$ (since there are 15 republics), when total capital is equally distributed among all republics.

TABLE 5.10

Measures of Regional Dispersion and Comparability
of Regional Distribution of Industrial Branches:
1961 and 1974

| | | $H\left(s_i\right)$ | | |
|---|---|---|---|---|
| | $\lambda\left(s_i\right)$ | 1961 | 1974 | 1974 as a Percentage of 1961 |
| All industry | .045 | 1.812 | 1.935 | 106.8 |
| Ferrous metallurgy | .116 | 1.433 | 1.464 | 102.2 |
| Fuels | .112 | 1.911 | 1.874 | 98.1 |
| Electric power | .097 | 1.867 | 2.124 | 113.8 |
| Machine-building and metalworking (MBMW) | .046 | 1.423 | 1.568 | 110.2 |
| Chemicals | .102 | 1.529 | 1.871 | 122.4 |
| Wood and paper | .027 | 1.151 | 1.115 | 96.9 |
| Construction materials | .086 | 1.953 | 2.203 | 112.8 |
| Light industry | .136 | 2.085 | 2.392 | 114.7 |
| Food | .088 | 2.087 | 2.340 | 112.1 |
| Other branches | .074 | 1.842 | 1.786 | 97.0 |

Source: $\lambda(s_i)$ and $H(s_i)$ as defined in the text, equations (3) and (4), were calculated on the basis of data from James W. Gillula, The Regional Distribution of Fixed Capital in the U.S.S.R., Foreign Economic Report no. 17 (Washington, D.C.: U.S. Bureau of the Census, Foreign Demographic Analysis Division, 1980), Tables B-1 and B-2.

The values of $\lambda(s_i)$ show that the distribution of fixed capital among republics changed most during this period in the light industry, fuels, ferrous metallurgy, and chemicals branches. However, the $H(s_i)$ coefficients for 1961 and 1974 indicate that this change was in the direction of greater dispersion among republics in the chemicals and light industry branches, while fixed capital in the fuels branch was even more concentrated in a few republics in 1974 than in 1961. These trends are also reflected in changes in the location quotients based on fixed capital given in Table 5.11. Although there was a continuing high degree of specialization in light industry in Moldavia, Latvia, Lithuania, and three of the Central Asian republics (all had location quotients of 2.0 or more in 1974), nine of the location quotients for this branch were closer to 1.0 in 1974 than in 1960. For chemicals there were large increases in the location quotients for Belorussia, Latvia, Lithuania, and Tadzhikistan, and again nine quotients were closer to 1.0 in 1974. Azerbaidzhan and Turkmenistan continued to have the highest degree of specialization in the fuels branch, although the bulk of fixed capital in this branch was increasingly concentrated in the RSFSR, the Ukraine, and Kazakhstan.

The branches that rank just behind the four mentioned above in both the extent of change in regional distribution and the increase in dispersion are electric power and construction materials. The development of these two branches is a prerequisite to the broader-based industrialization of any region, and their increasing dispersion during this period is evidence of an attempt to establish a base for such industrialization in all republics. Location quotients for electric power increased most in Kirgizstan, Moldavia, and Tadzhikistan, while those for construction materials increased most in three of the Central Asian republics, Lithuania, and Armenia. From this base, however, quite different paths toward further industrialization may be taken, as the analysis of location quotients on a republic-by-republic basis shows.

In order to analyze the overall extent of change in the industrial structure of republics, coefficients of the same form as equation (3) were calculated:

$$\lambda\left(s_r\right) = \sqrt{\frac{\sum\limits_{i}\left(s_{ir}^{t} - s_{ir}^{o}\right)^{2}}{\sum\limits_{i}\left(s_{ir}^{o}\right)^{2}}} \tag{5}$$

TABLE 5.11

Location Quotients for USSR and Republics Based on Fixed Capital in Industry: 1961 and 1974

1961

| | Ferrous Metallurgy | Fuels | Electric Power | MBMW | Chemicals | Wood and Paper | Construction Materials | Light Industry | Food | Other Branches* |
|---|---|---|---|---|---|---|---|---|---|---|
| USSR | 1.00 | 1.00 | 1.00 | 1.00 | 1.00 | 1.00 | 1.00 | 1.00 | 1.00 | 1.00 |
| RSFSR | .78 | .85 | 1.04 | 1.13 | 1.08 | 1.27 | .97 | 1.02 | .92 | 1.01 |
| Ukraine | 2.17 | 1.26 | .68 | .87 | .94 | .38 | .91 | .50 | 1.06 | .71 |
| Moldavia | n.a. | n.a. | .86 | .47 | .10 | .59 | 1.53 | 1.53 | 5.07 | .75 |
| Belorussia | .04 | .41 | 1.14 | 1.24 | .88 | 1.47 | 1.37 | 2.19 | 1.45 | .65 |
| Latvia | .15 | .25 | 1.15 | 1.02 | .37 | 1.61 | 1.20 | 2.20 | 2.42 | .46 |
| Lithuania | .03 | .24 | 1.07 | .88 | .08 | 1.22 | 1.72 | 2.55 | 2.69 | .64 |
| Estonia | n.a. | .85 | 1.51 | .64 | .43 | 1.26 | 1.20 | 2.14 | 2.07 | .55 |
| Georgia | 1.62 | .57 | 1.69 | .61 | .79 | .57 | 1.03 | 1.22 | 1.53 | .57 |
| Armenia | .07 | n.a. | 2.12 | .78 | 2.16 | .36 | 1.05 | 1.89 | 1.15 | 1.85 |
| Azerbaidzhan | .37 | 3.68 | .86 | .30 | .81 | .12 | .51 | .76 | .40 | .71 |
| Kazakhstan | .96 | 1.01 | 1.11 | .47 | .64 | .47 | 1.51 | .70 | .74 | 2.95 |
| Uzbekistan | .09 | .79 | 1.47 | .71 | 1.25 | .36 | 1.34 | 2.72 | .92 | 1.70 |
| Kirgizstan | n.a. | 1.68 | .72 | .79 | .02 | .47 | 1.04 | 1.97 | 1.57 | 1.65 |
| Tadzhikistan | n.a. | .37 | 1.84 | .39 | .06 | .34 | 1.99 | 4.49 | 1.23 | 1.57 |
| Turkmenistan | n.a. | 3.15 | .70 | .33 | 1.19 | .19 | 1.08 | 1.39 | .89 | .67 |

1974

| | | | | | | | | | | |
|---|---|---|---|---|---|---|---|---|---|---|
| USSR | 1.00 | 1.00 | 1.00 | 1.00 | 1.00 | 1.00 | 1.00 | 1.00 | 1.00 | 1.00 |
| RSFSR | .86 | .94 | .99 | 1.13 | 1.00 | 1.33 | .93 | .91 | .86 | 1.00 |
| Ukraine | 2.01 | 1.18 | .83 | 1.00 | .87 | .31 | .88 | .69 | 1.13 | .51 |
| Moldavia | n.a. | n.a. | 1.45 | .66 | .06 | .66 | 1.36 | 2.42 | 4.43 | .54 |
| Belorussia | .03 | .59 | 1.11 | 1.11 | 1.99 | .92 | 1.33 | 1.82 | 1.11 | .32 |
| Latvia | .25 | .16 | 1.19 | .97 | .84 | 1.33 | 1.23 | 2.25 | 2.49 | .51 |
| Lithuania | .05 | .12 | 1.43 | .94 | .85 | 1.31 | 1.71 | 2.00 | 2.25 | .43 |
| Estonia | n.a. | 1.03 | 1.92 | .53 | .37 | 1.29 | 1.16 | 1.56 | 2.24 | .30 |
| Georgia | 1.14 | .36 | 1.29 | .60 | 1.04 | .63 | 1.28 | 1.62 | 2.01 | .88 |
| Armenia | .02 | n.a. | 1.47 | .98 | 1.52 | .32 | 1.46 | 1.64 | 1.32 | 1.72 |
| Azerbaidzhan | .35 | 2.56 | .83 | .39 | 1.07 | .20 | .64 | .89 | .89 | .54 |
| Kazakhstan | 1.41 | 1.09 | 1.18 | .42 | .69 | .31 | 1.40 | .82 | .79 | 2.49 |
| Uzbekistan | .09 | .74 | 1.31 | .64 | 1.35 | .31 | 1.83 | 2.42 | .94 | 1.56 |
| Kirgizstan | .02 | .76 | 1.56 | 1.08 | .02 | .24 | 1.26 | 2.49 | 1.67 | 1.09 |
| Tadzhikistan | n.a. | .30 | 2.59 | .42 | .65 | .29 | 1.56 | 2.73 | 1.28 | .66 |
| Turkmenistan | n.a. | 3.74 | .88 | .17 | 1.09 | .10 | 1.41 | 1.60 | .75 | .35 |

n.a. = Not applicable.

*"Other branches" includes nonferrous metallurgy, glass industry, and other activities not elsewhere classified.

Source: James W. Gillula, The Regional Distribution of Fixed Capital in the U.S.S.R., Foreign Economic Report no. 17 (Washington, D.C.: U.S. Bureau of the Census, Foreign Demographic Analysis Division, 1980), Tables B-1 and B-2.

181

While the coefficient defined in equation (3) measures the comparability of the distribution by republic of fixed capital in a particular
branch at two points in time, $\lambda$ ($s_r$) measures the comparability of
the branch distributions of capital in different years for a particular
republic.  Values of this coefficient for all republics are given in
Table 5.12.  The extent of structural change was greatest in republics that had some of the highest growth rates of industrial fixed
capital during this period—Kirgizstan, Tadzhikistan, Belorussia,
Lithuania, and Moldavia.  In fact, there is a positive correlation
between the ranking of republics by the value of $\lambda$ ($s_r$) and by the
growth of fixed capital in industry from 1961 to 1974 ($r_{sp}$ = 0.64).

TABLE 5.12

Structural Change and Overall Growth of Fixed Capital in
Industry for USSR and Republics: 1961-74

| | $\lambda$ ($s_r$) | Average Annual Growth of Industrial Fixed Capital (percent) |
|---|---|---|
| USSR | .201 | 9.5 |
| RSFSR | .175 (14) | 9.2 (12) |
| Ukraine | .240 (11) | 8.9 (13) |
| Moldavia | .400 (5) | 13.2 (2) |
| Belorussia | .448 (3) | 13.6 (1) |
| Latvia | .259 (8) | 9.5 (11) |
| Lithuania | .407 (4) | 12.2 (5) |
| Estonia | .363 (6) | 10.3 (9) |
| Georgia | .246 (9) | 7.3 (14) |
| Armenia | .187 (13) | 10.8 (8) |
| Azerbaidzhan | .244 (10) | 5.2 (15) |
| Kazakhstan | .267 (7) | 12.4 (4) |
| Uzbekistan | .234 (12) | 12.0 (7) |
| Kirgizstan | .637 (1) | 12.2 (6) |
| Tadzhikistan | .588 (2) | 12.6 (3) |
| Turkmenistan | .168 (15) | 9.9 (10) |

Note: Numbers in parentheses show the ranking of republics
by the corresponding indicator.
Source: Calculated according to equation (5) in the text on the
basis of data from James W. Gillula, The Regional Distribution of
Fixed Capital in the U.S.S.R., Foreign Economic Report no. 17
(Washington, D.C.: U.S. Bureau of the Census, Foreign Demographic Analysis Division, 1980), Tables B-1 and B-2.

Structural change in Kirgizstan involved growing specialization in light industry as well as increases in the branch shares of fixed capital in electric power and construction materials. This republic also had a larger increase in the location quotient for machine-building and metalworking than any other southern republic. In Tadzhikistan the relative degree of specialization in light industry declined sharply, but the location quotient for this branch still remained the highest among all branches in the republic as well as the highest among the light industry location quotients for all republics. In the other two Central Asian republics, where the overall extent of structural change was much less, light industry continued to have the highest location quotient in Uzbekistan and the second highest in Turkmenistan, which had an increasing specialization in fuels.

Extractive industry also had a large, and in some cases, growing, role in three southern republics other than Turkmenistan. Kazakhstan and Armenia continued to have the two highest location quotients for "other branches" because of the inclusion of nonferrous metallurgy in this branch, and there was a sharp increase in the quotient for ferrous metallurgy in Kazakhstan. Azerbaidzhan continued to have a high degree of specialization in fuels. Although the location quotients for seven of the ten branches in this republic were closer to 1.0 in 1974 than in 1960, most of these changes were very small. Thus, the very low rate of growth of total industrial capital in Azerbaidzhan cannot be attributed solely to the relative decline of its fuel industry.

Among the European republics the greatest overall structural change took place in Belorussia, where seven of the ten location quotients were closer to 1.0 in 1974 than in 1961, the most pronounced exception to this trend being a sharp increase in the quotient for chemicals. In Moldavia, Latvia, and Lithuania the highest degree of specialization continued to be in the food and light industry branches, and Estonia deviated from this pattern only in that it also had a location quotient in electric power exceeding that in light industry in 1974. The location quotient for the food industry in Moldavia reflects the highest degree of specialization in a single branch in any republic.

There was less structural change in the RSFSR than in all but two other republics during the period considered here. The highest degree of specialization in the republic continued to be in wood and paper and in machine-building and metalworking. The location quotients for each of these two branches were higher than the corresponding quotients for all other republics in 1974. Although the RSFSR's specialization in the wood and paper branch is strongly influenced by considerations of natural resource location, this would seem to be a less important factor in the case of machine-building. Substantial shares of the basic metals used in the republic's machine-building industry are shipped in from other republics, primarily the Ukraine and Kazakhstan. Certainly other factors, such as the availability of skilled personnel and perhaps defense considerations, underlie this continuing concentration of machine-building in the RSFSR.

Nonetheless, the unequal regional distribution of machine-building capacity is an issue of growing concern to spokesmen for less developed republics, who see the development of machine-building as a necessary prerequisite to breaking the pattern of narrow specialization in low-technology, low-wage branches in their economies.[12] With the exception of Kirgizstan and Armenia, little progress has been made toward this end, as the measures of dispersion and comparability for machine-building and metalworking in Table 5.10 show. There was less overall change in the distribution of this branch among republics than for any other except wood and paper. In 1974 only wood and paper and ferrous metallurgy had lower coefficients of dispersion than machine-building and metalworking.

The regional location policy for the machine-building industry may also be questioned from the standpoint of considering relative factor availability in location decisions. As the summary of location quotients above showed, most of the labor-surplus southern republics continued to have a high degree of specialization in the most labor-intensive branch, light industry. In fact, the combined share of the Central Asian republics and Kazakhstan in fixed capital in light industry increased from 10 percent of the USSR total in 1961 to 14 percent in 1974. However, machine-building and metalworking, which is the second most labor-intensive branch among the ten distinguished here,[13] is much less developed in these republics.

An analysis of the capital/labor ratios in individual branches of industry for all republics reveals some very interesting aspects of Soviet regional development policy. In Table 5.13 the capital/labor ratio in a given branch for each republic in 1974 is expressed as a percentage of the national capital/labor ratio for that branch. The most striking feature of this table is the wide variation among republics in capital/labor ratios in certain branches. Some of these interrepublic differences can be explained immediately by differences in the structure of production within a branch. For example, the low capital/labor ratio for fuels in the Ukraine, contrasted with the very high ratios in Turkmenistan and Azerbaidzhan, is largely due to the predominance of the more labor-intensive production of coal in the fuels industry of the Ukraine and the very

TABLE 5.13

Indexes of Capital/Labor Ratios in Branches of Industry for Republics Relative to the USSR: 1974

| | Industry Total | Ferrous Metallurgy | Fuels | Electric Power | MBMW | Chemicals | Wood and Paper | Construction Materials | Light Industry | Food | Other Branches |
|---|---|---|---|---|---|---|---|---|---|---|---|
| USSR | 100 | 100 | 100 | 100 | 100 | 100 | 100 | 100 | 100 | 100 | 100 |
| RSFSR | 99 | 95 | 115 | 103 | 104 | 95 | 110 | 105 | 101 | 98 | 98 |
| Ukraine | 91 | 97 | 57 | 99 | 93 | 85 | 48 | 72 | 73 | 90 | 63 |
| Moldavia | 75 | n.a. | n.a. | 94 | 74 | 22 | 67 | 74 | 98 | 136 | 43 |
| Belorussia | 77 | 27 | 119 | 87 | 87 | 120 | 67 | 94 | 103 | 80 | 35 |
| Latvia | 72 | 67 | 61 | 108 | 80 | 58 | 72 | 108 | 117 | 122 | 38 |
| Lithuania | 80 | 58 | 57 | 103 | 84 | 83 | 100 | 116 | 111 | 126 | 33 |
| Estonia | 107 | n.a. | 60 | 105 | 94 | 94 | 106 | 120 | 109 | 140 | 30 |
| Georgia | 100 | 87 | 78 | 92 | 107 | 100 | 82 | 89 | 99 | 111 | 87 |
| Armenia | 85 | 37 | n.a. | 111 | 87 | 92 | 91 | 98 | 85 | 115 | 111 |
| Azerbaidzhan | 164 | 78 | 252 | 69 | 110 | 124 | 69 | 109 | 86 | 114 | 84 |
| Kazakhstan | 148 | 175 | 117 | 82 | 94 | 140 | 84 | 125 | 104 | 95 | 178 |
| Uzbekistan | 113 | 97 | 199 | 100 | 97 | 187 | 84 | 119 | 145 | 97 | 121 |
| Kirgizstan | 88 | 18 | 73 | 106 | 101 | 116 | 48 | 91 | 130 | 119 | 69 |
| Tadzhikistan | 118 | n.a. | 89 | 198 | 107 | 147 | 68 | 122 | 120 | 101 | 71 |
| Turkmenistan | 194 | n.a. | 520 | 60 | 73 | 181 | 46 | 128 | 147 | 107 | 114 |

N.A. = Not applicable.

Sources: Calculated from values of fixed capital in James W. Gillula, The Regional Distribution of Fixed Capital in the U.S.S.R., Foreign Economic Report no. 17 (Washington, D.C.: U.S. Bureau of the Census, Foreign Demographic Analysis Division, 1980), Table B-2; and employment figures in Stephen Rapawy, "Regional Employment Trends in the U.S.S.R.: 1950 to 1975," in U.S. Congress, Joint Economic Committee, Soviet Economy in a Time of Change, vol. 1 (Washington, D.C.: U.S. Government Printing Office, 1979), pp. 608-11, except that additional significant digits in the employment data as originally reported in republic statistical handbooks were preserved.

capital-intensive production of oil and gas in the latter two republics. However, explanations for other differences are less obvious,
particularly in the light of patterns that emerge from these data.
We will return to this question below.

In the previous section—see equation (2)—the effect of branch
structure on the aggregate capital/labor ratio in material production
in each republic was analyzed by weighting its individual branch
ratios by the USSR branch shares of employment. The results of
similar calculations to determine the effect of branch structure on
the aggregate capital/labor ratio in industry for each republic are
given in Table 5.14. These figures must be interpreted with caution because of intrabranch structural differences of the type just
discussed.

The impact of branch structure on the aggregate capital/labor
ratio is not as consistent as might be expected. The hypothetical
capital/labor ratio was closer to the USSR value than the actual
ratio for only eight republics. However, the effect of structural
differences on the industrial capital/labor ratios of most southern
republics is evident. The actual ratio is higher than the hypothetical ratio in six of these republics, and the greatest differences
occur in the three republics with high concentrations of extractive
industry—Azerbaidzhan, Turkmenistan, and Kazakhstan.

Returning now to the question of interrepublic differences in
capital/labor ratios for a given branch, a comparison of each column of figures in Table 5.13 with the corresponding column of
location quotients in Table 5.11 reveals the following curious result: in several manufacturing branches capital/labor ratios tend
to be highest in those republics where the particular branch is a
sector of specialization. An intuitively appealing conclusion that
might be drawn from this result is that Soviet planners have pursued a capital-intensive approach to the development of the branches
that are of the greatest importance in the economy of a particular
republic. Such a conclusion certainly has an analogy in the observations of other Western scholars that the Soviets tend to "throw
capital" into high-priority branches of the national economy to
spur rapid growth of output. However, while there may be a certain degree of validity to such a characterization of Soviet regional
development strategy, a more careful analysis of this pattern for
each major branch of industry suggests that intrabranch structural
differences play an important role here as well.

In light industry the four Central Asian republics have the
highest capital/labor ratios, and three of these republics have the
highest degree of specialization in this branch. The three Baltic
republics have the next highest capital/labor ratios in light industry, and two of them rank just behind the Central Asian republics

# TABLE 5.14

Actual and Hypothetical Capital/Labor Ratios in
Industry for USSR and Republics: 1974
(thousands of rubles per employee)

|  | Actual | Based on USSR Branch Structure |
|---|---|---|
| USSR | 9.3 | 9.3 |
| RSFSR | 9.4 | 9.7 |
| Ukraine | 8.6 | 7.8 |
| Moldavia | 7.1 | 5.6 |
| Belorussia | 7.3 | 8.0 |
| Latvia | 6.9 | 7.8 |
| Lithuania | 7.6 | 8.0 |
| Estonia | 10.1 | 8.0 |
| Georgia | 9.4 | 8.9 |
| Armenia | 8.1 | 7.6 |
| Azerbaidzhan | 15.5 | 10.9 |
| Kazakhstan | 14.0 | 10.9 |
| Uzbekistan | 10.7 | 11.7 |
| Kirgizstan | 8.3 | 8.4 |
| Tadzhikistan | 11.2 | 10.4 |
| Turkmenistan | 18.3 | 13.4 |

Sources: James W. Gillula, The Regional Distribution of
Fixed Capital in the U.S.S.R., Foreign Economic Report no. 17
(Washington, D.C.: U.S. Bureau of the Census, Foreign Demo-
graphic Analysis Division, 1980), Table B-2; Stephen Rapawy,
"Regional Employment Trends in the U.S.S.R.: 1950 to 1975," in
U.S. Congress, Joint Economic Committee, Soviet Economy in a
Time of Change, vol. 1 (Washington, D.C.: U.S. Government
Printing Office, 1979), pp. 608-11.

in respect to location quotients for this branch. Part of the explanation for this result in Central Asia must lie in the fact that the initial processing of cotton and other fibers accounts for a large share of light industry in the region, and these operations have capital/labor ratios that are much higher than the average for all light industry. For example, in Uzbekistan cotton ginning accounted for 35 percent of fixed capital in light industry in 1970, and the capital/labor ratio in this subbranch was 3.8 times greater than that for all other light industry in the republic.[14]

Although this explanation weakens the "capital-intensive specialization" hypothesis stated above, it is of independent interest for its implications for development policy in Central Asia. Central Asian economists have argued for greater diversification of their economies on the basis of their natural resources, so as to alter the existing pattern under which most of their raw materials and processed fibers are shipped to European regions for the manufacture of cloth and clothing.[15] The evidence cited above indicates that such a diversified approach to development would also make it possible to expand employment in these labor-surplus regions at a capital cost per worker even lower than the light industry averages in these republics.

In the food industry Moldavia and the Baltic republics rank 1–4 by both the capital/labor ratio and the location quotient in 1974. The food industry in Moldavia is probably the best single example of a capital-intensive approach to development in a branch of specialization. Although this republic's food industry includes above-average shares of production of some products (such as wine) that are relatively more capital-intensive, intrabranch structural differences apparently are not the explanation for its high capital/labor ratio. One source on the Moldavian economy reports that in 1970 capital/labor ratios in the republic were higher than in the USSR as a whole in 14 of 16 subbranches of the food industry.[16] For the Baltic republics, however, at least one significant structural characteristics of their food industries has the effect of increasing the capital/labor ratio. The share of the fish products subbranch in total fixed capital in the food industry for each of these republics was at least twice as large as the corresponding share for the USSR as a whole in 1974, and the national capital/labor ratio in this subbranch was about 2.4 times greater than that for the food industry as a whole.[17]

The relation between capital intensiveness and degree of specialization is not as clear-cut in construction materials, but four republics—Kazakhstan, Uzbekistan, Tadzhikistan, and Turkmenistan—rank among the top five according to capital/labor ratios for this branch, and among the top six according to location quotients. The construction materials industry is not a branch of specialization in the same sense as the food or light industries, in that its predominance in these republics reflects their rapid rates of overall development rather than production for the national market (as is the case in the latter two branches). Nevertheless, the limited evidence available on the internal structure of the construction materials industry in these republics suggests that differences in the relative shares of subbranches are at best only a partial explanation of their relatively high capital/labor ratios in the construction materials branch as a whole.[18]

The final branch that should be considered in this discussion is the wood and paper industry. The RSFSR had the highest capital/labor ratio and one of the two highest location quotients for this branch. Lithuania and Estonia ranked second and third according to the former indicator, and third and fourth according to the latter. But Latvia, which had a very high location quotient, had a capital/labor ratio that was well below average. The high capital/labor ratios in the three republics that fit the pattern being examined are due largely to the greater share of pulp and paper production in their wood and paper industry. The capital/labor ratio in pulp and paper production was 3.4 times as great as the branch average for the entire wood and paper industry in the USSR in 1974.[19] The RSFSR also had a lower share of woodworking—the least capital-intensive subbranch—than any other republic.

From this brief survey of factors underlying interrepublic differences in capital/labor ratios in branches of industry it is clear that the hypothesis of a capital-intensive approach to development in branches of specialization has only limited validity. Intrabranch structural differences explain the high branch capital/labor ratios in many instances. Furthermore, the relatively high capital/labor ratios observed in many of the less developed republics are probably due in part to the fact that their rapid economic growth has necessarily been based more on the construction of complete new plants than on the expansion of existing plants, and the former is generally a more capital-intensive approach to increasing employment and output. However, focusing on the branch structure of republics in some detail has served to illustrate the variety of factors that can shape the aggregate demand for capital, and an understanding of such factors will be of growing importance for any attempt to anticipate Soviet responses to the competing demands of regions for larger shares of a volume of capital investment that will be growing more slowly in coming years.

SUMMARY

While the rapid growth of fixed capital in the USSR during the 15-year period considered here was accompanied by some substantial structural changes in the economy of the country as a whole, the major national trends in branch structure occurred in nearly all republics as well. Nearly all republics had an increase in the share of productive capital in total fixed capital, a decrease in the share of housing in nonproductive capital, and increases in the shares of industry and construction in productive capital. As a result, comparisons of the branch structure of the economies of individual republics with the structure of the national economy in years at the beginning and end of this period reveal little change in overall patterns of branch specialization in republics. From the standpoint of a division of the economy into the five major branches of material production, there was only a weak trend toward equalizing the shares of industry in the economies of republics, and there was continuing (in some instances increasing) relative specialization in agriculture in all the southern republics except Armenia. The greatest degree of structural change occurred in Belorussia and Lithuania—republics that ranked just below the Central Asian republics and Moldavia in respect to growth of productive fixed capital during this period.

Similarity in branch growth trends among republics was also evident in the fact that the value of capital per worker grew faster in agriculture than in industry in all republics. However, again with respect to agriculture, the development pattern in most southern republics (including Moldavia) differed from that in the RSFSR and other European republics. The capital/labor ratio in agriculture generally grew faster in the latter group of republics, where there was an absolute decline in agricultural employment, than in the former group, where employment in agriculture increased.

Structural change within industry was marked by an increase in the dispersion among republics of two branches that are of fundamental importance in the economic development process: electric power and construction materials. Among other producers' goods branches, the regional distribution of fixed capital changed most substantially in the chemicals branch. There was much less change in the distribution of the machine-building and metalworking and wood and paper branches, which remained heavily concentrated in the RSFSR. The less developed southern republics retained a high degree of specialization in the light industry and/or food branches, and in some cases in extractive branches.

Capital/labor ratios in individual branches of industry differ greatly among republics. In several manufacturing branches these ratios tend to be highest in those republics where the particular branch is a sector of specialization. However, in many instances these high capital/labor ratios are explained by structural differences within the given branch for the republics concerned.

The study of structural differences in the economies of republics has important implications for a number of basic issues in Soviet regional development policy that have been mentioned only briefly here. Perhaps the most significant is the question of the determinants of Soviet industrial location policy. As Wagener's analysis has shown, Soviet location decisions are governed by a number of factors in addition to considerations of economic efficiency. The continuing high degree of specialization observed in the economies of the southern republics may be explained in part by relative factor availability, but a further rationale can be inferred from the indirect results of this policy. Very high percentages of the output of these branches of specialization—such as fuels, ores, and products of the light and food industries—are shipped to other regions, and even where certain heavy industry branches have been developed, a large share of their output is exported. These republics in turn have continued to rely heavily on imports from other regions to satisfy their needs for capital goods.[20] Thus, the policy of encouraging specialization at the expense of diversification has created strong trade ties and has served to keep these republics highly dependent on the rest of the USSR.

NOTES

1. The Soviet study referred to here is A. K. Zakumbaev, Ekonomicheskoe razvitie soiuznykh respublik i raionov (faktornyi analiz) (Alma-Ata, 1977). The capital stock estimates used in this paper were derived from this and other Soviet sources as described in James W. Gillula, The Regional Distribution of Fixed Capital in the U.S.S.R., Foreign Economic Reports no. 17 (Washington, D.C.: U.S. Bureau of the Census, Foreign Demographic Analysis Division, 1980). All values of fixed capital used in this paper are in constant 1955 prices, gross of depreciation at the end of the year cited.

2. See, for example, Alastair McAuley, Economic Welfare in the Soviet Union: Poverty, Living Standards, and Inequality (Madison: University of Wisconsin Press, 1979), pp. 112-14.

3. Daniel L. Bond, "Multiregional Economic Development in the Soviet Union: 1960-1975" (Ph.D. diss., University of North Carolina at Chapel Hill, 1979), p. 79.

4. James W. Gillula, "The Economic Interdependence of Soviet Republics," in U.S. Congress, Joint Economic Committee, Soviet Economy in a Time of Change, vol. 1 (Washington, D.C.: U.S. Government Printing Office, 1979), pp. 630-36.

5. Of note in this regard, however, is the fact that quite different conclusions about industrialization trends in the USSR are obtained when the units of analysis are the major economic regions rather than republics. See Gillula, "The Economic Interdependence . . . ," pp. 621, 653; and Matthew J. Sagers and Milford B. Green, "Industrial Dispersion in the Soviet Union: An Application of Entropy Measures," Soviet Geography, December 1979, pp. 572-75.

6. Further evidence of this is that there is a negative correlation for republics ($r = -0.67$) between the capital/labor ratio in agriculture and agriculture's share of employment in the sphere of material production in 1975.

7. Hans-Juergen Wagener, "Rules of Location and the Concept of Rationality: The Case of the U.S.S.R.," in V. N. Bandera and Z. L. Melnyk, eds., The Soviet Economy in Regional Perspective (New York: Praeger, 1973).

8. Data on the structure of industrial capital for all republics have not appeared in national statistical handbooks since 1974, and no data on employment by branch of industry have been published in handbooks for the USSR or republics since 1975.

9. The values of fixed capital in ten branches of industry used in these calculations were taken from Gillula, The Regional Distribution . . . , Tables B-1 and B-2. It should be noted that the branch distributions from national statistical handbooks used in making these estimates refer to enterprises on an independent balance (na samostoiatel'nom balanse), and thus exclude a small proportion of capital included in the industry totals to which these percentages were applied, but this difference should not affect the conclusions drawn here on the basis of these data. See ibid., sec. IV-A.

10. This coefficient was used in an analysis of regional structural differences in A. G. Granberg, ed., Mezhotraslevye balansy v analize territorial'nykh proportsii SSR (Novosibirsk, 1975), p. 299.

11. This coefficient was used in an analysis of the regional dispersion of industry in the USSR in Sagers and Green, "Industrial Dispersion . . . ," pp. 569-71.

12. See, for example, A. K. Zakumbaev, Ekonimicheskoe razvitie soiuznykh respublik i raionov (Alma-Ata, 1977), pp. 181, 183.

13.  For the USSR as a whole in 1974, the capital/labor ratios in light industry and in machine-building and metalworking were 30 percent and 53 percent, respectively, of the ratio for all industry (based on values of fixed capital from Gillula, The Regional Distribution . . . , Tables B-1 and B-2, and employment figures from Narkhoz 75, p. 188).

14.  Calculated from data in Kh. Dzhuraev, Promyshlennost' Uzbekistana: Tempy, struktura, effektivnost' (Tashkent, 1974), p. 264.

15.  For example, only 5 percent of all textile raw materials produced in Uzbekistan are currently processed to the stage of final goods, and about 70 percent of all cotton fabrics consumed in Uzbekistan are imported from other republics.  See the abstracts of articles from Voprosy ekonomiki i planirovanie otraslei narodnogo khoziaistva Uzbekistana (Tashkent, 1979) included in "Referativnyi zhurnal: Geografiia, 07E," Geografiia SSSR no. 3 (March 1980): 48, and no. 4 (April 1980): 45.

16.  N. P. Frolov, ed., Razvitie i razmeshchenie proizvoditel'nykh sil Moldavskoi SSR (Moscow, 1972), p. 16.

17.  The capital shares for the Baltic republics were calculated from TsSU, Narodnoe khoziaistvo SSR v 1974 g. (Moscow, 1973), p. 199 (publication hereafter cited as Narkhoz).  Capital/labor ratios for fish products and the food industry as a whole are based on data from the 1972 input–output table for the USSR in Dimitri M. Gallik, Gene D. Guill, Barry L. Kostinsky, and Vladimir G. Treml, "The 1972 Input-Output Table and the Changing Structure of the Soviet Economy," in U.S. Congress, Joint Economic Committee, Soviet Economy in a Time of Change, vol. 1 (Washington, D.C.: U.S. Government Printing Office, 1979), pp. 449, 451.

18.  Cement production is the only subbranch with a capital/labor ratio that deviates substantially from that for construction materials as a whole.  According to data from the 1972 input–output table for the USSR, the capital/labor ratio in cement was 3.1 times greater than the construction materials average.  However, in two of the four republics for which data are available—Kazakhstan and Uzbekistan—the share of cement in fixed capital in construction materials was only slightly higher than the corresponding share for the USSR. Dzhuraev, Promyshlennost' Uzbekistana, p. 231; and R. D. Trubnikova, "Uroven' i effektivnost' razvitiia otrasli, obsluzhivaiushchikh khoziaistvo regiona," in Effektivnost' regional'noi ekonomiki Kazakhstana (Alma-Ata, 1977), pp. 138-39.

19.  Calculated from Narkhoz 74, pp. 188, 199.

20.  See Gillula, "The Economic Interdependence . . . ," pp. 640-52.

# II

# ECONOMIC DEVELOPMENT IN INDIVIDUAL REGIONS IN THE USSR

# 6

# THE EUROPEAN USSR

## F. E. Ian Hamilton

This chapter analyzes the European USSR, long the leading region in most fields of Soviet endeavor. Outstanding as a producer of agricultural crops and manufactures, the region also dominates the Soviet economy in control functions, research and development, transport, trade, tourism, and recreation. Although the area is little larger than East Siberia and substantially smaller than the Far East, its location endows the European region with major natural and human advantages, embodying the most favorable regional combination in the USSR of climate, soils, hydrology, and geology for agriculture, mining, power generation, and transportation; the greatest access to ice-free seas for international trade and military endeavor; and adjacency to the remainder of the "old continent" of modern culture, civilization, and technology.

Historically the region has exhibited the greatest continuity in settlement and urbanization, development, and socioeconomic integration, both in terms of legacies from the pre-Revolutionary period and under Soviet government. Politically, since 1917 this region may be said to have been a testing ground for some of the major tenets of Soviet ideology. In particular it is the arena for the implementation of policies for socioeconomic development, for cultural advancement, for full employment, and for equality of opportunity regardless of nationality, in the face of the interaction between the ethnic majority—the Russians—and the whole gamut of non-Russian ethnic minorities from the largest (the Ukrainian nation) to the smallest groups (such as the Komi, Osetian, and Neneto peoples).

As defined in this chapter, the European USSR comprises 12 of the country's 19 economic regions and embraces six of its non-Russian Soviet Socialist Republics (SSRs) as well as a significant

part of the Russian Soviet Federated Socialist Republic (RSFSR).
Indeed, the region in effect contains a large Russian-dominated
core surrounded by an almost continuous "crescent" of mainly or
substantially non-Russian peripheral areas. The core includes six
economic regions of the RSFSR: the Northwest (centered on Leningrad), the Central (with Moscow as its hub), the Volga-Viatka (center at Gorkii), the Povolzh'e or Volga (major cities are Kuibyshev,
Volgograd, Kazan', Saratov, and Ufa), the Central Chernozem (or
Black Earth—center at Voronezh), and the North Caucasus (center
at Rostov). To the west and south lies a tier of SSRs. From north
to south they are Estonia, Latvia, and Lithuania, which form the
Baltic economic region; Belorussia and Moldavia, which are separate economic regions in their own right; and the Ukraine, which
comprises three economic regions.

However, the economic regions of the RSFSR contain an arc
of areas inhabited by ethnic minorities. On the west and north are
the Karelian ASSR, Nenets Autonomous Oblast, and Komi ASSR
in the Northwest region. On the east, along the western flanks of
the Urals, lie the Udmurt ASSR and Komi-Permiak National Oblast
(Kama River area), and the Mari, Chuvash, Mordovian, Bashkir,
and Kalmyk ASSRs in the middle and lower Volga Basin. Along the
North Caucasus foreland in the south are the Dagestan, Chechen-
Ingush, North Osetian, and Kabardino-Balkar ASSRs and the
Karacheevo-Cherkess and Adygei autonomous oblasts.

The region is larger in territory than all independent world
nations outside the Soviet Union, except Canada, the People's
Republic of China, the United States, Brazil, and Australia—in that
order. This huge area, nevertheless, embraces only one-quarter
of all Soviet territory. The region contains two-thirds of all Soviet
people (an estimated 178 million in 1979)—more than in any other
country except the People's Republic of China, India, and the
United States.


FUNCTIONAL IMPORTANCE

Proper assessment of the importance to the Soviet Union of
its European lands cannot be couched only, or even mainly, in
terms of area and number of people. Rather, the qualitative features of territory and population, their value as resources, and the
dynamics of their engagement in the development process are the
true indexes of the socioeconomic significance of the region.
Tables 6.1 and 6.2 set out in summary form selected indexes of
trends in the scale and relative importance of production in the
European USSR since 1940. Broadly speaking, three characteristics

## TABLE 6.1

Indexes of the Growth and Changing Importance of Industrial Production: European USSR, 1940-75

| European Soviet Production of | 1940 | 1960 | 1970 | 1971 | 1975 |
|---|---|---|---|---|---|
| **Energy** | | | | | |
| Electric power | | | | | |
| Installed capacity (mill. kw) | 8.6 | 42.7 | 98.5 | 106.8 | n.a. |
| % of the USSR | 76.8 | 64.0 | 59.3 | 60.8 | |
| Production (bill. kwh) | 38.1 | 180.0 | 459.3 | 497.4 | 567.1 |
| % of the USSR | 78.3 | 61.6 | 62.1 | 62.1 | 58.1 |
| Petroleum (mill. tons) | 6.8 | 111.8 | 245.0 | 250.9 | 247.4 |
| % of the USSR | 21.8 | 75.6 | 69.4 | 66.5 | 53.9 |
| Natural gas (bill. cu. m.) | 0.7 | 37.5 | 131.0 | 136.2 | 111.0 |
| % of the USSR | 21.9 | 82.7 | 66.1 | 64.1 | 42.9 |
| Coal (mill. tons) | 105.8 | 269.6 | 205.7 | 312.6 | 314.4 |
| % of the USSR | 73.7 | 52.9 | 48.9 | 48.8 | 45.9 |
| **Metallurgy** | | | | | |
| Iron ore (mill. tons) | 21.5 | 67.3 | 138.3 | 145.2 | n.a. |
| % of the USSR | 71.9 | 63.5 | 70.7 | 71.5 | |
| Steel ingots (mill. tons) | 12.5 | 36.1 | 65.8 | 67.3 | 74.5 |
| % of the USSR | 68.3 | 55.3 | 56.7 | 55.7 | 54.7 |
| Rolled steel products (mill. tons) | 7.8 | 23.3 | 45.4 | 47.5 | n.a. |
| % of the USSR | 68.5 | 53.3 | 56.3 | 56.4 | |

(continued)

Table 6.1, continued

| European Soviet Production of | 1940 | 1960 | 1970 | 1971 | 1975 |
|---|---|---|---|---|---|
| Chemicals | | | | | |
| Caustic soda (mill. tons) | 0.15 | 0.64 | 1.6 | 1.66 | n.a. |
| % of the USSR | 78.9 | 83.0 | 82.5 | 82.0 | |
| Fertilizers (mill. tons) | 2.2 | 8.3 | 38.8 | 42.4 | n.a. |
| % of the USSR | 68.8 | 59.7 | 70.0 | 69.0 | |
| Synthetic fibers (mill. tons) | 0.011 | 0.169 | 0.51 | 0.56 | n.a. |
| % of the USSR | 100.0 | 79.6 | 81.1 | 82.3 | |
| Machinery | | | | | |
| Metal-cutting machines (thou. units) | 53.5 | 131.1 | 174.2 | 166.0 | n.a. |
| % of the USSR | 91.5 | 84.1 | 86.1 | 80.1 | |
| Tractors (thou. units) | 23.0 | 188.4 | 368.5 | 376.7 | n.a. |
| % of the USSR | 72.7 | 78.9 | 80.3 | 79.8 | |
| Tractor-drawn plows and seeders (thou. units) | 40.6 | 168.7 | 230.0 | 231.9 | n.a. |
| % of the USSR | 67.8 | 64.6 | 61.3 | 61.5 | |
| Combine-harvesters (thou. units) | 12.8 | 51.2 | 80.9 | 82.7 | n.a. |
| % of the USSR | 100.0 | 85.1 | 81.5 | 81.1 | |
| Timber and paper | | | | | |
| Lumber (mill. cu. m.) | 73.3 | 147.0 | 153.0 | 152.0 | 194.8 |
| % of the USSR | 62.0 | 56.2 | 51.1 | 50.9 | 50.1 |
| Cellulose (mill. tons) | 0.39 | 1.63 | 3.47 | 3.63 | n.a. |
| % of the USSR | 73.8 | 71.6 | 67.8 | 47.1 | |
| Paper and cardboard (mill. tons) | 0.8 | 2.44 | 4.99 | 5.24 | n.a. |
| % of the USSR | 83.1 | 75.7 | 74.5 | 74.0 | |

|  | | | | | |
|---|---|---|---|---|---|
| **Building materials** | | | | | |
| Cement (mill. tons) | 4.4 | 27.6 | 59.5 | 61.6 | 70.6 |
| % of the USSR | 78.9 | 60.6 | 62.5 | 61.4 | 61.3 |
| **Consumer goods** | | | | | |
| Cotton cloth (mill. m.) | 3,726.7 | 5,645.0 | 6,508.6 | 6,727.5 | 6,826.0 |
| % of the USSR | 94.3 | 88.4 | 87.0 | 87.2 | 86.9 |
| Woolen cloth (mill. m.) | 114.9 | 321.2 | 447.7 | 460.8 | n.a. |
| % of the USSR | 95.8 | 93.9 | 90.2 | 89.4 | n.a. |
| Silk cloth (mill. m.) | 65.3 | 707.5 | 975.1 | 970.9 | n.a. |
| % of the USSR | 84.5 | 87.3 | 78.5 | 76.3 | n.a. |
| Shoes (mill. pr.) | 177.6 | 316.0 | 494.7 | 499.9 | 494.0 |
| % of the USSR | 84.1 | 75.4 | 73.1 | 73.6 | 72.2 |
| Radios and radio equipment (mill. units) | 0.16 | 2.1 | 4.65 | 5.33 | n.a. |
| % of the USSR | 100.0 | 51.5 | 59.5 | 60.6 | n.a. |
| Refrigerators (mill. units) | 0.004 | 0.52 | 2.38 | 2.60 | n.a. |
| % of the USSR | 100.0 | 97.6 | 57.5 | 57.1 | n.a. |
| Washing machines (mill. units) | — | 0.58 | 3.14 | 2.36 | n.a. |
| % of the USSR | — | 64.8 | 59.9 | 58.1 | n.a. |
| Meat (mill. tons) | 1.06 | 3.17 | 5.3 | 6.14 | n.a. |
| % of the USSR | 70.7 | 71.9 | 74.2 | 74.9 | n.a. |
| Butter (mill. tons) | 0.13 | 0.54 | 0.72 | 0.75 | n.a. |
| % of the USSR | 58.1 | 72.5 | 74.1 | 73.5 | n.a. |

n.a. = not available.
Source: TsSU, Narodnoe Khoziaistvo SSSR 1922–1972 (Moscow, 1972), pp. 142 ff. (hereafter Narkhoz).

of the regional economy emerge quite clearly: a great increase in production has occurred in the European region, particularly in industrial sectors, but also—though to a significantly lesser degree—in agriculture; these increases have enabled the region to continue its traditional dominance of Soviet economic activity; and in the 1970s the relative share of the European region in Soviet production stabilized, after several decades of decline. These three features express the relatively limited or generally markedly decelerating degrees of locational shift in the spatial pattern of Soviet economic activity from the western and European to the eastern and Asiatic USSR, despite most impressive developments in many economic sectors in the east.

As Table 6.1 indicates, the European USSR accounted for more than half the total output of the major industrial products listed, except for natural gas, coal, and (marginally) timber. Indeed, in per capita terms the region significantly "underproduces" relatively few items: oil, nonferrous metals, and the simpler or more bulky capital and household goods, such as steel, cement, tractor-drawn plows and seeders, radios, refrigerators, and washing machines. Since 1975 there has been a dramatic shift eastward only in the case of one major product—oil, as a result of the tremendous expansion of output from the West Siberian field. In most other sectors the relative shift has been little more than marginal. Significantly, the European USSR maintains special supremacy in the field of manufactures, notably engineering, electrical and electronic products, chemicals, textiles and clothing, footwear, and processed foods. A wide range of Soviet manufactures is virtually entirely localized within the European region: automobiles, trucks, buses, trolleybuses, railway and subway cars, color television sets, tape recorders, cameras, and a variety of machinery.

The general trends in the regional economy over time are also clear: rapid and large-scale expansions in European regional industrial production have nevertheless yielded a parallel decline in the share of Soviet output, as a result of faster growth in other regions. Rates of absolute output increase and of relative decline vary, but broadly they have characterized the geography of Soviet industrial activity since the Revolution. The European dominance of energy (coal, electricity, hydrocarbon fuels), raw materials (timber), and basic manufactures (steel, cement) has been eroded more rapidly than has its role in the output of more sophisticated and higher-value manufactures because of different sectoral growth rates in other regions. Some new consumer products were introduced fairly rapidly, however, in new factories located outside the European USSR after World War II: radio equipment in the 1950s and refrigerators in the 1960s (see Table 6.1). By contrast, the most traditional of European Russian industries—textiles—shows the greatest location (in this sense, interregional) inertia.

Not all trends, though, are either regular or in the same direction. The European region became a relatively more important producer in the 1960s and 1970s of certain products, especially in the chemicals (such as synthetic fibers), engineering (such as tractors), and food processing (such as dairy and meat products) industries. Greatest fluctuation has been recorded by the petroleum and natural gas industries: the European USSR rose rapidly to preeminence in the 1950s and 1960s but lost its dominant position in the 1970s. Indeed, the total output of oil and gas in the region has begun to decline. Such a trend, however, is not yet a widespread feature of the European Soviet industrial economy as a whole, although the production of coal, steel, and cotton textiles leveled out in the 1970s. More typical is likely to be the maintenance of the region's long-term position in manufacturing, particularly since the growth rate of the Soviet economy as a whole is slowing significantly.

Table 6.2 summarizes certain key indexes of the importance of the European USSR in agriculture. The total area of farmland within the region currently exceeds 190 million hectares. Though equal to only 35 percent of all Soviet agricultural land, its real significance lies in its combination of comparatively high fertility, adequate water supply, and favorable annual accumulated temperatures.[1] The European USSR boasts almost 60 percent of the country's arable land and 90 percent of its hay-producing meadow, despite the marked decrease in the regional share of Soviet farmland in the 1950s following the rapid extension of cultivation into non-European semiarid areas beyond the Urals during the Khrushchev period. As is apparent from Table 6.2, the European USSR also experienced substantial extension of its farm area, by almost 18 million hectares in that period, through a combination of increased drainage of waterlogged areas in the northwest, and more widespread irrigation and extended cultivation of semiarid steppes in the southeast. However, the continued preeminence of the region lies primarily in the comparative quality of the land and substantially improved farm practice.

Production figures for major Soviet crops support such a conclusion and indicate above-average yields. The region contributes more than 70 percent of all Soviet grain, 74 percent of the vegetables, 87 percent of potatoes, and 97 percent of the sugar beets (see Table 6.2). Two-thirds of the country's fruit production from state and collective farms originates from areas west of the Urals and north of the Caucasus, despite favorable regional conditions for such crops, including wine and table grapes, in

TABLE 6.2

Indexes of Agricultural Change: European USSR, 1940-71

| | Total Sown Arable Land (mill. ha.) | | | Production (mill. tons) 1970-71 | | | | Yields (metric centners per ha.) | | | | | | | |
|---|---|---|---|---|---|---|---|---|---|---|---|---|---|---|---|
| | | | | | Sugar | | | Grains | | Sugar Beets | | Potatoes | | Vegetables | |
| | 1940 | 1965 | 1970 | Grains | Beets | Potatoes | Vegetables | A | B | A | B | A | B | A | B |
| USSR | 150.6 | 209.1 | 223.7 | 186.8 | 78.9 | 96.8 | 21.2 | 8.6 | 15.6 | 146 | 237 | 99 | 120 | 91 | 138 |
| European USSR | 109.3 | 124.9 | 125.51 | 128.2 | 73.2 | 80.4 | 15.5 | n.a. | n.a. | n.a. | n.a. | n.a. | n.a. | n.a. | n.a. |
| RSFSR | | | | | | | | | | | | | | | |
| Northwest | 3.8 | 2.8 | 2.9 | 1.2 | — | 3.8 | 0.73 | 6.8 | 12.9 | — | — | 118 | 157 | 61 | 252 |
| Central | 13.1 | 13.9 | 13.9 | 9.5 | — | 15.0 | 2.13 | 7.8 | 14.2 | 85 | 139 | 118 | 123 | 90 | 163 |
| Volga-Viatka | 6.4 | 6.6 | 6.5 | 4.9 | 0.3 | 5.9 | 0.63 | 9.2 | 12.6 | — | 102 | 81 | 116 | 101 | 156 |
| Central Chernozem | 8.6 | 10.9 | 10.9 | 11.3 | 12.1 | 4.3 | 0.70 | 8.7 | 19.9 | 98 | 171 | 83 | 101 | 93 | 110 |
| Povolzh'e | 21.1 | 27.9 | 27.9 | 28.5 | 2.7 | 7.8 | 1.36 | 7.5 | 15.6 | 59 | 137 | 50 | 130 | 71 | 154 |
| N. Caucasus | 12.5 | 16.2 | 15.8 | 20.8 | 5.8 | 1.8 | 1.78 | 10.4 | 24.5 | 174 | 252 | 48 | 99 | 74 | 115 |
| Estonia | 0.9 | 0.77 | 0.9 | 0.9 | — | 1.4 | 0.13 | 11.5 | 21.3 | — | — | 147 | 178 | n.a. | n.a. |
| Latvia | 1.9 | 1.55 | 1.6 | 1.6 | 0.23 | 1.9 | 0.20 | 12.1 | 23.1 | n.a. | n.a. | 151 | 160 | n.a. | n.a. |
| Lithuania | 2.5 | 2.4 | 2.4 | 2.5 | 0.55 | 2.5 | 0.28 | 9.4 | 26.6 | n.a. | n.a. | 129 | 148 | n.a. | n.a. |
| Belorussia | 5.2 | 6.0 | 6.2 | 5.4 | 0.8 | 12.3 | 0.62 | 8.0 | 21.4 | n.a. | n.a. | 128 | 130 | n.a. | n.a. |
| Moldavia | 2.0 | 1.9 | 1.9 | 2.2 | 2.6 | 0.3 | 0.63 | 10.8 | 29.3 | 89 | 287 | n.a. | n.a. | n.a. | n.a. |
| Ukraine | 31.3 | 33.8 | 34.1 | 39.4 | 46.1 | 23.4 | 6.23 | 12.4 | 23.4 | 159 | 280 | 101 | 99 | 74 | 115 |

A = 1940; B = 1970.

n.a. = not available.

Sources: <u>Narkhoz</u>, various years.

Transcaucasia and Central Asia. Figures for yields show the European region's higher productivity per hectare. By Soviet standards, farms in the Central Chernozem and North Caucasus economic regions and in the entire belt of western, non-Russian republics between the Baltic and the Black Seas excel in grain yields. These republics, with the Northwest and Povolzh'e economic regions, also lead in potato yields, while the Ukraine and Moldavia have high sugar beet yields. Although European supremacy in livestock production is not quite so marked, it is impressive: about 73 percent of Soviet milk, 70 percent of eggs, 68 percent of meat, and 44 percent of wool come from the region's farms.

## ECONOMICS AND THE FACTORS OF DEVELOPMENT AND CHANGE

Viewed in the perspective of the years since the Revolution, the dominance of the western region was destined to be eroded and to be replaced by a spatially more "balanced" or "even" distribution—a much wider diffusion—of economic activity. In broad terms the period of Soviet administration has largely seen a significant "match" between policy and natural resource potentials at the macrogeographic levels.

First, Soviet regional development policy—rooted in Lenin's principles for electrification and industrial location and later refined or extended in the 1920s and 1930s by Gosplan and economics experts close to this approach—determined that industry, in particular, should be allocated among regions in greater accordance with the geographic distribution of natural resources.

Second, over time, various combinations of economic, social, ethnic, and strategic considerations have interacted with the more persistently dominant allocations of most investment to group "A" heavy industries—which are relatively more energy- and material-intensive—to support the rationale, if not the implementation, of such a policy.

Third, the larger part of known Soviet natural resources, at least for industry, lay—and still lie—in the eastern regions: upward of 80 percent of all energy resources, whether coal (over 90 percent), hydroelectric power (over 80 percent), or hydrocarbon fuels (at least 60 percent); virtually all significant nonferrous metals; and, with the exception of potash and apatite, most non-metallic minerals used in the chemicals industries.

Clearly, the situation in the early 1900s, when 96.5 percent of all Russian factory industry was localized in the European area, was destined never to return after the Revolution. And the constantly

declining contribution that the European region has made to the
Soviet economy since the 1920s—despite phenomenal regional growth
by any yardstick—stands as broad testimony to the success of policy implementation in the harnessing and the processing of natural
resources in other regions.

This said, however, one can argue justifiably that Soviet
policy aspirations, almost throughout peacetime, have exceeded the
real scales and rates of development achieved outside the European
USSR in most economic sectors. Indeed, generally speaking, the
"East-West problem of planning and implementing spatial change
in the USSR has mostly been a struggle for the containment of economic growth in the Western region. Such a situation remains true
despite three groups of factors that have militated against development there: apparent periodic policy "neglect" of the European
area, especially when eastern development is being accelerated:
Khrushchev's extension of arable land into Kazakhstan and West
Siberia rather than intensification of farming in the existing European lands is a case in point; the impact of shorter-term external
factors having relatively longer-term internal (Soviet) consequences:
in particular, the devastation of much of the area southwest of the
Leningrad-Stalingrad (now Volgograd) line during the Nazi occupation of 1941-44; and the effects of long-term constraints on
European-regional development, notably evident in the growing
scarcities of energy, water, and other resources.

Bearing these "anti-processes" in mind, it is clear in historical perspective that the continuity in the functional preeminence
of the European USSR results largely from the interaction of
decision-making processes and the region's positive balance of
developmental advantages. Above all, the region contains the hub
of the Soviet Union, Moscow, undoubtedly the world's most powerful center of politicoeconomic control. Its decision makers must
interact, in addition, with more numerous decision makers operating in both more numerous and more influential centers within the
European region than exist within any other Soviet region—if not,
indeed, within all other regions and republics combined. These
"provincial" decision makers, moreover, can wield collectively a
greater range of real or perceived ideological, national-ethnic,
social, and economic arguments in favor of development in the
area than can their counterparts from other regions. Moreover,
the European region suffers from fewer of the country's widespread
"antiresources"—permafrost, aridity, marshland, and desolate
mountains, all of which are associated with extreme regional labor
deficiencies and high development threshold costs—and it suffers
them both less acutely and less extensively than do other regions.
Taken together, these two broad groups of factors basically result

in a convergence of powerful decision-making processes and of developmental advantages that have tended to sustain, rather than to weaken, the position of the European USSR in the investment bargaining process.

Perhaps even more important, the diversity and complexity of the subregional economies that make up the Western region as a whole expose it less sensitively than other Soviet regions to the consequences of marked fluctuations (or "campaigns") in national structural or regional policies. For example, vacillation in investment-location emphasis between greater regional structural specialization and greater regional self-sufficiency, or between more "economic" and more "ethnic" areas for development, generally have less impact on growth in the European USSR than they do anywhere else. In other words, development to satisfy almost any criterion of Soviet policy usually means some, if not substantial, new construction or expansion within the European region, whereas elsewhere it frequently entails more choice between non-European regions.

Not surprisingly, the balance sheet of regional advantages and disadvantages is complex. Space permits no more than a broad outline of the "accounts." Although an attempt is made to separate items on the ledger, they interact almost inseparably to share the real, and largely unique, European Soviet regional development environment. Broadly, one can group them under the following headings: the supply of the factors of production; costs; market demand; transport and accessibility; control functions; the "scientific and technical revolution"; and international integration. (An important aspect of human welfare is discussed in a separate chapter of this volume.)

Supply of Factors of Production

Supply considerations relate to the availability of the natural, human, and capital resources to support the region's economic life. The natural resource endowment of the European USSR exhibits wide diversity in the types of resources available, their scale, and their quality. By Soviet standards—but certainly not by world standards—the per capita reserves of nonrenewal industrial resources in the region are low. As a result of long-term, rising, and still often the highest regional rates of extraction, those reserves are declining faster, certainly, than in the eastern USSR. For instance, at current rates of mining, the proven coal deposits of the European region will remain productive for some 240 years, while total proven and workable Soviet reserves may well last for upward of 500 years. Nonetheless, this should not obscure two fundamental facts: the region has long enjoyed the benefit of adequate supplies of a wide range of nonrenewable, as well as renewable, resources; and only recently have the sustained rate, scale, and diversity of economic development begun to convert the region into one of deficit, particularly for energy.

Indeed, the industrialization of the European USSR, especially the growth there of Group "A" "heavy" or "capital-goods" industries, has been facilitated preeminently by the availability of abundant coal, oil, gas, iron ore, manganese, mineral salts, apatite, timber, and—not least—water. Besides adequate supplies, further advantages have been the complementarity of resources in type and quality as well as in location, thus permitting both the substitution of one source for another to achieve sustained growth when existing "traditional" sources set constraints, and the development of diverse industrial sectors in several subregions within the European USSR.

Coal, of course, has been the backbone of the regional economy. Two major fields—the Donbas and the Moscow—delivered 25 million tons in the early 1920s, 104 million tons in 1940, and more than 265 million tons in 1976. Mining commenced at the difficult subarctic Pechora field just before World War II, and the field produces more than 20 million tons today. By far the most significant field is, of course, the Donbas. Currently it supplies 70 percent of the European regional and one-third of all Soviet coal (about 230 million tons). Although its coking coals are consumed primarily by metallurgical industries within the Donbas, its other high-quality bituminous coals are shipped to industries throughout the European USSR, except for the central Volga Basin, which receives some shipments from the eastern Urals. The Moscow and Pechora fields complement the Donbas and meet highly concentrated industrial and urban thermal power station demand mainly in the Central and Northwest regions, respectively, thereby freeing much-needed railway carrying capacity between Kursk and Moscow. Without these coal resources the postwar scale of development of the iron and steel and engineering industries in the European USSR would have been impossible.

Complementing coal as a source of energy and as raw materials are the region's oil and natural gas. Oil production commenced in the western Ukraine as far back as 1859, but until the major development of the Volga field in the 1950s, most oil and gas consumed within the region was shipped from its Caucasian and Caspian Sea margins, from Groznyi and Baku. The latter, traditionally the main producer, now supplies 50 million tons of oil annually—double its 1940 capacity—while output from the Volga

field has been raised from 1.8 million to almost 220 million tons
in the same period.  Although, by and large, these quantities have
been sufficient to sustain the rapid growth of chemical industries
in the European USSR, increased oil exports and the lower quality
of oils, from the Volga field especially, have begun to act as severe
constraints on regional supply, necessitating greater flows of West
Siberian oil into the region.

European natural gas supplies are relatively more favorable,
not only in quantity but also in their more widespread location:
about equal supplies come from the Volga and Ukrainian (Shebelinka)
fields (15-20 percent of Soviet, 30 percent of European regional
supplies), while the Krasnodar-Stavropol' (North Caucasian) field
supplies about 25 and 40 percent, respectively.  Although gas,
like oil, may be readily piped over long distances, this greater
diversity of sources has resulted in fewer pipeline bottlenecks than
has been the case with oil supplies, which go from the one Volga
field to both Soviet and East European markets.

Electrification in the European region has been the prime
force not only in regional industrialization but also in facilitating
overall Soviet technical progress, as well as modernization in
agriculture and transport.  Fortunately, power generation in the
region has enjoyed the advantage of easy access to both adequate
and diversified sources of electricity that have proved to be both
complementary and competitive substitutes.  While this has played
an active role in reducing the rise in power costs, its significance
perhaps lies mainly in opportunity cost terms:  the harnessing of
alternative sources—especially waterpower and natural gas—has
released major coal and oil supplies for use as raw materials in
chemicals and as metal-reduction agents in steel and metal-foundry
industries.  Diversification of the power base commenced in the
1920s under the GOELRO plan.  Although Donbas and Moscow coals
remained the main sources of thermal-power generation, electricity
prior to World War II came in increasing quantities from peat-
burning stations around Kalinin and Shatura (north and east of
Moscow, respectively) and hydroelectric power stations on the
upper Volga (Dubna, Uglich, and Rybinsk) and at the Dnieper bend
(Zaporozh'e).

Since 1950 further diversification has taken place, and while
coal is still the major electricity-generating source in the European
USSR, cheaper and more convenient energy sources have been
tapped more vigorously.  In particular natural gas from the North
Caucasus and Ukraine has been introduced into new stations or has
replaced coal in older thermal power stations, especially in the
Central Chernozem, Central, Baltic, Belorussian, Northwest
(Leningrad), and Southwest (Ukrainian) economic regions.  Since

1954 nuclear power stations have made their appearance, mostly in the Central and Central Chernozem regions, again to relieve pressure on coal transport. Far more significant, however, is the power supplied from the "cascades" of hydroelectric power stations that, from 1954 to 1974, converted the Dnieper River within the Ukraine and the Volga River between Gorkii and Volgograd virtually into two series of man-made lakes.

One of the major deficiencies in the European region's industrial base is the almost total absence of major nonferrous metals. In a sense, however, this is a less critical factor in the regional economy, since nonferrous metallurgy is a highly capital-intensive and power-intensive sector that does not generate large-scale local multiplier effects, and would impose very serious strains on the energy supply and environment in this populous, urbanized region. Moreover, small quantities of refined metal, supplied from neighboring regions such as the Urals, impose only limited burdens on Soviet railways—certainly by comparison with energy transport. The only notable nonferrous metal resource of the region is bauxite, mined to the east of Leningrad around Boksitogorsk and, more recently, Pikalevo. Until the 1950s supplies sufficed to support alumina-aluminum industries in the European USSR. Subsequently, however, the comparatively rapid growth of aluminum production to serve the aerospace industry has increasingly outstripped the capacity of these mines by a widening margin. The largest plants in the region now depend wholly upon imports: the Volgograd aluminum plant obtains alumina from Hungary, while the Zaporozh'e complex processes raw bauxite transported by sea from Greece and from Guinea.

Quite the opposite situation exists with respect to ferrous metallurgy. The region is richly endowed with the larger part of the Soviet Union's comparatively high-quality proven reserves— reserves that at current extraction rates can support steelmaking for at least 450 years. Iron ore mining exhibits the same subregional European pattern as does steelmaking: high concentration in one subregion (the Donbas-lower Dnieper area) with significant deposits elsewhere. Ukrainian ore output has been raised from 20 million tons in 1940 to more than 125 million tons in 1980, but represents a decreasing proportion of Soviet iron ore production (from two-thirds to little more than half). The proportion of European Soviet iron and steel capacity that is dependent on Ukrainian ore has declined even more sharply (as capacity has expanded), from about 96 percent in 1940 to about 50 percent in 1980. These two trends result largely from two sets of developments. The first is the greatly increased commitment of ore, especially from the huge Krivoi Rog mines, to export, mainly to support the growth of East European steel industries. From 1949 to 1979, for example, this producer supplied 100 million tons of ore to steelworks in Polish Upper Silesia.[2] The second is the rapid growth of iron ore mining in the European RSFSR, which, since 1970, has surpassed both Siberia and the Urals to become the second largest supplier in the USSR. Output rose from 1 million tons in 1940 to more than 45 million tons in 1980. The "traditional" European Russian source of iron ores, along the Tula-Lipetsk axis, has been eclipsed since the 1950s by the development of major mines in the Kola Peninsula, to supply the Northwest region's integrated steelworks at Cherepovets, and by the even greater exploitation of the ores of the Kursk magnetic anomaly. Ore from the latter is being shipped to an expanded works at Lipetsk, which is likely to become the largest integrated steel plant in the European USSR.

Although delays in the decision to construct major new steel capacity near the Kursk magnetic anomaly have resulted from divided planning, political, and economic opinions about key investment allocations between the Asiatic and European USSR, a very real practical constraint is water supply. For the Kursk area lies in the Central Chernozem, on the margins of the "moisture-deficient" USSR. This is a broadening wedge of country stretching eastward from southern Moldavia through the southern and most of the eastern Ukraine to embrace the Central Chernozem and North Caucasus regions and the Povolsh'e south of Kuibyshev. These areas rely heavily on river water supplies carried from the moisture-surplus central and northern subregions, by the Dnieper, Don, and Volga systems. Were this supply not available, the concentrated urban-industrial use of water in the larger cities, and the Donbas-Dnieper bend in particular, would have rapidly depleted groundwater and artesian well supplies long ago. As it is, even with good river supplies, the competition among agricultural, industrial, and urban uses of water has become serious enough throughout a broad belt between the Moscow-Gorkii line on the north and the Odessa-Volgograd line on the south to cause periodic shortages.

In addition, within this zone industrial pollutants from the chemicals, metallurgical, and mining industries critically reduce the availability of pure or high-quality water for farming purposes, especially in the southern part of the region, where irrigation is either essential or desirable. Indeed, agriculture in the European region faces the general constraint imposed by the "maldistribution" of physical environment that results from the poor spatial association between growing temperatures and adequate water supplies. On the one hand, areas lying broadly north of a line from

Brest through Gomel' in Belorussia to Iaroslavl' have excess
moisture, marshland, and lakes, and the climate is unfavorable
for the ripening of many crops. And industry in such areas can be
adversely affected by the winter freeze. But the warmest southern
European areas with the best chernozem and brown-earth soils are
those liable to moisture deficiency. Tremendous industrial demands in these areas, especially between Krivoi Rog and Volgograd,
would have been impossible to meet without the construction of
multipurpose dams on the Dnieper, Volga, and Don. Al this, however, is not to say that more northern areas do not suffer water-
supply problems. Moscow, lying close to the watershed of these
three rivers, has seriously depleted artesian water.[3] And Leningrad's unhealthy "Venetian" situation is of long standing.[4]

A critically important factor of production within the European
region is its large and skilled labor force. Outside the region the
only areas of the Soviet Union that still possess labor reserves
sufficient to support labor-intensive agriculture and industries are
Transcaucasia and Central Asia. None, however, can rival the
European USSR either in the numerical strength of the regional
labor force or in its skills. From the 1920s to the 1960s a highly
significant factor contributing to Soviet economic growth overall
was the increased employment of labor in the European USSR in
nonfarm occupations. Since the 1960s the emphasis has been shifted
to increased labor productivity as the labor market at the broad
regional and national levels has become tighter. However, with the
extremely high capitalization of most activities necessary in the
development of the eastern regions of the RSFSR to offset acute
labor shortages there, one can expect the European region to gain
further in development through its favorable thresholds for improved productivity from a far larger labor force. Nevertheless,
one should not be misled into thinking that labor supply has been,
or is, adequate everywhere in the European region all the time.
The picture is varied.

First of all, population has increased relatively slowly since
the 1920s. Although voluntary and involuntary transfers of labor
to develop Siberia, the Far East, and the Virgin Lands have undoubtedly depressed the rate of population growth west of the Urals,
a far more significant factor has been high periodic loss of life.
World War I, the Revolution and the Civil War, the elimination of
kulaks, and the purges of the 1930s all took their toll of people of
productive age. Yet that loss was small compared with the 20 million killed during World War II. The consequences for the European region are readily apparent from Table 6.3. Even 14 years
after the end of World War II, the region contained slightly fewer
people than in 1940, despite the relatively stable annual rate of

natural increase of 13-16 per 1,000 between 1945 and 1959. Marginally, too, population was reduced in the western Ukraine, Belorussia, and Lithuania by Polish emigration in 1945, following the international boundary changes, but the major factor in the regional demographic picture remains the direct war losses and subsequent lost births.

It has been estimated that the actual shortfall of population from the expected peacetime population living in the Moscow city region alone is currently 5-10 million people as a result of World War II.[5] In general a large excess of women over men has resulted in lower marriage and birth rates, with working people currently in the 25-40 and over-50 age groups in abnormally short supply. Table 6.3 clearly shows that the legacies of war were felt throughout all the economic regions of the European RSFSR (save the North Caucasus and Povolzh'e, which in part escaped Nazi occupation), the Southwest (in the Ukraine), and Belorussia.

Peacetime population growth has been substantial, and since the mid-1960s has been marginally augmented by the net return flows of migrants from the Asiatic USSR. Nevertheless, a markedly declining birth rate slowed regional population growth dramatically in the 1970s and, as employment growth continued at a high rate in nonfarm (and hence urban-centered) occupations, the demand for labor was met mostly by rural-urban migration (and by commuting) and by the increased engagement of women in the productive process, as much on the farm as off it. Although increased mechanization in agriculture has facilitated these trends, on balance most larger cities within the European region suffer labor shortages. The causes go beyond population constraints per se. Contributory factors are that the substitution of capital equipment, whether mechanical or automated, has proceeded too slowly in both farm and nonfarm sectors, with the result that labor productivity has risen, but not by enough, and that the control has been imposed on permanent migration into larger cities, such as Moscow, Leningrad, Kiev, and Kharkov.

Urban labor scarcity became a sufficiently serious constraint on economic growth for Gosplan to set its research group, SOPS (Council for the Organization of Productive Forces), the task of finding out whether and where labor surpluses existed in the European region. The resulting study clearly showed that labor resources were unevenly employed.[6] While labor shortages hampered further growth in larger cities, hundreds of smaller towns in predominantly rural regions had been bypassed not only by the mainstream of industrialization but also by the more powerful attractive force of urbanization from major cities.

TABLE 6.3

Population Growth and Change: European USSR, 1940-77
(thousands)

| | 1940 | 1959 | 1970 | 1977 |
|---|---|---|---|---|
| USSR | 194,077 | 208,827 | 241,720 | 257,824 |
| European RSFSR | 82,282 | 80,180 | 88,810 | n.a. |
| Northwest | 11,204 | 10,865 | 12,157 | n.a. |
| Center | 27,044 | 25,718 | 27,652 | n.a. |
| Volga-Viatka | 8,848 | 8,252 | 8,348 | n.a. |
| Central Chernozem | 9,043 | 7,769 | 7,998 | n.a. |
| Povolzh'e | 15,649 | 15,975 | 18,374 | n.a. |
| North Caucasus | 10,494 | 11,601 | 14,281 | n.a. |
| Ukraine | 41,340 | 41,923 | 47,126 | 49,300 |
| Donets-Dnieper | 16,387 | 17,766 | 20,057 | n.a. |
| Southwest | 19,982 | 19,082 | 20,689 | n.a. |
| South | 4,971 | 5,075 | 6,380 | n.a. |
| Belorussia | 9,046 | 8,056 | 9,002 | 9,414 |
| Baltic republics[a] | 5,865 | 6,612 | 7,580 | n.a. |
| Lithuania | 2,925 | 2,711 | 3,128 | 3,342 |
| Latvia | 1,886 | 2,093 | 2,364 | 2,512 |
| Estonia | 1,054 | 1,197 | 1,356 | 1,447 |
| Moldavia | 2,468 | 2,885 | 3,569 | 3,885 |
| European USSR[b] | 144,050 | 143,950 | 160,530 | |

n.a. = not available.

[a]Figures for 1959, 1970, and 1977 include the population of Kaliningrad oblast of the RSFSR.

[b]Includes relevant parts of the Urals economic region.

Sources: Narkhoz for various years.

Table 6.4 presents data on recent trends in the proportions of rural population living in the various republics, regions, and oblasts of the European USSR. Such data are only rough guides to the distribution of latent or real labor reserves. First, the proportion of rural population is itself only an indirect index—in the absence of Soviet occupational data by oblasts (let alone raions)—of the relative importance of farm versus nonfarm occupations. In particular, they give no indication of variations among oblasts in agricultural labor productivity, land-use intensity, rural population densities, rural-urban commuting, or age-sex structure—all of

TABLE 6.4

Percentages of Rural Population: Selected Oblasts
of European USSR, 1959-77

|  | 1959 | 1970 | 1977 |
|---|---|---|---|
| RSFSR | 48 | 38 | 31 |
| Northwest | 35 | 27 | n.a. |
| Arkhangel'sk | 47 | 34 | 27 |
| (Nenets AO) | (54) | (45) | (40) |
| Vologda | 65 | 52 | 28 |
| Leningrad oblast* | 50 | 39 | 36 |
| Murmansk | 8 | 11 | 11 |
| Novgorod | 62 | 47 | 37 |
| Pskov | 73 | 57 | 46 |
| Karelian ASSR | 37 | 31 | 23 |
| Komi ASSR | 41 | 38 | 29 |
| Central | 41 | 29 | n.a. |
| Briansk | 65 | 53 | 42 |
| Vladimir | 43 | 32 | 26 |
| Iaroslavl' | 42 | 30 | 23 |
| Ivanovo | 34 | 25 | 20 |
| Kalinin | 56 | 43 | 35 |
| Kaluga | 63 | 48 | 39 |
| Kostroma | 60 | 47 | 37 |
| Moscow oblast* | 44 | 31 | 27 |
| Orel | 76 | 61 | 47 |
| Riazan' | 70 | 53 | 42 |
| Smolensk | 68 | 52 | 40 |
| Tula | 40 | 29 | 22 |
| Volga-Viatka | 61 | 47 | n.a. |
| Gorkii | 48 | 35 | 28 |
| Kirov | 63 | 45 | 36 |
| Mari ASSR | 72 | 59 | 46 |
| Mordov ASSR | 82 | 64 | 55 |
| Chuvash ASSR | 76 | 64 | 55 |
| Central Chernozem | 73 | 60 | n.a. |
| Belgorod | 80 | 65 | 50 |
| Voronezh | 65 | 54 | 46 |

(continued)

Table 6.4, continued

|  | 1959 | 1970 | 1977 |
|---|---|---|---|
| Kursk | 80 | 67 | 53 |
| Lipetsk | 70 | 56 | 45 |
| Tambov | 76 | 61 | 41 |
| Povolzh'e | 54 | 43 | n.a. |
| Astrakhan' | 48 | 39 | 32 |
| Volgograd | 46 | 34 | 28 |
| Kuibyshev | 38 | 28 | 22 |
| Penza | 67 | 56 | 47 |
| Saratov | 46 | 35 | 28 |
| Ulianovsk | 64 | 48 | 37 |
| Bashkir ASSR | 62 | 52 | 43 |
| Kalmyk ASSR | 79 | 66 | 23 |
| Tatar ASSR | 58 | 48 | 38 |
| North Caucasus | 57 | 50 | n.a. |
| Krasnodar Krai | 51 | 53 | 49 |
| (Adygei AO) | (68) | (60) | (53) |
| Stavropol Krai | 69 | 58 | 51 |
| (Karachaevo-Cherkessy AO) | (77) | (67) | (58) |
| Rostov | 43 | 37 | 31 |
| Dagestan ASSR | 70 | 65 | 61 |
| Kabardino-Balkar ASSR | 60 | 52 | 42 |
| Severo-Osetian ASSR | 47 | 36 | 32 |
| Checheno-Ingush ASSR | 59 | 58 | 56 |
| Ukraine | 54 | 45 | 39 |
| Donets-Dnieper | 37 | 30 | n.a. |
| Voroshilovgrad | 21 | 17 | 15 |
| Dnepropetrovsk | 30 | 24 | 20 |
| Donetsk | 14 | 13 | 11 |
| Zaporozh'e | 43 | 34 | 28 |
| Kirovograd | 70 | 56 | 49 |
| Poltava | 70 | 60 | 51 |
| Sumy | 68 | 56 | 50 |
| Kharkov | 38 | 31 | 26 |
| Southwest | 71 | 62 | n.a. |
| Vinnitsa | 83 | 75 | 67 |
| Volyn' | 74 | 68 | 62 |

|              | 1959 | 1970 | 1977 |
|--------------|------|------|------|
| Zhitomir | 74 | 65 | 57 |
| Zakarpatskaia | 71 | 70 | 63 |
| Ivano-Frankovsk | 77 | 69 | 65 |
| Khmelnitskii | 81 | 73 | 66 |
| Kiev oblast* | 74 | 64 | 56 |
| L'vov | 61 | 53 | 48 |
| Rovno | 83 | 72 | 67 |
| Ternopol' | 83 | 77 | 71 |
| Cherkassy | 77 | 63 | 56 |
| Chernigov | 78 | 65 | 57 |
| Chernovtsy | 74 | 65 | 63 |
| South | 51 | 43 | n.a. |
| Crimea | 35 | 35 | 33 |
| Nikolaev | 60 | 47 | 39 |
| Odessa | 53 | 44 | 39 |
| Kherson | 60 | 46 | 40 |
| Belorussia | 69 | 57 | 47 |
| Brest | 76 | 65 | 56 |
| Vitebsk | 68 | 54 | 45 |
| Gomel' | 72 | 60 | 50 |
| Grodno | 77 | 67 | 59 |
| Minsk oblast* | 81 | 73 | 66 |
| Mogilev | 69 | 57 | 46 |
| Lithuania | 51 | 50 | 42 |
| Latvia | 44 | 38 | 33 |
| Estonia | 44 | 35 | 31 |
| Moldavia | 78 | 68 | 62 |
| Kaliningrad oblast | 35 | 27 | 23 |

*Cities of Leningrad, Moscow, Kiev, and Minsk are omitted.

Parentheses indicate subdivision of the preceding administrative unit.

n.a. = not available.

Sources: Narkhoz for various years.

which are variables in labor supply. Second, one must adopt a very arbitrary percentage figure in judging whether an area may contain a labor surplus. Under current technological conditions, however, one can hazard a guess that labor reserves still exist in areas that substantially exceed the RSFSR average of 30 percent rural population, particularly since this figure is high by the standards of regions of advanced economic development in Western Europe and North America. Here, therefore, the arbitrary figure of 40 percent is adopted to indicate the very minimum of areas with rural labor reserves in the European USSR.

Table 6.4 shows clearly that an extensive belt of the better agricultural areas of the southern USSR contains rural populations that still exceed 40 percent of the total population: Moldavia; the west, central, and northern Ukraine (north of an Odessa-Kharkov line); the North Caucasus; the Central Chernozem region (marginally); and adjacent southern oblasts of the Central (Moscow) region like Briansk, Orel, and Riazan'.

The SOPS study led, in part, to a greater emphasis in the Ninth (1971-75) and Tenth (1976-80) Five-Year Plans on the allocation of investments to secondary and tertiary activities, especially the more labor-intensive, in smaller towns and more rural areas of the region. It is too early to judge the effectiveness of this policy in hastening the absorption of rural labor reserves. Nevertheless, development has diffused an absolute decline in the rural population in all areas of the European USSR since at least the mid- or late-1960s, though a relative decrease has been apparent everywhere since 1959 (see Table 6.4). Indeed, the impact of urbanization in this period is especially noticeable in the sharp decline in the proportion of rural populations in a central belt that comprises the Central Chernozem and much of Volga-Viatka, Orel, and Riazan' oblasts, though outliers occur elsewhere, notably in the areas farther from the main metropolitan centers of Leningrad and Moscow than from Novgorod, Pskov, and Vologda oblasts.

Indeed, Table 6.4 suggests the operation of two factors in the economic environment: the more effective employment of rural labor reserves in nonfarm work since 1959, and the absorption by that more effective employment of a much larger surplus of rural labor (from areas with more than 40 percent rural population in 1959, which, in the early 1960s, extended virtually over the entire European USSR). The exceptions were few. Apart from the major cities, only the Donbas, the Tula area, and the European North (Karelian and Komi ASSRs, Murmansk) did not have rural labor reserves. In the future, labor supply will become a more stringent constraint on regional development.

Costs

Productivity lies at the heart of issues relating to cost, whether interpreted narrowly as product-plus-delivery and investment cost, or widely as both social and economic cost. On either score the European Soviet economic "landscape" forms an intricate mosaic. For even if we must ignore hidden or "artificial" cost variations that arise from arbitrary or subsidized input, product, or service pricing and from zonal (regional) pricing, the pattern of real regional cost advantages and disadvantages is still difficult to unravel. In the most general terms the European regional disadvantages within the country are higher production costs, especially of natural resources and standardized manufactures, and higher unit investment costs of modernizing older, smaller-scale plant. On the other hand, the regional advantages lie in lower delivery costs on foods and manufactures, closer contact with the capital and consumer markets for quality and custom-made products, and lower investment costs in welfare and social infrastructure. Only an indication of the many complexities can be given here.

Higher production costs arise in more economic sectors in the European region than elsewhere, and stem from several factors. One of the most common expressions of higher costs is the higher level of manning—and hence lower labor productivity—a factor of particular significance when the "wage fund" is a major variable in the economics of most enterprises. Usually, though, higher labor inputs per unit of output reflect other, deeper causes related to organization, lower levels of capitalization, "inherited" or outdated plant, smaller operational scales, and less favorable physical properties of mineral deposits. For example, the European region's agriculture is dominated to a greater extent than in most other Soviet regions by collective (kolkhoz) as opposed to state (sovkhoz) farms. And since labor productivity is higher on the sovkhozy than on the kolkhozy by margins of 5-60 percent for nearly all crop and livestock products, the European USSR generally is less competitive on this score. However, some areas in the region have the highest labor productivity in the USSR for certain crops—for example, the southern Ukraine and North Caucasus in grain and the Baltic republics in milk production, while the Donets-Dnieper, North Caucasus, and Central Chernozem can rival Central Asia and Kazakhstan in sugar beet productivity per worker, regardless of farm type. Yet often the higher yields per hectare and the lower wages in the European USSR—certainly by comparison with the eastern RSFSR—combine to compensate partially or totally for lower labor productivity.

The same cannot necessarily be said, for instance, for the production of industrial minerals. Differences in coal production costs are often increased, rather than reduced, by physical and technological conditions. By far the most expensive coal in the USSR is raised to the pitheads of European mines. Labor productivity is the lowest in the country for several reasons. All coal is shaft-mined, which increases manning levels and costs of ventilation and water pumping. Although these conditions also exist in mines in Karaganda and the Kuzbas, the latter do not have the disadvantages of more disturbed geological conditions and relatively thinner seams or worked-out thicker seams—situations commonly found in the Donbas and Moscow Basin. Yet the major factor is that many thick seams in the east can be extracted at very low cost by highly mechanized strip-mine methods. Under conditions of scarce equipment supply, the areas in the east where mechanization would have greatest impact (especially in view of the labor shortage) received priority over European mines. Thus one ton of coal from the European mines costs 10-70 percent more than the Soviet average. With the single exception of deep-mined far eastern coal, the eastern regions can produce coal that at the pithead costs 5-30 percent below average from shaft mines and 45-75 percent below average from open-cast mines.

Partly for these reasons, oil and gas have been substituted progressively for coal in the supply of energy to the European USSR. And that tendency is reinforced by the highest efficiencies of hydrocarbon fuels in general. It is reckoned that production costs of Volga oil are one-sixth, and of European natural gas one-thirtieth, the costs of producing their coal equivalents. That unfettered substitution has not occurred is a function of the scale of the growth in demand for all energy sources in general and of the inability of pipelines to carry larger supplies from the Volga and West Siberian fields in particular. Similarly, hydroelectric power is more expensive in the European region than further east: investment costs of dams and reservoirs and generating costs in Siberia are only one-third to one-eighth of those on the Volga and Dnieper systems. Yet again regional demand, and bottlenecks and losses in transmission from other regions, necessitated the development to the full of power facilities on European rivers.

Despite the relative proximity, and hence low delivery costs, of iron ore from Krivoi Rog and coking coal from the Donbas, Ukrainian steelworks produce pig iron and steel at costs that exceed those at plants in the Urals and Kuzbas by 25-40 percent and 50 percent, respectively. Until Kursk ores were supplied in significant quantities, steel output at the Tula and Lipetsk plants cost up to three times per ton more than that produced at Urals and

Siberian plants. Since interregional differences in coking coal costs account for most of these variations (iron ore cost differentials are far smaller), expanded capacity at Lipetsk using Kursk ores probably will not be able to produce steel at prices below those at Ukrainian plants.

The disadvantages the European region suffers in the costs of generating energy and of producing basic commodities are made up partly or wholly in other ways. Savings on the assembly, production, and distribution costs of more sophisticated manufactures is one way. The relatively dense network of factories served by railways, roads, and navigable waterways in the region is by far the best economic environment for the increasingly complex inter-industry, interplant, and interenterprise linkages demanded by increasingly long and intricate chains of industrial and agro-industrial production. At times this tendency to manufacturing localization has been stimulated by the relative ease of supplying regionally deficit inputs (such as oil) and cheaper standardized inputs (such as steel and nonferrous metal sheets) from the Urals, West Siberia, and Kazakhstan. Moreover, labor rates are kept down in the European region by lower costs of living that stem from relatively favorable climate and relatively cheap food supplies.

A further factor is the generally lower investment costs, though this advantage is by no means straightforward. As Table 6.1 shows, the European region, except in 1960, has consistently had a smaller share of Soviet electricity-generating capacity than it has of Soviet electricity production. Although the difference is not great, it indicates higher levels of capacity use in the European region, suggesting greater investment efficiency. In large measure this stems from the dominance there of coal- and gas-fired stations that can operate all year and can come into production in shorter gestation periods (in contrast with the large hydroelectric stations in the East that have long gestation periods and can be affected in winter by frozen rivers and reservoirs).

Also, by comparison with the central and southern European USSR, the construction and engineering costs of new investment projects (industries, canals, railways, city buildings [including housing]) rise by 160 percent, to the northeast of Leningrad (southern Karelian and Komi ASSRs), to 575 percent, in the Arctic and subarctic areas of the eastern regions. These high costs result from labor shortages, high labor turnover, excessive demand for power supply, remoteness and poor transport, poor physical conditions (such as marshes, mountains, earthquakes, and water problems), permafrost, polar nights, and climatic harshness.

An offsetting factor is that in many sectors—from coal mining through electric power to metal and food processing—the European region has older and often smaller-scale plants and facilities than do regions of more recent industrialization. While expansion of such plants often may be cheaper in the short run than construction of new plants on virgin sites, longer-term inefficiency of such capital investment may well express itself in higher unit costs of production. One should note, however, that the European USSR contains a large number of plants, especially in the chemicals, electronics, and aerospace industries, that have been constructed since 1960 and are equipped with the most modern machinery in the country. Also, plants in the eastern regions of earliest industrialization—especially the Urals and, to a lesser degree, along the Trans-Siberian Railway and in the Kuzbas in West Siberia— suffer the problems of outdated equipment and inefficiency that older European facilities do.

Finally, the real longer-term costs of huge projects (more typical in Siberia) are often immeasurably higher than anticipated because of the serious time lags in construction and, hence, in coming on stream, particularly where interindustry linkages are involved. Under these conditions the more incremental growth of older European facilities and construction of smaller-scale new plants ensures more rapid and smoother additions to supply, with fewer negative chain reactions on investment costs and production costs.

Market Demand

One of the most fundamental factors that has helped to offset the planners' negative reaction to higher production costs in the European USSR, especially in making interregional investment allocation decisions, has been the general excess of demand over supply, virtually across the whole range of goods and services in the Soviet economy. The consequences are several.

First, the rapid growth in market requirements has resulted in much locational inertia and continued growth in the European USSR. The tremendous pressure on investment supply, with resultant capital scarcity, has put a premium on the need for "incremental" and "plant replacement" investments at older plants, in existing economic infrastructure (especially transport facilities), and on social-urban infrastructure in more populated areas. These needs have had to be balanced against the need for large investments in projects and cities on virgin sites—usually in other regions. A consequence has been continuing higher levels of labor intensity in the European USSR.

Second, ceteris paribus, in a market economy buoyant demand fuels inflation. In the USSR price control has not only restricted inflation, and so yielded more steady levels of capital accumulation, but has also meant complex systems of interregional subsidies. Were evidence at hand, it would probably reveal the complexity of subsidy and profit in the economic sectors of the European region.

Nevertheless, some generalizations can be made. The most fundamental economic attribute of the European USSR within the Soviet economy has been its leading role as a region of capital surplus. Traditionally that surplus has been funded by taxation on two sectors in which the region excels: agriculture and consumption. The growth of European Soviet manufacturing, especially of finished goods, has raised the contribution of this sector to capital supply. However, some of the financial "surplus" must be absorbed within the European region itself because of its more than "fair" share of outdated or inefficient plants and unprofitable collective farms. In particular the European heavy industries, especially coal and steel, require regional subsidization—although what contribution the East European importers of Ukrainian iron ore and coal make to such a subsidy must remain a subject for debate.

On the other hand, the European USSR highly localizes consumer goods industries such as the traditional textile, clothing, and shoe industries; and the new, fast-growing electrical, plastics, and automotive industries carry the highest turnover taxes on sales. One can argue that the very large proportion of Soviet cars exported offers a hard-currency "subsidy" to regional production, as well as a source of repayment of (foreign) capital investments made in the European region and elsewhere. Broadly, too, one can argue that without the maintenance of higher levels of labor intensity and older equipment in the European USSR, the interruptions in supply and in meeting market demand would cause greater costs to the Soviet economy than would the loss to eastern regions of the large-scale capital investments required there in resource development, basic processing, and capital goods manufacturing. In other words, the high level of demand and insulation from world competition "justify" the subsidization of higher-cost European regional production.

Third, and of critical importance, is the scale and structure of regional market demand, particularly for products that gain weight or bulk in manufacture, are perishable, fragile, or of low value in relation to weight, and hence are awkward or costly to transport. Not surprisingly, therefore, the European USSR retains a large proportion of industries supplying agriculture with fertilizers, more complex machinery, and livestock feed, as well as of food and beverage industries serving urban markets. With 60 percent of the Soviet population living south and west of a line connecting Leningrad, Ufa, Volgograd, Stavropol', and Novorossiisk, the labor supply and consumer market combination operates to retain a localization of production within this region of consumer goods; capital goods industries in which interindustry and interplant linkages are critical; "urban market" capital goods such as cement, public transport vehicles, office, scientific, and hospital equipment; and "custom-made" goods in general.

Transport and Accessibility

The European area enjoys many advantages in the critically important area of transport. Its railway, road, waterway, pipeline, electricity grid, and oceanic port systems are almost unrivaled in carrying capacity and density of network. Relevant transport indicators are given in Table 6.5. Few areas, let alone people, are more than 80 kilometers from a railhead in the European area, whereas elsewhere that is the rule, not the exception. Because demand for transport continually outstrips the supply of capacity, these networks are complementary alternatives rather than competitive substitutes. Moreover, climate permits the uninterrupted use of transport facilities for longer periods of the year than is possible further east. Most fundamental, though, is the shorter average distance between supply origins and market destinations, a factor that arises from the denser transport network, the denser distribution of production and consumption points, and the greater degree of connectivity in the transport networks. These factors result in lower real transport costs, more regular supplies, and the ability to hold smaller stocks. Nevertheless, the transport system is always overloaded, and access to capacity is often fraught with delays and safety problems.

Steps have been taken in all Five-Year Plans to raise transport carrying capacities. New railways have been constructed, particularly to link more recently opened resource supplies with the main network (for example, the Pechora and Vorkuta branch), to improve interregional integration by providing shorter links and to relieve existing overloaded routes (such as the Gorkii-Leningrad and Baltic republics-Donbas railways). More important has been rail electrification on all main routes, which has approximately trebled their carrying capacities. Since World War II, however, much of the growth in the movement of energy within (and to) the European USSR has been through pipelines (for oil and gas) and new electricity transmission grids. This development has been of

TABLE 6.5

Indicators of Transport Provision: Selected Republics, 1975

| | Percentage of RSFSR Rail Freight Tonnage | | Rail Network Density | | Road Network Density | |
| | Outbound | Inbound | Km per 100 sq. km Area | Km per 1,000 Population | Km per 100 sq. km Area | Km per 1,000 Population |
|---|---|---|---|---|---|---|
| European RSFSR | 73.3 | 76.0 | | | | |
| Estonia | | | 2.2 | 0.7 | 57.0 | 18.2 |
| Latvia | | | 3.8 | 1.0 | 38.0 | 9.0 |
| Lithuania | | | 3.0 | 0.6 | 51.0 | 10.3 |
| Belorussia | | | 2.6 | 0.6 | 31.7 | 7.1 |
| Moldavia | | | 3.3 | 0.3 | 30.3 | 2.7 |
| Ukraine | | | 3.6 | 0.5 | 34.7 | 4.3 |
| Soviet average | | | 0.6 | 0.5 | 6.0 | 5.4 |

Sources: Narkhoz for various years.

greater significance than the shift of bulkier materials like stone, sand, and gravel and fertilizers onto navigable waterways. Road transport has been taking on the increased distribution of lighter manufactures, especially to industrial, wholesale, and retail consumers in the major European urban regions of the USSR.

All these trends have relieved the railways of excess freight and have not reduced actual freight flows, although recently the latter have begun to stabilize in volume. Rail freight tonnage originating in the European RSFSR rose from 380 million tons in 1950 to 1,206 million tons in 1970. In these ways the improved quality of transport has enabled the European region to cushion some of the rise in pithead and factory-gate production costs and has made many more smaller towns more accessible to larger centers.

Control, Research, and Development

In recent years in the Western world, the significance for regional development of the information-processing, administrative, and research and development (R&D) functions has become more fully recognized. This awareness has resulted from the relatively rapid growth of this sector combined with its comparative labor intensity, high skills, high pay, and locational stability. Little attention has been devoted to these issues in the USSR, largely because the high degree of central planning and the close integration of political, social, military, and economic functions appear to simplify the issue. Indeed, Soviet statistics show only a very small increase in the employment of personnel engaged in "state administration, the management of co-operative and state organizations, finance and social security" between 1940 and 1972: from 2.1 million to 2.35 million, representing a drop in the percentage of total employment from 3 to 2 percent. In part this reflects the creation, prior to 1940, of an adequate centralized system.

What statistics do not tell us, however, is the proportion of employees in the manufacturing, transport, and service sectors, in particular, who are actually in control and information-processing jobs, although it is known that in general nonproduction workers in the administration, social security, and economic sectors increased as a proportion of all workers from 5.8 percent in 1940 to more than 7.5 percent in the mid-1970s. (There was, however, a relative decrease from 6.1 percent in 1950 to 5.8 percent in 1960, but a rapid rise to 6.3 percent by 1965 following Khrushchev's reorganization of Soviet regional administration—the sovnarkhoz period—and the emphasis on more qualitative and decentralized economic management under Brezhnev.) By contrast, there is no mistaking the Soviet attention to the "scientific and technical revolution": the number of employees engaged in scientific R&D and information-processing that feed "control" rose from 360,000 in 1940 to 3.8 million in 1976.

It is difficult to quantify the precise role of the European region in this process. One thing is clear, nevertheless: the region is more than proportionately dominant in control and R&D within the Soviet economy. That dominance stems from two complementary processes: centralization in the Moscow region of both USSR and RSFSR control, information-processing, and R&D functions, and federal decentralization of some of these functions to the six national republics (the Ukrainian, Belorussian, Estonian, Latvian, Lithuanian, and Moldavian SSRs) and the 12 autonomous republics within the European RSFSR (the Karelian, Komi, Mari, Mordov, Chuvash, Bashkir, Kalmyk, Tatar, Dagestan, Kabardino-Balkar, Severo-Osetian and Chechino-Ingush ASSRs).

Centralization in Moscow is the most important single factor. Not only does this city localize more than 11 percent of all Soviet administrative and financial control personnel and more than 21 percent of all scientific and R&D employees;[7] the significance of the functions they perform surpasses those undertaken by others elsewhere. Yet, in addition, Moscow oblast localizes a large number of R&D facilities that, for reasons of labor scarcity, security, or regional planning goals, are located at some distance from, yet near to, the metropolis. The nuclear research installations at Duban and Serpukhov are two examples.

The spatial pattern within the European region can be established only indirectly, in the absence of oblast and city occuaptional data. Thus, other indexes must be used to expose the pattern. The best index for which data are available—particularly on information-processing and R&D functions—is the number of specialists with higher educational qualifications who are employed in the subregional economies of the European region. Data for 1970 indicate that the region as a whole localized almost 77 percent of all such employment in the USSR—clearly well above average. The intra-European regional pattern is no less instructive,although no intra-republic data is available for the non-Russian republics (see Table 6.6).

Within the RSFSR the localization in Moscow is clear—it has almost four times the Soviet average of highly qualified personnel—but Leningrad is also outstanding. Elsewhere specialists are well spread among cities, factories, mines, farms, and other enterprises throughout the region, though most oblasts fall below the Soviet average. Indeed, even in oblasts with leading industrial enterprises and larger cities, only average or below-average

TABLE 6.6

Distribution of Specialists with Higher Educational Qualifications
Working in the USSR Economy: 1970
(number per 1,000 population)

| Area | Number | Area | Number |
|---|---|---|---|
| Northwest | 40 | Volga-Viatka | 23 |
| Arkhangel'sk | 21 | Gorkii | 26 |
| Vologda | 18 | Kirov | 18 |
| Leningrad city | 77 | Mari ASSR | 23 |
| Leningrad oblast | 20 | Mordov ASSR | 20 |
| Murmansk | 29 | Chuvash ASSR | 20 |
| Novgorod | 20 | | |
| Pskov | 20 | Central Chernozem | 22.5 |
| Karelian ASSR | 25 | Belgorod | 20 |
| Komi ASSR | 24 | Voronezh | 28 |
| | | Kursk | 18 |
| Central | 44.5 | Lipetsk | 22 |
| Briansk | 19 | Tambov | 20 |
| Vladimir | 23 | | |
| Iaroslavl' | 25 | Povolzh'e | 25.5 |
| Ivanovo | 23 | Astrakhan' | 24.5 |
| Kalinin | 20 | Volgograd | 28 |
| Kaluga | 26 | Kuibyshev | 34 |
| Kostroma | 20 | Penza | 21 |
| Moscow city | 101 | Saratov | 30.5 |
| Moscow oblast | 25 | Ulianovsk | 22 |
| Orel | 22 | Bashkir ASSR | 18.5 |
| Riazan' | 22 | Kalmyk ASSR | 20 |
| Smolensk | 21 | Tatar ASSR | 26 |
| Tula | 26 | | |
| | | Urals | 22.5 |
| North Caucasus | 25 | Kurgan | 17 |
| Krasnodar krai | 24 | Orenburg | 20 |
| Stavropol' | 24 | Perm' | 21 |
| Rostov | 30 | Sverdlovsk | 25 |
| Dagestan ASSR | 18 | Cheliabinsk | 24 |
| Kabardino-Balkar ASSR | 26 | Udmurt ASSR | 23 |
| Severo-Osetian ASSR | 34 | | |
| Chechino-Ingush ASSR | 19 | Other republics | |
| | | Ukrainian SSR | 28 |
| | | Belorussian SSR | 26 |
| | | Lithuanian SSR | 26 |
| Average RSFSR1 | 30 | Moldavian SSR | 22 |
| | | Latvian SSR | 32 |
| Average USSR | 28 | Estonian SSR | 34 |

Source: Narkhoz 22-72, pp. 499ff.

numbers of specialists are employed. Gorkii, Volgograd, Voronezh, and the Urals cities are cases in point. This seems to suggest that Moscow and Leningrad are supreme in the higher-order control, information-processing, and R&D functions, while second-order, routine, or lower-order innovative functions are dispersed among even the largest industrial cities. Only Kuibyshev appears to be an exception, possibly reflecting its highly capital-intensive industries. Although the Ukraine shows only an average incidence of specialists, there are surely marked differences between the rural west and the industrial east and center, though Kiev is probably outstanding.

As with other indicators, however, the south-north gradation from the poor supply in Moldavia to above-average supply in Latvia and Estonia repeats itself, indicating a key reason why interrepublic wage rates differ. At the other extreme the density of qualified specialists is comparatively low in oblasts that are in the "shadow" of major metropolitan centers, are dominantly rural, are inhabited by ethnic minorities, or are locationally peripheral to the main European transport/urban-industrial system: Vologda, Briansk, Kirov, Kursk, the Bashkir ASSR, Dagestan ASSR, and Chechino-Ingush ASSR. Indeed, only the Karelian and Komi ASSRs can boast a "respectable" level of specialists among the ASSRs.

International Factors

Historically, trade via the Barents, Baltic, and Black seas was a significant factor in capital accumulation in the European region, though it also provided a channel for foreign exploitation of resources. Soviet development policy, however, strongly emphasized "continentality," a self-sufficiency dependent upon powerful industrialization of interior regions at a distance from ports, coasts, or foreign frontiers. Nevertheless, it can be argued that since World War II the importance of international economic linkages has been growing steadily, if slowly, but in recent years has shown marked acceleration. The need for Soviet access to the world's oceans has never been greater, nor has its capacity to exploit that access.

In terms of accessibility, the European USSR is the preeminent region of the country, despite the two major disadvantages of the costs of icebound approaches for up to six months of the year to such northern ports as Leningrad, Riga, Tallinn, and Arkhangel'sk, and the more strategic disadvantage of access to open oceans only via the "closed" Baltic and Black seas or via distant Murmansk. With Kaliningrad and Lithuanian ports on the Baltic, and Odessa on the Black Sea, open virtually all year, the European region has better access to the sea for trading and fishing than any other region, except the sensitive Far East coastlands bordering on China. The Arctic Ocean is frozen for up to eight months, and much of the Pacific coast is icebound for half of the year. Unfortunately, Soviet statistics on traffic, commodity flows, and fish landings at the country's ports are not published. There is no doubt, however, that rising Soviet maritime-defense and trade interests have dictated accelerated Soviet investment in ports since 1950. The Soviet merchant fleet has grown tenfold, and now represents more than 8 percent of gross world tonnage, compared with 2.5 percent in 1950. Fish landings rose in the same period from 1.7 million to 8 million tons.

Ports, for commerce and defense, now are a more significant factor in regional development than at any time since the Revolution. Although the construction of facilities around the Sea of Okhotsk and along the coasts of Kamchatka and Maritime Krai in the Far East have been relatively impressive, the greatest port expansion has occurred in the European region. Urban population figures are an indirect index of this growth. Statistics from the 1959 and 1970 censuses and the 1978 population estimates for cities suggest that a majority of ports have expanded at rates above the Soviet average (see Table 6.7). The exceptions are the relatively more icebound or larger-city ports of Leningrad, Tallinn, and Riga. Other larger ports—notably Odessa, Murmansk, and, prior to 1970, Arkhangel'sk-Severodvinsk—have expanded at or above the average urban growth rates. Generally, however, it is the Ukrainian and Azov Sea ports that have experienced the most rapid growth, particularly the smaller ones like Nikolaev and Kherson. The tendency for more rapid development of smaller ports, however, is also evident on the Baltic, especially Klaipeda, as pressure on wharfage and urban infrastructure causes bottlenecks in the larger or more "military" ports. One fact can demonstrate the development importance to the European region of port expansion. Between 1959 and 1970 the port complex of Arkhangel'sk-Severodvinsk grew by as many people (about 150,000) as did the largest and most favorably situated Far East port, Vladivostok. (By comparison, Odessa gained 230,000 inhabitants.)

These trends clearly express the economic significance of major regional variations in accessibility to the sea from centers of population, production, and consumption. Whereas far fewer than 10 million people live within 1,000 kilometers of the Far East ports, almost 200 million live within the same distance of all European ports combined. The latter are much more accessible in terms of time and cost via a relatively dense network of railways,

TABLE 6.7

Indexes of Industrial Growth: USSR and Selected Republics, 1940–72

| | 1945 | 1950 (1940 = 100) | 1960 | 1972 | 1972 (1950 = 100) | 1972 (1960 = 100) |
|---|---|---|---|---|---|---|
| USSR | 92 | 173 | 524 | 1,190 | 687 | 227 |
| RSFSR | 106 | 175 | 494 | 1,064 | 608 | 215 |
| Northwest | 37 | 129 | 369 | 717 | 556 | 194 |
| Central | 75 | 150 | 397 | 742 | 495 | 187 |
| Volga-Viatka | 164 | 221 | 616 | 1,422 | 643 | 231 |
| Central Chernozem | 35 | 112 | 437 | 1,079 | 963 | 247 |
| Povolzh'e | 179 | 259 | 902 | 2,305 | 890 | 256 |
| North Caucasus | 41 | 116 | 351 | 799 | 689 | 228 |
| Ukraine | 26 | 115 | 365 | 832 | 723 | 228 |
| Donets-Dnieper | 27 | 110 | 332 | 699 | 635 | 211 |
| Southwest | 29 | 135 | 463 | 1,190 | 881 | 257 |
| South | 20 | 104 | 370 | 947 | 910 | 256 |
| Baltic republics | 51 | 281 | 1,115 | 2,949 | 1,049 | 264 |
| Lithuania | 40 | 191 | 1,030 | 3,117 | 1,631 | 302 |
| Latvia | 47 | 303 | 1,099 | 2,726 | 900 | 248 |
| Estonia | 73 | 342 | 1,150 | 2,779 | 813 | 241 |
| Belorussia | 20 | 115 | 425 | 1,251 | 1,087 | 294 |
| Moldavia | 44 | 206 | 899 | 2,496 | 1,211 | 278 |

Source: Narkhoz 22–72, pp. 134–35.

TABLE 6.8

Population Growth in Port Cities in the European USSR: 1959-78
(thousands)

| | | | | Rate of Growth | |
|---|---|---|---|---|---|
| | | | | 1970 1959 | 1978 1970 |
| USSR urban population | 99,990 | 135,990 | 159,590 | 136 | 117 |
| Port cities | | | | | |
| White and Barents seas | | | | | |
| Arkhangel'sk-Severodvinsk | 336.8 | 487.2 | 580.0 | 145 | 119 |
| Murmansk | 221.9 | 308.6 | 376.0 | 139 | 122 |
| Baltic Sea | | | | | |
| Leningrad | 3,321.2 | 3,949.5 | 4,425.0 | 119 | 112 |
| Tallinn | 281.7 | 362.7 | 415.0 | 129 | 115 |
| Riga | 580.4 | 731.8 | 816.0 | 126 | 112 |
| Ventspils | 27.4 | 40.5 | 50.0 | 148 | 123 |
| Liepaia | 71.5 | 92.9 | 105.0 | 130 | 112 |
| Klaipeda | 89.9 | 140.0 | 174.0 | 156 | 124 |
| Kaliningrad | 203.6 | 296.9 | 358.0 | 146 | 120 |
| Black and Azov seas | | | | | |
| Odessa | 664.1 | 891.5 | 1,040.0 | 134 | 117 |
| Nikolaev | 235.5 | 331.0 | 448.0 | 141 | 135 |
| Kherson | 157.9 | 260.7 | 325.0 | 165 | 125 |
| Kerch | 98.1 | 127.6 | 154.0 | 130 | 121 |
| Kerdiansk | 65.2 | 100.1 | 120.0 | 153 | 120 |
| Zhdanov | 283.6 | 416.9 | 475.0 | 147 | 114 |
| Taganrog | 202.0 | 254.1 | 285.0 | 126 | 112 |
| Rostov-on-Don | 599.5 | 788.8 | 921.0 | 132 | 117 |
| Novorossiisk | 93.4 | 132.7 | 155.0 | 142 | 116 |

Sources: Narkhoz for various years.

roads, navigable waterways, and pipelines. Thus it is not only the port facilities that have caused port-city expansion but also the industrial processing of imported materials or oceanic (ship-building) or export-oriented manufacturing using port facilities.

Such expansion cannot be divorced from the closer economic integration of the European USSR with the neighboring regions of East-Central Europe through the Council for Mutual Economic Aid (CMEA). Nor should one forget the local effects of the enormous expansion of "land ports" to handle the vast quantities of Soviet raw materials being exchanged for heavy manufactures at frontier rail junctions between the Soviet broad-gauge and East European standard-gauge railroads. The most important impact of this integration is being felt more widely in the European USSR through the need for new factory buildings and extensions to existing plants required by the growth in scale, complexity, and diversity of international industrial linkages.

There is little doubt that industrial production in the more backward and rural western regions of the European USSR has been accelerated by CMEA integration. As the data in Table 6.8 suggest, industrial expansion since 1950 has accelerated (relative to the rest of the European region) in the western areas adjoining East-Central Europe: Belorussia, Lithuania, Moldavia, and the south-western and southern Ukraine. East European demands for iron ore and coal have probably contributed to the sustaining of industrial growth in the Donets-Dnieper and Central Chernozem areas, and the major steel expansion in the latter region is certainly related to the wider CMEA steel market. By contrast, industrial growth in the Povolzh'e—which, like the western areas, is significantly above the average European and Soviet levels—is closely linked to wider Soviet international integration: oil exploitation to serve CMEA and the automotive and chemical industries using Western technology.

NOTES

1. Annual accumulated temperatures are the sum of the mean daily temperatures for the period when they exceed $10^{\circ}C$.
2. Ore exports generally, however, rose from 3.2 million tons in 1950 to more than 40 million tons annually in the 1970s.
3. F. E. I. Hamilton, The Moscow City Region (Oxford: Oxford University Press, 1976), p. 12.
4. R. A. French and F. E. I. Hamilton, The Socialist City: Spatial Structure and Urban Policy (London: Wiley and Son, 1979), ch. 2.

5. Hamilton, The Moscow City Region, p. 14.

6. SOPS, Pati razvitiia malykh i srednikh gorodov tsentral'nykh ekonomicheskikh raionov SSSR (Moscow, 1967).

7. Hamilton, The Moscow City Region, p. 14.

# 7

## THE ASIATIC RSFSR

### F. Douglas Whitehouse and David S. Kamerling

The most important regional problem confronting the Soviet Union today is the triangular distribution of the nation's resources: fuel and energy supplies in Asiatic Russia,[1] increments to the supply of labor in Central Asia, and the bulk of the population and established industrial capacity and socioeconomic infrastructure in the European USSR.[2] This geographic chimera presents Soviet leaders and planners struggling with a slowly growing economy, with difficult choices in allocating finite investment resources among these three macro regions. At the core of the problem is the growing concentration of energy resources in the east, away from the major energy consumers in the west. The focus of this chapter, therefore, is the evolving role of the Asiatic RSFSR in this economic triad as the 1980s begin, and the implications for the future direction of the region's development. Although other aspects of the economy will be examined, the role of Asiatic Russia in Soviet energy development will be of paramount importance.

The important decisions for the Asiatic RSFSR during the foreseeable future will revolve around two key issues: in what sequence the natural resources of the region will be developed, and to what degree Siberia and the Far East will experience only limited, specialized development as a raw material resource base rather than a more diversified, complex type of development. To some extent these questions have already been answered. Raw material extraction and processing—especially of fuels—will continue to dominate the economic development of these eastern regions at least through the 1980s. But advocates of more diversified development of Asiatic Russia will push their views, stressing development based on the availability of low-cost energy, savings in transportation costs, and greater productivity. In particular they will advocate the location

of energy-intensive industries in the region as an alternative to
sending energy from surplus areas in the eastern regions to deficit
areas in the west.

Whatever decisions are made, they will be strongly affected
by the interplay of regional constraints—environment, location, and
level of development—and important national trends, in particular
the Soviets' growing energy problems, the declining increments to
the labor force, and the increasing competition for limited capital
investment as economic growth slows. Asiatic Russia's demands
will be challenged within the decision-making hierarchy by "lobby-
ists" from other regions as Soviet leaders seek to optimize the allocation of resources. The results of this decision-making process
will have a lasting effect on the future path of growth and development for both Asiatic Russia and the rest of the nation.

Regional research on the Soviet Union is hampered by the lack
of systematic regional data, especially below the republic level.
The availability of regional data was particularly limited during the
period prior to 1958. More recently the flow of regional data was
greatly reduced by the Soviets after 1975, probably because of the
economic problems they have been experiencing. Where possible,
systematic regional data will be supplemented with "fragmented"
data, bits and pieces culled from various sources. The emphasis
will be on the relative position of Asiatic Russia within the Soviet
economy rather than on its absolute contribution. In this context it
is important to remember that the Asiatic RSFSR encompasses a
very large area and summary statistics for the entire region mask
great internal diversity. As a partial solution to this traditional
problem of scale, data for the three major economic regions that
constitute Asiatic Russia—West Siberia, East Siberia, and the Far
East—will be presented whenever possible.[3]

## SOVIET REGIONAL DEVELOPMENT
## POLICY IN ASIATIC RUSSIA

Soviet regional development policy in Asiatic Russia has been
guided by consideration of the frequently overlapping factors of
ideology, strategy, and economics. The impact of ideology on regional development policy was greatest in the period prior to World
War II.[4] Concern for the need to implement often contradictory and
poorly understood "Marxist principles of industrial location," especially those relating to the goal of equalizing regional levels of development, resulted in efforts to provide Asiatic Russia with a more
fully developed industrial structure.[5] This policy was most clearly
manifested in the development of the Kuznetsk Basin and in construction of a steel plant at Komsomol'sk during the 1930s.

Equalization of regional levels of development remained an official tenet of Soviet policy until 1972, when Brezhnev declared the problem solved.[6] Although some of the evidence is contradictory and inconclusive, reviews of studies of regional inequality in the Soviet Union suggest that despite the long-term ideological commitment to the goal of reducing regional inequality and despite the significant improvements that have been made in the level of living in all regions, including the eastern ones, the Soviet Union continues to exhibit a substantial degree of socioeconomic regional inequality.[7]

During the post-World War II period the productivity of industrial investment in the eastern regions was consistently below that of other regions even though Asiatic Russia received a proportionately greater share of investment per capita.[8] In effect, development in the Asiatic RSFSR was being subsidized by the older, industrialized western regions. I. S. Koropeckyj points out that while the net result of this post-World War II location policy was to substantially increase the absolute amount of industry in the eastern regions, it "corrected only slightly . . . the territorial imbalance in regard to shares in total industrial output and output per capita."[9] He concludes that other factors, especially political (defense/strategic) considerations, must have played an important role in the decision to locate industry in Asiatic Russia.

Strategic considerations centered primarily on the desire to disperse industry away from the major industrial centers of the European USSR in order to reduce the vulnerability of the Soviet industrial base. Many industries now located in the eastern regions were originally evacuated to Siberia during World War II. More recently Soviet concern about China has played a part in Soviet development of Asiatic Russia, especially the decision to build the Baikal-Amur Mainline Railroad (BAM), which is located 150 kilometers or more north of the Trans-Siberian Railroad and the Chinese border.

Although ideological and strategic factors have played a role in the development of the Asiatic RSFSR, the economic factor has been by far the most important. This region has often been called one of the world's last great storehouses of natural resources, a well-deserved description. The history of Soviet development of Asiatic Russia has been characterized largely by the fits and starts of major investment programs designed to tap these resources and by the subsequent development these programs have spawned.

The development of the Kuznetsk Basin is a prominent example of this pattern. Industrial development of the Kuzbas began in the 1930s with the Ural-Kuznetsk Combine. Complementary flows of iron ore from the southern Urals moved east while coal from the Kuzbas moved west, establishing the basis for major iron and steel centers in each region. Today the Kuznetsk Basin is the major industrial center for all of Asiatic Russia. It has a well-developed, self-sufficient iron and steel industry, as well as large metalworking, machine-building, and chemical sectors.

During the mid-1950s economic development in southwestern Siberia was affected by the Virgin Lands scheme. Later the effort to tap the hydroelectric potential of the major Siberian rivers began with the construction at Bratsk of the first of several dams on the Angara-Ienisei system that have provided the basis for development of capital- and energy-intensive industries such as aluminum refining and pulp and paper (cardboard) production. The discovery of petroleum, and later natural gas, sparked large-scale investment in Tiumen' Oblast for exploration, extraction, and transportation of these resources. More recently these deposits have formed the basis for a major expansion of the Siberian chemical industry with the construction of chemical plants at Tobol'sk and Tomsk.

Finally, construction of the BAM, which began in 1974 and probably will not be completed until sometime after 1985, is expected to stimulate development within its zone of influence in East Siberia and the Far East, mainly by providing access to previously inaccessible resources. [10] This pattern of development has resulted in an industrial structure strongly oriented toward the exploitation of natural resources and development of some associated heavy industry, but very little toward investment in infrastructure and social overhead capital.

The importance of Asiatic Russia's resources in the Soviet economy has increased steadily as the quality and quantity of many of the traditional European sources of energy, especially coal and petroleum, have declined. [11] Undoubtedly one of the most critical problems facing Soviet leaders today is how to bring together most efficiently, either as raw materials or in the form of electric power, the energy resources of the Asiatic RSFSR and the industrial energy consumers concentrated in the European USSR. As a result the development of Asiatic Russia is no longer just an ideologic, strategic, or economic option; it has become an economic imperative.

CONSTRAINTS TO DEVELOPMENT

While the lure of eastern resources is great, the Soviets are continuously and severely hampered in their efforts to tap them by three interrelated constraints—harsh environment, remote location, and low level of development—each of which adds to the cost of regional development.

## Harsh Environment

The impact of the harsh environment in the eastern regions on economic activity is manifested in various ways.[12] Undoubtedly most of the problems can be traced to the cold weather associated with the continental climate that envelops most of the region. The severity of the cold is increased by the presence of a series of mountain ranges east of the Ienisei River. Temperatures below $40^\circ$ C. occur throughout the region during the winter. Over two-thirds of the region is underlain with permafrost, a situation that requires specialized construction techniques in order to avoid structural damage due to the shifting that occurs as the top layer repeatedly thaws and freezes. In addition, much of the area in northern Tiumen Oblast, where the rich oil and natural gas reserves are concentrated, turns into a veritable swamp during the summer as the permafrost melts. According to Iu. Sobolev, the overall corrective coefficient for construction-installation operations in the BAM zone, which includes consideration of climate and other environmental factors, is 1.3 for Irkutsk Oblast, 2.2 for Zeia Raion in Amur Oblast, and 3.1 for the southern Iakutsk ASSR, as compared with costs in the central industrial regions.[13]

The cold climate and short growing season restrict the development of agriculture throughout most of the area, making it partially dependent on food imports, especially of fruits and vegetables. The productivity of machinery also is greatly affected by the cold temperatures. According to one Soviet author, the time between major overhauls for tractors and the service life of motor vehicles are reduced by 50 percent during the winter, and the performance of excavators, even in southern Siberia, is reduced by 25-30 percent.[14] This problem has led to repeated calls for development of equipment specially designed for northern climates. Academician A. G. Aganbegian has estimated that the annual losses due to trucks not being adapted to the harsh environment of the Asiatic RSFSR exceeds 500 million rubles per year.[15]

## Remote Location

Development of important eastern resources is also limited by the vast distances separating these resources from consumers in the west and by their location in inaccessible, nearly uninhabited wilderness. Pipelines carrying oil and natural gas to Moscow consumers from Tiumen' Oblast—a relatively close-in area of Asiatic Russia—exceed 3,000 kilometers in length. Equally impressive are the rail distances separating cities in Asiatic Russia from cities in the

industrialized heartland in the west (see Table 7.1). Even within
the Asiatic RSFSR itself, intercity distances are quite great. It is
partly because of the great distances involved that the area east of
Lake Baikal has become relatively isolated and more strongly
oriented toward the Pacific, while areas west of Lake Baikal remain oriented toward the European areas.[16]

TABLE 7.1

Asiatic RSFSR: Selected Railroad Distances

| Between | km | Between | km |
|---|---|---|---|
| Vladivostok and L'vov | 10,565 | Novosibirsk and Moscow | 4,148 |
| Vladivostok and Moscow | 9,216 | Vladivostok and Irkutsk | 3,228 |
| Irkutsk and Moscow | 5,068 | Irkutsk and Novosibirsk | 1,840 |

Source: J. P. Cole and F. C. German, A Geography of the
USSR (London: Butterworths, 1970), p. 205.

The problem of distance adds greatly to the cost of using eastern resources. For example, although the cost of producing coal in
the Kuznetsk Basin in 1977 was almost 50 percent less than in the
Donets Basin, the cost of transporting Kuznetsk coal to the west
substantially reduced the difference in the cost of the two coals upon
delivery in Moscow (see Table 7.2). The cost of producing coal in
the Kansk-Achinsk Basin, 2.5 rubles per metric ton of standard
coal equivalent, is even less than in the Kuznetsk Basin. But so far
the Soviets have not been able to transport Kansk-Achinsk coal by
rail—it is prone to spontaneous combustion—or to develop the technology required for long-distance transmission of electricity produced locally from Kansk-Achinsk coal. The latter problem must
also be resolved before much of Asiatic Russia's hydroelectric power
potential can be fully utilized.

Low Level of Development

Because the eastern regions generally have been looked upon
by Soviet planners as a storehouse of natural resources to be drawn
upon as needed, rather than as an area for comprehensive economic

## TABLE 7.2

### Asiatic RSFSR: Comparative Cost of Coal
(rubles per metric ton of standard coal equivalent)

|  | Production Cost | Delivered Cost at Moscow |
|---|---|---|
| Kuznetsk Basin | 9.0 | 20.4 |
| Donets Basin | 17.7 | 22.0 |
| Eastern advantage | 8.7 | 1.6 |

Source: Central Intelligence Agency, USSR: Coal Industry Problems and Prospects (Washington, D.C.: CIA, 1980), pp. 10-11.


## TABLE 7.3

### Asiatic RSFSR: Development of Transportation
(density = km/1,000 sq. km.)

|  | Railroads | Hard-Surface Roads | Inland Waterways | Composite Index |
|---|---|---|---|---|
| USSR | 6.0 | 25.3 | 6.5 | 100.0 |
| Central industrial | 26.6 | 87.1 | 13.2 | 293.0 |
| West Siberia | 2.7 | 6.3 | 12.6 | 44.0 |
| East Siberia | 1.7 | 5.9 | 5.8 | 22.0 |
| Far East | 0.9 | 2.4 | 4.2 | 29.0 |

Notes: Density is about 1970; composite index is probably about mid-1960s.

Sources: Density—A. D. Danilov, V. V. Kistanov, and S. I. Ledovskikh, Ekonomicheskaia geografiia SSSR (Moscow: Vysshaia Shkola, 1976), p. 246; composite index—Leslie Dienes, "Investment Priorities in Soviet Regions," Annals of the Association of American Geographers, September 1972, p. 442.

development, investment in transportation infrastructure and social overhead capital (housing, schools, medical care facilities) has been neglected, even in areas that have experienced substantial investment in industry. This policy has resulted in a relatively low level of development throughout the region that makes present and future exploitation of the region's resources more difficult and more costly—the more so as the pinch on the USSR's human and capital resources tightens in the 1980s.

The remote locations of Asiatic Russia's resources and its poorly developed transportation system form one of the most severe bottlenecks to the region's development.[17] These constraints place a heavy burden on existing facilities and limit the cost effectiveness of resource development. One of the primary reasons for investing in construction of the BAM was to open up an area of approximately 1.5 square kilometers to resource exploitation. Yet this leaves most of East Siberia and the Far East largely inaccessible except by air. Railroad density throughout Asiatic RSFSR is less than 3 kilometers per 1,000 square kilometers, compared with 25 or more kilometers in the main industrialized regions of the European west (see Table 7.3). Put another way, over 50 percent of the area is at least 200 kilometers from the nearest railroad.[18] Moreover, in those southern areas of Asiatic Russia that are relatively well served, the railroad system is already overburdened and unable to handle the current load efficiently.

Hard-surface roads are even more rare than railroads in Asiatic Russia. The region is relatively well endowed with rivers that provide access to many areas in summer and serve as truck highways in the winter, but their north-south orientation reduces their utility. Access to the region from the sea, despite its very long coastline, is restricted by ice, especially along the Arctic coast, although the Soviets have been able to extend the shipping season through the use of icebreakers. The combination of distance and the lack of adequate transportation facilities will exacerbate problems facing Soviet leaders and planners in the 1980s as dependence on these remote sources of fuel and energy becomes even greater. As Leslie Dienes puts it, there is "no ready solution to the energy-transportation dilemma that will confront Soviet leaders during the next decade."[19]

Problems relating to the availability of labor, which reflect the interplay of the constraints of environment, location, and level of development, will also vex Soviet planners. Asiatic Russia, with its relatively small population, is a labor-deficit area, especially in the skilled manpower required by the capital-intensive extractive industries that characterize much of eastern development. Although Asiatic Russia accounts for nearly 57 percent of the territory of the

Soviet Union, its share of the population has remained relatively
stable since 1959 at somewhat under 11 percent (see Table 7.4).
The relationship between territory and population is even more
tenuous than the aggregate figures suggest, because the bulk of the
population and associated socioeconomic development is concentrated in a relatively narrow band in the southern part of the region
roughly parallel to the path of the Trans-Siberian Railroad. In contrast, most of the resources needed by the Soviet economy, particularly the petroleum and natural gas reserves, are located in the
sparsely settled regions north of the main zone of population.

TABLE 7.4

Asiatic RSFSR: Population
(percent USSR)

|  | 1959 | 1970 | 1979 |
|---|---|---|---|
| Asiatic Russia | 10.8 | 10.5 | 10.6 |
| West Siberia | 5.3 | 5.0 | 4.9 |
| East Siberia | 3.1 | 3.1 | 3.1 |
| Far East | 2.3 | 2.4 | 2.6 |

Sources: 1959 and 1970—TsSU, Itogi vsesoiuznoi perepisi
naseleniia 1970 goda, vol. 1 (Moscow, 1972); 1979—see "Vsesoiuz-
naia perepis naselenia," Vestnik statistiki (1980): no. 2, pp. 12-14.

To lure workers to this area, Soviet planners have had to offer
substantial wage incentives that vary both geographically and sectorally within the region.[20] According to A. G. Aganbegian, writing in
late 1979, the average regional wage coefficients applicable to the
most populated areas of West and East Siberia were only 1.15 and
1.20, respectively.[21] However, the regional wage coefficient in
1978 for construction workers in the BAM zone, a much less hospitable region, was 1.7 times that in the central region of the European USSR.[22] The coefficient rises as one moves north and east.
A Western analysis of Soviet data that considers both the remoteness of the site and labor costs suggests that the additional cost of
construction in the Asiatic RSFSR varies from 120 to 250 percent
more than the cost in the central region, although the majority of
construction probably occurs in zones with a regional coefficient of
only 1.2 to 1.3.[23] In addition, workers in the most harsh environ-

ments—regions of the Far North and areas equated with them—who have been on the job for at least six months are eligible for substantial additional bonuses of up to 300 rubles per month, based on their salary and length of time in the area.[24]

Unfortunately, the higher wages do not entirely cover the higher cost of living in this region. G. Mil'ner estimates the cost of living in Siberia and the southern part of the Far East to be 35-50 percent higher than the southern regions of the European RSFSR, while the level of income is only 15-30 percent higher. Moreover, the higher wages apply mainly to extractive industries. In the machine-building industry, for example, the average wage is actually lower than the average for the Russian Republic.[25]

Although the use of wage incentives and other inducements, such as appeals to patriotism, have enabled the Soviets to attract large numbers of workers to major projects in Asiatic Russia, they have been unable to keep them in the region. The labor turnover rate in Siberia is about 50 percent higher than in the European part of the country, and the resulting losses run into hundreds of millions of rubles each year.[26] About half of the workers originally recruited to work on the BAM in 1974 left after completing their three-year commitment. They were generally replaced by relatively inexperienced and poorly qualified young people.[27]

The fundamental cause of the high rate of labor turnover in the Asiatic RSFSR is the lack of established socioeconomic infrastructure and basic amenities throughout most of the region. Housing, schools, health care, and other services, as well as food and other retail goods, are in relatively short supply, especially in the more remote areas. According to R. Vitebskii, the cost of developing the necessary social infrastructure in Siberia is two to four times greater than for the center of the European part of the country.[28] Aganbegian claims that each worker in the North costs the state 17,000 rubles a year more than the same worker in European regions of the country because of increased wages, more expensive services, losses from turnover, and the like.[29] Sobolev's estimate of 11,000-13,000 rubles is lower, but still reflects clearly the additional costs incurred.[30]

In determining the optimal allocation of resources, Soviet planners must weigh the high cost of development in Asiatic Russia resulting from the regional constraints discussed above against positive factors encouraging further economic development within the region. Certainly the most important positive factor is the availability of large quantities of fuel and other resources. The tension between the positive and negative factors underlies the debate over the proper direction of development—specialization or diversification—and resolution of this tension will ultimately determine the structure of the economy of Asiatic Russia. The rest of this chapter is devoted to a consideration of these topics.

ASIATIC RUSSIA IN NATIONAL PERSPECTIVE

The economic structure of Asiatic Russia reflects, both geographically and sectorally, the influence of the three regional constraints—environment, location, and level of development. As noted
earlier, most economic activity is restricted to the southern flanks
of the three economic regions; exceptions indicate the location of important natural resources. Nonetheless, much of the region remains
virtually uninhabited wilderness, its economic potential existing only
as a vision of the future in the minds and plans of Soviet leaders.

Agriculture

Agriculture plays a relatively unimportant role in the economy
of the eastern regions. The three economic regions contain over 50
percent of the nation's total land area but only 11.9 percent of all
agricultural land and a somewhat greater percentage of the nation's
arable land (14.3 percent). Over 50 percent of the agricultural land
is located in the former Virgin Lands area adjacent to the Kazakh
Republic.

In general, Asiatic Russia is a food-deficit region. Its relative share of the USSR's grain production fluctuates between 12 and
15 percent in response to local and national weather conditions. The
region's share of USSR meat production fell from 10.7 percent in
1950 to 9.1 percent in 1975, resulting in an obvious regional deficit.
The region's share of milk production declined during the same
period from 12.3 percent to 10.5 percent. On the other hand, the
region has become nearly self-sufficient in egg production, its share
of production climbing from 8.9 percent in 1960 to 10.5 percent in
1975. The Asiatic RSFSR experiences its greatest deficit in the production of fruits and vegetables. The region is almost totally dependent on imports for its supply of fruits, but is able to supply at least
some of its requirements for vegetables. Asiatic Russia produced
only 7.0 percent of all vegetables (except potatoes) in 1975. Its
share in the production of potatoes, a staple in the Russian diet, was
9.9 percent, less than its share of the population.

Asiatic Russia accounted for only 9.5 percent of the total value
of agricultural production in the Soviet Union in 1975, about one percentage point less than its share of the population (see Table 7.5).
Agricultural productivity for the region, both per capita and per
hectare, was below the average for the USSR, although considerable
internal regional variation exists. This variation is partly explained
by differences in the structure of agriculture in the three economic
regions—West Siberia and, to a lesser extent, East Siberia are

dominated by the existence of very large state farms engaged in grain production, whereas farming in the Far East tends more toward smaller farms engaged in market garden agriculture. The relative cost of production for several major agricultural products also exhibits considerable intraregional variation (see Table 7.6). Collective farms (kolkhozes) in all three regions are less efficient relative to the national average for all collective farms. State farms (sovkhozes) exhibit a similar tendency for the majority of agricultural products. In all cases the cost of production rises rapidly from west to east.

TABLE 7.5

Asiatic RSFSR: Indexes of Agricultural Production, 1975

| | Percent USSR | Productivity per Capita | Rubles per Hectare |
|---|---|---|---|
| USSR | 100.0 | 100.0 | 100.0 |
| Asiatic Russia | 9.5 | 90.6 | 80.4 |
| West Siberia | 5.3 | 108.5 | 81.5 |
| East Siberia | 2.7 | 86.1 | 64.2 |
| Far East | 1.6 | 61.6 | 129.0 |

Sources: TsSU, Narodnoe khoziaistvo SSSR v 1974 g. (Moscow: Statistika, 1975), p. 9 (publication hereafter cited as Narkhoz); and, TsSU, Narodnoe khoziaistvo RSFSR v 1974 g. (Moscow: Statistika, 1975), p. 7 (publication hereafter cited as Narkhoz RSFSR).

These data reflect not only the obvious environmental constraints on agriculture in the eastern regions, but also the relative neglect of agriculture there. According to Aganbegian, only one-fifth the national average of fertilizer is applied per hectare in Siberia, and the region also lags in the availability of agricultural machinery and support industries.[31] These characteristics undoubtedly apply also to the Far East. It is doubtful that the Soviet leadership will decide to invest additional amounts of scarce capital in the improvement of agriculture in Asiatic Russia, especially with the current emphasis on improving agriculture in the non-chernozem zone of the European RSFSR. Thus, Asiatic Russia will probably remain a net importer of food for the foreseeable future.

TABLE 7.6

Asiatic RSFSR: Relative Cost of Production of Major
Agricultural Products, 1978
(USSR = 100)

| | USSR (rubles/ton) | West Siberia | East Siberia | Far East |
|---|---|---|---|---|
| **Grain** | | | | |
| Kolkhoz | 61 | 125 | 134 | 144 |
| Sovkhoz | 70 | 104 | 120 | 181 |
| **Potatoes** | | | | |
| Kolkhoz | 91 | 108 | 115 | 159 |
| Sovkhoz | 113 | 88 | 98 | 154 |
| **Milk** | | | | |
| Kolkhoz | 247 | 103 | 121 | 143 |
| Sovkhoz | 272 | 97 | 113 | 164 |
| **Eggs** | | | | |
| Kolkhoz | 81 | 105 | 115 | 123 |
| Sovkhoz | 61 | 89 | 98 | 130 |
| **Vegetables** | | | | |
| Kolkhoz | 106 | 153 | 145 | 128 |
| Sovkhoz | 97 | 81 | 125 | 169 |

Note: "Grain" does not include corn.
Sources: Narkhoz 78, pp. 265, 281; Narkhoz RSFSR 78, pp. 141, 145.

Forestry

In contrast with agriculture, Asiatic Russia plays a disproportionately large role in the production of Soviet forest products. The eastern regions contain about 80 percent of the Soviet Union's forest resources, although much of this forest area remains inaccessible. The region's share of commercial timber cut has been increasing steadily, rising from slightly over 25 percent of the total USSR output in 1960 to nearly 35 percent in 1975. The wood-processing industry has been lured to Siberia by the availability of cheap electric power and water.[32] Led by the giant plant at Bratsk, pulp production has risen to nearly one-fourth of the nation's total production. On the other hand, paper production, which requires more processing, has remained concentrated outside Asiatic Russia, in close proximity to demand. Because of the relative weight loss involved, and the availability of cheap energy (hydropower), it is much less expensive to ship pulp than timber to western paper mills.

A significant contribution to the development of the forest products industry in the eastern regions has been provided through foreign assistance. Japan, in three agreements signed since 1968, has provided machinery and credits in exchange for roundwood and pulp.[33] The CMEA countries are providing assistance in the construction of the Ust'-Ilimsk pulp mill, and North Korean laborers are helping to resolve labor shortages in some logging areas.[34] The major problems restricting the further growth of the forest products industry in the Asiatic RSFSR are the high cost of equipment, including importation of Western technology, and the long distance between eastern supply of forest products and European demand. The completion of the BAM is not expected to substantially affect the regional distribution of this industry. Neither local nor foreign (primarily Japanese) demand for forest products is expected to increase rapidly, and the break-even point for shipping wood products west remains at Krasnoiarsk.

Industry

Industrial development in Asiatic Russia has been heavily oriented toward the extractive industries and hydroelectric power. Although the area contributed only 10 percent of total Soviet industrial production in 1975, it accounted for roughly one-third of Soviet oil, coal, and timber production, and nearly one-fifth of the nation's electric power output (see Table 7.7). Extractive industries accounted for about 19 percent of the gross production of Siberia's industry in 1967-75, more than double the contribution of this sector to industry for the USSR as a whole.[35] Similarly, in 1975 industrial production personnel constituted 15 and 23 percent of total employment in West and East Siberia, respectively—well above the 10 percent average for the country.[36]

The industrial employment structure of the three regions of the Asiatic RSFSR reflects the peculiarities of each region's natural resource base (see Table 7.8). The share of employment in the fuel sector in West Siberia has generally remained at about twice the national average, an indication of the importance of these industries to the region and the country. In machine-building and metallurgy the employment shares are slightly above the USSR average in West Siberia, reflecting the importance of the Kuznetsk Basin, but remain well below average in the other two regions. On the other hand, East Siberia and, to a lesser extent, the Far East have an unusually large share of industrial employment in the timber industry. Only the Far East has an employment share in the food industry above that of the nation,

TABLE 7.7

Asiatic RSFSR: Industrial Production, 1975
(percent USSR)

|  | Percent |
|---|---|
| Total production | 10.2 |
| Electric power | 18.2 |
| Petroleum | 30.6 |
| Natural gas | 13.8 |
| Coal | 34.0 |
| Steel | 10.0 |
| Chemical fibers | 11.8 |
| Metal-cutting tools | 2.3 |
| Fertilizers | 3.1 |
| Rolled ferrous metals | 9.7 |
| Timber | 35.0 |

Sources: Adapted from Alan B. Smith, "Soviet Dependence on Siberian Resource Development," in U.S. Congress, Joint Economic Committee, Soviet Economy in a New Perspective (Washington, D.C.: U.S. Government Printing Office, 1976), p. 482; and N. N. Nekrasov, Regional'naia ekonomika (Moscow: Ekonomika, 1978), p. 156.

largely the impact of the important Pacific coast fishing industry. Further evidence of the importance of natural resources in the economy of Asiatic Russia is provided by Theodore Shabad, who lists 18 minerals for which the regional share of production is estimated to be above 50 percent.[37] Included in this group are aluminum, nickel, tin, platinum group metals, and two large earners of foreign exchange: gold and diamonds.

Fuel and Energy Resources

For the Soviet economy the most important natural resources in Asiatic Russia are fuel and energy. The European industrial

This section is based largely upon Leslie Dienes and Theodore Shabad, The Soviet Energy System (Washington, D.C.: V. H. Winston and Sons, 1979); Dienes, "The Regional Dimensions"; Robert G. Jensen, ed., "Soviet Energy Policy and the Hydrocarbons: Comments and Rejoinder," Discussion Paper no. 7, AAG Project (Washington, D.C.: AAG, 1979); and Theodore Shabad, "News Notes," SG:RT, April 1980, pp. 241-56.

TABLE 7.8

Asiatic RSFSR: Employment in Major Branches of Industry, 1960 and 1970
(percent)

| Branch of Industry | 1960 | | | | 1970 | | | |
|---|---|---|---|---|---|---|---|---|
| | USSR | West Siberia | East Siberia | Far East | USSR | West Siberia | East Siberia | Far East |
| Electric power engineering | 2 | 2 | 3 | 3 | 2 | 2 | 3 | 3 |
| Fuel | 7 | 14 | 6 | 8 | 5 | 10 | 5 | 6 |
| Heavy metallurgy | 5 | 5 | 1 | 1 | 4 | 4 | 1 | 1 |
| Chemicals and oil technology | 3 | 4 | 3 | 1 | 4 | 6 | 3 | 1 |
| Machine-building and metalworking | 32 | 35 | 19 | 25 | 38 | 41 | 23 | 29 |
| Forest products | 12 | 12 | 29 | 20 | 9 | 10 | 26 | 17 |
| Construction materials | 7 | 6 | 7 | 7 | 7 | 5 | 8 | 7 |
| Light industry | 17 | 11 | 9 | 7 | 16 | 10 | 10 | 9 |
| Food | 9 | 8 | 8 | 20 | 9 | 8 | 7 | 17 |

Source: N. C. Kistanova, Regional'noe ispol'zovaniie trudovykh resursov (Moscow: Nauka, 1978), p. 43.

center is already struggling with an increasing energy deficit that can be made up only by increasing imports from the eastern regions. Asiatic Russia possesses 64 percent of Soviet coal reserves and over 50 percent of the coking coal reserves. Natural gas reserves in the region in 1975 were estimated at 18.2 trillion cubic meters, slightly over 70 percent of total USSR reserves. Both the absolute and the relative figures should increase as exploration continues throughout the Asiatic RSFSR. Oil reserves are considered a state secret, but it seems safe to assume, on the basis of current and anticipated production trends, that the eastern regions also contain the majority of petroleum resources.[38]

More important, Asiatic Russia's share in the production of these resources has been growing since 1960, and especially for oil and natural gas since 1970 (see Table 7.9). The most dramatic increase among the hydrocarbons has occurred in petroleum production, mostly in Tiumen' Oblast. The chief contributor to this growth in 1970-75 was the supergiant Samotlor field, which provided 55 percent of the entire Soviet growth in oil production for that period. At the same time the share of petroleum in total Soviet energy output was rapidly increasing. By 1976 petroleum accounted for 43.6 percent of energy production and 36.9 percent of "apparent gross consumption."[39] Petroleum had also become a major export item and the leading Soviet earner of foreign exchange.

The cost of development of the West Siberian oil fields has been enormous—about 25 billion rubles during the 10th Five-Year Plan (1976-80) alone—in part because of the high cost of transportation.[40] Regardless of the cost involved, however, the problem confronting Soviet planners in the 1980s with respect to petroleum is how to increase West Siberian oil production, at least enough to offset declines in older producing areas, and to maintain current national production levels. With no new supergiant field like Samotlor yet discovered, the Soviets must develop many smaller deposits in even more remote areas, at great cost. Most Western experts are not very optimistic, and a decline in both West Siberian and total Soviet oil production, which seems likely within the next few years, could cause severe dislocations throughout the Soviet economy.

A dramatic increase also has occurred in Asiatic Russia's share in the production of natural gas. Tiumen Oblast provided more than half of the increase in Soviet natural gas production between 1970 and 1979. Currently, only Medvezh'e and Urengoi, of the four known supergiant fields, are producing. These natural gas fields are even more distant than the major Siberian oil fields from the consuming areas. The Soviets have encountered major problems

TABLE 7.9

Asiatic RSFSR: Energy Production, 1950–79
(percent USSR)

| Year | Coal | Oil | Gas | Hydro | Electricity |
|------|------|-----|-----|-------|-------------|
| 1950 | 26.5 | 2.6 | 1.6 | n.a. | 11.1 |
| 1960 | 28.0 | 1.1 | 0.8 | 13.9 | 14.9 |
| 1970 | 31.9 | 9.6 | 5.6 | 67.0 | 17.8 |
| 1975 | 34.5 | 30.8 | 13.8 | 85.0 | 18.2 |
| 1979 | 36.9* | 48.8 | 31.4 | n.a. | 18.1* |

*1978

n.a. = not available.

Sources: Narkhoz RSFSR 64, p. 61; Narkhoz 65, p. 170; Leslie Dienes and Theodore Shabad, The Soviet Energy System (Washington, D.C.: V. H. Winston and Sons, 1979), pp. 46–47, 70–71, 110–11; Theodore Shabad, "News Notes," SG:RT, April 1980, pp. 242, 245, 248.

in transporting equipment and supplies to the gas fields and laying the large-diameter pipelines in the region because of environmental constraints. Unlike petroleum, which is expected to reach peak production soon, output of natural gas should continue to increase during the 1980s. Soviet gas reserves in the Asiatic RSFSR are extensive, and prospects are good for even further additions to these reserves from other areas within the region. Iakutsk natural gas, however, will primarily be exported through Pacific ports rather than sent to ease energy problems in the European areas.

The share of gas in Soviet energy production should continue to increase. In contrast with petroleum, for which supply is a problem, transportation will be the major roadblock to the future delivery of Siberian natural gas to European consumers. Natural gas pipelines deliver much less energy than oil pipelines of similar size, and the demands created by the need to ship ever larger amounts of gas from remote Siberian fields will place a severe strain on the economy. Much of the demand for pipe and equipment will have to be met by foreign imports and paid for with foreign exchange earned from the export of natural gas.[41]

Among the hydrocarbons coal has shown the least growth in terms of Asiatic Russia's share of Soviet production. On the other hand, the lower production cost associated with eastern coal, much of which can be strip-mined, and the declining quantity and quality of coal in other regions suggest that this resource will continue to increase in importance through the 1980s. Current production in the eastern regions is centered in the Kuznetsk Basin. About 55 percent of Siberian coal production came from the Kuzbas in 1978. The Kuzbas is also a major producer of coking coal, much of it sent to consumers in regions outside Asiatic Russia, especially the Urals. The Soviets are currently in the process of developing coal production in the Kansk-Achinsk coal basin, which contains over one-fourth of Soviet coal reserves.[42] These two coal basins, which contain 52 percent of Soviet coal reserves, will become increasingly important in Soviet energy production. The Soviets are also developing the South Iakutsk coal deposits at Neriungri, but, like Iakutsk natural gas, this coal is destined largely for export to Japan and for use within the local regional economy.

Coal from Asiatic Russia will have to play an important role in solving the energy problems facing the European areas. As with natural gas, the Soviets face major transportation difficulties that must be overcome if Siberian coal is to fulfill its role. Two possibilities exist. One is to ship increasing amounts of coal to the west by rail. However, the lines that would be used are already over-burdened, and a large increase in coal shipments would require major investment in new railways or, possibly, slurry pipelines. The alternative, especially for Kansk-Achinsk coals, which are subject to spontaneous combustion, is to transform the coal into electricity at thermal power plants and send the energy west in that form. As noted earlier, however, the Soviets lack the technology for the transmission of electricity over the long distances involved.

It is in the production of hydroelectric power that the Asiatic RSFSR has its greatest comparative advantage. In 1975 the region produced 18.2 percent of all electric power but 85 percent of the electricity produced from hydropower. Nearly 50 percent of the generating capacity for the central Siberian power grid is obtained from hydropower. The Soviet Union has built (or is building) a series of large dams on the Angara-Ienisei system—Bratsk, Ust'-Ilimsk, Saiano-Shushensk, and Krasnoiarsk—and is in the process of developing the hydroelectric power of the Far East, an energy-deficit region, with construction of the large Zeia and Bureia dams. These projects are too far away to transmit electricity to the European regions of the USSR. Instead, the inexpensive power they produce has been used by the Soviets as the basis for locating energy-intensive aluminum refining and wood products industries in East Siberia.

## ENERGY, CAPITAL INVESTMENT, AND
## INTERREGIONAL CONFLICT

The growing demand for fuel and energy resources provided the impetus for the increasing share of capital investment allocated to Asiatic Russia during the 1970s (see Table 7.10). Within the region West Siberia, and more particularly Tiumen' Oblast, with its enormous oil and gas deposits, has been the chief beneficiary. East Siberia's share of total Soviet capital investment has stabilized at around 4.5 percent after declining from a high of 5.5 percent in the early 1960s as massive investment in hydroelectric power development has slowed. Investment in the BAM and development of Pacific transportation facilities are largely responsible for the slight increase in the share of capital investment in the Far East.

The cost of exploration, production, and distribution of fuel and energy is a capital-intensive venture under any circumstances, but is even more so in Asiatic Russia because of higher costs imposed by the constraints of environment, location, and low level of development. The Soviets, however, have had little choice but to invest heavily in Asiatic Russia's fuel and energy resources. Traditional sources located closer to the industrial heart of the nation generally have been declining in quality and quantity, particularly during the 1970s, while demand for energy in these western regions has been growing. A significant increase in the contribution of atomic power and other "exotic" forms of energy production to the European area's energy supply remains at best a hope for the end of this century.

Thus, future Soviet demand for energy will be met increasingly from the fuel and energy resources of Asiatic Russia, requiring the allocation of large annual increases in capital investment to West and East Siberia. If growth in total Soviet investment continues to decline, the rest could be a relatively rapid increase in the share of capital investment allocated to the Asiatic RSFSR. Such a trend would sharply reduce the availability of capital to other areas of the country and would probably provoke considerable interregional conflict over future investment allocation. [43]

Underlying any conflict over regional resource allocation is the issue of the future path of economic development in Asiatic Russia. Soviet authors agree that economic development in the region must, as in the past, be based on the extraction and processing of raw materials—timber, minerals, coal, oil, and natural gas—and the production of energy. Differences exist, however, in the degree to which these authors favor general diversification of the economy of the eastern regions based on the development of energy and natural resources, as opposed to strict specialization within a narrow range of energy-related activities. [44]

TABLE 7.10

Asiatic RSFSR: Capital Investment, 1950-78
(percent USSR)

| Year | Asiatic Russia | West Siberia | East Siberia | Far East |
|---|---|---|---|---|
| 1950 | 14.4 | 5.4 | 4.0 | 5.0 |
| 1958 | 15.6 | 6.7 | 4.7 | 4.3 |
| 1960 | 16.6 | 6.6 | 5.7 | 4.3 |
| 1961 | 16.5 | 6.5 | 5.5 | 4.4 |
| 1962 | 16.3 | 6.4 | 5.4 | 4.6 |
| 1963 | 16.4 | 6.6 | 5.7 | 4.2 |
| 1964 | 16.1 | 6.3 | 5.5 | 4.3 |
| 1965 | 15.0 | 6.0 | 4.9 | 4.1 |
| 1966 | 15.1 | 6.1 | 4.9 | 4.1 |
| 1967 | 15.5 | 6.4 | 4.8 | 4.2 |
| 1968 | 15.5 | 6.3 | 4.7 | 4.4 |
| 1969 | 15.3 | 6.1 | 4.7 | 4.5 |
| 1970 | 15.3 | 6.3 | 4.6 | 4.5 |
| 1971 | 15.7 | 6.6 | 4.6 | 4.5 |
| 1972 | 15.8 | 6.9 | 4.5 | 4.4 |
| 1973 | 15.9 | 7.2 | 4.4 | 4.3 |
| 1974 | 16.1 | 7.2 | 4.5 | 4.4 |
| 1975 | 16.8 | 7.4 | 4.6 | 4.7 |
| 1978* | 17.7 | | | |

*Planned.

Sources: Narkhoz 67, pp. 616, 626; Narkhoz 75, p. 513; Narkhoz RSFSR 65, p. 374; Narkhoz RSFSR 71, pp. 296-97; Narkhoz RSFSR 74, pp. 360-61; Narkhoz RSFSR 75, pp. 328-29; estimate for 1978 from A. I. Rezchikov, "Razvitie material'no-teknicheskoi bazy stroitel'stva na Vostoke," Ekonomika stroitel'stva (1978): no. 10, pp. 24-25.

Those authors favoring limited development point out that although Asiatic Russia's natural resources have the lowest costs of extraction, the higher costs of transportation, wages, and infrastructure greatly reduce this advantage. From their point of view, development in the eastern regions should focus narrowly on extraction of natural resources and energy-intensive semiprocessing of raw materials. Finished products should be manufactured in the western industrialized regions, where a pool of skilled labor and a fully developed industrial base already exist.[45]

Advocates of a more diversified development of Asiatic Russia's economy agree that future development should be tied to natural resources and energy. But, in addition, they advocate developing other aspects of the economy in support of these activities.[46] Supporters of economic diversification argue that labor productivity, gross industrial output per capita, and per capita national income produced are greater in Asiatic Russia than for the USSR as a whole, and that the payback period on investment is shorter in this region than in others. This latter point may be true for some narrowly defined projects. However, in an area where construction costs are much higher than the national average, transportation infrastructure is minimal, and other social overhead capital is virtually nonexistent, the payback period for comprehensive investment projects would likely be much longer than that associated with modernization of existing facilities in the European areas of the country.

Granberg, speaking only about Siberia, offers an interesting reply to those who complain that further investment in Siberia beyond that necessary to obtain raw materials and energy only means even greater subsidization of the region, primarily by the European areas. According to Granberg, the current structure of centrally planned domestic prices, as compared with world market prices, artificially understates Siberia's proportional contribution to the country's national income and gross social product. If world market prices were used, Siberia would shift from having a net regional balance-of-trade deficit with the rest of the country of 3 billion rubles to a positive balance of 8-9 billion rubles.[47] This general relationship also applies to extractive industries in the Far East. The wholesale price reform scheduled to go into effect on January 1, 1982, should help resolve this imbalance by increasing the price of eastern resources.[48]

Much of the argument of authors favoring diversified development has emphasized two elements. First, the industrial structure of Asiatic Russia should be broadened in direct support of its primary industrial specialization in raw material extraction, energy production, and energy-intensive semimanufacturing. G. Kurbatova, for instance, advocates an increase in the size and diversity of the Siberian machine-building capacity that serves the regional economy, such as mining equipment.[49] She points out that approximately 85 and 73 percent of the need of West and East Siberia, respectively, for machinery must be met by imports from outside the region. Kurbatova anticipates that locating more machine-building capacity in Siberia would reduce transportation costs and have a stabilizing effect on the labor force.

Second, advocates of diversification argue that without greater attention to development of social infrastructure and an improvement in the standard of living, Asiatic Russia will continue to experience severe labor problems in terms of both shortages and turnover. According to Aganbegian, housing availability in Siberia averages 10-20 percent less than in the European parts of the country, and the accommodations are qualitatively inferior. Moreover, the lag is even greater in the area of personal services such as health care, preschool facilities, and retail merchandising.[50]

Not only is the social infrastructure of Asiatic Russia poorly developed in comparison with that of the center, but, according to R. Vitebskii, the level of services supplied to the regional population needs to be 10-20 percent higher than in the center in order to retain the population. Because of the growing importance of these regions to the economy, Vitebskii believes that investment in infrastructure in Asiatic Russia must grow 1.5-2.5 times faster than in the European parts of the country.[51] This view accords with Aganbegian's statement that, for the good of the entire country, the growth rate of the economy of West and East Siberia over the long run should be 20-40 percent higher than that for the national economy.[52] At a time of decreasing growth of capital, it is unlikely that such a proposal would draw much support from leaders in other regions that already have a fully developed infrastructure supporting an existing industrial base.

## TPKs AND FUTURE DEVELOPMENT OF ASIATIC RUSSIA

At present, Soviet planners appear to be trying to strike a compromise between regional specialization in extractive industries and energy production, on the one hand, and greater diversification of the industrial base, on the other. Thus, while investment in Tiumen' oil and natural gas is continuing at a high rate, a major new chemical industry complex based on these resources is under construction at Tobol'sk. Also, the Saian dam will produce electricity for an energy-intensive aluminum plant but, within the same area, the Soviets are building a railroad car plant at Abakan and are forming an electrical equipment industry at Minusinsk. Similarly, along with plans to open up the Kansk-Achinsk coal fields and to expand coal mining in the Kuzbas, the Soviets are building the country's largest plant for the production of large excavators at Krasnoiarsk.

Regardless of which policy is followed—specialization or diversification, or some combination of the two—future development of the natural resources of Asiatic Russia will require enormous sums of money at a time when the growth of investment will be slowing, increments to the labor force declining, and oil production stagnating or in decline. Interregional and intersectoral competition for scarce resources will increase as the effects of these stringencies spread throughout the economy and force Soviet leaders to make hard decisions concerning the future allocation of capital investment and the location of production capacity.

According to Soviet planners, an important method that can be used to plan the future development of Asiatic Russia and that also addresses the conflict between resource stringencies (specialized development) and diversification of industry is concentration of investment in the region in a series of territorial production complexes (TPKs). [53] This approach has received tacit official approval, as reflected in the joint Central Committee-Council of Ministers planning decree of July 1979. [54]

Although Soviet writers have been unable to agree on the definition of a TPK, the basic elements are clear. [55] A TPK usually consists of a group of interrelated industries formed on the basis of one or more natural resources of national importance within a relatively compact area. The group of industries is usually dominated by one large industry that provides the basis for a set of forward and backward linkages among all the industries.

By concentrating investment, and thus economic development, within a relatively small area, Soviet planners expect TPKs to achieve significant economic efficiencies through external economies of scale in both economic and social infrastructure. This should result in substantial savings in the cost of developing Asiatic Russia's resources. O. A. Nekrasov estimates that concentrating investment in a TPK rather than dispersing the funds among several areas reduces the total cost of construction for all elements within the complex by 20 percent. [56] In addition, by concentrating investment in social infrastructure within a relatively small area, Soviet planners hope to raise the local standard of living and thus help reduce labor turnover. In practice, however, the Soviet press continues to be filled with complaints about the quality of life throughout Asiatic Russia, including TPKs.

The effectiveness of TPKs as the basis for an investment strategy has been seriously weakened in the past by severe management problems. [57] In general, there has been no strong central authority charged with development of each TPK. This fact has left their development subject to conflict between ministries and local authorities in the competition for scarce resources. Without a single decision-making entity, the integrated, planned nature of TPKs rapidly breaks down. Ministries may unilaterally change their plans concerning the construction of an enterprise in a TPK. Infrastructure construction inevitably lags far behind construction of industry, since it doesn't contribute directly to plan fulfillment. Even when a TPK appears to have a centralized authority in charge, as occurred in Bratsk, it suffers from the same kinds of problems that plague all Soviet industry in the eastern regions—labor turnover and lack of equipment and supplies.

There appears to be general agreement among Soviet authors that successful implementation of a TPK-oriented investment strategy requires the introduction of a TPK "project manager" with full authority over the construction and development of the TPK. The July 1979 planning decree may be a first step in this direction, perhaps concentrating the necessary authority within Gosplan.[58]

Although it is impossible to know precisely what direction Soviet development of Asiatic Russia will take in the long run, the short-term picture is relatively clear. When the Eleventh Five-Year Plan for 1981-85 is announced, it is highly probable that it will designate continued development of selected TPKs as an important goal for the plan period. Such a step would be consistent with the emphasis placed on long-range plans and the targeted-program approach to regional planning in the July 1979 planning decree.[59] It also seems likely that because of their growing economic and energy problems, the list of TPKs will not be expanded from those included in the past.

The West Siberian TPK will be allocated the lion's share of investment for the production of the oil and natural gas that is absolutely essential to the Soviet economy. This TPK is much too large, however, to serve as a focus for diversified development. Construction in this region will consist of relatively isolated projects, such as the petrochemical complex at Tobol'sk, and the large regional electric power station at Surgut, which will use casing head gas as a power source.

The major focuses for truly diversified development are likely to be the Saian TPK and the Kansk-Achinsk TPK. The former is named for a dam being built on the Ienisei River that will supply electric power to an aluminum plant planned for the area. This TPK is located in one of the most environmentally benign regions of Asiatic Russia. The region also produces coal, iron ore, and other minerals, and has a relatively well developed transportation network. More than 100 industrial enterprises have been projected for construction within the Saian TPK by 1990, including the previously mentioned railroad car plant at Abakan and the electrical equipment plants at Minusinsk. Although the commitment of various ministries to build these plants has varied through time, the Saian TPK should undergo considerable industrial diversification and development during the coming years.

The Kansk-Achinsk TPK will be developed during the 1980s on the basis of open-pit extraction of brown coal and large coal-fired electric power stations. These stations will provide energy for local industries and will transmit electricity at least as far west as the Kuzbas, which will then be able to use its own higher-quality coal for purposes other than electric power generation. The city of Krasnoiarsk, which already has a well-established industrial base, will serve as the focal point for further industrial development.

Two other TPKs that are more limited in scope, but probably will receive attention, are the Bratsk-Ust'-Ilimsk and the South Iakutsk TPKs. Bratsk and Ust'-Ilimsk are both based on the availability of inexpensive hydroelectric power and the energy-intensive wood products industries. Bratsk also has an aluminum plant; a similar project planned for Ust'-Ilimsk has apparently been shelved. The construction of a third dam at Bogucharny is under way, but at present there does not appear to be sufficient demand to justify it.

The South Iakutsk TPK is just beginning to be formed. At present its major reason for existence is the availability of coal, more particularly high-quality coking coal, although other minerals, including iron ore, are found in the area. It is currently the only officially designated TPK in the Far East.

The Bratsk-Ust'-Ilimsk and South Iakutsk TPKs illustrate another aspect of Soviet regional development policy in Asiatic Russia: the use of foreign help to develop resources. In the case of Ust'-Ilimsk, the pulp industries are being developed with help from the CMEA countries; the Japanese are paying a large share of the cost of developing the South Iakutsk TPK. In each case the sponsoring countries receive payment in kind once production begins. This type of agreement is understandably most appealing to the Soviets, who have an abundance of natural resources in the Asiatic RSFSR but limited capital and labor with which to develop them. In many cases the Soviets are willing to delay development of resources until foreign investment can be secured. For instance, the development of the extensive Udokan copper deposits will not occur in the foreseeable future without foreign assistance because the Soviets are able to supply their own copper needs from other sources.

Each of the five TPKs discussed above was mentioned specifically in the directives for the Tenth Five-Year Plan. Given the country's economic and energy problems, including a large backlog of unfinished construction, it seems unlikely that the Soviets will embark on any major new development project in Asiatic Russia during the next five-year plan, particularly because of the need to satisfy investment demands from other regions. Primary emphasis will probably be given to developing the already existing industrial capacity at these TPKs. If the Eleventh Five-Year Plan were to mention any new TPK for Asiatic Russia, perhaps the most likely candidate is the Kuznetsk Basin, where coal production is being expanded and a strong industrial base already exists. This endeavor would be appealing because investment in infrastructure and new industry could be kept to the minimum.

A similar case can be made for Komsomol'sk in the Far East. Because of the great distances separating the Far East from the main industrial and population centers of the country, this region appears to be developing almost independently of the rest of the country. Although it remains an important region strategically, much of its economic activity is oriented eastward toward the Pacific coast, whereas the other economic regions of Asiatic Russia remain largely oriented toward the western areas. Only goods with a high value, such as gold and diamonds, can stand the cost of transportation from the Far East region to Moscow. There is almost no possibility for the Far East to contribute to the solution of the country's energy problems in the 1980s except by trying to achieve regional energy self-sufficiency. The completion of the Zeia and Bureia dams will greatly contribute to this and, along with other resources, may form the basis for further industrial diversification within the region.

Soviet writers frequently talk about developing a string of TPKs along the BAM; some even seem to consider the BAM itself a TPK.[60] The Soviets have great hopes for the BAM. They expect it to provide access to a wide variety of resources within its zone of influence, many of which will be destined initially for export via the Pacific rather than for shipment to the industrialized west. Future development along the BAM, however, will be very costly, and probably will not occur to any great extent before the 1990s. When it is completed, however, the chief beneficiary of the BAM may be Komsomol'sk. This city, which already had an established industrial base and links to the Pacific, has now been linked to the BAM, and thus has gained access to a major new resource area.


SUMMARY AND CONCLUSION

It seems certain that the role of Asiatic Russia as the provider of Soviet raw materials and energy will be enhanced in the 1980s and that the share of capital investment allocated to Asiatic Russia will rise, at least during the early part of the 1980s, as the Soviets struggle with their energy problems and the slowing growth of capital and labor. The eastern regions are well-endowed with the kinds of fuel and energy resources that will be in greatest demand, but the severity of the regional constraints to economic development within Asiatic Russia present many problems and place a large additional burden on the Soviet economy. Nonetheless, the Soviets have no choice but to develop the fuel and energy resources in the eastern regions. This necessity will probably lead to increased interregional competition for scarce resources. It will also leave relatively less investment capital available for diversification of the economy of Asiatic Russia. What little there is, will probably be directed toward a few TPKs that will serve as the focuses for investment.


NOTES

1. For purposes of this chapter, the terms Asiatic Russia, Asiatic RSFSR, and eastern regions refer to the West Siberia, East Siberia, and Far East economic regions. Siberia refers only to the first two economic regions.

2. The basic parameters of this geographical dilemma are well known. See, for instance, NATO, Regional Development in the USSR: Trends and Prospects (Newtonville, Mass.: Oriental Research Partners, 1979); V. N. Bandera and Z. L. Melnyk, eds., The Soviet Economy in Regional Perspective (New York: Praeger, 1973); Leslie Dienes, "Investment Priorities in Soviet Regions," Annals of the Association of American Geographers, September 1972, pp. 437-54; Robert G. Jensen, "Soviet Regional Development Policy and the 10th Five-Year Plan," Soviet Geography: Review and Translation (hereafter SG:RT), March 1978, pp. 196-201; A. A. Mints, "A Predictive Hypothesis of Economic Development in the European Part of the USSR," SG:RT, January 1976, pp. 1-28; Theodore Shabad, Basic Industrial Resources of the USSR (New York: Columbia University Press, 1969).

3. Any regional study leaves itself open to various charges concerning the scale of analysis and choice of regional units. These decisions are always inherently subjective and often are guided by pragmatic problems of data collection and availability. The decision to include data for the economic regions is a compromise between those who would prefer a smaller scale of analysis and the stated objectives of the present volume.

4. Theodore Shabad, "The BAM, Project of the Century," in U.S. Congress, Joint Economic Committee, The Soviet Economy in a Time of Change (Washington, D.C.: U.S. Government Printing Office, 1979), p. 165.

5. Soviet principles of industrial location are discussed in F. E. Ian Hamilton, "Spatial Dimensions of Soviet Economic Decision Making," in Bandera and Melnyk, The Soviet Economy in Regional Perspective, pp. 235-60; and George A. Huzinec, "Soviet Decision-Making in Regional Planning and Its Potential Impact on Siberian Resource Exports," Discussion Paper no. 17, Association of American Geographers Project on Soviet Natural Resources in

the World Economy (Washington, D.C.: AAG, 1979). (Hereafter AAG Project.)

6. _Pravda_, December 22, 1972.

7. David S. Kamerling, "Regional Inequality of Social Indicators in the Soviet Union: The Examples of Health and Education" (M.A. thesis, Syracuse University, 1975); Roland J. Fuchs and George J. Demko, "Geographic Inequality Under Socialism," _Annals of the Association of American Geographers_, June 1979, pp. 304-18.

8. Dienes, "Investment Priorities in Soviet Regions," p. 446.

9. I. S. Koropeckyj, "Industrial Location Policy in the U.S.S.R. During the Postwar Period," in U.S. Congress, Joint Economic Committee, _Economic Performance and the Military Burden in the Soviet Union_ (Washington, D.C.: U.S. Government Printing Office, 1970), p. 276.

10. See Theodore Shabad, "Siberian Resource Development in the Soviet Period," in Theodore Shabad and Victor L. Mote, eds., _Gateway to Siberian Resources (The Bam)_ (Washington, D.C.: Scripta, 1977), pp. 1-61.

11. Nuclear power is expected to provide a growing share of the electricity needs of the European industrialized areas as the century progresses. Its use in Asiatic Russia will be limited to remote, isolated locations. Peat and oil shale production is concentrated in a band of oblasts between Leningrad and Gor'kii and in Estonia, respectively.

12. For an extensive review of environmental constraints in Asiatic Russia, see Victor L. Mote, "Environmental Constraints to the Economic Development of Siberia," Discussion Paper no. 6, AAG Project (Washington, D.C.: AAG, 1978).

13. Iu. Sobolev, "Narodnokhoziaistvennaia programma osvoeniia zony BAM," _Planovoe khoziaistvo_ (1978): no. 7, pp. 77-84.

14. A. I. Shrago, "Nauchno-tekhnicheskii potentsial mashinostrotel'nikh preapriiatnii Sibiri," _Vestnik mashinostroveniia_ (1980): no. 1, pp. 66-68.

15. A. G. Aganbegian, "Dorogo, no . . . deshevle," _Material-tekhnicheskoe snabzhenie_ (1980): no. 2, pp. 14-19.

16. Shabad, "Siberian Resource Development in the Soviet Period," p. 52.

17. A. G. Granberg, "Sibir' v narodno-khoziaistvennom komplekse," _Ekonomika i organizatsiia promyshlennogo proizvodstva_ (hereafter EKO) (1980): no. 4, pp. 83-106.

18. _Atlas razvitiia khoziaistva i kul'tury SSSR_ (Moscow: GUGK, 1967), pp. 82-83.

19. Leslie Dienes, "The Regional Dimensions of Soviet Energy Policy (With Emphasis on Consumption and Transport)," Discussion Paper no. 13, AAG Project (Washington, D.C.: AAG, 1979), p. ii.

20. G. Mil'ner, "Problems of Ensuring the Supply of Labor Resources for Siberian and Far Eastern Regions," Problems of Economics, June 1979, pp. 82-97.

21. A. G. Aganbegian, "Ekonomicheskie problemy razvitiia Sibiri," Ekonomika i matematicheskie metody (1979): no. 5, pp. 837-50.

22. I. P. Tsyganova, "Dolgii put' k Udokan," EKO (1978): no. 4, pp. 15-17.

23. Central Intelligence Agency, Ruble-Dollar Ratios for Construction (Washington, D.C.: CIA, 1976).

24. A. Smoliarchuk, "L'goty severianam," Trud, October 12, 1979, p. 4.

25. Mil'ner, "Problems of Ensuring . . .," pp. 88-89.

26. Aganbegian, "Ekonomicheskie problemy," p. 849.

27. V. Perevedentsev, "Chelovek na BAMe," Sovetskaia kul'tura, January 30, 1979, p. 3.

28. R. Vitebskii, "Regional'nye razlichiia v zatratakh na infrastrukturu," Voprosy ekonomiki (1978): no. 9, p. 53.

29. A. G. Aganbegian, "Utsenivat' po konechnym rezul'tatam," EKO (1976): no. 3, pp. 4-16.

30. Sobolev, "Narodnokhoziaistvennaia programma osvoeniia zony BAM."

31. Aganbegian, "Ekonomicheskie problemy," p. 845.

32. Shabad, "Siberian Resource Development," p. 21.

33. Richard L. Edmonds, "Siberian Resource Development and the Japanese Economy: The Japanese Perspective," Discussion Paper no. 9, AAG Project (Washington, D.C.: AAG, 1979), pp. 8-10.

34. Brenton M. Barr, "Soviet Timber: Regional Supply and Demand, 1970-1990," Arctic, December 1979, pp. 322-23.

35. T. B. Baranova, "Osnovnye pokazateli razvitiia promyshlennosti Sibiri v sedmoi-deviatoi piatiletkakh," Izvestiia sibirskogo otdeleniia Akademii nauk SSSR, Seriia obshchestvennykh nauk (1979): no. 1, pp. 28-33.

36. B. P. Orlov, "Ot Kuzbassa do BAMa," EKO (1977): no. 5, pp. 61-76.

37. Theodore Shabad, "Siberia and the Soviet Far East: Exploitation Policies in Energy and Raw Materials Sector. A Commercial Assessment," in NATO, Regional Development in the USSR, p. 155.

38. Leslie Dienes and Theodore Shabad, The Soviet Energy System (Washington, D.C.: V. H. Winston and Sons, 1979), passim.

39. Ibid., p. 34.

40. Aganbegian, "Ekonomicheskie problemy," p. 844.

41. Dienes, "The Regional Dimensions," pp. 47-53.

42. A lead editorial in Planovoe khoziaistvo claims that the mining of Kansk-Achinsk coal costs three to four times less than mining Donetsk coal. Planovoe khoziaistvo (1978): no. 11, pp. 3-6.

43. Granberg, "Sibir' v narodno-khoziaistvennom komplekse."

44. For a discussion of the East-West question, see Dienes, "Investment Priorities"; David A. Drach, "Tapping the Energy Wealth of Siberia: A Case Study of the Kansk-Achinsk Coal Basin," Discussion Paper no. 51 (Syracuse, N.Y.: Department of Geography, Syracuse University, 1978), pp. 8-20.

45. For recent articles supporting limited development in Asiatic Russia and favoring greater investment in the established industrial areas, see N. V. Alisov, "Spatial Aspects of the New Soviet Strategy of Intensification of Industrial Production," SG:RT, January 1979, pp. 1-6; Iu. G. Seliukov, "Locational Factors of Machine Manufacturing in the Soviet North," SG:RT, May 1979, pp. 310-20.

46. See the various pieces by "Siberia-firsters" Aganbegian and Granberg cited in this chapter. The term is Gertrude Schroeder's.

47. Granberg, "Sibir' v narodno-khoziaistvennom komplekse," p. 73. The relationship between central prices and the increase in the cost of raw materials is discussed in Iu. Iakovets, "Dvizhenie tsen mineral'nogo syr'ia," Voprosy ekonomiki (1975): no. 6, pp. 3-13.

48. N. T. Glushkov, "O razrabotke novykh optovikh tsen," Ekonomicheskaia gazeta (1980): no. 17, pp. 7-8.

49. G. Kurbatova, "Problemy razvitiia mashinostroeniia v Sibiri," Planovoe khoziaistvo (1980): no. 3, pp. 32-39.

50. Aganbegian, "Ekonomicheskie problemy," p. 849.

51. Vitebskii, "Regional'nye razlichiia . . .," p. 53.

52. Aganbegian, "Ekonomicheskie problemy," p. 843.

53. For western reviews of the Soviet concept of TPKs, see Richard E. Lonsdale, "The Soviet Concept of the Territorial-Production Complex," Slavic Review, September 1965, pp. 466-78; Violet Conolly, "The Territorial Production Complex in Siberia and the Far East," Munich, Germany, Radio Liberty Research, July 1976; G. J. R. Linge, Gerald J. Karaska, and F. E. Ian Hamilton, "An Appraisal of the Soviet Concept of the Territorial Production Complex," SG:RT, December 1978, pp. 681-95; George A. Huzinec, "Some Initial Comparisons of Soviet and Western Regional Development Models," SG:RT, October 1976, pp. 552-65.

54. In the decree Gosplan is instructed to review plans for TPKs and to exercise supervision over them, without regard to the departmental subordination of the enterprises and organizations making up the complex. CDSP, August 22, 1979, pp. 4-5.

55. See V. Nikol'skii, "A Typology of Regional Production Complexes," SG:RT, February 1973, pp. 92–100; A. Ie. Probst, "Territorial Production Complexes," SG:RT, February 1977, pp. 195–203; Mark K. Bandman, "Territorial'no-proizvodstvennie kompleksy," Obshchestvennye nauki (1979): no. 6, pp. 68–79.

56. O. A. Nekrasov, "Ekonomicheskie problemy khoziaistvennogo osvoeniia Sibiri i Dal'nego Vostoka," Vestnik moskovskogo universiteta, Seriia ekonomika (1978): no. 6, pp. 3–15.

57. V. P. Gukov et al., "Voprosy predplanovykh issledovanii i planirovaniia formirovaniia territorial'no-proizvodstvennykh kompleksov," Izvestiia sibirskogo otdeleniia Akademii nauk SSSR, Seriia obshchestvennykh nauk (1978): no. 1, pp. 3–11.

58. "Pravovoe regulirovanie kompleksnogo razvitiia territorii," Khoziaistvo i pravo (1979): no. 12, pp. 83–85.

59. A. I. Chistobaev and Iu. N. Bazhenov, "Programmno-tselevoi podkhod v territorial'nykh issledovaniiakh: Neobkhodimost' i napravleniia ispol'zovaniia," Izvestiia vsesoiuznogo geograficheskogo obshchestva (1980): no. 1, pp. 11–17.

60. V. S. Katargin and L. I. Iurkevich, "Territorial'no-proizvodstvennye kompleksy tsentral'noi chasty zony BAM," Izvestiia Akademii nauk SSSR, Seriia ekonomicheskaia (1977): no. 5, pp. 95–106.

# 8

## UKRAINE

### Ihor Gordijew and I. S. Koropeckyj

The Ukraine was one of the founding republics of the USSR. Its
economic experience under Soviet rule has been rather uneven. Reconstruction following World War I and the Civil War was very speedy,
especially during the New Economic Policy period, when the Kiev government enjoyed extensive decision-making powers and economic policy for the entire USSR was more consumer-oriented. This period
was succeeded by a quarter-century of Stalin's rule, punctuated by
World War II. Under the dictator rapid industrialization in the whole
of the USSR was largely dependent, during the late 1920s and the
early 1930s, on the performance of the heavy industry and the agriculture of the Ukraine. Collectivization of the Ukraine's agriculture,
to extract the "surplus" for industrialization, had tragic consequences
for its inhabitants: millions of people perished from starvation during the 1932-33 famine.

To add to the already difficult living conditions, World War II
was fought largely on Ukrainian soil, and left behind incalculable
human losses and material destruction. Postwar reconstruction,
still under Stalin's heavy hand, concentrated on industrial projects
and did little to alleviate the hardships being endured by the Ukrainian
population. Even though the Khrushchev and Brezhnev periods brought
substantial improvements in the standard of living of the entire Soviet
population, they were not particularly conducive to the expansion of
the economy of the Ukraine relative to other Soviet republics. The
leadership concentrated its attention on the development of other regions than the Ukraine, and such development has often been at the
Ukraine's expense.

This chapter focuses on the economic history of the Ukraine
since World War II and aims to discuss the Ukraine's economic development against the background of the Soviet economy as a whole.

This focus has necessitated the exclusion from consideration of the impact of Soviet-type economic arrangements on the Ukraine's performance, because they apply equally to all the constituent union republics. Our attention will be concentrated on the following aspects of the Ukraine's postwar experience: growth in its labor force and capital stock; growth in overall output and in the two principal sectors, industry and agriculture; growth in factor productivity; some selected problems currently facing the Ukrainian economy; the Ukraine's financial relations with the rest of the USSR; and a brief comparison of its economy with those of its Central European COMECON neighbors.

For our purposes, "the Ukraine" refers to the territory of the postwar Ukrainian SSR. Following the procedure usually accepted in regional studies, we shall use indicators for the USSR inclusive of the Ukraine; in so doing we shall find that because of the Ukraine's substantial weight in various USSR totals, differences between them are less pronounced than would have been the case if indicators for the USSR were calculated to exclude the Ukrainian component. Our discussion will cover the period from 1950, the year when, according to official statements, postwar reconstruction was completed, through 1978. Whenever the data cited in this chapter commence in a year later than 1950 or terminate with a year prior to 1978, the reason is the absence of the necessary data.

GROWTH IN RESOURCE SUPPLIES

The Ukraine covers approximately 2.7 percent of the territory of the USSR. Its prewar territory was about 36 percent smaller than now, owing to the incorporation during World War II within its present boundaries of Ukrainian ethnic lands that previously belonged to Poland, Romania, and Czechoslovakia. [1] Administratively the Ukraine is subdivided into 25 oblasts consisting of 477 raions. For planning purposes these oblasts are grouped into three major economic regions. In 1978 the Donets-Dnieper region accounted for 36.7 percent of the republic's territory and for 42.5 percent of its population, the South-Western region contributed 44.9 percent of the territory and 43.2 percent of the population, and the Southern region accounted for the remaining 18.4 percent of the territory and 14.3 percent of the population.

By 1980 the Ukraine's population had reached 50 million. [2] However, the share of the Ukraine in the total USSR population has been continuously declining. Within present territorial boundaries this share has been at the following percentages: 1913, 22.2; 1940, 21.3; 1950, 20.5; 1959, 20.0; 1970, 19.5; 1979, 19.0. [3] The reason for the lower weight of the Ukraine's population in the USSR is no doubt attributable to the consequences of World War II. Some estimates indicate that the Ukraine's prewar population increased by about 9.5 million (30.8 percent) following the incorporation of the western Ukraine within the USSR in 1939 and 1940.[4] But the Ukraine's World War II population losses were staggering, and have been estimated at 11 million persons.[5] As a result the population of the Ukraine decreased by 11 percent between 1940 and 1950. These war losses were not made up during the postwar period. Thus, while the population of the USSR as a whole increased by 47.0 percent during the period 1950-79, that of the Ukraine rose by only 36.0 percent. Taking the entire 1940-79 period, the cumulative increase for the Ukraine was 20 percent, while for the USSR (within comparable borders) it amounted to 35 percent.[6]

Between the census years of 1959 and 1970, net immigration accounted for about 10 percent—an average of 50,000 persons per annum—of the total population increase in the Ukraine.[7] The majority of the immigrants came from the Russian Federation, and they outnumbered persons emigrating from the Ukraine (primarily to the RSFSR and the Central Asian republics). As a consequence of this process, the percentage of persons of Russian origin in the total population of the Ukraine increased between 1959 and 1970 from 16.9 to 19.4 percent, and rose to 21.1 percent in 1979.[8] They tend to settle predominantly in urban and highly industrialized areas of the southeastern and southwestern Ukraine.[9]

Urbanization of the Ukrainian population is rising. The proportions of urban and rural population were 33.9 percent and 66.1 percent, respectively, in 1940; by 1979 the urban share had risen to 61.3 percent and the rural share had dropped to 38.7 percent. This trend is similar to the experience of the USSR as a whole, for which the share of urban population over the same period increased from 32.5 percent to 62.3 percent. The bulk of the population of the Ukraine resides in medium-size cities. Kiev, the largest city and the capital of the Ukraine, boasts a population of 2,144,000, followed by Kharkov, Dnieprodzerzhinsk, Odessa, and Dniepropetrovsk, all with populations exceeding 1 million.

In terms of its sex distribution, the Ukrainian population has not yet recovered from World War II losses, as evidenced by the fact that the proportion of females to males was 54.2 to 45.8 percent in 1978.[10] The proportion of females is especially high in the older cohorts. Population growth in the Ukraine has been among the lowest in the Soviet republics. For example, its natural population growth has been estimated at 0.52 percent and its actual growth at 0.53 percent for 1975, compared with the corresponding rates of 2.90 percent and 2.88 percent, respectively, for Tadzhikistan.[11]

Average family size in the Ukraine in 1979 was 3.3 persons.[12] Since rising levels of industrialization and urbanization, coupled with shortages of housing and nurseries, adversely affect family size, and since there is no prospect that these factors will change in the foreseeable future, average family size in the Ukraine most likely will not increase.

In 1970, 26,192,000 (55.6 percent) of the total Ukrainian population were classified as belonging to the able-bodied category (ages 16–59 for males and 16–54 for females),[13] compared with 54.0 percent for this group within the USSR as a whole. Growth of this age group between 1959 and 1975 exceeded the Ukraine's population growth. Children up to the age of 14 years accounted for 23.1 percent of the Ukraine's population in 1975. During the same year, persons of pensionable age amounted to 11.4 percent of the total among males and to 24.0 percent among females.[14] In conformity with trends in other developed countries, a process of population aging is evident in the Ukraine, since the percentage of pensionable males was only 8.2, and that for females 17.7, in 1959, rates considerably lower than those cited for 1975.[15]

Between 1950 and 1975 employment in state and cooperative enterprises rose from 13,567,000 to 23,331,000 (52 percent of the latter figure were women).[16] This change implies a 2.2 percent annual growth rate in the Ukraine, and is identical with the USSR rate of growth for employment in that period. But because of lower population growth in the Ukraine, compared with the USSR as a whole, the same growth rate in employment for the former means higher work participation rates than for the USSR. Table 8.1 presents data on the sectoral distribution of employment in the Ukraine for 1950, 1960, and 1975, and the shares of employment for the Ukraine in the corresponding USSR totals. As can be seen, the share of agricultural employment declined dramatically, while the share of industry, and even more so of service sectors, increased. These structural changes were more pronounced during 1960–75 than in 1950–60. Between 1950 and 1960 employment in industry grew at 4.9 percent per annum, in agriculture at 2.5 percent, and in other sectors at 4.1 percent. The corresponding growth rates for 1960–75 were 3.3, -1.1, and 4.2. In such service sectors as health, education, and communications, females constitute the predominant share of the work force.[17]

Employment shares for the various sectors of material and nonmaterial production within the Ukrainian economy, while varying as a proportion of their respective USSR totals within ranges that have equaled or fallen slightly short of the Ukraine's population ratio in the USSR total, remained relatively stable over 1950–75. Two exceptions need to be noted. First, although employment in various

TABLE 8.1

Growth and Sectoral Distribution of Employment in the Ukraine,
and Its Share in the USSR: 1950-75
(percent)

| | 1950 | | 1960 | | 1975 | | |
|---|---|---|---|---|---|---|---|
| | Distri-bution | Ukraine as Percent of USSR | Distri-bution | Ukraine as Percent of USSR | Distri-bution | Ukraine as Percent of USSR | 1975 (1950 = 100) |
| Total employment | 100.0 | 19.9 | 100.0 | 20.3 | 100.0 | 19.8 | 172.0 |
| Industry | 18.5 | 16.4 | 23.7 | 17.9 | 28.3 | 19.4 | 263.1 |
| Agriculture and forestry | 53.9 | 23.2 | 43.7 | 25.4 | 27.3 | 24.4 | 87.1 |
| Transportation and communications | 5.8 | 17.1 | 6.9 | 16.7 | 8.5 | 18.4 | 248.0 |
| Construction | 4.4 | 18.2 | 6.3 | 17.2 | 7.9 | 17.5 | 311.6 |
| Trade, public catering, material-technical supply, and sales and procurement | 4.5 | 18.2 | 5.0 | 18.3 | 7.3 | 19.3 | 279.4 |
| Housing, communal economy, and personal services | 1.6 | 16.2 | 1.8 | 16.4 | 3.0 | 18.4 | 315.8 |
| Health services | 2.8 | 18.8 | 4.0 | 19.9 | 4.9 | 19.8 | 297.1 |
| Education, culture, art, science, and scientific services | 5.3 | 17.1 | 6.6 | 16.5 | 9.6 | 16.5 | 311.5 |
| Government administration | 2.5 | 18.2 | 1.3 | 17.3 | 1.7 | 17.4 | 117.4 |
| Credit, insurance, and other | 0.6 | 17.0 | 0.7 | 16.7 | 1.4 | 16.8 | 423.1 |

Source: Stephen Rapawy, "Regional Employment Trends in the USSR: 1950 to 1975," in U.S. Congress, Joint Economic Committee, Soviet Economy in a Time of Change (Washington, D.C.: U.S. Government Printing Office, 1979), Table 1.

sectors of nonmaterial production grew at a rate faster than that experienced in industry, only the latter's share in the USSR total increased noticeably—by three percentage points—over the period under review. We shall have occasion to return to this point later in this chapter, since it has an important bearing on the entire postwar economic experience of the Ukraine. Second, the share that agricultural employment in the Ukraine constitutes in total agricultural employment in the USSR markedly exceeds the Ukraine's population ratio in the USSR total. The collective farm sector is particularly prominent in Ukrainian agriculture, accounting for almost one-third of the corresponding USSR total. [18] It follows that the Ukraine has remained specialized in agriculture within the USSR, a role it performed before the Revolution.

Between 1950 and 1975 industrial employment in the Ukraine increased from 2,509,000 to 6,602,000—more than 2.5 times. Information about structural changes in this sphere of employment is available for 1960-75 only (see Table 8.2). Employment in branches that have been important in the Ukraine for a long time—fuels (mainly coal mining) and ferrous metallurgy—grew at a rate less than overall industrial employment, which increased 63 percent between 1960 and 1975. In fact, employment in the fuels branch declined by 13 percent, reflecting structural changes within this branch. Compared with the relevant branches for the USSR, the share of these two branches combined declined from 24.3 to 15.3 percent between 1960 and 1975.

This relative decline clearly illustrates the continuing shift of heavy industry from the European part of the USSR—predominantly from the Ukraine—to the Asiatic regions, a process that began before World War II. Among the various industry branches, chemicals and machine-building deserve special mention because growth in their output tends to embody technological progress. The combined share of these two branches in total industrial employment in the Ukraine increased from 31.5 to 44.3 percent. Their share increased as well in the corresponding USSR employment by 2.8 percentage points. No significant shifts took place in employment in the remaining industrial branches during the period under discussion.

Major occupational changes have taken place in the Ukrainian work force during the postwar period. As a rule these changes facilitated increases in labor productivity. Between the 1959 and 1970 censuses the percentage of blue-collar nonagricultural workers increased as a proportion of the total work force from 39.5 to 51.8, and that of white-collar workers rose from 15.5 to 23.2 percent, while, as noted earlier, there was a decrease in the share of agricultural employment. [19] At the same time the proportion of persons engaged in mental work increased from 16.7 to 24.4 percent of the

## TABLE 8.2

Growth and Sectoral Distribution of Employment in Ukrainian
Industry and Its Shares in USSR: 1960 and 1975

(percent)

| | 1960 | | 1975 | | |
|---|---|---|---|---|---|
| | Distribution | Ukraine as Percent of USSR | Distribution | Ukraine as Percent of USSR | 1975 (1960 = 100) |
| Total | 100.0 | 17.9 | 100.0 | 19.4 | 162.8 |
| Electric power | 1.5 | 14.9 | 1.7 | 16.2 | 188.1 |
| Fuels | 14.7 | 38.1 | 7.9 | 36.3 | 87.0 |
| Ferrous metallurgy | 9.6 | 37.1 | 7.4 | 35.8 | 126.3 |
| Chemical and petrochemical | 2.7 | 13.6 | 4.7 | 17.7 | 288.0 |
| Machine-building and metalworking | 28.8 | 16.2 | 39.6 | 18.9 | 223.8 |
| Timber, woodworking, pulp and paper | 6.4 | 9.7 | 4.7 | 11.2 | 119.9 |
| Construction materials | 8.3 | 21.5 | 6.9 | 21.3 | 135.5 |
| Light industry | 12.7 | 13.3 | 12.8 | 16.5 | 164.0 |
| Food industry | 11.1 | 20.8 | 9.9 | 21.7 | 145.0 |
| Other | 4.2 | 12.9 | 4.3 | 14.8 | 168.2 |

Source: Stephen Rapawy, "Regional Employment Trends in the USSR: 1950 to 1975," in U.S. Congress, Joint Economic Committee, Soviet Economy in a Time of Change (Washington, D.C.: U.S. Government Printing Office, 1979), Table 2.

total, while the proportion of those occupied primarily in manual work decreased from 83.5 to 75.6 percent.[20]

These changes were, of course, the result of higher levels of education among the population. For example, the percentage of employees with higher and special higher education increased from 15.6 to 25.1 percent between 1960 and 1977. In this respect educational levels in the Ukraine were equal to those for the USSR.[21] However, with regard to scientific personnel, the Ukraine's share lagged behind unionwide standards. Although the number of scientific personnel increased 8.3 times between 1950 and 1977, the Ukraine's share of the total pool of such workers for the USSR as a whole experienced little change during this period, rising from 13.8 to 14.1 percent—well below the Ukraine's population share in the USSR total. There appear to be no immediate prospects for improvement in this situation, because the number of Ukrainian graduate students in 1978 accounted for only 13.5 percent of the USSR total.[22] Needless to say, this circumstance is liable to exert a negative effect on the rate of technological progress in the Ukrainian economy.

Turning now to a consideration of the Ukraine's nonlabor resources, it may be noted that while the Ukraine accounts for 2.7 percent of the USSR's total territory, its share of land used for agricultural purposes amounts to 7.6 percent, and rises to 15.4 percent for area sown to crops.[23] The fertility of the Ukrainian soil, much of it belonging to the black earth category, has been renowned for centuries. Availability of coal, iron ore, various nonferrous ores, natural gas, and various other mineral deposits facilitated development of a modern economy in the Ukraine. Furthermore, such factors as moderate climate, availability of sea coast, and proximity to Western Europe influenced favorably the growth of its economy throughout history.

Data on fixed capital in the Ukrainian economy are available in some detail only for the period 1960-75.[24] Figures on the growth of fixed capital, its sectoral distribution, and the shares of various components in the relevant unionwide totals are presented in Table 8.3. The total stock of fixed capital for the Ukrainian economy as a whole almost tripled during the period under review. The fixed capital of the material production sectors increased much more rapidly than that of the service sector. Construction, a sector of the material sphere, experienced the highest rate of growth, registering an increase of 6.5 times; agriculture, not surprisingly, occupied last place. Housing, accounting for approximately two-thirds of fixed capital and classified as belonging to the nonmaterial sector of production, displayed the lowest growth rate of the material and nonmaterial sectors combined.

TABLE 8.3

Growth and Sectoral Distribution of Fixed Capital in the Ukraine
and Its Shares in USSR: 1960 and 1975
(percent)

| | 1960 | | 1975 | | |
|---|---|---|---|---|---|
| | Distribution | Ukraine as Percent of USSR | Distribution | Ukraine as Percent of USSR | 1975 (1960 = 100) |
| Total | 100.0 | 19.1 | 100.0 | 17.2 | 284.9 |
| Material production | 54.8 | 18.3 | 65.4 | 17.4 | 339.6 |
| Industry | 25.9 | 19.1 | 32.4 | 17.5 | 355.8 |
| Agriculture | 14.4 | 20.8 | 14.4 | 18.3 | 285.0 |
| Transportation and communications | 10.6 | 15.9 | 12.6 | 16.8 | 339.6 |
| Construction | 1.0 | 10.6 | 2.3 | 13.2 | 648.2 |
| Trade, distribution, and other material production | 2.9 | 16.8 | 3.7 | 18.6 | 356.3 |
| Nonmaterial production | 45.2 | 20.2 | 34.6 | 16.9 | 218.4 |
| Housing | 33.8 | 20.7 | 21.9 | 17.4 | 185.0 |
| Other nonmaterial | 11.4 | 18.6 | 12.7 | 16.1 | 317.4 |

Source: James W. Gillula, The Regional Distribution of Fixed Capital in the USSR (Washington, D.C.:
Bureau of the Census, Foreign Demographic Analysis Division, 1980), Tables A-1, A-3.

In relation to the USSR, the Ukraine's share in the total fixed capital decreased by two percentage points during the 15 years under consideration. Some decline in relative share was evident in the majority of the Ukraine's economic sectors. Sectors of material production other than industry and agriculture constituted exceptions; their shares in the fixed capital of the corresponding sectors of the USSR increased by one to three percentage points during this period. Industry's share declined by almost two points, and that of agriculture by 2.5 points. Sectors of nonmaterial production, especially housing, suffered reductions in capital stock shares that were even more pronounced than in industry or agriculture.

More detailed information on the fixed capital stock of industry branches for 1960-74 is given in Table 8.4. The highest growth rates during this period took place in chemicals, electric power generation, and light industry, none of them particularly prominent within the industrial structure of the Ukraine. Branches in which the Ukraine has traditionally specialized—ferrous metals, fuels, and food processing—registered below-average growth in capital stock. As a result a tendency toward a more balanced structure of Ukrainian industry is evident. Compared with their respective Soviet counterparts, the shares of fixed capital assets of most industrial branches declined in the Ukraine. The only exceptions were electric power generation and machine-building.

In summary, in comparison with the USSR, the growth of the Ukraine's labor force since World War II has been faster than that of its capital stock, particularly in such major economic sectors as industry, agriculture, and housing. Since the central planners could hardly affect the supply of labor, but had almost complete control over the supply of capital, this investment policy shows clearly that economic development and population welfare in the Ukraine were of low priority to the Soviet leadership. (For discussion of this point, see the last section of this chapter, "Financial Relations and Alternative Institutional Arrangements.")

GROWTH OF NATIONAL INCOME,
INDUSTRY, AND AGRICULTURE

The nature of postwar development in the Ukraine is best understood when considered against the background of the destruction of much of its economy during World War II, which inflicted extremely heavy losses upon the Ukraine. Its resource-rich territory was a prime target for both Nazi Germany and the Soviet government. Some of the most destructive battles of World War II were fought on Ukrainian territory. Owing to the deficiency of arms,

# TABLE 8.4

Growth and Distribution of Fixed Capital in Ukrainian Industry,
by Branch and Share in the USSR: 1960 and 1974

(percent)

| | 1960 | | 1974 | | |
|---|---|---|---|---|---|
| | Distribution | Ukraine as Percent of USSR | Distribution | Ukraine as Percent of USSR | 1974 (1960 = 100) |
| Total | 100.0 | 19.1 | 100.0 | 17.8 | 327.9 |
| Ferrous metallurgy | 21.7 | 41.4 | 19.7 | 35.7 | 297.7 |
| Fuels | 19.7 | 24.1 | 14.9 | 21.0 | 248.1 |
| Electric and thermal power | 9.1 | 13.0 | 14.0 | 14.7 | 504.6 |
| Machine-building and metalworking | 17.4 | 16.6 | 21.0 | 17.7 | 395.8 |
| Chemicals | 4.9 | 17.9 | 8.1 | 15.5 | 542.3 |
| Wood and paper | 2.5 | 7.2 | 1.5 | 5.4 | 196.9 |
| Construction materials | 5.9 | 17.3 | 5.1 | 15.6 | 283.4 |
| Light industry | 2.3 | 9.5 | 3.1 | 12.2 | 442.4 |
| Food industry | 10.8 | 20.2 | 8.9 | 20.0 | 270.2 |
| Other | 5.7 | 13.6 | 3.7 | 9.1 | 212.8 |

Source: James W. Gillula, The Regional Distribution of Fixed Capital in the USSR (Washington, D.C.: Bureau of the Census, Foreign Demographic Analysis Division, 1980), Tables B-2, B-3.

277

ammunition, and other military supplies at the disposal of the Red Army, and the reluctance of many of its soldiers to defend the Stalin regime, the German army was able to overrun much of the Ukraine shortly after the outbreak of war.

Before retreating, the Soviet authorities succeeded in evacuating a substantial amount of various types of movable equipment previously located in the Ukraine. Some of the machinery and factories were reassembled at considerable distances from the front and were commissioned either as new enterprises or as additions to existing ones. In addition, substantial quantities of the fixed capital of the Ukraine were destroyed by the Soviet authorities either prior to their retreat or during their evacuation. Many workers were evacuated along with their enterprises, either by themselves or accompanied by their families. It appears that none of the equipment was returned to the Ukraine, though most of the workers came back after the war.

Owing to this large-scale destruction of the Ukraine's production capability, the Germans were, in general, unable to utilize Ukrainian resources for their war effort. Only a small fraction of Ukrainian factories, mainly those in food processing, were put into operation. Apart from a few exceptions in the eastern Ukraine, where land was distributed among the peasants for private cultivation, the Germans retained the kolkhoz system intact in order to mobilize urgently needed food supplies more easily. Like the Red Army before them, the Germans applied a "scorched earth" policy in the Ukraine before retreating in 1943–44 under the pressure of the Red Army onslaught.

By the time of the Red Army's return, the Ukrainian economy lay virtually in ruins. According to the findings of a Soviet government committee charged with the task of assessing war damage, 714 cities and 28,000 villages had been destroyed in the Ukraine.[25] Ten million people had become homeless as a result. About 38 million square meters (50 percent of urban living space) had been rendered unusable. Many public buildings, including churches, cultural establishments, and local government utilities, had been destroyed. Some of these buildings were of great historical value as unique relics of the past. Agriculture had suffered the loss of 422,000 kolkhoz structures and of the bulk of its machinery, equipment, and livestock (for example, 2.8 million horses, 5.0 million head of cattle, and 5.4 million sheep had been killed or removed from the Ukraine). Transportation had ceased to function. All railroad bridges, 50 percent of rail tracks, and the majority of the buildings servicing transportation needs and rolling stock had been destroyed.

But it was the Ukrainian population that suffered the most severe losses. The conduct of war, evacuation, and various other war-related activities caused losses in the Ukraine that have been estimated, as noted earlier, at 11 million persons. The committee of inquiry into war damage attributed the entire blame for the losses and the destruction to Germans. But in view of the "scorched earth" policy of the Soviet troops in 1941, sabotage activities by Red guerrillas behind German lines, and the actions of the advancing Red Army upon its return to the Ukraine in 1943-44, one may apportion the blame for the atrocities committed on the Ukrainian population and economy equally between the Nazi leadership and the Soviet leaders.

Following the extensive war devastation, reconstruction of the Ukrainian economy proceeded apace. Official data claim that by 1950 the Ukrainian economy had regained prewar output levels. While no doubt somewhat exaggerated, this claim has to be viewed in the light of two significant considerations. First, the usual postwar "reconstruction effect" should not be disregarded. This was reinforced by the replacement of equipment and machinery that had been destroyed (much of which was obsolete) by more modern capital assets obtained by the USSR from Germany and its allies as war reparations. Second, the bulk of the resources earmarked by the Soviet leadership for reconstruction was channeled toward the rehabilitation of producer-goods rather than consumer-goods industries. Since the former were more modern and efficient than the latter, this investment policy was conducive to the maximization of overall industrial growth rate.

Data on the growth in the net material product (NMP) in the Ukraine since 1956 and of the net output of the principal economic sectors (as available) since 1960 are presented in Table 8.5. Before proceeding with an analysis of the trends revealed by the data, two reminders are in order. First, the NMP concept differs from the usual and more comprehensive indicator—gross national product—in that it excludes, in addition to depreciation, the output of the sectors of nonmaterial production, such as services and government activities. Second, there is widespread agreement among Western students of the Soviet economy that official Soviet indexes of NMP and industrial output are biased upward. For example, according to official statistics NMP in the USSR increased 13.8 times between 1950 and 1975, whereas painstaking calculations by Western scholars show an increase (in GNP) of no more than 5.6 times over the same period.[26] Unfortunately, no Western estimates of the growth in total output have been computed as yet for the Ukraine, forcing us to rely on official Soviet statistics for our analytical conclusions.

Between 1956 and 1978 the Ukraine's NMP rose 3.9 times, somewhat below the increase for the USSR as a whole (4.2 times).[27] For the entire USSR, and for the Ukraine separately, a slowing down

TABLE 8.5

Growth Rates of Net Material Product in the Ukraine,
by Economic Sectors: 1956–77
(percent)

|  | 1956–65 | 1965–70 | 1970–77 |
|---|---|---|---|
| Net material product | 7.8 | 6.8 | 4.8 |
| Industry | n.a. | 9.9 | 6.3 |
| Agriculture | n.a. | -0.2 | -0.3 |
| Transportation and communications | n.a. | 8.0 | 6.7 |
| Construction | n.a. | 7.0 | 3.1 |
| Trade, public catering, material-technical supply, and sales and procurement | n.a. | 8.2 | 6.0 |

n.a. = not available.

Sources: TsSU, Narodnoe Hospodarstvo Ukrains'koi RSR v 1970 R. (Kiev, 1971, p. 395 (hereafter Narkhoz Ukraine); Narkhoz Ukraine 77, p. 288.

in the rate of growth in NMP has occurred since 1960. During the period 1956–65 the rate of growth was slightly higher for the Ukraine than for the USSR—7.8 and 7.4 percent per annum, respectively. But in subsequent periods there was a deceleration in the rate of increase in this indicator in both the USSR and the Ukraine, somewhat more pronounced for the latter than for the former. For 1965–70 the relevant growth rate was 7.8 percent for the USSR and 6.8 percent for the Ukraine, and for 1970–78 it was 5.5 and 4.6 percent, respectively. The decrease in growth rate was experienced by all sectors of the Ukrainian economy. This slowdown in the Soviet economy is usually explained by a decrease in the rates of resource growth and factor productivity, and by increased transfers of high-quality resources to defense requirements. These considerations most likely apply with equal force to the Ukraine.

As a result of a fairly similar performance in all sectors of the Ukrainian economy in terms of the NMP indicator, no significant structural changes took place during the 17-year period for which data are available (see Table 8.6). The only noteworthy distribution increases are a two-point rise in trade and related activities and a one-point increase in transport and communications, at the expense

TABLE 8.6

Distribution of Net Material Product in the Ukraine,
by Sector, and Shares in the USSR Totals: 1960–77
(percent)

| | 1960 | | 1970 | | 1977 | |
|---|---|---|---|---|---|---|
| | Distri-bution | Ukraine as Percent of USSR | Distri-bution | Ukraine as Percent of USSR | Distri-bution | Ukraine as Percent of USSR |
| Net material product | 100.0 | 18.6 | 100.0 | 18.9 | 100.0 | 18.1 |
| Industry | 48.1 | 17.2 | 50.0 | 18.5 | 47.8 | 17.0 |
| Agriculture | 25.9 | 23.6 | 25.3 | 21.6 | 23.7 | 24.3 |
| Transportation and communications | 4.4 | 15.6 | 4.8 | 16.0 | 5.6 | 16.3 |
| Construction | 10.0 | 18.6 | 9.2 | 16.7 | 9.3 | 15.5 |
| Trade, public catering, material-technical supply, and sales and procurement | 11.5 | 17.9 | 10.7 | 18.3 | 13.6 | 17.5 |

Sources: Narkhoz Ukraine 70, p. 395; Narkhoz Ukraine 77, p. 288; TsSU, Narodnoe khoziaistvo SSR v 1970 g. (Moscow: TsSU, 1971), p. 534 (publication hereafter cited as Narkhoz); Narkhoz 78, p. 386.

of the remaining sectors. Industry continues to account for one-half, and agriculture for approximately one-quarter, of total Ukrainian NMP. However, the peculiarities of Soviet statistical procedures have to be kept in mind when considering the structure of output. Official Soviet methodology attributes the bulk of nonlabor return, the "surplus," accruing in agriculture primarily to industry, where the products with agricultural inputs are sold to consumers. As a result the share of industry in national income is biased upward while that of agriculture is depressed.[28]

The somewhat faster growth of NMP for the USSR economy as a whole relative to the Ukraine, mentioned earlier, is also evident in Table 8.6. During the period under discussion, the shares of the Ukrainian NMP and of most of its sectors declined relative to the USSR totals. The only observable increases are those in agriculture, mainly because of a more bountiful harvest in the Ukraine than in the rest of the USSR in 1977, and in transport and communications (for reasons that are unclear).

Industrial growth is considered in the USSR to be the mainstay of economic development. Not surprisingly, therefore, industry is found to have grown faster than any other economic sector in the Ukraine. During 1950-77 its growth rate in the Ukraine slightly exceeded that of the USSR (11.3 versus 10.9 times). Nevertheless, the Ukraine was unable to regain its prewar position of relative industrial prominence within the USSR. Relative to 1940, industrial output in 1977 was 13.0 times greater in the Ukraine, and 18.8 times greater in the USSR.

Data in Table 8.7 present information on the postwar growth in the gross output of Ukrainian industry, its branch distribution, and branch shares in their respective USSR totals. Growth was quite high, but is undoubtedly overstated because of the underlying official methodology. Much lower growth rates are given by an approach more nearly comparable to that used in Western countries. Thus, while the official index shows a growth rate in gross output for 1946-71 of 14.6 percent per annum, the calculation based on net output shows a growth rate of about 11.0 percent.[29]

Both official and Western-type indexes of Ukrainian industrial growth look less impressive when three additional considerations are taken into account. First, the overall growth rate of industrial output, as well as of individual industrial branches, declined markedly after 1965. Significant retardation is evident in the output growth of fuels, ferrous metals, and food processing, all branches in which the Ukraine has traditionally specialized.

Second, the structure of Ukrainian industry remains unbalanced (a problem to be discussed later). Expressed as proportions of branch output totals for the USSR as a whole, the Ukraine's

# TABLE 8.7

Growth Rates, Distribution, and Shares of USSR Industrial
Output, by Branch: Ukraine, 1950-77

(percent)

| | Growth Rate | | 1975 | |
| --- | --- | --- | --- | --- |
| | 1950-65 | 1965-77 | Distribution | Ukraine as Percent of USSR |
| Total | 11.1 | 7.3 | 100.0 | 18.6 |
| Electric power | 14.0 | 7.7 | 2.6 | 17.3 |
| Fuel | 7.7 | 3.3 | 5.6 | 18.3 |
| Ferrous metals | 9.6 | 4.1 | n.a. | 41.9 |
| Chemicals and oil refining | 17.7 | 11.6 | 6.1 | 16.4 |
| Machine-building and metalworking | 15.5 | 11.6 | 28.1 | 18.8 |
| Timber, woodworking, and celluloid | 6.8 | 6.0 | 2.7 | 10.9 |
| Construction | 14.5 | 6.8 | 4.0 | 18.1 |
| Glass, porcelain, and china | 11.0 | 9.7 | n.a. | n.a. |
| Light industry | 9.3 | 8.1 | 11.3 | 14.1 |
| Food | 9.5 | 4.5 | 22.5 | 22.0 |

n.a. = not available.

Sources: Narkhoz Ukraine 77, p. 82. The Ukrainian shares were derived from absolute data for the total in the Ukraine (97,277,000,000 rubles) and in the USSR (523,439,000,000 rubles)—James W. Gillula, "Regional Interdependence and Economic Development in the USSR" (Ph.D. diss., Duke University, 1978), p. 153—and from the official branch distribution—Narkhoz Ukraine 75, p. 197. The share for ferrous metals is for 1967 and was derived from P. V. Voloboi and V. A. Popovkin, Problemy terytorial'noi spetsializatsii i kompleksnoho rozvytku narodnoho hospodarstva Ukrains'koi RSR (Kiev, 1972), p. 120.

283

shares in ferrous metals (the figure in Table 8.7 refers to 1967) and the food industry are in excess of its population ratio within the Soviet counterpart. On the other hand, output shares in light industry and wood and related products are considerably below its population ratio. In the remaining branches there is a fairly close correspondence between output shares and the population ratio.

Third, output of inferior quality is a disease endemic to Soviet economic performance. A few examples will illustrate the extent of the problem in the Ukraine.[30] In 1978, 90 percent of the overall output of light industry was below prescribed standards. About one-quarter of all the equipment employed in the metalworking branch was occupied in repair work. During the mid-1970s outlays on the repair of machinery, equipment, and transport facilities exceeded those on investment in new machinery and equipment.

Agriculture, thanks to excellent climatic and soil conditions, has historically been very important within the overall structure of the Ukrainian economy. Even after half a century of Soviet emphasis on rapid industrialization, it still accounted for 40 percent of the Ukraine's GNP in 1970[31] and, as noted earlier, has continued to employ more than one-quarter of its work force in recent years. In terms of institutional arrangements, kolkhozes are more common than sovkhozes in the Ukraine when the relative weights of these two types of agricultural enterprise are compared with their shares for the USSR as a whole. The number of kolkhozes in the Ukraine represented 26.2 percent, and that of sovkhozes 10.2 percent, of their respective numbers in the USSR in 1977. Enterprises jointly set up by kolkhozes, sovkhozes, and various nonagricultural organizations have become increasingly numerous in the Ukraine; they accounted for more than one-third of such organizations in the USSR in 1977.[32] The private sector continues to contribute a substantial share of various types of agricultural produce in the Ukraine. For example, while in 1977 this sector had only 1.5 percent of the sown area, it accounted for 64.2 percent of the total potato crop, 25.6 of vegetables, 32.0 of meat and lard, 26.9 of milk, and 42.5 of eggs.[33] The importance of the private sector has tended to rise in years when performance in the socialized sector has been poor, since at such times the leadership has usually relaxed constraints on private activity.[34]

Selected indicators of the postwar development of Ukrainian agriculture are presented in Table 8.8. As was the case with industry, a definite deceleration in the growth rate has occurred since 1960 with pronounced fluctuations from year to year. For example, net output increased by 26.9 percent between 1963 and 1964, and declined by 19.6 percent between 1974 and 1975.[35] As far as structural movements are concerned, the output of the livestock sector grew at a slightly faster rate than that of crop cultivation during the period under review. As a result the share of the former in the total gross output of Ukrainian agriculture increased from 47.9 to 51.1 percent between 1950 and 1976-78, while that of crop cultivation declined from 52.1 to 48.9 percent.[36]

TABLE 8.8

Growth Rates of Gross Output of Ukrainian Agriculture,
by Branch, and Shares in the USSR Totals: 1950-78
(percent)

| | Growth Rate | | | Ukraine as Percent of USSR | |
|---|---|---|---|---|---|
| | 1950-60 | 1961/65–1971/75 | 1971/75–1976/78 | 1950 | 1976/78 |
| Total | 4.5 | 3.1 | 1.5 | 23.7 | 23.5 |
| Crops | 3.8 | 2.7 | 1.8 | 23.7 | 24.7 |
| Animal products | 5.8 | 3.4 | 1.2 | 24.1 | 22.5 |

Sources: Narkhoz Ukraine 77, pp. 141–42; Narkhoz 78, pp. 198–99.

The last two columns in Table 8.8 deserve special attention. They show that the share of the Ukraine in the total output of USSR agriculture exceeded its share in the USSR population by four to five percentage points during the second half of the 1970s. This achievement was the more remarkable in view of the fact that Ukrainian agriculture received only around 20 percent of the Soviet output of mineral fertilizers during the 1960s and the 1970s, and had—for example, in 1978—at its disposal only 15.9 percent of all tractors and 12.1 percent of the combine harvesters used in the USSR.[37] Moreover, the Ukraine was able to retain its relatively preeminent position in Soviet agriculture during the postwar period despite a considerable increase in sown area and massive agricultural investment in other republics—for example, in the Virgin Lands and the Nonchernozem region. The creditable output performance shows the continued high fertility and productivity of Ukrainian agriculture.

As a result of the speedy reconstruction and the comparatively vigorous rate of growth of its economy during the postwar period, the Ukraine may be ranked among the more developed countries in the world. Owing to the specificity of Soviet conditions, this statement applies with greater force to the expansion of productive capacity than to the welfare of the population. A comprehensive comparison in terms of GNP magnitudes can be made only for 1970, the sole year for which this indicator of economic performance was estimated for the Ukraine and other union republics on the basis of Western methodology. [38] It may be assumed that no significant changes occurred during the 1970s with respect to the relative position of the Ukraine.

In 1970 the Ukraine's GNP amounted to 69.5 billion rubles and, among union republics, was second only to that of the RSFSR, which was three times larger. [39] Compared with the GNP of the economically weakest republic, Turkmenia, that of the Ukraine was almost 32 times larger. GNP per capita in the Ukraine was close to the unionwide average, and ranked fifth among the 15 republics, following the three Baltic republics and the RSFSR. The per capita magnitude for the Ukraine exceeded by almost two times that of the least developed republic, Tadzhikistan. If we distinguish between material production, on the one hand, and services and the government sector, on the other, we find that the Ukraine was relatively more developed with respect to the former. The output of material production per capita in the Ukraine exceeded the USSR-wide average by 2.8 percent. Conversely, the indicator of nonmaterial production per capita fell short of its unionwide counterpart by almost 15 percent. Since the level of service output has a direct impact on public welfare, the relative underdevelopment of the nonmaterial production sector in the Ukraine suggests that the needs of its population are relatively poorly served. (This matter is discussed in greater detail in Chapter 4.)

To permit a comparison between the Ukraine and countries outside the USSR, the ruble values of the Ukraine's GNP were converted in the study cited above into 1970 U.S. dollars. When thus converted, the Ukraine's GNP in that year was found to equal $94.5 billion and to average $2,100 per head. The data that follow are intended to indicate the proportion of the Ukraine in the total and per capita GNP of selected Western countries in 1970. [40]

|  | Aggregate | GNP per capita |
|---|---|---|
| USA | 9.9 | 43.5 |
| West | 50.3 | 65.8 |
| France | 53.0 | 57.1 |
| United Kingdom | 64.3 | 76.0 |
| Italy | 88.4 | 102.2 |

The Ukraine is seen to occupy a position approximately equal to that
of Italy but otherwise considerably behind most of the advanced countries in the world. When compared with the European socialist countries in terms of aggregate GNP, the Ukraine is ahead of all of them;
and on a per capita basis it is exceeded only by the German Democratic Republic and Czechoslovakia to the extent of some 10 percent,
whereas it leads Hungary, Poland, Bulgaria, Romania, and Yugoslavia by a considerable margin.

PRODUCTIVITY GROWTH

A survey of the Ukraine's postwar economic experience would
be incomplete without an analysis of growth in the productivity of its
resources and a comparison between the Ukraine and the USSR in
this respect. Since, in view of the Soviet price structure, a study
of static efficiency would not be very meaningful, we shall concentrate on trends in productivity growth. Data from Chapter 3 will be
used for this purpose. There, as well as in the present chapter,
"productivity growth" means the difference between the growth rate
in net output and the growth rate in labor and capital, combined with
the aid of a variant of the Cobb-Douglas production function. In
other words, the difference is meant to indicate the extent to which
the growth in output has resulted from factors other than increases
in labor and capital. These factors could be improvements in the
quality of the labor force and capital as well as in institutional arrangements or economies of scale.

Table 8.9 provides information on the productivity growth in
NMP and in the two basic sectors of the economy for three subperiods. From the data themselves, it may be observed that with
respect to total output, there was a tendency for productivity growth
in the Ukraine to decelerate during the postwar period, from 3.0 to
1.6 percent between the early 1960s and the 1970s. This was in line
with trends in the entire USSR economy, for which the corresponding figures declined from 4.0 to 1.9 percent. Furthermore, it
should be noted that starting with the second half of the 1960s, the
Ukraine's position deteriorated relative to the USSR as a whole in
regard to productivity growth. We also observe that the growth
rates of combined factor inputs and of output were approximately
the same for the Ukraine and the USSR over the entire 15-year
period. However, after 1965 resource, and even more so output,
growth proceeded at a lower pace in the Ukraine than it did in the
USSR as a whole.

The behavior patterns of both inputs and output in Ukranian
industry were similar to those for the USSR. Reflecting these trends,

productivity growth in Ukrainian industry increased between the
first and the second halves of the 1960s by more than one percentage
point, then declined during the 1970s by almost two percentage points.
However, relative to the USSR, productivity growth in Ukrainian industry began to decline after 1965.

TABLE 8.9

Total Factor Productivity Growth in the
Ukraine and the USSR: 1960-75
(percent)

| | 1960-65 | | 1965-70 | | 1970-75 | |
|---|---|---|---|---|---|---|
| | Ukraine | USSR | Ukraine | USSR | Ukraine | USSR |
| Net Material Product | | | | | | |
| Output | 7.4 | 6.7 | 6.7 | 7.8 | 4.7 | 5.7 |
| Resources | 4.4 | 4.5 | 3.6 | 3.8 | 3.1 | 3.8 |
| Factor productivity | 3.0 | 2.2 | 3.1 | 4.0 | 1.6 | 1.9 |
| Industry | | | | | | |
| Output | 10.0 | 9.0 | 9.9 | 9.8 | 6.6 | 7.8 |
| Resources | 6.5 | 6.6 | 5.3 | 4.9 | 3.8 | 3.8 |
| Factor productivity | 3.5 | 2.4 | 4.6 | 4.9 | 2.8 | 4.0 |
| Agriculture | | | | | | |
| Output | 1.9 | 2.1 | -0.2 | 2.1 | -2.8 | -3.9 |
| Resources | 0.8 | 0.9 | -0.4 | 0.1 | 0.6 | 1.6 |
| Factor productivity | 1.1 | 1.2 | 0.2 | 2.0 | -3.4 | -5.5 |

Sources: See sources to Tables 3.2 and 3.4 and text of
Chapter 3.

The trends in productivity growth in Ukrainian agriculture
during 1960-75 were as follows. During the 1960s agricultural production in the Ukraine grew at a slower pace than in the USSR. During the 1970s this growth was negative in both the Ukraine and the

USSR as a whole. The decline was slightly less for the Ukraine:
-2.8, compared with -3.9 percent per annum for the USSR. The resource increment in agriculture was lower for the Ukraine than for
the USSR during the whole period under review. The trend was com-
posed of two parts: labor in the Ukraine decreased somewhat less
than in the USSR, and capital increased (but relatively less). It is
evident, therefore, that in this respect the experience of Ukrainian
agriculture was similar to that of its industry. As a result productivity growth in the Ukraine was slightly lower than for the USSR
during the 1960s. However, this trend was reversed during the
1970s. This was no doubt due, apart from other factors, to the
massive investment by the Soviet government in the non-chernozem
regions of the European RSFSR, where, however, the anticipated
increase in agricultural output has not yet materialized.[41]

A detailed explanation of the reasons for the decline in productivity growth within the Ukrainian economy and its major sectors,
particularly compared with USSR trends after 1965, would require a
special study. Nevertheless, some relevant considerations can be
outlined briefly. Since the productivity growth indicator is a composite of output and input trends, both of the components will be discussed separately.

Taking output first, it is reasonable to suppose that the lower
growth of the Ukrainian economy, and of its industry in particular,
relative to the USSR is in part attributable to Soviet price-setting
procedures. Newly produced goods, particularly those intended for
the consumer market, are usually released at prices higher than
those of existing substitutes. Branches such as light industry and
civilian machine building are particularly vulnerable to this practice. Food processing is less affected because, for political reasons, food prices are not allowed to rise. Ukrainian industry spe-
cializes in ferrous metals, fuels, and food processing, branches in
which price increases tend to be minimal. Since the data in Table
8.9 are based on the official Soviet index, it is possible that for this
reason the growth rate in the output of Ukrainian industry is understated when compared with its counterpart for the USSR as a whole.

Next, turning to the input side, it is conceivable that structural changes, in terms of resource transfers to sectors in which
output increments per ruble of inputs are lower than in other sectors,
could be exerting a downward pressure on productivity growth. But,
according to both Western[42] and Soviet[43] sources, these considerations were not particularly significant in the Ukrainian economy as a
whole after World War II. In contrast, structural changes appear to
be beneficial for productivity growth in the industrial sector. Thus,
a Soviet econometric study[44] finds that greater attention to the development of the chemical and machine-building branches, at the

expense of the fuels, ferrous metals, and light industry branches, has been conducive to the overall productivity growth of Ukrainian industry.

Some of the factors mentioned below are often put forward by Soviet authors as adversely affecting productivity growth in the Ukraine. Although they are normally mentioned in connection with development in industry, it is possible to argue that they are applicable to the entire economy. Among the factors influencing productivity patterns are rising machinery and equipment costs;[45] long gestation periods for new capital construction;[46] rising costs of environmental protection,[47] a consideration that is of greater relevance in the more densely populated Ukraine than in the sparsely settled regions of the Asiatic USSR; increases in the cost of mining coal[48] and ores (in which the Ukraine has specialized) as a result of the depletion of more suitably located deposits; and deterioration in the quality of physical inputs and technological obsolescence in ferrous metallurgy.[49] It is highly probable that all of these factors, especially the first two, affected productivity growth in the USSR economy and its industrial sector in the same direction. However, for reasons that require thorough investigation, the above factors may have exerted a stronger depressing influence on the performance of the Ukrainian economy.

Furthermore, preceding discussion suggests the operation of two additional factors that may have contributed directly to the relative slowing down in productivity growth within the Ukrainian economy compared with the rest of the USSR. First, modern economic growth depends to a great extent on technological progress, which is itself a product of research activity by scientists. If an invention is made elsewhere, and a particular region wishes to take advantage of it, teams of scientists are needed in order to adapt the new technology to local conditions.[50] As mentioned earlier, the Ukraine has a fairly low proportion of the USSR's pool of scientific manpower. This relative shortfall in scientific know-how may exert a retarding influence on technological progress in the Ukrainian economy. Second, the share of investment outlays (as a proportion of the USSR total) to meet the needs of the Ukrainian economy, of its industry and agriculture in particular,[51] has been declining consistently in recent years. The result of such a policy must be a reduction in the amount and type of new capital that can be introduced. Since new machinery and equipment embody technological progress, there was a reduction in innovational opportunities in the Ukrainian economy as compared with regions of the USSR where above-average growth has been taking place.

Although the factors discussed above may have affected productivity growth adversely in the Ukrainian economy exclusively, or more so in that economy than in the rest of the USSR, they do not explain why this slowdown became particularly pronounced after 1965. The following considerations may be relevant to this problem. Judging from the statements made by various Soviet Ukrainian political leaders and economists, their republic's resources were particularly efficiently utilized between the mid-1950s and 1965.[52] This coincides more or less with the period when the economic powers of regional authorities in the USSR, including those in Kiev, were far more extensive than they had been during Stalin's rule or after the reintroduction of branch planning in 1965, followed by gradual concentration of decision making in the hands of the Moscow planners. These recentralization tendencies became particularly strong during the 1970s, as the draft of the new Soviet Constitution was discussed. The Constitution, introduced in 1978, contains for the first time an article whose practical import is the virtual elimination of any lingering elements of separateness of the national economies of individual union republics.[53] It may, therefore, be suggested that the relatively greater decline in productivity growth in the Ukraine, as compared with the corresponding indicators for the USSR as a whole, after 1965 may have been associated with the almost complete subordination of the economic interests of the republic to those of the entire union.

## SOME CURRENT PROBLEMS IN THE UKRAINIAN ECONOMY

Despite some unquestionable successes that the Ukrainian economy has chalked up during the decades following World War II, there are a number of problems urgently requiring solutions. Let us focus our attention on some of the more pressing among them. Along with many other countries in the world, the Ukraine has experienced shortages of fuel and energy. As shown earlier, between 1956 and 1977 the NMP of the Ukraine grew at an annual rate of 6.6 percent, while its gross industrial output rose at 9.4 percent between 1950 and 1977.[54] Growth in electricity generation was on the order of 11.2 percent, and fuel output averaged a rate of increase of 5.7 percent from 1950 to 1977.[55]

Normally one would expect fuel and energy output to exceed the growth rate of the entire economy or at least of industry, but this obviously was not the case for the Ukraine. The situation was aggravated by the export of Ukrainian coal and natural gas to other parts of the USSR (the Baltic republics, Belorussia, and the RSFSR), as well as of coal (coking coal in particular) and electricity to other socialist countries.[56] In its turn the Ukraine has imported considerable amounts of crude oil from the RSFSR, but this seems to have been insufficient to meet the rising internal demand. Energy-saving equipment and processes have been introduced on an increasing scale in the Ukrainian economy in order to avoid a fuel crisis. Nevertheless, fuel shortages have contributed to a decline in the annual rate of growth of fuel consumption, from 7.4 percent during the 1950s to 5.1 percent during the 1960s, and the decline is expected to continue to between 4 and 5 percent during the 1970s and the 1980s.[57]

The Ukrainian leadership and planners in Kiev are well aware of the magnitude of this problem and have, on a number of occasions (without much success), demanded from the Moscow authorities higher investment allocations for the expansion of energy and fuel production.[58] However, in view of the unfavorable natural conditions prevailing in the mining of coal, the main energy supplier for the Ukraine, it is doubtful whether a sufficiently large expansion of output could now be achieved. In order to prevent the inadequate supply of fuels from becoming an obstacle to further growth of the Ukrainian economy, it would be advisable to suspend all fuel exports from the Ukraine for some time to come. Furthermore, a greater effort should be mounted to develop facilities for generating nuclear energy in the Ukraine; at present the effort is confined to the construction of only two plants (at Chornobyl' and Trypillia). Finally, imports of electricity and crude oil from other regions of the USSR should be stepped up.[59]

A structural imbalance inherited from pre-Revolution times continues to plague the Ukrainian economy. Compared with the structures of well-developed Western economies, in the Ukraine heavy industry and agriculture occupy relatively high shares in GNP terms, while the consumer goods branches and the service sector are rather underdeveloped.[60] Imbalances also exist within individual economic sectors. For example, among agricultural branches livestock husbandry is insufficiently developed as compared with crop cultivation. The imbalances are particularly serious in industry. The Ukraine continues to specialize in the output of various extractive and heavy-industry branches, such as coal and iron ore mining, ferrous metallurgy, the production of raw materials for the chemical industry, some construction materials, metal-intensive machine-building, and sugar refining. In contrast, the Ukraine lags behind in the output of labor-intensive subbranches of machine-building, chemicals, nonferrous metallurgy, wood processing, paper, and light industries.[61]

This structure came into being during the initial industrialization stages in the Ukraine, more than 100 years ago, and has persisted into the present. It was evidently efficient under the scarcity relationship prevailing in those times, and was even of paramount usefulness as an instrument in the industrialization of the entire tsarist empire. However, the survival of this kind of structure into the present hinders the maximization of aggregate output and reduces the welfare of the population below its potential. Not only is the inefficient structure harmful to the Ukraine, but it is contrary to the interest of the USSR as a whole. [62]

The former low-cost industries of the Ukraine—coal, for example—have been producing, roughly since World War II, at costs exceeding the USSR average. In contrast, products of various labor-intensive branches (instrument-making, electrical and radio equipment, synthetic fibers, products of the rubber and light industries) could now be manufactured more cheaply in the Ukraine than in some other regions of the USSR. Efficiency demands that resources should now be gradually withdrawn from the various material- and energy-intensive branches and shifted into the labor-intensive branches. [63]

Furthermore, Ukrainian agriculture deserves greater attention. Increased investment allocations to this sector would, judging from experience in other countries, result in additional output even with a smaller labor force. The labor thus released could then be employed in the expanding branches of industry and in the service sector of the economy.

But cost-of-production levels cannot serve as the sole criterion for structural changes of the economy; other factors should be taken into account as well. A faster rate of development of the various labor-intensive branches in the Ukraine would relieve the continued exploitation of nonreplaceable mineral resources that are more intensively mined in the Ukraine than in the rest of the USSR;[64] provide employment opportunities for underemployed and unemployed labor in its less developed regions, primarily in the western Ukraine, an area from which young people are forced to emigrate to other Soviet republics because of inadequate employment opportunities;[65] lessen the demand for additional investment, fuels, and water; prevent economic stagnation or even retardation following the exhaustion of mineral resources (as happened in Azerbaidzhan following the depletion of oil reserves there); and, finally, increase the supply of consumer goods to the public.

The structural imbalances discussed above are accompanied by—and may, indeed, be regarded as the cause of—regional imbalances in the level of economic development within the Ukraine. Owing to the availability of the necessary raw materials for the growth of the favored branches of heavy industry, the Donets-Dnieper region is by far the most developed in the Ukraine. The development of the Southern region, which contains a favorable mix of industrial, agricultural, and resort activities, is at a level

approximately average for the entire Ukraine. On the other hand,
the South-Western region, in which agriculture is still the predominant sector, is the least developed. This region contains oblasts
that were industrially backward prior to their incorporation into the
USSR during World War II. Since then some of them have experienced spectacular industrial progress. For example, between 1940
and 1978 industrial output in the L'vov Oblast increased 58 times;
that of Rovno, 41 times; and that of Zakarpatskaia Oblast 45 times
(since 1946). For the entire Ukraine this increase was only 14
times.[66] Despite the progress in the less developed western Ukraine,
interoblast differences are still pronounced. During the 1960s the
proportion between the most developed and least developed oblast, in
terms of a composite index consisting of output, fixed capital, and
employment indicators, was 1:2.3.[67]

Judging, however, from data on retail sales per capita, there
has been a tendency toward some equalization of consumption levels
among the various oblasts of the Ukraine. According to one study,
the coefficient of variation of food retail sales decreased from 36.5
to 21.6 percent, and for consumer goods other than food items it
fell from 21.3 to 15.0 percent between 1960 and 1975.[68] However,
differences in retail sales levels per capita remain substantial. For
example, in 1977 total consumer goods purchased per capita in the
developed Donetsk oblast exceeded by 24.7 percent the level of the
corresponding indicator in the weakly developed Chernovtsy oblast.[69]
It should be noted that the private agricultural sector is often quite
substantial in extent in the less developed regions of the USSR and
the consumption of foods in these regions would tend to be especially understated by the official retail sales index.

These and other deficiencies evident in the Ukrainian economy
could have been eliminated or at least ameliorated if the Kiev government had had a freer hand in pursuing economic policies of its
own choosing. As it is, that government has continuously had to
subordinate the interests of the Ukrainian economy to those of the
USSR (as the latter were perceived by the Moscow leadership). A
crucial aspect of this powerlessness of the Kiev government was the
outflow of investable funds from the Ukraine for the development of
other regions of the USSR. As noted earlier, output in the principal
sectors of the Ukrainian economy—industry and agriculture—grew
primarily as a result of increments in the labor force, since the
rate of the growth of capital was lagging behind that for the USSR as
a whole. As a result, production processes in the Ukraine have been
increasingly labor-intensive and less capital-intensive than in the
rest of the Soviet economy, with consequences such as a reduced
ability to introduce new technology and lower adaptability of the
Ukraine's economic structure to technological changes.

## FINANCIAL RELATIONS AND ALTERNATIVE
## INSTITUTIONAL ARRANGEMENTS

It is perhaps best to link discussion of the Ukraine's financial relations with the rest of the USSR to consideration of hypothetical alternative institutional and political status arrangements for the Ukraine and its economy. This is because an insight into interregional transfers may shed some light on the opportunity cost to the Ukraine of present institutional arrangements in reference to which alternatives could be evaluated. Even abstracting from poorly substantiated claims presented by Soviet sources that the Ukraine has gained unprecedented economic benefits as a result of its membership of the USSR,[70] the more general view that has been propounded by some Western observers is best summarized as follows:

Statistical computations purporting to show that Russia withdraws more wealth from the national republics than it puts into them are not convincing, because they usually do not take into account the cost of administration and defense which these republics would have to bear if they were independent. They are indeed no more realistic than Marxist statistics adduced to show imperialistic exploitation of colonies by capitalist countries.[71]

It is further argued that if economic considerations were the determining factor in such matters, nationalism would not exist, because it is inherently an economic absurdity.[72]

Ignoring the debatable nature of the statement that "Marxist statistics" regarding "imperialistic exploitation" are unrealistic, it may be noted that existing budgetary and redistributive arrangements in the USSR are by no means "neutral" between various regions and classes of society. In connection with the latter, we need only mention the point that agriculture and the peasant class throughout the USSR, and collective farm members in particular regions, have contributed substantially toward Soviet industrialization. Various observers have remarked, for example, that it cannot possibly be said that the sacrifices imposed on the peasants in the Soviet Middle East republics match those borne by the Russians and Ukrainians.[73] Even Soviet economists admit that the Ukraine contributed significantly toward the development of Imperial Russia;[74] that it has been the foundry, the smithworks, the "coal and metal base" of industrialization within the USSR in general and in other Soviet republics in particular;[75] that in addition to bearing the heavy costs connected with post-World War II reconstruction, it has—over a long period—supported much of the USSR's defense potential.[76]

In the section dealing with the growth of resource supplies,
we observed that the capital endowment situation in the Ukraine
showed that a low priority was being placed by the Soviet leadership
on expanding the Ukrainian economy.  This point will now be elabo-
rated as one illustration of the financial relationship between the
Ukraine and the rest of the USSR.  The slower growth rates in the
fixed capital assets of the Ukraine as compared with the USSR as a
whole are explicable by the investment policies pursued by the central planners.  These, in turn, are closely linked with the redistributive activities of the central government through the price
mechanism and the state budget.

The magnitude of these excessive contributions of the Ukraine
to the needs of the USSR as a whole can be estimated by various
methods.  Studies of the relationship between the Ukrainian and
union budget have most often been used for this purpose.  They show
that national income transfers from the Ukraine to other regions of
the USSR have been taking place virtually since the incorporation of
the Ukraine into the USSR.  According to various Western and Soviet
estimates, these transfers, which are equivalent to the excess of
national income produced over national income utilized in the Ukraine,
varied between 10 and 20 percent of the NMP of the Ukraine.[77]  A
recent Western source[78] places this national income loss at an average of 11 to 14 percent per year during 1961-72, while two Kiev
economists estimate it at 15.2 percent between 1959 and 1969.[79]
Regardless of differences in these estimates, which result from the
differences in methodologies and availability of data, there is no
doubt that the Ukraine experienced continuous and significant loss of
its national income to other parts of the USSR.

The loss of a part of the Ukraine's national income no doubt
reduced both consumption and investment in this republic.  It is difficult to show the effect on consumption with the available statistics.
On the other hand, the following data on the Ukraine's share in the
total USSR investment during the postwar period reflect this national
income outflow.[80]

| 1946-50 | 19.3 | 1966-70 | 16.6 |
| 1951-55 | 16.5 | 1971-75 | 15.9 |
| 1956-60 | 17.0 | 1976-78 | 15.1 |

As can be seen, these shares were consistently lower than the
Ukrainian shares in the total output and population of the USSR.
The immediate postwar period, when the Ukraine's share approxi-
mated its population share, is an exception.  Moreover, the investment percentage has been falling in recent years, so that by 1978 it
stood at 15 percent—suggesting a rather bleak outlook for the future
of the Ukrainian economy.

Furthermore, an analysis of budget data reveals that, but for investments by collective farms and by the population from their own sources, the percentage would have been even lower.[81] This relatively low allocation of investment to the Ukraine has been taking place despite the Ukraine's considerable contribution toward the accumulation of investment funds within the USSR as a whole. One estimate indicates that in 1970, for example, the Ukraine contributed 24.8 percent of the total differential rent for the USSR and 18.5 percent of the total returns on capital.[82] The Ukrainian labor force also adds to this fund. The latter contribution arises from the fact that labor productivity in the Ukrainian economy—for example, in agriculture—is sometimes higher than the average for the USSR, while labor remuneration for such work is determined by the central planners at levels that approximate the average for the USSR as a whole. No attempt has yet been made to estimate the surpluses arising from these differences between remuneration and productivity of the Ukrainian labor force.

Finally, in the most speculative portion of our study, we turn from that which we have tried to ascertain as "being" to that which "might have been." Peter Wiles has addressed himself to the question of "how rich and how well developed would the Ukraine have been without Soviet rule?"[83] The interested reader is referred to Wiles's stimulating and perceptive treatment of the subject. Considerations of space allow us to make only a few remarks.

While such resource-poor republics as Moldavia have few alternatives under any regime as to how they might utilize their meager resources and how they should specialize, the Ukraine finds itself in a different position. Possessing a rich soil, minerals, fuels, and other raw materials, as well as a skilled labor force in numbers and of qualities that made it the granary and smithworks of both the Russian Empire and the USSR, the Ukraine, if it had been independent, could have used these resources to evolve a pattern of production and specialization that would have differed from the present configuration. This comparative abundance and versatility of the Ukraine's resources makes an extrapolation of their potential uses difficult.

A comparison with the Ukraine's Central European COMECON neighbors may provide an insight into the problem. In terms of population and land area, the Ukraine is the largest among them. Its population density is low when compared with that of the German Democratic Republic, Czechoslovakia, and Hungary.[84] When we rank the internal distribution of the NMP of each of the seven countries (Bulgaria, Czechoslovakia, the German Democratic Republic, Hungary, Poland, Romania, and the Ukraine), the industrial sector in the Ukraine is in last place, while agriculture is in first place. Transport and communications, construction, trade, and other activities occupy a middle position (fourth rank). On this ranking the Ukraine possesses the most agrarian of the economies being compared.

The finding that the Ukraine is relatively less industrialized than other COMECON countries is confirmed by ranking data on the percentage distribution of the population engaged in various sectors of the economy, since on this indicator Ukrainian industry and construction are last. [85] Romania and Poland, however, have higher shares of their population engaged in agriculture. Ukrainian agriculture is second after Poland's in the share of fixed assets employed by that sector, but its industry has a greater proportion of fixed assets than do the industries of Poland and Hungary. [86]

A more precise indication of the Ukraine's industrial specialization is obtained by considering employment shares and then their ranks within the industrial sector of the COMECON countries and the Ukraine. [87] A comparison of ranks shows that the Ukraine's ferrous metallurgy and construction materials branches occupy first place, while the second rank goes to fuels and machine-building and metalworking. Despite its preeminent position in agriculture, however, the Ukraine's food processing industry ranks only fourth in the COMECON group. Strikingly, its light industry branch is last in this classification of rankings.

Most of the problems that beset the Ukrainian economy discussed earlier—such as an observed disharmony between the development of producer-goods and consumer-goods production, an imbalance between branches producing finished output and those producing raw materials, fuel, and semifabricates, excessive levels of materials and capital use in contrast with underutilization of labor resources, excessive rates of extraction of minerals and fuels, shortages of water for industrial purposes—must be attributed to the role of the producer of mostly extractive and intermediate goods that it has been the lot of the Ukrainian economy to fill for many decades. There is little doubt that the present political status of the Ukraine makes it the object of planning objectives that subordinate, and therefore sacrifice, the interests of its residents for the achievement of aims of a much larger agglomeration. This much has been recognized—however grudgingly—even by Soviet economists. [88]

Experience of the COMECON countries that have not been formally incorporated within the USSR indicates that even if the Ukraine were socialist but enjoyed the status of its Central European neighbors, it would have had a much more balanced economy. Its agriculture would probably not be as prominent in its NMP; and even though heavy industry and mining would still occupy significant positions, the light and food industries, which on the whole are more labor-intensive, would surely be more developed than they are now.

Finally, not being forced to lose a substantial share of its national income, an independent Ukraine, whether capitalist or socialist, would be able to assure a higher growth rate of its entire economy and a higher welfare level for its population.

NOTES

1.  Two other changes must be taken into account when comparing the Ukraine's prewar and postwar territories: the Moldavian ASSR, which was part of the prewar Ukraine, was transformed into a separate administrative entity, the Moldavian SSR, after World War II; and in 1954 the Crimea was detached from the RSFSR and incorporated in the Ukraine.

2.  This chapter was prepared prior to the publication of all results of the 1979 census.

3.  TsSU, Narodnoe khoziaistvo SSR v 1978 g. (Moscow, 1979), p. 10 (publication hereafter cited as Narkhoz); Godfrey S. Baldwin, Population Projections by Age and Sex for the Republics and Major Economic Regions of the USSR 1970 to 2000 (Washington, D.C.: U.S. Government Printing Office, 1979), p. 3, Table A.

4.  This increase was derived by comparing the population of the Ukraine as of January 17, 1939, within its prewar boundaries and the population total on January 1, 1940, adjusted for the incorporation of the western Ukraine. See TsUNKhU, Sotsialisticheskoe stroitel'stvo Soiuza SSR (1933-1938 gg.) (Moscow, 1939), p. 9; TsSU, Narodnoe khoziaistvo Ukrainskoi SSR v 1977 G. (Kiev, 1978), p. 7 (hereafter Narkhoz Ukraine).

5.  Stephan G. Prociuk, "Human Losses in the Ukraine in World War I and II," Annals of the Ukrainian Academy of Arts and Sciences in the U.S. 13 (1977), p. 49.

6.  Baldwin, Population Projections . . ., p. 3, Table A; Narkhoz 78, p. 10.

7.  V. S. Zhuchenko et al., eds., Demograficheskoe razvitie Ukrainskoi SSR (Kiev, 1977), p. 157).

8.  Narkhoz Ukraine 70, p. 39; Narkhoz 60, p. 18; TsSU, Naselenie SSSR (Moscow, 1980), p. 28.

9.  Zhuchenko et al., Demograficheskoe razvitie . . ., pp. 164-65.

10.  Narkhoz Ukraine 77, p. 12.

11.  Baldwin, Population Projections . . ., pp. 37, 53.

12.  TsSU, Naselenie SSSR, p. 17. In 1970 the average family size was 3.4 persons (3.3 in urban and 3.6 in rural areas). Narkhoz Ukraine 75, p. 13.

13. TsSU, Itogi vsesoiuznoi perepisi naseleniia 1970 goda, vol. 2 (Moscow, 1972), pp. 12, 20.

14. Baldwin, Population Projections . . ., p. 103.

15. TsSU, Itogi vsesoiuznoi perepisi naseleniia 1959 goda, vol. 2 (Moscow, 1963), p. 30.

16. Stephen Rapawy, "Regional Employment Trends in the USSR: 1950 to 1975," in U.S. Congress, Joint Economic Committee, Soviet Economy in a Time of Change (Washington, D.C.: U.S. Government Printing Office, 1979), Table 1.

17. Ibid., Table 3.

18. Ibid., Table 2.

19. Zhuchenko et al., Demograficheskoe razvitie . . ., p. 86.

20. Ibid., p. 90.

21. Narkhoz Ukraine 77, p. 277; Narkhoz 78, p. 377.

22. Narkhoz 74, p. 145; Narkhoz 78, pp. 90, 93.

23. Narkhoz Ukraine 77, pp. 160-62; Narkhoz 78, pp. 211, 213, 216.

24. James W. Gillula, The Regional Distribution of Fixed Capital in the USSR (Washington, D.C.: Bureau of the Census, Foreign Demographic Analysis Division, 1980), Tables A-1, A-3.

25. A. A. Nesterenko et al., eds., Ocherki razvitiia narodnogo khoziaistva Ukrainskoi SSR (Moscow, 1954), pp. 446-51.

26. Narkhoz 78, p. 33; Rush V. Greenslade, "The Real Gross National Product of the USSR, 1950-1975," in U.S. Congress, Joint Economic Committee, Soviet Economy in a New Perspective (Washington, D.C.: U.S. Government Printing Office, 1976), p. 271, Table 1.

27. Narkhoz Ukraine 70, p. 395; Narkhoz 70, p. 533; Narkhoz 78, p. 385.

28. For example, according to the official methodology, agriculture in 1970 accounted for 25.3 percent of NMP, while industry and other sectors of material production contributed the remaining 74.7 percent. Allocation of the returns to factors of production other than labor within the sectors of the economy where these returns originate gives a somewhat different result: agriculture, 45.5 percent; industry and the remaining sectors of material production, 54.5 percent. See I. S. Koropeckyj, "National Income of the Soviet Union Republics in 1970: Revision and Some Applications," in Zbigniew M. Fallenbuchl, ed., Economic Efficiency in the Soviet Union and Eastern Europe, vol. 1 (New York: Praeger, 1975), Tables 11.7, 11.8.

29. See Roman Senkiw, "The Growth of Industrial Production in Ukraine, 1945-71" (Ph.D. diss., University of Virginia, 1974), p. 247.

30. P. Bahrii, "Efektyvnist' vyrobnytstva iak faktor zbalanso-vanosti narodnoho hospodarstva," Ekonomika Radians'koi Ukrainy (1979): no. 5, p. 13.

31. Koropeckyj, "National Income . . .," Table 11.8.

32. Narkhoz Ukraine 77, pp. 185, 189, 193; Narkhoz 78, pp. 261, 268, 275.

33. Narkhoz Ukraine 77, pp. 160, 176, 179.

34. David W. Carey, "Soviet Agriculture: Recent Performance and Future Plans," in U.S. Congress, Joint Economic Committee, Soviet Economy in a New Perspective (Washington, D.C.: U.S. Government Printing Office, 1976), p. 593.

35. Daniel L. Bond, "Multiregional Economic Development in the Soviet Union: 1960-1975" (Ph.D. diss., University of North Carolina at Chapel Hill, 1979), Table A-2.

36. For a discussion of specialization in Ukrainian agriculture, see I. Stebelsky, "Ukrainian Agriculture: The Problems of Specialization and Intensification in Perspective," in P. J. Potichnyj, ed., Ukraine in the Seventies (Oakville, Ontario: Mosaic Press, 1975).

37. Narkhoz 78, pp. 236, 209.

38. Koropeckyj, "National Income . . . ."

39. Ibid., Tables 11.1, 11.8.

40. For sources and methodology for these calculations, see ibid., pp. 321-25.

41. This investment accounted for 14.8 percent of total agricultural investment in the USSR during 1971-75 and was scheduled to rise to 20.4 percent, according to provisions in the Tenth Five-Year Plan, during 1976-80. See Carey, "Soviet Agriculture," p. 594.

42. Stanley H. Cohn, "Economic Growth," in I. S. Koropeckyj, ed., The Ukraine Within the USSR: An Economic Balance Sheet (New York: Praeger, 1977), p. 75. Cohn, too, finds a decline in productivity growth in the Ukraine relative to the USSR. His numerical results differ slightly from the present estimates owing to a different data base and methodology.

43. O. Iemel'ianov, "Tendentsii formuvannia i faktornyi analiz vykorystannia osnovnykh fondiv v narodnomu hospodarstvi Ukrains'koi RSR," Ekonomika Radians'koi Ukrainy (1979): no. 6, p. 28.

44. Ibid., p. 29.

45. Bahrii, "Efektyvnist' vyrobnytstva . . .," p. 11.

46. Iemel'ianov, "Tendentsii formuvannia . . .," p. 30.

47. Ibid.

48. Leslie Dienes, "Minerals and Energy," in I. S. Koropeckyj, ed., The Ukraine Within the USSR (New York: Praeger, 1977), p. 161.

49. S. Aptekar and Iu. Dolhorukov, "Reservy chornoi metalurhii URSR," Ekonomika Radians'koi Ukrainy (1979): no. 5, p. 13.

50. Regressing the rate of growth in the number of scientific personnel on the rate of growth in productivity for all union republics for 1960-75 gives a "b" coefficient equal to 0.56 (3.06), significant at the 5 percent level, which indicates a strong statistical relationship between these two variables. The calculation was carried out using data from Chapter 3 and from various issues of Narkhoz.

51. The Ukraine's shares in the corresponding USSR totals were as follows:

|             | 1956-60 | 1961-65 | 1966-70 | 1971-75 | 1976-77 |
| ----------- | ------- | ------- | ------- | ------- | ------- |
| Industry    | 18.3    | 17.9    | 17.7    | 16.9    | 16.3    |
| Agriculture | 18.7    | 18.5    | 17.5    | 16.7    | 15.4    |

Sources: Narkhoz Ukraine 77, p. 255; Narkhoz 78, p. 343.

52. See I. S. Koropeckyj, "Economic Prerogatives," in I. S. Koropeckyj, ed., The Ukraine Within the USSR (New York: Praeger, 1977), p. 23.

53. Article 16 states that the Ukrainian economy is "a constituent part of a unified economic complex that comprises all aspects of social production, distribution, and exchange on the territory of the USSR." See Konstytutsiia (Osnovnyi Zakon) Ukrains'koi Radians'koi Sotsialistychnoi Respubliky.

54. Narkhoz Ukraine 70, p. 395; Narkhoz Ukraine 77, p. 288.

55. Narkhoz Ukraine 77, p. 82.

56. P. V. Voloboi and V. A. Popovkin, Problemy terytorial'noi spetsializatsii i kompleksnoho rozvytku narodnoho hospodarstva Ukrains'koi RSR (Kiev, 1972), pp. 175-78.

57. Dienes, "Minerals and Energy," p. 175.

58. For an example of such complaints, see Koropeckyj, "Economic Prerogatives," p. 21.

59. Dienes, "Minerals and Energy," pp. 174 ff.

60. As observed earlier, agriculture in 1970 accounted for 40 percent of the Ukraine's GNP; during the early 1970s this proportion stood at the following levels for some of the highly industrialized countries: United States, 4 percent; United Kingdom, 3 percent; France, 5 percent; German Federal Republic, 3 percent; and Italy, 8 percent. See United Nations Secretariat, Statistical Yearbook (New York: United Nations, 1976), pp. 674-75, 681-82.

61. Voloboi and Popovkin, Problemy terytorial'noi spetsializatsii . . . , p. 127.

62. Ibid., pt. iii.

63. Ibid., pt. iv.

64. Ibid., p. 187.

65. Koropeckyj, "Economic Prerogatives," pp. 21-22.

66. V. Horodnii, "Ekonomichnyi rozkvit zakhidnoukrains'kykh zemel' v iedynii Ukrains'kii Radians'kii derzhavi," Ekonomika Radians'koi Ukrainy (1979): no. 9, p. 23.

67. According to a composite indicator developed by Voloboi and Popovkin, Problemy terytorial'noi spetsializatsii . . ., p. 221 (based on the gross output of industry and agriculture, fixed assets in these two sectors, electricity consumption, industrial and agricultural employment per 1,000 of the population, all expressed in per capita terms), the following was the ranking, in descending order, of the Ukrainian oblasts in 1967 with respect to the level of their economic development: Dniepropetrovsk, Zaporozhe, Donetsk, Voroshilovgrad, Kharkov, Kherson, Crimea, Kiev, Nikolaev, Odessa, Poltava, Sumy, L'vov, Kirovograd, Chernigov, Cherkassy, Zhitomir, Vinnitsa, Chernovtsi, Khmel'nitskii, Rovno, Ivano-Frankovsk, Volyn', Ternopol', Zakarpatskaia. The above ranking did not differ significantly from that prepared for 1962 by M. Palamarchuk and S. Bazhan, "Pytannia metodyky doslidzhennia rivniv ekonomichnoho rozvytku raioniv," Ekonomika Radians'koi Ukrainy (1965): no. 1-2.

68. O. Kocherha and O. Rudavs'kyi, "Osnovni tendentsii zhladzuvannia rehional'nykh vidminnostei spozhyvannia neprodovol'chykh tovariv v Ukrains'kii RSR," Ekonomika Radians'koi Ukrainy (1979): no. 8, pp. 48-49.

69. Narkhoz Ukraine 77, pp. 9, 342.

70. Ia. A. Tikhonov, Radians'ka Ukraina (Kiev, 1979), p. 11.

71. R. Pipes, "'Solving' the Nationality Problem," in J. L. Nogee, ed., Man, State and Society in the Soviet Union (New York: Praeger, 1972), p. 509.

72. Ibid., p. 510.

73. Alec Nove and J. A. Newth, The Soviet Middle East: A Model for Development (London: Allen and Unwin, 1967), p. 114.

74. Voloboi and Popovkin, Problemy teryterial'noi spetsializatsii . . ., p. 110.

75. Ibid., p. 212; P. Horodens'kyi, "Vyrivniuvannia ekonomiky respublik—zakonomirnist' nashoho rozvytku," Ekonomika Radians'koi Ukrainy (1965): no. 11, p. 75.

76. Voloboi and Popovkin, Problemy terytorial'noi spetsializatsii . . ., pp. 213, 212.

77. For a list of various estimates of these transfers, see Z. L. Melnyk, "Capital Formation and Financial Relations," in I. S. Koropeckyj, ed., The Ukraine Within the USSR (New York: Praeger, 1977, p. 288, Table 10.7.

78. James W. Gillula, "The Economic Interdependence of Soviet Republics," in U.S. Congress, Joint Economic Committee,

Soviet Economy in a Time of Change (Washington, D.C.: U.S. Government Printing Office, 1979), p. 634.

79. A. S. Iemel'ianov and F. I. Kushnirskii, Modelirovanie pokazatelei razvitiia ekonomiki soiuznoi respubliki (Moscow, 1974), p. 141; various issues of Narkhoz Ukraine.

80. Narkhoz Ukraine 77, p. 247; Narkhoz 78, pp. 338, 349.

81. The table below provides a summary view over the 1918-78 period of the composition of total investment for both the USSR as a whole and the Ukraine, and the shares of state, collective farm, private housing, and total investment of the Ukraine in the corresponding categories for the USSR.

| Investment | USSR | Ukraine | Ukraine as Percent of USSR |
|---|---|---|---|
| Total | 100.0 | 100.0 | 16.1 |
| State | 87.7 | 81.2 | 14.9 |
| Collective farm | 9.1 | 13.8 | 24.5 |
| Private housing | 3.2 | 5.0 | 25.4 |

Sources: Derived from Narkhoz 78, p. 73; URSR v tsyfrakh 1978, p. 73.

82. Koropeckyj, "National Income of the Soviet Union Republics in 1970," p. 302, Table 11.4, and p. 309, Table 11.6.

83. Peter Wiles, "Comparison with Some Alternatives," in I. S. Koropeckyj, ed., The Ukraine Within the USSR (New York: Praeger, 1977).

84. Various issues of Narkhoz Ukraine and SEV, Statisticheskii iezhegodnik stran-chlenov Sovieta ekonomicheskoi vzaimopomoshchi— 1979 (Moscow, 1979); relevant tables (1977 data).

85. When 1977 data for the Ukraine were not available—as in this case—1975 data were used for both the Ukraine and the COMECON countries.

86. Data are for 1975.

87. Data are for 1975.

88. The conflict between the "global optimum" or "general state interests," on the one hand, and a "local optimum" or the needs of the republic, on the other, is never explicitly stated; the reader must derive his or her own conclusions by implication—the admission that there is a "local" as against a "global" optimum. See for example, Voloboi and Popovkin, Problemy terytorial'noi spetsializatsii . . ., pp. 46, 48, 135, 185. In this connection see a review article by Ihor Gordijew, "Regional Economics from the Standpoint of a Member Republic," Annals of the Ukrainian Academy of Arts and Sciences in the U.S. 13, no. 35-36 (1977).

# 9

## MOLDAVIA

### Ihor Ghordijew

The land now called Moldavia has been subject over time to a series of territorial and name changes. The Moldavian Soviet Socialist Republic (MSSR), which lies in the extreme southwest of the USSR, was established by the Soviet government in August 1940. It covered 33,700 square kilometers and had a population of 2,468,000 in that year.[1] The MSSR replaced the Moldavian Autonomous Soviet Socialist Republic (MASSR), set up in October 1924 as part of the Ukrainian Soviet Socialist Republic.[2] The Soviet government's 1940 decision quadrupled Moldavia's size, moved its capital from Tiraspol' to Kishenev, and raised it to "union" status. Despite this enlargement, Moldavia remains (after Armenia) the second smallest union republic within the USSR, occupying only 0.15 percent of the USSR's territory. With a population of 3,948,000 in 1979 (an increase of 60 percent over 1940), Moldavia has ranked eighth in population size among the union republics for a number of years, but has the highest density—over 117 persons per square kilometer, compared with the union average of 11.8 persons per square kilometer. Moldavia's population is still predominantly rural, although between 1940 and 1979 the urban population increased 4.7 times while the rural population rose by only 12 percent.[3] In 1979 the population was 61 percent rural and 39 percent urban.

Along with other front-line republics, Moldavia suffered a population decline during World War II. Factor equipment and collective and state farm assets were transported out of Moldavia to the Urals, Siberia, and Central Asia. The cost of war damage to the Moldavian economy is given as 11 billion rubles,[4] while that sustained by its industry and agriculture is estimated by Soviet sources to have been around 800 million rubles. Among other losses, about 100,000 horses and 130,000 head of cattle had to be written off, and 15 percent of the vineyards, 25 percent of the orchards, and all nursery gardens were destroyed. In urban and rural areas over 30,000 private dwellings and public buildings were burned or demolished.[5] The population was subjected to severe material deprivation, aggravated shortly after the conclusion of World War II by a drought leading to starvation. Agricultural output in 1945 and 1946 was in many instances below 50 percent of prewar levels,[6] and the 1945 level of industrial output was only 44 percent of that in 1940.[7]

## TRENDS IN NATIONAL INCOME AND OTHER ECONOMIC INDICATORS

Between 1960 and 1977, Moldavia's gross social product (GSP) at current prices rose fourfold, compared with a rise of 3.1 times for the USSR as a whole. Over the same period Moldavia's national income went up 3.4 times, while that for the USSR as a whole increased by 2.8 times. As data in Table 9.1 show, industry occupies first place, and agriculture second place, in Moldavia's GSP.[8] The fact that Moldavia is still a predominantly agrarian economy is indicated by the fact that only around 1970 did industry displace agriculture as the largest contributor to national income. Moreover, Moldavia has accounted for about 2.5 percent in the agricultural component of USSR national income for many years, while its share in the total national income has ranged between 1.0 and 1.3 percent (see Table 9.2). When coupled with Moldavia's share in the USSR's population (about 1.5 percent), those ratios may be taken as a benchmark range within which we would expect many of the indicators of the Moldavian economy to fall. They may also be used as rule-of-thumb measures of the equity of distributional policies pursued by the Soviet authorities in Moscow in relation to Moldavia's residents.

Data on Moldavia's financial relations with the rest of the USSR are rather sketchy. Its budget is the principal document from which we may gleam some fragmentary information. Between 1960 and 1978 budget revenue increased almost sixfold. The principal sources were deductions from turnover taxes and from enterprise profits, the former growing at almost double the rate for total budget revenue, compared with barely a fourfold increase in profit deductions. These trends led to a doubling of the share of turnover tax deductions from 22.7 percent in 1960 to 45.4 percent of total revenues in 1978, and a reduction in the share of profit deductions from about one-third to under one-quarter over the

TABLE 9.1

Percentage Shares of Various Sectors in Moldavia's Gross Social Product
and National Income: 1960–77

(percent)

| Sector | Gross Social Product | | | | | National Income | | | | |
|---|---|---|---|---|---|---|---|---|---|---|
| | 1960 | 1965 | 1970 | 1975 | 1977 | 1960 | 1965 | 1970 | 1975 | 1977 |
| Industry | 50.27 | 53.71 | 55.90 | 56.50 | 56.5 | 36.60 | 35.56 | 40.74 | 39.01 | 39.95 |
| Agriculture | 30.87 | 30.35 | 26.14 | 25.37 | 25.1 | 41.72 | 45.83 | 38.01 | 36.08 | 34.36 |
| Transport and communication | 2.33 | 2.00 | 2.19 | 2.26 | 2.3 | 2.56 | 2.37 | 2.70 | 3.04 | 3.09 |
| Construction | 10.02 | 8.41 | 9.82 | 9.79 | 9.1 | 8.21 | 6.60 | 7.90 | 9.57 | 8.77 |
| Trade and other | 6.51 | 5.53 | 5.95 | 6.08 | 7.0 | 10.91 | 9.44 | 10.65 | 12.30 | 13.83 |
| Total | 100 | 100 | 100 | 100 | 100 | 100 | 100 | 100 | 100 | 100 |

Sources: Derived from data in Sovetskaia Moldavia k 60–letiu velikogo oktiabria (Kishinev, 1977), p. 23 (hereafter Mold. 60); and TsSU, Narodnoe Khoziaistvo Moldavskoi SSR v 1978 G. (Kishinev, 1979), pp. 16, 153 (publication hereafter cited as Narkhoz Moldavia).

## TABLE 9.2

### Moldavia's Gross Social Product and National Income as Shares of the USSR: 1960-77

(percent)

| Sector | Gross Social Product | | | | | National Income | | | | |
|---|---|---|---|---|---|---|---|---|---|---|
| | 1960 | 1965 | 1970 | 1975 | 1977 | 1960 | 1965 | 1970 | 1975 | 1977 |
| Industry | 0.80 | 1.03 | 1.00 | 1.09 | 1.12 | 0.73 | 0.90 | 0.96 | 0.92 | 0.99 |
| Agriculture | 1.89 | 2.18 | 1.85 | 2.23 | 2.13 | 2.14 | 2.66 | 2.10 | 2.67 | 2.76 |
| Transport and communication | 0.54 | 0.57 | 0.63 | 0.66 | 0.69 | 0.51 | 0.52 | 0.58 | 0.60 | 0.63 |
| Construction | 0.96 | 1.07 | 1.07 | 1.14 | 1.14 | 0.86 | 0.93 | 0.92 | 1.04 | 1.01 |
| Trade and other | 0.90 | 1.12 | 1.17 | 1.22 | 1.30 | 0.96 | 1.19 | 1.16 | 1.20 | 1.24 |
| Total | 0.99 | 1.21 | 1.14 | 1.24 | 1.27 | 1.05 | 1.31 | 1.20 | 1.24 | 1.26 |

Sources: Derived from data in Sovetskaia Moldavia k 60-letiu velikogo oktiabria (Kishinev, 1977), p. 23 (hereafter Mold. 60); TsSU, Narodnoe Khoziaistvo Moldavskoi SSR v 1978 G. (Kisseine, 1979), pp. 16, 153 (publication hereafter cited as Narkhoz Moldavia).

same period.[9] This experience did not tally with that of the consolidated USSR budget, in which the relative weight of turnover tax revenues fell from 40.7 percent in 1960 to 31.6 percent in 1978, while that of receipts from state enterprise profits rose from 24.2 to 29.6 percent over the same period.[10]

Even though subventions to Moldavia's budget from the union budget have usually exceeded payments into the union budget, Moldavia's budget expressed as a percentage of the budgets of all the republics combined has constituted a smaller fraction than its share in total Soviet population. In 1950, Moldavia's budget revenue constituted 1.2 percent of combined republic budget revenues, declined to slightly below 1 percent around 1965, and regained the 1950 ratio by 1970.[11] Its budget revenues are planned to reach 1.34 percent of the total for 1980.[12] Although this ratio is still below Moldavia's share in the total population, the republic may receive a larger share of allocations from the union budget. But there are no data on this matter.

Tables 9.3 and 9.4 provide available data on the structure of employment in Moldavia. The data in Table 9.3 indicate that during 1960-78 the share of the economically active population in the "material sphere" of the economy declined by about 10 percent, with a corresponding increase in the share of the nonmaterial sphere. Within the material sphere the share of agriculture, which includes collective farm members and those self-employed in private plot gardening, dropped steadily and rapidly, while the shares of other branches rose correspondingly. Industry and construction together engaged between one-sixth and slightly over one-quarter of Moldavia's population during 1960-78, while agriculture and forestry combined gave sustenance to almost two-thirds of the population in 1960 and just over 41 percent in 1978. The former share has risen rapidly, at the expense of employment on collective farms and private plots.[13]

Compared with the USSR as a whole, Moldavia's level of industrialization, as shown by labor source data, is still well behind—though slowly gaining. For industry and construction Moldavia's shares relative to those in the USSR were 52 percent in 1960, 59 percent in 1970, and 67 percent in 1978. For agriculture and forestry, in contrast, Moldavia's position was reversed—the ratio of its share to the corresponding USSR sectors was 1.67 in 1960 and around 2 in subsequent years.

Turning to state employment in Moldavia (for which detailed data are available up to 1975 only), we see that throughout 1960-75 industry employed between 26 and 28 percent of the state labor force (see Table 9.4). In contrast with the Ukraine, where the share of state agriculture has been rather low and stable in recent

# TABLE 9.3

Population Engaged in the Economy: USSR and Moldavia, 1960–78

(percent)

| | 1960 | | 1965 | | 1970 | | 1975 | | 1978 | |
|---|---|---|---|---|---|---|---|---|---|---|
| | USSR | Mold. | USSR | Mold. | USSR | Mold. | USSR | Mold. | USSR | Mold. |
| Industry and construction | 32.0 | 16.7 | 36.0 | 19.2 | 38.0 | 22.8 | 38.0 | 25.0 | 39.0 | 26.1 |
| Agriculture and forestry | 39.0 | 65.1 | 31.0 | 57.4 | 25.0 | 50.1 | 23.0 | 44.3 | 21.0 | 41.2 |
| Transport and communication | 7.0 | 3.3 | 8.0 | 4.6 | 8.0 | 5.4 | 9.0 | 6.0 | 9.0 | 6.6 |
| Trade, etc. | 6.0 | 3.3 | 6.0 | 4.4 | 7.0 | 5.6 | 8.0 | 6.5 | 8.0 | 6.9 |
| Adjustment* | -1.0 | +0.9 | -1.2 | +0.1 | -0.9 | -0.8 | -2.8 | -1.2 | -2.6 | -1.3 |
| Material sphere | 83.0 | 89.3 | 79.8 | 85.7 | 77.1 | 83.1 | 75.2 | 80.6 | 74.4 | 79.5 |
| Health, education and culture, art and science | 11.0 | 8.0 | 14.0 | 10.8 | 16.0 | 12.2 | 16.0 | 13.6 | 17.0 | 14.4 |
| Credit, insurance, and administration | 2.0 | 1.2 | 2.0 | 1.3 | 2.0 | 1.7 | 2.0 | 1.9 | 2.0 | 1.9 |
| Other | 3.0 | 2.4 | 3.0 | 2.3 | 4.0 | 2.2 | 4.0 | 2.7 | 4.0 | 2.9 |
| Adjustment* | +1.0 | -0.9 | +1.2 | -0.1 | +0.9 | +0.8 | +2.8 | +1.2 | +2.6 | +1.3 |
| Nonmaterial sphere | 17.0 | 10.7 | 20.2 | 14.3 | 16.9 | 16.9 | 24.8 | 19.4 | 25.6 | 20.5 |
| Total | 100.0 | 100.0 | 100.0 | 100.0 | 100.0 | 100.0 | 100.0 | 100.0 | 100.0 | 100.0 |

*The adjustments are due to the fact that the classification of employment subcomponents differs slightly from the totals given for the material and nonmaterial spheres in the statistical sources consulted.

Sources: TsSU, Narodnoe khoziaistvo SSR v 1970 g. (Moscow: TsSU, 1971), p. 515 (publication hereafter cited as Narkhoz); Narkhoz 72, p. 501; Narkhoz 77, p. 375; Narkhoz 78, p. 363; Mold. 60, p. 123; Narkhoz Moldavia 78, pp. 143–44; Sovetskaia Moldavia k 50-letiu velikogo oktiabria (Kishinev, 1967), pp. 161, 163–64 (hereafter Mold. 50.

TABLE 9.4

Distribution of State Employment: Moldavia, 1960–75

| | 1960 | | 1965 | | 1970 | | 1975 | |
|---|---|---|---|---|---|---|---|---|
| | Rank | Percent | Rank | Percent | Rank | Percent | Rank | Percent |
| Industry | 1 | 27.9 | 1 | 27.2 | 1 | 27.5 | 1 | 25.6 |
| Agriculture | 6 | 9.0 | 3 | 12.5 | 2 | 13.5 | 2 | 20.0 |
| (state farms) | | (7.2) | | (11.0) | | (12.8) | | (18.2) |
| Forestry | 13 | 0.7 | 13 | 0.5 | 13 | 0.5 | 13 | 0.5 |
| Transport | 3 | 9.8 | 4 | 9.6 | 6 | 8.9 | 6 | 7.9 |
| Communication | 12 | 1.4 | 12 | 1.2 | 11 | 1.5 | 11 | 1.4 |
| Construction | 4 | 9.8 | 6 | 9.2 | 4 | 10.5 | 4 | 9.4 |
| Trade | 5 | 9.1 | 5 | 9.4 | 5 | 9.8 | 5 | 9.4 |
| Housing | 10 | 2.6 | 9 | 2.6 | 9 | 2.3 | 8 | 2.6 |
| Health | 7 | 8.8 | 7 | 7.2 | 7 | 6.4 | 7 | 5.8 |
| Education, culture, and art | 2 | 12.7 | 2 | 13.1 | 3 | 12.7 | 3 | 11.4 |
| Science | 11 | 1.7 | 10 | 2.4 | 10 | 2.2 | 10 | 1.8 |
| Credit and insurance | 14 | 0.5 | 14 | 0.4 | 14 | 0.4 | 14 | 0.5 |
| Administration | 9 | 2.8 | 11 | 2.3 | 8 | 2.5 | 9 | 2.5 |
| Others | 8 | 3.2 | 8 | 3.3 | 12 | 1.3 | 12 | 1.2 |
| Total | | 100.0 | | 100.0 | | 100.0 | | 100.0 |

Sources: Narkhoz 70, p. 515; Narkhoz 75, p. 537; Mold. 50, p. 163.

years, the share of state agricultural employment in Moldavia more than doubled between 1960 and 1975, when it accounted for 18.2 percent of the total state labor force, almost entirely on state farms. Primarily because of the growth in the share of agricultural employment in the state sector, the combined relative share of the remaining sectors—even that of industry—has tended to decline. Total state employment in Moldavia has risen much more rapidly than in the USSR as a whole, and the relative share of state agriculture is double that in the USSR.

Table 9.5 provides data on total capital investment in Moldavia during 1946-78, along with data on the three sources of financing it—the state, collective farms, and the population (for private housing). As in the Ukraine, the share of investment outlays by the state in Moldavia is substantially below the union average (66 percent as against 88 percent), while the shares of investment financed by collective farms and by the population far exceed the union average (34 percent as against 12 percent). As a result, Moldavia's share of total USSR state investment is well below 1 percent, while its share of collective farm investment is more than 3 percent. In accord with its relatively more rural character, the share of private investment is relatively large. Both sets of data indicate that collective farms and the population in Moldavia have borne a disproportionate share of the investment burden.

TABLE 9.5

Aggregate, State, Collective Farm, and Private Housing
Investment: USSR and Moldavia, 1946-78

| | USSR | | Moldavia | | Moldavia |
| | Billion Rubles | Percent | Billion Rubles | Percent | as Percent of USSR |
|---|---|---|---|---|---|
| State | 1,566.1 | 87.8 | 12.608 | 65.9 | 0.81 |
| Collective farms | 164.0 | 9.2 | 5.480 | 28.6 | 3.34 |
| Private housing | 52.6 | 3.0 | 1.043 | 5.5 | 1.98 |
| Total | 1,782.7 | 100.0 | 19.131 | 100.0 | 1.07 |

Sources: Narkhoz 75, p. 502; Narkhoz 78, p. 338; Mold. 60, p. 112; Narkhoz Moldavia 78, p. 128.

INDUSTRY

Data cited earlier have shown the large and growing role of industry in the Moldavian economy, whether assessed as share of total product or of total employment. The 45-fold expansion in gross industrial output between 1940 and 1978 is quite high (when compared with a 60 percent increase in population), although growth started from a very low base. Moldavia's industrial growth was more than twice as fast as the USSR average, and was the second highest among the republics (after Lithuania). During 1946-77 the state invested 3,483,000,000 rubles in Moldavian industry (30.3 percent of the total investment in the Moldavian economy).[14] This amount was well under 1 percent of total state investment in industry for the USSR as a whole. During 1946-60 this share amounted to as little as 0.2 to 0.5 percent, rising to 0.6 and 0.7 percent in recent years. Despite its much smaller share of investment, Moldavian industry has been able to contribute about 1 percent to the industrial component of Soviet GSP and national income.

Information on the structure of industrial employment is available for the period 1960-75.[15] Because of lack of the requisite natural resources, Moldavia does not have branches for fuels and metallurgy. Employment is concentrated in three branches: light industry, food industry, and machinery and metalworking. In 1960 the food and light industries accounted for 57 percent of total industrial employment, and in 1975 their share was 50 percent. In contrast, the share of the machinery branch rose from 12 percent to 27 percent. The only other major employers are the timber, woodworking, and paper branches and the construction materials branch; together they accounted for 25 percent of the total in 1960 and 15 percent in 1975.

Information on the distribution of fixed assets within Moldavian industry shows that although the light industry branch employs the highest proportion of the industrial force, it has a low proportion of fixed assets.[16] This branch and the food branch account for 1.8 percent and 2.3 percent, respectively, of the total USSR employment in these branches—considerably higher shares than the share of Moldavian population in the USSR total. These indicators show that Moldavia tends to specialize in consumer goods production, especially food, a natural consequence of the predominance of agriculture in its economy.

AGRICULTURE

In 1977, Moldavia contributed 2.3 percent of the total gross value of output of agriculture,[17] about the same as its share in

total national income and rural population. Moldavia has only 0.5
percent of the agricultural land of the USSR and 0.8 percent of
arable lands and sown acreage. In recent years crops have provided two-thirds of its total agricultural gross output, and livestock has provided one-third. The corresponding shares for the
USSR as a whole are approximately 45 and 55 percent, respectively.[18] Agricultural production in Moldavia rose about one-third
more rapidly during 1940-78 than in the USSR as a whole. The
private component, though slowly diminishing, made up around 20
percent of gross agricultural output. Its share in the livestock
sector was 38 percent in 1960 and 27 percent in 1977, and about
15 percent in the crop sector in both years.[19]

TABLE 9.6

Relative Share of Moldavia in USSR Production of
Selected Products: Averages for Five-Year
Periods, 1960-65 to 1978
(percent)

|  | 1960-65 | 1966-70 | 1971-75 | 1978 |
|---|---|---|---|---|
| Grapes | 27.2 | 22.8 | 23.2 | 10.0 |
| Other fruit | 6.8 | 10.1 | 9.8 | 5.2 |
| Wine | 4.1 | 10.2 | 8.3 | 6.6 |
| Canned foods (all types) | 8.4 | 9.3 | 9.5 | 7.8 |
| Canned fruits and vegetables | 9.9 | 16.0 | 18.2 | 15.0 |
| Vegetable oil | 5.5 | 5.6 | 5.2 | 4.3 |
| Refined sugar | 3.1 | 3.2 | 3.6 | 3.8 |

Sources: N. P. Frolov, ed., Istoriia narodnogo khoziaistva
Moldavskoi SSR 1959-1975 (Kishinev, 1978), p. 103; TsSU, Narodnoe
Khoziaistvo SSSR v 1978 G. (Moscow, 1979) (hereafter Narkhoz),
pp. 184, 189, 233, 247-48; Narkhoz Moldavia 78, p. 59.

In Moldavia, as in the Ukraine, but unlike the USSR as a
whole, collective farms have provided the major source of funds
for investment in agriculture. While for the USSR the percentage
shares of state and collective farm investment in total agricultural
investment during 1946-77 were 61.2 and 38.8 percent, respectively, they were 37.3 percent and 62.7 percent in Moldavia.[20]

Thus, state investment in Moldavian agriculture as a proportion of total state investment in Soviet agriculture for this period represented 1.33 percent; that by Moldavian collective farms, 3.46 percent. The two categories combined made up 2.15 percent of total agricultural investment in the USSR over the 31-year period.[21]

Although crops predominate in Moldavia's agriculture, some subbranches of livestock raising, such as swine and poultry, exceed the 1-1.3 percent levels in the USSR totals. The most important crops are "technical" crops (tobacco, grapes). Areas sown to "technical" crops in Moldavia in 1977 constituted as much as 2.72 percent of such areas for the USSR as a whole—well above the percentage sown to grain crops in that year (0.7 percent of USSR grain areas). The highly significant contribution of certain intermediate-type agricultural products in Moldavia's economy can be assessed by considering their share (in both raw and processed form) in the respective USSR totals (see Table 9.6). Moldavia is reputed to occupy first place in the cultivation of grapes and to be the third largest producer of wine and tinned foods. Although it does not specialize in the cultivation of potatoes (usually accounting for only 0.3-0.4 percent of the USSR total), its gross harvests of vegetables and sunflower seeds have attained comparatively high proportions of USSR totals—4.2 and 5.7 percent, respectively.

COLLECTIVE AND STATE FARMS

Between 1960 and 1978 the number of collective farms in Moldavia diminished by about 25 percent (from 552 to 422), but the size of the average farm in terms of sown area has remained around 1,500-3,000 hectares. Moldavian collective farms made up 1.2 percent of the USSR total in 1960 and 1.6 percent in 1977. However, Moldavia's share in total collective farm employment was much larger, rising from 2.0 to 3.4 percent in that period. Like the Ukraine, Moldavia's share of the USSR's collective farmers considerably exceeds its share of the population.

The "indivisible" assets of collective farms in Moldavia have been around 3.0 percent of their Soviet counterpart. These assets include school and hospital buildings as well as dwellings and structures for both production and consumption purposes that are financed from collective farm resources. The share of preschool establishments, school buildings, and hospital facilities commissioned by collective farms in Moldavia in recent years has been in excess of 3 percent of USSR totals (the overall figure for the commissioning of assets by collective farms in Moldavia in 1977 as a proportion of the USSR was 3.8 percent). Because of the shortage of construction materials and equipment for nonstate purposes in particular, such social overhead items are likely to be of substandard quality when compared with similar facilities built by the state. In 1977 the fixed and working assets of Moldavian collective farms constituted 1.9 percent of USSR collective farm assets. However, Moldavian collective farm perennial plantings, mainly grapevines, made up a phenomenal 27.7 percent of the USSR total.[22]

Between 1960 and 1978 the number of state farms in Moldavia grew from 61 to 291—4.8 times.[23] Despite this growth their share of the total number of state farms in the USSR (about 1 percent) did not change much, Moldavia's state farms have had a growing share of the USSR's sown area—from 0.11 percent in 1960 to 0.37 percent in 1978. The average size of state farms in terms of hectares sown per farm ranged from a low of about 1,200 hectares in 1960 to a high of nearly 1,900 hectares in 1965. During the 1970s it was around 1,500 hectares, about half the size of the average Moldavian collective farm. The share of state farm output in the total output of state and collective farms increased from under 10 percent in 1960 to 30 percent in 1978.

The fixed and working assets of Moldavia's state farms, when viewed as a proportion of the corresponding categories of assets for USSR state farms as a whole, appear to be in rough correspondence with the proportion of Moldavian state farms in the USSR total. In 1977, for example, the fixed and working assets of Moldavia's state farms were 1.43 percent; when broken down into the two principal components, fixed capital and working capital, the percentages were 1.63 and 0.94, respectively. The relatively high share of fixed assets evidently is due mainly to the large areas of berry and grapevine plantings. Moldavian state farms had 1 percent of the power capacity available to state farms in the USSR. However, while power per hectare of sown land was high—owing to the relatively small proportion of sown areas cultivated by Moldavia's state farms—power per worker was lower even than that in the Ukraine.


PRODUCTIVITY GROWTH

With respect to national income (net material product), the growth of productivity in Moldavia decelerated rapidly from 4.9 percent to 1.1 percent per annum between the early 1960s and the first half of the 1970s. The deterioration in Moldavia's position relative to the USSR set in during the second half of the 1960s.[24] During the preceding five-year period productivity growth in

Moldavia had exceeded the USSR average by almost two percentage points. The growth rates of combined factor inputs and of output were somewhat higher for Moldavia than for the USSR over the entire period 1960-75. However, during 1965-70 the difference between the rate of growth in output and in factor inputs narrowed dramatically to well below half the average for the USSR.

In the industrial sector the growth in both inputs and output was higher than in the entire Soviet industry, as was the growth of factor productivity. During 1960-75 the latter rose at an average annual rate of 4.4 percent in Moldavia, compared with 3.8 percent in Soviet industry as a whole. As in the USSR, productivity growth fell sharply in Moldavian industry—from an average of 7.3 percent in 1960-65 to 4.3 percent in 1965-70 and to 1.9 percent in 1970-75.

Similar trends prevailed in Moldavian agriculture, where output, inputs, and productivity increased much more rapidly than in the USSR. For the period as a whole, productivity in this sector in Moldavia grew at an average annual rate of only 0.1 percent, but in the USSR as a whole productivity growth was negative. This lackluster performance, though better than either that of the USSR as a whole or of the Ukraine, resulted at least in part from unfavorable weather conditions in 1969, 1970, 1972, and 1975.[25] There is evidence also that the share of the intermediate materials in the gross value of Moldavian agriculture is rising, with a corresponding decline in the net output component.[26] Between 1960 and 1975 the ratio of output to capital in Moldavian agriculture dropped from 1.79 to 0.66 rubles per ruble of fixed assets[27] (63 percent). In industry this decrease amounted to 31 percent during the same period.[28]

THE STANDARD OF LIVING

This section briefly examines selected aspects of changes in the level of living of the Moldavian population. (More extensive data are provided in Chapter 4.) In housing—as with a number of other indicators—Moldavia's experience parallels fairly closely that of the Ukraine, on a scale that is appropriate to their relative sizes. The ratio of 1.26 percent of useful dwelling space commissioned in Moldavia during 1946-77 as a proportion of the USSR total was below Moldavia's population ratio. Over the same period state financing of the commissioning of dwellings (0.72 percent) was very low indeed. State employees, however, have financed useful dwelling space (1.35 percent) at about Moldavia's population share level. Dwelling construction in rural areas by collective farms and their members has barely kept pace with their proportion in the corresponding USSR category.[29]

The stock of school buildings in Moldavia constituted 1.23 percent of the corresponding USSR total in 1977 and accommodated 1.76 percent of USSR pupils,[30] a sign of relative overcrowding. Collective farms continue to play a prominent role in commissioning new schools. For example, in 1977 they put into operation 25 percent of the schools commissioned in Moldavia in that year.[31] Data on secondary, special, and higher educational establishments and enrollments show ratios below its 1.5 percent population ratio. In health care facilities Moldavia has done somewhat better. For example, the number of hospital beds as a share of the USSR total in 1977 was equal to the population ratio, but the share of sanatoriums, rest homes, and resorts was surprisingly low (0.6 percent).[32]

The standard of living of the citizens of Soviet republics is determined to a considerable extent by the level of wages and supplements from "communal consumption funds." Data in Table 9.7 show that the average monthly wages of all workers and employees, as well as supplements, in Moldavia were well below those in the Ukraine and the RSFSR. In 1977 the two combined in Moldavia were roughly 80 percent of the average in the RSFSR and 90 percent of that in the Ukraine.[33] Wage levels for each sector of the Moldavian economy, except health and welfare, credit, and government insurance and administration, were below those for the corresponding sectors in the Ukraine.[34]

TABLE 9.7

Average Monthly Wages of Workers and Employees,
and Supplements from Communal
Consumption Funds: 1977
(all sectors; rubles)

|  | Moldavia | Ukraine | RSFSR |
| --- | --- | --- | --- |
| Average monthly wage of workers and employees, all sectors | 129.8 | 143 | 163 |
| Supplements from communal consumption funds | 46.5 | 53 | 58 |
| Average monthly wages and supplements | 176.3 | 196 | 221 |

Sources: Narkhoz Moldavia 78, p. 146; TsSU, RSFSR v tsifrakh v 1977 G. (Moscow, 1978), p. 73; Narkhoz Ukraine 77, p. 290.

With respect to retail trade activities in Moldavia, except for the number of service and retail outlets and the value of service sales—which are in proportion to Moldavia's population ratio—and a comparatively high level of nonfood sales in Moldavia's urban areas, the rest of the indicators are both below Moldavia's population ratio and below union standards per 10,000 population.[35]

Comparisons of the levels of various economic indicators for Moldavia in recent years with those for Central European member countries of COMECON reinforce the conclusion that Moldavia is a somewhat underdeveloped agrarian economy.[36] For example, comparing Bulgaria, Czechoslovakia, the German Democratic Republic, Hungary, Poland, and Romania with Moldavia, we find that industry's share in net material product is the lowest in Moldavia. Conversely, agriculture contributes to Moldavian net material product a share more than double those in the economies of the COMECON countries. This conclusion is also supported by the sectoral distribution of employment in the various countries. Data on branch employment show that the share of the food industry in Moldavia's industrial labor force is some two to three times greater than in the other countries.

In conclusion, we address the hypothetical question of an alternative economic and political status for Moldavia and the possible impact on its economy. Considering its size and location, an independent status is highly improbable under any but the most unrealistic of assumptions. All that can be said is that even an independent Moldavia—whether socialist or capitalist—would, because of the limited range of natural resources at its disposal, have few economic specialization options. It would still be a predominantly agrarian economy. Indeed, because of the industrialization bias of socialist governments, it would be even more agrarian if it were capitalist than it is at present. If it were an independent socialist state, it likely would pursue policies that would stress industrialization, possibly to an even greater extent than at present, as most COMECON member countries have done. An independent Kishenev socialist or capitalist government would certainly try to maximize its "objective function" without as much regard for the interests of an entity such as the USSR as is the case at present. In other words, the interests of Moldavia would not be treated as subordinate to those of a larger entity, as subsystem interests.

It is more probable, however, that because of its size and location Moldavia would be incorporated within either the Ukraine or Romania—as it has been at various times in the past. One may speculate that if incorporated in either a socialist Ukraine or Romania, it would be less developed than it is at present, since its contemporary union republic status, however insignificant in itself, gives it a slightly greater leverage in Moscow against Kiev than if it were completely incorporated within another union republic. Furthermore, an incorporation within Romania might deprive Moldavia of easy access to the raw materials and to products manufactured within the USSR.

Only "reality" could test the validity of the suppositions expressed above.


NOTES

1. Both tsarist Russia and the Soviet government have had territorial acquisitions in this area of Eastern Europe. For a discussion of the Soviet-Romanian dispute over Bessarabia and Bukovyna, see A. Motyl, "The Problem of Bessarabia and Bukovyna: The Intersection of the Sino-Soviet and Soviet-Rumanian Disputes," Journal of Ukrainian Graduate Studies 2, no. 1 (Spring 1977): 32-48.

2. MASSR's population was 615,500 in 1933. N. L. Meshcheriakov, ed., Malaia sovetskaia entsiklopediia, vol. 7 (Moscow, 1938), p. 14. Since Moldavia was incorporated into the Ukrainian SSR before 1940, it will not be considered separately in that period.

3. The population and territory data are taken from various issues of TsSU, Narodnoe khoziaistvo SSR v . . . g. (Moscow; hereafter cited as Narkhoz).

4. I. I. Bodiul, Sovetskaia Moldavia (Moscow, 1978), p. 31.

5. Sovetskaia Moldavia k 50-letiu velikogo oktiabria (Kishinev, 1967), pp. 6-7. Hereafter cited as Mold. and year.

6. Mold. 60, p. 61.

7. Mold. 50, p. 34.

8. But it should also be noted that owing to Soviet national income accounting practices involving some double-counting and the attribution of turnover tax collections in their entirety to industry, the share of industry's contribution tends to be exaggerated in the various aggregate output concepts.

9. TsSU, Narodnoe Khoziaistvo Moldavskoi SSR v 1978 G. (Kishinev, 1979), pp. 225-26 (publication hereafter cited as Narkhoz Moldavia).

10. Narkhoz 72, pp. 724-25; Narkhoz 78, pp. 533-34.

11. Gosudarstvennyi biudzhet SSSR i biudzhety soiuznykh respublik 1961-1965 gg. (Moscow, 1966), pp. 72, 166; Gosudarstvennyi biudzhet SSSR i biudzhety soyuznykh respublik, 1966-1970 gg. (Moscow, 1972), pp. 78, 173.

12. Ekonomicheskaia gazeta (1979): no. 50, p. 3.

13. See Narkhoz 70, pp. 405, 515; Narkhoz 75, pp. 441, 537; Mold. 50, pp. 163-64; Mold. 60, p. 123; Mold 78, pp. 92, 143-44. State employment data on the required basis are not available beyond 1975.

14. Data on investment in Moldavian industry are available on a basis that does not show separately the amounts placed in industrial-type investment by collective farms.

15. Stephen Rapawy, "Regional Employment Trends in the USSR: 1960 to 1975," in U.S. Congress, Joint Economic Committee, Soviet Economy in a Time of Change, vol. 1 (Washington, D.C.: U.S. Government Printing Office, 1979), pp. 608-11.

16. N. P. Frolov, ed., Istoriia narodnogo khoziaistva Moldavskoi SSR 1959-1975 (Kishinev, 1978), p. 150.

17. Narkhoz Moldavia 78, p. 64; Narkhoz 78, pp. 198-99.

18. Narkhoz Moldavia 78, pp. 64-65, 97-98.

19. Narkhoz 78, p. 196.

20. Narkhoz Moldavia 78, pp. 132-33.

21. Narkhoz 78, pp. 128, 131-33.

22. In 1977, Moldavia's collective and state farms cultivated 6.8 percent of the USSR's fruit and berry plantings and 22.2 percent of grapevine plantings. Since the absolute data for these items were not given separately for state farms for the USSR as a whole—though they were available for Moldavian state farms—it was not possible to calculate the share of fruit, berry, and grapevine plantings for Moldavian state farms as a proportion of the corresponding USSR totals. Narkhoz 77, pp. 240-41, 81-82, 98.

23. Narkhoz Moldavia 78, p. 63; Narkhoz 78, p. 276. This figure does not include enterprises described as "state-farm factories."

24. For data and methodology, see Chapter 3. Additional calculations were made on the basis of these data.

25. Frolov, ed., Istoriia . . . Moldavskoi SSR . . . , p. 327.

26. Ibid., p. 244.

27. Ibid., p. 283.

28. Ibid., p. 187.

29. Derived from data in Narkhoz 77, p. 411; Narkhoz Moldavia 78, p. 155.

30. Narkhoz 77, p. 493.

31. Ibid., p. 423.

32. Ibid., p. 442.

33. Narkhoz Moldavia 78, p. 125.

34. Narkhoz Ukraine 77, p. 274.

35. Narkhoz 77, pp. 451, 455, 456, 473, 474, 478.

36.  The sources used in these comparisons are various editions of <u>Narkhoz Moldavia</u>, <u>Narkhoz</u>, <u>Statisticheskii iezhegodnik stran chlenov Soveta Ekonomicheskoi Vzaimopomoshchi</u>.  The terminal years for which comparisons are being made are 1960-77 or 1978, as available at the time of writing.

# 10

## BELORUSSIA AND BALTICS
### Juris Dreifelds

INTRODUCTION

The Baltic republics and Belorussia have rarely been considered a single economic region, although they have similarities
in soil conditions, climate, land utilization, and, to some extent,
industrial specialization. Estonia, Latvia, Lithuania, and Belorussia undeniably form what a <u>Pravda</u> correspondent described as
"a very compact geographic quartet," and they are becoming increasingly involved in common programs of scientific, environmental, and industrial cooperation.[1] The latest and most significant development in this regard was the creation in 1976 of a permanent council and eight commissions to oversee, coordinate, and
guide specialization in separate branches of light industry.[2]
It is evident from the many changes in Soviet classification
of regions that there is no permanent, single, best way of grouping
republics and oblasts. Soviet economic geographers have spent much
time debating various aspects of proper regionalization without coming to any final conclusions.[3] At the most basic level a region,
according to one Soviet definition, should designate an area "with
more or less uniform natural conditions whose productive forces
and economic objectives tend in a particular direction."[4] Currently the three Baltic republics and the Kaliningrad Oblast form
one region, and Belorussia forms another.[5] For many years prior
to 1962, however, Belorussia and the Baltic republics were joined
in one of 13 large regions that were used, at least nominally, by
Gosplan in its territorial planning.[6]
It is interesting to note that N. N. Kolosovski of the Department of Economic Geography of Moscow University disputed the
rationale of the pre-1962 grouping of Belorussia with the Baltic
republics:

In singling out as a unit the Baltic and Belorussia there
was again a consolidation of territories whose economies were developing in different directions. The
economy of the Baltic republics is based not only on
skilled cadres but also on their coastal location.
Whereas the first element also exists in Belorussia,
as it does, incidentally in northern and central Russia,
the second element, an extremely important one for
the Baltic is completely absent. On the other hand,
Belorussia has a developed lumber industry, but in
the Baltic there is none to speak of. The further development of Belorussia's agriculture is linked to the
solution of complex reclamation problems. This element also sharply distinguishes Belorussia from the
Baltic republics.[7]

Indeed, Belorussia is a landlocked republic, and the Baltic
states, with their many ports, are a significant outlet and entry
point for Soviet trade. Nevertheless, forests cover nearly the
same proportion of territory in both areas, and the Baltic republics
are just as dependent on land drainage for agricultural improvement as Belorussia is. Rather than precluding a final judgment on
the merits or drawbacks of grouping Belorussia with the Baltic
republics, the following data and analysis will provide a detailed
overview of the similarities and differences within the four cul-
turally different areas, thus allowing for independent assessment.
   It should be emphasized from the beginning that Soviet republics cannot be seen as independent economic units, or even as
members of a true federation. Practically, republics do not have
independent budgets or taxes, and their exclusive jurisdiction, even
at the theoretical level, is minimal.[8] Production specialization by
individual regions apparently is determined by considerations of
"rational division of labor" within the context of the USSR as a
whole and by "overriding national interests" as calculated by those
at the highest level of Party and administration.[9] Most often,
rational division of labor refers to the optimal utilization of favorable factors of production present in a given region or republic.[10]
Factors cited as determinants of specialization include availability
and type of natural resources, economic geographical situation,
manpower characteristics, historical traditions, and historically
accumulated production and nonproduction assets.[11] National interests, on the other hand, implicitly include considerations of
rapid economic growth, regional equalization, balanced development, and military security.
   One of the more important questions about Soviet regional
economic development is the degree to which specialization and

living conditions have been skewed both positively and negatively by membership in the "unified Soviet economic complex." Soviet leaders and economists constantly reiterate only the benefits gained by cooperative sharing of assets throughout the Soviet Union. Augusts Voss, first secretary of the Communist Party in Latvia, has summarized this common theme well:

> Today nobody in the whole world, not even our opponents or enemies, can assert that the separate nations of our land working in isolation could have achieved such significant gains in economic and cultural development in the past few decades. The pooling of efforts is a powerful factor in increased development. Through mutual cooperation, sister nations are able to resolve with unprecedented energy both "their own," that is local, regional and national problems as well as union wide responsibilities thus gaining unparalleled success.[12]

On the other hand, complex arrangements of regional economic sharing can have drawbacks, either real or perceived. For obvious reasons, discussions of drawbacks are not officially encouraged within the USSR. Only rarely, when leaders attack the national narrow-mindedness of certain individuals or groups, can one perceive the existence of discontent about current economic arrangements. Outside the Soviet Union criticism is much more pronounced. It is often asserted that republics could have achieved higher levels of economic and welfare development on their own rather than as members of the Soviet Union.[13]

This chapter will analyze in relative detail the economic resources and specialization of Estonia, Latvia, Lithuania, and Belorussia. It will attempt to assess some of the major consequences of economic specialization and growth for the welfare and demographic profile of the population, and for the natural environment. It also will estimate in a general way the areas of specialization that would most probably be developed if each of the republics were independent, and will evaluate the degree of possible skewing introduced into these economies because of integration into the Soviet Union. Finally, in order to assess alternative options of development for the republics of this region, a brief comparison will be made with the economy and living standards of neighboring Finland, a country that until World War II had an economic profile closely similar to that of Estonia and Latvia.

It should be noted that this four-republic region, with the exception of eastern Belorussia, was subject to Communist state planning and regimentation more than 20 years later than other

parts of the Soviet Union. The Baltic states were forcibly annexed
by the USSR in 1940, and were fully integrated into the Soviet system only after World War II. The western section of Belorussia
was a part of Poland until 1939, when it was occupied by the Red
Army and attached to Soviet Belorussia.[14] The entire region was
held by the Nazis from about 1941 to 1944. This three-year occupation, together with intensive war operations, resulted in devas-
tating losses to the economy and population.[15]

## GEOGRAPHIC AND DEMOGRAPHIC CHARACTERISTICS

The Baltic-Belorussian region has received little attention in
Western economic publications. Perhaps one of the reasons is the
seemingly small size of its territory and population in comparison
with the rest of the USSR. The region's 382,000 square kilometers
(147,000 square miles) form only 1.7 percent of the total Soviet
land mass, and its 16.5 million inhabitants account for only 6.5
percent of the Soviet population. Yet, in comparative terms, its
territory is larger than that of Japan, the German Federal Republic, or the United Kingdom, and its population is almost the same
size as that of the German Democratic Republic, and larger than
that of the Netherlands, Hungary, or Czechoslovakia.[16]

Significant geographic and demographic variations among the
four republics should be mentioned to caution against tempting
generalizations. The size of population and territory increases
from north to south, with Belorussia being larger than the other
three republics combined. Over half the territory of Lithuania,
but only a third of the area of Estonia, is suitable for farming.
Surprisingly, all four republics are equally endowed with agricultural land (if considered on a per capita basis). While the Baltic
republics, taken as a whole, have a forested area proportionately
similar to that of Belorussia (33.3 percent and 32.7 percent), Latvia
is significantly more forested than Lithuania.

Demographic differences are also important. The rate of
urbanization is highest in Estonia and lowest in Belorussia, diminishing sequentially from north to south. A north-to-south pattern
prevails in the proportion of the labor force engaged in agriculture,
with Estonia having the lowest proportion and Belorussia the highest.

Birth rates today are equally low for all four republics, although in previous decades Lithuania and Belorussia had far higher
rates than Estonia or Latvia, resulting to some degree in problems
of underemployment and emigration. The 1979 census highlighted
another demographic divergence: Lithuania and Belorussia, with
about 80 percent native ethnic stock, are more homogeneous than

TABLE 10.1

Selected Geographic, Demographic, and Economic Data for Belorussia, the Baltic Republics, and the USSR: Selected Years, 1970–79

| | Year | Unit | Belorussia | Lithuania | Latvia | Estonia | USSR |
|---|---|---|---|---|---|---|---|
| Total area | 1977 | 1,000 sq. km. | 207.6 | 65.2 | 63.7 | 45.1 | 224,022 |
| Forest area | 1973 | percent | 32.7 | 26.4 | 38.3 | 36.1 | 34.4 |
| Farm area | 1975 | percent | 47.7 | 56.1 | 40.1 | 34.6 | 24.7 |
| | | 1,000 ha. | 9,893 | 3,655 | 2,554 | 1,560 | 552,600[a] |
| | | ha. pc | 1.1 | 1.1 | 1.0 | 1.1 | 2.1 |
| Total population | 1979[b] | 1,000 | 9,560 | 3,398 | 2,521 | 1,466 | 262,436 |
| Urban population | 1979 | percent | 55 | 61 | 68 | 70 | 62 |
| Population in capitals | 1979 | 1,000 | 1,276 | 481 | 835 | 430 | 8,011 |
| | | percent | 13.3 | 14.2 | 33.1 | 29.3 | 3.1 |
| Average family size | 1979 | no. | 3.3 | 3.3 | 3.1 | 3.1 | 3.5 |
| Titular nationality[c] | 1979 | percent | 79.4 | 80.0 | 53.7 | 64.7 | n.a. |
| Population density | 1979 | per sq. km. | 46.1 | 52.1 | 39.6 | 32.5 | 11.7 |
| Birth rate | 1977 | per 1,000 | 15.8 | 15.5 | 13.6 | 15.1 | 18.1 |
| Death rate | 1977 | per 1,000 | 9.0 | 9.8 | 12.2 | 11.8 | 9.6 |
| Natural increase | 1977 | per 1,000 | 6.8 | 5.7 | 1.4 | 3.3 | 8.5 |
| Employed in economy[d] | 1975 | per 1,000 | 482 | 482 | 510 | 496 | 461 |
| In industry | 1975 | per 1,000 | 128 | 139 | 163 | 162 | 134 |
| In agriculture | 1975 | per 1,000 | 141 | 121 | 97 | 80 | 101 |
| Female share of labor force[e] | 1977 | percent | 53 | 51 | 54 | 54 | 51 |
| National income produced[f] | 1975 | rubles pc | 1,550 | 1,676 | 1,910 | 1,846 | 1,428 |
| National income produced[g] | 1970 | rubles pc | 1,092 | 1,336 | 1,574 | 1,587 | 1,194 |
| Gross agricultural output | 1977 | rubles pc | 692 | 803 | 635 | 745 | 477 |
| Crops | 1977 | rubles pc | 282 | 250 | 185 | 224 | 216 |
| Livestock | 1977 | rubles pc | 410 | 553 | 449 | 520 | 261 |

(continued)

Table 10.1, continued

| Livestock products | Year | Unit | Belorussia | Lithuania | Latvia | Estonia | USSR |
|---|---|---|---|---|---|---|---|
| Meat | 1977 | kgs. pc | 95 | 140 | 105 | 125 | 57 |
| Milk | 1977 | kgs. pc | 692 | 841 | 746 | 838 | 366 |
| Eggs | 1977 | kgs. pc | 290 | 271 | 278 | 317 | 235 |
| Grain | 1977 | kgs. pc | 701 | 860 | 614 | 855 | 755 |
| Gross industrial output | 1975 | rubles pc | n.a. | 2,142 | 2,617 | 2,785 | 2,009 |
| Producer goods | 1975 | rubles pc | n.a. | 1,248 | 1,483 | 1,671 | n.a. |
| Consumer goods | 1975 | rubles pc | n.a. | 894 | 1,134 | 1,114 | n.a. |
| Fixed capital | 1975 | rubles pc | n.a. | 4,924 | 6,132 | 7,101 | n.a. |
| Capital investments | 1977 | rubles pc | 437 | 474 | 501 | 497 | 472 |

pc = per capita.

n.a. = not applicable/not available.

aThis figure is for 1977.

bAll 1979 demographic data taken from Soviet census of January 1979. TsSU, Naselenie SSSR (Moscow, 1980), pp. 3-30.

cThis refers to the share of native ethnic stock as a percentage of the total population in the republic.

dIncludes kolkhozes except fishing kolkhozes. For Estonia, table refers to all agricultural work.

eExcludes kolkhoz and private labor.

fBaltic data for 1975 is in Latvijas PSR Ministru Padomes Centrala Statistikas Parvalde, Latvijas PSR tautas saimnieciba 1975 gada (Riga, 1976), p. 53 (publication hereafter cited as Latvijas saimnieciba). USSR figure calculated from TsSU, Narodnoe khoziaistvo SSR v 1977 g. (Moscow, 1978), p. 404 (publication hereafter cited as Narkhoz). Belorussian figure calculated on basis of 1,092 rubles pc in 1970 and a 142 percent increase in pc national income 1970-75. TsSU, Narodnoe khoziaistvo Belorusskoi SSR v 1975 g. (Minsk, 1976), p. 169 (publication hereafter cited as Narkhoz Belorussia).

gNational income pc for 1970 is in TsSU, Narodnoe khoziaistvo Latviiskoi SSR v 1971 g. (Riga, 1972), p. 56 (publication hereafter cited as Narkhoz Latvia).

hFigures are for the end of 1975.

the two northern republics. In 1979 only 53.7 percent of the population in Latvia was Latvian, and 64.7 percent of the population in Estonia was Estonian. (For a summary of geographic and demographic factors, see Table 10.1.)

The republics of the region are among the most productive in the Soviet Union. Their produced national income per inhabitant in 1975 was above the USSR average. Even Belorussia surged ahead of the average in 1970-75. On a per capita basis Lithuania has the highest indexes for gross agricultural output, whereas Estonia and Latvia are more advanced in industrial production. The two northern republics reflect the USSR pattern in the proportional contribution of industry and agriculture to the national income. In the two southern republics, especially Lithuania, a disproportionately large contribution is still being made by the agricultural sector.

TABLE 10.2

Distribution of Net Material Product, by Major Sectors of
the Economy: Belorussia, Baltic Republics, USSR, 1974
(percent)

|  | Belorussia | Lithuania | Latvia | Estonia | USSR |
|---|---|---|---|---|---|
| Net material product | 100 | 100 | 100 | 100 | 100 |
| Industry | 47.0 | 37.9 | 55.3 | 51.4 | 52.7 |
| Agriculture | 26.1 | 33.4 | 17.9 | 20.6 | 18.4 |
| Transport and communications | 4.2 | 4.4 | 5.3 | 5.8 | 6.1 |
| Construction | 10.6 | 12.4 | 8.9 | 9.5 | 11.0 |
| Trade, service, and other | 12.1 | 11.9 | 12.6 | 12.7 | 11.8 |

Sources: Narkhoz Belorussia 75, p. 170; Ekonomika Litovskoi SSR 75, p. 220; Latvijas saimnieciba 75, p. 41; Eesti rahvamajandus 75, p. 241; Narkhoz 74, p. 574.

330 / ECONOMICS OF SOVIET REGIONS

## NATURAL RESOURCES AND ECONOMIC SPECIALIZATION

For a very long time the natural resources of the Baltic-Belorussian region were limited to land, timber, and water, with very meager mineral wealth. An economic geography textbook on the USSR claimed, as late as 1976, that "One of the outstanding characteristics of the region is the extreme poverty of its industrial resource base," and that "The potential for industrial growth has always been, and remains, rather limited."[17] This assertion, however, is somewhat misleading. In the 1970s there was a turn-around in the natural assets of the region, and now oil, gas, potash, phosphates, and salt are changing, in part, the character of the region's economic base.

### Agriculture

Despite the new mineral discoveries and high rates of industrialization and urbanization in the region, agriculture is still one of the principal resources in all four republics. In 1977 the region accounted for 3.15 percent of total agricultural land, but produced 9.6 percent of total Soviet agricultural output. Undeniably, the direct role of agriculture in total gross output, national income, and employment has diminished considerably since 1950. Nevertheless, in 1974 agriculture provided 33.4 percent of the net material product in Lithuania, 26.1 percent in Belorussia, 20.6 percent in Estonia, and 17.9 percent in Latvia. But even in Latvia the impact of farming was larger than the above statistics would indicate. In that republic agriculture, together with related and dependent industries and services, was responsible for over one-third of gross output and one-third of total employment.[18]

The mainstay of agriculture in the region is clearly animal husbandry and dairying, although much attention is also paid to cereal and root crops. Official statistics about the division of agricultural output do not fully reflect the preeminent status of livestock farming because most of the field crops in the region are utilized for animal feed.[19] In all four republics the structure of crops indicates a preponderance of traditional feed grains, such as barley and oats. Potatoes, sugar beets, and corn also are largely used for feedstuff.[20] (See Table 10.3.)

Climate, soil, and topography have contributed to the increasing orientation to animal farming, and have made grain cultivation very expensive and labor-intensive. The Baltic-Belorussian region is one of the most humid in the entire USSR, receiving 600-800

millimeters of precipitation per year. As a Soviet specialist has
noted, "The damp climate favors the growth of natural meadows and
the cultivation of fodder grasses."[21] The high rainfall, general
cloudiness, cool temperatures, and limited growing season have
restricted the growing of hard wheat and corn, but have favored the
cultivation of hardy and moisture-tolerant barley, oats, rye, potatoes, and flax.[22] The high precipitation has heavily affected soil
ecology. Much of the mineral and organic content of the already im-
poverished glacial-origin soils is regularly dissolved and leached
out; hence, fields have to be treated frequently with large quantities of fertilizer, and have to be limed in order to neutralize
residual acidity and allow the beneficial growth of soil micro-
organisms.[23]

The high water table and poor drainage have necessitated expensive investments in water amelioration projects involving laying
of drainage pipes, straightening of natural streams, digging of
drainage ditches, and construction of polder dams. Large areas
still remain to be drained, especially in Belorussia. Nevertheless,
in 1977 the four republics had an amazingly disproportionate share
of drained land in the USSR. Little Lithuania alone held 16.0 percent, Belorussia 16.3 percent, Latvia 11.3 percent, and Estonia
6.4 percent of the Soviet total.[24] In Latvia water amelioration
projects absorbed 31 percent of all investments in agriculture
between 1966 and 1970.[25] In 1975 these outlays were still claiming
31.8 percent of agricultural investments in Latvia, 25.0 percent in
Lithuania, 22.9 percent in Belorussia, and 18.8 percent in Estonia.[26] Drained land in many cases is far more productive than
regular land; hence a continuation of amelioration programs should
result in increased harvest yields. In addition, the earlier drying
of fields in spring lengthens the growing season and minimizes the
dangers of late frosts. Not all land reclamation programs have
been successful, however. The draining of large sections of the
vast Polesye wetlands of southern Belorussia has not provided
"desired results," especially in sandy soils. In fact, productivity
in that region has decreased rather than increased.[27]

A peculiarity of the climate is that the heaviest precipitation
usually occurs at harvest time, in August and September. This
hinders mechanized grain harvesting, leads to grain drooping, and
forces heavy investment outlays in grain-drying structures and
ventilation systems. In some years the biggest problem is not
humidity but excessive dryness. In fact, small-scale irrigation
and sprinkling systems have been constructed in scattered localities,
especially in Belorussia.

The land in the region is part of an extensive plain, with few
promontories rising over 300 meters above sea level. The micro-

## TABLE 10.3

Production of Major Agricultural Products and Their Relative Weight as a Percentage
of the USSR Total: Belorussia and Baltic Republics, 1977

| | Belorussia | | Lithuania | | Latvia | | Estonia | | Region |
|---|---|---|---|---|---|---|---|---|---|
| | Total | Percent | Total | Percent | Total | Percent | Total | Percent | Percent |
| Agricultural land (million ha., Nov. 1977) | 9.8 | 1.77 | 3.6 | 0.65 | 2.5 | 0.45 | 1.5 | 0.27 | 3.15 |
| Gross agricultural output (million rubles, 1973 prices) | 6,534 | 5.29 | 2,690 | 2.18 | 1,600 | 1.30 | 1,082 | 0.88 | 9.64 |
| Total grain production (1,000 tons) | 6,618 | 3.38 | 2,881 | 1.47 | 1,547 | 0.79 | 1,243 | 0.64 | 6.28 |
| Wheat | 421 | | 621 | | 240 | | 138 | | 1.54 |
| Rye | 2,059 | | 297 | | 132 | | 35 | | 29.68 |
| Barley | 3,150 | | 1,503 | | 915 | | 839 | | 12.16 |
| Oats | 775 | | 225 | | 213 | | 179 | | 7.57 |
| State purchase of grain (1,000 tons) | 1,403 | 2.06 | 315 | 0.46 | 257 | 0.38 | 128 | 0.19 | 3.09 |

| | | | | | | | | | |
|---|---|---|---|---|---|---|---|---|---|
| **Other products (1,000 tons)** | | | | | | | | | |
| Potatoes | 11,314 | 13.61 | 1,912 | 2.30 | 1,404 | 1.69 | 1,156 | 1.39 | 19.0 |
| Sugar beets (industrial use) | 1,356 | 1.45 | 766 | 0.82 | 335 | 0.36 | — | — | 2.64 |
| Flax fiber | 105 | 21.64 | 19 | 3.92 | 4 | 0.82 | 2 | 0.41 | 26.80 |
| Vegetables (excl. potatoes) | 637 | 2.64 | 242 | 1.00 | 178 | 0.74 | 102 | 0.42 | 4.80 |
| Fruit (incl. grapes) | 429 | 2.81 | 106 | 0.69 | 21 | 0.14 | 26 | 0.17 | 3.81 |
| **Livestock (1,000)** | | | | | | | | | |
| Cattle | 6,494 | 5.89 | 2.136 | 1.94 | 1,385 | 1.26 | 826 | 0.75 | 9.82 |
| Cows | 2,688 | 6.40 | 887 | 2.11 | 584 | 1.39 | 329 | 0.78 | 10.69 |
| Pigs | 4,158 | 6.59 | 2,326 | 3.69 | 1,275 | 2.02 | 891 | 1.41 | 13.72 |
| Poultry | 32,300 | 4.06 | 11,500 | 1.44 | 8,400 | 1.06 | 5,100 | 0.64 | 7.20 |
| **Livestock products** | | | | | | | | | |
| Meat (1,000 tons) | 895 | 6.09 | 466 | 3.17 | 266 | 1.81 | 184 | 1.25 | 12.33 |
| Milk (1,000 tons) | 6,534 | 6.90 | 2,852 | 3.01 | 1,880 | 1.99 | 1,215 | 1.28 | 13.18 |
| Eggs (million) | 2,741 | 4.49 | 918 | 1.50 | 700 | 1.15 | 456 | 0.75 | 7.88 |

Source: Narkhoz 77, pp. 222-62.

topography is extremely variable, with large areas covered by un-
dulating drumlins and moraines formed by receding glaciers. About
one-third to one-half of the land area is hilly, which presents difficulties for mechanized crop cultivation, creates soil erosion hazards, and limits the size of individual fields.[28] Field size also is
affected by the patchy topography of swamps, streams, lakes,
small forests, isolated farmsteads, and roads.

An Estonian geographer has indicated that for proper mechanized harvesting, the minimum size of field and cultivated meadow
should be at least 20 hectares.[29] Actual average field size in
Estonia and Latvia is about 3 hectares. In Belorussia average field
size varies from 2.2 hectares in Vitebsk Oblast to 8.8 hectares in
Gomel Oblast.[30]

As a result of the various climatic, soil, and topographic
factors, the cost of grain production in all four republics is much
higher than the Soviet average. In 1977, for example, the production cost of grain in kolkhozes was from 35 to 78 percent above the
Soviet average. In contrast with grain, however, production costs
for milk, eggs, cattle, and even vegetables were lower than the
Soviet average. (See Table 10.4.)

Average trends, of course, cover a broad spectrum of localized conditions. To be sure, there are pockets of fertile and flat
land, especially in the scattered clay belts, that produce high yields
of grain and sugar beets, as well as animal products at comparatively low cost. Other areas are unprofitable for almost all types
of farming. The variability of local conditions has forced the state
to set differentiated purchasing prices for milk, meat, and other
commodities, but these differentials apparently are not significant
enough to stem the exodus of people from poorer farming areas.[31]
Moreover, with increased investments in farming, production costs
have gone up for most food items. State purchasing prices have
not kept a systematic pace with these changes.[32] In some cases
prices have, in fact, become dysfunctional, leading to conditions of
low rentability, and even to losses on products that are regional
specialties, such as potatoes and milk, but leading also to high
rentability for grain.[33]

Certain trends in agriculture may lead to increased productivity in the future. Many animals are now fattened in "animal factories." Chickens and hogs especially are serviced by conveyor
belts at minimum cost and expenditure of labor.[34] All this is leading to further narrow specialization and to the creation of inter-
farm associations, organizations, and enterprises within different
areas of each republic.

But as yet the rate of growth of agricultural output has lagged
far behind the growth rates of other sectors of the economy. Agri-

## TABLE 10.4

Production Costs, Selected Agricultural Commodities in Kolkhozes and Sovkhozes:
Belorussia, Baltic Republics, USSR, 1977
(rubles per metric ton)

| | Belorussia | | Lithuania | | Latvia | | Estonia | | USSR | |
|---|---|---|---|---|---|---|---|---|---|---|
| | Kol. | Sov. | Kol. | Sov. | Kol. | Sov. | Kol. | Sov. | Kol. | Sov. |
| Grain | 88 | 100 | 90 | 100 | 116 | 120 | 98 | 105 | 65 | 82 |
| Sugar beets | 39 | 45 | 38 | 46 | 34 | 39 | — | — | 27 | 36 |
| Potatoes | 69 | 76 | 101 | 102 | 104 | 104 | 77 | 85 | 92 | 111 |
| Vegetables | 93 | 74 | 92 | 110 | 83 | 74 | 81 | 64 | 108 | 101 |
| Cattle | 1,601 | 1,710 | 1,499 | 1,654 | 1,455 | 1,502 | 1,303 | 1,335 | 1,639 | 1,868 |
| Hogs | 1,716 | 1,671 | 1,496 | 1,580 | 1,335 | 1,297 | 1,135 | 1,073 | 1,505 | 1,424 |
| Sheep | 2,083 | 2,038 | 1,935 | 2,301 | 1,718 | 1,900 | 1,704 | 1,519 | 1,196 | 1,245 |
| Milk | 218 | 236 | 208 | 225 | 215 | 216 | 206 | 197 | 235 | 262 |
| Eggs | 71 | 47 | 57 | 62 | 66 | 61 | 55 | 49 | 76 | 61 |
| Wool | 8,305 | 9,264 | 9,223 | 11,876 | 9,753 | 11,430 | 10,085 | 11,068 | 5,904 | 5,971 |

Source: Narkhoz 77, pp. 275, 291.

culture has not only been subject to the vagaries of nature, labor deficits, and pricing inefficiencies, but its total output has been seriously affected by the diminishing effort of the private sector. The private sector appears to be no longer willing or able to contribute its former share of total product in spite of the recent dramatic change in attitude and policy toward private production by Party and state officials.[35]  (See Table 10.5.)

Estonia has long been in the vanguard of agricultural productivity and a model for the plans and goals set by other republics. In the mid-1960s its productivity lead was attributed to higher rates of mineral fertilizer application, more available energy and tractors, more widespread land drainage and liming, and better pay and better "agricultural production technology."[36] Differences in agricultural conditions between Estonia and the other three republics narrowed appreciably during the 1970s, but in 1977, Estonia was still ahead in most categories of farm productivity (except vegetable growing).[37]

Without a doubt, much potential for improvement in agriculture exists, even in Estonia, if productivity figures there are compared with the output figures of certain countries in the West. Dairy products account for the largest share of agricultural output in all four republics, but average milk yield per cow in Estonia in 1977 was only 8,042 pounds, compared with 11,660 pounds in the United States.[38] A successful American dairy farmer was quoted by the New York Times as saying, "A farmer can't be fussing around with a lazy old cow that only produces 10,000 pounds a year."[39] Obviously farmers in the Baltic republics and Belorussia have to make do with very many cows having comparatively great lactation inertia.

The relatively low levels of overall agricultural production in the USSR also help explain the continued reliance in the region on locally grown expensive grain. Apparently grain must be grown, since it still is not being produced in sufficient quantities in the USSR.[40] If Soviet agriculture ever produces enough for its needs, a reorientation of agricultural practices might occur, and the Baltic-Belorussian region could produce livestock on local grass and hay, and on cheap grain from the Ukraine.

The food industry is dependent to a large extent on local farm produce, although fish and Cuban sugarcane are also important inputs. The most significant food items include processed meat, sausages, butter, milk products (yogurt, powdered milk, ice cream), cheese, canned goods, sugar, confectionery, and beer. (See Table 10.6.)

TABLE 10.5

The Share of Private Production in Agriculture: Belorussia, Baltic Republics, USSR, 1965–75
(percent)

| | Belorussia | | | Lithuania | | | Latvia | | | Estonia | | | USSR | | |
|---|---|---|---|---|---|---|---|---|---|---|---|---|---|---|---|
| Commodities | 1965 | 1970 | 1975 | 1965 | 1970 | 1975 | 1965 | 1970 | 1975 | 1965 | 1970 | 1975 | 1965 | 1970 | 1975 |
| Grain | 2 | 1 | 1 | 10 | 11 | 9 | 2 | 1 | 2 | 5 | 5 | 3 | 2 | 1 | 1 |
| Potatoes | 57 | 54 | 51 | 73 | 68 | 71 | 60 | 60 | 60 | 42 | 39 | 30 | 63 | 65 | 59 |
| Vegetables | 66 | 61 | 53 | 83 | 77 | 71 | 64 | 58 | 48 | 58 | 53 | 44 | 41 | 38 | 34 |
| Meat (dressed wt.) | 53 | 37 | 31 | 51 | 38 | 31 | 47 | 35 | 28 | 35 | 29 | 20 | 40 | 35 | 31 |
| Eggs | 81 | 70 | 51 | 77 | 61 | 49 | 51 | 34 | 28 | 58 | 37 | 29 | 67 | 53 | 39 |
| Wool | 40 | 31 | 17 | n.a. | n.a. | n.a. | n.a. | n.a. | n.a. | 87 | 96 | 94 | 20 | 19 | 20 |
| Milk | 47 | 41 | 36 | 51 | 46 | 40 | 43 | 39 | 34 | 36 | 31 | 24 | 39 | 36 | 31 |
| Livestock | 1966 | 1971 | 1975 | 1965 | 1970 | 1975 | 1965 | 1970 | 1975 | 1965 | 1970 | 1975 | 1966 | 1970 | 1975 |
| Cattle | 33 | 25 | 21 | 39 | 35 | 32 | 32 | 27 | 24 | 24 | 21 | 17 | 30 | 26 | 23 |
| Cows | 50 | 46 | 40 | 51 | 47 | 43 | 39 | 36 | 31 | 32 | 27 | 21 | 42 | 39 | 34 |
| Pigs | 54 | 44 | 37 | 47 | 35 | 27 | 38 | 25 | 15 | 24 | 15 | 7 | 31 | 25 | 19 |
| Sheep and goats | 52 | 43 | 32 | 76 | 97 | 83 | 84 | 86 | 76 | 90+* | 90+* | 90+* | 24 | 23 | 21 |
| Poultry | 84 | 75 | 61 | 81 | 69 | 56 | 57 | 41 | 27 | 64 | 47 | 28 | n.a. | n.a. | n.a. |

n.a. = not available.

*An exact percentage cannot be calculated because total numbers for state and private holdings include sheep and goats together, but state holdings refer only to sheep.

Sources: Narkhoz Belorussia 75, pp. 83, 85, 101; Ekonomika Litovskoi SSR 75, pp. 104, 108, 126, 139–40; Ekonomika Litovskoi SSR 70, pp. 148, 170; Latvijas saimnieciba 75, pp. 173, 179, 210–11; TsSU, Narodnoe khoziaistvo Estonskoi SSR v 1971 g. (Tallinn, 1972), pp. 162, 177–79 (publication hereafter cited as Narkhoz Estonia); Narkhoz 70, pp. 352–53; Narkhoz 74, p. 399; Eesti rahvamajandus 75, pp. 142, 157–59.

TABLE 10.6

Processing of Major Food Items in Belorussia and Baltic Republics, and Their Percentages of USSR Total: 1975

| | Unit | Belorussia | Percent of USSR | Lithuania | Percent of USSR | Latvia | Percent of USSR | Estonia | Percent of USSR | Region Percent of USSR |
|---|---|---|---|---|---|---|---|---|---|---|
| Meat, all categories | 1,000 t. | 586.2 | 5.9 | 331.2 | 3.4 | 193.2 | 2.0 | 130.1 | 1.3 | 12.6 |
| Sausages | 1,000 t. | 136.3 | 4.6 | 53.9 | 1.8 | 50.6 | 1.7 | 39.5 | 1.3 | 9.5 |
| Butter | 1,000 t. | 88.1 | 7.2 | 49.4 | 4.0 | 34.6 | 2.8 | 28.0 | 2.3 | 16.3 |
| Milk products | 1,000 t. | 904.5 | 3.6 | 508.0 | 2.0 | 444.7 | 1.8 | 308.6 | 1.2 | 8.7 |
| Cheese | 1,000 t. | 28.4 | 5.1 | 14.7 | 2.6 | 15.4 | 2.7 | 10.7 | 1.9 | 12.3 |
| Canned goods | mil. std. tins | 549.2 | 3.8 | 273.9 | 1.9 | 339.2 | 2.3 | 259.8 | 1.8 | 9.7 |
| Sugar | 1,000 t. | 248.9 | 2.4 | 203.2 | 2.0 | 256.1 | 2.5 | — | — | 6.8 |
| Confectionery | 1,000 t. | 138.4 | 3.2 | 56.6 | 1.3 | 44.7 | 1.0 | 43.2 | 1.0 | 6.6 |
| Beer | mil. decaliters | 19.6 | 3.4 | 13.5 | 2.4 | 8.3 | 1.5 | 6.9 | 1.2 | 8.5 |

Sources: Narkhoz Belorussia 75, p. 51; Ekonomika Litovskoi SSR 75, pp. 67–68; Latvijas saimnieciba 75, p. 131; Eesti rahvamajandus 75, pp. 105–08; Narkhoz 77, p. 191.

Forests

Trees cover a significant portion (about one-third) of the
Baltic-Belorussian region. Only Georgia and the RSFSR have a
higher percentage of forested land. Regional wood reserves, however, are dwarfed by the vast expanses of timberland in northern
and western Russia, and consequently account for only 1.6 percent
of total Soviet holdings, and 4.0 percent of all wood harvested. [41]

The annual cut of timber today is somewhat below full potential because of the residual effects of severe war devastation and
burning, postwar overcutting, and the 1967 and 1969 hurricanes
that damaged many stands along the Baltic Sea. [42] Thus, a very
high proportion of the timber crop is immature, and much of the
local wood comes from thinning and improvement cuts. The age
distribution of stands in Latvia highlights the dimensions of the
problem. For optimal conditions all four timber age groups should
be of about equal magnitude, but in 1978 the youngest age category
claimed 33.7 percent, and the immature stands 49.4 percent, of
all forests. The maturing and mature groups represented 17 percent of the total. [43] In Estonia, in 1969, the two oldest groups
accounted for only 16 percent of all timber holdings. [44]

Scotch pine and Norway spruce form the bulk (over 60 percent) of all trees grown. Regional growing conditions for these are
close to ideal, and if normal age structures of stands are ever
reestablished, output of wood should increase substantially. [45]

The volume of wood could also be increased by upgrading
forestry practices, by increasing soil fertilization, and especially
by draining wet forest lands. While much has been done in this
direction, potential for improvement is still considerable. [46]

Better utilization of available wood is another avenue for improvement. At present a high proportion of harvested wood is
burned for fuel. As late as 1977, 43.5 percent of wood in Latvia,
38.5 percent in Lithuania, 21.4 percent in Estonia, and 15.6 percent in Belorussia was used for combustion. The average rate for
the USSR was 21 percent. [47] As yet only about half of every tree is
being exploited. Roots, branches, bark, needles, and leaves are
usually left behind to rot. [48] Many suggestions have been made for
more intensive and economical use of wood resources by increasing
the amount used for fiberboard, particle board, and pulp production. [49] There is also interest in the wider use of deciduous trees
for pulp and paper production. [50] Tree wastes and wood fibers can
be transformed into edible yeasts, needle flour, perfumes, pharma-
ceuticals, and fertilizer. [51] It may still be of interest to note that
a 1965 analysis of the equivalent ruble value obtained from 1,000
solid meters (cubic meters) of timber indicated that Estonia, with

TABLE 10.7

Wood and Wood Products, and Their Relative Weight as Percent of USSR Total: Belorussia and Baltic Republics, 1975 and 1977

| | Unit | Belorussia | Percent of USSR | Lithuania | Percent of USSR | Latvia | Percent of USSR | Estonia | Percent of USSR | Region Percent of USSR |
|---|---|---|---|---|---|---|---|---|---|---|
| *1977* | | | | | | | | | | |
| Wood | 1,000 cu. m. | 6,251 | 1.7 | 2,599 | 0.7 | 3,862 | 1.0 | 2,451 | 0.7 | 4.0 |
| Firewood | 1,000 cu. m. | 974 | 1.2 | 756 | 0.9 | 1,680 | 2.1 | 524 | 0.7 | 4.9 |
| Sawnwood | 1,000 cu. m. | 3,030 | 2.8 | 1,041 | 1.0 | 863 | 0.8 | 733 | 0.7 | 5.2 |
| Paper | 1,000 t. | 178 | 3.3 | 124 | 2.3 | 169 | 3.1 | 106 | 1.9 | 10.6 |
| *1975* | | | | | | | | | | |
| Cellulose (pulp) | 1,000 t. | | | 53 | 0.8 | 46 | 0.7 | 117 | 1.7 | |
| Cardboard | 1,000 t. | 158 | 4.7 | 121 | 3.6 | 19 | 0.6 | 11 | 0.3 | 9.2 |
| Fiberboard | 1,000 sq. m. | 28,962 | 7.1 | 17,804 | 4.4 | 9,031 | 2.2 | 3,450 | 0.8 | 14.5 |
| Presswood (chipwood) | 1,000 cu. m. | 256 | 6.4 | 107 | 2.7 | 70 | 1.8 | 48 | 1.2 | 12.0 |
| Glued plywood | 1,000 cu. m. | 229 | 10.4 | 27 | 1.2 | 134 | 6.1 | 36 | 1.6 | 19.4 |
| Matches | 1,000 std. boxes | | | 240 | | 765 | | 936 | | |

Sources: Narkhoz 77, pp. 172-75; Narkhoz Belorussia 75, p. 35; Ekonomika Litovskoi SSR 75, p. 66; Latvijas saimnieciba 75, p. 126; Eesti rahvamajandus 75, pp. 96-97.

340

15,600 rubles, was faring better than the Sovet average of 10,800 rubles, but much worse than Finland (27,200 rubles), the German Federal Republic (37,800 rubles), and Canada (41,300 rubles).[52]

The number of people employed in forestry operations is small in comparison with numbers in other branches of the economy. In 1974 forestry accounted for about 47,000 people, less than 1 percent of all workers and employees in the region. At the same time this number formed 10.5 percent of total forestry workers in the USSR.[53]

Today local wood and large quantities of imported wood are processed into pulp and paper, plywood, fiberboard, and matches.[54] Wood-related industries provide employment for about 10 percent of the industrial labor force in the region (See Table 10.7.)

Little growth in wood-related industries is expected in the future.[55] Wood processing requires much energy, raw materials, and water. Only water is available in sufficient quantities. Raw materials can be imported, but to import one cubic meter of wood from Siberia costs twice as much as using wood near the source of processing.[56] Moreover, woodworking and pulp and paper mills have received severe criticism for high and apparently intractable pollution levels that are interfering with other uses of natural resources and are creating health hazards.[57]

Water and Hydroelectricity

Water remains one of the least appreciated natural resources. Many industries have been located in the Baltic republics and Belorussia because of their need for large quantities of clean water for production, cooling, and waste disposal. Plants producing synthetic fibers, pulp and paper, processed food, thermal and atomic electricity, and many chemicals must be located near rivers or large bodies of water. The water balance of the region is very high, especially when considered on a per capita basis. Latvia, for example, has 16,000 cubic meters of fresh water per inhabitant, whereas the Ukraine has only 1,000 and Moldavia has 347.[58] In total volume the Baltic area has an annual water flow of 49 square kilometers, Belorussia has 38, and the Ukraine has 51.[59]

Water itself can be an important factor of production. A significant although diminishing share of electricity in the region comes from the exploitation of hydro energy. Hydroelectricity has been most important in Latvia, where it accounted for over 80 percent of local electric capacity and 71 percent of consumption in 1975.[60] The Baltic republics have a total yearly hydroelectric potential of about 6.2 billion kilowatt hours, of which 3.9 billion

(63 percent) are estimated to exist in Latvia.[61] The major source of this large capacity is the Daugava River (Western Dvina), which flows from the RSFSR through Belorussia and into the Gulf of Riga. It already sustains three large stations in Latvia and has potential for four others, two of which are planned for Belorussia.[62] The total annual potential of the river, as calculated by the All-Union Hydroenergy Project Institute (Gidroenergoproekt) is 4.6 billion kilowatt hours.[63]

In 1975 only about 53 percent of Latvia's potential hydro resources were being utilized, although by 1979 one of the existing stations had been expanded and a new station had been put into operation.[64] In 1960 a medium-size hydroelectric station was built on the Nemunas in Lithuania, but the contribution of hydroelectricity in that republic diminished from 33.2 percent in 1960 to 5.8 percent in 1970 as a result of the extremely rapid growth of thermal generating stations.[65] In 1967, Lithuanian rivers were estimated to have a combined capacity of only 600,000 kilowatts.[66]

The Narva in Estonia is also exploited for hydroelectricity, but its share in total generated power is very small. Belorussia, similarly, is dependent mostly on thermal electricity. The Belorussian hydroelectric potential has been estimated at about 3 billion kilowatt hours a year, but by 1972 only about 2 percent of this potential was being utilized.[67]

Even if the entire hydroelectric potential of the Baltic republics were tapped, it would be equal to only about 17.7 percent of total 1978 Baltic electricity production.[68] Nevertheless, the value of hydroelectricity in the Baltic is much higher than actual capacity might indicate, because it is relatively cheap and costs decrease rapidly after amortization. Also, hydropower potential can be stored and utilized during peak demand periods within the northwest electricity grid system.[69]

Peat

The topography of the region is dotted with swamps that have, in the course of thousands of years, accumulated a valuable energy-producing material: peat. Extensive deposits of peat are found in all four republics, but the most significant reserves lie in Belorussia, which in 1975 produced about 17.2 percent of all Soviet fuel peat, compared with 3.5 percent of the total in Latvia, 1.9 percent in Estonia, and 1.9 percent in Lithuania.[70] Close to 90 percent of fuel peat is utilized to stoke furnaces of communal heating plants and thermal electric stations. It should be noted that until the construction of a natural gas pipeline in the region in the

1960s, peat was the major fuel for heating and electricity generation in Belorussia, Latvia, and Lithuania.[71] The relative position
of peat, however, has declined rather rapidly in the total fuel
budget of the region. In Belorussia it accounted for 67 percent of
fuels in 1960, 37 percent in 1965, and 25 percent in the late 1960s.[72]
In Lithuania the decline was equally rapid: from 26 percent in 1960
to 5 percent in 1970.[73] In 1975 peat made up 86.2 percent of all
fuel in the heating industry in Latvia and 35.8 percent of fuel in
thermal electricity production, but its share in the total fuel balance
was only 6.4 percent.[74] The large Riga thermal electric station
continues to operate on peat, but because of the fuel's bulk and low
heat value, the station required a daily supply of 232 peat-loaded
railroad cars in 1975.[75]

Peat is also used as a mulch and agricultural fertilizing agent.
It has been found to have good insulating properties, and has been
assessed as a valuable raw material for the chemical industry.[76]
The costs of producing peat from widely scattered bogs are high in
comparison with other fuels. However, the overall fuel situation
in the region and the USSR precludes the abandonment of this resource, although some people have argued that it is too valuable to
burn.[77]

Minerals and Oil

Many traditional local natural resources are utilized in the
construction industry. The region contains ample clay for bricks,
limestone for cement, slate for roofing, gravel and sand for ad-
mixtures, and gypsum for paneling. Most of this material is used
locally because of its large bulk and high transportation costs.
However, over 40 percent of Latvian slate is exported.[78] Similarly, exports from Estonia include 90 percent of ground limestone,
78 percent of roofing materials, 30-35 percent of cement and
fiberglass, 23 percent of asbestos, and 13 percent of lime.[79] The
building materials industry employs 5-8 percent of all industrial
workers in the area.[80] In addition, sand and clays are the basis
for the glass, porcelain, and china industries, which provide employment for about 20,000 people.[81]

There are also deposits of a different kind that are changing
the industrial profile of the region. Oil shale from Estonia has
been a source of oil and gas since the 1920s, and its wide use in
thermal electric stations has alleviated the electricity shortfalls of
the northwest regional grid.[82] Oil shale is not widely distributed,
and Estonia produces about three-quarters of the total mined in the
USSR.[83] The first gas pipeline from the oil shale fields at Kohtla-

Jarve in northern Estonia, opposite Finland, was constructed to Leningrad in 1948, and five years later a pipeline was built to Tallinn.[84]

The reserves of economically usable oil shale have been estimated at 8.6 billion tons, which is equivalent to about 1.7 billion tons of oil.[85] In 1974 two giant thermal electric plants consumed about 20 million tons—73 percent of the total production of 27.3 million tons of shale.[86] The chemical industry is also dependent on oil shale for at least 40 different types of products.[87] The usefulness of oil shale is limited by the high costs of oil extraction in comparison with other sources. Nevertheless, the former chairman of the Presidium of the Estonian Supreme Soviet, Artur Vader, stated in 1972: "The economic structure of the Estonian SSR is determined to a great degree by the oil shale industry."[88]

Until the mid-1960s Estonia was the only republic in the region to have economic deposits of hydrocarbons, but then oil was struck in Belorussia and, a few years later, in Lithuania. In the latter republic the volume of oil produced is still insignificant, although a Lithuanian promotional booklet claimed reserves of "hundreds of millions of tons of high-quality oil," and a Soviet economist stated, "Taking into account the known oil deposits, one is justified in regarding the Baltic Depression as a new oil-bearing province of major importance."[89]

In Belorussia oil production in 1975 was 1.6 percent of the Soviet total (almost 8 million tons), and gas production was 568 million cubic meters.[90] The oil and gas in this region are particularly valuable because they are easily accessible, lie in the middle of an area of high energy consumption, and have a low sulfur content. While all industry in Belorussia increased 2.94 times in 1965-75, the chemical and petrochemical industries increased 8.9 times.[91] Moreover, Belorussia produced 15.9 percent of the total chemical fibers and threads in the USSR in 1975.[92] A large part of this growth, however, was planned prior to the new oil discoveries, and chemical production is still based in part on imported hydrocarbons.

Vast deposits of phosphorites, potash, and salt have further spurred the development of the chemical industry, particularly in Belorussia but also in Estonia and Lithuania. Belorussia is the leading republic within the USSR in the production of potash, with reserves of about 40 billion tons.[93] It also has large deposits of phosphates. Both of these resources are essential ingredients in mineral fertilizers, so it is not surprising that Belorussia was responsible for over 12.2 percent of all synthetic fertilizer production in the USSR in 1975.[94] Production of this vital agricultural material in Belorussia more than quintupled from 1965 to 1974.[95]

Lithuania and Estonia have much sought-after deposits of phosphorite, which is used in the production of superphosphate fertilizers.
The Estonian deposits have been estimated at 906 million tons.[96]

In addition to the widely publicized mineral resources, the
four republics have limited quantities of other underground wealth.
Belorussia has some combustible shale and coal.[97] Estonia processes uranium at Sillamae, but no public mention has been made
of whether this ore is local or imported.[98] And the Baltic countries have often been called "amberland" because of unique deposits
of petrified pine pitch now in great demand for jewelry and art-
work.[99]

### The Sea

A signal advantage of the Baltic republics is their seaside lo-
cation and year-round ports. A Soviet geographer claims that the
Baltic region "may be regarded as a natural harbor which serves the
Center of the European part of the USSR."[100]

In tsarist times Riga and Tallinn were ports of major significance, especially after the construction in the 1860s of railway links
with Moscow, Leningrad, Warsaw, and other centers of Russia.
Latvian ports handled 24.5 percent of all foreign trade of the empire
in 1913.[101] In 1973, Latvian ports were still important in sea trade,
although their overall volume share of Soviet sea-based external
trade was down to 10 percent.[102] In 1966 about 16 percent of all
Soviet external trade passed through Baltic republic ports.[103]

In 1978, Latvian ports handled 20 million tons of exports and
over 3 million tons of imports.[104] Almost 95 percent of this
freight was in transit—that is, it neither came from nor was
destined for Latvia.[105] Interestingly, a major transit customer is
Japan. The port of Riga has become the terminal point for Japanese
goods dispatched in containers from the Far East port of Nakhodka
and destined for Western Europe.[106] As a result of increased
traffic, the port of Riga is being expanded, and has already received a Yugoslav-built floating ship-repair dock, specialized
gantry cranes, and other lifting equipment.[107] A large, new
freight-container handling terminal is also being constructed on a
nearby island.[108]

The Latvian port of Ventspils has expanded rapidly, especially
since becoming the terminal port for the Volga-Urals crude-oil
pipeline in March 1968.[109] In 1974 the port's loading capacity was
increased with the addition of a third deep-water berth capable of
servicing "gigantic ocean tankers."[110] Ventspils has also become
one of the main exchange points for a unique long-term barter deal

between the American Occidental Petroleum Corporation and the USSR.[111] "Oxy" agreed to provide the Soviet Union with super-phosphoric acid in return for ammonia, potash, and urea. In addition, "Oxy" helped plan and build a giant industrial-chemical complex at Ventspils, increasing even more the strategic and economic importance of this all-season port.[112]

The ports of Tallinn in northern Estonia and Klaipeda (Memel) in Lithuania also have received considerable attention. Klaipeda is one of the major Soviet ports involved in building oceangoing vessels.[113] It is a base for deep-sea trawlers and an important outlet point for Soviet heavy oil, coal, and other dry cargo.[114] With the completion of the oil refinery at Mazeikiai, Lithuania, the port of Klaipeda most probably will increase in importance.[115] Tallinn, according to a Novosti Press publication of 1972, has also not yet reached its full potential, but will "soon" become one of the "largest Baltic ports."[116] Tallinn has traditionally received goods diverted from Leningrad during the winter.[117] It is a major center for sea tourism, and a regular tourist line runs several times a week from Helsinki.[118] Tallinn's harbor was deepened and renovated, and its berthing capacity increased, during the early 1970s.[119]

The development of ports has been paralleled by the development of republic-based sea fleets. The Latvian fleet contained 43 tankers and 35 dry cargo ships in 1973.[120] About 40 new ships were added between 1975 and 1980, including six West German-built, low-temperature gas tankers, each capable of handling 12,000 cubic meters of liquid ammonia, propane, butane, or other liquefied gas.[121] The Latvian fleet also contained many specialized "banana boats" for long-distance fruit hauling. On occasion these boats and their crews have been rented to firms from capitalist countries.[122] The Estonian fleet had about 75 "modern vessels" in the early 1970s.[123]

The Baltic region is ideally located for developing the fish industry. Although it accounts for about 14.3 percent of the fish catch of the USSR, only a small fraction of the fish are taken in local waters.[124] The modern trawler fleets spend most of their time in the North Atlantic, the Grand Banks, and areas near northwest Africa.[125] The Baltic ports provide many servicing facilities for fishing fleets and have become important bases for the fish-canning industry. It seems probable, however, that fish-related activities will diminish rather than grow, because of the constraints placed on international fishing by the extension of controlled sea boundaries to 200 miles.[126] While trade and fishing are the primary economic assets of Baltic ports, one should not ignore their usefulness for military bases and servicing. Liepaja and Ventspils, in particular, have been oriented to military needs. Obviously few details can be gleaned from Soviet public information sources on developments in this area. It is interesting to note, however, that Latvian ports have recently become bases for submarines carrying nuclear missiles.[127]

Most probably the overall significance of Baltic ports will increase in the near future because of growing Soviet external trade and because of a new trend in development that Theodore Shabad has characterized as the "shift toward seacoasts."[128] This shift, according to Shabad, is a "departure from the traditional interior continental location of economic activity," which had prevailed in the Soviet Union.[129]

Serious consideration was once given to the construction of a 2,430-kilometer Baltic-Black Sea canal from Klaipeda, Lithuania, through a complicated system of locks joining the Nemunas, Shchara, Yaselda, Pripet', and Dnieper rivers. In the early 1960s a Lithuanian economist noted, "This grandiose water route is expected to be completed by 1980."[130] The scheme was again mentioned in 1967.[131] No such route has been constructed, but the potential for a canal cannot be dismissed. If it is ever built, it seems certain that Klaipeda would become a truly important trade junction.

A final exploitable asset based on location and water resources should be considered. The Baltic republics have numerous sandy beaches and modern resorts. Pleasure sailing and sunbathing have become trademarks of the coastal area. With more leisure time, an increasing number of people from across the Soviet Union are spending their holidays in places such as Jurmala, Palanga, Neringa, and Tallinn. Tallinn was chosen as the site for the 1980 Olympic sailing events. Millions of visitors to these tourist areas spend significant sums of money, and may help to account for the larger per capita retail trade turnover in the three coastal republics.[132]

## LABOR

The availability of a skilled labor force has frequently been cited by Soviet sources as an important asset and a determining factor in the expansion of engineering and light industries in the region.[133] The Balts, especially, have inherited a work tradition similar to that of Germans and Scandinavians. Latvian industry was nurtured along in tsarist times by experienced German specialists and workers.[134] Industrial productivity at the turn of the century was found to be much higher in Riga than in most other Russian cities.[135] More recently certain impressionistic accounts of the higher work ethic in the Baltic have been noted. A Russian

journalist pointed out to <u>Washington Post</u> correspondent Anthony
Astrachan:

> The workers here [in Riga] are interested in cars, re-
> frigerators, days off as the workers in Minsk.  But they
> know they get these things by good work.  At the same
> time the engineers and managers here think more about
> maintaining the quality of work, of holding the workers
> to high standards.[136]

Labor productivity statistics have been used for comparison,
but such data can be very misleading because productivity depends
on mechanization and the efficiency of machinery as well as on work
discipline and worker ability.[137]
A Soviet geographer has claimed that the development of modern industry based on skilled labor provided the Baltic republics
with the highest gross industrial output per capita and the highest
rate of return on capital.  At the same time he indicated that the
labor advantages in the Baltic area, compared with other republics,
were quickly eroding:

> In view of the traditional skills of the population,
> Central Russia and the Baltic republics undoubtedly
> still have certain advantages in providing labor re-
> sources for industries that play a crucial role in tech-
> nical progress.  However, those advantages are
> gradually being eroded as the cultural level of ethnic
> groups in the USSR is being equalized and industrial-
> ization becomes more widespread.[138]

Not just the quality, but also the quantitiy, of available labor
is an important consideration in economic growth.  For several
decades the population of Belorussia, and to a lesser extent of
Lithuania, was underemployed.  The employment expanded rapidly
during the 1960s through new recruits from farming and household
work.  Many Belorussians, and to some extent Lithuanians, were
induced to move to other republics to find employment.[139]  The
abundance of labor apparently became one of the important considerations in locating machine-building and metalworking industries in
Lithuania:

> The specialization of Lithuania's engineering and metal-
> working industries and its place in the Soviet Union's
> system of the divisions of labor were determined by the
> circumstances that Lithuania was short of raw material
> resources but had surplus manpower.[140]

TABLE 10.8

Light Industry Products and Their Percentages of USSR Total:
Belorussia and Baltic Republics, 1977 and 1975

| | | Belorussia | Percent of USSR | Lithuania | Percent of USSR | Latvia | Percent of USSR | Estonia | Percent of USSR | Region Percent of USSR |
|---|---|---|---|---|---|---|---|---|---|---|
| **1977** | | | | | | | | | | |
| Hosiery | mil. prs. | 136 | 8.7 | 86 | 5.5 | 66 | 4.2 | 14 | 0.9 | 19.3 |
| Knitted underwear | mil. pcs. | 85 | 8.2 | 44 | 4.2 | 24 | 2.3 | 12 | 1.1 | 15.9 |
| Knitted outerwear | mil. pcs. | 39 | 8.2 | 15 | 3.1 | 18 | 3.8 | 5 | 1.1 | 16.2 |
| Leather footwear | mil. prs. | 42 | 5.7 | 9 | 1.3 | 10 | 1.4 | 6 | 0.8 | 9.2 |
| **1975** | | | | | | | | | | |
| Cotton fabrics | mil. sq. m. | 104.8 | 1.6 | 88.4 | 1.3 | 54.4 | 0.8 | 169.8 | 2.6 | 6.3 |
| Woolen fabrics | mil. sq. m. | 40.9 | 5.5 | 17.7 | 2.4 | 18.5 | 2.5 | 7.3 | 1.0 | 11.4 |
| Linen fabrics | mil. sq. m. | 83.7 | 10.7 | 22.4 | 2.9 | 18.1 | 2.3 | 6.4 | 0.8 | 16.8 |
| Silk fabrics | mil. sq. m. | 49.1 | 3.3 | 33.5 | 2.2 | 22.3 | 1.5 | 5.9 | 0.4 | 7.3 |
| Rubber footwear | mil. prs. | 6.2 | 3.1 | 10.2 | 5.2 | 13.4* | 6.8 | 1.9 | 1.0 | 16.1 |
| Carpets | mil. sq. m. | 7.7 | 12.2 | 1.4 | 2.2 | | | | | |

*For Latvia only, rubber footwear is listed under chemical industry output.

Sources: Narkhoz 77, pp. 180–85; Narkhoz Belorussia 75, p. 35; Ekonomika Litovskoi SSR 75, pp. 66–67; Latvijas saimnieciba 75, p. 128; Eesti rahvamajandus 75, pp. 100–04.

In Belorussia "rich labor resources" also have been cited as a reason for the trend toward production requiring much labor, such as electronics, instrument making, heavy machine building, textiles, and clothing.

The two northern republics have traditionally been labor-deficit areas, but they have specialized in labor-intensive engineering and light industry. The labor deficit created by these industries has largely been filled by the influx of workers from other republics. (See Table 10.8.)

GROWTH PATTERNS

In the first five years after the war, Soviet sources show Latvian and Estonian industrial output expanding at average annual rates of 46 and 36 percent, respectively. In the period 1971-75 the rates declined to a more modest 6.4 percent and 7.2 percent, and by 1978 were down to 2.7 and 3.1 percent, respectively.[141] In 1945-75 the two southern republics also were subject to rapid industrialization. Between 1940 and 1975 industrial gross output, according to Soviet statistics, increased about 21 times in Belorussia, 46 times in Lithuania, 37 times in Latvia, and 39 times in Estonia. (See Table 10.9.)

TABLE 10.9

Index of Gross Industrial Output: USSR, Belorussia,
and the Baltic Republics: 1940-75
(percent)

|  | USSR | Belorussia | Lithuania | Latvia | Estonia |
|---|---|---|---|---|---|
| 1940 | 100 | 100 | 100 | 100 | 100 |
| 1945 | 92 | 20 | 40 | 47 | 73 |
| 1950 | 173 | 115 | 191 | 303 | 342 |
| 1955 | 320 | 237 | 493 | 586 | 670 |
| 1960 | 524 | 425 | 1,030 | 1,099 | 1,150 |
| 1965 | 791 | 698 | 1,791 | 1,739 | 1,840 |
| 1970 | 1,190 | 1,300 | 3,117 | 2,726 | 2,779 |
| 1975 | 1,694 | 2,100 | 4,639 | 3,713 | 3,908 |

Sources: TsSU, Promyshlennost' SSSR (Moscow, 1964), pp. 31, 50-52; Eesti rahvamajandus 75, p. 77; Ekonomika Litovskoi SSR 75, p. 58; Narkhoz Belorussia 75, p. 46.

TABLE 10.10

Growth Indexes, Various Branches of Industry: Belorussia and
Baltic Republics, 1970 and 1975
(1965 = 100)

| | Belorussia | | Lithuania | | Latvia | | Estonia | |
|---|---|---|---|---|---|---|---|---|
| | 1970 | 1975 | 1970 | 1975 | 1970 | 1975 | 1970 | 1975 |
| All industry | 179 | 294 | 174 | 259 | 157 | 214 | 151 | 212 |
| Electroenergy | 190 | 335 | 214 | 282 | 217 | 245 | 169 | 245 |
| Fuels | 286 | 533 | 115 | 145 | 113 | 131 | 143 | 211 |
| Ferrous metallurgy | n.a. | n.a. | n.a. | n.a. | 159 | 246 | n.a. | n.a. |
| Chemical-petrochemical | 330 | 890 | 343 | 539 | 207 | 333 | 148 | 206 |
| Machine-building and metalworking | 200 | 402 | 228 | 411 | 172 | 266 | 178 | 292 |
| Wood and wood processing | 131 | 182 | 153 | 226 | 137 | 143 | 133 | 173 |
| Construction materials | 166 | 254 | 173 | 247 | 159 | 230 | 150 | 210 |
| Glass, porcelain, and china | n.a. | n.a. | 236 | 246 | 152 | 265 | n.a. | n.a. |
| Light industry | 176 | 237 | 162 | 214 | 156 | 195 | 147 | 180 |
| Food | 152 | 206 | 141 | 193 | 139 | 179 | 144 | 200 |
| Printing | n.a. | n.a. | 216 | 273 | 184 | 258 | n.a. | n.a. |

n.a. = not available.

Sources: Narkhoz Belorussia 75, pp. 46–47; Ekonomika Litovskoi SSR 75, p. 61; Latvijas saimnieciba 75, p. 89; Eesti rahvamajandus 75, pp. 81–82.

While the two northern republics slowed down in the 1970s, Lithuania and, especially, Belorussia maintained above-average industrial growth. In 1970-78, Belorussia had an industrial growth index of 205, compared with the USSR average of 166. In this same period Latvia had an index of 154, Estonia of 159, and Lithuania, of 174.[142]

The increase was not evenly spread in all branches of industry. In general, slower rates predominated in wood processing, food, and light industry. The most rapid growth occurred in machine building and metalworking, and, except for Estonia, in petrochemicals and chemicals. This pattern prevailed as well in the period 1965-75. (See Table 10.10.)

EFFECTS OF SOVIET DEVELOPMENT

The rapid pace of industrialization and development has left its imprint on the welfare of the population, on its demographic profile, and on the natural environment.

Standard of Living and Welfare

Most of the common indexes used to evaluate standard of living and welfare indicate levels above the Soviet average for the Baltic republics and somewhat below or close to that average for Belorussia. Only in certain types of education do the Baltic republics fall below the average. (See Table 10.11.)

Not all standard-of-living data are equally useful, however. The above commonly used indexes should, in many cases, be treated with caution. The intrinsic value of a high per capita national income has yet to be demonstrated, especially under conditions where production is assigned, prices are set, and profits are redistributed according to centrally determined plans. Average wages do not indicate whether benefits accrue equally to all ethnic groups within the republic. It is well known that managers usually earn more than low-grade workers. A sample study of Riga workers in 1967-68, for example, indicated that post-1945 immigrants from other republics formed 32 percent of the total work force but held 44 percent of managerial jobs.[143] Until more detailed data are published on ethnicity and income, one can only speculate about who earns most in the Soviet system. Per capita retail trade turnover is another confusing index. Apparently it indicates the value of goods bought in republic stores, but it does not indicate that these goods were bought by residents of the

republic. The deputy chairman of the Latvian State Planning Commission discussed the flawed value of this index in 1975:

> One cannot consider merely on the basis of average indi-
> cators that state and cooperative consumer trade in our
> republic is 43 percent above the Soviet average. One
> must consider various factors which bring this about
> including strongly developed tourism, visiting shoppers,
> a higher republican proportion of older and city people,
> [higher] levels of institutional and organization pur-
> chases, etc.[144]

There are other ways of appraising levels of welfare. Per
capita food consumption in the four republics is higher than the
Soviet average for meat, milk and milk products, and vegetables
and legumes. In terms of ideal Soviet norms, the Baltic republics
are overconsuming milk and milk products, and potatoes. Belorussia is above the ideal in potato and bread consumption.[145] (See
Table 10.12.)

Ownership of certain consumer durables appears to be higher
than average in Latvia and Lithuania, but generally lower than
average in Belorussia. (See Table 10.13.)

In a few areas, however, services and conditions of living
have not improved, or have declined since 1945. Living space is
still below the average of 1939.[146] In contrast with prewar conditions, much shopping time is spent lining up at various shops, and
many common necessities have become scarce. The number of
communications offices has declined, and there are fewer dentists
than in 1940.[147] Freedom of movement and travel abroad have been
severely restricted. Moreover, according to most eye witnesses,
maintenance of buildings and gardens is now far below prewar levels.


Demographic Consequences

The pace of economic development has affected several important demographic patterns. The surge of industrialization in
Belorussia and Lithuania has eased the problem of out-migration.
In fact, both republics are now experiencing a shortage rather than
a surplus of labor. In Latvia and Estonia the establishment of industries without regard to local labor reserves has created continuing labor shortages and, more important, has induced a vast
flow of in-migrants who have changed the ethnic composition of
these republics. Consequently, one of the primary objectives of
the two republics has been to raise industrial output by increasing

### TABLE 10.11

Indexes of Welfare and Standard of Living: Belorussia, Baltic Republics, USSR, Various Years, 1975-77

| | Year | Unit | Belorussia | Lithuania | Latvia | Estonia | USSR |
|---|---|---|---|---|---|---|---|
| Net material product[a] | 1975 | rubles pc | 1,550 | 1,676 | 1,910 | 1,846 | 1,428 |
| Average monthly money earnings of state employees | 1975 | rubles | 126.0 | 142.3 | 146.4 | 159.8 | 145.8 |
| Volume of services | 1977 | rubles pc | 26 | 31 | 45 | 39 | 24 |
| State and cooperative retail trade turnover | 1977 | rubles pc | 873 | 1,011 | 1,262 | 1,287 | 891 |
| Nonedibles | | | 423 | 497 | 652 | 634 | 423 |
| Edibles | | | 450 | 514 | 610 | 653 | 468 |
| Deposits in savings accounts | 1977 | rubles pc | 477 | 728 | 547 | 650 | 449 |
| Private automobiles[b] | 1977 | per 1,000 | n.a. | 50 | 45 | 61 | n.a. |
| Population age 10 years and over with more than primary school education | 1976 | per 1,000 (10+) | 543 | 464 | 557 | 553 | 570 |

| | | | | | | | |
|---|---|---|---|---|---|---|---|
| Children in preschool institutions | 1977 | per 1,000 | 44 | 38 | 40 | 55 | 49 |
| Students at secondary special institutes | 1977 | per 10,000 | 171 | 208 | 172 | 170 | 179 |
| Students at higher education institutes | 1977 | per 10,000 | 177 | 197 | 183 | 169 | 194 |
| Number of doctors | 1977 | per 10,000 | 31.9 | 33.9 | 41.0 | 38.9 | 34.5 |
| Number of hospital beds | 1976 | per 1,000 | 118.1 | 112.7 | 127.8 | 112.8 | 119.3 |
| Life expectancy at birth | c | | | | | | |
| Male | | years | 68 | 68 | 65.3 | 66 | 64 |
| Female | | years | 76 | 74 | 74.6 | 74 | 74 |

pc = per capita.

n.a. = not available.

aFor sources of net national product, see Table 10.1.

bVoprosy ekonomiki (1978): no. 7. Also in Current Digest of the Soviet Press 30, no. 33 (1978): 13.

cFor Belorussia the average age figures are for 1970–71—U.N. Statistical Office, Statistical Yearbook, 1977 (New York: U.N., 1978), p. 84; for Lithuania no actual date is given, but the figures appear to be for 1970—Jonas Pocius, ed., Present-Day Lithuania in Figures (Vilnius, 1971), p. 15; the Latvian figures refer to 1972-73—Latvijas saimnieciba 75, p. 369; the Estonian data are for 1965-66—Tõnu Parming and Elmar Järvesoo, eds., A Case Study of a Soviet Republic: The Estonian SSR (Boulder, Colo.: Westview Press, 1978), p. 46; the USSR figures are for 1971-72—U.N. Statistical Office, Statistical Yearbook, 1977, p. 84.

Sources: Narkhoz Belorussia 75; Ekonomika Litovskoi SSR 75; Latvijas saimnieciba 75; Eesti rahvamajandus 75; Narkhoz 75; Narkhoz 77; TsSU, The USSR in Figures for 1977 (Moscow, 1978); Latvijas saimnieciba 76.

## TABLE 10.12

Consumption of Staple Foodstuffs: Belorussia, Baltic Republics, USSR, and
USSR Ideal Norm, 1974 and 1975

(kg. per capita)

| | Belorussia (1975) | Lithuania (1974) | Latvia (1974) | Estonia (1975) | USSR (1975) | Soviet Ideal Norm[b] |
|---|---|---|---|---|---|---|
| Meat and meat products | 62 | 76 | 76 | 80 | 57[a] | 82 |
| Milk and milk products | 385 | 447 | 471 | 442 | 316 | 405 |
| Eggs (units) | 262 | 234 | 237 | 258 | 216 | 292 |
| Fish and fish products | 17.2 | 15.4 | 23 | 27.6 | 16.8 | 18.2 |
| Vegetable oil | 5.8 | 5.0 | 7.1 | 8.2 | 7.6 | 9.1 |
| Potatoes | 218 | 186 | 150 | 140 | 120 | 97 |
| Vegetables and legumes | 74 | 84 | 65 | 79 | 89 | 146 |
| Bread products | 141 | 108 | 108 | 104 | 141 | 110 |
| Sugar | 40.5 | 36.9 | 44 | 41.3 | 40.9 | 40 |

[a]The Statistical Office of the European Communities (Eurostat) provides a figure of 38 kilograms for the per capita consumption of meat (carcass weight) in the USSR in 1975. The comparable average for the nine Common Market countries is 82 kilograms per capita. Basic Statistics of the Community. 15th ed. (Luxembourg: Eurostat, 1977), p. 169.

[b]Taken from V. Zeile, "Tautas labklajibas paaugstinasanas un sabiedriskas razosanas strukturas pilnveidosanas," Padomju Latvijas komunists (1979): no. 3, p. 66.

Sources: Narkhoz Belorussia 75, p. 180; Ekonomika Litovskoi SSR 75, p. 234; Latvijas saimnieciba 75, p. 366; Eesti rahvamajandus 75, p. 252; The USSR in Figures for 1977 (Moscow, 1978), p. 202.

TABLE 10.13

Stock of Consumer Durables per 100 Population: Belorussia and Baltic Republics, Compared with USSR, 1975

| | Belorussia | | Lithuania | | Latvia | | Estonia | USSR |
|---|---|---|---|---|---|---|---|---|
| | No. | Pct. | No. | Pct. | No. | Pct. | | |
| Clocks and watches | 1,315 | 99.7 | 1,557 | 118.0 | 1,971 | 149.7 | n.a. | 1,319 |
| Radio sets and radio-gramophones | 196 | 85.2 | 285 | 123.9 | 339 | 147.4 | n.a. | 230 |
| Television sets | 188 | 87.4 | 204 | 94.9 | 256 | 119.1 | n.a. | 215 |
| Bicycles and mopeds | 201 | 128.8 | 236 | 151.3 | 199 | 127.6 | n.a. | 156 |
| Motorcycles and scooters | 26 | 104.0 | n.a. | n.a. | 43 | 172.0 | n.a. | 25 |
| Vacuum cleaners | 40 | 76.9 | n.a. | n.a. | 120 | 230.8 | n.a. | 52 |
| Sewing machines | 195 | 110.0 | n.a. | n.a. | 174 | 97.8 | n.a. | 178 |
| Refrigerators | 170 | 95.5 | n.a. | n.a. | 272 | 152.8 | n.a. | 178 |
| Washing machines | 147 | 77.8 | n.a. | n.a. | 259 | 137.0 | n.a. | 189 |
| Photo cameras | 71 | 92.2 | n.a. | n.a. | | | n.a. | 77 |

n.a. = not available.

Sources: Narkhoz Belorussia 75, p. 180; Ekonomika Litovskoi SSR 75, p. 233; Latvijas saimnieciba 75, p. 386; The USSR in Figures for 1977 (Moscow, 1978), p. 203.

productivity rather than the work force.[148]  Opposition to more industrialization has increased in both Estonia and Latvia, and lately
also in Lithuania.  The first secretary of the Communist Party in
Latvia, Augusts Voss, explicitly referred to this opposition in 1971:

> We cannot overlook the fact that one still meets national
> narrow-mindedness in some people.  They do not under-
> stand that Communist construction cannot be achieved
> without the tightest political, economic and cultural co-
> operation and without the mutual assistance of all peoples
> of the U.S.S.R.  They think for example that it would not
> benefit our republic to build some big industrial power,
> and other projects.  Why?  Because in connection with
> such construction, the size of the non-Latvian population
> would increase in Latvia and the national composition of
> the republic would be mixed.[149]

There have been few protests against continued economic expansion
in Belorussia.

The high concentration of inhabitants within Baltic capital
cities is another serious problem.  Riga, with the adjoining resort
area of Jurmala, holds 35 percent of the republic's total population.
This condition has apparently created a polarization in the economic
development of agriculture.  Areas close to Riga, in spite of poor
land quality, can profit from local demand.  Areas away from Riga
have few alternative markets.[150]  Tallinn holds 29 percent, and
Vilnius 14 percent, of the total population of their republics.[151]
Plans have been created in all three republics for a greater redistribution of the urban population by stopping growth in the metropolitan areas and by inducing expansion in smaller urban centers.[152]
In the rural areas of the Baltic republics, on the other hand, a program of resettlement and concentration of farmers from widely scattered farmsteads is under way, but progress appears to be slow.[153]

There are many other demographic problems familiar to most
residents of industrialized countries.  Urbanization and "modernization" have induced smaller families, lower birth rates, higher
divorce rates, and higher labor turnover.  All these changes have
had significant impact on style of living, production, and even national consciousness.[154]


Environmental Degradation

One of the most significant effects of rapid industrialization
has been the damage inflicted on the environment by air and water

pollution. The first signals of alarm about this problem were sounded in the mid-1950s, but despite volumes of laws, regulations, and directives, vary limited progress had been made in decreasing most forms of pollution by 1970. Air pollution control has been an exception, in part because of the replacement of sulfur-containing coal with clean natural gas and oil. Water pollution has been, and continues to be, a serious threat to health, economics, and aesthetics.

A Soviet Estonian geographer wrote in 1973: "Almost without exception, waste waters are discharged into open water-bodies with only an insignificant part being purified before discharge."[155] The Bay of Tallinn and the Gulf of Finland have become symbols of pollution catastrophe. In Latvia much criticism has been directed at the Sloka pulp and paper mill, whose effluent directly threatens the popular unionwide resort of Jurmala.[156] The nearby city of Riga is still dumping most of its wastes without even primary treatment. The combination of Riga sewage, Sloka industrial effluent, and high concentrations of oil has presented a serious threat to the biological viability of the Gulf of Riga.[157] In addition, dangerous chemicals in the gulf have created health hazards for local fish consumers and have led to the near extinction of many species of fish-eating birds.[158]

In Lithuania the most serious pollution levels are found at the mouth of the Nemunas River and in the Courish Lagoon, a part of the Baltic Sea.[159] Belorussia, with its newly acquired oil, has also suffered heavily.[160] Warnings about the dangers of pollution have come from many scientists and even from state officials. A Latvian deputy premier enumerated in a USSR Supreme Soviet speech the various shortcomings in pollution control found in Latvia, noting especially the reluctance of all-union enterprises to respect local environmental laws.[161] In Lithuania, 26 prominent people signed a memorandum in 1966 to oppose an oil refinery at Jurbarkas on the already polluted Nemunas River.[162] Three years later the plans for Jurbarkas had not been changed, but in the early 1970s a new refinery site was chosen.[163] Estonian scientists have recently protested the devastation of nature in their republic, especially the ecologically ruinous method of exploiting oil shale and phosphorite deposits.[164]

Some progress appears to have been made despite institutional inertia. The volume of untreated waste water in Latvia apparently decreased by 18 percent between 1970 and 1975.[165] Polluted water is slated to decrease by another 21 percent by 1980, and to be totally eliminated by 1990.[166] This goal is not likely to be achieved. Certain types of pollution are especially difficult to control, and probably will not be eliminated several decades after the 1990 deadline. Pollution coming from animal manure, pesticides, artificial fertilizers, herbicides, acid rain, and even city streets is a looming hazard that has stymied even the most dedicated environmentalists in the West, and will no doubt present the same difficulties for the Soviets. There is some basis for optimism in the future, however. The fundamental threat of pollution to the whole biosphere, regardless of ideological and state boundaries, has spurred East-West cooperation. Scientists from the Baltic states are among the most active participants—especially in efforts to revive the critically damaged Baltic Sea. [167]

Any balance sheet of credits and debits resulting from rapid industrialization will surely have to note the losses and debasement of the quality of life springing directly or indirectly from pollution. Closed recreation areas, lost fish and crayfish, the beauty of clear streams—all these cannot be calculated in rubles or in dollars. A short-lived public debate in Latvia about the construction of a huge hydroelectric dam that would flood one of the most beautiful areas of Latvia, containing rare species of plant and animal life and many archaeological, historical, and folk-myth areas, brought a perceptive insight from one of the participants:

> We should not forget that every undertaking has its own relevance within a wider context of life. Every percentage calculation is significant only within this broader framework. Today we are struggling for a better, more beautiful future. Electricity is therefore very necessary. However, electricity is only a means rather than an end. Can we truly admit that for the sake of a means we are willing to destroy that which already appears to us all as part of this end?[168]

## AUTONOMY AND ECONOMIC DEVELOPMENT

It is obviously impossible to determine what would have happened if the republics of the region had developed on their own rather than as integral parts of the Soviet system. One can only speculate and offer some general observations. It seems that the exploitation of natural resources and geographical assets would occur regardless of political system or form of economic association, although the intensity and scope of exploitation would probably differ. Agriculture, food processing, electroenergy, forestry and wood products, construction materials, glass and porcelain, and certain branches of light industry based on local materials would exist in all four republics. Shipping, fishing, and tourism would be stressed in the Baltic republics. Oil, oil shale, and peat would be processed for fuel and would form a base for the chemical industry in the republics where these resources are found. Local reserves of phosphorites, phosphates, potash, and shale would most probably be utilized for the chemical fertilizer industry. It also seems likely that some forms of electric engineering and light industry would have been developed in the Baltic republics to make use of a relatively educated labor force and favorable transportation distribution. In Estonia and Latvia in particular, the electric and textile industries were growing rapidly before the Soviet occupation.

Possible areas of slower development under autonomous conditions may be inferred from criticisms and statements by local leaders and economists as well as from an analysis of bottlenecks, such as fuel, power, and raw materials. The clearest statement on unwanted development was formulated by the Latvian Party and government leadership in 1958. These Latvian "autonomists" wanted to stop all immigration. They suggested that greater stress be placed on local rather than all-union needs, and that production of streetcars, railroad rolling stock, diesel engines, and oiling equipment for steel mills be discontinued in Latvia.[169] More recently, in 1971, Augusts Voss indicated that some "narrow-minded" people were opposed to big industrial projects in Latvia because these would entail even greater growth of the non-Latvian population.[170]

In parallel with the "narrow-minded" Latvians, but for slightly different reasons, a Soviet geographer criticized the overdevelopment of labor-intensive industries in the Baltic republics, "where the rate of natural increase is extremely low and labor resources had to be replenished by bringing in workers from other parts of the USSR."[171] One can state with a fair degree of certainty that under conditions of autonomy, Latvian and Estonian industrial growth would have been based on available local labor reserves in the same way that the Soviet Union has relied on its internal labor pool without allowing uncontrolled immigration from neighboring labor-surplus areas, such as China and India.

If the republics were independent, then no doubt supplies of raw materials for industry would be obtained from various countries, rather than just the Soviet Union. Accessibility to relatively cheap ocean shipping in the Baltic would allow much greater flexibility in buying materials at most favorable prices. This point of locked-in inefficiencies because of internal Soviet material exchange has been well described by a Western economist:

Even though light industry ranks second in the Baltic region in utilization of manpower and gross output, its material base is located in Central Asia (textiles), Kazakhstan, Ukraine and North Caucasus (hides and wool). The average distance over which materials and fuel (which account for 80-97 percent of factory costs) are transported is 1580-2250 km. In addition, the transportability of finished goods from the Baltic region is poor; on the average less than 50 percent of rail wagon capacity is utilized.[172]

The structure of industry—or more specifically, the large share of output provided by machine building and metalworking—might be different under autonomous conditions. Artur Vader, the chairman of the Supreme Soviet Presidium of Estonia, has implied that this would in fact be the case:

Under the tsarist regime the machine tool and metalworking industries in Estonia were represented by big industrial plants which worked on raw material and the output was intended for the Russian market. In bourgeois Estonia these industries dwindled down. If in 1913, when Estonia was part of the Russian Empire, the output of the large machine-building plants and iron works amounted to 33 percent of the gross industrial output of Estonia, then in 1939 the percentage was as low as nine.[173]

Vader pointed out that after the "re-establishment" of Soviet power, this branch of industry underwent a virtual boom, and by 1971 accounted for 20 percent of total industrial output and 22 percent of industrial workers. In Lithuania this particular branch employed 9.9 percent of industrial workers in 1937, but 34.7 percent in 1975.[174] In Latvia the tsarist-independence-Soviet pattern has been similar to that of Estonia. The branch accounted for 25.6 percent of industrial labor in 1913, 14.5 percent in 1940, and 34.8 percent in 1975.[175]

The nature of the Baltic relationship with the Soviet Union is even clearer when one considers the high proportion of inputs and outputs of this industry coming from and going to other republics. In Latvia in 1972, 62.4 percent of production inputs for the machine building and metalworking industry were imported, and about 68 percent of production output was exported.[176] This type of dependence appears to be growing rather than diminishing.[177] Even Soviet Latvian sources have noted the negative aspects of importing

metal and fuel for this industry.[178] A Soviet Lithuanian official
has also indirectly criticized the drawn-out lines of transportation
and heavy weight hauling, and has called for transport rationaliza-
tion and industry reorientation to lighter materials.[179]

One could assume that in independent republics greater stress
would have been placed on consumer goods than has been the case
in the Soviet Union. What effect this would have had on long-term
growth and capital accumulation is difficult to evaluate, but it seems
rather certain that a large share of industrial capital would have
come from outside sources. In view of the national pride of these
republics, it also seems likely that the bulk of investments would
not involve direct share ownership but, rather, portfolio investment.

Many factors can be cited that might conceivably limit the
growth and expansion of industry in any one of the republics under
autonomous conditions. Energy and fuel, especially, are considered scarce resources even today, with direct access to neighboring reserves. Estonia with its oil shale, Latvia with its hydro
energy, and Belorussia with its oil could certainly meet some, if
not most, of local power demands. Yet, as in the case of other
energy-poor and resource-poor countries, such as Japan, local
shortages can be obviated by imports.

Finally, it appears likely, in view of the experiences of the
European nations, that under free enterprise conditions the services sector of the economy would absorb a far larger share of the
labor force than has been the case in the Baltic republics and
Belorussia.

The question of skewing induced by the Soviet framework of
rational division of labor and all-union interests cannot be fruit-
fully analyzed in any great detail. Obviously no one can know the
exact course of development of these republics if history had been
different and they had remained unattached to the Soviet Union.
However, a comparison with a country that was at a more or less
equal stage of development prior to 1940, and that remained independent, might add more scope to our discussion.


FINLAND

Finland is the one neighboring country that before 1940 had
an economic structure generally similar to that of Estonia and
Latvia. In fact, economically Finland resembled the two northern
Baltic states more than the other Scandinavian countries. (See
Table 10.14.)

In 1940, Finland was essentially rural, with an urban population rate of 26.7 percent; Latvia had an urban rate of 35 percent,

TABLE 10.14

Distribution of Economically Active Population, by Main Sectors
of Employment: Baltic Republics and Scandinavia, 1930-35

| | Year | Agriculture | Industry | Commerce | Transportation and Communication |
|---|---|---|---|---|---|
| Estonia | 1934 | 67.0 | 15.5 | 4.5 | 2.5 |
| Latvia | 1930 | 65.9 | 13.5 | 5.3 | 3.5 |
| Lithuania | 1935 | 76.7 | 6.5 | 2.5 | 1.1 |
| Finland | 1930 | 64.6 | 14.6 | 4.5 | 3.0 |
| Sweden | 1930 | 35.6 | 31.7 | 10.9 | 6.6 |
| Norway | 1930 | 35.3 | 26.5 | 12.5 | 9.3 |
| Denmark | 1930 | 35.3 | 27.1 | 12.4 | 5.7 |

Source: Eesti Pank, Estonian Economic Year-Book for 1937 (Tallinn, 1938), p. 117.

and Estonia of 33.6 percent.[180] All three countries suffered the
ravages of war. Finland sustained heavy industrial damage and
casualties in the winter war of 1939-40 and during World War II.
In addition, it was forced to cede 12 percent of its most productive
territory to the USSR, to resettle a large number of refugees, and
to pay very large reparations to the Soviet Union.[181] Yet in spite
of these afflictions Finland reached prewar levels of production by
1947 without massive economic help or a large inflow of specialists
from the Russian or other Soviet republics.[182]

Today Finland is a viable, independent country pursuing its
own economic goals. There is no threat of imminent economic col-
lapse or pauperization of the population. In fact, Finland has
reached high levels of production and national income, and its standard of living and welfare system appear superior in most cases to
the levels reached in Soviet republics. A comparison of Finland
with Estonia and Latvia can perhaps indicate to a greater degree the
possible directions of development under autonomous conditions.

Present-day employment distribution indicates a much smaller
proportion of Finns in industry and agriculture, but a larger concentration in services, than is the case in the two Baltic republics.
(See Table 10.15.)

TABLE 10.15

Labor Force Distribution: Finland, Estonia, Latvia,
and the USSR, 1975 and 1976
(percent)

|  | Finland (1976) | Estonia (1975) | Latvia (1975) | USSR (1975) |
|---|---|---|---|---|
| Agriculture | 13 | 14.9 | 18.6 | 23.0 |
| Manufacturing and construction | 33 | 43.5 | 41.5 | 38.0 |
| Transportation and communications | 7 | 9.6 | 9.1 | 9.0 |
| Distribution and hotels | 14 | 9.0 | 8.8 | 8.0 |
| Finance and real estate | 5 | n.a. | n.a. | n.a. |
| Other | 28 | 23.0 | 22.0 | 22.0 |

Sources: The Economist, The World in Figures (London:
Economist, 1978), p. 219; Eesti rahvamajandus 75, p. 223;
Latvijas saimnieciba 77, pp. 212-13; TsSU, The USSR in Figures
for 1977 (Moscow, 1978), p. 173.

Industrial employment did not grow as rapidly in Finland as in Latvia and Estonia, but was about equal to the rate in the USSR. The total number employed in Finnish industry in 1938 was 228,987; by 1975 the number had grown 2.4 times to 552,425.[183] In contrast, industrial employment in Latvia increased 3.6 times, from 113,000 in 1940 to 405,000 in 1975.[184] The Estonian industrial labor force grew 3.2 times during the same period.[185] Clearly, the large number of Soviet immigrants provided most of the cadres for accelerated growth in the two republics.

In view of the extremely rapid growth in industrial labor, it is not surprising that Estonian and Latvian industrial output increased an average of 8.4 and 8.6 percent per year, respectively, from 1961 to 1975, while Finnish industrial output rose an average of 6.5 percent.[186] In the case of Finland allowance must be made for the early introduction of a five-day workweek and generally shorter work hours than exist in the Soviet Union.[187]

The national income per capita in Finland in 1976, as given by the prestigious British Economist, was equivalent to U.S. $5,351.[188] According to Soviet sources, the 1976 national income per capita in Latvia, using Soviet methodology, was U.S. $2,664.[189] To be sure, "capitalist" and Soviet methodologies of national income calculation do not provide directly comparable data. However, by applying the differential used by Soviet sources for recalculating 1972 Finnish national income, we find the comparable 1976 per capita national income in Finland to be U.S. $3,919, 47 percent above Latvian income.[190] This relatively high national income was achieved in Finland despite a dearth of many resources and with a comparatively lower rate of import dependence than was the case in Latvia. Finland imported 30 percent of all raw materials and semifinished products for industrial consumption, a far lower rate than the current 50 percent level in Latvia.[191]

Finland has little local fuel besides peat, and about 38 percent of its power in 1979 was generated hydroelectrically.[192] To offset energy shortfalls, construction of nuclear reactor stations has been started.[193] Finland has also had to rely on foreign capital for investments, but of total borrowed funds, the share of foreign loan capital was only 24.4 percent in 1973.[194]

Finally, it should be stressed that Finland has not been dependent on the export of raw materials; 98 percent of all its exports were provided by manufacturing industries.[195] In Finland livestock products account for over 80 percent of total agricultural output value, and dairying has become the main foundation of farming.[196] According to a Soviet agronomist, Finnish cows produce the world's highest volume of milk per centner of live weight (if calculated on the basis of standard 4 percent milk).[197]

in grain and potato yields per hectare, Finland appears to lag slightly behind Estonia, but is ahead of Latvia and certainly of the USSR.[198]

Indexes of the quality of life are probably a more useful form of comparison because, given the centralized system of redistribution, it is impossible to assess the intrinsic value of industrial and agricultural production in individual Soviet republics. At the same time one should be extremely cautious about the types of welfare indexes being compared. Statistics in areas of relative Soviet backwardness are not generally available, so there is a tendency to focus on standards publicized by the Soviets themselves. (See Table 10.16.)

The high number of doctors and hospital beds is one of the most publicized achievements of the Soviet Union and its republics. Undeniably the Finnish index of 13.3 doctors per 10,000 population is less than half of the Soviet index of 34.5, and only one-third of the Latvian index of 41.0. Similarly, there are more hospital beds per 1,000 inhabitants in Latvia, Estonia, and the USSR than in Finland.[199] However, life expectancy at birth in Latvia, Estonia, and the Soviet Union is below that of Finland.[200] The rate of infant mortality, one of the primary indexes of health advancement, is much lower in Finland than in Latvia or the USSR.[201] Of the 34,000 children born in Latvia in 1973, 538 died within their first year.[202]

Finland has maintained a lead in other health-related areas as well. Dentists are an obviously scarce resource in the USSR. In 1975, Estonia had a total of only 154, and Latvia had 285, compared with 3,254 in Finland.[203] The situation is somewhat better with pharmacists. Finland had 104 pharmacists per 10,000 population; Latvia had 102. But in Latvia only 37 percent of all pharmacists had a higher education.[204]

Finland is also significantly ahead of Latvia and Estonia in the number of people attending secondary vocational and, especially, higher educational institutes. In 1974–75 Finland had 24.3 students per 1,000 population in higher educational institutes; Latvia had 18.3, and Estonia had 16.9.[205]

Per capita food consumption of bread, potatoes, milk, and meat appears to be higher in the Soviet republics than in Finland. However, the Soviet classification of meat consumption appears to differ from the standard European method, and includes substances not characterized as meat by most Western countries. Thus the Soviet figure of 57 kilograms of meat per inhabitant is reduced to 38 kilograms by the Common Market statistics office. The same office provides a figure of 56 kilograms of meat consumption per inhabitant for Finland.[206]

TABLE 10.16

Statistical Overview of Finland, 1975

|  | Unit |  |
|---|---|---|
| Area | 1,000 sq. km. | 337 |
| Agricultural area | percent | 8.4 |
| Forest area | percent | 64.5 |
| Population (midyear) | 1,000 | 4,707 |
| Density | per sq. km. | 14 |
| Employed in economy | per 1,000 | 470 |
| Agriculture, forestry | per 1,000 | 70 |
| Industry | per 1,000 | 170 |
| Services | per 1,000 | 230 |
| Female share of labor force | percent | 46.8 |
| Consumption | kg. per capita | |
| Grain | | 75 |
| Rice | | 3 |
| Potatoes | | 77 |
| Refined sugar | | 45 |
| Vegetables | | 22 |
| Meat (dressed weight) | | 55 |
| Liquid milk | | 258 |
| Butter (pure fat content) | | 12 |
| Eggs in shell | | 11 |
| Fats and oil (pure fat content) | | 9 |
| Agricultural land | ha. per capita | .60 |
| Agricultural production | kg. per capita | |
| Grain | | 614 |
| Meat (dressed weight) | | 56 |
| Milk | | 656 |
| Passenger cars in use | units | 937,000 |
| (Jan. 1, 1975) | per 1,000 | 200 |
| Commercial vehicles in use | units | 140,000 |
| (Jan. 1, 1975) | per 1,000 | 30 |
| Television sets | 1,000 units | 1,261 |
| (Jan. 1, 1975) | per 1,000 | 269 |
| Telephones (Jan. 1, 1975) | 1,000 | 1,679 |
| | per 1,000 | 358 |
| Doctors | per 10,000 | 13.3 |
| Pharmacists | per 10,000 | 10.4 |
| Hospital beds | per 1,000 | 15.0 |
| Infant mortality | per 1,000 born | 10.5 |
| Life expectancy at birth | years | |
| Male | | 66.9 |
| Female | | 75.4 |
| Length of workweek | hours | 38.4 |
| Students in secondary vocational institutes (1974-75) | per 1,000 | 17.5 |
| Students in higher educational institutes (1974-75) | per 1,000 | 24.3 |

Sources: Statistical Office of the European Communities, Basic Statistics of the Community, 15th ed. (Luxembourg: Eurostat, 1977); U.N. Statistical Office, Statistical Yearbook, United Nations 1977 (New York: U.N., 1978), pp. 83-89, 95-96; The Europa Yearbook 1978, vol. 1 (London, 1978), p. 601.

Housing is another area receiving much Soviet publicity, but an analysis of the 1970s indicates that Finland has been building proportionately more housing space than the Soviet Union or the Baltic republics, and the gap between them appears to be increasing. In 1975, Finland built over two times more per inhabitant than the Soviet Union.[207] In addition, a cursory visual comparison of the quality of housing would leave no doubt as to which country has a greater variety of architectural styles, more privacy, and more pleasant landscaping.

The automobile age has barely begun in the USSR, and all the attendant services and hard-surface roads are several decades behind the levels found in Finland. In 1975, Finland had 937,000 passenger cars (200 vehicles per 1,000 population), which is three to four times more than in the Baltic republics.[208]

In telephone communications the Soviet Union is far behind Finland. For every 100 inhabitants Finland had 40.9 telephones in 1975, but Latvia had 15.0, Estonia 12.6, Lithuania 8.6, and Belorussia 5.7.[209]

The number, quality, and variety of services, hotels, restaurants, clubs, lounges, and other facilities are generally higher in Finland than in the Baltic republics. However, theaters, operas, concerts, and cinemas appear to be well developed in the Baltic republics.

The Soviet republics claim certain advantages over Finland. Their inflation rates until now have been much lower than in Finland. Unemployment does not exist, and transportation and housing costs are very low.

There is, of course, a vast range of possible comparisons, and in some realms quality becomes a subjective evaluation of what one feels is "better" or "worse." In conclusion, it is worth noting that more and more economists are stressing nonmeasurable aspects of the quality of life. For many Balts the incorporation of their countries into the Soviet Union cannot be compensated by economic growth, regardless of its scope and material benefits. Moreover, many Balts were subjected to terror and deportation during the 1940 occupation, and later during the 1948-49 collectivization drive. Belorussians also suffered heavily during their collectivization drive. It is surely rhetorical to ask how many lives one tractor is worth.

The example of Finland is useful to highlight the fact that the choices for the western Soviet republics are not necessarily limited to continued prosperity within the present system or economic disintegration and chaos outside this system, as many Soviet officials and economists have argued. There is another way—a way similar to that of Finland—which might involve fewer burdens on each individual citizen, and provide better social amenities and a higher standard of living. Moreover, to be master in one's own house would certainly help resolve the extremely explosive issue of unwanted immigration from other republics and of forced linguistic accommodation by non-Russian nationalities.

The natural resources, population characteristics, and geopolitical location, coupled with unhindered trade relationships with neighboring countries, could no doubt assure the economic viability, and even prosperity, of each of the four republics while giving them the intangible thing that many countries—including Russia itself—place in the forefront of all values: "freedom of choice."

NOTES

1. Pravda, February 8, 1978; translated in Current Digest of the Soviet Press 30, no. 6 (1978): 23. There has been close coordination between the Baltic republics and Belorussia on the production of agricultural machinery and electric apparatus. As Soviet sources point out, "such cooperation allows to rationally exploit production capacity and to expand production volume."
V. Purins and J. Jankevics, eds., Latvijas PSR geografija, 2nd ed. (Riga, 1975), p. 311. In 1959 both Belorussian and Latvian scientists were trusted with the responsibility of developing coordinated biological, biogenic, and pollution research on the Daugava (Western Dvina) River, which flows through both republics. Trudy vii nauchnoi konferentsii po izucheniiu vnutrennikh vodoemov Pribaltiki: Petrozavodsk, 1959 (Moscow and Leningrad, 1962), pp. 281–86.

2. Cina, August 5, 1978. Cina is the main Party and government daily newspaper in Latvia.

3. See the compendium of articles in the special volume on regionalization in Soviet Geography, May 1968.

4. N. Nekrasov, The Territorial Organization of Soviet Economy (Moscow, 1974), p. 20.

5. The current 18 Soviet economic regions vary in population from 3.2 million for Moldavia to 26.4 million for the Central Moscow region (1964). Moldavia has the smallest area of any region—33,700 square kilometers—whereas the Far East region has 6,215,900 square kilometers, or over 184 times more than the smallest region. V. Samsons, ed., Latvijas PSR maza enciklopedija, vol. 1 (Riga, 1967), pp. 456–57. A Latvian economist has pointed out that the four units of the Baltic territorial production complex are united by a common past history, common economic and geographical features, natural resources, basic economic directions, production cooperation in industry, and complementarity

of production specialization. V. Purins, "Latvijas PSR ekonomika-
musu valsts vienota tautsaimnieciska kompleksa neatnemama
sastavdala," Padomju Latvijas Komunists (1979): no. 7, p. 45.
(This periodical is henceforth cited as P.L.K.)

6. John P. Hardt, "Strategic Alternatives in Soviet Resources Allocation Policy," in U.S. Congress, Joint Economic
Committee, Dimensions of Soviet Economic Power, pt. 1 (Washington, D.C.: U.S. Government Printing Office, 1962), pp. 54-55.

7. N. N. Kolosovskii, "Voprosy ekonomicheskogo raioniro-
vaniia SSSR," Voprosy geografii (1959): no. 47. As quoted in Yu. G.
Saushkin and T. M. Kalashnikova, "Basic Economic Regions of the
USSR," in George J. Demko and Roland J. Fuchs, eds., Geographi-
cal Perspectives in the Soviet Union: A Selection of Readings
(Columbus: Ohio State University Press, 1974), p. 144.

8. In Estonia only 11.7 percent of industrial production was
nominally under republican control in 1975; 57.8 percent was under
joint control; and 30.5 percent was under all-union control. (Tallinn;
1976), p. 79. (This series is henceforth cited as Eesti zahvama-
jandus.) In Latvia the respective figures in 1973 were 11,53, and
36. Latvijas PSR Ministru Padomes Centrala Statistikas Parvalde,
Latvijas PSR tautas saimnieciba 1973 gada (Riga, 1974), p. 102.
(This series is henceforth cited as Latvijas saimnieciba.) All-union
control of industry for the USSR as a whole has been much higher
than in the Baltic republics. The share of union ministry output in
the total output has grown from 48 percent in 1969, to 50 percent in
1970, to 53 percent in 1974. TsSU, Narodnoe khoziaistvo SSSR v
1969 g. (Moscow: TsSU, 1970), p. 145. (This series is henceforth cited as Narkhoz); Narkhoz 70, p. 132; Narkhoz 74, p. 170.

9. Nekrasov, Territorial Organization, pp. 11-14.

10. Ibid., pp. 9-28; Purins, "Latvijas PSR . . . ," p. 41.

11. Nekrasov, Territorial Organization, p. 20. A geographer
from the Latvian Academy of Sciences states: "The most important
local factors that have influenced the present condition and character of the Latvian SSR economy include historically accumulated
material funds, natural conditions and resources, economic-
geographical conditions, qualified specialists and accumulated production skills." Cina, April 3, 1979. A group of Belorussian
geographers put it in more generalized terms: "The specialization
and distribution of Belorussian industry derive from a comprehensive analysis of physical, historical and economic conditions and
from existing skills among the population." See V. A. Dementiev,
N. T. Romanovskii, V. G. Siniakova, and I. I. Trukhan, "The
Development of Geography in Belorussia During 50 Years of Soviet
Rule," Soviet Geography (1968): no. 4, p. 268. Also see E. D.
Kobakhidze, "Economic-Geographic Peculiarities of Formation of

the Industrial Territorial Complexes of Union Republics," Soviet Geography (1977): no. 12, pp. 736-43; Purins, "Latvijas PSR . . . ," pp. 40-46.

12. A. Voss, "Vienotaja tautsaimnieciskaja kompleksa," P.L.K. (1978): no. 11, p. 21.

13. This theme is common in many of the articles and books written about the Baltic by former Baltic republic residents. See, for example, Elga Eliaser, Estonia Past and Present (Stockholm: Estonian Information Centre, 1959).

14. Nicholas P. Vakar, Belorussia, the Making of a Nation: A Case Study (Cambridge, Mass.: Harvard University Press, 1956), pp. 155-58.

15. Ibid., pp. 209-13; Bronius Akstinas, Glimpses of Lithuania (Vilnius, 1972), p. 112; Johannes Käbin, Estonia, Yesterday and Today (Moscow, 1971), p. 81; Latvian Soviet Socialist Republic (Moscow, 1967), p. 15; "Ta ir Baltkrievija," Zvaigzne (1977): no. 11, p. 2. The economic losses were, of course, inflicted to some extent by all combatants.

16. Narkhoz 74, p. 782.

17. John C. Dewdney, The USSR (Surrey, England: Unwin Brothers, 1976), pp. 194-96.

18. A Latvian economist has analyzed all the production and servicing organizations whose functional purpose is to produce and process consumer goods from agricultural raw materials. This agro-industrial complex, as he calls it, has five spheres:

1. Agricultural production.
2. The manufacture of producer goods for all branches of the agro-industrial complex (tractors and agricultural machinery, cattle feed machines, equipment for water amelioration, mineral fertilizers and plant-protection chemicals, and construction of nonresidential buildings for the agro-industrial complex.
3. The processing of agricultural products (meat and milk, flour and barley, food, footwear, textiles, and other industrial branches).
4. The production infrastructure, including servicing of machinery and personnel, road maintenance and transport, communication and computer services, scientific research, and planning.
5. The social infrastructure, which includes housing, social, and cultural services on farms, and the education and training of cadres.

E. J. Treijs, "Republikas agrari rupnieciskais komplekss," P.L.K. (1979): no. 8, p. 43. In the Soviet Union as a whole the agro-industrial complex accounted for 40 percent of all those employed in the state economy.

19. Cina, December 30, 1978. This high rate of grain utilization for cattle feed also can be seen from the differential between grain produced and grain sold to the state. In 1977 the region produced a total of 12,289,000 metric tons of grain, but sold the state only 2,103,000 tons (17.1 percent). See Table 10.3.

20. Narkhoz 74, p. 343; Veseliba (1974): no. 6, p. 28.

21. N. N. Baransky, Economic Geography of the USSR (Moscow, 1956), p. 318.

22. As can be seen in Table 10.3, Belorussia produced 21.6 percent of all Soviet flax fiber in 1977, although flax occupies less than 5 percent of all sown area there. Flax can adjust to a cool, moist climate and acidic soils. Paul E. Lydolph, Geography of the Soviet Union, 3rd ed. (Toronto: Wiley, 1977), p. 158.

23. In 1977 the average USSR application of mineral fertilizers per hectare of field was 30.8 kilograms. In Belorussia it was 259.8; in Lithuania, 225.4; in Latvia, 226.9; and in Estonia, 242.5. Narkhoz 77, p. 248. In Latvia over 70 percent of soils are acidic, and 45 percent of soils have to be limed. Purins and Jankevics, Latvijas PSR geografia, p. 231.

24. Narkhoz 77, p. 251.

25. Latvijas saimnieciba 75, p. 307.

26. Narkhoz Belorussia 75, pp. 145-46; Ekonomika Litovskoi SSR 75, pp. 186-87; Latvijas saimnieciba 75, p. 306; Eesti rahvama jandus 75, p. 209.

27. J. Kronitis, Dabas aizsardziba (Riga, 1977), p. 122.

28. In Latvia over 47 percent of the land is hilly, "hampering the formation of large fields," according to Purins and Jankevics, Latvijas PSR geografia, p. 228. The sloping of land in Lithuania has been analyzed in detail; very hilly areas with over 12 degree sloping occupy 9 percent of land, and 25 percent is somewhat hilly, with slopes ranging from 5 to 12 degrees. Only 53 percent of the land could be considered flat, with less than 2 degrees of sloping. S. S. Tarvilas and A. B. Basalikas, eds., Sovetskii Soyuz Litva (Moscow, 1967), p. 254. In Estonia "uplands" occupy 15 percent, and "wavy plains" 37 percent, of the land area. See Kallio Kildema, "Estonian Landscapes as a Basis for Ecosystems," in E. Kumari, H. Jänes, and O. Renno, eds., Man and Environment (Tallinn, 1973), p. 26.

29. Endel Vin, "On the Location of Agricultural Production in Estonia," in Kumari, Jänes, and Renno, eds., Man and Environment, p. 21.

30. L. I. Slizhanov, Sel'skoe rasselenie Belorussii (Minsk, 1974), pp. 8-9; V. Stroganovs, Lauksaimnieciskas razosanas

intensifikacija (Riga, 1973), p. 136; E. Varep, "The Landscapes of Estonia Throughout the Centuries," in Estonian Geographical Society, Estonia: Geographical Studies (Tallinn, 1973), p. 88. Varep claims the average field size is only 2.8 hectares. Another Estonian geographer states that the average is about 4 ha. Rein Ratas, "Role of Land Improvement in Shaping Agricultural Landscapes," in Kumari, Jänes, and Renno, eds., Man and Environment, p. 26.

31. In group I districts, where conditions are the worst, state purchasing prices were 18 percent higher than average in 1973. In group IV, where conditions are the best, state prices were 8 percent lower than average. In Lithuania differential prices are set for farming units rather than for entire districts. Cina, December 16, 1973. For details on Lithuania see Pravda, June 11, 1979. A study of population changes in Latvia from January 1967 to January 1968, by district, indicates a gain for the Central Zone, where the average income per working kolkhoznik was the highest, but a loss in the Eastern Zone, where the average income was the lowest.

|  | Average Income per Worker in Money and Product Equivalent (1970) | Rural District Changes of Population, Jan. 1967 to Jan. 1968 (1,000) |
|---|---|---|
| Central Zone | 1,316 | +4.5 |
| Northern Zone | 1,157 | +0.2 |
| Western Zone | 1,136 | -0.1 |
| Eastern Zone | 830 | -3.0 |
| Average for Latvia | 1,096 | +1.6 |

1970 income data, Latvijas saimnieciba 70, p. 514; population changes calculated from Latviia za godi sovetskoi vlasti 1967 (Riga, 1967), p. 31, and Padomju Latvijas tautas saimnieciba (Riga, 1968), p. 11.

32. In 1977 the average price per ton of milk in Latvia was 216 rubles. That year the average cost of production for one ton of milk in kolkhozes was 215.20 rubles, and in sovkhozes 215.90 rubles. Many farms had much higher production costs and were operating at a loss. In 1978 the milk prices were set at 232 rubles per ton. Cina, November 22, 1978.

33. The rentability of flax in Latvian kolkhozes in 1975 was minus 33 percent; of potatoes, minus 6 percent. Grain, on the other hand, had a positive rentability of 39 percent. Latvijas saimnieciba 75, p. 251.

34. In 1978 a turkey "factory" with a rearing capacity of 300,000 birds was constructed in Belorussia. A farm near Vitebsk

will produce 3 million broilers a year. It will be the fifth such chicken farm in the republic. Duck factories for 700,000-800,000 birds were constructed in 1978. As a result of placing agriculture on industrial foundations, egg production increased seven times from 1965 to 1978. Cina, July 27, 1978. In Lithuania industrial livestock and poultry farming is to become the main type of enterprise in the production of animal products "in the nearest future." J. Maniusis, Soviet Lithuania: Achievements and Prospects (Vilnius, 1977), p. 128. Similarly, in Estonia there are poultry farms with a capacity of over 200,000 chickens.

35. There are fewer people in agriculture, a situation that affects private production. In addition, people who have moved to rural centers find it unnecessary or difficult to continue private farming. A 1972 study in Latvia found that out of a sample of 766, over 71 percent planned to stop farming on private plots in the future because food products are readily available in stores, personal farming is uneconomical, average wages are high, or there are no readily available facilities. J. Porietis, Literatura un maksla, January 27, 1973. The slowdown of private agricultural production affects the food balance in two ways. First, less is sold to the state. Second, the farmer who provided much of his own food is now wholly dependent on state-supplied food. It is not surprising, then, that socialist competition has been introduced in the private sector with an assortment of prizes and awards for increased food deliveries. Cina, June 2, 1978. In 1978 the private sector provided 29 percent of all agricultural goods in Latvia, but as an editorial in Cina points out, "production in personal supplementary plots is dwindling." Cina, November 23, 1979. See also Elmar Järvesoo, "Private Enterprise in Soviet Agriculture in the 1970's," Journal of the Northeast Agricultural Economics Council (1974): no. 1, pp. 48-63. In fact, the new Soviet Constitution directs the state and kolkhozes to provide help and support for private farming. Cina, November 23, 1979.

36. A. Svikis, Padomju Latvijas sabiedriskais kopprodukts un nacionalais ienakums: 1959-1965 (Riga, 1967), pp. 99-100.

37. Narkhoz 77, pp. 229-60

38. Narkhoz Latvia 77, p. 102; New York Times, May 18, 1980.

39. New York Times, May 18, 1980.

40. P. Gulans, Latvijas ekonomika padomju socialistisko republiku savieniba (Riga, 1973), p. 65.

41. Narkhoz 74, pp. 253, 257.

42. Purins and Jankevics, Latvijas PSR geografia, p. 234; A. Jalovic, "Forests of the Belorussian SSR," Belorussian Review (1955): no. 1, pp. 107-20; O. Lugus, "The Level and Prospects of

the Forest Industry in the Estonian SSR," Eesti NSV teaduste akadeemia toimetised (1970): no. 1, p. 48.

43. M. Dzelmite, "Racionali izmantot mezu resursus," P.L.K. (1978): no. 10, p. 74.

44. Lugus, "The Level and Prospects . . . ," p. 53. In Lithuania only 6.5 percent of forests were mature, according to K. Kublys, "About Lithuanian Forests and Forestry," Eesti loodus (1972): no. 10 (English summary of Estonian-language article).

45. Purins and Jankevics, Latvijas PSR geografia, p. 103.

46. In Latvia over 45 percent of forested lands have too much moisture. By 1975 about 35 percent of overly moist lands had been drained, thus apparently adding an extra 1 million cubic meters of annual growth. Drainage can improve growth from three to four times for firs and two to three times for birch. Padomju jaunatne, February 4, 1975.

47. Narkhoz 77, p. 173.

48. Janis Rubens, "Mezs—zala saules noliktava," Zvaigzne (1978): no. 17.

49. Dzelmite, "Racionali . . . resursus," p. 75.

50. Cina, September 17, 1977.

51. G. Baltins and T. Ieva, Latvijas PSR ekonomikas sasniegumi un perspektivas (Riga, 1976), pp. 43, 55.

52. Lugus, "The Level and Prospects . . . ," p. 52.

53. Narkhoz 74, pp. 554-55.

54. In Estonia about 30-35 percent of all industrial timber is imported. Elmar Järvesoo, "The Postwar Economic Transformation," in Tõnu Parming and Elmar Järvesoo, eds., A Case Study of a Soviet Republic: The Estonian SSR (Boulder, Colo.: Westview Press, 1978), p. 159. Järvesoo also states that about 45 percent of raw material for paper manufacturing, 50 percent of plywood logs, 65-70 percent of poles, and 40 percent of mine props are imported (p. 162). In Latvia imports covered 38 percent of the demand for roundwood and "about a quarter" of all sawnwood. In addition, over 50 percent of required cellulose was imported. See Purins and Jankevics, Latvijas PSR geografia, p. 348; Baltins and Ieva, Latvijas . . . perspektivas, p. 55.

55. Maniusis, Soviet Lithuania, p. 123.

56. Dzelmite, "Racionali . . . resursus," p. 75.

57. The Sloka pulp and paper complex has been a particularly notorious water polluter, threatening the nearby resort area of union-wide importance at Jurmala. The process of complaints and litigation against the mill began in the mid-1950s, and by 1978 purification devices, although being built, still had not been completed. See Juris Dreifelds, "Implementation of Pollution Control Policy in Latvia: A Case Study of the Sloka Pulp and Paper Mill,"

forthcoming article in <u>Co-Existence</u> (Glasgow).  The Kehra pulp
and paper mill was contaminating the Yagala River in 1971.
<u>Sovetskaia Estoniia</u>, July 8, 1971.

58.  I. Grosvalds, Latvijas dzilu bagatibas (Riga, 1970),
p. 140.  In the Soviet Union the production of one ton of sugar requires 100 tons of water; one ton of steel requires 150; one ton of
paper, 250; and one ton of synthetic fibers, 600 tons of water.  See
Arvis Pope, "Udenssaimnieciba, tas uzdevumi un problemas,"
<u>Zinatne un tehnika</u> (1970): no. 1, p. 15.

59.  I. I. Dreier, "Vodnye resursy krupnykh ekonomicheskikh
raionov RSFSR i soyuznykh respublik," in A. M. Grin, ed., <u>Vodnye
resursy i ikh kompleksnoe ispolzovanie</u> (Moscow, 1968), p. 66.

60.  <u>Latvijas saimnieciba 75</u>, p. 141.

61.  Purins and Jankevics, <u>Latvijas PSR geografia</u>, p. 225.

62.  The height drop in the existing dams is 12.5 to 16.5
meters for the Riga hydroelectric station, 15.5 for Kegums, 40.0
for Plavinas.  Within Latvia the Jekabpils station will have a drop
of 15.5 meters, and the Daugavpils station, at present under construction, will have a drop of 21.5 meters.  In Belorussia the
Polotsk station will have a drop of 18.0 meters, and the Vitebsk
station 28.0 meters.  See Samsons, <u>Latvijas . . . enciklopedija</u>,
vol. 1, p. 356.

63.  Ibid.

64.  The Riga hydroelectric station came into production after
1975, with a capacity of 384,000 kilowatts.  The Kegums station was
enlarged from 72,000 to 264,000 kw.  The Plavinas station was
completed in the mid-1960s and has a capacity of 825,000 kw.  The
Daugavpils station is expected to have a capacity of 300,000 kw.
<u>Padomju Jaunatne</u>, August 28 and November 7, 1979.

65.  TsSU, <u>Promyshlennost' Litovskoi SSR</u> (Vilnius, 1973),
p. 93.

66.  Tarvilas and Basalikas, <u>Sovetskii Soyuz Litva</u>, p. 36.

67.  V. P. Borodina et al., <u>Soviet Byelorussia</u> (Moscow,
1972), p. 30.  Because of the very flat slope of Belorussia, the
costs per unit of electricity are high.  Moreover, to obtain any
kind of waterpower, huge areas of land would have to be flooded.
This is perhaps why the Vitebsk station on the Daugava, which
originally had been planned for completion by 1961, has not yet
been built.  The reservoir behind the dam was to cover 807 square
kilometers.  S. Kabys, "Belorussian Industry and the Sixth Five-
Year Plan," <u>Belorussian Review</u> (1956): no. 3, pp. 123-24.

68.  Data assembled by Theodore Shabad in <u>Soviet Geography</u>
(1979): no. 4, p. 267.

69.  The Daugava was the first river in the USSR used to produce peak-load electricity.  Samsons, <u>Latvijas . . . enciklopedija</u>,

vol. 1, p. 356. The Baltic republics, Belorussia, the Kaliningrad Oblast, and the Leningrad area are all integrated into an electricity grid system. Much of the surplus for this energy-short region is provided by thermal electric stations that burn Estonian oil shale.

70. Latvijas saimnieciba 75, p. 123; Eesti rahvamajandus 75, p. 93; TsSU, Ekonomika Litovskoi SSR 75 (Vilnius, 1976), p. 63; Promyshlennost Belorusskoi SSR (Minsk, 1976), p. 33; The Europa Yearbook 1979: A World Survey, vol. 1 (London, 1979), p. 1235.

71. Theodore Shabad, Basic Industrial Resources of the USSR (New York: Columbia University Press, 1969), pp. 201, 207-09.

72. Ibid., p. 201.

73. Henry Ratnieks, "Energy Situation in the Baltic," paper presented at the Sixth Conference on Baltic Studies, Toronto, May 1978, p. 8.

74. Latvijas saimnieciba 75, pp. 46-47.

75. Cina, February 1975. Peat contains about 2,700-3,200 gram calories per kilogram.

76. A full-page advertisement by Belorussia during Expo 67 declared that new methods had been developed for making peat "into protein carbohydrate, foodstuffs and growth stimulants, waxes and activated carbon and mould powder for plastics and insulation materials." The Gazette (Montreal), September 27, 1967.

77. G. Rozena, "Racionali Izmantot kudru un kudras atradnes," P.L.K. (1978): no. 11, p. 47.

78. Purins and Jankevics, Latvijas PSR geografia, p. 351.

79. Järvesoo, "The Postwar Economic Transformation," p. 168.

80. Ibid., p. 166.

81. Ibid.

82. Ibid., p. 163.

83. Artur Vader, "The National Economy of the Estonian SSR in the Economic System of the Soviet Union," in Estonia (Tallinn, 1972), p. 3. A thorough but somewhat dated analysis of the distribution, reserves, energy potential, and production of oil shale is in Jordan A. Hodgins, Soviet Power: Energy Resources, Production and Potentials (Englewood Cliffs, N.J.: Prentice-Hall, 1961), ch. 8.

84. Järvesoo, "The Postwar Economic Transformation," p. 135.

85. Ibid., p. 164.

86. Ibid., p. 165.

87. Vader, "The National Economy," p. 3.

88. Ibid., p. 4.

89. E. Danilevicius, Lithuania in Questions and Answers (Vilnius, 1970), p. 70; Nekrasov, The Territorial Organization . . . , p. 174.

90. Europa Yearbook 1979, pp. 1293, 1235.

91. Narkhoz Belorussia 73, p. 46.

92. Ibid., p. 47.

93. Vitaut Kipel, "Some Demographic and Industrial Aspects of Soviet Belorussia During 1965-1975," in George W. Simmonds, ed., Nationalism in the USSR and Eastern Europe in the Era of Brezhnev and Kosygin (Detroit: Wayne State University Press, 1977), p. 98.

94. Narkhoz Belorussia 75, p. 47.

95. Narkhoz 74, p. 234.

96. E. Kivimägi, "Phosphorite Reserves in Estonia," Eesti loodus (1971): no. 5 (from English summary at the end of journal).

97. Borodina et al., Soviet Byelorussia, p. 20.

98. Shabad, Basic Industrial Resources of the USSR, p. 213.

99. For example, a publicity pamphlet states: "The heavy waves of the Baltic Sea roll in slow succession. From time immemorial it has been called the amber sea: when a storm rages, pieces of amber are cast ashore." See Board of Foreign Tourism for the Council of Ministers of the USSR, Welcome to Riga (n.p., n.d.)

100. Baransky, Economic Geography of the USSR, p. 318.

101. Purins and Jankevics, Latvijas PSR geografia, pp. 448-50.

102. Ibid., pp. 456-57.

103. R. Blazis, "Padomju Baltijas republikas ekonom-geografu skatijuma," Zinatne un tehnika (1966): no. 4, p. 3.

104. Purins, "Latvijas PSR . . . sastavdala," p. 46.

105. Cina, April 3, 1979.

106. Cina, April 5, 1980; Dzimtenes balss, December 27, 1979.

107. Cina, February 2, 1977.

108. Dzimtenes balss, January 1, 1978.

109. Theodore Shabad, "News Notes," Soviet Geography (1968): no. 4, p. 335.

110. Purins and Jankevics, Latvijas PSR geografia, p. 457.

111. Theodore Shabad notes the terms of the deal in Soviet Geography (1978): no. 9, p. 500. The first shipments of this "barter arrangement" started in 1978, after the completion of a "seaside chemical terminal" at Ventspils.

112. Cina, April 6, 1980.

113. Augustine Idzelis, "Response of Soviet Lithuania to Environmental Problems in the Central Zone," Journal of Baltic Studies (1979): no. 4, p. 301.

114. Ibid.

115. Ibid.

116. Novosti Press, Estonian Soviet Socialist Republic (Moscow, 1972), p. 41.

117. Tamara Tomberg, Tallinn: A Tourist Guidebook (n.d., n.p.)

118. Intourist, Soviet Baltic Republics (n.p., n.d.)

119. Novosti Press, Estonian . . . Republic, p. 41.

120. Purins and Jankevics, Latvijas PSR geografia, p. 454.

121. Cina, April 5, 1980, and January 24, 1978.

122. Cina, April 5, 1980.

123. Novosti Press, Estonian . . . Republic, p. 41.

124. TsSU, Lietuvos TSR ekonomika ir kultura (Vilnius: TsSU, 1972), p. 37. The latest data on the fish catch are for 1970. In thousands of tons Belorussia had 9.0; Lithuania, 376.7; Latvia, 441.1; and Estonia, 305.1. Ibid.

125. R. S. Mathieson, The Soviet Union: An Economic Geography (New York: Barnes and Noble, 1975), p. 199.

126. Sovetskaia Estonia, November 11, 1979, announced that fish catches have been decreasing and that 1,300 qualified fishermen were forced to seek jobs elsewhere.

127. "The Baltic as a Missile Base," Manchester Guardian Weekly (U.K.), April 9, 1978 (overseas ed.).

128. Theodore Shabad, "Introduction: Soviet Regional Development Policy in the Tenth Five-Year Plan and Beyond," in NATO Economic Directorate, ed., Regional Development in the USSR: Trends and Prospects (Newtonville, Mass.: Oriental Research Partners, 1979), p. 22.

129. Ibid.

130. "Par baltijas dabas bagatibam, to tautsaimniecisko nozimi un izmantosanu," Vestis (1963): no. 5, pp. 128-29.

131. Novosti Press, Byelorussian Soviet Socialist Republic (Moscow, 1967), p. 44.

132. There are some 13 commercial resorts and health spas in the Baltic republics. For a list of their names and principal specialization, see John L. Scherer, ed., USSR Facts and Figures Annual, vol. 3 (Gulf Breeze, Fla.: Academic International Press, 1979), pp. 277-78. According to Purins and Jankevics, Latvijas PSR geografia, p. 278, the resort of Jurmala, Latvia, has a four-fold increase in population during summer (about 250,000 in 1973). A Latvian economist points out that the net inflow (saldo) of individually spent cash currency into the republic runs to about 100 million

rubles a year. He claims that this phenomenon should be carefully investigated, in order to better plan the distribution of retail goods on a territorial basis. Svikis, Padomju . . . 1959-1965, p. 181.

133. Most textbooks and articles dealing with engineering and light industry in the region stress the important role of the highly qualified work force. See, for example, Nikolajs Baibakovs, "PSRS—vienota saimnieciba," Zvaigzne (1972): no. 23, p. 7. Purins and Janovics, Latvijas PSR geografia, p. 302, indicates that a qualified work force has been the determining factor in the development of such branches as the electrotechnical industry, radio electronics, instrument-making and other specialized branches in Latvia.

134. Margers Skujeneeks, Latvija, zeme un eedzivotaji (Riga, 1927), p. 630.

135. Ibid.

136. Washington Post, November 22, 1970.

137. Quite commonly, even in comparisons of U.S. and Canadian workers, the same inference is made—if American workers produce more, then they must be more productive because of innate qualities.

138. E. D. Kobakhidze, "Economic-Geographic Peculiarities of Formulation of the Industrial-Territorial Complexes of Union Republics," Soviet Geography (1977): no. 12, p. 738.

139. See Ann Sheehy, "The National Composition of the Population of the U.S.S.R. According to the Census of 1979," Radio Liberty Research, RL 123/80, March 27, 1980, p. 17. The number of Lithuanians in Latvia increased from 22,900 in 1935 to 32,400 in 1959, and 40,600 in 1970. Latvijas saimnieciba 70, p. 11.

140. Maniusis, Soviet Lithuania, pp. 28-29.

141. Latvijas saimnieciba 68, p. 59; Latvijas saimnieciba 76, p. 84; Narkhoz Estonia 68, p. 55; Eesti rahvamajandus 75, p. 78; Narkhoz Latvia 78, pp. 41-42.

142. Narkhoz Latvia 78, p. 42.

143. B. Mezgailis and P. Zvidrins, Padomju Latvijas iedzivotaji (Riga, 1973), p. 365.

144. Elerts Abolins, "Labklajibas un pieprasijuma problemas piecgadu mija," Zvaigzne (1975): no. 17, p. 2.

145. Higher consumption of starchy foods is not, of course, necessarily beneficial or healthy. A Soviet Estonian scientist, Einar Vagane, found, on the basis of sample research of the Estonian population, that nourishment has become "too sweet and too rich in fats," "too poor in proteins," and "deficient in vitamins and foodstuffs containing minerals and bulk materials." Vagane points out that about 13 percent of the men and 25 percent of the women were at least 10 kilograms overweight. The quantity and content of

food are also blamed for the high rate of "degenerative diseases,"
which "considerably exceed" the average for the Soviet Union.
Einar Vagane, "On Changes in the Composition and Requirement of
Nutrition of the Population of Soviet Estonia," in Kumari, Jänes,
and Renno, eds., Man and Environment.

146. According to Latvijas saimnieciba 75, p. 411, the per
capita living space in 1939 was 17.8 square meters, but only 14.3
square meters in 1975.

147. In 1940, Latvia had 433 dentists, but in 1975 only 285.
Latvijas saimnieciba 75, p. 458. In Estonia there were 182 and
154 dentists for the same years. Eesti rabvamajandus 75, p. 352.

148. The campaign to hold the line on the growth of the industrial labor force is being waged in many labor-shortage areas. In
Latvia intensive or increased productivity factors, rather than extensive factors, accounted for 77 percent of the increase in industrial output between 1966 and 1970, 94 percent in 1971, 100 percent
in 1972 and 1973, 86 percent in 1974, and 94 percent in 1975. See
Latvijas saimnieciba 75, p. 109.

149. New York Times, March 21, 1971.

150. Cina, February 9, 1980.

151. Ibid.

152. See A. B. Margolin, V. L. Gerbov, and D. A. Golovkin,
Pribaltiiski ekonomicheskii raion (Moscow, 1970), pp. 280-90.

153. Sandra Janschewsky, "Agrotowns in Latvia," Radio
Liberty Research Bulletin, RL 17J/7J, April 25, 1975; Washington
Post, September 13, 1974.

154. See Yaroslav Bilinsky, "The Background of Contemporary Politics in the Baltic Republics and the Ukraine: Comparisons
and Contrasts," in Arvids Ziedonis, Jr., Rein Taagepera, and
Mardi Valgemäe, eds., Problems of Mininations: Baltic Perspectives (San Jose, Calif.: A.A.B.S., 1973), pp. 89-122; V. Stanley
Vardys, "Modernization and Baltic Nationalism," Problems of
Communism, September-October 1975, pp. 32-48; Thomas Remeikis,
"Political Developments in Lithuania, Latvia, Estonia Since 1964,"
in Simmonds, ed., Nationalism in the USSR and Eastern Europe,
Juris Dreifelds, "Latvian National Demands and Group Conscious-
ness Since 1959," ibid.

155. Enno Siirde, "Industrial Waste Waters and Their Treatment," in Kumari, Jänes, and Renno, eds., Man and Environment,
p. 53.

156. Dreifelds, "Implementation of Pollution Control Policy
in Latvia."

157. See A. I. Simonov and A. A. Justchak, "Recent Hydro-
chemistry Variations in the Baltic Sea in the USSR," in Anders
Akerblom, ed., 1st Soviet-Swedish Symposium on the Pollution of
the Baltic; Ambio Special Report, 1972, no. 1.

158. Georg Loogna, "Circulation of Carcinogens in the Human Environment," in Kumari, Jänes, and Renno, eds., Man and Environment, pp. 45-46.

159. Idzelis, "Response of Soviet Lithuania . . . ," pp. 299-300.

160. Sovetskaia Belorussia, April 20, 1972; Izvestia, Nov. 17, 1972.

161. Padomju Jaunatne, September 22, 1972.

162. The memorandum was submitted to the top Lithuanian Communist authorities on March 22, 1966. The highlights of the memorandum have been published in English: "Protest Against Soviet Industrialization Ills in Lithuania," Baltic Review (1967): no. 33, pp. 22-31.

163. Ratnieks, "Energy Situation in the Baltic," p. 7.

164. Aina Zarins, "Scientists Protest the Devastation of Nature in Estonia," Radio Liberty Research, RL 224/77, September 28, 1977.

165. L. Glazacheva and M. Tomass, "Saudzet udens resursus," P.L.K. (1977): no. 6, p. 70.

166. P. Strautmanis, "Lai daba kalpotu cilvekam," Veseliba (1974): no. 7, p. 2; P.L.K. (1976) no. 2, p. 15.

167. Cina, September 16, 1973. According to Skolotaju Avize, June 16, 1976, there is a "division of labor" concerning research on the Baltic Sea. The Lithuanian Academy of Sciences concentrates on hydrogeology. Estonian scientists are constructing mathematical models of sea processes, and the Latvian Academy of Sciences is dealing with biological problems and the dynamics of self-purification. For a comprehensive review of Baltic Sea pollution and scientific activity, see Aina Zarins, "The Baltic Sea: A Pointer for the United Nations Law of the Sea Conference," Radio Liberty Research Bulletin, RL 188/77, August 9, 1977.

168. Literatura un maksla, April 5, 1958.

169. For an analysis and discussion of the "autonomists" in Latvia, see Gundar Julian King, Economic Policies in Occupied Latvia: A Manpower Management Study (Tacoma, Wash.: Pacific Lutheran University Press, 1965), pp. 193-204.

170. New York Times, March 21, 1971.

171. Kobakhidze, "Economic-Geographic Peculiarities . . . ," p. 738. This geographer also criticized the "inadequate development" of high-skill machinery manufacturing in labor-abundant areas in Central Asia and Transcaucasus. Nekrasov, Territorial Organization, pp. 154-55, indicates another problem area: "In Byelorussia, as in some other areas of the European part of the USSR, the development of energy-consuming chemical industries does not make good sense because of the unfavourable fuel and energy balance in the macro-region."

172. Alexander Woroniak, "Regional Aspects of Soviet Planning and Industrial Organization," in V. N. Bandera and Z. L. Melnyk, eds., The Soviet Economy in Regional Perspective (New York: Praeger, 1973), p. 274.

173. Vader, "The National Economy . . . ," p. 4.

174. Maniusis, Soviet Lithuania, p. 19.

175. Latvijas saimnieciba 75, p. 102.

176. V. Purins and J. Jankevics, Latvijas P.S.R. Socialistiskaja darba dalisanas sistema (Riga, 1978), p. 48.

177. In 1970 about 40 percent of Latvian industrial production was exported. By 1972 the rate was 43 percent, and by 1979 about 50 percent. Imports generally approximate the export percentage. Narkhoz Latvia 71, pp. 49–50; Latvijas saimnieciba 75, pp. 66–67; Purins, "Latvijas PSR . . . sastavdala," p. 43.

178. Purins and Jankevics, Latvijas PSR socialistiskaja darba dalisanas sistema, p. 45.

179. Maniusis, Soviet Lithuania, pp. 130–31.

180. Eesti rahvamajandus 75, p. 27; Latvijas saimnieciba 75, p. 6; Facts About Finland (Helsinki, 1967), p. 10.

181. Finfacts Institute, ed., Finland as a Trading Partner (Helsinki: Finnish Foreign Trade Association, 1974), p. 11.

182. Ibid.

183. Central Statistical Office of Finland, Statistical Yearbook of Finland 1978 (Helsinki, 1979), p. 120.

184. Latvijas saimnieciba 75, p. 324.

185. Eesti rahvamajandus 75, p. 224.

186. Baltins and Ieva, Latvijas PSR . . . perspektivas, p. 14; Eesti rahvamajandus 68, p. 55, and 75, p. 78; Jyrki Malmio and Heikki Tulokas, "Finnish Industry: An Overview," Bank of Finland Monthly Bulletin (1977): no. 1, p. 21.

187. In 1973 average weekly hours per worker in manufacturing were 38.0 in Finland and 40.6 in the USSR. United Nations, Statistical Office, Statistical Yearbook 1974 (New York: U.N., 1975), p. 93.

188. The Economist, The World in Figures (London: Economist, 1978), p. 219.

189. Latvijas saimnieciba 77, p. 251.

190. Latvijas saimnieciba 77, p. 236, provides 1972 per capita national income data for Finland as $2,280, according to Western methodology, and $1,670, according to the methodology used in the USSR. While the exact differential might not apply for calculating 1976 data, it is useful for providing a degree of approximation.

191. Malmio and Tulokas, "Finnish Industry," p. 23.

192. The Statesman's Year-Book 1979-80 (London: Macmillan, 1979), p. 452.

193. Malmio and Tulokas, "Finnish Industry," p. 24.

194. Ibid., p. 27.

195. Ibid., p. 28.

196. Jussi Linnamo, Finland a Growing Economy (Helsinki, 1967), p. 29.

197. Raimonds Baltakmens, "Ka sasniegts pasaules rekords lopkopiba," Zinatne un tehnika (1969): no. 5, p. 32.

198. Statistical Yearbook of Finland 1978, p. 88; Eesti rahvamajandus 75, p. 146; Latvijas saimnieciba 75, p. 203; The USSR in Figures for 1977 (Moscow, 1978), pp. 118-19.

199. Compare Tables 10.11 and 10.16.

200. Ibid.

201. In Finland the rate of infant mortality was only 10.5 per 1,000 born in 1976. The USSR rate in 1974 was 27.7. U.N. Statistical Office, Statistical Yearbook 1977 (New York: U.N., 1978), p. 83. In Latvia the 1973 rate was 15.8. J. Krumins and P. Zvidrins, Padomju Latvijas iedzivotaju muza ilgums (Riga, 1976), p. 92.

202. Krumins and Zvidrins, Padomju . . . ilgums, p. 92.

203. Eesti rahvamajandus 75, p. 352; Latvijas saimnieciba 75, p. 458; Statistical Yearbook of Finland 1978, p. 299.

204. Latvijas saimnieciba 75, p. 465.

205. Compare Tables 10.11 and 10.16.

206. Compare Tables 10.12 and 10.16.

207. From 1965 to 1975 the newly constructed housing space per capita increased from .31 meter to .45 meter in Latvia, from .41 to .51 in Estonia, and from .53 to 1.06 in Finland. Statistical Yearbook of Finland 1978, p. 129; Narkhoz 77, p. 414.

208. Compare Tables 10.11 and 10.16.

209. Narkhoz Belorussia 75, p. 136; Ekonomika Litovskoi SSR 75, p. 170; Latvijas saimnieciba 75, p. 286; Eesti rahvamajandus 75, p. 192.

# 11

## TRANSCAUCASUS

### Oleg Zinam

BACKGROUND

Transcaucasia is one of 18 major economic regions established in the USSR in 1963.[1] It represents a distinct geographic region of the Soviet Union, separated from the North Caucasus by the Caucasian Mountains. Its western and eastern boundaries are the Black and Caspian seas, respectively, and in the south it borders on Turkey and Iran. Transcaucasia is the Soviet Union's oldest oil-producing region, the nation's only zone of wet subtropics, its second most important cotton-producing region, and a highly developed producer of wine and silk.[2] Here, in an area covering less than 1 percent of the Soviet Union's territory, one finds mountains covered by perennial snow, hot valleys, dry semi-deserts, and well-irrigated lands covered with subtropical vegetation.[3]

In 1978 the Transcaucasus, an area covering 0.83 percent of the USSR, had about 13.9 million people (about 5.3 percent of the total Soviet population). The region is divided into three union republics: Georgia, Azerbaidzhan, and Armenia. The Georgian SSR was formed in 1921; the Azerbaidzhan and Armenian republics, in 1920. In March 1922 all three were incorporated into the newly created Transcaucasian Socialist Federative Soviet Republic (ZSFSR), which lasted until 1936. Since then, separate republics have existed.[4]

The total area of Transcaucasia is slightly less than half of the state of California: the Georgian SSR is about half the size of the state of Georgia, Azerbaidzhan is almost as large as the state of Maine, and the Armenian SSR is slightly more than half as large as West Virginia. In 1978 the population of these republics was 5,041,000 for Georgia, 5,866,000 for Azerbaidzhan, and 2,950,000 for Armenia. The Georgian SSR incorporates the Abkhasian and Adzharian Autonomous Republics as well as the South Ossetian Autonomous Region.[5]

The Transcaucasian republics are non-Russian and non-Slav. They were gradually incorporated into the Russian Empire in the eighteenth and nineteenth centuries. Armenians, Georgians, and Azerbaidzhanis are people with the most ancient cultures in the Soviet Union. Their forefathers were known in the fourth century B.C. Before the nineteenth century, Georgians lived on a common territory and spoke the same language, but did not constitute a nation, which was formed only in the second half of the nineteenth century. In 1801 eastern Georgia became a part of Russia. The rest of Georgia was gradually incorporated into the Russian Empire. By 1878 this incorporation was completed.[6]

Armenians are among the most ancient people in the world. Armenia has existed since the time of the formation of the Greek and Roman civilizations. It has defended its distinctiveness and independence against numerous powerful enemies. In the fourteenth and fifteenth centuries Armenia was divided between Turkey and Persia. As a result of the Russian-Persian war of 1827-28 and the Russian-Turkish war of 1878, the eastern part of Armenia became a part of the Russian Empire and now is the Armenian SSR.[7]

Georgians and Armenians are traditionally Christians, and the Azerbaidzhanis are Muslims. Their language is close to Turkish. There are probably as many Azerbaidzhanis in Iran as in the Azerbaidzhan SSR. Azerbaidzhan was annexed to Russia in 1828 by the Treaty of Turkmanchaisk between Russia and Persia.

The Georgian Republic, situated in the western part of the Transcaucasus, produces about 95 percent of the Soviet output of tea and almost 100 percent of citrus fruits (lemons and tangerines). It also produces tobacco, wines, mineral waters, and aromatic oils. It has ample supplies of minerals, including coal, oil, and manganese. Among its industrial products are steel, motor cars, computers, electric locomotives, and machine tools. Georgia is also famed for its excellent resorts: Gagra, Sukhumi, Pitsunda, Borzhomi, Tshkaltubo, and Bakuriani.

The Azerbaidzhan SSR is located in the eastern part of Transcaucasus and is washed by the Caspian Sea. On the Apsheron Peninsula are some of the oldest Soviet oil fields. As oil supplies are depleted, floating installations are moved farther out to sea. Turbo and electric drills made in Baku are export items. The republic has a rapidly developing petrochemical industry. It also has numerous iron and steel machine-building and metalworking factories. Huge cotton fields are cultivated in the Kura Valley and in the lower reaches of the Araks. An extensive irrigation system has been built for this purpose. Its agriculture also produces tobacco, grapes, early vegetables, and fruits—dates, plums, pomegranates, quinces, and figs. In addition to oil, Azerbaidzhan has copper, magnetite, cobalt, and arsenic. Between 1899 and 1901, Russia was a top producer of oil in the world, ahead of the United States, which had held this position since 1859. At that time almost all Russian oil came from Azerbaidzhan.

The Armenian SSR is a mountainous land situated in the southern part of the Transcaucasus. It is the smallest of all union republics in terms of territory (0.13 percent of the USSR), yet it produces 0.8 percent of the Soviet Union's total industrial output. Endowed with a subtropical climate and an extensive irrigation system, Armenia produces good harvests of wheat, barley, corn, sugar beets, grapes, tobacco, peaches, apricots, figs, and pomegranates. Its mining industry produces copper, aluminum, zinc, molybdenum, and some rare metals. Its industrial production extends into electrometallurgy, electrochemistry, building materials, the production of machines and food, light industry based on hydroenergy, electronic automation equipment, and complicated measuring instruments.[8]

Transcaucasia with its distinct three nationalities—Georgians, Azerbaidzhanis, and Armenians—has existed for more than a century as part of a multinational state (the Russian Empire and, since 1921, the USSR) with one predominant majority, Russians. Moreover, Transcaucasians have a strong historical background of national identity. During the Soviet rule over Transcaucasus, the Kremlin's policy toward interregional equalization of economic development has undergone a gradual change. It has evolved from an early explicit commitment to equalization to a more vague and diffused concept of developing all regions and republics within the framework of major national objectives, such as fostering rapid industrial development, strengthening the nation's defense posture, and building a solid base for the future Communist society.

Within this general governmental policy, the Transcaucasian republics have shown rapid increases in agricultural and industrial production, and this economic growth has been accompanied by substantial improvement in the standard of living. However, in comparison with the nation as a whole and with the Russian Republic, the relative position of Transcaucasus, on a per capita basis, has deteriorated, partially because of its relatively rapid population growth.

Statistics indicate that from 1913 to 1978, the rate of population increase in the Transcaucasian republics was higher than in both the RSFSR and the USSR (see Table 11.1). During this 65-year period the RSFSR's share of the total population declined from 56.5 percent to 52.5 percent, while the percentage shares of the Georgian,

TABLE 11.1

Population of the USSR, RSFSR, and Transcaucasia: 1913-78
(thousands)

| Year | USSR | RSFSR | Georgian SSR | Azerbaidzhan SSR | Armenian SSR | Trans-caucasia |
|------|------|-------|--------------|------------------|--------------|----------------|
| 1913 | 159,153 | 89,902 | 2,601 | 2,339 | 1,000 | 5,940 |
| 1940 | 194,077 | 110,098 | 3,612 | 3,274 | 1,320 | 8,206 |
| 1960 | 212,564 | 118,971 | 4,110 | 3,832 | 1,834 | 9,776 |
| 1970 | 241,720 | 130,079 | 4,686 | 5,117 | 2,492 | 12,295 |
| 1978 | 260,020 | 136,532 | 5,041 | 5,866 | 2,950 | 13,857 |

Population as Percentage of the USSR

| | | | | | | |
|------|------|-------|--------------|------------------|--------------|----------------|
| 1913 | 100 | 56.48 | 1.63 | 1.47 | .62 | 3.73 |
| 1940 | 100 | 56.72 | 1.86 | 1.67 | .68 | 4.22 |
| 1960 | 100 | 55.96 | 1.93 | 1.80 | .86 | 4.60 |
| 1970 | 100 | 53.81 | 1.94 | 2.12 | 1.03 | 5.09 |
| 1978 | 100 | 52.51 | 1.94 | 2.26 | 1.13 | 5.33 |

Urban-Rural Population Ratios

| | | | | | | |
|------|------|-------|--------------|------------------|--------------|----------------|
| 1913 | 18:82 | 17:83 | 26:74 | 24:76 | 10:90 | 22:78 |
| 1940 | 33:67 | 34:66 | 31:69 | 37:63 | 28:72 | 33:67 |
| 1960 | 48:52 | 52:48 | 42:58 | 48:52 | 50:50 | 46:54 |
| 1970 | 56:44 | 62:38 | 48:52 | 50:50 | 59:41 | 51:49 |
| 1978 | 62:38 | 70:30 | 51:49 | 52:48 | 65:35 | 54:46 |

Relationship of Population to Territory in 1978

| | | | | | | |
|------|------|-------|--------------|------------------|--------------|----------------|
| 1,000 sq. km. | 22,402 | 17,075 | 69.7 | 86.8 | 29.8 | 186.3 |
| Pop. per sq. km. | 11.6 | 8.0 | 72.3 | 67.8 | 99.0 | 74.4 |
| % of USSR | 100 | 76.22 | 0.31 | 0.39 | 0.13 | 0.83 |

Source: TsSU, Narodnoe khoziaistvo SSR v 1977 g. (Moscow, 1978), pp. 42-43, 49, 54 (publication hereafter cited as Narkhoz).

Azerbaidzhan, and Armenian republics showed substantial increases: from 1.6 to 1.9, from 1.47 to 2.3, and from 0.62 to 1.3, respectively. For Transcaucasus as a whole, the share rose from 3.7 to 5.3 percent. The density of population in Transcaucasia is about 6.5 times higher than the density in the country as a whole. The region's urban-rural population ratios have changed significantly. In 1913, Georgia and Azerbaidzhan, with urban-rural ratios of 26:74 and 14:76, were ahead of Russia with its ratio of 18:82, while Armenia was much more rural with a ratio of 10:90. By 1978 the ratios had drastically changed in favor of the USSR as a whole and the RSFSR. Their urban-rural ratios were 62:38 and 70:30, while those of the Georgian, Azerbaidzhan, and Armenian republics were 51:49, 52:48, and 65:35, respectively.


INDUSTRY

Transcaucasia lacks many of the natural resources required for the development of modern industry. Yet, despite this relatively poor resource endowment, its republics have shown rapid industrial development. This outcome was partially due to the policies of the Soviet government, which stressed high rates of capital formation and placed high priority on industrialization. Before 1950 industrial production in Georgia and Armenia was growing faster than in the USSR as a whole, and agricultural production in all Transcaucasian republics grew much faster than the national average. By 1950 about a third of total investment was allocated to industry in Georgia and Armenia, and more than half in Azerbaidzhan. At that time Transcaucasia was still relatively underdeveloped, with more than half of its labor force engaged in agricultural production. Only since the mid-1950s have serious attempts been made to develop industries of national importance in the Transcaucasus.

Despite scarcities of raw materials and high transportation costs, Georgia and Azerbaidzhan have developed small steel industries. After World War II an iron and steel plant was built at Rustavi, Georgia. The Tkibuli and Tkvarcheli coal fields provide it with low-grade coal, and iron ore is supplied by the Dashkesan mines in Azerbaidzhan. Part of the steel output is used to manufacture oil pipelines for the ports of Tuapse and Batumi on the Black Sea. For more than a century Azerbaidzhan was known for its oil industry. Relatively slow industrial growth in Azerbaidzhan is partially compensated for by a sharp rise in the production of natural gas. Azerbaidzhan has developed substantial petrochemical and machine-building industries around these fuels. The Armenian machine-building industry, which produces motors, machine tools, electric equipment, and other machinery, represents a larger share of industrial output in Armenia than in the two other republics.

During the postwar period the region has seen the progressive promotion of new industries made feasible by modern technology. This technological advance is manifested by the spread of gas and oil pipelines and electrical transmission lines, and the emergence of efficient small-scale plants: local steel plants, food-processing factories, nonferrous metal concentrators, and other manufacturing plants. As a result, both the union and the republics of Transcaucasia benefit from much more diversified economies and a much higher standard of living.[9]

The postwar period also witnessed a significant structural change in Transcaucasian industry: a shift from predominant production of consumer goods to a diversified product mix including capacities for machinery production. Between 1950 and 1975 the shares of light and food industries in total industrial output for Georgia and Armenia dropped from 68.2 and 61.0 to 59.8 and 42.0 percent, while the shares of machinery and metalworking industries rose from 8.9 and 5.9 to 12.7 and 27.8 percent, respectively. In comparison, in 1975, for the USSR as a whole, the respective percentages were 33.9 and 27.8. In terms of employment, in 1975, Transcaucasian light industry employed 25 percent of the industrial labor force, compared with 15 percent for the whole country. About 24 percent of the industrial labor force in Georgia and Azerbaidzhan was employed in the machine-building industry. For Armenia it was 40 percent (or about the same as for the USSR as a whole).[10]

A summary of growth rates of total industrial output in selected years between 1913 and 1977 is shown in Table 11.2. Using 1913 as a base (1913 = 1), Armenia's industrial output, with an index of 312 in 1977, grew more than twice as fast as the industrial outputs of the USSR and the RSFSR, with indexes of 145 and 144, respectively, while Georgia and Azerbaidzhan lagged behind with indexes of 134 and 57. Considering the period 1940-77, Armenia in 1977 made a good showing with an index of 36, while Georgia and Azerbaidzhan performed less well with 13 and 9.6, compared with 19 for the USSR and 17 for the RSFSR. Since 1970 rates of growth of industrial production have been fairly close. Azerbaidzhan and Armenia, with indexes of 174 and 169, were ahead of the USSR (with 159) and the RSFSR (with 156), while Georgia with 157 held an intermediate position.

Although these official statistics show an impressive growth of industrial output, they do not give a complete picture of relative interregional performance. Republics starting with a very low base can show spectacular increases. Alec Nove and J. A. Newth remind

# TABLE 11.2

Growth Rates of Total Industrial Output:
USSR, RSFSR, Transcaucasia, 1913–77

| Year | USSR | RSFSR | Georgian SSR | Azerbaidzhan SSR | Armenian SSR |
|------|------|-------|--------------|------------------|--------------|
| | | | (1913 = 1) | | |
| 1913 | 1 | 1 | 1 | 1 | 1 |
| 1940 | 7.7 | 8.7 | 10 | 5.9 | 8.7 |
| 1965 | 61 | 62 | 56 | 24 | 107 |
| 1970 | 92 | 92 | 85 | 33 | 184 |
| 1975 | 131 | 131 | 118 | 49 | 266 |
| 1977 | 145 | 144 | 134 | 57 | 312 |
| | | | (1940 = 1) | | |
| 1940 | 1 | 1 | 1 | 1 | 1 |
| 1965 | 7.9 | 7.2 | 5.5 | 4 | 12 |
| 1970 | 12 | 11 | 8.4 | 5.5 | 21 |
| 1975 | 17 | 15 | 12 | 8.3 | 31 |
| 1977 | 19 | 17 | 13 | 9.6 | 36 |
| | | | (1970 = 100) | | |
| 1970 | 100 | 100 | 100 | 100 | 100 |
| 1975 | 143 | 142 | 139 | 150 | 144 |
| 1977 | 159 | 156 | 157 | 174 | 169 |
| Growth Rate of Labor Productivity in Industry | | | | | |
| | | | (1940 = 100) | | |
| 1940 | 100 | 100 | 100 | 100 | 100 |
| 1965 | 372 | 399 | 239 | 242 | 315 |
| 1970 | 492 | 535 | 316 | 307 | 412 |
| 1975 | 657 | 719 | 416 | 412 | 523 |
| 1977 | 706 | 773 | 452 | 451 | 568 |
| As Percentage of the RSFSR | | | | | |
| 1940–65 | | 100 | 59.9 | 60.7 | 78.9 |
| 1965–70 | | 100 | 59.1 | 57.4 | 77.9 |
| 1970–75 | | 100 | 57.9 | 57.3 | 72.7 |
| 1975–77 | | 100 | 58.4 | 58.3 | 73.5 |

Source: Narkhoz 78, pp. 122, 128.

us of this phenomenon in their statement that "Even the opening of a medium-sized textile mill in the thirties had the effect of multiplying severalfold the very modest output of the Central Asian republics, Armenia and Georgia."[11]

With respect to productivity, output per worker in industry in the Transcaucasian republics advanced considerably less rapidly than in the USSR and the RSFSR between 1940 and 1977. In the lower part of Table 11.2, the growth rates of industrial labor productivity are shown in index form with 1940 as a base. By 1977 the growth of industrial output per worker, compared with the rate for the RSFSR, was 58.4 percent in Georgia, 58.3 percent in Azerbaidzhan, and 73.5 percent in Armenia. However, the gap has been greatly reduced. Since 1970, relative to the RSFSR, the growth of industrial labor productivity has been 99.3, 102.1, and 95.8 percent for the Georgian, Azerbaidzhan, and Armenian republics, respectively.

Output of electricity is an important indicator of economic development. In 1913, Azerbaidzhan used four times more kilowatt-hours per capita than the USSR as a whole, while Georgia and Armenia consumed only about half as much as the USSR (see Table 11.3). After substantial electrification efforts, by 1940, Azerbaidzhan used twice as much electricity per person as the USSR, Armenia about 20 percent more, and Georgia about 85 percent more. Since then per capita use of electricity in the Transcaucasian republics, relative to the USSR, has declined considerably. In 1977, in comparison with the USSR, the indexes per capita for Georgia, Azerbaidzhan, and Armenia were 53.8, 61.2, and 84.5 percent, respectively. When compared with the RSFSR, the ratios are even lower: 46.0 percent for Georgia, 52.3 for Azerbaidzhan, and 72.1 for Armenia.

Vsevolod Holubnychy compared per capita use of electricity in all Soviet republics in 1913, 1940, and 1965, and concluded that "vast differences exist in the levels of electrification and in the general consumption of energy between the RSFSR and the other Soviet republics," and that "the gap between the electrification of Russia and the non-Russian republics, taken together, increased rather than decreased."[12] According to his findings, in 1913, Azerbaidzhan used slightly more than three times more kilowatt-hours per capita than the RSFSR; in 1940, only twice as much, and in 1965 about 86 percent of the Russian Republic. In the same years the corresponding percentages for Georgia were 51.7, 74.6, and 50.7; for Armenia they were 34.7, 107.0, and 50.0. The most rapid decline in per capita use of electric energy was observed in Azerbaidzhan, primarily as a result of the decline in the republic's oil industry.

A similar trend can be discerned in data on capital investment related to growth and total output. Holubnychy's study indicates that

TABLE 11.3

Output of Electricity: USSR, RSFSR, Transcaucasia, 1913–77
(kwh per capita)

| Year | USSR | RSFSR | Georgian SSR | Azerbaidzhan SSR | Armenian SSR | Transcaucasus |
|------|------|-------|--------------|------------------|--------------|---------------|
| 1913 | 12.5 | 14.7 | 7.6 | 48.2 | 5.1 | 23.2 |
| 1940 | 250 | 284 | 212 | 571 | 304 | 353 |
| 1965 | 2,207 | 2,639 | 1,338 | 2,265 | 1,320 | 1,734 |
| 1970 | 3,066 | 3,613 | 2,134 | 2,345 | 2,448 | 2,204 |
| 1977 | 4,459 | 5,222 | 2,400 | 2,731 | 3,766 | 2,829 |
| | | | As Percentage of the USSR | | | |
| 1913 | 100 | 117.6 | 60.8 | 385.6 | 40.8 | 185.6 |
| 1940 | 100 | 113.6 | 84.8 | 228.4 | 121.6 | 141.2 |
| 1965 | 100 | 119.6 | 60.6 | 102.6 | 59.8 | 78.6 |
| 1970 | 100 | 117.8 | 69.6 | 76.5 | 79.8 | 71.9 |
| 1977 | 100 | 117.1 | 53.8 | 61.2 | 84.5 | 63.4 |
| | | | As Percentage of the RSFSR | | | |
| 1913 | 85.0 | 100 | 51.7 | 327.5 | 34.7 | 157.8 |
| 1940 | 88.0 | 100 | 74.6 | 201.0 | 107.0 | 124.3 |
| 1965 | 83.6 | 100 | 50.7 | 85.8 | 50.0 | 65.7 |
| 1970 | 84.9 | 100 | 59.1 | 64.9 | 67.8 | 61.0 |
| 1977 | 85.4 | 100 | 46.0 | 52.3 | 72.1 | 54.2 |

Source: Narkhoz 78, pp. 10–11, 142.

during 1918-60, per capita investment in both industry and all state
and cooperative enterprises was, in general, higher in the RSFSR
than in other republics. In his words, "The RSFSR has enjoyed
clear priority in the allocation of investment per capita: it has received considerably more per capita from the USSR treasury than
other republics, and this inequality increased over time."[13] These
findings apply to the Transcaucasian republics, except Azerbaidzhan
(because of its important oil industry). This general trend is confirmed in I. S. Koropeckyj's comparison of per capita industrial investment by republics, during 1951-58, with per capita industrial
investment in the USSR as a base: 65.5 percent for Georgia, 142.3
for Azerbaidzhan, and 72.7 for Armenia. Comparable indexes for
1959-65 are 58.2, 98.3, and 90.4 percent. For the RSFSR these
indexes are even lower (54.4 and 50.8 for Georgia, 118.2 and 87.9
for Azerbaidzhan, and 60.4 and 78.0 for Armenia).[14]

The trend in total per capita investment in the USSR, the
RSFSR, and the Transcaucasus between 1940 and 1977 is shown in
Table 11.4. In 1940, with the USSR as a base, Georgia, Azerbaidzhan, and Armenia scored 112.1, 154.5, and 115.2 percent.
With the RSFSR as a base, the indexes were 94.8, 130.8, and 97.4
percent. By 1977 these indexes had declined to 65.4, 59.9, and
73.2 percent in terms of the USSR and to 55.9, 51.2, and 62.5 percent in terms of the RSFSR. The comparison of total capital investment between 1928-32 and 1956-60 made by Holubnychy reveals a
similar but weaker trend before 1960. His findings show a decline
in the share of two Transcaucasian republics in percent of total capital investment for the USSR—from 1.8 to 1.1 percent for Georgia
and from 2.1 to 1.6 percent for Azerbaidzhan—and no change in the
relative share of Armenia (about 0.6 percent for both periods).[15]

The trends in levels of per capita industrial production in the
Transcaucasian republics relative to both the USSR and the RSFSR
from 1940 to 1977 reveal, in general, a steady decline until 1975 and
some stabilization between 1975 and 1977 at a comparatively low
level of performance. In 1940 the republics of Georgia, Azerbaidzhan,
and Armenia had per capita industrial outputs equal to 85.0, 107.2,
and 57.5 percent, respectively, of the value of per capita industrial
output of the RSFSR. Percentages relative to the USSR were 89.4,
112.5, and 60.2. By 1975 these indexes were 57.4, 40.6, and 67.6
percent relative to the RSFSR and 65.9, 46.6, and 77.7 percent relative to the USSR. The greatest decline was recorded in Azerbaidzhan,
while Armenia showed some improvement in relative position.

Yet, by 1958 all the Transcaucasian republics had a lower per
capita industrial product than the average for the country and the
Russian Republic. Koropeckyj's indexes for 1940, 1958, and 1965,
expressed in terms of the USSR, have been incorporated into Table

TABLE 11.4

Per Capita Capital Investment: USSR, RSFSR, Transcaucasia, 1940–77
(rubles)

| Year | USSR | RSFSR | Georgian SSR | Azerbaidzhan SSR | Armenian SSR | Transcaucasus |
|---|---|---|---|---|---|---|
| 1940 | 33 | 39 | 37 | 51 | 38 | 43 |
| 1965 | 244 | 262 | 171 | 183 | 239 | 189 |
| 1970 | 334 | 368 | 235 | 231 | 327 | 252 |
| 1975 | 445 | 518 | 264 | 280 | 344 | 288 |
| 1977 | 474 | 555 | 310 | 284 | 347 | 307 |
| | | | As Percentage of the USSR | | | |
| 1940 | 100 | 118.2 | 112.1 | 154.5 | 115.2 | 130.3 |
| 1965 | 100 | 107.4 | 70.1 | 75.0 | 98.0 | 77.5 |
| 1970 | 100 | 110.2 | 70.4 | 69.2 | 97.9 | 75.4 |
| 1975 | 100 | 116.4 | 59.3 | 62.9 | 77.3 | 64.7 |
| 1977 | 100 | 117.1 | 65.4 | 59.9 | 73.2 | 64.8 |
| | | | As Percentage of the RSFSR | | | |
| 1940 | 84.6 | 100 | 94.8 | 130.8 | 97.4 | 110.3 |
| 1965 | 93.1 | 100 | 65.3 | 69.8 | 91.2 | 72.1 |
| 1970 | 90.8 | 100 | 63.9 | 62.8 | 88.9 | 68.5 |
| 1975 | 85.9 | 100 | 51.0 | 54.1 | 66.4 | 55.6 |
| 1977 | 85.4 | 100 | 55.9 | 51.2 | 62.5 | 55.3 |

## Per Capita Industrial Output
### (rubles)

| | | | | | | |
|---|---|---|---|---|---|---|
| 1940 | 167 | 159 | 142 | 179 | 96 | 149 |
| 1965 | 1,205 | 1,067 | 722 | 588 | 833 | 690 |
| 1970 | 1,734 | 1,529 | 1,038 | 711 | 1,257 | 946 |
| 1975 | 2,395 | 2,086 | 1,374 | 973 | 1,620 | 1,257 |
| 1977 | 2,596 | 2,270 | 1,528 | 1,094 | 1,829 | 1,408 |
| **As Percentage of the USSR** | | | | | | |
| 1940 | 105.6 | 100 | 89.4 | 112.5 | 60.2 | 93.7 |
| 1965 | 112.9 | 100 | 67.7 | 55.1 | 78.1 | 64.7 |
| 1970 | 113.4 | 100 | 67.9 | 46.5 | 82.2 | 61.9 |
| 1975 | 114.8 | 100 | 65.9 | 46.6 | 77.7 | 60.2 |
| 1977 | 114.4 | 100 | 67.3 | 48.2 | 80.6 | 62.0 |
| **As Percentage of the RSFSR** | | | | | | |
| 1940 | 100 | 95.2 | 85.0 | 107.2 | 57.5 | 89.2 |
| 1965 | 100 | 88.5 | 59.9 | 48.8 | 69.1 | 57.3 |
| 1970 | 100 | 88.2 | 59.9 | 41.0 | 72.5 | 54.6 |
| 1975 | 100 | 87.1 | 57.4 | 40.6 | 67.6 | 52.5 |
| 1977 | 100 | 87.4 | 58.9 | 42.1 | 70.5 | 54.2 |

Sources: Narkhoz 77, p. 359; Narkhoz 78, pp. 10-11, 122; I. S. Koropeckyj, "Industrial Location Policy in the USSR During the Postwar Period," in U.S. Congress, Joint Economic Committee, Economic Performance and Military Burden in the Soviet Union (Washington, D.C.: U.S. Government Printing Office, 1970), p. 286.

11.4.[16] In a comparable study Holubnychy arrived at considerably
lower indexes for the Transcaucasian republics as percentages of
the RSFSR. His indexes for Georgia, Azerbaidzhan, and Armenia
were 37, 80, and 48 for 1940; 32, 42, and 46 for 1958; and 29, 31,
and 53 for 1965.[17]

AGRICULTURE

Transcaucasia, with its subtropical climate, long growing
season, high rainfall in its western part, and extensive irrigation
in the drier east, produces a great variety of agricultural products.
It is a leading producer of tropical fruits in the USSR. It grows almost all of the tea, about 16 percent of all fruits and berries (including 25 percent of all grapes), about 5.7 percent of all cotton, and 4
percent of all wool. It also grows excellent tobacco, potatoes, and
a variety of vegetables. Grain is grown on half of the sown acreage
in Georgia and Azerbaidzhan, and on 40 percent in Armenia. The
region must import a considerable quantity of grain. The eastern
part of the region is very dry, and requires extensive irrigation.
Over half of the lands in Armenia and 70 percent in Azerbaidzhan
are irrigated. In the Colchis lowland of western Georgia, a considerable amount of land has been reclaimed and many marshes have
been drained.

A comparatively large part of agricultural output in Transcaucasia is produced by the private sector. In 1975, in Georgia, 51
percent of the vegetables, 64 percent of the fruits and berries, 64
percent of the meat, 46 percent of the wool, 54 percent of the milk,
and 43 percent of the eggs were privately produced. In total, about
46 percent of the gross value of agricultural output in Georgia was
in this category. In terms of labor, 40 percent of agricultural employment in Georgia was in the private sector. In Armenia and
Azerbaidzhan the private-sector share exceeded the national average for eggs, milk, and wool. In terms of livestock herds, the private share was over 50 percent in Georgia, about 40 percent in
Azerbaidzhan, and 33 percent in Armenia, compared with about 20
percent in the Soviet Union as a whole. Moreover, in Georgia in
1976, 14 percent of retail sales of food were at collective farm markets, contrasted with about 4.5 percent for the Soviet Union.[18]

Agricultural production in the Transcaucasian republics has
grown more rapidly than in the USSR and the RSFSR. During the
period 1913-77 total agricultural production in Georgia rose three
times as fast, and in Azerbaidzhan and Armenia more than twice as
fast, as in the RSFSR. On a per capita basis, however, only Georgia
exceeded the national average. Data relating to average agricultural

outputs for 1966-70, 1971-75, and 1976-77 are presented in Table
11.5. For these recent periods the growth in Transcaucasia is considerably higher than in the USSR and the RSFSR. Between 1966-70
and 1976-77, average annual agricultural production in the USSR,
RSFSR, Georgia, Azerbaidzhan, and Armenia increased by 21.3,
13.0, 46.4, 73.3, and 44.8 percent, respectively. Yet the Transcaucasian republics contributed proportionately less than their population share, as did the RSFSR. In 1977 the RSFSR, Georgia, Azerbaidzhan, and Armenia contributed 46.7, 1.6, 1.5, and 0.6 percent
of the country's agricultural output, while their populations represented 52.5, 1.9, 2.6, and 1.1 percent of the total. On a per capita
basis in 1977, agricultural output was 88.9 percent of the national
average in the RSFSR, 92.7 percent in Georgia, 74.6 percent in
Azerbaidzhan, and 59.7 percent in Armenia.

However, as Nove and Newth have pointed out, one should not
underestimate the contribution of Transcaucasia to the Soviet economy. A considerable part of the region is mountainous, with little
precipitation. Yet where cultivation is possible, crops are grown
that could not be produced in other parts of the Soviet Union: tea,
tobacco, citrus fruits, and grapes. The USSR greatly relies on
these agricultural crops because they reduce imports.[19]

ECONOMIC GROWTH AND STRUCTURAL CHANGE

According to official statistics, between 1950 and 1978 gross
industrial output grew at average annual rates of 8.2, 9.9, and 7.4
percent in Georgia, Armenia, and Azerbaidzhan, respectively. At
these rates per capita industrial output in Georgia and Armenia rose
more than sixfold, and in Azerbaidzhan it more than tripled. During
the same period agricultural production in all Transcaucasian republics expanded more than threefold. On a per capita basis all three
republics fell short of the national average in industrial production,
and in agriculture only Georgia exceeded it.

During 1960-78, Georgia and Armenia exceeded the national
average in terms of the growth of per capita national income, while
Azerbaidzhan lagged behind. On a per capita basis, national income
per capita grew at 5.5 percent in Georgia and Armenia, and at about
3 percent in Azerbaidzhan, compared with 6.3 percent for the USSR.
Despite these relatively high rates of growth of industrial and agricultural production and national income, the Transcaucasian republics are lagging behind the national average in levels of economic
development. In 1975 the level of national income per capita in
Georgia was about 75 percent of the national average; in Armenia,
83 percent; and in Azerbaidzhan, about 66 percent. Although all

TABLE 11.5

Indexes of Agricultural Production and Gross Agricultural Output:
USSR, RSFSR, Transcaucasia, 1913–77 and 1966–77

| Year | USSR | RSFSR | Georgian SSR | Azerbaidzhan SSR | Armenian SSR |
|---|---|---|---|---|---|
| 1913 | 100 | 100 | 100 | 100 | 100 |
| 1940 | 141 | 126 | 252 | 156 | 156 |
| 1965 | 252 | 235 | 551 | 317 | 428 |
| 1970 | 309 | 293 | 709 | 402 | 541 |
| 1975 | 317 | 288 | 829 | 540 | 636 |
| 1977 | 347 | 308 | 951 | 626 | 713 |
| | | | As Percentage of the RSFSR | | |
| 1913–40 | | 100 | 200 | 123.8 | 123.8 |
| 1940–65 | | 100 | 234.5 | 134.9 | 182.1 |
| 1965–70 | | 100 | 241.9 | 137.2 | 184.6 |
| 1970–75 | | 100 | 287.8 | 187.5 | 220.8 |
| 1975–77 | | 100 | 308.8 | 203.2 | 231.5 |

400

Gross Agricultural Output
(in comparable 1973 prices, million rubles)

| Ann. Avg./Yr. | USSR | RSFSR | Georgian SSR | Azerbaidzhan SSR | Armenian SSR | Transcaucasus |
|---|---|---|---|---|---|---|
| 1966–70 | 100,394 | 49,986 | 1,252 | 1,040 | 516 | 2,808 |
| 1971–75 | 113,736 | 54,448 | 1,488 | 1,389 | 627 | 3,504 |
| 1976–77 | 121,808 | 56,500 | 1,833 | 1,802 | 747 | 4,382 |
| 1976 | 120,081 | 55,293 | 1,715 | 1,782 | 728 | 4,225 |
| 1977 | 123,535 | 57,708 | 1,950 | 1,822 | 766 | 4,538 |
| **As Percentage of the USSR** | | | | | | |
| 1966–70 | 100 | 49.8 | 1.2 | 1.0 | 0.5 | 2.8 |
| 1971–75 | 100 | 47.9 | 1.3 | 1.3 | 0.6 | 3.1 |
| 1976–77 | 100 | 46.4 | 1.5 | 1.5 | 0.6 | 3.6 |
| 1976 | 100 | 46.0 | 1.4 | 1.5 | 0.6 | 3.5 |
| 1977 | 100 | 46.7 | 1.6 | 1.5 | 0.6 | 3.7 |
| **As Percentage of the RSFSR** | | | | | | |
| 1966–70 | 200.8 | 100 | 2.5 | 2.1 | 1.0 | 5.6 |
| 1971–75 | 208.9 | 100 | 2.7 | 2.6 | 1.2 | 6.5 |
| 1976–77 | 215.6 | 100 | 3.2 | 3.2 | 1.3 | 7.7 |
| 1976 | 217.2 | 100 | 3.1 | 3.2 | 1.3 | 7.6 |
| 1977 | 214.1 | 100 | 3.4 | 3.2 | 1.3 | 7.9 |

Sources: Narkhoz 77, p. 205; Narkhoz 78, p. 198.

three republics improved their relative position in the 1970s in respect to agricultural production and national income, and Georgia and Azerbaidzhan did so in terms of industrial production, the relative position of the region as a whole deteriorated.

As economic development in the Transcaucasus has progressed, composition of the labor force and national output has changed. In 1950 slightly over 50 percent of the labor force was employed in agricultural activities. Since then it has experienced a considerable decline in the share of the labor force engaged in these activities. By 1975, in Georgia and Azerbaidzhan, about 40 percent of labor was still occupied in agriculture; in Armenia the figure was only 30 percent. The nonagricultural production sector expanded in all three republics, with most rapid increases in Armenia. Moreover, the services sector in Transcaucasus was expanding faster than the national average. In 1975 the region had a larger share of the labor force in services than did the Soviet Union as a whole.

Structural changes in output were most rapid in Armenia. Between 1960 and 1975 the agricultural sector declined from 12.7 to 9 percent, the manufacturing sector rose from 75.7 to 77.6 percent, and the service sector showed an increase from 11.6 to 13.4 percent. During the same period, in Georgia, the shares of output changed from 31.7 to 28.6, from 51.7 to 51.8, and from 18.6 to 19.6 in the primary, secondary, and tertiary sectors, respectively. The slowest changes occurred in Azerbaidzhan, where during 1965-75 the agricultural sector retained its share of about 25 percent of the national income, the manufacturing share dropped from 59 to 57 percent, and the services sector slightly increased its share. By this measure Georgia and Azerbaidzhan were less industrialized than the USSR as a whole, and Armenia was relatively more so. In general the pace of structural change in Transcaucasus was slower in the postwar period than in other countries at a comparable level of economic development.

Since per capita output in both industry and agriculture in Transcaucasia is lower than in the USSR and the RSFSR, their relative per capita national incomes naturally reflect these differences. Per capita national income data are given in Table 11.6. Relative to the RSFSR, per capita national income indexes for Georgia, Azerbaidzhan, and Armenia were 67.6, 70.1, and 84.5 percent in 1960. In 1977 they were 64.4, 48.2, and 84.2 percent, respectively, representing a slight decline for Georgia, a considerable decline for Azerbaidzhan, and a very slight decline for Armenia. Since the Russian Republic improved its per capita income position during 1960-77 relative to the USSR as a whole, the indexes of the Transcaucasian republics, in terms of the USSR, are more favorable: 80.2 for Georgia, 60.4 for Azerbaidzhan, and 104.8 percent for Armenia in 1977.

The data in Table 11.6 show that considerable differences in per capita income exist between the RSFSR and the Transcaucasian republics, and that these differences have been increasing in Georgia and Azerbaidzhan while remaining more or less stable in Armenia. Indexes of national income computed by other writers for the period 1958-65 agree with these findings.[20] Some of the indexes of Gertrude Schroeder's study were used in the computation given in Table 11.6.[21] The indexes for per capita national income in 1965 computed by Koropeckyj,[22] with the RSFSR as a base, and for 1970 by Alexander Woroniak, who used the USSR as a base,[23] are not much different from indexes in this table.

A comparison of indexes of per capita industrial production and per capita national income reveal that the former are lower than the latter. Koropeckyj has found a high degree of correlation between these two sets of variables and a decline in both indexes for the Transcaucasus between 1961 and 1965. The present findings are in agreement with Koropeckyj's generalization that "since the level of national income determined the level of consumption, an inference is justified that the welfare of population has been becoming more unequal among republics in recent years."[24] Among the Transcaucasian republics, only Armenia kept its relative (and inferior) position to the RSFSR in terms of per capita industrial production and per capita national income. Azerbaidzhan suffered a much greater decline than Georgia, mainly because of its high rate of population growth.

Since wages are the largest element in national income, comparison of levels of wages is also of interest. Data are available for average monthly wages of the state labor force (omitting collective farmers and private incomes). Between 1960 and 1978, in terms of the RSFSR, Georgia showed a decline from 90.1 to 79.8 percent, and Azerbaidzhan a decline from 90.5 to 82.1 percent. Armenia recorded a slight increase from 90.7 to 91.1 percent. Yet all the Transcaucasian republics had lower average monthly wages than the Russian Republic. As percentages of the USSR, the indexes for 1978 were 83.8, 86.3, and 95.6 for Georgia, Azerbaidzhan, and Armenia, respectively. (See Chapter 4 in this volume.) In the view of one investigator, "wage differences among the republics were surprisingly narrow" and "are largely the result of centralized fixing of wages and salaries throughout the state sector." These differences can be partially explained by the relative importance of various branches within the republics and by the "deliberate regional differentiation of wages by means of coefficients designed to allow for differences in climatic conditions and the cost of living."[25]

Holubnychy has found that between 1940 and 1965, average wages in the Russian Republic were higher than in all other republics combined. However, the difference in percentage of the RSFSR

TABLE 11.6

Per Capita National Income and Its Ratio to Per Capita Industrial
Gross Output: USSR, RSFSR, Transcaucasia, 1960–77

| Year | USSR | RSFSR | Georgian SSR | Azerbaidzhan SSR | Armenian SSR | Transcaucasia |
|---|---|---|---|---|---|---|
| | | | In Rubles | | | |
| 1960 | 679 | 762 | 515 | 534 | 644 | 547 |
| 1965 | 842 | 969 | 659 | 571 | 804 | 652 |
| 1970 | 1,199 | 1,378 | 885 | 667 | 1,125 | 843 |
| 1975 | 1,435 | 1,787 | 1,104 | 847 | 1,470 | 1,072 |
| 1977 | 1,562 | 1,944 | 1,252 | 944 | 1,637 | 1,203 |
| | | | As Percentage of the USSR | | | |
| 1960 | 100 | 112.2 | 75.8 | 78.6 | 94.8 | 80.6 |
| 1965 | 100 | 115.1 | 78.3 | 67.8 | 95.5 | 77.4 |
| 1970 | 100 | 114.9 | 73.8 | 55.6 | 93.8 | 70.3 |
| 1975 | 100 | 124.5 | 76.9 | 59.0 | 102.4 | 74.7 |
| 1977 | 100 | 124.5 | 80.2 | 60.4 | 104.8 | 77.0 |
| | | | As Percentage of the RSFSR | | | |
| 1960 | 89.1 | 100 | 67.6 | 70.1 | 84.5 | 71.8 |
| 1965 | 87.1 | 100 | 68.0 | 58.9 | 82.9 | 67.3 |
| 1970 | 87.0 | 100 | 64.2 | 48.4 | 81.6 | 62.2 |
| 1975 | 80.3 | 100 | 61.8 | 47.4 | 82.3 | 60.0 |
| 1977 | 80.3 | 100 | 64.4 | 48.6 | 84.2 | 61.9 |

Ratios of Per Capita Industrial Gross Output and Per Capita National Income

### As Percentage of the USSR

| | | | | | |
|---|---|---|---|---|---|
| 1960 | 100:100 | 113.1:112.2 | 72.4:75.8 | 64.3:78.6 | 81.2:94.8 | 70.8:80.6 |
| 1965 | 100:100 | 112.9:115.1 | 67.7:78.3 | 55.1:67.8 | 78.1:95.5 | 64.7:77.4 |
| 1970 | 100:100 | 113.4:114.9 | 67.9:73.8 | 46.5:55.6 | 82.2:93.8 | 61.9:70.3 |
| 1975 | 100:100 | 114.8:124.5 | 65.9:76.9 | 46.6:59.0 | 77.7:102.4 | 60.2:74.7 |
| 1977 | 100:100 | 114.4:124.5 | 67.3:80.2 | 48.2:60.4 | 80.6:104.8 | 62.0:77.0 |

### As Percentage of the RSFSR

| | | | | | |
|---|---|---|---|---|---|
| 1960 | 100:100 | 84.4:89.1 | 64.0:67.6 | 56.8:70.1 | 71.8:84.5 | 62.6:71.8 |
| 1965 | 100:100 | 88.5:87.1 | 59.9:68.0 | 48.8:58.9 | 69.1:82.9 | 57.3:67.3 |
| 1970 | 100:100 | 88.2:87.0 | 59.9:64.2 | 41.0:48.4 | 72.5:81.6 | 54.6:62.2 |
| 1975 | 100:100 | 87.1:80.3 | 57.4:61.8 | 40.6:47.4 | 67.6:82.3 | 52.5:60.0 |
| 1977 | 100:100 | 87.4:80.3 | 58.9:64.4 | 42.1:48.6 | 70.5:84.2 | 54.2:61.9 |

Sources: Narkhoz 70, p. 534; Narkhoz 78, p. 386; Gertrude E. Schroeder, "Regional Differences in Incomes and Levels of Living in the USSR," in V. N. Bandera and Z. L. Melnyk, The Soviet Economy in Regional Perspective (New York: Praeger, 1973), p. 169. Ratios from Table 11.2 and upper panel of this table.

declined: in 1940 the average for all non-Russian republics was 82.6, while in 1965 it was 93.6 percent.[26] Data for 1960-78 show that only Armenia experienced a slight narrowing of differentials, while the difference between the RSFSR and the other two Trans-caucasian republics continued to increase. In sum, the differences between the Transcaucasian republics and the RSFSR are largest in per capita industrial output, somewhat smaller in per capita national income, and smallest in average monthly wages of workers and employees.

LIVING STANDARDS

In respect to average annual wages of the state labor force, in 1978 Transcaucasia ranked below the national average and its position has been deteriorating since then. The relative positions of Georgia, Azerbaidzhan, and Armenia declined from ninth, eighth, and seventh in 1960 to fourteenth, thirteenth, and tenth in 1978, respectively. Although average wages in Transcaucasia were at the bottom of the scale, savings per capita in 1978 were higher than the national average and higher than in the RSFSR and the Central Asian republics (see Table 4.2 in this volume). In per capita personal income (money incomes from all sources plus income in kind from private agriculture), the Transcaucasus fell below the national average, with only the Central Asian republics lagging behind in 1978 (see Table 4.1). The same is true for real per capita consumption (see Table 4.3).

Relative to the USSR, both per capita personal incomes and per capita consumption levels in the Transcaucasian republics fell somewhat between 1960 and 1978. A similar pattern applies to per capita retail sales. The region is below the national average and is above only the Central Asian republics (see Table 4.5). In terms of per capita urban housing space, the region as a whole is below the national average. Georgia, however, holds a high relative position in this area. Georgians have a high propensity to invest in private housing. In 1978, in Georgia, 41 percent of urban housing was private, in contrast with 24 percent for the USSR as a whole.[27] Between 1960 and 1978 the number of doctors per capita in the Trans-caucasus slowly increased, yet relative to the USSR and the RSFSR, its superiority was declining. In terms of hospital beds, however, the region occupied the lowest position in the nation (see Table 4.6).

On measures of educational attainments, the Transcaucasian republics show up well, especially Georgia. Ethnic Georgians are better-educated than other nationality groups living in their republic (see Table 4.7), while in Armenia and Azerbaidzhan the Russians show higher educational attainments than the native population.

In an earlier study of per capita expenditures on education by the republics covering 1940, 1946, 1950, and 1955, Nove and Newth found that in 1940, in the republics of the "Soviet Middle East" (Kazakhstan, Uzbekistan, Kirgizstan, Tadzhikistan, Turkmenistan, Georgia, Azerbaidzhan, and Armenia), per capita expenditures on education were 35 percent above the USSR average, and that by 1955 the difference had declined to 13 percent. Between 1940 and 1955, for the Transcaucasian republics, the indexes (as percentages of the USSR) show declines for Georgia from 165.2 to 128.6, for Azerbaidzhan from 147.2 to 118.3, and for Armenia from 196.6 to 150.9. In the authors' words, "the average expenditure on schooling remains 20-50 percent above the USSR's average even in 1955."[28]

Holubnychy's data for 1960 and the indicators of educational attainments in Table 4.7 show some leveling of these differences between the Transcaucasian republics and the RSFSR between 1960 and 1976. His comparisons of per capita expenditures on social and cultural measures for 1940, 1956, and 1960 show an unmistakably declining trend in indexes for the Transcaucasus (expressed in percentages of the RSFSR). For these selected years, Georgia shows 143.8, 108.7, and 94.5; Azerbaidzhan 134.9, 101.0, and 83.7; and Armenia 159.0, 123.1, and 99.2.[29] In the 1970s the indexes continued to decline at a slower rate for Georgia and Azerbaidzhan, while for Armenia they slowly increased.

To cover some selected cultural activities, Holubnychy's data for 1964 were compared with the same activities in 1977 (see Table 11.7). In 1964 the Transcaucasian republics were far behind the Russian Republic in terms of copies of newspapers read, books published, visits to movies, number of children in summer camps, students in higher education, and books in public libraries.[30] By 1977 all three republics were still behind the RSFSR, with some relative deterioration in publication of books, students in higher education (except in Azerbaidzhan), and books in public libraries, and some improvement in visits to movies, children in summer camps, and (except for Armenia) copies of newspapers read. In general, conventional indicators of standards of living in the Transcaucasian republics are far below the average for the Soviet Union as a whole. The region ranks below all other regions except Central Asia, which is at the bottom of the scale.

The republics do not collect taxes from their populations and, therefore, do not have their own funds to finance cultural activities. And since the allocation of funds for this purpose in the Soviet Union is highly centralized, it is not easy to overcome the "suspicion that some national cultures are being short-changed and gradually squeezed into oblivion while the Russian culture is being subsidized at their expenses."[31] Khrushchev himself confirmed the existence

TABLE 11.7

Selected Cultural Activities: USSR, RSFSR, Transcaucasia, 1964 and 1977
(per 1,000 population)

| Year | | USSR | RSFSR | Georgian SSR | Azerbaidzhan SSR | Armenian SSR | Transcaucasia |
|---|---|---|---|---|---|---|---|
| | | | | Copies of Newspapers Read | | | |
| 1964 | RSFSR = 100 | 82.5 | 100 | 56.0 | 40.0 | 53.0 | 49.0 |
| 1977 | RSFSR = 100 | 72.8 | 100 | 66.8 | 44.2 | 41.9 | 52.0 |
| 1964 | USSR = 100 | 100 | 121.2 | 67.9 | 48.5 | 64.2 | 59.4 |
| 1977 | USSR = 100 | 100 | 137.3 | 91.7 | 60.6 | 57.6 | 71.4 |
| | | | | Books Published | | | |
| 1964 | RSFSR = 100 | 74.0 | 100 | 38.0 | 35.0 | 46.0 | 38.4 |
| 1977 | RSFSR = 100 | 66.8 | 100 | 33.9 | 22.3 | 34.4 | 29.1 |
| 1964 | USSR = 100 | 100 | 135.1 | 51.4 | 47.3 | 62.2 | 51.9 |
| 1977 | USSR = 100 | 100 | 149.7 | 50.7 | 33.4 | 51.4 | 43.6 |
| | | | | Visits to Movies | | | |
| 1964 | RSFSR = 100 | 84.8 | 100 | 48.0 | 44.0 | 59.0 | 48.6 |
| 1977 | RSFSR = 100 | 96.6 | 100 | 59.4 | 59.4 | 37.8 | 54.8 |
| 1964 | USSR = 100 | 100 | 117.9 | 56.6 | 51.9 | 69.6 | 57.3 |
| 1977 | USSR = 100 | 100 | 103.6 | 61.5 | 61.5 | 39.2 | 56.8 |

Children in Summer Camps

| | | | | | | | |
|---|---|---|---|---|---|---|---|
| 1964 | RSFSR = 100 | 79.4 | 100 | 35.0 | 44.0 | 35.0 | 36.8 |
| 1977 | | 91.8 | 100 | 46.0 | 153.6 | 50.7 | 70.8 |
| 1964 | USSR = 100 | 100 | 125.9 | 44.1 | 55.4 | 44.1 | 46.3 |
| 1977 | | 100 | 108.9 | 50.1 | 167.2 | 55.2 | 77.1 |

Students in Higher Education

| | | | | | | | |
|---|---|---|---|---|---|---|---|
| 1964 | RSFSR = 100 | 88.8 | 100 | 95.0 | 90.0 | 74.0 | 85.6 |
| 1977 | | 89.4 | 100 | 77.5 | 89.4 | 80.3 | 81.2 |
| 1964 | USSR = 100 | 100 | 112.7 | 107.0 | 101.4 | 83.4 | 96.4 |
| 1977 | | 100 | 111.8 | 86.7 | 100.0 | 89.7 | 90.8 |

Books in Public Libraries

| | | | | | | | |
|---|---|---|---|---|---|---|---|
| 1964 | RSFSR = 100 | 95.5 | 100 | 86.0 | 89.0 | 86.0 | 86.6 |
| 1977 | | 93.3 | 100 | 83.4 | 64.0 | 70.6 | 73.8 |
| 1964 | USSR = 100 | 100 | 104.7 | 90.0 | 89.0 | 90.0 | 89.8 |
| 1977 | | 100 | 107.2 | 89.4 | 68.6 | 75.6 | 79.2 |

Sources: Narkhoz 77, pp. 494, 499, 509, 518, 524, 528, 529; Vsevolod Holubnychy, "Some Economic Aspects of Relations Among the Soviet Republics," in Erich Goldhagen, ed., Ethnic Minorities in the Soviet Union (New York: Praeger, 1968), p. 105.

of "a wholly inexplicable gap between the appropriations for some of the republics."[32]

Judging by the measures derived from official statistics, the level of living in Azerbaidzhan is about 66 percent of the national average, while in Georgia and Armenia it is 10-15 percent below the national average. However, the official data do not fully reflect economic conditions in the USSR. It is well known that the Soviet Union has a "second economy" that comprises a wide variety of semilegal and illegal economic activities: black markets, cheating, illegal production, bribery, theft, and other abuses. Since these activities were widespread in the Transcaucasian republics, the latter might have been much better off than official statistics reveal.

Gertrude Schroeder, who has made recent studies of these activities, found that there is no way to measure the impact of these activities quantitatively; other republics have similar activities, and there is no way to establish that Transcaucasia has a disproportionate share of them; and the illegal activities are primarily redistributive and do not add greatly to the supply of goods and services included in real per capita consumption. She legitimately concludes that "The regional incidence of 'second economy' activities is not such as to appreciably alter our perception of relative levels of living reflected in official data."[33]

## COMPARISONS WITH NEIGHBORING COUNTRIES

Since large numbers of Armenians live in Turkey and many Azerbaidzhanis in Iran, a comparison of standards of living in Transcaucasus and these neighboring nations is of some interest. Such a comparison is of added significance because Iran and Turkey are predominantly market economies, while the Transcaucasian republics are developing within the framework of a highly centralized socialist country with many characteristics of a "command economy."

Nove and Newth have asserted that the republics of the Soviet Middle East, if permitted to operate in a free-enterprise setting, would not have had the rapid industrialization they actually experienced within the framework of the USSR's command economy. In their view, these republics benefited "not only from being a part of a much larger whole, but also, or even particularly from the fact that the Government of the USSR had an industrializing ideology, equated progress with industry, and paid special attention to the development in formerly backward areas."[34]

Per capita national income of the USSR in 1962 was estimated by Nove and Newth at $836, and average per capita income in the Transcaucasian republics at about $600. This level is favorable in comparison with $149 for Turkey, $267 for Spain, and $292 for Greece in the same year.[35] Nove and Newth conclude that the Transcaucasian republics "have plainly benefited from the Russian connection." According to them, "The Soviet ideological commitment to . . . combating backwardness in the national republics caused a diversion of capital to those areas which, on strictly economic grounds, would have provided a higher return elsewhere."[36] Referring to Transcaucasus, Nove and Newth concluded that "no reasonable person can doubt that industrial growth would have been less rapid without Russian capital and Russian skills."[37]

According to a World Bank report, in 1977 gross national product per capita was $1,110 for Turkey and $2,160 for Iran, compared with $3,020 in the USSR.[38] Applying the relative indexes of the Transcaucasian republics' per capita national incomes in terms of the USSR, the estimates of per capita gross national product for Georgia, Azerbaidzhan, and Armenia would amount to $2,422, $1,824, and $3,164, respectively—about two or three times larger than Turkey's per capita gross national product. In comparison with Iran, Georgia's per capita gross national product is about 11 percent higher, Azerbaidzhan's 16 percent lower, and Armenia's about 46 percent higher. Moreover, per capita gross national product during 1960-78 grew at 4.3, 4.0, and 7.9 percent per annum for the USSR, Turkey, and Iran. If the assumption is made that per capita gross national product in Transcaucasia grew at the same rate as national income, then the rate of growth in Georgia, Azerbaidzhan, and Armenia can be estimated at 4.8, 2.6, and 5.1 percent, respectively. Growth in Iran was much higher than in all three republics, while Turkey's growth ranked below Georgia and Armenia but above Azerbaidzhan.

Since Nove and Newth's study, the difference in per capita income between the Transcaucasian republics and their neighbors has declined considerably, eroding the empirical basis for their argument of the advantages of development under a socialist system. In addition, between 1960 and 1978, Iran's per capita gross national product grew considerably faster than Transcaucasia's, while Turkey's grew at about the same rate. Yet some other socioeconomic indicators still show the relative backwardness of Turkey and Iran in comparison with Transcaucasia in terms of urbanization, literacy, and education. The paucity of empirical data and the complexity of theoretical analysis make this type of comparison a difficult task.

CONCLUDING REMARKS

Undoubtedly, Transcaucasia has experienced rapid economic development within the framework of the Soviet economy. Both agricultural and industrial production have increased in absolute and per capita terms. This was especially true for the period between 1960 and 1978. In terms of levels of living, measured by several available indicators, the Transcaucasian republics have enjoyed significant improvements. However, in relative terms, compared with per capita indicators for the USSR as a whole, the region's position has not improved and has even deteriorated somewhat, partially because of a more rapid growth of population. In terms of living standards, Georgia and Armenia are ahead of Azerbaidzhan. The standard of living in the Georgian and Armenian republics is comparable with that of Kazakhstan and the western republics, while Azerbaidzhan ranks with the Central Asian republics.

Findings for the postwar period indicate that interregional differences between the Transcaucasian republics and both the USSR and the RSFSR tended to increase in magnitude. This widening of differentials can be perceived as a result of a basic conflict between the ideological commitment of the Soviet leadership to interrepublic and interregional equalization of economic development and the realities of domestic and international power relationships that require both rapid overall industrial development of the nation and continual expansion of its military might. Historical evidence indicates that the long-run desideratum of interregional equalization had to yield to the overwhelming needs of bolstering the industrial and military power of the nation as a whole.

Specific development in the Transcaucasian republics can be properly understood only within this general analytical framework, as a special case of a broader and much more general problem. Since Transcaucasia did not represent an area of priority in the postwar period, from the point of view of defense, the productive resources that could have been allocated to it were used elsewhere, mostly in the RSFSR. Changing defense needs have led to shifts of emphasis in industrial development from the eastern Urals and western Siberia, before World War II, to the Ural and Volga region during the period of the cold war, and in more recent years to Kazakhstan, eastern Siberia, and the Far East in response to the looming danger from China.[39] Within this context, "The location of the Transcaucasian republics," says Koropeckyj, "does not require their economic buildup for strategic reasons. Because of mountainous terrain and because of the weakness of neighboring countries, this region has never . . . been an invasion route into Russia."[40]

From the economic point of view, the Transcaucasian republics do not represent major "growing points" that tend to be developed first to speed up the process of overall industrialization of the nation. This is another reason why resources were allocated to more industrially developed republics and not to Georgia, Azerbaidzhan, and Armenia. The relationship between the economic development of a country and its interregional inequality is a complex one, and, as observed by several theorists, tends to take the shape of an inverted U: in the early stages of industrialization, the inequality among the regions tends to increase, and after a certain degree of maturity in the developmental process is reached, starts decreasing. Perhaps in the 1960s and 1970s the USSR was still slowly moving toward this maturity, but had not yet reached it. Thus divergence among the republics was, on the whole, increasing. In the long run, however, after the Soviet economy reaches maturity and the pressing military needs to strengthen other critical areas are satisfied, the trend observed in this study may slowly reverse itself and the differentials may start shrinking.

In terms of economic development and standards of living, Transcaucasia is below the average level of the USSR but slightly better off than its Middle East neighbors, Iran and Turkey. From a purely economic point of view, the region benefited from the Soviet policy of industrialization and modernization that was pursued despite a dearth of natural resources needed for that objective. Within the republics, allocation of resources was more in conformity with comparative advantages. Georgia allocated much larger shares of investment to its subtropical agriculture than did the other republics. As oil supplies diminished in Azerbaidzhan, the dominance of its industrial sector started to decline. The rapidly growing labor force in all three republics and their natural endowments led to the channeling of above-average shares of investment to the light and food industries. The region also benefited from a large market for its surplus products and from favorable prices for its specialized crops: tea, semitropical fruits, and cotton. In return the region obtained grain, needed manufactures, and energy.

The most interesting question of whether Transcaucasia benefited from income transfers from the rest of the country and the closely related question of economic "exploitation" cannot be settled with present knowledge. In a recent study James Gillula concludes that during 1961-75, Georgia and Armenia benefited from income redistribution because their national income used exceeded the national income produced. He also found that Azerbaidzhan contributed to the rest of the USSR, though its ratio of produced to used incomes declined during this period.[41] The study is not conclusive because the income data depend on irrational and changing product prices and the arbitrary way in which turnover taxes are recorded. Especially surprising is that Azerbaidzhan, a relatively backward republic, could contribute income to the rest of the Soviet Union, except in accounting terms, because of the "peculiarity of its product mix, the arbitrary pricing thereof, and the random incidence of turnover tax allocation."[42]

Finally, the ultimate question in comparative economics — whether and to what extent the three republics of Transcaucasia would develop differently if they were independent nations—is beyond the reach of scholars. One primary reason for the incorporation of Transcaucasia into the Russian Empire was the danger of its extermination by powerful neighbors in the south. Assuming that the threat was removed by the time of the emergence of the USSR, it is still doubtful whether they would have been able to attain the same level of development as today, given their relatively poor natural resources and the low initial level of economic and technological development. This is, of course, a purely economic assessment that in no way diminishes the crucial importance of such values as national independence, preservation of cultural identity, and freedom of choice.

NOTES

1. A. N. Lavrishchev, Ekonomicheskaia geografiia SSSR (Moscow, 1965), pp. 28-33.

2. G. N. Cherdantsev, N. P. Nikitin, and B. A. Tutykhin, Ekonomicheskaia geografiia SSSR (Moscow, 1957), p. 155.

3. N. I. Lialikov, Ekonomicheskaia geografiia SSSR (Moscow, 1958), p. 277.

4. Cherdantsev et al., Ekonomicheskaia geografiia SSSR, p. 162.

5. USSR 77: Sixty Soviet Years (Moscow, 1977), pp. 32-33.

6. Cherdantsev et al., Ekonomicheskaia geografiia SSSR, pp. 161. 172, 173.

7. Soviet Life (1978): no. 11, p. 32.

8. USSR 77, pp. 32-33; Soviet Life (1978): no. 11, pp. 32-33; Cherdantsev et al., Ekonomicheskaia geografiia SSSR, p. 214.

9. R. S. Mathieson, The Soviet Union: An Economic Geography (New York: Harper & Row, 1975), pp. 23-24.

10. TsSU, Narodnoe khoziaistvo SSR v 1975 g. (Moscow, 1976), p. 197 (publication hereafter cited as Narkhoz); Stephen Rapawy, "Regional Employment Trends in the USSR," in U.S. Congress, Joint Economic Committee, Soviet Economy in a Time of Change (Washington, D.C.: U.S. Government Printing Office, 1979), pp. 608-10.

11. Alec Nove and J. A. Newth, The Soviet Middle East: A Model for Development? (London: Allen and Unwin, 1967), p. 39.

12. Vsevolod Holubnychy, "Some Economic Aspects of Relations Among the Soviet Republics," in Erich Goldhagen, ed., Ethnic Minorities in the Soviet Union (New York: Praeger, 1968), p. 74.

13. Ibid., pp. 76-78.

14. I. S. Koropeckyj, "Industrial Location Policy in the USSR During the Postwar Period," in U.S. Congress, Joint Economic Committee, <u>Economic Performance and the Military Burden in the Soviet Union</u> (Washington, D.C.: U.S. Government Printing Office, 1970), p. 255.

15. Holubnychy, "Some Economic Aspects . . .," p. 82.

16. Koropeckyj, "Industrial Location Policy . . .," p. 286.

17. Holubnychy, "Some Economic Aspects . . .," p. 73.

18. <u>Zaria vostoka</u>, July 25, 1976; <u>Narkhoz 78</u>, p. 432; <u>Narkhoz Georgia 77</u>, p. 176.

19. Nove and Newth, <u>The Soviet Middle East</u>, p. 55.

20. Holubnychy, "Some Economic Aspects . . .," p. 69.

21. Gertrude E. Schroeder, "Regional Differences in Incomes and Levels of Living in the USSR," in V. N. Bandera and Z. L. Melnyk, eds., <u>The Soviet Economy in Regional Perspective</u> (New York: Praeger, 1973), p. 169.

22. Koropeckyj, "Industrial Location Policy . . .," p. 249.

23. Alexander Woroniak, "Regional Aspects of Soviet Planning and Industrial Organization," in Bandera and Melnyk, <u>The Soviet Economy</u>, p. 269.

24. Koropeckyj, "Industrial Location Policy . . .," p. 249.

25. Schroeder, "Regional Differences . . .," pp. 172, 174.

26. Holubnychy, "Some Economic Aspects . . .," p. 94.

27. <u>Narkhoz 78</u>, p. 394.

28. Nove and Newth, <u>The Soviet Middle East</u>, pp. 84, 85.

29. Holubnychy, "Some Economic Aspects . . .," p. 103.

30. Ibid., p. 105.

31. Ibid., p. 103.

32. N. S. Khrushchev, speech at the Twentieth Congress of the CPSU, quoted in Holubnychy, "Some Economic Aspects . . .," p. 104.

33. Gertrude Schroeder Greenslade, "Transcaucasia Since Stalin—The Economic Dimension," paper presented at the Kennan Institute, Washington, D.C., April 1980 (Occasional Paper no. 101), pp. 15, 16. Also see Schroeder Greenslade's paper "Regional Dimensions of the 'Second Economy' in the USSR," presented at the Kennan Institute, January 1980.

34. Nove and Newth, <u>The Soviet Middle East</u>, p. 45.

35. Ibid., p. 43.

36. Ibid., p. 122.

37. Ibid., p. 114.

38. World Bank, <u>World Development Report, 1979</u> (Washington, D.C.: World Bank, 1979), p. 12.

39. Koropeckyj, "Industrial Location Policy . . .," p. 284.

40. Ibid., p. 269.

41. James W. Gillula, "The Economic Interdependence of Soviet Republics," in U.S. Congress, Soviet Economy in a Time of Change, p. 634.

42. Schroeder Greenslade, "Transcaucasia Since Stalin," p. 20.

# 12

## CENTRAL ASIA AND KAZAKHSTAN
### Ian M. Matley

Until 1961, Soviet planners looked on Central Asia and Kazakhstan as one macroregion. This was probably due to the concept of Kazakhstan as a region with a population of basically Central Asian origin. However, their separation into two economic regions recognizes their diverse characteristics and different directions of economic development and regional specialization.

Definition of the Central Asian region in political terms is relatively simple. It consists of the Uzbek, Tadzhik, Turkmen, and Kirgiz Soviet Socialist Republics. Physically, the area of the region is less easy to delineate. Its southern border with Iran, Afghanistan, and China is fairly well defined by the mountain ranges and rivers, although the Chinese dispute the alignment of the border in the Pamir area. The northern border with Kazakhstan, however, is drawn to reflect the ethnic composition of the population and, for the most part, does not follow any natural feature. It can, in fact, be argued that the logical northern boundary of the Central Asian region should run through the center of the Kazakh Republic. The ethnic composition of the population, the physical environment, and the economy of southern Kazakhstan are more closely linked to the Central Asian republics than they are to those of northern Kazakhstan.

In 1971, 43.0 percent of the total population of the seven southern oblasts and the capital of the republic were Kazakhs, compared with only 24.4 percent in the ten northern oblasts.[1] Southern Kazakhstan has the same desert and semi-desert environment as the adjoining areas of Central Asia, and much of its agriculture is based on irrigation. Northern Kazakhstan, on the other hand, has a population consisting largely of Russians, Ukrainians, and Germans, a grassland environment similar to that of the southern part of West Siberia, and an agricultural economy based mainly on wheat production.

The industry of northern Kazakhstan is more strongly linked to that of West Siberia and the Urals than to Central Asia. The different character of northern Kazakhstan compared with the areas to the south led the Soviet authorities in 1960 to group five northern oblasts together as the Tselinyi krai with the possible intention of joining it to the West Siberian region of the RSFSR.[2] The krai, however, was abolished in 1965 and the boundaries of Kazakhstan have remained unchanged. In 1956 and 1963, Uzbekistan received some land from Kazakhstan to facilitate the development of irrigation.

Although the detachment of the southern area of Kazakhstan and its inclusion with the Central Asia republics would create a more logical and satisfactory region for the purpose of economic analysis, Soviet statistical data and economic information are generally issued for republics or major economic regions. Although some statistics are available by oblasts, there are gaps in the coverage of Kazakhstan at that level, and for the purpose of this study Kazakhstan will be considered as one region, distinct from Central Asia.

## CENTRAL ASIA: AGRICULTURE AND INDUSTRY

### Agriculture

Central Asia diverges in many ways from the other economic regions of the Soviet Union. Its borders contain natural environments that are not found in other parts of the country. Much of the region has a desert and semi-desert climate, with temperatures that can reach as high as 47°C. or as low as -33°C. The aridity of the region is reflected in the low precipitation totals, which in general average below 200 millimeters a year (and in some areas less than 100 millimeters). In particular, much of the territory of Turkmenistan is covered by the sands of the Karakum Desert, and northern Uzbekistan and part of southern Kazakhstan contain the Kyzylkum Desert. The western part of the region consists of extensive plains, but toward the east the terrain becomes more hilly as one approaches the foothills of the ranges of high mountains that extend from the great knot of the Pamirs in the southeast and cover much of the eastern part of the region.

Precipitation levels in the mountains are much higher than on the plains, and in some areas the mountains are high enough to be covered with snow and ice all year. They are thus a good source of water. Several major rivers, such as the Amu Dar'ia, the Syr Dar'ia, the Murgab, and the Tedzhen, have their source in the Central Asian mountains. These and other rivers form the major source of water for irrigation and other purposes, and areas watered by the rivers, especially where they emerge from the mountains, form the major settled parts of the region. The mountains themselves offer little opportunity for human settlement except in the valleys, such as the Fergana and the Chu. Mountain pastures, although of less importance than in the past, are still used for the grazing of livestock, especially in Kirgizstan.

The soils of Central Asia vary in quality. Those of the desert areas are mainly of poor quality and are salinized in places. Alluvial soils are found along the major rivers, and form a good base for irrigated agriculture. The foothills of the mountains are covered with loess soils of excellent quality. In general, conditions for agriculture in Central Asia are good. The climate is sunny, the growing season is long, and there are many areas of fertile soils. The provision of water for irrigation is the main limiting factor. Fortunately, the major areas of good soils are close to the main sources of water.[3]

The basic agricultural specialization of Central Asia is cotton. Since the introduction of American cotton in the 1880s, the irrigated areas of the region have been greatly expanded by various schemes, of which the most important are the Golodnaia Steppe and Murgab projects.[4] By 1913, 543,000 hectares of the region were producing 646,000 tons of cotton, some 87 percent of total Russian cotton production. By 1976 the area planted with cotton had increased to 2,623,000 hectares and production had reached 7,439,000 tons, some 90 percent of total Soviet cotton production. All cotton is produced on irrigated land, and in 1976 it occupied 54.6 percent of the 4,801,500 hectares of sown irrigated land in Central Asia. This proportion may not seem large, but it must be remembered that cotton is grown in rotation with alfalfa and corn or sorghum. In 1976, 23.7 percent of the sown irrigated area was under fodder crops and 15.8 percent under grain (including wheat, corn, and rice). The remaining irrigated land was sown with potatoes, vegetables, and sugar beets, the last being grown mainly in Kirgizstan.[5]

Production of grain is relatively unimportant by national standards. In 1976, Central Asia produced 3,924,000 tons of grain, which amounted only to 1.8 percent of total Soviet grain production. About two-thirds of this grain came from irrigated land. More significant is the production of fruit and vegetables, both of which amounted to more than 10 percent of total Soviet production in 1976.[6] Production of sugar beets, however, is small by national standards.

Livestock herding in Central Asia is traditionally associated with nomadism, but little remains of this old way of life. At present livestock raising is based mainly on the provision of fodder crops. However, Central Asia's 5.8 million head of cattle make up only about 5 percent of the national total. Sheep and goats are more important, and total some 25 million (17 percent of the Soviet total). Production of wool in 1976 amounted to 17.5 percent of total national production, while production of meat and milk was only 4.2 and 3.4 percent, respectively, of the Soviet total.[7]

The picture of the agriculture of Central Asia that emerges from the study of the evidence is of a type associated with arid lands and relying on irrigation. The irrigated lands are utilized mainly for the production of a specialized industrial crop that is rotated with fodder crops and grain. Production of vegetables and fruit is relatively important. Grain is of little importance, and is grown on both irrigated and nonirrigated land. Livestock raising is of minor importance, except for the herding of sheep and goats from which a modest production of wool is obtained.

Industry

Central Asia lacks good supplies of coal and oil, but is fortunate in its reserves of natural gas and its hydroelectric power potential.[8] Bituminous coal is found in the mountains north of the Fergana Valley and in eastern Kirgizstan, while lignite of poor quality is extracted by surface mining in the Angren area of Uzbekistan and south of the Fergana Valley in Tadzhikistan. Quantities produced are small. In 1975, Central Asian production of coal of all types was 10.2 million tons, only 1.5 percent of total Soviet production.[9] Supplies are far from sufficient for regional needs, and coal is imported from northern Kazakhstan and western Siberia. Oil is found in western Turkmenistan near the Caspian coast, in the Fergana Valley, and near Termez in southern Uzbekistan. Production in 1975 totaled 17.4 million tons, of which 15.6 million tons came from the Turkmenian oil fields. Central Asia supplies only 3.6 percent of total Soviet production.[10] However, enough oil is produced to justify the development of a refining industry at Krasnovodsk and Neftezavods in Turkmenistan and in the Fergana Valley.

Natural gas reserves are large, and constitute one of the major resources of the Central Asian region. There are two main areas of production. The first is near Bukhara in western Uzbekistan, where production started in 1959. Pipelines were built to export gas to the Urals and to the Moscow region. Regional pipelines convey gas to Tashkent, Dushanbe, Frunze, Alma-Ata, and the Fergana Valley. The second area is in northeastern Turkmenistan and near Mary, where one of the largest fields is located. A major pipeline leads to the Moscow region and a regional one to Ashkhabad. Total production of natural gas was 89.7 billion cubic meters in 1975, of which 51.8 billion cubic meters came from Turkmenistan. About 31 percen of total Soviet production comes from Central Asia, a major contribution to the total energy supply of the country.[11]

Apart from its value to other regions, Central Asian gas forms the most economical source of energy for the region itself. Central Asian coal mined by the open-cast method costs as much as Donets Basin coal, while shaft-mined coal costs twice as much. The use of natural gas reduces the necessity of developing expensive coal mines and reduces the import of coal from the Kuznets Basin, while also cutting consumption of oil.[12] The further development of West Siberian gas to supply the European part of the Soviet Union will release further supplies for Central Asian industry.[13]

Central Asia occupies third place in the Soviet Union for hydroelectric potential after East Siberia and the Far East regions.[14] Several electric power stations have been constructed, of which the largest is the Nurek dam and station on the Vakhsh in Tadzhikistan, with a planned capacity of 2.7 million kilowatts. There are three smaller stations on the same river. A large power station at Toktogul, on the Naryn River in Kirgizstan, has a capacity of 1.2 million kilowatts. Several more stations on the same river are planned. The Charvak power station, on the Chirchik River near Tashkent, has a capacity of 600,000 kilowatts and is the largest of a string of small stations along the river. In 1970, 21 percent of Central Asia's electric power came from hydroelectric stations.[15]

Apart from these hydroelectric power stations there are large thermal stations at Tashkent and the other republic capitals, as well as at Navoi, Mary, Bezmein, and Chardzhou, and a number of smaller ones at other sites. About 62 percent of fuel used in these power stations in 1969 was natural gas, 23 percent was coal, and 15 percent was oil. All power stations in Turkmenistan and Tadzhikistan operate on gas, while in Uzbekistan some 20 percent, and in Kirgizstan some 74 percent, run on coal.[16]

Production of electric power in Central Asia in 1976 amounted to 50.3 billion kilowatt-hours, about 4.5 percent of total Soviet production. Almost 70 percent of total regional production was in Uzbekistan.[17] Further construction of gas-powered stations, especially in Turkmenistan, and of hydroelectric stations in Tadzhikistan should increase power production significantly.

Central Asia is not rich in metallic ores suitable for heavy industry. There is no iron ore nor manganese. The most important metallic ore deposit is copper, found in the mountains southeast of Tashkent. The ore is processed at Almalyk. Molybdenum, lead, and zinc are mined in conjunction with copper. Other deposits of the same metals are found elsewhere in the region. Most of the lead is smelted at Chimkent in Kazakhstan. Tungsten is mined in western Tadzhikistan and in Samarkand Oblast. Antimony and mercury are found in northern Tadzhikistan and Kirgizstan, and uranium is mined in the Almalyk area. Gold is mined in the same area and in the Kyzylkum Desert.

No statistics are available for production of these metallic ores, but it is clear that some of them are of national significance. Central Asia is the leading producer of antimony in the Soviet Union and the second in production of mercury.[18] It is an important producer of tungsten and molybdenum.[19] Output of copper, lead, and zinc is important, but is less than in Kazakhstan.[20] Uranium production is no doubt of considerable importance.

Nonmetallic ores occur in considerable variety. One of the most important is sulfur, which is found mainly in southeast Turkmenistan. Sulfur is also obtained from the processing of natural gas. A unique source of mineral salts is the Kara-Bogaz-Gol, a landlocked bay of the Caspian Sea, where sodium sulfate, sodium chloride, bromine, iodine, magnesium, potassium, and other salts are obtained. Central Asia has about half the total reserves of sodium chloride of the Soviet Union.[21] Deposits of salts occur in other parts of the region. Fluorspar is mined at several locations and is used in the electrolysis of aluminum. Local deposits of kaolin, nepheline, alunite, and possibly bauxite may be used in future as sources of alumina. Kaolin is mined in conjunction with coal at Angren.

Many of these minerals form the basis for processing and manufacturing industries. A large oil refinery is located at Krasnovodsk and another is under construction at Neftezavodsk near Chardzhou, both in Turkmenistan. The latter refinery will be linked with a major petrochemicals plant. Neftezavodsk will obtain oil by pipeline from western Turkmenistan and possibly also from West Siberia. Turkmenian oil may be piped to the Fergana Valley, where two major refineries and a nitrogen fertilizer plant are located. At present, oil is transported to these refineries by rail.[22]

Natural gas is used not only as a source of energy, but also as a raw material for the chemical industry. There is a large nitrogen chemical plant at Chirchik, near Tashkent and nitrogen fertilizer plants at Navoi, in the Fergana Valley, and at Kalininabad in Tadzhikistan. Sulfur is recovered from natural gas at a plant in Mubarek, south of Navoi.

The quality of Central Asian coal is too poor for the development of a major regional iron and steel industry. There is no iron ore in the region. The only ferrous metallurgical plant is located at Bekabad, south of Tashkent, where steel is produced with coal brought from northern Kazakhstan and West Siberia and pig iron and scrap from Magnitorgorsk in the Urals, the Kuznets Basin, and Karaganda in Kazakhstan. In 1975 the Uzbek Republic produced

409,000 tons of steel.[23] The Bekabad plant was constructed in 1946, with the aim of providing a local supply of steel. Its proximity to the Farkhad hydroelectric power station on the Syr-Dar'ia makes possible the use of electric furnaces, with a consequent saving of coal. The Bekabad plant produces only 15-20 percent of the steel requirements of the region.[24]

The nonferrous metallurgical industry of the region has been developed on a more solid basis of local raw materials. A major industrial complex for the complete processing of copper has been established at Almalyk. Sulfuric acid, obtained as a by-product of the process, is used along with phosphate rock from Kazakhstan and ammonia from the Chirchik chemical plant to produce ammonium phosphate. Natural gas is used in the smelting of copper. Zinc and molybdenum also are processed in the Almalyk complex. Another metallurgical plant is located at Chirchik, where molybdenum and tungsten products are manufactured.

Mention should be made of the growing aluminum industry, although it is not based primarily on local raw materials. The fluorspar mined in Central Asia is not an ore of aluminum, although it is used in the electrolysis of the metal, and is mostly exported to other regions. A plant at Regar in southern Tadzhikistan produces aluminum from alumina from the Urals, using power from the Nurek hydroelectric plant. Even with the importation of raw materials, costs of production at the plant are two times lower than those of plants in the European part of the Soviet Union. The possibility of obtaining supplies of bauxite from the processing of kaolin, mined along with coal at Angren, is regarded as practical.[25]

Nonmetallic minerals form the basis for a developing chemical industry. The deposits of the Kara-Bogaz-Gol are processed at nearby Bekdash, and iodine and bromine are produced at Nebit-Dag, Gaurdak, and Cheleken. A recently constructed plant at Iavan, south of Dushanbe in Tadzhikistan, is planned to become one of the largest chemical complexes in Central Asia and will produce calcium carbide, calcinated soda, chlorine, and polychlorinated resin. It will use local reserves of sodium chloride and carbon, and electric power from the Nurek dam. However, the most important branch of the Central Asian chemical industry is the production of fertilizer. Apart from nitrogen fertilizer, discussed above, phosphate fertilizers are produced at Kokand, Samarkand, and Chardzhou, and there are plans for development of potash fertilizer plants in Turkmenistan and elsewhere. In 1976, Central Asia produced 6.7 million tons of chemical fertilizer, 7.2 percent of total Soviet production.[26] Although this proportion may seem low, it should be realized that the Uzbek SSR occupies fourth place among the Soviet republics in production of fertilizers, and that most of the fertilizer is consumed within the region. Production of insecticides and herbicides is also considerable, mainly at a plant at Fergana. Central Asia is the main producer of defoliants in the country.[27] The growth of the Central Asian chemical industry is a direct result of the regional specialization in cotton-growing.

The residue of cotton processing—the lint, husks, and stalks— forms a useful raw material for the manufacture of acetate fibers at Namangan, and of alcohol, glucose, yeast, and other products at factories in Iangiiul and Andizhan. Citric acid is obtained from the leaves of the cotton plant.

Although the region produces large amounts of natural fiber, there is a considerable production of artificial fibers. Plants in Fergana and Navoi manufacture rayon from cotton cellulose, and further plants are planned to produce other types of artificial fibers. The production of plastic tubes for irrigation equipment is also being developed, with plants located at Dzhizak, Mary, and Iavan.

Apart from the utilization of the by-products of the cotton plant in the chemical industry, the processing of cotton fiber and the manufacture of cotton thread and textiles forms a relatively important branch of Central Asian light industry. However, most of the cotton leaves the region after its initial processing. Over 100 cotton-ginning plants exist in the region, and in 1976 they produced 2.3 million tons (90 percent of the Soviet Union's production of cotton fiber).[28] The manufacture of cotton thread and material is concentrated mainly in the Tashkent textile combine, the largest in the Soviet Union, employing about 20,000 workers.[29] Other plants are located in Fergana, Frunze, Dushanbe, Ashkhabad, Mary, and Osh. Of the 7,809.9 million meters of cotton textiles produced in the Soviet Union in 1975, only 423.3 million meters (5.4 percent) came from Central Asia.[30] About half of this production came from the textile combine in Tashkent. These figures highlight the fact that Central Asian cotton production is not basically intended as a raw material for local industry. Other branches of light industry include the production of silk fiber, of which the region is a major supplier, and of clothing and footwear (both modest industries).

The engineering industry of Central Asia has two major characteristics of note: it is based on imported metal, and it is highly specialized. As might be expected, this specialization is closely linked to the requirements of the cotton-growing industry. Because of the labor-intensive nature of cotton harvesting, the development and manufacture of cotton-picking machines has been particularly stressed. Machinery of this type is manufactured at the large agricultural machinery plant (Tashsel'mash) in Tashkent. Tractors also are produced in Tashkent. Other specialized machinery for the cotton industry includes seeding machines, cultivators, trailers for the transport of cotton, equipment for cotton-ginning plants, and irrigation equipment, such as ditching machines and pumps. Equipment for the gas, oil, and chemical industries also is manufactured.

## FUTURE DEVELOPMENT OF THE ECONOMY

The above review of the present state of Central Asian agriculture and industry enables certain conclusions to be drawn and gives indications for directions of future development. The most important branch of the regional economy is cotton-growing. To support the growing of cotton, various other industries produce specialized machinery, chemical fertilizers, insecticides, and herbicides. Cotton is ginned, cottonseed is pressed for oil, and the fibers are spun into thread and made into textiles and clothing. Central Asian industry is linked strongly to cotton, and the region is virtually self-supporting in the production of equipment for the cotton industry. Other branches of agriculture and industry are relatively poorly developed, and there is no evidence of attempts to diversify the regional economy. In other words, Central Asia exhibits a high degree of regional specialization. Along with this specialized complex of industries goes the production of the main regional source of energy, natural gas, which, like cotton, forms a major export of the region. The existence of natural gas (rather than coal or oil) in large quantities will obviously be an important influence on the direction of development of regional industry.

Indications are that the production of cotton will be expanded in the future. The area sown to cotton in Central Asia increased from 2,435,000 hectares in 1970 to 2,623,000 hectares in 1976. In Turkmenistan the down area rose by 94,000 hectares during that period. The 7.7 percent increase in the sown area of cotton was made possible by a 15.6 percent increase in the area of irrigated land during 1970-76. In Turkmenistan the rate of increase of irrigated land was 31.6 percent.[31] Such increases are due to the development of major irrigation projects, such as the Murgab and Tedzhen oases, supplied by the Kara-Kum Canal. The pumps of these irrigation schemes are powered by electricity from the large power station at Mary, which uses natural gas as fuel. These Turkmen projects are continuously being enlarged.[32] During the 1960s the major expansion in irrigated land took place in Uzbekistan, where the Golodnaia Steppe scheme received priority and resulted in an increase in regional cotton-growing capabilities, although not as large as originally hoped.[33] The rate of increase of irrigated land in Uzbekistan has been around the regional average for the last few years. On the other hand, Tadzhikistan and Kirgizstan have not increased their irrigated areas significantly. There are plans for further expansion of the irrigated lands of the Zeravshan Valley and the Karshi Steppe, near Bukhara, and at Termez on the Amu-Dar'ia.

Deliveries of fertilizer to Central Asian agriculture increased by 33.9 percent between 1970 and 1976. In Turkmenistan deliveries increased by 46 percent. Although these increases were less than the national average of 70.3 percent during the same period (deliveries in the RSFSR rose by 87.9 percent), they resulted in an increase in yields of cotton per hectare in the region from 24.9 centners per hectare in 1966-70 to 27.5 in 1976. A decrease in yields in Turkmenistan during this period, probably due to the rapid expansion of cotton sowing without sufficient fertilizer, was offset by an increase in yields of about 5 centners per hectare in the longer-established cotton-growing areas of Uzbekistan, such as the Fergana Valley.[34] All indicators are that the expansion of irrigated land and cotton-growing will continue, and there are no signs of any attempts to diversify Central Asian agriculture.

Central Asian industry will likewise continue to specialize in servicing the cotton-growing and cotton-processing industries. The supply of iron and steel for these industries is likely to raise some problems because of the lack of a sound regional ferrous metallurgical base. Cost factors support the importation of metals from other regions rather than the importation of machinery. The transportation of farm machines in the 1960s cost three times more than the movement of a corresponding quantity of metal.[35] Nevertheless, it would seem most logical to develop those types of industries that can operate on natural gas, consume relatively small quantities of steel, and utilize the abundant manpower of the region. However, the degree of specialization already achieved in the manufacture of machinery and equipment for the cotton-growing industry is a virtual guarantee that this type of industry will continue, and no doubt expand, in the future. The possibility of expansion of the regional iron and steel industry is limited, and the importation of metals from other regions will continue.

The chemical industry operates on a more solid basis of local raw materials, and its orientation to the cotton-growing industry will ensure its continuous growth. The petrochemical industry will see some further development based on Turkmen oil, and natural gas will continue as a major raw material for the industry.

The role of natural gas in the development of Central Asian industry in general, and its export to other regions, should continue. Indications are that potential reserves (about 20 percent of total Soviet reserves) should be sufficient for all forms of industrial use, even for energy-consuming industries, within the region, and still allow for exports. However, future plans should include the possibility of declining supplies from established fields and the necessity of obtaining gas from smaller fields and at greater depths.[36] Natural gas is cheaper than electricity to transport over long distances, and the present use of Central Asian gas as fuel for power stations and industry in the Urals region and other locations in the European part of the country would seem to be the optimum allocation of this resource.

The nonferrous metals industry should continue to expand, although its role in the Soviet economy is small compared with that of other regions, such as the Urals or Kazakhstan. With the further growth of the electric power industry and the successful development of regional sources of aluminum ore, the aluminum industry, now in its infancy, should see some expansion. However, it is never likely to be of great national significance.

The location and distribution of Central Asian industry will also exert some influence on its future development. First, Central Asia is to a great extent isolated by its distance from the rest of the country. It is 1,600 kilometers by rail from Tashkent to Orenburg in the Urals region, and almost 1,800 kilometers to Krasnovodsk on the Caspian Sea. Coal or pig iron from Karaganda in Kazakhstan must travel some 1,400 kilometers to the steel plant at Bekabad. Transportation costs for war materials or finished goods to and from the region are high, a fact that must influence planning decisions.

Second, industry is highly concentrated within the region. The main area of concentration is the Tashkent region and the Fergana Valley in Uzbekistan—the southeastern part of the region. There is also some industry at Bukhara and Samarkand in the Zeravshan Valley, and in the north at Urgench and Nukus on the Amu-Dar'ia. Uzbekistan accounts for about two-thirds of total Central Asian industrial production. In Tadzhikistan most industry is located close to Dushanbe, and in Kirgizstan it is in the Frunze area or on the fringes of the Fergana Valley. The completion of the Toktogul dam in the west-central part of the country may influence this distribution somewhat. The location of industry in Turkmenistan is more widespread than in the other republics. Apart from a concentration of industry around Ashkhabad, there are industrial complexes at Mary and Chardzhou, based on supplies of natural gas, at Krasnovodsk and the oil fields and salt deposits of the Caspian coast, and in the north at Tashauz on the Amu-Dar'ia.

This uneven distribution of industry is due to several factors, the most important of which is the availability of water. The considerable areas of deserts form large empty spaces on the economic map of Central Asia. The mountainous areas in the south and east of the region are not conducive to agricultural or industrial develop-

ment, with the exception of mining and the construction of hydroelectric dams. Because of the importance of cotton-growing to
many branches of the regional economy, it is not surprising that the
most important areas of cotton-growing are close to the major concentrations of industry. The need for water and labor also plays a
part in explaining this close proximity of industry and agriculture.
There are no indicators that any change in the basic distribution of
industry is likely to take place in the foreseeable future, unless new
deposits of raw materials or sources of energy are discovered. An
expansion of irrigated land is, however, taking place, which may
lead to some changes in the distribution of agricultural activities
and of population.

## DEMOGRAPHIC CHARACTERISTICS OF THE REGION

Any discussion of the future of the Central Asian economy
would not be realistic without taking into account the demographic
trends that are characteristic of the region and that differ considerably from those of most other regions of the Soviet Union. The
total population of the region at the census of 1959 was 13,682,000
(6.6 percent of the total population of the Soviet Union), and by the
census of 1970 it had reached 19,792,000 (8.2 percent of total Soviet
population). In 1977 regional population was estimated at 24,158,000
(9.4 percent of total Soviet population). During the 18-year period
the population of Central Asia rose by 76.6 percent, compared with
a rise of 23.5 percent for the population of the Soviet Union and of
15.4 percent for the population of the RSFSR.[37]
This dramatic rise in population is due to high rates of natural
increase combined with migration from other regions. In 1976 the
regional birth rate was 34.9 per 1,000 and the death rate 7.9 per
1,000, giving an annual rate of increase of 2.70 percent. The highest rate of growth was in the Tadzhik Republic, with 2.97 percent,
followed by the Uzbek Republic with 2.82 percent. In the same year
the rate of growth for the Soviet Union was 0.89 percent.[38] These
rates of increase are for the total population of all ethnic groups in
the region and the republics; the rate of increase for the indigenous
population is higher than for the emigrants from the European part
of the Soviet Union, a point that will be discussed later.
The main question raised by this rapid rise in regional population is whether the structure and rate of growth of the regional economy are capable of providing employment for the increasing number
of people entering the work force, or whether some degree of migration to other regions may be necessary. The problem of Central
Asian manpower is linked to the question of Soviet manpower in

general, a subject that has received considerable attention in recent years.[39] At present there are few Central Asians living outside their region. Of the 9,195,093 Uzbeks in the Soviet Union in 1970, only 76,240 lived outside of Central Asia or Kazakhstan, and other Central Asians showed an equally low rate of migration.[40] Although views differ as to likely developments, it is generally agreed that this region is faced with serious economic and social problems unless some outlet is provided for the surplus labor force.[41] There are three solutions to this problem: rapid development of the regional economy, control of population growth, and emigration of workers to other regions.[42] Robert Lewis, Richard Rowland, and Ralph Clem have studied the possibility of absorbing the surplus labor force in an expanding regional economy, and do not consider it feasible. Expansion of employment in the agricultural sector would involve either the curtailment of mechanization and the use of more labor-intensive methods of farming, or rapid expansion of the irrigated area. Unless this is done, the increasing amount of surplus rural manpower could not be absorbed.[43] They see no evidence to support the possibility of any great future growth of Central Asia's irrigated area.[44] Likewise, they do not believe that the growth rate of Central Asian industry is great enough to ensure absorption of the surplus manpower in rural areas.[45] Investment in regional industry has been low.[46]

The above points need careful consideration because they lie at the heart of the question of the future economic development of Central Asia. First, Lewis, Rowland, and Clem are correct in identifying the Central Asian population and labor problem as primarily affecting the rural population. As they point out in another study, during the periods of rapid industrialization before and after World War II, the skilled jobs in the factories of the cities of Central Asia were taken by Russians and other outsiders. In 1970 there were 3 million Russians in the region and more than 500,000 other Slavs. Russians formed 15.1 percent of the total population. Most of them lived in urban centers. About 30 percent of the urban populations of the Uzbek, Tadzhik, and Turkmen republics were Russians, while in the Kirgiz Republic the figure was over 51 percent.[47] Thus, a significant part of the urban labor force consisted of Russian immigrants.

At the same time 77 percent of the Uzbeks living in their own republic were located in rural areas, while in the Kirgiz Republic over 85 percent of the Kirgiz were classified as rural.[48] It is this indigenous rural population that has exhibited the highest rate of growth. The gross reproduction ratio in the urban centers of Uzbekistan in 1969-70 was 1.8, while in the rural areas it was 3.57. In 1970 the birth rates per 1,000 of the main constituent ethnic groups living in Uzbekistan were 19.3 for the Russians, 23.0 for the Ukrainians, and 39.2 for the Uzbeks.[49] If the trends of 1969-70 continue, the populations of the Central Asian republics in the year 2000 will constitute 15.8 percent of the population of the Soviet Union, compared with 8.2 percent in 1970.[50] At present there are no signs of any significant drop in regional birth rates.

The question of providing work for an increasing rural labor force is linked to the possibilities of increasing the irrigated area of the region, the degree of mechanization of agriculture, and the future development of rural industries. As mentioned above, the area of irrigated land in the region increased during 1970-76 by 15.6 percent. Rowland, Lewis, and Clem underestimated the regional rate of growth of irrigation in their analysis.[51] Turkmenistan increased its irrigated area by 31.6 percent during this period, and the more populous Uzbekistan showed an increase of 16.2 percent. During 1975-76, in fact, the irrigated area of Uzbekistan grew at a rate of 4.2 percent, and that of Turkmenistan increased at a rate of 3.3 percent.[52] Unless problems of soil salinization or waterlogging are removing land from agricultural use, it seems that the area of irrigated land is increasing at a rate sufficient to create considerable local employment.

As Rowland, Lewis, and Clem point out, Soviet policy has been devoted for many years to increasing mechanization of agriculture.[53] It is claimed that in 1974 there were 27,000 mechanical cotton pickers operating in Uzbekistan, and that many farms in the Virgin Lands used no manual labor for harvesting.[54] Application of energy to aid labor on collective farms, state farms, and mixed agricultural enterprises in Central Asia in 1976 amounted to 428.3 horsepower per 100 hectares of sown area, compared with 209 horsepower for the whole country and 242 horsepower for the Ukraine. However, the application of energy per worker was relatively low in the same year, amounting to 10.9 horsepower, compared with 18.1 horsepower for the Soviet Union and 36.6 horsepower in Kazakhstan. Only Transcaucasia had a lower rate, with 5.6 horsepower per worker.[55] Thus, the application of energy to Central Asian agriculture is high in terms of the sown area, but relatively low in terms of labor.

Another indicator is the figure for the mechanization of cotton harvesting in the Soviet Union in 1976: 49 percent of the total volume of work. This figure is the lowest for various agricultural operations, but nevertheless is greater than the figure of 43 percent given for 1975 and of 32 percent for 1970. There are no indications that future growth of mechanization of the cotton industry will be limited. It should be noted that the two major operations in cotton-growing that employ large numbers of workers are harvesting and weeding.

Thus, any increase in their mechanization will substantially reduce labor requirements. It would seem that at present there is still considerable use of manual labor in Central Asian agriculture, especially in the older, established farming areas, but trends indicate a higher degree of mechanization in the future.

Rural industry in Central Asia is confined mainly to the cleaning of cotton in local cotton gins. There is no handicrafts industry to compare with that of the rural areas of India or Pakistan and no indication that rural industries will be able to absorb any significant surplus labor.

The possibilities of future absorption of at least part of the increase in the rural labor force in Central Asian agriculture seem better than is suggested by Rowland, Lewis, and Clem. The rate of absorption will be controlled by the ability of the authorities to maintain the rate of expansion of irrigated land and by some delay in the complete mechanization of regional agriculture. It is impossible to forecast the long-term trends in either of these areas, but it would seem that in the 1980s, at least, the problem of surplus rural labor could be alleviated by implementation of these policies.

Although Central Asians have shown less inclination to move to urban centers than is the case in other regions of the Soviet Union, the absorption of large numbers of surplus rural workers can be efficiently achieved only by increased employment opportunities in industry. Rowland, Lewis, and Clem do not believe that Central Asian industry exhibits a level of growth sufficient to achieve this. They point to an average annual rate of industrial growth in the region of 8 percent in the period 1965-70, and say that a rate of 9-13 percent a year would be necessary.[56] They also indicate that Soviet planners intend to achieve industrial growth by means of increased labor productivity rather than by an increased labor force.[57] In order to maximize economic development, industrial investment should be increased in labor-surplus regions, but this has not happened in Central Asia. They think that this low level of investment is due to the lack of natural resources for heavy industry and the region's isolation from the rest of the country.[58]

The average annual rate of industrial growth in Central Asia given by Rowland, Lewis, and Clem for 1965-70 is based on rates of growth for individual republics ranging from 12 percent for Kirgizstan to 8 percent for Tadzhikistan and Turkmenistan and only 6 percent for Uzbekistan. Since Uzbekistan is the main industrial producer in the region, they estimate the regional rate at 8 percent a year.[59] The figures for 1970-75 do not show any improvement over those of 1965-70. Although the rate of growth of Uzbek industry rose by over 2 percent per annum, the rates of growth of Kirgiz and Tadzhik industry dropped considerably, resulting in an annual rate of growth for the whole region of less than 8 percent, [60] less than the necessary rate specified by Rowland, Lewis, and Clem.

The low level of industrial investment in Central Asia is substantiated by the available data. The first impetus toward the industrialization of Central Asia came during World War II, when factories were evacuated from the European part of the country. After the war priority was given to reconstruction of industry in the European west. Any movement of industry eastward during the 1950s was primarily to Siberia and Kazakhstan, and it was only in the 1960s that attempts were made to increase the rate of industrial growth in the Central Asian republics. [61] This increased attention to the industrial development of the region did not produce dramatic results. Leslie Dienes showed that in the 1960s Central Asia suffered from low per capita investment and relatively low capital return and productivity. [62] This was in spite of the fact that capital investment in Central Asia increased by 46.7 percent during 1965-70, more than 2 percent above the national average. However, during 1970-75 an increase of only 37.7 percent was recorded, about 2 percent below the national average. [63] There are no signs of any crash program of industrial development for Central Asia.

There is likewise no indication of any attempts to introduce a birth control program in the region, a measure that Lewis, Rowland, and Clem consider as already too late to have much effect in the near future. [64] Their view is that there is no alternative to future migrations of Central Asians to other regions of the Soviet Union in order to obtain employment. [65]

Factors that tend to weaken this prediction of out-migration are the low levels of education and working skills of the Central Asian population, their poor command of Russian, the reluctance of many to move even to cities within their own region, and the fact that much of the regional population consists of women and children. [66] The views of the opponents of the out-migration theory are summarized by Michael Rywkin, who thinks that there will be no large-scale out-migration to other regions, and that the problem of surplus labor will be solved by increased migration from rural areas to the cities, the development of labor-intensive light industry, some restrictions on Siberian workers moving to climatically superior Central Asia, and the more rapid development of irrigation. As the indigenous population becomes better-trained and the urban populations contain more Muslims, European workers in the region may begin to leave, thereby creating more skilled jobs for local people. [67]

It is impossible to predict the policy that will be adopted by Soviet authorities to manage the Central Asian labor force problem. It is clear that something will have to be done: either more rapid industrialization and urbanization, or movements of Central Asians to other parts of the Soviet Union. Those who view as an unlikely development the migration of a poorly educated, unskilled Muslim labor force with a way of life different from that of the inhabitants of the urbanized areas of the West, should remember the similar movement of North Africans and Turks to Western Europe and Pakistanis to Great Britain. These developments may not have been desirable, but they took place. The pressures of regional unemployment may force the same type of movements in the Soviet Union, a solution that may be cheaper in the short run than increasing industrial investment in a region that presents few real attractions for development as a major industrial base.

## ALTERNATIVE POSSIBILITIES FOR DEVELOPMENT: THE EXAMPLE OF PAKISTAN

The debate on the question of whether Central Asia is a colony has already been conducted by Alec Nove and J. A. Newth.[68] There are aspects of the region—such as its ethnic composition, its emphasis on cotton-growing, the subordinate place held in regional administration by Central Asians (as opposed to Russians), and the low level of industrial development—that are similar to the situation in many colonies in the past. On the other hand, Central Asians receive the same wages as any other ethnic group for the same work, attempts are being made to improve levels of education, and investment in the region has come from Russia.[69] However, there is one fact that cannot be denied: the direction of the economic development of the region is not decided by the Central Asians themselves, but by Moscow. The interests of the Soviet Union as a whole are placed before regional interests and desires. Thus, it is possible that Central Asia might have developed in a different fashion if it had been an independent country or, more likely, a number of independent countries. However, we shall assume that the whole region would form a single political unit. One method of assessing the possible direction of development of such an independent state is to compare it with a similar state that was once a colony and has followed its own independent policy for some time. At the same time an assessment of the comparative levels of development achieved by Central Asia and by a neighboring state can be made.

There are three independent countries, either contiguous or close to Soviet Central Asia, that have certain features in common: Iran, Afghanistan, and Pakistan. All have a basically Muslim population, contain several ethnic groups, and have somewhat similar climates. However, Iran and Afghanistan do not have the large areas of irrigated land that are found in both Central Asia and

Pakistan. Iran has benefited from its large oil reserves and has developed an economy that is not easily comparable with that of Central Asia. Afghanistan has few good areas for agriculture because of its predominantly mountainous nature. It has no railroads, and a very low level of urbanization. Pakistan, on the other hand, has large areas of plains watered by the Indus River and its tributaries, resulting in the development of a good agricultural base similar to that developed along the Amu-Dar'ia and other rivers of Central Asia. It has mountain and desert areas, as does Central Asia. Unlike its neighbors, Pakistan has a colonial past that resulted in an emphasis on cotton-growing and the development of irrigation schemes by the British comparable with the Russian efforts in Central Asia.

The main problem of comparison between the two regions lies in the difference in sizes of territory and population. The total area of Pakistan is 804,000 square kilometers, compared with the much larger area of 1,277,000 square kilometers of Central Asia, but a proportionately larger area of Central Asia consists of desert and mountains. The population of Pakistan—72.4 million in 1976—is considerably larger than Central Asia's 23.5 million in the same year. This population is supported by an irrigated area approximately three times as large as that of Central Asia, resulting in roughly comparable conditions in the rural areas.

During the period of British control, when Pakistan formed part of India, the northern plains, watered by the Indus and its tributaries, were developed as areas of irrigated cotton-growing. Several major barrages and canals were constructed, some of them now on Indian territory. Since independence in 1947 the irrigation system has been expanded considerably, including the increased use of wells to tap the large subsoil water reserves. The irrigated area has expanded from 11.8 million hectares in the mid-1960s to 14.5 million hectares in 1977-78.[70] In particular, the Thal project on the upper Indus has contributed over 500,000 hectares to the irrigated area in recent years, and there are several similar projects. However, about 41,000 hectares of cultivated land are lost every year due to waterlogging and salinization.[71] In 1978 about 6 million hectares were waterlogged and 7.9 million hectares were salinized. A major program has been launched to control these problems.[72] The seriousness of this loss of valuable agricultural land is demonstrated by the above figures, and suggests that Central Asia may face similar problems of the same magnitude. In the 1960s serious salinization problems were admitted in Uzbekistan, although it is claimed that since 1968 control of salinization in the Golodnaia Steppe has greatly improved.[73] The Pakistani experience demonstrates the limits on the development of irrigation without a large capital expenditure on drainage systems.

Agricultural production in Pakistan follows a pattern somewhat similar to that of Central Asia. Cotton is the main cash and export crop and occupied 1.9 million hectares, 13.0 percent of the total area sown to principal crops (14.4 million hectares) in 1976-77.[74] This is a smaller proportion than in Central Asia, where 39.5 percent of the total sown area was devoted to cotton. Two grain crops together occupied a much larger area than cotton. The area under wheat amounted to 6.4 million hectares in 1976-77 (44.4 percent of the total area of major crops), and rice occupied 1.7 million hectares (11.9 percent of the total area of major crops). Other grains, mainly sorghum and corn, occupied about 1.9 million hectares. About 10.1 million hectares (69.7 percent of the total area of major crops) was devoted to food grains,[75] compared with 32.5 percent of the total sown area occupied by grain crops in Central Asia in 1976.

These figures suggest that growing food crops receives a higher priority in Pakistan than in Central Asia. Pakistan aims not only at self-sufficiency in wheat, but at the export of wheat and rice.[76] A major obstacle to the achievement of this goal is the low yields of the major crops. The 10.1 million hectares of grain lands produced some 14 million tons of food grains in 1977-78, with an average yield of just under 1,400 kilos per hectare. The much smaller grain area of Central Asia (2.2 million hectares) in 1976 produced 3.9 million tons of grain, with an average yield of 1,800 kilos per hectare (18 centners per hectare). The 1.8 million hectares of Pakistan's cotton land produced about 570,000 tons of cotton, with a yield of about 317 kilos per hectare. Central Asia's cotton-growing area of 2.6 million hectares produced 7.4 million tons, with an average yield of 2,750 kilos per hectare (27.5 centners per hectare).[77] The high priority of cotton-growing in Central Asia is clearly demonstrated by these comparative figures. The difference in yields is largely explained by the patterns of fertilizer application. In Pakistan consumption of fertilizer in 1977-78 reached 680,000 nutrient tons. In 1975-76, 48 percent of fertilizer consumed went to wheat, 16 percent to cotton, and 12 percent to rice. In Central Asia consumption of fertilizer in 1976 amounted to 1.6 million nutrient tons.[78] Most of this fertilizer was applied to cotton. Application of fertilizer per hectare of cropped land thus amounts to about 37 nutrient kilos per hectare in Pakistan and about 241 nutrient kilos per hectare in Central Asia.

There is little of significance to note in the different patterns of livestock holding in the two regions. Pakistan had 25.5 million head of cattle (including 10.6 million head of buffalo) in 1976, compared with Central Asia's 5.8 million in the same year. Buffalo are not only important draft animals, but also supply a large proportion of Pakistan's milk and meat. Central Asia had more sheep in 1976—23.9 million, compared with 18.9 million in Pakistan. As noted above, the production of good-quality wool is a minor area of agricultural specialization in Central Asia. In Pakistan about half the wool produced is used in the carpet and rug industry, and the rest is exported. The quantities involved are small. Pakistan has more goats than sheep, about 21.7 million in 1976. Goats are destructive grazers, and the Pakistan authorities are attempting to ensure that they are all stall-fed. They provide meat, milk, and skins, and the better varieties produce fine hair. Goats in Central Asia are relatively unimportant, totaling 1.5 million in 1976. It should be noted that Pakistan has achieved a notable rate of growth in numbers of sheep, goats, and poultry in recent years.[79]

The above facts lead to two main conclusions. First, if Central Asia were an independent country, it would probably concentrate to a much greater extent on growing food crops in order to feed its increasing population, with a smaller land area and less fertilizer being devoted to cotton-growing. The highly specialized agriculture of Central Asia is made possible by the fact that it is a region of a larger political and economic unit that provides a guaranteed market for its products and encourages its specialization. In return the region is provided with food supplies and other necessities, including fertilizers. Pakistan must rely on selling its crops on the world market, and faces the competition of other producers and the vagaries of world prices. It must pay ever-increasing prices for fuel and fertilizer, and must seek foreign aid in order to carry out many of its projects. It is continually faced with the problem of feeding a rapidly growing population. These are the conditions that Central Asia would have to face as an independent country.

The second conclusion to be drawn is that Central Asian agriculture is more productive than that of Pakistan, mainly because of greater inputs of fertilizer and technology. Crop yields are considerably lower in Pakistan than in Central Asia. However, one should remember that yields in Pakistan are particularly poor even compared with similar areas, such as the East Punjab of India or Egypt. The cotton yield is only 40 percent of that of Egypt.[80] Apart from the problem of fertilizer and pesticide supplies, the land tenure system in Pakistan has hindered agricultural progress, despite the land reforms of 1959 and 1972. More than 75 percent of farms are less than ten acres in size. These are problems that, of course, Central Asia does not have. Pakistan also has fewer tractors than Central Asia: 71,000 in 1977-78, compared with Central Asia's 238,000 in 1976.[81] In 1971 only 3 percent of the total cultivable area was plowed by tractors.[82] Although lack of mechanization may result in low labor productivity, it may be a benefit in providing employment for a rural labor force that has little opportunity to find work in industry.

Industrial development in Pakistan lags behind that in Central Asia, and has a different structure. Nevertheless, it is possible to compare the industrialization of the two regions fairly easily because the resource bases are somewhat similar. The level of urbanization is higher in Central Asia: 40 percent of the population lived in urban centers in 1977, compared with 27 percent in Pakistan in the same year. [83] However, Pakistan's major cities are larger than those of Central Asia. In 1977 the populations of Karachi and Lahore were 3.5 million and 2.2 million, respectively; Tashkent, the largest city of Central Asia, had 1.7 million.

Pakistan lacks good supplies of coal. Production amounts to about 1.3 million tons annually, much of it being lignite of poor quality. Its main use is in brick kilns. Because of the problem of spontaneous combustion, the lignite cannot be easily transported, and thus is of little use for power production. There is only one coal-fired power station in the country, although a second one is planned. [84] The quality of Central Asian coal is better, and production is almost ten times as great as that of Pakistan. Proven coal reserves in Central Asia are about three times larger than those of Pakistan.

Oil is in poor supply in Pakistan, although the possibilities of future finds are promising. Production amounted to about 500,000 tons in 1977, and 87 percent of the country's oil requirements have to be imported. Pakistan's oil situation compares unfavorably with Central Asia's 17.4 million tons produced in 1975. [85] There are several refineries for processing domestic and imported oil, and expansion is planned.

Pakistan's most important source of mineral energy is natural gas. A large natural gas field was discovered along with oil in the north, and other fields are being developed. A field recently discovered in Baluchistan is thought to be one of the largest in the world. The major field at Sui is connected by a pipeline to Karachi, and also supplies many other areas of the country. The gas is used for the manufacture of fertilizers.

The production of natural gas amounted to 5,574 million cubic meters in 1976-77, an amount that met about 33 percent of total commercial energy needs. About 36 percent of production was consumed by the power industry. However, since the use of gas in power production is regarded as uneconomic, it is planned to develop its use in the petrochemical and fertilizer industries, and possibly to export it. [86] Although Pakistan's production of natural gas is less than Central Asia's 89,691 million cubic meters in 1975, the possibilities of expansion are considerable.

The major source of energy in Pakistan is hydroelectric power. The best sites for development are in the mountain areas of the north, where several major dams provide water for power production and irrigation. It is unlikely that the full potential of the region will be developed, owing to the high cost of dams and other problems. Nevertheless, expansion of hydroelectric power is continuing. In 1976-77 the total generation of electric power amounted to 8.7 billion kilowatt-hours, 59 percent of which came from hydroelectric sources. Total production may reach 10 billion kilowatt-hours in 1977-78. In 1976-77 about 40 percent of electric power produced was consumed by industry, and 26 percent by agriculture. A small nuclear plant is in operation at Karachi, and a larger one is planned to supply the northern region with extra power. Pakistan seems committed to the further development of nuclear power as a substitute for natural gas and oil. [87]

Central Asia's electric power production of 50.3 billion kilowatt-hours in 1976 is considerably larger than that of Pakistan, and on a per capita basis is much more impressive, amounting to 1,837 kilowatt-hours per person, compared with 150 kilowatt-hours in Pakistan in 1977. Nevertheless, Pakistan has substantially increased its total production of electricity in recent years. In 1967 per capita production was only 47 kilowatt-hours. It is hoped to reach 800 kilowatt-hours per capita in the year 2000. [88]

Pakistan has a variety of minerals, many of which are mined for domestic use and for export. Iron ore is found in several locations, but much of it is of poor quality. There are plans for beneficiation and pelletization of some ores. A newly discovered field in Baluchistan promises to be of better quality, and may supply about half the country's requirements. [89] Because of the lack of a major iron and steel industry, production is small at present. Chromite is the most important of the minerals mined, all of it exported. Other mineral products are antimony ore, fluorite, and bauxite. There is no aluminum industry. Rock salt, salts from salt lakes, gypsum, asbestos, and kaolin are also produced. Discoveries of lead, manganese, and uranium offer some promise for future exploitation. [90]

In comparison with Central Asia, Pakistan has somewhat the same mix of industrial raw materials, but production and known reserves are smaller. However, there is little doubt that Central Asia has developed its resources to a greater extent than has Pakistan. The development of Central Asia's resources by the Soviet government has proceeded as part of a larger national plan for modernization and industrialization. Even if Central Asia has received less investment and attention than some other regions of the Soviet Union, the national drive for the exploitation of all available resources has left its mark on the regional economy. Pakistan is still a Third World country, and is struggling with problems of economic organization and of obtaining investment capital to develop its resources.

In terms of industrial development Pakistan lags behind Central Asia. The iron and steel industry consists of a few small plants that process imported scrap. A heavy industrial complex was built in the north with Chinese aid. It has a foundry, and manufactures heavy machinery. A major iron and steel plant is being built with Soviet aid at Karachi, and another is planned near the Kalabagh iron ore field. None of these projects is large.

The engineering industry is small. The Renault Company is collaborating in the construction of a truck manufacturing plant, and Massey Ferguson is helping to plan a tractor factory with an ultimate output of 20,000 tractors a year. There is a shipbuilding industry of some importance at Karachi that is equipped with foundries and can build medium-size ships and undertake repairs. Even with the future development of these projects, Pakistan's metallurgical and engineering industries will not match those of Central Asia in capacity or production.

The chemical fertilizer industry has received considerable attention in recent years, and several new plants have been built. It is hoped that the country will be self-sufficient in nitrogenous fertilizers by 1982-83. New factories are planned to reduce the gap between present production of phosphate fertilizers and the demand. Total production of all types of fertilizers reached 833,000 tons in 1975-76, compared with 6.6 million tons in Central Asia in 1976.[91]

The most important industry in Pakistan, in terms of production and exports, is the textile industry, particularly cotton textiles and yarns. The cotton textile industry employs around 150,000 persons, more than 33 percent of all those employed in large-scale industry.[92] Production of cotton textiles amounted to 520.4 million square meters in 1975-76, compared with about 350 million square meters in Central Asia in 1975.[93] The cotton textile industry is particularly suitable for a country that produces the raw material in considerable quantities and that must find employment for a large unskilled and semiskilled labor force. If Central Asia had been an independent country, the cotton textile industry probably would have been much more developed, at the expense of the more specialized branches of the engineering industry. Kazi Ahmad suggests priorities for the development of Pakistan's industries that might well have been those for Central Asia under other circumstances: the textile industry; the chemical industry, based on salts and natural gas; the leather industry; the consumer goods industry; and industries using imported raw materials that are essential to the economy and national security, such as the steel industry.[94]

The greatest difference between the Pakistani and Central Asian economies, however, lies in the importance of cottage and small-scale industry in the former. In 1977 about 73 percent of the population of Pakistan lived in rural areas, with agriculture as the main occupation. The villages in which most of them live are more or less self-sufficient. Not only are there blacksmiths, carpenters, potters, and weavers, but the farmers themselves manufacture textiles, leather goods, carpets, utensils, and other items. Cottage industries, in fact, still supply the bulk of Pakistan's manufactured goods.[95] The Pakistani authorities see cottage industries as an essential part of the economy, providing employment and extra income for the large rural population in a country with little surplus capital for investment.[96] Cottage industries are not necessarily primitive. They produce such varied goods as tennis rackets, field hockey balls, silver and gold items, steel cutlery, surgical instruments, embroidery, and furniture.

This type of small-scale industry does not exist to any extent in Central Asia. Before the advent of the Russians there had been a local metalworking industry, but it suffered from the import of Russian metal articles. The local manufacture of textiles was not encouraged by the Russians, who wished no competition with their own products. The only small-scale industries left of importance were silk, carpets, and leather.[97] During the Soviet period most of these industries moved from the cottage to the factory. Although cottage and other types of small-scale industry would no doubt provide considerable employment in rural areas, there is no real possibility that they will be redeveloped in the region. In view of the Soviet devotion to the principles of development of large-scale industry, such a move would be seen as retrogressive.

There is no doubt that Central Asia has moved further than Pakistan along the road of industrialization and modernization. Apart from the higher levels of development of natural resources and greater levels of industrial production of similar goods, the standard of living is higher in Central Asia. In 1970 the GNP per capita in U.S. dollars in Turkmenistan was 1,400, in Kirgizstan 1,346, in Uzbekistan 1,144, and in Tadzhikistan 1,083.[98] In 1971-72 the GNP per capita in Pakistan was U.S.$163.[99] The total GNP of Uzbekistan in 1970 was U.S.$13.5 billion, compared with U.S.$10.3 billion for Pakistan in 1971-72.[100] By 1975-76, Pakistan's GNP per capita was more than double the 1971-72 figure, but was still considerably less than the 1970 figure for Central Asia. Even if the level of living is lower in the Central Asian republics than in other republics of the Soviet Union, as was demonstrated by Gertrude Schroeder's four indicators for 1965,[101] this low level is relative only to the other Soviet republics. A similar study of the same indicators for Pakistan and many other developing countries would certainly be in favor of Central Asia.

Central Asia has both gained and lost by its incorporation into the Soviet Union. As part of a larger political and economic unit whose rulers have emphasized industrialization and the development of modern technology, its agriculture and industry have gained. Most of the available mineral deposits have been exploited, power resources developed, agriculture supplied with fertilizer and machinery, and new factories built. Even if, on the social side, housing has been less than adequate, the medical and educational facilities of the region have experienced considerable development. The losses to Central Asia are less tangible. The economic structure of the region has been molded to fit the requirements of the larger whole, and has developed differently from that of an independent country such as Pakistan. However, as long as Central Asia remains part of the Soviet Union, and if it is adequately rewarded for its contributions to the whole, this may not necessarily be a disadvantage. The real loss is the lack of self-determination for the peoples of Central Asia. In contrast with their neighbors in Iran, Afghanistan, and Pakistan, their fate does not lie in their own hands. At a time when the Muslim world seems to be experiencing a resurgence of religious fervor and Muslim countries are attempting to establish their identity and strengthen their links with one another, the Soviet Central Asians must stand on the sidelines, as observers. They have lost the possibility of playing a major role in any grouping of countries in a larger Central Asian context.

It is difficult to assess the feelings of the average inhabitant of Central Asia toward his or her situation. The Muslim religion has been crushed, contact with fellow Muslims in neighboring countries has been discouraged, and cultural identity has been threatened by Russification. The Central Asian has seen the best jobs in the republics, both political and economic, held by outsiders. On the other hand, life is more secure, with better medical care and the chance of obtaining a higher level of education than is available to many of the peoples of the neighboring countries. The future course of events in Central Asia will be of great interest and significance, not only for the foreign observer but also for the Soviet Union as a whole.


KAZAKHSTAN

As discussed at the beginning of this chapter, Kazakhstan can be most logically viewed as two regions, a Central Asian south, with an environment and population similar to that of the neighboring Central Asian republics, and a northern region with many of the characteristics of the adjacent regions of the RSFSR. The southern oblasts can, in fact, be regarded as the northern fringe of the Central Asian region. They are isolated from the northern oblasts by a vast area of desert and semi-desert that is crossed only by three widely spaced railroad routes. Thus the southern oblasts are linked more strongly to Central Asia than to the rest of the Kazakh Republic, and much of southern Kazakhstan's agriculture, mining, and industry is complementary to that of Central Asia. The northern oblasts have developed an economy that is more similar to that of West Siberia. The extensive grasslands of the region have been developed as major grain-producing areas, and coal and other mineral deposits have formed the basis for the growth of a major industrial region. The development of agriculture and industry in Kazakhstan must, thus, be considered in the context of these two divergent regions of the republic.

The southern oblasts of Kazakhstan have an irrigated agriculture similar to that of Uzbekistan. Because of the shorter growing season in Kazakhstan, cotton plays a smaller role in the region's irrigated agriculture than it does in Central Asia, and grain, sugar beets, and fruit and vegetables are more important. Grain is also grown by dry-farming methods on the areas of fertile loess soils.[102] In 1976 the total area of irrigated land in Kazakhstan was 1.7 million hectares, of which 1.4 million were sown. Grain occupied 36.5 percent of the sown area, and industrial crops 14.1 percent. Since about 39 percent of the area sown to industrial crops consisted of sugar beets, it can be assumed that the remaining area (8.6 percent of the total sown irrigated area) was sown to cotton. In the same year 55.7 percent of the total sown irrigated area of the Central Asian republics was devoted to cotton.[103] Production of cotton in Kazakhstan amounted only to 310,000 tons in 1976, less than any single cotton-growing republic except Kirgizstan.[104] Thus, cotton is not a major product of Kazakh agriculture.

The development of agriculture on the steppes of northern Kazakhstan began in the eighteenth century with the settlement of the rich chernozem soils by Russians from the west. Further settlement continued during the nineteenth century, and was reinforced by the deportations of Volga Germans and other groups to the region during World War II. However, the main impetus to the development of large-scale grain farming in the region came in the 1950s with the Virgin Lands scheme. Between 1954 and 1958 over 20 million hectares of virgin and fallow land were plowed.[105] Although variable precipitation and low yields prevented the Virgin Lands scheme from being as successful as planned, the region has become a major producer of grain for the Soviet Union. In 1976 about 88 percent of the 35.6 million hectares of sown area in Kazakhstan was located in the 11 northern oblasts of the region, and 72.5 percent of this area was sown to grain.[106] In 1976 the total area sown to grain in Kazakhstan—25.5 million hectares (20 percent of the total grain area of the Soviet Union)—produced 29.8 million tons of grain (13 percent of total Soviet production). These figures suggest low yields per hectare and, indeed, the yield of grain in Kazakhstan in 1976 was 11.7 centners per hectare. This was the lowest figure for all Soviet republics except Tadzhikistan.[107] About 72 percent of the total Kazakh grain harvest consisted of wheat, and 21 percent of barley.[108]

The low yields for Kazakh grain, compared with the Ukrainian yields of 27.9 centners per hectare in 1976, suggest that the region's grain-growing is still based on extensive farming methods with little application of fertilizer, as was the practice during the initial period of the Virgin Lands scheme. This supposition is borne out by the fact that the application of fertilizer per hectare of plowed land in Kazakhstan in 1976 amounted to 14.5 kilos, compared with 246 kilos in Uzbekistan and 109.6 kilos in the Ukraine.[109] Uzbek cotton and Ukrainian wheat have priority over Kazakh grain. Although Kazakhstan has only one tractor per 153 hectares of sown land, compared with one per 87 hectares in the Ukraine, Kazakhstan is better supplied with grain-harvesting combines, having 113,600 in 1976 (16.6 percent of the national total), compared with 81,700 in the Ukraine. (The sown areas of the two republics are approximately equal.)[110] The use of harvesting combines on a large scale in Kazakhstan is necessitated by the number of large sovkhozy. The average size of the 1,984 sovkhozy in Kazakhstan in 1976 was 15,588 hectares of sown area, compared with the national average of 5,680 hectares. The Ukraine had 2,087 sovkhozy, but their average size was only 3,475 hectares of sown area.[111]

The livestock industry of Kazakhstan has national significance. In 1976 the region produced 537,600 tons of meat, 6.4 percent of the national total. Although less than 33 percent of Ukrainian production, it was about the same as that of Belorussia.[112] There were 7.6 million head of cattle and 33.8 million sheep. Kazakhstan had about 24 percent of all the sheep in the Soviet Union, and produced 100,900 tons of wool (23.3 percent of total Soviet production).[113] Although the livestock industry of Kazakhstan originated with the herds of the nomadic Kazakhs, at present 63.5 percent of cattle and 74.1 percent of sheep and goats are the property of state farms.[114] As in the case of grain-farming, livestock herding is a large-scale industry carried out predominantly by state farms.

Kazakhstan's energy resources are different in composition from those of Central Asia. The main source of energy is the bituminous coal basin of Karaganda. Although mining at Karaganda began on a large scale in the 1930s, it was the demand for coal during World War II that resulted in a rapid increase in production. At present it is third in production after the Donbas and the Kuzbas. In 1976 the Karaganda mines produced 47.4 million tons of coal, of which about 33 percent was coking coal. The equally large coal basin at Ekibastuz, in northeastern Kazakhstan, produced 46.2 million tons of coal in the same year. This coal cannot be used for coking, but is good for production of steam. It is one of the cheapest coal-mining areas in the Soviet Union, since the seams can be worked by open-pit methods. Most of Ekibastuz coal goes at present to power stations in the Urals region. In 1976, Kazakhstan produced 93.7 million tons of coal, 13.2 percent of total Soviet production. There are several other deposits of sub-bituminous coal that may be utilized in large thermal power stations.[115]

Kazakhstan's oil production is quite impressive. In 1975, Kazakh production was 23.9 million tons. Although this amounts to only 4.9 percent of total Soviet production, it is the largest amount produced by any republic apart from the RSFSR. Most of it comes from the Gur'ev and Mangyshlak fields on the Caspian Sea. Although a pipeline carries Mangyshlak oil to refineries at Kuibyshev, the high paraffin content of the oil makes its transportation by pipeline difficult, and has retarded development of the field.[116] Production of natural gas is small, and is dwarfed by that of Uzbekistan and Turkmenistan.

Most of Kazakhstan's electric power production comes from thermal stations. A large plant using Ekibastuz coal is located at Yermak, and further plants are planned for construction at the coal fields themselves. In 1976 the republic produced 55.6 billion kilowatt-hours, 5 percent of total national electric power production. Of this amount only 4.8 million kilowatt-hours (8.8 percent) came from hydroelectric power stations.[117] The main hydroelectric plants are at Ust'-Kamenogorsk and Bukhtarma on the Irtysh, and on the Ili near Alma-Ata. Conditions for development of hydroelectric power are not favorable except in the east and south of the region. In 1976 production of electric power per capita in Kazakhstan was 3,858 kilowatt-hours, compared with 2,459 kilowatt-hours in Uzbekistan and the national average of 4,330 kilowatt-hours.[118] Further development of electric power rests largely on the use of reserves of sub-bituminous coal rather than on water power or natural gas. Some of this power may be transmitted to other regions. As in Central Asia, there are no nuclear power stations under construction at present.

Kazakhstan is fortunate in having reserves of iron ore relatively close to the major coal fields. The republic contains about 11.5 percent of the iron ore reserves of the Soviet Union, the most important deposit being the Turgai Basin in Kustanai Oblast, in the north. Other deposits are at Karazhal, south of Karaganda; near Pavlodar;

and in southern Kazakhstan.[119] Production of iron ore in 1976 was 22.7 million tons, 9.5 percent of total Soviet production.[120] The republic is also a major producer of manganese, mined near Dzhezkazgan and occupies third place in the Soviet Union in terms of manganese reserves. It also has the largest deposits of chromite in the country. The mines at Khrom Tau, near Aktiubinsk, yield about 85 percent of the Soviet Union's total production.[121]

The proximity of these ferrous minerals to the coal deposits of Karaganda has encouraged the development of a major iron and steel industry. In the early 1960s the Karaganda integrated metallurgical complex began operations. Since then the plant has been expanded, and there are plans for further growth. In particular the combine produces metal for the automobile industry, and the Togliatti factory already is a customer. Rolled steel for various branches of the engineering industry is also produced.[122] In 1975, Kazakhstan produced 3.6 million tons of pig iron and 4.9 million tons of steel (both about 3.5 percent of Soviet production).[123] Although the Kazakh iron and steel industry cannot be compared with those of the Ukraine or the Urals, the Karaganda plant is nevertheless one of the major new Soviet metallurgical plants. The Irtysh-Karaganda Canal, opened in 1972, brings sufficient quantities of water to Karaganda not only for industrial purposes, but also for development of irrigated agriculture to supply the growing urban population of the area. Coal supplies seem sufficient not only to support growth of the local iron and steel industry, but also to maintain deliveries to the Urals region.

In spite of the great significance of the iron and steel industry to the Kazakh economy, nonferrous metallurgy is more important.[124] Kazakhstan has particularly large reserves of copper and polymetallic ores. Dzhezkazgan is the major center for production, and has the largest copper reserves in the Soviet Union.[125] A concentrator, refinery, and other processing plants have been built in the area. Copper is mined in other locations, including Balkhash. Polymetallic ores containing copper, lead, zinc, and other metals are mined and processed at several places. Lead and zinc are particularly important in the Altai Mountain region of eastern Kazakhstan, and Ust'-Kamenogorsk has become a major center of nonferrous metallurgy. In the south, Chimkent has an important lead industry. Bauxite is mined in Kustanai Oblast and is sent to an alumina plant in Pavlodar. Because of the lack of a well-developed power base, aluminum metal is not produced locally; the alumina is sent to aluminum plants in Siberia.[126] Apart from the above-mentioned metallic ores, Kazakhstan has important reserves of gold, silver, titanium, molybdenum, barite, and other rare metals. Kazakhstan is, thus, a major supplier of a number of nonferrous metals to Soviet industry, and has a more varied metallic resource base than any of the Central Asian republics.

Kazakhstan also supplies the Soviet Union with a number of important chemical raw materials. The phosphorite deposits of southern Kazakhstan contain about 33 percent of the Soviet Union's reserves of raw material for the manufacture of phosphate fertilizer.[127] Several plants have been built to process phosphorite, including the fertilizer plant at Dzhambul. Some Kazakh phosphorite is processed at fertilizer plants in Central Asia. In 1976, Kazakhstan produced 5.8 million tons of fertilizer, about the same as Uzbekistan.[128] As noted above, applications of fertilizer per unit area are much lower in Kazakhstan than in Central Asia; and with a sown area almost double that of Uzbekistan, Kazakhstan's fertilizer production is insufficient for the requirements of the region.

A large borax deposit is mined and processed in western Kazakhstan, and about 25 percent of the Soviet Union's asbestos comes from near Aktiubinsk. In general, the Kazakh chemical industry, like the nonferrous metals industry, provides the Soviet Union with a number of minerals that are in short supply in other regions or are of strategic value.

Soviet geographers and planners see Kazakh industry as consisting of several major complexes: the central Kazakhstan fuel, iron and steel, and chemical complex, centered on Karaganda; the eastern Kazakhstan nonferrous metallurgical complex; the Pavlodar-Ekibastuz power, metallurgical, chemical, and heavy-engineering complex; the Turgai mining complex; and the southern Kazakhstan oil and gas chemical complex.[129] The Pavlodar-Ekibastuz complex is the main center of heavy engineering in the republic. It is well supplied with power, has good transportation links, and is the center of a productive agricultural region. It already has a number of nonferrous and ferrous metallurgical plants, and Pavlodar has a large tractor factory. The complex is heralded as an example of the rational development of regional resources.[130]

Although 56.2 percent of the NMP of the Kazakh Republic in 1975 came from industry,[131] there is little diversification of regional industry, which is concentrated mainly in metallurgy and chemicals. Production of engineering products, apart from farm machinery, is low. Likewise, there has been no notable development of light industry. In 1975, Kazakhstan produced 96.7 million running meters of cotton material, compared with 223.1 million in Uzbekistan. In spite of the large number of sheep in the republic, it produced only 14.1 million running meters of wool material in 1975, some 2.6 percent of total Soviet production.[132]

The structure and location of Kazakh industry results from several factors. Most of the industrial raw materials and the best agricultural soils are concentrated in the northern oblasts of the republic. This area is close to the important industrial regions of the

Volga, Urals, and West Siberia—and, in fact, is a southward extension of them. The railroad network of northern Kazakhstan provides a relatively good link between the major Kazakh industrial complexes and the rest of the Soviet Union, in contrast with the areas of southern Kazakhstan and Central Asia. Northern Kazakhstan is essentially a supplier of power, fuel, metals, and chemicals to other regions of the Soviet Union. Thus regional industry has not concentrated to any extent on production of finished goods.

Northern Kazakhstan does not face the problem of rapid growth of the indigenous population that southern Kazakhstan and Central Asia have. The composition of the population of the northern oblasts is characterized by a predominance of Russians, Ukrainians, and Germans, with Kazakhs in the minority. Of the 7.9 million inhabitants of the 11 northern oblasts in 1970, 3.7 million (47 percent) were Russians and 2.1 million (26 percent) were Kazakhs. Ukrainians and Germans made up 9.8 and 8.1 percent of the population, respectively. Various other non-Central Asian groups, notably Tatars and Belorussians, formed the balance of the population.[133] Kazakhstan exhibited a much larger migration balance than any of the Central Asian republics in the period 1961-70, with total immigrants outnumbering emigrants by 602,000 in 1961-65 and 90,000 in 1966-70, compared with 77,000 and 69,000 for Uzbekistan during the same periods.[134]

Although some of the earlier immigrants probably settled on sovkhozy in the Virgin Lands, many must have moved to urban centers. In 1977 about 54 percent of the total population of Kazakhstan lived in urban centers, compared with 44 percent in 1959. The level of urbanization in Kazakhstan is higher than in Uzbekistan, where only 39 percent of the population in 1977 was classed as urban.[135] In 1970, 58.4 percent of the urban population of the republic consisted of Russians, and only 17.1 percent were Kazakhs.[136] In the same year 70 percent of the 730,000 inhabitants of Alma-Ata were Russians, and only 12 percent were Kazakhs.[137] The movement of outsiders into Kazakh cities is not confined only to the industrial centers of the north.

One result of this large number of outsiders who have settled in Kazakhstan is a relatively low rate of population increase for the whole republic. In 1976 the annual rate of population growth for Kazakhstan was 1.71 percent, compared with 2.82 percent for Uzbekistan and 2.97 percent for Tadzhikistan.[138] A projection of the estimated percentage change in the work force (population aged 20-29) in Kazakhstan between 1970 and 1990 suggests a probable increase of 87.8 percent, compared with 182.4 percent for Central Asia and 42.8 percent for the Soviet Union.[139] The problem of providing employment for this growing population is not so serious as in Central Asia.

Despite the influx of large numbers of outsiders, some industrial jobs in Kazakhstan have been filled by native peoples. This trend has been much more noticeable in Kazakhstan than in Central Asia. In 1959, 48.6 percent of the employed indigenous population of Kazakhstan were in nonagricultural work, compared with 29.1 percent in Uzbekistan and 33.4 percent in Turkmenistan.[140] In 1970 there were 94.0 specialists with higher and secondary education per 1,000 population aged 16-59 in Kazakhstan, compared with 75.7 in Uzbekistan and 79.9 in Turkmenistan.[141] Although these figures are, in general, less than for other major ethnic groups in the Soviet Union, they indicate a higher level of specialized education and industrial employment for Kazakhs than for the indigenous inhabitants of the Central Asian republics. The greater level of industrial employment of Kazakhs in their own republic may result in a more satisfactory balance of industrial and agricultural employment than is found in the Central Asian region.

The future of Kazakhstan's economy would seem to lie in the further development of grain farming and of the major industrial complexes. Greater intensification of Kazakh wheat-growing through the increased use of fertilizer may increase yields and production, but the northern areas of the republic still remain an area of variable precipitation and potential problems, with the specter of dust-bowl conditions always present if overcultivation takes place. The exploitation of the industrial raw materials of the republic, and the growth of the major complexes based on them, would seem to be the logical path to follow. Even if Kazakhstan were an independent state, its location would virtually compel it to act as a supplier of energy, raw materials, and metals to the surrounding regions. It would, in fact, have to play the role of an Asian Canada to the industrialized Soviet Union.

## NOTES

1. TsSU, Itogi vsesoiuznoi perepisi naseleniia 1970 goda, vol. 4 (Moscow, 1973), pp. 232-51.
2. Paul E. Lydolph, Geography of the U.S.S.R. (New York: John Wiley and Sons, 1970), p. 271.
3. Further information on the physical environment of Central Asia is in Ian M. Matley, "The Population and the Land," in Edward Allworth, ed., Central Asia: A Century of Russian Rule (New York and London: Columbia University Press, 1967), pp. 112-30.
4. Ian M. Matley, "The Golodnaya Steppe: A Russian Irrigation Venture in Central Asia," Geographical Review 60 (July 1970): 328-46; and "The Murgab Oasis: The Modernization of an Ancient

Irrigation System," <u>Canadian Slavonic Papers</u> 17 (Summer and Fall 1975):417-35.

5. TsSU, <u>Narodnoe khoziaistvo SSSR za 60 let</u> (Moscow, 1977), pp. 304, 310. (Hereafter <u>Narkhoz za 60 let.</u>)

6. Ibid., pp. 308, 314, 322.

7. Ibid., pp. 334, 335, 339, 340.

8. Basic information on the resources of Soviet regions is in Theodore Shabad, <u>Basic Industrial Resources of the U.S.S.R.</u> (New York and London: Columbia University Press, 1969).

9. TsSU, <u>Narodnoe khoziaistvo SSSR v 1975 g.</u> (Moscow: TsSU, 1976), p. 243. (Hereafter <u>Narkhoz 75.</u>)

10. Ibid., p. 240.

11. Ibid., p. 241.

12. N. Nekrasov, <u>The Territorial Organization of Soviet Economy</u> (Moscow, 1974), p. 220.

13. K. N. Bedrintsev et al., <u>Sredneaziatskii ekonomicheski raion</u> (Moscow, 1972), p. 9.

14. Ibid.

15. Ibid., p. 79.

16. Ibid., p. 74.

17. <u>Narkhoz za 60 let</u>, p. 202.

18. Bedrintsev, <u>Sredneaziatskii ekonomicheski raion</u>, p. 10.

19. Lydolph, <u>Geography of the U.S.S.R.</u>, p. 325.

20. Ibid., pp. 324-25.

21. Bedrintsev, <u>Sredneaziatskii ekonomicheski raion</u>, p. 82.

22. Lydolph, <u>Geography of the U.S.S.R.</u>, pp. 323-24.

23. <u>Narkhoz 75</u>, p. 245.

24. Lydolph, <u>Geography of the U.S.S.R.</u>, p. 324.

25. Bedrintsev, <u>Sredneaziatskii ekonomicheski raion</u>, p. 94.

26. <u>Narkhoz za 60 let</u>, p. 214.

27. Bedrintsev, <u>Sredneaziatskii ekonomicheski raion</u>, p. 84.

28. <u>Narkhoz za 60 let</u>, p. 246.

29. Bedrintsev, <u>Sredneaziatskii ekonomicheski raion</u>, p. 121.

30. <u>Narkhoz 75</u>, p. 285.

31. <u>Narkhoz za 60 let</u>, pp. 304, 328.

32. Matley, "The Murgab Oasis," p. 434.

33. Matley, "The Golodnaya Steppe," pp. 342-46.

34. <u>Narkhoz za 60 let</u>, pp. 325, 310.

35. A. E. Probst, <u>Razmeshchenie sotsialisticheskoi promyshlennosti</u> (Moscow, 1962; English ed., Warrington: Crossfield and Sons, 1963), p. 32, table 13.

36. A. E. Probst, <u>Voprosy razmeshcheniia sotsialisticheskoi promyshlennosti</u> (Moscow, 1971), p. 228.

37. <u>Narkhoz za 60 let</u>, p. 42.

38. Ibid., p. 73.

39. A summary and discussion of recent writings on the subject is in Michael Rywkin, "Central Asia and Soviet Manpower," Problems of Communism 28 (January–February 1979):1–13.

40. TsSU, Itogi vsesoiuznoi perepisi naseleniia 1970 goda, vol. 4, pp. 9, 13–15.

41. Rywkin, "Central Asia and Soviet Manpower," p. 4.

42. Robert A. Lewis, Richard H. Rowland, and Ralph S. Clem, Nationality and Population Change in Russia and the U.S.S.R. An Evaluation of Census Data, 1897–1970 (New York and London: Praeger, 1976), p. 356.

43. Ibid.

44. Ibid., pp. 356–57.

45. Ibid., p. 367.

46. Ibid., p. 370.

47. Robert A. Lewis, Richard H. Rowland, and Ralph S. Clem, "Modernization, Population Change and Nationality in Soviet Central Asia and Kazakhstan," Canadian Slavonic Papers 17 (Summer and Fall 1975):293.

48. TsSU, Itogi vsesoiuznoi perepisi naseleniia 1970 goda, vol. 4, pp. 208, 288.

49. A. Ia. Kvasha, Populiarnaia demografiia (Moscow, 1977), pp. 71–72.

50. Ibid., p. 73.

51. Lewis, Rowland, and Clem, Nationality and Population Change in Russia and the U.S.S.R., p. 357.

52. Narkhoz za 60 let, p. 328.

53. Lewis, Rowland, and Clem, Nationality and Population Change in Russia and the U.S.S.R., p. 356.

54. S. Tatur, From the Great Fergana to the Kara-Kum Canal (Moscow, 1976), p. 35.

55. Narkhoz za 60 let, p. 157.

56. Lewis, Rowland, and Clem, Nationality and Population Change in Russia and the U.S.S.R., pp. 367–68.

57. Ibid., p. 370.

58. Ibid., pp. 370–71.

59. Ibid., p. 368.

60. Narkhoz 75, p. 203.

61. Ann Sheehy, "Some Aspects of Regional Development in Soviet Central Asia," Slavic Review 31 (September 1972):556–57.

62. Leslie Dienes, "Investment Priorities in Soviet Regions," Annals of the Association of American Geographers 62 (September 1972):437–54.

63. Narkhoz za 60 let, p. 443.

64. Lewis, Rowland, and Clem, Nationality and Population Change in Russia and the U.S.S.R., p. 358.

65. Ibid., p. 369.

66. Referred to in Rywkin, "Central Asia and Manpower," p. 6.

67. Ibid., p. 12.

68. Alec Nove and J. A. Newth, The Soviet Middle East: A Model for Development? (London: Allen and Unwin, 1967), pp. 113-25.

69. These points are discussed in ibid., pp. 113-18.

70. Kazi S. Ahmad, A Geography of Pakistan (London: Oxford University Press, 1972), p. 51; Rafique Akhtar, ed., Pakistan Year Book 1978 (Karachi and Lahore: East and West, 1978), p. 299. (Hereafter Pakistan 1978.)

71. Ahmad, A Geography of Pakistan, p. 67.

72. Pakistan 78, pp. 308-09.

73. Matley, "The Golodnaya Steppe," p. 344; Sergei Tatur, The Hungry Steppe Becomes a Land of Plenty (Moscow, 1974), p. 23.

74. Pakistan 78, p. 315. The total area of principal crops is a more useful indicator than the total cropped area, which is not clearly defined.

75. Ibid. Other major crops are sugarcane, rape and mustard, and gram (chickpea).

76. Ibid., p. 298.

77. Figures calculated from Pakistan 78, pp. 300-03, 315, and Narkhoz za 60 let, pp. 303, 308-10.

78. Pakistan 78, p. 304; Statistics Division, Ministry of Finance, Pakistan Statistical Yearbook 1976 (Karachi: Manager of Publications, 1977), p. 41; Narkhoz za 60 let, p. 325.

79. Pakistan 78, pp. 309-10; Narkhoz za 60 let, pp. 334-36; Ahmad, A Geography of Pakistan, pp. 102-03.

80. Azimusshan Haider, Economic History of the Region Constituting Pakistan from 1825 to 1974 (Karachi: Afro-Asian Research Centre, 1975), p. 89.

81. Pakistan 78, p. 299; Narkhoz za 60 let, p. 295.

82. Haider, Economic History . . . , p. 88.

83. Narkhoz za 60 let, pp. 53-54; Pakistan 78, p. 43; direct comparison of rural and urban populations in both countries is difficult because of different definitions.

84. Pakistan 78, pp. 474, 493.

85. Ibid., pp. 498, 494. Oil production is calculated on the basis of figures for July 1976-March 1977 and July 1977-March 1978; Narkhoz 75, p. 240.

86. Ahmad, A Geography of Pakistan, pp. 115-16; Pakistan 78, pp. 493-94, 500.

87. Ahmad, A Geography of Pakistan, p. 72; Pakistan 78, pp. 494, 504-05, 507-08.

88. Pakistan 78, p. 491; Narkhoz za 60 let, p. 117.

89. Pakistan 78, pp. 475-76.

90. Ahmad, A Geography of Pakistan, pp. 117-22.

91. Pakistan 78, pp. 344-45; Pakistan Statistical Yearbook 1976, p. 58.

92. Ahmad, A Geography of Pakistan, p. 137.

93. Pakistan Statistical Yearbook 1976, p. 51; Narkhoz 75, p. 285. Production of cotton textiles in square meters is calculated approximately from the figures given for production in running meters.

94. Ahmad, A Geography of Pakistan, p. 124.

95. Ibid., pp. 126-27.

96. Ibid., p. 126.

97. Matley, "The Population and the Land," pp. 309, 310, 312, 314.

98. I. S. Koropeckyj, "National Income of the Soviet Union Republics in 1970: Revision and Some Applications," in Zbigniew M. Fallenbuchl, ed., Economic Development in the Soviet Union and Eastern Europe (New York: Praeger, 1975), p. 323.

99. Pakistan Statistical Yearbook 1976, p. 144.

100. Koropeckyj, "National Income . . .," p. 322; Pakistan Statistical Yearbook 1976, p. 144.

101. Gertrude E. Schroeder, "Regional Differences in Incomes and Levels of Living in the U.S.S.R.," in V. N. Bandera and Z. L. Melnyk, eds., The Soviet Economy in Regional Perspective (New York: Praeger, 1973), pp. 187-90.

102. Lydolph, Geography of the U.S.S.R., p. 349.

103. Narkhoz za 60 let, p. 329.

104. Ibid., p. 310.

105. Matley, "The Population and the Land," p. 305.

106. TsSU, Narodnoe khoziaistvo Kazakhstana v 1976 g. (Alma-Ata, 1977), p. 71. (Hereafter Narkhoz Kazakhstan 76.)

107. Narkhoz za 60 let, pp. 303, 308, 309.

108. Narkhoz Kazakhstan 76, p. 75.

109. Narkhoz za 60 let, p. 327.

110. Ibid., pp. 295, 296, 303.

111. Ibid., pp. 356, 371.

112. Ibid., p. 259.

113. Ibid., pp. 334, 336, 340.

114. Ibid., p. 371.

115. Narkhoz Kazakhstan 76, p. 47; Narkhoz za 60 let, p. 206; Lydolph, Geography of the U.S.S.R., p. 356.

116. Narkhoz 75, p. 240; Lydolph, Geography of the U.S.S.R., p. 357.

117. Narkhoz za 60 let, p. 202; Narkhoz Kazakhstan 76, p. 45.

118. Narkhoz za 60 let, p. 117.

119. E. Turkebaev, B. Dvoskin, and K. Isentaev, Problemy regional'noi ekonomiki Kazakhstana (Alma-Ata, 1977), p. 49.

120. Narkhoz Kazakhstan 76, p. 47; Narkhoz za 60 let, p. 210.

121. Lydolph, Geography of the U.S.S.R., p. 359.

122. Turkebaev, Dvoskin, and Isentaev, Problemy . . . Kazakhstana, p. 52.

123. Narkhoz 75, p. 245.

124. Turkebaev, Dvoskin, and Isentaev, Problemy . . . Kazakhstana, p. 45.

125. Shabad, Basic Industrial Resources . . ., p. 288.

126. Lydolph, Geography of the U.S.S.R., p. 361; Turkebaev, Dvoskin, and Isentaev, Problemy . . . Kazakhstana, pp. 48-49.

127. Turkebaev, Dvoskin, and Isentaev, Problemy . . . Kazakhstana, p. 62.

128. Narkhoz za 60 let, p. 214.

129. Nekrasov, The Territorial Organization . . ., pp. 213-14.

130. Ibid., p. 216; Lydolph, Geography of the U.S.S.R., p. 363.

131. Turkebaev, Dvoskin, and Isentaev, Problemy . . . Kazakhstana, p. 36.

132. Narkhoz 75, p. 285.

133. TsSU, Itogi vsesoiuznoi perepisi naseleniia 1970 goda, vol. 4, pp. 232-50.

134. Rywkin, "Central Asia and Manpower," p. 11.

135. Narkhoz za 60 let, p. 44.

136. TsSU, Itogi vsesoiuznoi perepisi naseleniia 1970 goda, vol. 4, p. 266.

137. Ibid., p. 233.

138. Narkhoz za 60 let, p. 73.

139. Lewis, Rowland, and Clem, Nationality and Population Change in Russia and the U.S.S.R., p. 372.

140. Ibid., p. 339. Rywkin, "Central Asia and Manpower," p. 9, table 2, suggests that the proportions of employed indigenous workers in industry rose to 63 percent in Kazakhstan and 39 percent in Uzbekistan by 1970. His 1959 figures, however, differ somewhat from those given by Lewis, Rowland, and Clem.

141. Lewis, Rowland, and Clem, Nationality and Population Change in Russia and the U.S.S.R., p. 337.

# INDEX

Asiatic RSFSR: coal resources, 253; development alternatives, 235-36; development level, 240, 242; distances, 239-40; electric power, 253; environment, 239; food deficit, 245; forestry, 247; geopolitical considerations, 237; natural resources, 237; production cost, 240

Astrachan, A., 348

Azerbaidzhan: agricultural employment, 44; development level, 5; employment rate, 32; fixed capital, 158, 159, 168, 169, 175, 179, 183, 184; food consumption, 133; geopolitical considerations, 104; labor supply, 21; labor supply potential, 36; inputs growth, 99; output growth, 96; personal incomes, 119, 121, 122; productivity growth, 111; real consumption, 130; services, 136, 140; specialization, 387; structural changes, 390; working age population, 20

Baikal-Amur Magistrale, 6, 237, 242, 254, 261

Baku, 208, 390

Baldwin, G. S., 38

Baltic republics: agricultural resources, 331; comparison with Finland, 363-65; collective farmers incomes, 123, 126; climate, 331; consumer durables, 136; dairy products, 8; dairy products costs, 219;

employment growth, 27-32; environmental destruction, 358-59; fish industry, 346; fixed capital, 186, 188; food consumption, 132; forests, 339; geopolitical considerations, 104; inputs growth, 99; labor shortages, 353; lack of autonomy, 361; minerals, 343-44; peat, 342; personal incomes, 121; population growth, 99; productivity growth, 111; real consumption, 130; as a region, 330-31; services, 137; transportation, 224; welfare, 145-48, 149

Bashkir ASSR, 4, 198, 227

Belorussia: agricultural resources, 330-31; climate, 331; communal services, 140-42; education, 142-44; fixed capital, 158, 160, 166, 168, 169, 175, 176, 179, 182, 183, 190; food consumption, 131-32; forests, 339; geopolitical considerations, 105; incomes, 121; inputs growth, 99; labor availability, 6; labor shortages, 353; lack of autonomy, 360-61; minerals, 342; nonfood consumption, 133, 137; output growth, 96; peat, 342; productivity growth, 111; R&D, 227; urban population, 137; welfare, 145

Bond, D. L., 93, 94, 111

Brezhnev, L. I., 4, 121, 226, 267